OXFORD STUDIES
IN THE
SYNOPTIC PROBLEM

STUDIES IN THE
SYNOPTIC PROBLEM

By Members of
The University of Oxford

EDITED BY

W. SANDAY D.D.
Lady Margaret Professor of Divinity

Wipf & Stock
PUBLISHERS
Eugene, Oregon

Wipf and Stock Publishers
199 West 8th Avenue, Suite 3
Eugene, Oregon 97401

Studies in the Synoptic Problem
by Members of the University of Oxford
By Sanday, William
ISBN: 1-59244-479-2
Publication date 1/16/2004
Previously published by Oxford University Press, 1911

THE FOUR EVANGELISTS
(From MS. in the Domschatz at Aachen; see pp. xxvi, 18)

CONTENTS

	PAGE
INTRODUCTORY	vii

W. SANDAY, D.D., LL.D., LITT. D.
    I. THE CONDITIONS UNDER WHICH THE GOSPELS WERE WRITTEN, IN THEIR BEARING UPON SOME DIFFICULTIES OF THE SYNOPTIC PROBLEM . 3

SIR JOHN C. HAWKINS, BART., M.A., D.D.
    II. THREE LIMITATIONS TO ST. LUKE'S USE OF ST. MARK'S GOSPEL :
        1. The Disuse of the Marcan Source in St. Luke ix. 51–xviii. 14 29
        2. The Great Omission by St. Luke of the Matter contained in St. Mark vi. 45–viii. 26 . 61
        3. St. Luke's Passion-Narrative considered with reference to the Synoptic Problem . . 76
    III. PROBABILITIES AS TO THE SO-CALLED DOUBLE TRADITION OF ST. MATTHEW AND ST. LUKE . 95

B. H. STREETER, M.A.
    IV. ON THE ORIGINAL ORDER OF Q . . . 141
    V. ST. MARK'S KNOWLEDGE AND USE OF Q . . 165
    VI. THE ORIGINAL EXTENT OF Q 185
    VII. THE LITERARY EVOLUTION OF THE GOSPELS . 209
    VIII. ON THE TRIAL OF OUR LORD BEFORE HEROD: A SUGGESTION 229
    [See also Appendix, p. 425]

W. C. ALLEN, M.A.
    IX. THE BOOK OF SAYINGS USED BY THE EDITOR OF THE FIRST GOSPEL 235
    X. THE ARAMAIC BACKGROUND OF THE GOSPELS . 287

Contents

J. VERNON BARTLET, M.A., D.D. PAGE
    XI. THE SOURCES OF ST. LUKE'S GOSPEL . . 315

W. E. ADDIS, M.A.
    XII. THE CRITICISM OF THE HEXATEUCH COMPARED WITH THAT OF THE SYNOPTIC GOSPELS . 367

N. P. WILLIAMS, M.A.
    XIII. A RECENT THEORY OF THE ORIGIN OF ST. MARK'S GOSPEL 389

APPENDIX (B. H. STREETER)
    SYNOPTIC CRITICISM AND THE ESCHATOLOGICAL PROBLEM 425

INDEX 437

ADDENDA AND CORRIGENDA

Essay I. Page 7, lines 2 and 3 from foot, *for* Jesus *read* John
Essay II. Page 43, line 11. *for* ὅλη *read* ὅλῃ
    Page 66, lines 15-17, *for* by Mt . . . used to be. *read* by Lk and by Mt, if Lk used it before Mt (which would now be considered more possible than it used to be).
    Page 71, line 10, *for* Mt *read* Mk
Essay IV. Page 146, line 24, *for* 146 *read* 89.
Essay V. Page 178, line 19, *for* reproduce *read* reproduces
Essay VI. Page 192, line 32, *for* breast *read* womb
Essay VII. Page 216, line 8, *for* three companions *read* one of the companions
In Essay XI the symbol S is used both in a wider and in a narrower sense, according to the context, to denote Luke's 'special source' either as inclusive or exclusive of the Q element in it (QL).

Synoptic Problem.   *March*, 1912.

INTRODUCTORY

FOR some considerable time past (since 1894) a class has been in the habit of meeting in the 'lodgings' of the Lady Margaret Professor which we have called a 'Seminar', though it has not been quite like the gatherings known by that name on the Continent. The subject of study has been the Synoptic Problem. But as this larger class has alternated with a smaller (usually upon a subject of Textual Criticism), the number of meetings has only been three in each term or nine in the year. It will therefore be understood that progress has been very leisurely.

The Seminar has lived through some four or five generations of Oxford life, and it has been attended for the most part by graduates and special students; so that a certain proportion of the members have naturally been 'birds of passage', who have stayed for a year or so and have then gone. But it has been the peculiar happiness of this Seminar that it has had a permanent nucleus of members who have been faithful to it from the very first This has been the case with three of the seven contributors to the present volume, Sir John C. Hawkins, Dr. Vernon Bartlet, and Mr. Willoughby C. Allen, who left us two years ago—just as the volume was being planned—to take up the higher dignity of Principal of the Hostel which is now about to be replaced by Egerton Hall, and Archdeacon of Manchester. Mr. B. H. Streeter has also been a very regular and active member since he joined us. Mr. Addis came for several years, but has now been called away to parochial work in London. Mr. N. P. Williams joined us recently, but has been another of our active members. It has been a special regret to me not to include among our fraternity Mr. C. Badcock, a very earnest student, who was also an original member and attended for a number of years until he was lost to us through ill health, which I fear still continues. I must needs at once wish, and not wish, that we could have kept as a contributor Mr. F. Lenwood of Corpus and Mansfield Colleges; but he had to obey the more heroic call of Missions. It is something for the Seminar to feel that it too has made its sacrifices in that great cause. We have twice, I think, had lady members for a few meetings.

It has been our custom to take the Synoptic Gospels section by section, with Tischendorf's handy *Synopsis Evangelica* as our basis, but of course calling in the many excellent *Synopses* that are in use, especially Rushbrooke and Wright and, among the Germans, Huck. We have taken the section, and have had reports upon it from one or two leading commentaries, usually beginning with the very close and careful treatment of Dr. Bernhard Weiss; we have then discussed it freely among ourselves over the table.

In this process opinion has gradually ripened—individual opinion, that is, rather than collective; for we have never sought to fix a corporate opinion, beyond the natural unforced convergence of individual minds. And at last the time seemed come when we might provisionally bring to a head our own studies, and in the same tentative manner give them to the world, by the publication of a joint volume.

With this brief historical *résumé* of the genesis of our book, I will now go on to give some account of its contents, taking the essays or groups of essays in their order.

It will be understood that even to one who has taken part in the proceedings of the Seminar from the first, as I have done, it is a new experience to have these ripened

Introductory (*Essay I*)

opinions of his colleagues set before him in black and white. We shall probably all need some little time to adjust our own bearings on the many points that are raised. It will therefore be only a first provisional survey that I can offer. But I will do what I can.

The essay which as it happens stands actually first, had its place determined for it by its subject-matter, as being preliminary to the rest. It is an attempt to correct in advance some mistakes which may very naturally be made, and to substitute in the mind of the student a right picture for a wrong one of the way in which the Evangelists sat down to their task, from the double point of view of internal or mental conditions and of external or mechanical. With regard to the former, the conception that we form must not be too self-conscious; it must not be stiff and artificial. The object of the Evangelists is just to tell a story — to tell over again the same story — with motives indeed, but not with any deliberately fixed mode of procedure. They were not hampered by literary conventions; they neither aimed at using the same language, nor did they consciously and of set purpose aim at varying their language. They just let the pen run on easily and naturally. They were not what we should call 'critical'; i.e. they were not on their guard against certain simple influences and tendencies which lie sufficiently upon the surface. In the first essay no attempt was made to pursue these influences and tendencies further into detail; the object only was to describe the general attitude of the Evangelists so far as it affected literary freedom of composition. The student who desires to define for himself more exactly the nature of this freedom in its subtler relations may be referred to Sir John Hawkins, *Horae Synopticae*[2], pp. 114-38, or he will find it frequently illustrated in the course of the present volume; for the succession of influences and tendencies as they came into play at different periods of time, I would commend him especially to a singularly clear and convincing sketch in Mr. Streeter's Essay (VII, pp. 210-27).

It was the purpose of the first essay rather to lay stress on the external conditions, as having been less insisted upon by other writers, and less habitually taken into account in the tracing of particular phenomena to their causes. This was perhaps more true some years ago, when the essay was originally written, than it is to-day (see, for instance, an allusion in Dr. Stanton's *Gospels as Historical Documents*, ii. 153). But it might be well if a sense of these mechanical conditions entered into the picture which every student forms for himself at the outset of his studies and keeps before his mind as they proceed.

The full title given to the first essay is 'The Conditions under which the Gospels were written, in their bearing upon some difficulties of the Synoptic Problem'; and at the end of the essay the opportunity was taken to illustrate the principles laid down, by applying them to certain special cases which have exercised the ingenuity of students for a long time and have given rise to a variety of hypotheses. It was not intended to put forward the explanations suggested as the whole and sole account of all the phenomena, but only to claim for them a place — and perhaps a rather prominent place — among the causes that have been at work. Besides other references that were given for the treatment of the coincidences between Matthew and Luke as against Mark, mention should have been made of that by Dr. Stanton, *op. cit.*, pp. 207-19. I am afraid that I am inclined to differ from Dr. Stanton, as well as from Mr. N. P. Williams at the end of this volume, in rejecting the idea of earlier and later editions of our Second Gospel, the one containing and the other not containing the section Mk vi. 45-viii. 26. I agree rather with Sir John Hawkins (pp. 60-74) in believing that the Second Gospel lay before St. Luke substantially in the form in which we have it

Introductory (*Essays II, III*)

now, and that the section in point was deliberately omitted by St. Luke for the reasons given by Sir John Hawkins, combined with the general considerations stated on p. 25 f.

The essay which comes first is a sort of hors-d'œuvre. It was on all grounds right and fitting that the main series of Essays should be headed by the senior member of our body, who has not only been the mainstay of the Seminar from the first but has also given to the Synoptic Problem a degree of close and continuous attention that has not been possible to others among us. But there is the special advantage in his heading the list of essays, with Mr. Streeter's contribution next in order, that in this way we are taken at once to the heart of the problem with a powerful statement of the views that may be described as generally current—in other words, of the 'Two-Document Hypothesis'. Other views are expressed, and ably expressed, in this volume; and it does not follow that the 'prerogative vote' always carries the day; but I think we shall wish the prerogative vote to be where it is. And I also think it a distinct advantage that the Two-Document hypothesis should have a full statement first. The two dissentients are Archdeacon Allen (Essay IX) and Dr. Bartlet (Essay XI). But I hope to show, when I come to these essays, that the dissent is only partial; and indeed I am myself inclined to mediate between the different positions. It would be a pity if the total margin of difference within the two covers of this book were supposed to be greater than it is. It is true that, by the time we have done, we shall still leave a good many questions unresolved, i.e. not brought to an absolute decision. But a case will have been stated for the different views; and I think it will be seen that the margin of difference is not so very large. In any case I believe that it is not large enough to justify the scepticism which exists in some quarters, as though the whole problem would never be brought to a conclusion—that is, a relatively probable conclusion.

The character of Sir John Hawkins's work is well known: its concreteness and definiteness, always supported by carefully chosen examples; its exactness and trustworthiness of detail—the amount of thought that has evidently been given to each item, as Mark Pattison said of Bishop Butler, 'every brick in the building has been rung before it has been laid'; its extreme sobriety and caution, never overstepping the limits of proof, and always scrupulously discriminating degrees of proof; the clear distinction that is observed between assured results and speculative probabilities or possibilities. I cannot help hoping that something of these qualities will be found to run through our book as a whole (see in particular p. 186, and compare p. 59).

The first of Sir John Hawkins's essays (Essay II) is a sort of trident or fork with three prongs. It deals with three limitations to the broad general principle that the Gospel of St. Luke is based upon the earlier Gospel of St. Mark. The first of these limitations is what Sir John believes to be the complete disuse of the Marcan source in the so-called 'Great Interpolation', Lk ix. 51–xviii. 14. The second is St. Luke's omission of the well-marked section, Mk vi. 45–viii. 26. The third is not concerned with insertion or omission, but points to a much greater freedom in the use of the fundamental document throughout the last section in which it is employed, the Passion-narrative of Lk xxii. 14–xxiv. 10.

The first of these I should have been inclined to describe as a 'discovery' of Sir John's, if he had not himself pointed out (p. 34) that Mr. F. H. Woods had been to some extent before him; and I think it will be agreed that a strong case is made out for it. The second I am myself inclined to regard as a classical treatment of the subject. But when we come to the third, I should have to express a certain amount of

Introductory (*Essays II, III*)

doubt — not so much as to the main proposition, that in this section the Second Gospel has been used with greater freedom than elsewhere, as with reference to the incidental hypothesis or theory suggested on pp. 90-94.

Sir John explains that his own views have undergone a change in connexion with this head. And, as at present advised, I should be inclined to agree with his earlier views rather than with those which he holds at present. He refers by anticipation to what he conveniently calls 'the three-document hypothesis', which (though under another name) is more fully expounded by Dr. Bartlet. Sir John is inclined to hold aloof from this hypothesis. And I am aware that in this Mr. Streeter is disposed to agree with him—which is rather like a conjunction of ℵ and B. Nevertheless I should (for the present at least) range myself rather with Dr. Bartlet on the other side.

At least I cannot say that the view put forward by Sir John — interesting as it is — carries conviction. Stress is laid upon the fact that St. Luke is described in Philem. 24 as a 'fellow-worker' with St. Paul. It is inferred that he was largely occupied in preaching the Gospel that St. Paul preached. We know that in that Gospel the Crucifixion and the Resurrection held a prominent place; and it is — quite naturally — assumed that they would have an equally prominent place in the preaching of St. Luke. Thus St. Luke would be led to repeat the same story many times, and would be able to set it down in writing from memory, and without much referring to documents.

I must allow myself time to weigh this hypothesis more carefully, and in particular to consider the exact nature of the difference pointed out between the freedom used in this section and in others. But I confess that, at the first blush, the suggestion (for so Sir John himself describes it, p. 94) does not seem to me to account for the phenomena as we find them. The most important features for our purpose are those specially added by St. Luke: such for instance as the charge of forbidding to give tribute to Caesar (Lk xxiii. 2), the trial before Herod, mockery by Herod's soldiers, the reconciliation of Herod and Pilate, the second hearing before Pilate, the address to the Daughters of Jerusalem, the fuller details about the two malefactors, an added name to the mention of the women (xxiv. 10), the walk to Emmaus and what follows. It will be observed at once that these are all historical details, for the most part of secondary importance. Not one among them has any doctrinal significance. In other words, we should say that St. Luke's additions are *narrative for narrative's sake*, not narrative for the sake of doctrine. I am glad to see that Sir John takes note that 'Luke's longest insertion, that relating to the appearance before Herod, must be admitted to have been made by him with no homiletic purpose, but to have been a result of his special interest in, and perhaps connexion with, the Herodian family and household (Lk iii. 1, viii. 3, xxiv. 10; Acts xiii. 1)'. But it is not only 'the longest insertion'; the added details generally are of the same character. And that character would be naturally accounted for if St. Luke had access to some special source of information. They do not seem to deal with the special doctrinal teaching of St. Paul.

Sir John Hawkins's second essay (III) deals with the reconstruction of the second document Q. We have had recently similar reconstructions from such eminent scholars as Wellhausen and Harnack. But I am sure that this very independent and methodical exposition will be welcomed. It has all the peculiar excellence of Sir John's work in the steady progressive advance from the more to the less assured, and the careful discrimination of grades of probability. It is a special pleasure to me to find that Sir John still pleads for the recognition of the connexion between the hypothetical document Q and the *Logia* of Papias;

Introductory (*Essays IV–VIII*)

I am also glad to see the list on pp. 132-4 of passages from a single Gospel which are regarded as having the highest claims to be considered portions of Q. At the head of this list stands the section Mt v. 17-48, followed especially by other portions of the Sermon on the Mount, and of the discourse against the Pharisees. In this estimate I should entirely concur.

It is probably true that the part of the Synoptic Problem which is threshed out most completely in our volume is that which is concerned with the second fundamental document Q. Sir John Hawkins devotes to this some forty-three pages; Mr. Streeter devotes to it in all very nearly seventy pages (besides incidental allusions in Essay VII); Mr. Allen's discussion of the subject extends over fifty-three pages; and the question is also directly contemplated in Dr. Bartlet's essay (XI). I believe there is hardly an aspect of the question that is not considered more or less fully; and I can certainly say for myself that I have never been conscious of having such a complete presentment of it before. The discussions by Sir John Hawkins and Mr. Streeter fall well within the limits of what may be called the view generally current among scholars. The theories of Mr. Allen and Dr. Bartlet fall a little (though in substantial result not very much) outside them. When it is remembered that the essays were written concurrently, and in practical independence of each other, I believe that the outcome will be felt to be satisfactory; and I should not be surprised if the agreement would have been greater still if the writers of the later essays had had the earlier essays before them. For I confess that to myself the earlier group (III–VI) comes with great and cumulative force. If Sir John Hawkins lays the foundation, the fabric erected upon it by Mr. Streeter seems to be very solid and compact, clamped together (I might say) by iron bands throughout its whole extent. I do not think that I need go further into the details of this; I would invite the reader to work through the essays at close quarters for himself.

But I feel it to be at once a duty and a pleasure to call attention to what seems to me to be the remarkable excellence of Mr. Streeter's summarizing essay (VII) on 'The Literary Evolution of the Gospels'. I do not remember to have seen, within anything like the same compass, a picture at once so complete, so sound, and (to my mind) so thoroughly scientific, of the whole course of development in the Apostolic and sub-Apostolic age in its bearing upon literary composition in general and the composition of the Gospels in particular. It is a real evolution, and an evolution conceived as growth, in which each stage springs naturally, spontaneously, and inevitably out of the last. I shall in future always refer to this essay when I desire either to refresh or to correct the picture present to my own mind.

It is not without reluctance that I have come round to the conclusion advocated by Mr. Streeter in Essay V, that St. Mark already possessed a knowledge of Q. This involves the complication, so often laid to the charge of the theory of Dr. Bernhard Weiss, that it implies the use of Q by the later Evangelists twice over, once through the medium of Mark, and a second time independently. This is a complication that one would gladly avoid if one could. But I have for some time had before my mind arguments similar to those put forward by Mr. Streeter, and in the form in which he states them they seem to compel assent. I should also accept the proposition very much in the limited and qualified way in which Mr. Streeter puts it. I do not think that Q was used by St. Mark regularly and systematically, as the later Evangelists used his own narrative; but he must have known of its existence, and reminiscences of it seem to have clung to him and from time to time

Introductory (*Essays IX, X*)

made their way into his text. Allowance should, however, be made for the possibility of what may be called real doublets as well as literary doublets. I believe that similar sayings were spoken by our Lord more than once. For instance, I cannot think that the important discussion about Marriage and Divorce in Mk x. 2–12 merely grew out of the saying probably recorded by Q (Mt v. 32, cf. Lk xvi. 18). I believe that these are distinct sayings spoken on different occasions.

I am altogether glad that our volume includes Mr. Allen's Essay (IX). I think the reader will agree with me that it is an able and independent piece of work. If I venture to express an opinion about it, it must be taken as just an individual opinion and nothing more. As editor, it is my duty to lay what we have done before the public impartially. In that capacity I would invite the reader to judge for himself. But if I am to attempt to describe the effect upon me of Mr. Allen's essay as compared with that of the preceding group upon the same subject, it would be something of this kind. The essay seems to me to state in a fresh and forcible form the objections that may be taken, and that ought to be taken, to the current reconstructions of Q. All advance in knowledge is gained by the patient weighing of arguments *pro* and *con*. It is far better that the arguments on each side should be stated in uncompromising terms. Mr. Allen has done this for the arguments *against* the current view of Q. His arguments happen to be directed more particularly against Harnack, because when he sat down to write Harnack's was the most conspicuous and the best presentment of the current view available. I do not feel called upon to try to strike a balance between the two opposing theories. Before I could do so at all judicially, I should have to read Harnack's book afresh. But in any case it seems to me that Mr. Allen's statement fully deserves attention. It would not, I think, exactly impress one as a last word; but I should say that it was a case that ought to be heard before the last word could be spoken. But as it is, coming to this essay from those which precede it, my impression is that the difficulties raised—and they are all real difficulties—have been met and answered. I give that as my impression for what it is worth. It will be for the reader to verify it, or not, from his own experience.

I ought perhaps to emphasize the distinction, pointed out on p. 242, between the 'Book of Sayings' as reconstructed by Mr. Allen and the Second Source (Q) of Sir John Hawkins and Mr. Streeter. They start from different principles; the former from that of collecting together Sayings as such, the latter from the matter common to St. Matthew and St. Luke that is not found in St. Mark. The principle in the one case turns upon similarity of subject-matter, in the other case upon literary analysis. And yet the final result is not widely different. If the larger conception of Q outlined by Sir John Hawkins on pp. 132 ff. is compared with Mr. Allen's actual reconstruction on pp. 242-72, the principal difference will be the omission of the preliminary matter connected with the preaching of the Baptist, the Baptism, and the Temptation. It must be confessed that it is a natural instinct which led Mr. Allen to omit these as not quite homogeneous with the rest. But we are in danger of judging too much by the standard of our later conception of what constitutes a Gospel. That conception is really derived from St. Mark. But in all probability Q was composed before St. Mark, when the whole idea of written reminiscences of the Life of Christ was still fluid. The difference could not be better expounded than it is by Mr. Streeter on pp. 210-20. In the light of that exposition it seems to me that the prima facie strangeness of the contents

Introductory (*Essay XI*)

of Q disappears. But I do not wish to beg the question. Readers must judge for themselves.

While he was with us, Mr. Allen was always the authority to whom we appealed on any question of Semitic idiom. He was possessed of a special knowledge of Syriac, Aramaic, and Hebrew upon which we did not often draw in vain. It was for this reason that I begged him to contribute an essay on 'The Aramaic Background of the Gospels'; and the result now lies before us. We must leave it for the specialists to judge. But I believe that it will be felt to be at once clear, circumspect, and judicious.

This brings me to another strong and detailed essay, by Dr. Bartlet. Once again, whether Dr. Bartlet's results are accepted or not, I believe it will be felt that the question or group of questions before him has been grappled with earnestly and closely. I spoke above (p. xiii), perhaps rather too loosely, of his theory as though it roughly corresponded with the 'three-document hypothesis' adumbrated by Sir John Hawkins. As a matter of fact Dr. Bartlet does add a third group of written material to the two groups (Mark and Q) of which we have hitherto been speaking. But he himself calls his theory a 'two-document' hypothesis of St. Luke's Gospel alone. He really recasts the conception of Q, and he is not even sure that it ever had a substantive existence in writing (pp. 315 n., 323). The two documents for him are Mark and a somewhat larger 'special source', having already embedded in it the substance of what we have hitherto been describing as Q. It is under this second head that the peculiarities of Dr. Bartlet's conception mostly come. He does not even identify his Q with *Logia*, but regards *Logia* as included in it.

I am a little inclined to regret the use of the symbol Q,

which in the rest of our volume has a fairly fixed connotation, for this comparatively new entity postulated by Dr. Bartlet. The nearest precedent for such a use would I suppose be found in the writings of Dr. Bernhard Weiss. But Dr. Bartlet goes even beyond this precedent, and uses terms in a rather different sense even from Dr. B. Weiss. Both writers speak of the 'Apostolic source or tradition'; but Dr. Bartlet is fond of the phrase 'common or basal apostolic tradition' (pp. 314, 323, 326). Now I believe that when Dr. B. Weiss speaks of the 'Oldest or Apostolic source' he has in his mind the work of St. Matthew apparently referred to by Papias. But I understand that Dr. Bartlet is shy of this identification (p. 362); he seems to mean by Q something like the general Apostolic teaching, defined in particular directions (QM, QMk, QL, *loc. cit.*). But I confess that I could have wished that some other symbol had been chosen.

Speaking for myself, I am inclined to deprecate the whole of this reconstruction. I am well content with the conception of Q as we have it, and as it is defined in the previous essays. I am afraid I do not see that there is any gain in 'simplicity', but rather the contrary.

It is really easy for me to define my own attitude towards Dr. Bartlet's essay. From the part relating to Q I find myself compelled (provisionally at least) to dissent; but in the part relating to the special source of St. Luke (in Dr. Bartlet's notation S), there is a great deal that I cordially welcome. The summary on pp. 350–4 (so far as Q is not involved) seems to me in every way admirable. I am specially glad to see the stress that is laid on the homogeneity of the peculiar matter of St. Luke. I fully believe myself in its Jewish-Christian and strictly Palestinian origin. It seems to me a valuable suggestion that 'S was a peculiar form of written memoirs elicited by our Third Evangelist *ad hoc*, not immediately for the literary

Introductory (*Essay XI*)

purpose to which he finally put it, but rather as a permanent record of the most authentic tradition to which it had been his lot to obtain access, for use in his own work as an evangelist or catechist of the oral Gospel' (p. 351). I can altogether go along with the view that St. Luke probably collected this material during his two years' stay at Caesarea (Acts xxiv. 27, compared with xxi. 17 and xxvii. 1); I could quite believe with Harnack, Mr. Streeter, and Dr. Bartlet that his chief informants were Philip the Evangelist and his four daughters, with perhaps (through them) other members of the Caesarean circle. This hypothesis would I think cover and explain many phenomena both in the Third Gospel and in the Acts. But I agree with Dr. Bartlet that the information derived in this way probably lay before St. Luke in writing. The interval between his stay at Caesarea and the publication of his Gospel can hardly have been less than some fifteen years; and I doubt if the freshness, precision, and individual touches which characterize S could well have been preserved otherwise than by writing.

Over all this ground Dr. Bartlet has in me a wholehearted ally. The only point in regard to S from which I am inclined to dissent is its supposed inclusion of Q material. I am aware that on this head I should have myself to be on the defensive. It has been to me rather strange that so many of the advocates of a special source as underlying the Third Gospel have accepted this inclusion. So Feine, who was the first to put forward the hypothesis of a special source (1891), Johannes Weiss in the eighth edition of Meyer's Commentary (1892), Dr. V. H. Stanton (1909), and now Dr. Bartlet. But I confess that to me this form of the theory seems to defeat a part at least of the object for which it was propounded. There are really two main reasons for believing in a special source to which St. Luke had access and the other Evangelists had not.

One is, to be a receptacle for the greater part of the matter found in this Gospel alone (some of it may be isolated remnants of Q). The reason for believing in a single source is the common character that runs through it. So far all supporters of the theory are agreed. But the second reason—which to my mind is no less important—is to account for the peculiar individualisms of St. Luke in passages common to him especially with St. Matthew. The phenomenon that has to be explained is why some of these parallels (e. g. in the Sermon on the Mount) should be so close, while others are so divergent. Why, in particular, should the two versions of the Beatitudes differ so widely? By far the simplest explanation seems to me to be that, in an instance like this, two of the Evangelist's documents overlapped, and he followed his own document and not the other. It is conceivable that the shape in which the Beatitudes appear in St. Matthew may be partly due to the Evangelist himself. But even so, it is difficult to think that St. Luke was following the same original, though in other parts of the Sermon he pretty certainly was doing so. Everything is clear if we suppose that he had another version before him. But if QL was already part of S he had no such other version. We should have, quite unnecessarily, to push the divergence further back, and to suppose that some previous writer had already compared and combined two distinct traditions. We should have to do this when our object is to economize stages as much as possible. For my own part therefore I believe that St. Luke was the first to carry out the fusion.[1]

It seems to me that the two halves of Dr. Bartlet's argument are separable, and that it is possible to accept the one (the distinction of a special source in St. Luke) without the other (the additional process of a previous

---

[1] This point was made by Mr. C. Badcock at an early stage in our proceedings.

Introductory (*Essay XII*)

fusion of this source with any form of Q). But I have already acknowledged, and I gladly repeat, that on the side on which I differ from him Dr. Bartlet has a considerable body of opinion in his favour. I only cannot help thinking that the broad and simple argument against that particular view is clearer and stronger than any of those that can be adduced for it.

If I were to attempt at this point to sum up the net result for the Synoptic Problem of the investigations contained in this volume, it would be something of this kind. None of the theories propounded—unless it were Mr. Allen's—is (to the best of my belief) in the strict sense new. The positions mainly defended by Sir John Hawkins and Mr. Streeter are held by a considerable majority of scholars. Dr. Bartlet, if he would forbear to press his (as I must needs think) somewhat elusive conception of Q—which has perhaps its nearest approach to support in Dr. A. Wright—would have behind him a compact group of influential names (notably Johannes Weiss and Dr. Stanton). The modification that I should myself desire would, I think, be most nearly in accord with the views of Dr. B. Weiss. This further position, in regard to the special source used by St. Luke, certainly cannot as yet be regarded as established. But I should like to ask whether it is not possible to rally round the clear and sharply drawn definition of Q as it is presented to us in the earlier essays, and so pass on to the closer testing of the supplementary hypothesis of St. Luke's special source.

These conclusions, or steps towards conclusions, are all concerned with main branches of the problem. Archdeacon Allen's second essay (X) and the essays of Mr. Addis and Mr. N. P. Williams (XII and XIII) might be called subsidiary to the main problem. They have to do with portions of the problem that are capable of being isolated from the rest. We were glad to avail ourselves of the special knowledge of Mr. Allen, and in like manner we had recourse to the experience in another field of Mr. Addis. His *Documents of the Hexateuch* in two volumes (1892 and 1898) is a standard work upon the subject; and Mr. Addis in his essay gives us the benefit of his previous studies. I believe it will be felt that in doing so he has cleared up not a little popular misconception. We are brought fully abreast of modern knowledge in relation to the Hexateuch, and the degree to which the literary analysis of the one set of documents furnishes a parallel for that of the other is accurately defined. It is true that Mr. Addis takes a wider range than most of the other essayists, and enters into historical as well as literary questions; but his treatment of both subjects will be interesting to many readers. He refers (pp. 375 ff.) to a doubt expressed by Sir W. M. Ramsay as to the results of the process of literary analysis. Mr. Addis discusses the validity of these doubts in their bearing upon the Pentateuch and Hexateuch; and I may take the opportunity of confirming what he there says with reference to the Synoptic Gospels. I do not think that we have really had any hesitation on this head in the Seminar. On the contrary, I believe that the longer we have worked at the subject and tested our methods, the greater is our confidence in them within the limits to which they are legitimately applicable. No one has had a more constant eye to those limits than Sir John Hawkins, and yet the sureness of touch which distinguishes his essays and the two editions of *Horae Synopticae* after some sixteen years of steady and unremitting work speaks for itself. I believe that we should all share in the same confidence, each within his measure.

The last essay, by Mr. N. P. Williams, pushes rather

Introductory (Essay XIII)

further than had been done in the body of the book the question as to the unity of the Second Gospel—the question, that is, how far it may be presumed to be the work of the same author at the same time, or how far it may be possible to trace different and successive stages in its composition. Mr. Williams, as coming to his task with a shorter experience than his colleagues, naturally preferred to limit his subject by treating it with reference to a single typical example of the kind of theory that had to be considered. The theory chosen for examination was that of E. Wendling in his shorter pamphlet *Urmarcus* (1905) and his longer work *Die Entstehung des Marcusevangeliums* (1908). Mr. Williams has expounded the theory with much lucidity, and with a fullness that will be welcome to those who desire to have the opportunity of testing it for themselves. I, for one, cannot help agreeing with the general impression that the grounds on which any such 'three-stratum hypothesis' can be made to rest are highly subjective and precarious. Mr. Williams himself reduces the theory to very modest dimensions. He thinks that two sections, Mk vi. 45–viii. 26 and ch. xiii, may have been added to the Gospel in a second or third edition, perhaps by St. Mark himself. On both points he would have the weighty support of Dr. V. H. Stanton. For myself, I doubt whether the Gospel was ever issued without these sections; and that mainly for this reason. It seems to me that the argument of Sir John Hawkins (pp. 61–74 *inf.*) at once proves as conclusively as we can expect the Marcan origin of the section vi. 45–viii. 26, and suggests probable reasons for its omission by St. Luke. But if the section was added to the Gospel, even by St. Mark himself, it must have been so added between the point at which the Gospel was used by St. Luke and that at which it was used by the editor whom we call St. Matthew. According to the hypothesis it was still absent from the copy which lay before the one Evangelist and present in that which lay before the other. And yet these two copies closely resembled each other, and were already some degrees removed from the autograph (see pp. 21–3). In other words, we shall be driving a wedge in the history of the text just where a wedge is not wanted.

The Appendix is really an additional essay, contributed by Mr. Streeter after the rest of the book was in pages. It may be interesting to compare it with a volume recently issued by Prof. E. von Dobschütz of Strassburg, *The Eschatology of the Gospels* (London, 1910). This volume, which is a reprint of a Congress paper and of four articles published in *The Expositor*, covers much the same ground with Mr. Streeter's essay and presents considerable similarity of treatment, though the two were quite independent of each other. Prof. von Dobschütz does not exactly note the progressive development pointed out by Mr. Streeter, but comes very near doing so; and the two writers will, I think, be found to be in substantial agreement.

It should be said that the Indexes are the work of the Rev. D. C. Simpson, Lecturer at St. Edmund Hall, who takes an active part in our work. We are indebted to Herr Alphons Dürr of Leipzig for permission to reproduce the photograph which serves as frontispiece; it is taken from the volume entitled *Die Trierer Ada-Handschrift*, mentioned on p. 18.

It may perhaps be thought that I have written a little too freely about the work of my colleagues in this volume. I feel sure that they at least will forgive me. For what I have written has been only as it were in continuation of the spirit which has animated all our discussions. We have been accustomed to a sort of running debate; and just as the several essayists have taken advantage of this opportunity to bring to a head views which they have formed in the course of that debate, so also have I ventured to bring to a head such general conclusions as suggest themselves to me, to go forth along with the work in which we have been engaged together and to share in its fortunes.

W. SANDAY.

OXFORD,
September, 1910.

I

THE CONDITIONS UNDER WHICH THE GOSPELS WERE WRITTEN, IN THEIR BEARING UPON SOME DIFFICULTIES OF THE SYNOPTIC PROBLEM

Rev. WILLIAM SANDAY, D.D.
LL.D., Litt. D.; F.B.A.

Lady Margaret Professor of Divinity and Canon of Christ Church
Chaplain in Ordinary to H.M. the King

SYLLABUS.

Presuppositions of the Inquiry.

I. *Characteristic forms of difference between the First Three Gospels.*

Examples.

1. General problem raised by these.
2. Particular problems.
   (*a*) Secondary or divergent features in Mk.
   (*b*) Omissions in Lk.

II. *Conditions under which the Synoptic Gospels were written.*

1. Psychological conditions.
   (i) The Evangelists are not copyists but historians.
   (ii) And yet the Gospels are not exactly histories.
2. External conditions.
   (i) The writing and use of books, in their bearing upon freedom of reproduction.
   (ii) The copying and transmission of texts, in their bearing upon
       (*a*) the agreements of Mt Lk against Mk.
       (*b*) the omission by St. Luke of Mk vi. 45–viii. 26.

THE CONDITIONS UNDER WHICH THE GOSPELS WERE WRITTEN, IN THEIR BEARING UPON SOME DIFFICULTIES OF THE SYNOPTIC PROBLEM

WE assume what is commonly known as the 'Two-Document Hypothesis'. We assume that the marked resemblances between the first Three Gospels are due to the use of common documents, and that the fundamental documents are two in number: (1) a complete Gospel practically identical with our St. Mark, which was used by the Evangelists whom we know as St. Matthew and St. Luke; and (2) a collection consisting mainly but not entirely of discourses, which may perhaps have been known to, but was probably not systematically used by St. Mark, but which supplied the groundwork of certain common matter in St. Matthew and St. Luke.

The first document contains 661 verses, the length of our St. Mark in the Revised Text. We can measure this exactly, because the document itself has come down to us as our Second Gospel. All but at most some 50 verses, out of 661, have been actually incorporated in the other two Gospels. The other document we cannot measure exactly, because in its original form it has perished. We may take provisionally the estimate of Sir John Hawkins (*Hor. Synopt.*[2], p. 110), who assigns to this document some 191 (or 218) verses of St. Matthew and 181 (or 208) verses of St. Luke. For the purpose of this essay it is indifferent whether we accept this reconstruction of the document or the alternative put forward by Mr. W. C. Allen in the present volume (Essay IX). I also keep an open mind as to the possibility of to some extent combining the two theories by adding to the common matter of St. Matthew and St. Luke some of the sections peculiar to the First Gospel, which may have been omitted by the author of the Third. The common matter of Matthew and Luke is a fixed nucleus in both theories, though the nature and history of the document are differently conceived. We call the second document in Sir John Hawkins's reconstruction (which is shared by many other scholars) Q; in Mr. Allen's special reconstruction we shall perhaps do well to call it L. But, as I have said, for the purpose of this essay the distinction need not be considered.

The above may be taken as a rough outline of the documentary theory of the origin of the Synoptic Gospels.

It will be obvious that this theory explains easily and naturally the multitude of resemblances which the Three Gospels present to each other. But after all this is only half the problem. The real difficulty of the Synoptic Problem arises, not from the resemblances only, nor yet from the differences only, but from the remarkable combination and alternation of resemblance and difference. The strong point of the documentary theory is the satisfactory way in which it accounts for the resemblances; its weak point—or at least the point at which the strain upon it is most felt—is when we come to deal with the differences. And the main purpose of the present essay is to suggest that in the particular direction which I am going to follow is to be found the simplest and most satisfactory solution of a group of difficulties which on a comparison of the Three Gospels are raised by the points in which they differ.

The opposite of a documentary theory of the origin of the First Three Gospels would be an oral theory: in other words, the view that our Gospels as we have them are not based upon earlier written documents, but that until the time at which they were committed to writing the substance of them had been transmitted orally.

I. Conditions under which Gospels were written

Now, just as it is the strong point of the documentary theory to account for agreements, so also is it the strong point of the oral theory to account for differences. And it is true that the differences between the Three Gospels are of such a kind as to suggest oral transmission. This has been hitherto the chief stumbling-block in the way of the acceptance of the documentary hypothesis. And it is a testimony to the strength of the arguments for the use of written materials that the majority of scholars accept that use in spite of all apparent indications to the contrary. It is, however, not enough to do this; we cannot really rest until all the phenomena are accounted for, not one set alone but both sets, however much they may seem to be opposed.

Our first duty, then, will be to try to form an idea of the nature of the differences which subsist between the Gospels. When we have done this, we may go on to consider how they may best be explained.

I. THE CHARACTERISTIC FORMS OF DIFFERENCE BETWEEN THE FIRST THREE GOSPELS.

No one has described more exactly or classified more successfully these phenomena of difference than Sir John C. Hawkins (*Horae Synopticae*², pp. 67–80), and I shall use his data freely in what follows. The most significant cases of difference are not those in which the divergence is complete, but those in which it is only partial. Sir John points out that 'we not infrequently find the same, or closely similar, words used with different applications or in different connexions, where the passages containing them are evidently parallel'. And then he naturally and rightly remarks that it is not at all difficult to see how variations such as these might have arisen in the course of oral transmission. Particular words 'might linger in the memory, while their position in a sentence was forgotten: and in some cases they might become confused with other words of similar sound'.

The kind of facts that we meet with are these.

i. **The same or similar words are used in different senses or with a different reference.**

For instance: In Mk xi. 3 (corrected text) the two disciples who are sent on before to fetch the ass which our Lord was to ride on His entry into Jerusalem are told that, if they are questioned as to what they are doing, they are to answer, 'The Lord hath need of him; and straightway he will send him back hither': meaning that the ass would very soon be returned. In Mt xxi. 3 the version is, 'The Lord hath need of them (i.e. the ass and the colt): and straightway he (i.e. the owner) will send them': meaning that the owner would at once let them go. In the one case it is the Lord who will send the ass back: in the other case it is the owner who will send the ass[es] without delay.

In Mk iv. 19 there are the words εἰσπορευόμεναι, 'entering in,' and συμπνίγουσι, 'choke': 'the cares of the world ... entering in choke the word' (cf. Mt xiii. 22 sing.). In Lk viii. 14 the same words are used of the men represented by the seed sown among thorns: these as they go on their way i.e. in course of time—συμπνίγονται, 'are choked' by the cares.

In Mk xii. 20 the word ἀφῆκεν is used of the woman married to seven brothers, the husband dying '*leaves* no seed'; in Mt xxii. 25 the husband, having no seed, ' leaves' his wife.

ii. **Sometimes the same or similar words are assigned to different speakers.**

For instance: In Mk vi. 14, Mt xiv. 2, Herod himself says that John the Baptist was risen from the dead; in Lk ix. 7 others say it in his hearing.

In Mk x. 21 Jesus says to the young ruler, 'One thing thou lackest' (ἕν σε ὑστερεῖ: cf. Lk xviii. 22 ἔτι ἕν σοι λείπει); in Mt xix. 20 the ruler puts it as a question, 'What do I lack?' (τί ἔτι ὑστερῶ;).

In Mk xv. 36 it is the man who offers our Lord the sponge soaked in vinegar who says 'Let be; let us see

I. Conditions under which Gospels were written

whether Elijah cometh to take him down'; in Mt xxvii. 49 it is not the man who says this, but the crowd of bystanders.

iii. **In one Gospel we sometimes have in the form of a speech what in another is part of the narrative, and in one Gospel we have a question where in another there is a direct statement.**

For instance: In Mk v. 30 the Evangelist writes, 'And straightway Jesus, perceiving in himself that the power proceeding from him had gone forth, turned him about in the crowd, and said, Who touched my garments?' In Lk viii. 46 Jesus says, 'Some one did touch me: for I perceived that power had gone forth from me.'

In Mk xiv. 1 the Evangelist states that 'after two days was the feast of the passover', whereas in Mt xxiv. 1, 2 Jesus says to His disciples, 'Ye know that after two days the passover cometh.'

In Mk xiv. 49 'This is done that the scriptures might be fulfilled' are words of Christ; in Mt xxvi. 56 it is a comment of the Evangelist's.

The question in Mk iv. 21, 'Is the lamp brought to be put under the bushel?' becomes in Lk viii. 16 the statement 'And no man, when he hath lighted a lamp, covereth it with a vessel'.

The question (Mk vi. 37), 'Shall we go and buy two hundred pennyworth of bread, and give them to eat?' disappears in the condensed paraphrase of the other Gospels, and is fused with the previous suggestion 'Send them away, that they may ... buy themselves somewhat to eat'.

Mk viii. 12, 'Why doth this generation seek a sign? verily I say unto you, There shall no sign be given unto this generation,' corresponds to Mt xvi. 4, 'An evil and adulterous generation seeketh after a sign; and there shall no sign be given unto it, but the sign of Jonah.' But the Matthaean version is really a conflation of two distinct documents.

iv. **Other conspicuous examples of diverse application.**

In Mt iii. 5, 'All the region round about Jordan' (i.e. the inhabitants of the region) went out to Jesus; in Lk iii. 3 Jesus ' came into all the region round about Jordan'.

In Mk vi. 19, 20 Herodias desired to kill John but could

not, because Herod feared him; in Mt xiv. 5 Herod desired to kill John but feared the multitude.

In Mk vi. 3 we read, 'Is not this the carpenter, the son of Mary?' In Mt xiii. 55 'Is not this the carpenter's son? Is not his mother called Mary?'

In Mk x. 18 (= Lk viii. 19), 'Why callest thou me good?' becomes in the best text of Mt xix. 17 'Why asketh thou me concerning that which is good?' The Marcan version is undoubtedly the more original; the Matthaean appears to be due to the First Evangelist.

v. **A special class of variations is formed by the cases of inversion of order, which are somewhat frequent.**

For instance: In Mt iv. 5-10, Lk iv. 5-12, there is a transposition of the second and third Temptations, the pinnacle of the temple and the high mountain.

Mt xii. 41, 42, Lk xi. 31, 32: 'The men of Nineveh' and the 'queen of the south' change places.

In the most probable text of Lk xxii. 17-19, the Cup is represented as given before the Bread, and not as in Mt, Mk.

On transpositions in general see especially Mr. Streeter in Essay IV.

The above are all examples—many of them striking examples—of the freedom with which the Evangelists reproduced the matter that lay before them. In all the cases in which Mk is involved we believe his version to be the original, and the variants in the other Gospels are deviations from the original. And these deviations are so free that we cannot be surprised if they have been often thought to point to oral transmission. It is true that they do point to just that kind of unconscious or semi-conscious mental action—lapses of memory, rearrangement of details, and the like—which is characteristic of oral transmission. But it would, I think, be a mistake to draw from these data the sweeping inference that, prior to our present Gospels, the substance of their contents had been transmitted not otherwise than orally. The conclusion would be too large for the premises. We shall see presently what I believe to be

I. Conditions under which Gospels were written

the right conclusion. In the meantime we will note these examples of free reproduction as a difficulty in the way of the Two-Document hypothesis with which we started. In any case they are phenomena which, upon that hypothesis, require to be satisfactorily accounted for.

And then, besides this general difficulty, there are two particular difficulties, which also appear to conflict with the hypothesis.

(*a*) The first is the problem of *secondary or divergent features in Mk.*

For a long time past the existence of these features has been a leading *crux* of the Synoptic Problem. It is very generally agreed that the 'most assured result' of the investigations which have been going on for the best part of a century, and with concentrated energy for the last fifty or sixty years, has been the proof of what is commonly called 'the priority of St. Mark'; in other words, the proof that our St. Mark actually lay before the authors of the First and Third Gospels and was used by them in the construction of their own works. The assumption that this was the case explains the whole phenomena far better than any other hypothesis that has been suggested.

At the same time it must not be thought that the phenomena are perfectly homogeneous. There is a great preponderance of data pointing towards the conclusion just stated; but, after all, it is a *preponderance* of evidence and not a compact mass of details pointing all the same way. There still remains a residuum of cases in which the usual relation of the documents to each other is not sustained. And this residuum of cases it is which constitutes the difficulty of which I am speaking.

In the first place there are a few rather prominent examples in which the text of St. Mark as we have it does not appear to be prior to that of one or both of the two companion Gospels.

For instance, the saying 'I was not sent but unto the lost sheep of the house of Israel' (Mt xv. 24) has nothing corresponding to it in Mk; and yet on internal grounds the presumption would be strongly in favour of its genuineness. In other respects, too, the section in which these words occur is somewhat peculiar.

Again, in Mt xxiv. 29, '*Immediately* after the tribulation of those days,' the word 'immediately' is not found in the parallel text Mk xiii. 24; and yet we may be pretty sure that it is original, because it would seem to be contradicted by the event.

But, apart from these few and rather special cases, there are a number of expressions in which the two presumably later Gospels (Mt, Lk) combine together against the presumably earlier (Mk). This inverts the usual relationship, and may well seem at first sight to be inconsistent with the priority of Mk altogether.

Sir John Hawkins (*Hor. Syn.*², p. 210 f.) has collected twenty or twenty-one rather notable examples of this phenomenon; and Dr. E. A. Abbott has printed in full the whole collection, numbering in all about 230 examples, as an appendix to his book *The Corrections of St. Mark* (*Diatessarica*, Part II), London, 1901. These lists, especially the longer, are perhaps subject to some deductions, of which we shall speak later. But in any case the instances are too numerous to be entirely the result of accident.

(*b*) Another question arises as to *omissions*.

In particular, why has St. Luke omitted a rather long section of St. Mark (Mk vi. 45-viii. 26)? A common view is that this section is omitted by St. Luke because it contains duplicates—a second Feeding, a second Storm at Sea—as well as in part discussions (like that about eating with unwashen hands) which would not interest St. Luke's Gentile readers. Dr. Plummer (*Comm. on St. Luke*, p. xxxviii) notes in reply to the first point that there are various places in which St. Luke has not avoided duplicates, so that some further explanation seems to be required.

I. *Conditions under which Gospels were written*

These still outstanding difficulties of the Synoptic Problem, and more particularly of the Two-Document hypothesis, have been described so far in a way that is of course quite summary. We will try to state them with a little more precision before we have done. I would only ask the reader to bear in mind the general character of these difficulties, in order that he may be in a position to judge how far the explanations which are about to be offered can really be said to meet them.

I would venture to lay it down that explanations, in order to be satisfactory, should be simple. And the chief recommendation of those which I am going to submit is that they are, I hope, both simple and real—*verae causae*, not drawn from a state of things that is purely imaginary, but from the actual conditions under which we have strong reason to believe that the Gospels were written.

When we speak of 'conditions' we have in view conditions of two kinds: (1) those consisting in the mental or psychological attitude of the writer towards his task; and (2) those consisting in the external circumstances in which his task had to be discharged.

II. THE CONDITIONS UNDER WHICH THE SYNOPTIC GOSPELS WERE WRITTEN.

(1) **Psychological Conditions.**

We are concerned at present, not with the individual Evangelists, but with the Evangelists as a class. The characteristics of the individual writers will come up for consideration in other parts of this volume (see especially Essay VII, by Mr. B. H. Streeter). Our present inquiry has to do with the Gospels, and more particularly the Synoptic Gospels, as a group by themselves. And our first duty is to correct an impression that may easily be formed in regard to this group.

We are so accustomed to a close comparison of the Synoptic texts, and those texts do in fact often present so close a resemblance to each other, that we are apt to think of the writers as though they were simply transcribing the documents which lay before them. But that was not the way in which they thought of themselves.

(i) *The Evangelists are not copyists but historians.*

The Evangelists thought of themselves not merely as copyists but as historians. They are not unconscious of a certain dignity in their calling. They are something more than scribes, tied down to the text which they have before them. They considered themselves entitled to reproduce it freely and not slavishly. They do not hesitate to tell the story over again in their own words.

At the same time, when we describe them as historians, we must think of them as belonging to a naïve and not very highly developed literary type. Historical writing varies according to the scale on which it is planned and the complexity of the authorities of which it takes account. We must put aside altogether an ideal constructed in view of the abundant materials of modern times. More often than not an Evangelist would only have a single authority before him. We may believe that the author of the Fourth Gospel was acquainted with the works of all his predecessors, though he did not deliberately base his own work upon theirs, and though his attitude towards them was quite independent. But the Gospel of St. Mark was a first attempt in its own particular kind. In this case we may believe that the writer knew of the existence of a previous document (Q), and allowed his work to be in some degree shaped by this knowledge. This seems to be the best way of explaining the comparatively summary character of the opening paragraphs; and it would also account for the preponderance of narrative over discourse—if the earlier

I. Conditions under which Gospels were written

document consisted mainly of discourse, the later writer would naturally wish to supplement its contents rather than to repeat them. There is reason to think that the tradition is true which represents him as deriving his own material chiefly from the public preaching of St. Peter. Besides this, he would doubtless be affected by the body of floating tradition which circulated amongst all the greater Churches. This tradition would be for the most part oral; whether St. Mark made use of any written document may remain, at least for our present purpose, an open question (see Essay XIII, by Mr. N. P. Williams). In the case of St. Matthew (i.e. our present First Gospel), the two chief constituent elements are St. Mark's Gospel and Q. These sometimes overlap each other, with the effect of producing the phenomenon known as 'Doublets' (on which see Sir John Hawkins, *Hor. Synopt.*^{2}, pp. 80–107). If any further written sources need be assumed in addition to these, they were probably not extensive. If we study the First Evangelist's treatment of St. Mark, it resolves itself for the most part into (*a*) free rearrangement for the sake of effectiveness of teaching, and (*b*) simple abridgement. St. Luke has rather more peculiar matter, and with him the peculiar matter is rather more considerable and rather more important. As an historical work his Gospel is a degree more elaborate than those of his companions. Accordingly, there is perhaps in his case a little more of the blending or fusion of different authorities. He has a somewhat higher ambition in the matter of style. In a word, he approximates rather more nearly to the ancient secular historian; and he shows that he is conscious of doing so, partly by the language of his preface, and partly by such features of his Gospel as his attempts to connect the events which he narrates with the larger framework of the world's history (Lk ii. 1, 2, iii. 1, 2, &c.). In this respect, however, he should not be judged by too severe a standard. He had not the advantages that (e. g.) Josephus had, of living at the centre of the empire, in personal intercourse with the court, and with access to the best authorities. Even with the help of public inscriptions and the like, it cannot have been an easy matter for a provincial like St. Luke to fix exact synchronisms. It is something to be able to say that in recent years, especially through the investigations and influence of Sir W. M. Ramsay, his credit has steadily risen.

(ii) *And yet the Gospels are not exactly histories.*

St. Luke is thus most nearly akin to the secular historians. It was very much their ideals which guided his hand. But even he to some extent, and his companions still more, had a further object in view. They were not content to narrate facts simply as facts. They all three—or we may say all four, for the statement is true most conspicuously and avowedly of the Fourth Gospel (Jn xx. 31)—had an eye not only to the facts but to something to be believed as growing out of the facts. Even St. Luke has an eye to this retrospectively; he writes to strengthen the confidence of his patron Theophilus in the truths in which he had been instructed. St. Mark indicates his object when he calls his work 'the gospel of Jesus Christ, the Son of God'; and this would still hold good, even if with a small but early group of textual authorities (ℵ*, Iren. 1/3 Orig. *pluries* Bas.) we were to omit the last clause, which only defines more explicitly the meaning of that which precedes; 'the gospel of Jesus Christ' is the good news of One who is believed in as Son of God. St. Matthew indicates his object when he so frequently points out the fulfilment of ancient prophecy. The purpose of the Evangelists is thus in part homiletic, though it is embodied in an historical form, and though the story is left as a rule to have its own effect.

I refer to the point here, chiefly in order to give a

I. *Conditions under which Gospels were written*

complete and not misleading impression of the frame of mind in which the Evangelists approached their task. For the more immediate bearings of this essay, it is of less importance. Our direct concern is with the difficulties of the Synoptic Problem; and in regard to these, the attitude of the writers comes in as a determining factor so far as it explains the nature and degree of the freedom with which they reproduced their documents. What has been said will perhaps go some way to explain this freedom. It shows us the Evangelists, not as painfully transcribing the older texts on which they relied (such as Mk and Q), or feeling themselves in any way called upon to reproduce them verbally, but as setting to work in a spirit independent and yet on the whole faithful, not punctilious and yet not wilfully capricious and erratic, content to tell their story very much as it came, sometimes in the words of their predecessors and sometimes in their own. This is the kind of picture that we should be led to form for ourselves from a combined study of the antecedent probabilities of the case and of the facts as we have them. It happens that we are in an exceptionally favourable position for this part of our inquiry. For the whole of the Triple Synopsis all three documents are extant—not only the two later Gospels, but the original which the writers worked up into their own compositions; so that we can see exactly what changes they introduced and in most cases can form a shrewd guess as to the reason which led to their introduction. In the net result the Evangelists come out as very human, not as actuated by the Machiavellian motives which at one time it was the fashion to attribute to them, as neither pedants nor yet wantonly careless, influenced a little by their wishes and their feelings, but not to such an extent as seriously to affect their credit. The examples given above of the degree of freedom which they allowed themselves are in this sense extreme that they are at least selected from among the more striking of their kind; and the reader will be able to judge for himself how far the general estimate based upon them is justified.

We have, however, as yet only considered one half of our problem. We must go on to the other half; and, if I am not mistaken, we shall find our results confirmed from another side or sides.

(2) **External Conditions.**

(i) *The writing and use of books, in their bearing upon freedom of reproduction.*

We have had to correct one impression which the inexperienced student may unconsciously or semi-consciously form for himself; and now we shall have to correct another impression of the same kind. When we think of composing a book, and still more when we think of compiling a book in the way in which the later Gospels at least were compiled, it is natural to us to picture to ourselves the author as sitting at a table with the materials of which he is going to make use spread out before him, his own book in which he is writing directly in front of him, and the other writings a little further away in a semicircle, each kept open at the place where it is likely to be wanted; so that the author only has to lift his eyes from his manuscript as he writes to his copy, and to transfer the contents from its pages to his own. In such a case it would be only natural to reproduce what lay before the eye with a considerable degree of accuracy. But it happens that this picture, if it were applied to the writing of the Gospels, would be in almost every feature wrong.

The ancients had tables, but they did not use them for the same miscellaneous purposes that we do. They used them for eating; they used them as a stand for vases or statuary; they used them for paying out money. But

I. Conditions under which Gospels were written

I am not aware of any evidence that they were used for other purposes than these.[1]

The ancients had books; but they were not *at this time* (i.e. when the Gospels were composed) like our own books. They were rolls, and rather lengthy rolls, with the writing in short vertical columns across them, as a rule less than a foot high. They were therefore rather cumbrous, and not quite easy to keep open at a particular place. Again, I am not aware of a single representation of the book-roll so kept open. There are many representations of a writer or student making use of books (i.e. of rolls); but to the best of my belief these are always, or almost always, contained in a sort of round canister (*capsa*) or square box (*scrinium*) which stands upon the ground.[2] Birt lays this down as the all but universal rule (op. cit., p. 254), and the exceptions which he notes are hardly exceptions. Under such conditions it is not at all likely that the roll would be taken out and referred to more often than could be helped.

The ancients had desks; but they were not like our desks on a writing table. They were quite small, like the reading desks that we attach to the arm of an armchair. As a rule they are affixed to a raised stand, which is independent of other furniture. Sometimes the writer sits at such a desk, more especially in the later examples from the fourth century onwards, when the *codex*, or book proper, had

---

[1] Cf. Th. Birt, *Die Buchrolle in der Kunst* (Leipzig, 1907), p. 2. Perhaps as the facts stated in this essay coincide closely with those given in Birt's excellent volume, it may be right to say that the rough draft of the essay was written some years before the book appeared, but of course with help from Birt's older work, *Das antike Buchwesen* (Berlin, 1882), and Wattenbach's *Schriftwesen im Mittelalter*[3] (Leipzig, 1896); also from Dr. Kenyon's *Handbook to the Textual Criticism of the N. T.* (1901), *Palaeography of Greek Papyri* (1899), and other recent literature. But I have been glad to introduce a few illustrations from Birt's new book, which is the most complete and detailed.

[2] 'In allen Darstellungen, die wir kennen gelernt, steht die Buchschachtel am Boden.'

superseded the roll. But in the earlier examples the writer is usually represented with the roll open simply upon his knees. So Virgil (*ap.* Birt, p. 178), who, however, is not writing but only holding a roll and has a desk at his side. So, more distinctly, an Evangelist in Pal. Soc., ser. I, pl. 44 (where the book is a *codex*). There are several examples of Evangelists at work in Beissel's *Vaticanische Miniaturen*, 1893 (pll. v, ix, x, xi); and more in the sumptuous reproduction of the copy of the Gospels written for Ada, sister of Charles the Great (*Die Trierer Ada-Handschrift*, 1889, pll. 10, 15, 16, 17, 20, 23, 26, 29, 32, 33, 36). Plate 23 of this work, from an Evangeliarium in the Domschatz at Aachen, is reproduced as a frontispiece to the present book.

What is the effect of all this on the problem more immediately before us? It enables us, I think, to realize more exactly the process involved in the construction of a narrative on the basis of older materials. A modern, if he were doing this, would have the document he was using constantly under his eye. There would be hardly any interval of time between the perusal of its text and the reproduction of it in writing. The copy would be followed clause by clause and almost word by word. Given physical accuracy of sight and an average power of attention, the rest of the process would be almost mechanical. With the ancient writer it would be otherwise. He would not have his copy before him, but would consult it from time to time. He would not follow it clause by clause and phrase by phrase, but would probably read through a whole paragraph at once, and trust to his memory to convey the substance of it safely from the one book to the other.

We see here where the opening for looseness of reproduction comes in. There is a substantial interval between reading and writing. During that interval the copy is not before the eye, and in the meantime the brain is actively, though unconsciously, at work. Hence all those slight

I. *Conditions under which Gospels were written*

rearrangements and substitutions which are a marked feature in our texts as we have them. Hence, in a word, all those phenomena which simulate oral transmission. There is a real interval during which the paragraph of text is carried in the mind, though not a long one. The question may be not one of hours or days but only of minutes. We cannot indeed lay down a rigid rule to which all use of books would strictly conform. We must leave a margin for the habits of the particular writer. One man would trust his memory, and run the risk of trusting his memory, for a longer period than another. All we need assume is that there would be some interval, some period; enough to account for, or to help to account for, the phenomena of free reproduction which, as a matter of fact, we find. The cause we are considering is elastic within certain limits. I believe that it will be found to meet all that we want.

The phenomena of variation (as between Mk and the succeeding Gospels) in the texts that have come down to us do not require for their explanation any prolonged extension of time or diffused circulation in space; they might be described in homely phrase as just so many 'slips between the cup and the lip'.

(ii) *The copying and transmission of texts, in their bearing upon (a) the agreements of Mt Lk against Mk.*

The question as to the agreements of Mt Lk against Mk in the Triple Synopsis takes us into another region, but still a region connected with the production and transmission of books.

This question of the coincidences between Mt Lk in places where Mk is extant is of great importance. There is a complete collection of these coincidences at the end of Dr. E. A. Abbott's *Corrections of Mark* (London, 1901) which is a valuable basis for study. It has been already said that the examples (many of them simple, but many also complex) given by Dr. Abbott number in all about 230. These examples, as constituting a problem in regard to the relation between Mk and his successors, are doubtless subject to some reduction. It may be questioned whether in all the cases the writers are even professing to reproduce the same text.

Mr. C. H. Turner has recently called attention (in *Journ. of Theol. Studies* for January, 1909, pp. 175 ff.) to two other causes which will account for some of the examples besides that of which we are about to speak. It might well be thought that some of the agreements are so slight and easy to account for that they might be set down as accidental, that they are obvious corrections of St. Mark arising in each of the two later Gospels independently of each other. And then, allowance may also be made for the possibility (on which Mr. Turner specially enlarges) that we have not yet got back to the true text of one or other of the Gospels, and that when we have done so, the double coincidence against St. Mark will be found to disappear. Besides these, there is yet a third cause to which I should be inclined to ascribe some of the most complex of the examples noted by Dr. Abbott. The later Evangelists certainly used St. Mark; but they also used the second document Q; and I suspect that in some of the cases there has been an overlapping of the two documents. This overlapping of documents is a phenomenon that certainly happened sometimes. It is by means of it that I should account for some cases of marked divergence between Mt and Lk in places where both Evangelists were using Q. The simplest way of explaining the divergence (as compared with the no less marked identity in other places) is to suppose that the same passage occurred not only in Q but in St. Luke's special source (or in one of his sources) in a somewhat different form. St. Luke will then have preferred the form in his own source to that of Q. A conspicuous example

I. *Conditions under which Gospels were written*

would be the treatment of the Beatitudes. The same sort of thing may well have happened in the case of the parallels to Mk iii. 19–21, 23–26; iv. 30–32; vi. 7–13, 31–34; viii. 12, 29; ix. 19, and a few others.

But I believe that by far the greater number of the coincidences of Mt Lk against Mk are due to the use by Mt Lk—not of an *Ur-Marcus* or older form of the Gospel, but —*of a recension of the text of Mk different from that from which all the extant MSS. of the Gospel are descended.*

I reject the idea of an *Ur-Marcus*, or older form of the Gospel, because the great majority of the coincidences seem to me to belong to a later form of text rather than an earlier. And I call this form of text a recension, because there is so much method and system about it that it looks like the deliberate work of a particular editor, or scribe exercising to some extent editorial functions.

This appears to come out clearly from Dr. Abbott's classification of the corrections. We may give this in Dr. Abbott's own words:—

> They are, almost entirely, just such modifications of Mark's text as might be expected from a Corrector desirous of improving style and removing obscurities.
>
> (i) In about twelve instances Matthew and Luke adopt corrections defining subject or object. For example, where Mark omits the subject (leaving it to be understood as 'they', 'people', &c.) Matthew and Luke supply 'the disciples', &c. . . .
>
> (ii) In about fifteen instances they correct in Mark the abrupt construction caused by the absence of a connecting word. . . .
>
> (iii) In about thirteen instances they correct Mark's historic present. This number does not include the corrections of Mark's use of 'says' applied to Jesus (see (v)).
>
> (iv) In about twelve instances they substitute the participle (e.g. 'saying') for the indicative with 'and' (e.g. 'and he says'), or for the relative and for the subjunctive, e.g. 'whosoever has', which is changed to 'those having', &c.
>
> (v) In about twenty-three instances they substitute for

Mark's 'says (λέγει)' the word 'said (εἶπεν)', or correct Mark's imperfect 'used to say' or 'began to say' (ἔλεγεν, more rarely ἤρξατο λέγειν). . . .

(vi) In at least thirty instances Matthew and Luke agree in adopting the idiomatic Greek connecting particle (δέ)—commonly and necessarily (though most inadequately) rendered by the English 'but'—instead of the literal translation of the Hebrew 'and', i.e. καί . . . .

(vii) Another class of corrections includes improvement of Greek construction or style, by softening abruptness, of a different kind from that mentioned above . . . changing interrogatives into statements, introducing μέν . . . δέ, ἀλλά, or other particles, and altering Hebraic or vernacular words or phrases. In a few instances the correction may be made in the interests of seemliness, rather than of style. . . .

(viii) In some cases, and notably in the use of the exclamatory 'behold', Matthew and Luke appear to agree in returning to the Hebrew original (*op. cit.*, pp. 300-304).

The number and the recurrence of these phenomena is evidently due to design, and not to accident. What appears to have happened is something of this kind. Neither our present Gospel, even in the best text, nor the copies used by St. Matthew and St. Luke were exactly what St. Mark wrote. All our extant copies, whether of the Received Text or of those constructed upon the most highly critical principles, are descended from a single copy which, although very near to St. Mark's autograph, is not to be identified with it. A few mistakes or slight modifications had already crept in. In like manner, the copies used by Mt Lk were not St. Mark's autograph. Into them, too, changes had been introduced, and that with considerable freedom. And it happens that, while these two copies— the copies used by Mt Lk—were closely allied to each other, indeed we may say probably sister MSS., they belonged to a different family or different line of descent from that other important copy from which the great mass of our extant authorities is descended.

I. *Conditions under which Gospels were written* 23

This is easily exhibited in the form of a diagram.

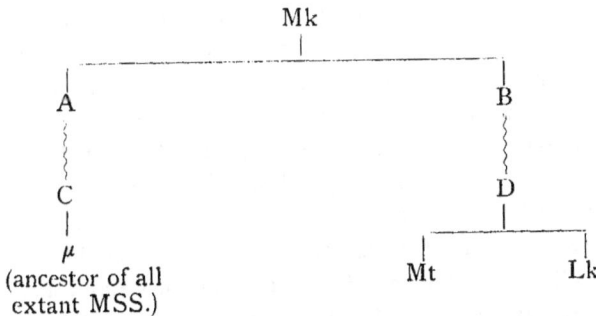

The question may be asked how it came about that these copies which were used by St. Matthew and St. Luke have not (like the A group) left descendants that have survived to the present day. It is never difficult to account for a MS. of this period perishing, and perishing without offspring. The books of this date were almost all written upon papyrus, and papyrus is a frail material; and the Christian book must have been much used and exposed to accidents of many kinds. But there was a special reason why those two copies should perish unregarded. The moment the two longer Gospels of St. Matthew and St. Luke were written, the shorter Gospel of St. Mark was at a discount. In early times it was always the Gospel least used and least quoted. The two longer Gospels incorporated the greater part of St. Mark; and therefore the possessor of either of them possessed practically the substance of St. Mark as well: and so that Gospel fell into comparative, though of course not complete, disuse.

We can form two interesting inferences as to the divergent families or lines of descent derived from St. Mark's autograph. One is, as I have just said, that the parent of our extant authorities was very near to the autograph, and represents it closely. The other is, that on the line of perhaps four or five copies intervening between St. Mark's autograph and the copies used by Mt Lk one at least must have been the work of a person with literary tastes and habits, who did not hesitate to improve the text before him and make it more correct and classical. This process of improvement went so far that I have ventured to call it a 'recension'. It was a recension perpetuated in just those two copies, but which after giving birth to them came to an abrupt end.

It is a remarkable fact that those two copies should have been so like each other, and it puts us upon questions which we are not able to answer. There is every reason to think that tradition is right in placing the origin of St. Mark's Gospel at Rome. But, apart from this curious connecting link, we know of nothing that would naturally bring the authors of the First and Third Gospels together. It is natural to suppose that the First Gospel was written not far from the outskirts of Palestine, at such a place, say, as Damascus or Antioch. And it is equally natural to associate St. Luke's Gospel with that part of the mission field in which the Evangelist seems to have been most at home —from Greece in the West to Antioch in the East. Is it possible that after the death of St. Paul and the destruction of Jerusalem St. Luke made his way once more to Caesarea, where he had spent the two years of St. Paul's captivity, or to Antioch? Two sister copies of St. Mark's Gospel might quite easily have been brought thither, or from St. Luke's copy another copy may have been made, which fell into the hands of the compiler of the First Gospel. It is, however, well to remember that at this time all roads led to Rome.

(b) The omission by St. Luke of Mk vi. 45–viii. 26.

There remains only the little puzzle about the omission by St. Luke of the contents of Mk vi. 45–viii. 26. Sir John Hawkins has written at length about this (Essay II. 2). Perhaps I may be allowed to say that, so far as my judge-

I. Conditions under which Gospels were written 25

ment goes, I agree entirely with his conclusions. He has stated, as I conceive, very happily the reasons which led St. Luke to omit this particular section—that is, always assuming that he found that he had to omit something. It is only on this last point that I have one small remark to offer, which falls strictly within the subject of this essay. The Gospels were written each on a separate roll of papyrus. These rolls were, roughly speaking, of the same kind of average length. This became a general rule for literary compositions dating from the Alexandrian critics of the second century B.C. There was a sort of recognized average length for a book, i.e. for the whole of a small composition or for a subdivision of a larger one.¹ The so-called 'books' of the *Iliad* and *Odyssey*, of Herodotus and Thucydides, were conventional divisions imposed upon the ancient poems and histories by the scholars of Alexandria after the fact.² But the later works, written after their time, were usually composed 'to scale'. The reason was that the materials for writing, the blank rolls of papyrus, were cut into convenient lengths, ranging within certain accepted limits. This was the meaning of the word τόμος, which in its origin had nothing to do with 'ponderous tomes'; it meant simply a 'cut' or 'length' of papyrus.³

Now, if we take Westcott and Hort's text, which is not encumbered with footnotes, we observe that St. Matthew occupies about 68 pages, St. Mark (without the last 12 verses) not quite 41, St. Luke about 73, St. John about 53 (not including the *pericope adulterae*), while the Acts occupies very nearly 70 pages. Dr. Kenyon has calculated that the Gospel of St. Mark would take up about 19 feet of

---

[1] 'Für verschiedene Litteraturgattungen waren verschiedene Buchmaxima oder Formate üblich oder obligat' (Birt, *Das antike Buchwesen*, p. 288).

[2] *Op. cit.* pp. 443 ff.

[3] Τόμος = 'abgeschnittene *charta papyracea*' (*op. cit.* p. 35). 'Denn es ist hervorzuheben, dass gerade er (τόμος) klarer und schärfer als alle anderen die Papyrusrolle und nur sie allein bezeichnete' (*Ibid.*).

an average-sized roll, that of St. John 23 feet 6 inches, St. Matthew 30 feet, the Acts and St. Luke's Gospel about 31 or 32 feet. The last figures are larger than those for any of the existing MSS. mentioned (Hyperides 28 feet; Iliad 25 feet; Mimes of Herodas about the same; Odyssey 24 feet [1]). I have little doubt that St. Luke was conscious of being pressed for space, and that he felt obliged to economize his materials. Something had to be omitted, and for the motives which led to the choice of this particular section I cannot do better than refer the reader to Sir John Hawkins's paper.

The suggestions made in this essay are all very simple. It is just their simplicity which has had the chief attraction for me: as a rule, the simpler the cause, provided it is adequate, the more likely it is to be true. And I cherish the hope that the connexions of effect and cause propounded may have the advantage of being, within their limits, adequate as well as simple. The essay will have served its purpose if it enables any of its readers to form for themselves a more exact conception of the processes which gave shape to the Gospels as we have them, and of the influences of various kinds to which they were due.

[1] Kenyon, *Handbook to Textual Criticism of N. T.*, p. 29.

II

THREE LIMITATIONS TO ST. LUKE'S USE OF ST. MARK'S GOSPEL

1. The Disuse of the Marcan Source in St. Luke ix. 51–xviii. 14.
2. The Great Omission by St. Luke of the Matter contained in St. Mark vi. 45–viii. 26.
3. St. Luke's Passion-narrative considered with reference to the Synoptic Problem.

III

PROBABILITIES AS TO THE SO-CALLED DOUBLE TRADITION OF ST. MATTHEW AND ST. LUKE

Rev. Sir JOHN CAESAR HAWKINS, Bart.
M.A., D.D.
Honorary Canon of St. Albans

SYLLABUS

The facts as to this 'great interpolation' into Mark's order. Comparison of the 'lesser interpolation' in Luke vi. 20–viii. 3. Examination of the only apparent correspondences with Mark, viz. those found

1. in eight Lucan doublets,

2. in nine other short sayings which Luke places differently from Mark,

3. in three longer passages (Luke x. 25–8; xi. 15, 17–23; xiii. 18, 19).

Tentative suggestions as to the source or sources which Luke may have here used instead of Mark.

THREE LIMITATIONS TO ST. LUKE'S USE OF ST. MARK'S GOSPEL[1]

1. THE DISUSE OF THE MARCAN SOURCE IN ST. LUKE IX. 51–XVIII. 14.

RATHER more than three-fourths of St. Matthew's Gospel, viz. 816 verses out of 1068, and rather more than two-thirds of St. Luke's Gospel, viz. 798 verses out of 1149, may be taken as generally supporting the now prevailing opinion that the compilers of those two Gospels used the Gospel of St. Mark—pretty nearly, if not quite, as we have it—not only as one of their most important sources, but as a framework. It is true that even in these major portions of their works they make many additions to the Marcan narrative in the way of introductions, conclusions, and both long and short insertions. They also make a few omissions from it, by far the most important being 'St. Luke's great omission' dealt with in the second of these Studies; and St. Luke makes an occasional substitution of more or less parallel matter. But *they do not desert its arrangement and order*, with the exception of some brief transpositions, most of which occur in Luke xxii–xxiii, and are therefore considered in the third Study, which relates to St. Luke's Passion-narrative.

That general statement, however, does not apply to what forms nearly a quarter of the First Gospel, viz. Mt viii–xiii, containing 252 verses, nor to what forms nearly one-third of the Third Gospel, viz. Lk ix. 51–xviii. 14,

---

[1] The first and third of these Studies are mainly reprinted, by the Editor's permission, from the *Expository Times* of 1902–4.

containing 350 verses (omitting xvii. 36 as spurious). Of neither of those two large departments of the Gospels bearing the names of Matthew and Luke can it be said that much account is there taken of the Marcan arrangement and order.

But though in that respect those two lengthy sections may be classed together, there is also an essential difference between them. On the one hand, it can hardly be doubted that in Mt viii–xiii the compiler had our Mark, or its general equivalent, before him, for there at least 108 verses, being more than two-fifths of the 252, are substantially parallel to Mark, and as a rule it is the latter which exhibits the chief signs of originality. In those chapters of Matthew therefore, the main task of students of the Synoptic Problem is to discover the reasons which induced Matthew (meaning the compiler of the First Gospel) here, and here only, to break up his Marcan source, and to rearrange it among other materials, instead of merely inserting those materials into it as it stood.[1] On the other hand, when we begin to examine Lk ix. 51–xviii. 14 in connexion with its parallels, the question soon arises whether the Marcan source is used there at all; and it is the chief object of this Study to show

---

[1] It has often been shown (very clearly in Allen's *Commentary*, pp. xiii–xvii and notes *passim*) that Matthew's main object here was to collect his Marcan and other materials into five blocks, of which three (corresponding roughly to chaps. v–vii, x, and xiii) should contain teaching of Jesus in its fundamental, missionary, and parabolic aspects, a fourth (chaps. viii–ix) should give specimens of His 'mighty works', and the remaining one (chaps. xi–xii) should show the reception which His words and works met with. As Von Soden well says, 'Each of these five great compositions shows an arrangement that has been well thought out' (*Early Christian Literature*, E. T., p. 184). And again, 'The author of these compositions is without doubt a born teacher. His arrangement, by which the reader gains an insight into the Life of our Lord from every standpoint, is masterly in the extreme' (p. 188). But, adds Von Soden, 'he has no interest in the historical connexion of events' (p. 194); and 'the occasions of the utterances of our Lord are to [him] matters of indifference' (p. 195). For a discussion of the specially difficult questions suggested by the arrangement in the fourth block (Mt viii–ix) I venture to refer to the *Expository Times*, vols. xii, pp. 471 ff., and xiii, pp. 20 ff.

II. 1. St. Luke's Use of St. Mark's Gospel

that the answer to that question must almost certainly be in the negative. For out of the 350 verses there are but 35—exactly one-tenth—which contain any parallels to Mark either in substance or in phraseology. And it will also be found that, with the exception of a few brief phrases, which shall be carefully noticed and scrupulously weighed as we proceed, the whole of the Lucan matter in these 35 verses, or parts of verses, which is parallel to Mark is also parallel to the First Gospel, between which and the Third Gospel there was undoubtedly some communion of sources. Is it not, then, very unlikely that Luke made such very slight use here of the Marcan source which he elsewhere uses so abundantly? Is it not more reasonable to suppose that, for whatever reason, he made no use of it at all, so that these 350 verses—including even the 35—were drawn up in complete independence of it, except, of course, so far as echoes of its doubtless familiar phraseology may have lingered in the memory?

Before entering upon the arguments for this view which this 'great interpolation' of Luke's—as it has well been termed from its relation to the Marcan order—itself supplies, it will be worth while to observe the analogy of that one of the insertions in the previous part of the Gospel which is so much longer and so much more varied in its contents than the rest of them, that it has sometimes been distinguished from them by being called Luke's 'lesser interpolation'. Certainly that analogy, so far as it goes, gives support to the hypothesis that Luke in his great interpolation wrote quite independently of Mark. For there is very strong evidence that he did so in his lesser interpolation. That section of the Gospel extends from chap. vi. 20 to viii. 3 (it seems to be sometimes taken as commencing at vi. 12, but surely vv. 12-19 are to be taken as parallel to Mk iii. 7-19, although there is an inversion of order for the purpose of providing an introduction to Luke's Sermon on the Level

Place), and thus contains 83 verses. Now in the whole of it there is nothing at all, either in words or substance, which is also found in Mark without Matthew, and only three short passages in which there is anything parallel to both Mark and Matthew. And as to two of these passages, we find that the 'setting' is completely different in Luke and Matthew from what it is in Mark. (1) The first of them is a very interesting and instructive case. We find that the five words, ᾧ μέτρῳ μετρεῖτε μετρηθήσεται ὑμῖν, are identical in Mk iv. 24, Mt vii. 2, Lk vi. 38, except that in Luke the right reading is almost certainly ἀντιμετρηθήσεται. But then we further find as to the contexts of those words and the purposes for which they are introduced, that while, like the words themselves, these are identical in Matthew and Luke, they are completely different in Mark. It seems then that, either in one of those two connexions or the other, the words can only be what I have above called an echo of familiar phraseology lingering in the memory, and applied to a matter to which it did not originally belong. And here, as sometimes elsewhere in reports of *discourse*, it is the Marcan connexion that gives the impression of being the less original; which happens to be the case also with the three other words, καὶ προστεθήσεται ὑμῖν, which Mark subjoins to the five words just quoted, but which have a more suitable environment and a clearer meaning in Mt vi. 33 and Lk xii. 31. (2) The second passage is the quotation from Mal iii. 1, ἰδοὺ (Mt and perhaps Mk ἐγὼ) ἀποστέλλω κτλ., which is recorded in Mt xi. 10, Lk vii. 27 as spoken by Jesus after the message from John in prison, but which Mark (i. 2) uses as an introduction to his account of the Baptist's preaching in the wilderness. And it is remarkable that the verb κατασκευάσει is used by all three writers, instead of the ἐπιβλέψεται of the LXX.[1]

---

[1] They also agree in substituting ἀποστέλλω for ἐξαποστέλλω, ὅς for καί, and σου for μου after πρὸ προσώπου. As Plummer (on Lk vii. 27) says,

(3) The third case of parallelism between all three Synoptists is of a different kind, for here Matthew and Mark agree generally against Luke. It consists in the use of a few words, of which ἀλάβαστρον μύρου and the name Σίμων are the only distinctive and important ones, both in Luke's account of the anointing by the sinful woman in the house of the Pharisee (vii. 36 ff.), and in Matthew's and Mark's accounts of the anointing by Mary at Bethany (Mt xxvi. 6 ff., Mk xiv. 3 ff.). But these resemblances between the two narratives are so very largely outweighed by the differences between them as to the time and place of the action and the teaching founded upon it, as to make it clear that any influence of the one upon the other can only have been very indirect. It may safely be concluded then, from an examination of these three passages, that though the first and second of them may prove, and apparently do prove, some real community of sources between Luke and Matthew, there are no adequate proofs of any such community between Luke and Mark in the 83 verses extending from Lk vi. 20 to viii. 3.

It may be taken then as morally certain that in Luke's previous and shorter interpolation into the Marcan order he laid aside entirely his usual Marcan source. And if so, we shall be to some extent predisposed to find the same independence of Mark in the later and much longer interpolation made by the same Evangelist. But here the circumstances of the case are considerably more complicated. For in Lk ix. 51–xviii. 14 there are, as has been said, no less than 35 verses or parts of verses which show more or less likeness to our Second Gospel, and which therefore might conceivably be derived from it; and it has been admitted that these verses contain a few words and short phrases found in

'the passage was one of the commonplaces of Messianic prophecy, and had been stereotyped in an independent Greek form before the Evangelists [or, we may add, Q] made use of it.'

Mark and Luke exclusively, which was not once the case in the lesser interpolation. But, nevertheless, I think it can be shown, by a close and careful examination of these verses, that the evidence which they supply is very decidedly against any derivation from Mark. Since making such an examination for myself, I have noticed that the Rev. F. H. Woods, in *Studia Biblica*, ii, pp. 75-8, has made some similar observations in support of the same conclusion; but as my investigation of the passages has been more minute and detailed than his could be in his general and comprehensive essay, I think it may be of use even to students of the subject who are well acquainted with that extremely valuable contribution to the literature of the Synoptic Problem.

The 35 verses or parts of verses in question may be most conveniently considered in three classes—I. Doublets (occupying 13 verses or parts of verses). II. Brief sayings of a similar kind to those found as doublets (9 verses). III. Three important passages of other kinds (13 verses).

I.

Doublets are almost always of primary importance in the investigation of sources. And the fact that nine of Luke's eleven doublets[1] have one of their members in this division of his Gospel, though it is less than one-third of the length of the whole Gospel, is perhaps in itself somewhat significant: it seems to suggest that Luke was here for some reason adopting a different procedure as to the use of sources from that which he adopted elsewhere. One of these nine, indeed, has both its members (Lk xiv. 11 and xviii. 14) in this same division, so it has no bearing upon our present inquiry. The remaining *eight Lucan doublets* are as follows:—

---

[1] I have displayed and discussed the eleven in *Horae Synopticae*[2], pp. 99 ff.; the two which have neither of their members in the great interpolation are Lk viii. 18 with xix. 26, and ix. 46 with xxii. 24.

II. 1. St. Luke's Use of St. Mark's Gospel

No. 1 Lk x. 4, 5, 7, 10, 11		Lk ix. 3, 4, 5	which	Mk vi. 6-11
No. 2 ,, xi. 33	form	,, viii. 16	passages	,, iv. 21
No. 3 ,, xi. 43	doublets	,, xx. 46	are	,, xii. 38, 39
No. 4 ,, xii. 2	with the	,, viii. 17	respec-	,, iv. 22
No. 5 ,, xii. 9	following	,, ix. 26	tively	,, viii. 38
No. 6 ,, xii. 11, 12	passages	,, xxi. 14, 15	parallel	,, xiii. 11
No. 7 ,, xiv. 27	respec-	,, ix. 23	in posi-	,, viii. 34
No. 8 ,, xvii. 33	tively,	,, ix. 24	tion to	,, viii. 35

No. 1 has been entered because it is technically a doublet, but I should not attach very much weight to it as evidence for a plurality of sources. For the two occasions referred to are so similar in nature, and the earlier of them had been put into writing so shortly before the latter (if the parts of the Gospel which include chaps. ix. 1-5 and x. 1-11 were composed at the same time, which we shall afterwards see to be by no means certain [1]), that Luke might easily reproduce in chap. x forms of expression which he remembered from having transcribed them in chap. ix. How closely connected these two discourses were in his mind seems to come out in chap. xxii. 35, where the words $\beta αλλάντιον$ and $ὑποδήματα$ are referred to as belonging to the charge to the Twelve, whereas he had only recorded them as addressed to the Seventy.

Bearing in mind this qualification as to one of the eight doublets, let us try to estimate their evidence, and the amount of weight that should be attached to it. Now doublets prima facie suggest the use of two sources, and they do so with a force which increases largely with their frequency; for it is very unlikely that a compiler—especially one who laid claim to accuracy and orderliness ($ἀκριβῶς$ $καθεξῆς$ $γράψαι$ Lk i. 3)—would repeatedly let himself use twice over materials derived from a single source, though he might, inadvertently or otherwise, do so once in a way.[2] He would be much more likely to draw similar

[1] See pp. 56, 58 below.
[2] There seem to be two instances of this in Matthew, viz. the doublets in vii. 16-18 and xii. 33-5, and in x. 22 (a and b) and xxiv. 9 b, 13 (*Hor. Syn.*[2], pp. 84 and 86).

materials, or in the case of short sayings admitting of different applications it might even be identical materials, from two distinct authorities. So the obvious inference from the occurrence of these eight members of doublets is that Luke in his Gospel had the use of at least two sources. But we can infer something more as to this particular department of the Gospel. For from the uniformity with which that member of the doublets which does not occur in the great interpolation agrees in position with a similar passage in Mark there result the two further probabilities as to one of these sources—(a) that it corresponded closely with our Second Gospel, and (b) that it was not made use of by Luke in this division of his Gospel. And these probabilities are confirmed and strengthened by the two following observations upon the doublets :—

(i) In five out of the eight cases, viz. in Nos. 3, 4, 5, 7, 8, the member of the Lucan doublet which corresponds to Mark in position is also considerably more similar to Mark in wording than is the member of it which occurs in the interpolation. The same is the case in the more complicated but (as has been pointed out) less certainly significant No. 1. In No. 2 the Marcan passage has about an equal resemblance to the two Lucan passages, the agreement as to $\kappa\lambda\acute{\iota}\nu\eta$ in one case being balanced by that as to $\mu\acute{o}\delta\iota o s$ in the other. As to No. 6—which next to No. 1 has the weakest claim to rank as a doublet—the preponderance of agreement is undoubtedly on the other side ; but, after making full allowance for that one case, there is on the whole a very large balance of evidence in favour of connecting with Mark, on the ground of language as well as on the ground of order and position, that half of the eight Lucan doublets which occurs elsewhere than in Lk ix. 51–xviii. 14.

(ii) It is further to be observed that in the 13 verses or parts of verses which have come under our consideration as

II. 1. St. Luke's Use of St. Mark's Gospel

forming these members of doublets, there is hardly anything which belongs to Mark and Luke without having a parallel in Matthew, and which therefore implies a Marcan source. I can find only two items of this kind. (*a*) There is a slight difference which nearly all MSS. keep up in No. 1, where Luke in x. 7 (and so in ix. 4 except in א) has μένετε as in Mk vi. 10, whereas in Mt x. 11 we find μείνατε. (*b*) And in No. 6 the τὸ πνεῦμα τὸ ἅγιον of Mk xiii. 11 and the τὸ ἅγιον πνεῦμα of Lk xii. 12 agree against the τὸ πνεῦμα τοῦ πατρὸς ὑμῶν of Mt x. 20. But such a reference to God as the 'Father of' men is a predominantly and almost exclusively Matthaean habitude (Matthew 20 times, Mark 1, Luke 3). And the coincidence of Mark and Luke in the employment of the usual epithet of the Divine Spirit, which occurs 3 times elsewhere in Mark and 12 times elsewhere in Luke, besides 41 times in Acts, and which had doubtless grown to be a familiar religious expression since its use in Ps l. (li.) 13 and Is lxiii. 10, 11 LXX as the adjectival rendering of the Hebrew genitives קָדְשֶׁךָ and קָדְשׁוֹ, cannot count for much as an indication of a direct Marcan origin of Lk xii. 11, 12. Those verses may be ascribed with far greater confidence to the collection of discourses which Matthew and Luke so often use in common.

II.

Our examination of these doublets, all of which have occurred in sayings of Jesus, seems to show that the members of each of them which are found in Lk ix. 51–xviii. 14 came to Luke quite independently of the Marcan source. In whatever degree that view is accepted as probable, it will lend probability to the further supposition that the same account is to be given of *certain other sayings of a like brief kind*, which also are found in this division of Luke, and which also are there placed in a totally different position from that which is assigned to them in Mark, but which do not happen to have such parallels in other parts of Luke as would qualify them to be classed as doublets.

There are nine such sayings, each of them occupying a single verse—

No. 1	Lk xii. 1	are re-spectively placed quite differently from the similar sayings in	Mk viii. 15	which respectively are exactly parallel in position to the very similar sayings in	Mt xvi. 6
No. 2	,, xii. 10		,, iii. 28, 29		,, xii. 31, 32
No. 3	,, xiii. 30		,, x. 31		,, xix. 30
No. 4	,, xiv. 34		,, ix. 50		
No. 5	,, xvi. 18		,, x. 11		,, xix. 9
No. 6	,, xvii. 2		,, ix. 42		,, xviii. 6
No. 7	,, xvii. 6		,, xi. 23		,, xxi. 21
No. 8	,, xvii. 23		,, xiii. 21		,, xxiv. 23
No. 9	,, xvii. 31		,, xiii. 15, 16		,, xxiv. 17, 18

In No. 4 the last column had to be left empty; for, although this saying is also given by Matthew (v. 13), he places it in a third—and seemingly the best—connexion. Between that connexion and Luke's it may be possible to trace some amount of parallelism, since the duties entailed by Christian discipleship were the general subject on both occasions; but Mark's setting is totally different, the saying being attached by him to the mysterious πυρὶ ἁλισθήσεται in a discourse which had taken an eschatological turn.

The above list of passages, like the previous list of doublets, gives a prima facie impression of Luke's independence of Mark, which an examination of the verses in detail confirms and strengthens in two respects—

(i) We find here, again, that the verbal similarities are in a large majority of cases greater between the Marcan and Matthaean than between the Marcan and Lucan versions of the sayings. This preponderance is very decided in Nos. 1, 3, 5, 7; it also exists, though to a smaller extent, in Nos. 2, 8, 9. In the remaining two cases, Nos. 4 and 6, something considerable will have to be said on the other side; but in No. 6 the exclusively Marco-Lucan correspondences which will presently be noticed are balanced, if they are not outbalanced, by the exclusively Marco-Matthaean correspondences τῶν πιστευόντων and ὀνικός (a word found nowhere else¹); so that No. 4, the only entry which does not show the sayings in Mark and Matthew as parallel to one another in position, is the only one which shows them as less like to one another in phraseology than the sayings in Mark and Luke.

(ii) It happens that the two verses of Matthew referred to as parallels in Nos. 5 and 7 are members of doublets in Matthew. And an examination of these Matthaean doublets lends support—in the first case very strong support—to the view that there had been some community of sources between Luke and Matthew, but none between Luke and Mark. (*a*) In No. 5 the passage named as both parallel and very similar to Mk x. 11 is Mt xix. 9, which forms a doublet with Mt v. 32. Now the verse which immediately precedes Lk xvi. 18 enforces the permanence of the law in words closely corresponding (note especially κερέα) with the like enforcement near the commencement (Mt v. 18) of the section of the Sermon on the Mount which contains Mt v. 32. This fact very strongly suggests that Mt v. 32 and Lk xvi. 18 have the same origin (presumably in Q), while Mt xix. 9 came separately from the other (presumably Petrine) source which lies before us in Mark. And this is only one of several Matthaean doublets as to which the same two distinct lines of descent can be traced with very considerable probability. (*b*) The case connected with our No. 7 is not one of the strongest of these, but it deserves mention. The words of Matthew (xxi. 21) there entered as parallel with Mk xi. 23 form a doublet with Mt xvii. 20; and the occurrence of ὡς κόκκον σινάπεως in Mt xvii. 20 and Lk xvii. 6 exclusively cannot but suggest here again a common origin for these two passages, while Mt xxi. 21 and Mk xi. 23 seem to be accounted for by the Marcan source. But Luke's substitution of the 'sycamine tree' (cf. οὐ μόνον τὸ τῆς συκῆς Mt xxi. 21) for the 'mountain', which forms

¹ Except in the papyri; three instances of its occurrence there are given by Moulton and Milligan in *Expositor*, VII. x. p. 92 (July 1910).

the illustration in the other three passages, makes the inference less clear and certain than in the case of No. 5.

We have now to notice in these nine verses the verbal coincidences between Mark and Luke only which can be quoted against the latter's complete disuse of the former as a source. Three of them are of real importance. In No. 4 it may be called practically impossible that Mark (ix. 50) and Luke (xiv. 34) can accidentally and independently both (α) have prefaced the saying with καλὸν (Luke καλὸν οὖν) τὸ ἅλας, and also (β) have introduced into it the verb ἀρτύειν, which only occurs once besides in the New Testament (Col iv. 6 ἅλατι ἠρτυμένος). And (γ) though it is not so near to being impossible, it is very highly improbable, that in No. 6 the use of περίκειται in Mk ix. 42, Lk xvii. 2 against κρεμασθῇ in Mt xviii. 6 was a mere accidental coincidence.

The four other verbal coincidences which follow seem to me to be 'negligible quantities', as being such expressions as writers, using the freedom which generally characterizes the Synoptists, might be expected to introduce anywhere. But it may be well to add them, if only to show that they have not been forgotten. (δ) It is true that in No. 2 Mark and Luke have εἰς τὸ πνεῦμα as against Matthew's κατὰ τοῦ πνεύματος (Mk iii. 29, Lk xii. 10, Mt xii. 32); but the significance of that coincidence almost or quite disappears when we remember (a) that κατά in the sense of against is a favourite usage with Matthew, being employed by him 14 times against 6 times in Mark and 3 times in Luke; and (b) that Matthew alone of the three had not been using the verb βλασφημεῖν, which carries after it the preposition εἰς in Dan iii. 96 (29) LXX, and in Bel 9 Theod., as well as in Mark and Luke here, but which is never followed by κατά either in the Greek O.T. or N.T. (ε) In No. 6, again, we have (besides the really important περίκειται already noted) the change of preposition from Mark's and Luke's εἰς τὴν θάλασσαν to Matthew's ἐν τῷ πελάγει τῆς θαλάσσης; but that is merely the result of the requirements of the three different verbs that had been used (Mk βέβληται, Lk ἔρριπται, Mt καταποντισθῇ). And similarly πελάγει is a rhetorical amplification suitable to the forcible καταποντισθῇ. (ζ) In No. 8, again, there is a trifling, and doubtless a fortuitous, agreement between Mark and Luke only, in that Mark has ὧδε followed by ἐκεῖ (xiii. 21) and Luke has ἐκεῖ followed by ὧδε (xvii. 23), whereas Matthew has ὧδε both times (xxiv. 23; cf. Ex ii. 12 LXX). (η) Once more, in No. 9 Mark and Luke, unlike Matthew, insert εἰς τά before ὀπίσω. But in doing so they were only adopting a fairly common usage which is employed again by Luke himself in ix. 62, and which is found also in Jn vi. 66, xviii. 6, xx. 14, and at least 17 times in LXX, exclusive of 5 places in which the reading is doubtful.

In examining then (13 + 9 =) 22 of the 35 verses in which the three Evangelists have any common subject-matter (there being none in which Mark and Luke stand alone), we have found only three really uncommon and outstanding expressions in which Mark and Luke agree against Matthew; and two more will have to be added to them from the remaining 13 verses.

These 13 verses are found in three passages, two of which are longer and more complex than any that have been hitherto discussed, and all of which deserve careful and minute attention, for it is from them chiefly that a cursory reader might gain the impression that Luke's disuse of the Marcan source was not entire in this division of his Gospel, and that consequently what we have here is not simply and completely a 'great interpolation' into the Marcan *Grundschrift*.

1. *Luke* x. 25–8.

This passage, which is the earliest of the three, has to be brought into comparison with Mk xii. 28–34, with which

Mt xxii. 34-40 is exactly parallel in position and in general substance. For the two latter passages describe one of four brief discussions which appear to be represented as occurring consecutively on the Tuesday before the death of Jesus (Mt xxii. 15-46, Mk xii. 13-37 ; cf. Lk xx. 20-44). But Luke has there three only of those discussions, for he omits the question of the scribe (Mark) or Pharisaic lawyer (Matthew) as to the first or great commandment, and the reply which that question received. His only account of such a dialogue is that given in the passage now before us (x. 25-8), which forms part of the great interpolation. But the contrasts between it and the Marco-Matthaean account are very considerable : (*a*) the incident is attributed to a much earlier time and to a quite different locality, and it leads up to the Parable of the Good Samaritan ; (*b*) the lawyer does not, as in Mark and Matthew, ask about the 'first' or 'great commandment', but (as in Mk x. 17, Lk xviii. 18, and cf. Mt xix. 16) about the way to ' inherit eternal life ' ; and (*c*) by the interrogative form of the response to the lawyer, he himself is made to be the quoter of the well-known passage from Deuteronomy, which in Mark and Matthew forms the direct reply given by Jesus. These three alterations—or, at any rate, the first and third of them—could hardly have been made by a writer who had the Marcan document before him as one of his sources, and who relied upon it, and especially upon its order, as Luke did usually. And they constitute divergences which very far outweigh three Marco-Lucan correspondences which have now to be noted and allowed for.

(*a*) One of these correspondences is not verbal, but consists in the fact that the inquirer receives in the Second and Third Gospels some commendation, in the former for his intelligent appreciation of the statement by Jesus of the two great commandments (νουνεχῶς ἀπεκρίθη Mk. xii. 34), and in the latter for his own correct statement of them (ὀρθῶς ἀπεκρίθης Lk x. 28). In Matthew's narrative there is no commendation; but this omission is sufficiently accounted for by his tendencies 'to give a very dark picture of the Pharisees', and to regard the Scribes as identical with them.[1]

The other two correspondences are verbal; they both occur in one verse, Lk x. 27 compared with Mk xii. 30. (β) One of them is rather important. To the three elements in man's being which are to be exercised in the love of God these two Evangelists add a fourth, viz. ἐξ ὅλης τῆς ἰσχύος σου (Mark) and ἐν ὅλῃ τῇ ἰσχύϊ σου (Luke). This coincidence is not very likely to have been accidental, although it is possible that the use of ἰσχύς in this connexion may have come naturally to both writers from a reminiscence of its occurrence in 4 (2) Ki xxiii. 25, where in the Deuteronomic language used in extolling the character of Josiah, ἰσχύς is adopted as the rendering of מְאֹד, instead of δύναμις, as in Dt vi. 5. (γ) The other such correspondence is certainly insignificant. It is true that Mark and Luke agree in having ἐξ ὅλης τῆς καρδίας σου against Matthew's ἐν with the dative, but this is only because the two former adhere more closely than the latter to the usage of prepositions in Dt vi. 5, LXX. It may be well to place that passage side by side with these quotations, adding to them the scribe's reply in Mk xii. 33, which is practically a second quotation in that Gospel, so that the numerous variations may be clearly seen; though indeed there is no passage of the O. T. in quotations from which we should so little expect to find variations as the leading portion of the familiar 'Shema' (Dt vi. 4-9, xi. 13-21; Nu xv. 37-41).

[1] See Allen, *St. Matthew*, pp. lxxviii and 240, for proofs of these tendencies.

Dt vi. 5	Mt xxii. 37	Mk xii. 30	Lk x. 27	Mk xii. 33
ἀγαπήσεις Κύ-	ἀγαπήσεις Κύ-	ἀγαπήσεις Κύ-	ἀγαπήσεις Κύ-	τὸ ἀγαπᾶν αὐ-
ριον τὸν Θεόν	ριον τὸν Θεόν	ριον τὸν Θεόν	ριον τὸν Θεόν	τὸν ἐξ ὅλης
σου ἐξ ὅλης τῆς	σου ἐν ὅλῃ καρ-	σου ἐξ ὅλης	σου ἐξ ὅλης	καρδίας καὶ ἐξ
διανοίας σου καὶ	δίᾳ σου καὶ ἐν	καρδίας σου καὶ	καρδίας σου καὶ	ὅλης τῆς συ-
ἐξ ὅλης τῆς	ὅλῃ τῇ ψυχῇ	ἐξ ὅλης τῆς	ἐν ὅλῃ τῇ	νέσεως καὶ ἐξ
ψυχῆς σου καὶ	σου καὶ ἐν ὅλῃ	ψυχῆς σου καὶ	ψυχῇ σου καὶ	ὅλης τῆς ἰσχύος
ἐξ ὅλης τῆς δυν-	τῇ διανοίᾳ σου.	ἐξ ὅλης τῆς δια-	ἐν ὅλῃ τῇ ἰσχύι	. . . περισσό-
άμεώς σου.		νοίας σου καὶ	σου καὶ ἐν ὅλῃ	τερόν ἐστιν
		ἐξ ὅλης τῆς	τῇ διανοίᾳ σου.	κτλ.
		ἰσχύος σου.		

To which passages may be added for further comparison, 4 (2) Ki xxiii. 25, above referred to: ὃς ἐπέστρεψεν πρὸς Κύριον ἐν ὅλῃ καρδίᾳ αὐτοῦ καὶ ἐν ὅλῃ ἰσχύι αὐτοῦ καὶ ἐν ὅλῃ ψυχῇ αὐτοῦ (so in B ; in A ἰσχύι and ψυχῇ are transposed).

On the whole, then, and after giving due weight to the coincidence as to ἰσχύς, there is no sufficient ground for supposing that Luke was here using Mark as one of his authorities. It seems much more reasonable to assume either (a) that the two writers were referring to two distinct incidents—and it is by no means unlikely that the Shema, which as an often-repeated formula 'undoubtedly belongs to the time of Christ' (Schürer, *H. J. P.*, ii. 2, p. 77 ; cf. p. 84), might more than once enter into His discussions with Jewish νομικοί[1]—or else (b) that one incident had in the course of oral tradition been deflected into these two forms.

On the other hand, and by way of contrast, it deserves notice that while Matthew agrees with Mark as to the time and place of this incident, the verbal correspondences between him and Luke only are very considerable, viz. νομικός[2] (used here only by Matthew, but often by Luke), πειράζων (for which, however, Luke characteristically has

---

[1] There is also now reason for supposing that this might have been the case even as to the *two* great commandments ; for Dr. Charles has shown in his edition of the *Testaments of the XII Patriarchs*, which he dates in B.C. 109-106, that 'Love the Lord and your neighbour' may have been known in Judaea as a summary of duties before the Christian era (Introd., pp. xcv and lxxix). But see also Plummer's *St. Matthew*, pp. xxxiv ff.

[2] But νομικός in Matthew is omitted by Syr^{sin} 1 e arm; and it seems probable that 'the critical texts of the future will remove' this agreement between Matthew and Luke (C. H. Turner in *J. T. S.*, x. 178).

ἐκπειράζων), διδάσκαλε, and ἐν τῷ νόμῳ, besides the use of ἐν with ψυχῇ and διανοίᾳ, which more than balances the Marco-Lucan use of ἐξ with καρδίας which has been mentioned. These identities seem sufficient to show either that Matthew and Luke were influenced by some non-Marcan source, or else that one of them was familiar with the other's Gospel in some form. There is not much here to guide us towards a decision between these alternatives, but that the former of them is by far the more probable will, I think, be suggested by the analogy of the passage which we have next to consider.

2. *Luke* xi. 15, 17–23.[1]

These seven verses have to be brought into comparison with Mk iii. 22–7. And it is at once evident that the verbal resemblances in which Mark and Luke stand alone are of the slightest kind. There are but three of them at the utmost. (a) There is the use of ἐπί for 'against' twice in Mk iii. 24, 25, and in Lk xi. 17, where Matthew (xii. 25) has κατά; but we have already seen that κατά with this meaning is a favourite usage of his (see above, p. 40, on Lk xii. 10, and cf. especially Mt x. 35 with Lk xii. 53); and even he agrees with the others in having ἐφ' ἑαυτόν in the very next verse (xii. 26 = Mk iii. 26 = Lk xi. 18). (β) There is the parallel use of the participial forms εἰσελθών in Mk iii. 27 and ἐπελθών in Lk xi. 22; but this little grammatical resemblance can count for nothing in comparison with the mass of exclusively Marco-Matthaean identities

---

[1] It is generally assumed that Luke places this incident and discourse much too late. But it should be noticed that in Mk iii. 22 there are no words of connexion with what had gone before; indeed this discussion with the Pharisees has seemed to many to break the connexion between the references to the relatives of Jesus in verses 21 and 31 ff. And in Mt xii. 22 ff. it forms one of several incidents leading to anti-Jewish controversy, which Matthew may have collected from records of different occasions.

which distinguish the records of this saying about the 'strong man armed'. (γ) And it is not impossible that ὅτι λέγετε κτλ. in Lk xi. 18 may be a reminiscence of Mark's brief concluding comment, ὅτι ἔλεγον κτλ., in iii. 30, or vice versa.

But to most people it will seem far more probable that none of these three little similarities betoken a common source. At any rate, it will be admitted that their testimony in favour of the dependence of Luke upon Mark would be outweighed by any fairly good arguments for the independence of the two accounts. And a careful study of those accounts in their relation to the parallel passage of Matthew (xii. 24–30) will be found to supply such an argument.

That study may be best commenced by a reference to the incident of asking for a sign, which in Matthew follows upon, and in Luke is actually bound up with, the controversy which produced this 'defensive discourse' (as it has been aptly named) on the subject of casting out demons. We find that Matthew, and he alone, has *two* accounts of such a request for a sign and of the answer with which it was met, one of those accounts being found in Mt xvi. 1, 4 (verses 2 and 3 are almost certainly spurious), and being parallel to, and presumably derived from, Mk viii. 11, 12, and the other occurring here (Mt xii. 38–40), and being parallel to Lk xi. 16 and 29 f. So those two incidents which come before us in Mark and Luke respectively, and are by them attributed to different occasions, are treated by Matthew as doublets, which may be taken as an indication that he drew them from two distinct sources. He does not, however, take this course as to the 'defensive discourse' which is now under our consideration; for although it happens that he does twice record miracles which might have led up to such a discourse (with Mt xii. 22, 23 cf. Mt ix. 32–4, remembering that v. 34 is bracketed by WH as perhaps a 'Western non-interpolation'[1]), he does not twice append any sayings of this defensive kind. Probably it may have seemed to him too distinctive and striking a discourse to have been delivered twice—or at any rate too distinctive and striking to need to be recorded twice in the Gospel. So, instead of giving in one place the Marcan account and in another place the account (probably from Q) used by Luke, he combines or 'conflates' them into a single account here. That this was almost certainly the genesis of the Matthaean passage as we have it, may be seen most conveniently and convincingly in Rushbrooke's *Synopticon*, or less easily in any ordinary Harmony of the Gospels (though, indeed, the arrangement of these parallel passages by Tischendorf in secs. 47 and 91 of his *Harmonia Evangelica* is not as simple and helpful as usual). For the following phenomena will be observed in the course of a close comparison of Mt xii. 24-30, Mk iii. 22-7, Lk xi. 15, 17-23 :—

i. Mark's record is considerably the shortest of the three, the number of words being in Matthew 136, in Mark 98, in Luke 139.

ii. The chief cause of this disparity in length lies in three entire verses which are found almost word for word in Matthew and Luke, so that they must have had a common origin, but to which Mark has no parallel at all (Mt xii. 27, 28, and 30, Lk xi. 19, 20, and 23).

iii. And, besides those three complete verses, Matthew has some detached words and phrases which are found also in Luke but not in Mark, and as to which it is hard to believe that they were all adopted independently by the compilers of the First and Third Gospels, viz. (*a*) εἰδὼς ... αὐτῶν (with ἐνθυμήσεις in Matthew here as in ix. 4, and with διανοήματα in Luke); (*b*) the participial forms μερισθεῖσα in Matthew, and διαμερισθεῖσα in Luke; (*c*) the verb

[1] Syr^sin omits it, besides D a k.

ἐρημοῦν, which is found in N. T. only here and in Rev xvii. 16, xviii. 16, 19; and (*d*) the interrogative form of the sentence πῶς σταθήσεται ἡ βασιλεία αὐτοῦ;

iv. And Matthew further agrees with Luke in introducing this discourse by means of the record of a miracle which had just been wrought, whereas Mark only speaks of it as resulting from the inference which 'scribes which came down from Jerusalem' had drawn from such miracles generally. The exclusive agreement of Matthew and Luke in this point is particularly noteworthy, because as a rule such agreement is not found to exist in records of acts, but only in records of discourses.

v. On the other hand, it is with Mark rather than with Luke that Matthew agrees as to the period of the ministry in which this discourse was spoken, though he is not here following Mark's order exactly.

vi. And Matthew's ver. 29 corresponds almost precisely with Mark's ver. 27 in the presentation of the little parable of the 'strong man armed', while Luke's vv. 21, 22 differ very widely from them,[1] as has been already noticed (p. 45).

vii. The use of Mark by Matthew is further supported by the fact that they both subjoin immediately to the verses now under consideration the passage on the blasphemy against the Holy Spirit (Mt xii. 31, 32, Mk iii. 28, 29), and their versions of it agree not only exactly in position but generally in form and substance, the few and easily accounted for exceptions being (*a*) the absence in Matthew of the plural υἱοὶ τῶν ἀνθρώπων, which, though common in the O.T., is almost disused in the N.T., being found besides only in Eph iii. 5; (*b*) the expansion by him of Mark's εἰς τὸν αἰῶνα into the then familiar Jewish eschatological terms οὔτε ἐν τούτῳ τῷ αἰῶνι οὔτε ἐν τῷ μέλλοντι (see Schürer,

---

[1] Matthew agrees with 23 words or parts of words out of the 26 words used by Mark, but with only 7 words or parts of words of the 33 words used by Luke.

II. 1. St. Luke's Use of St. Mark's Gospel

H. J. P., ii. 2, p. 177, and especially the references there to *Pirqe Aboth*, and 4 Esdras;[1]) and (c) his omission of the profound saying ἔνοχός ἐστιν αἰωνίου ἁμαρτήματος, the difficulty of which is proved by the later introduction of a *facilior lectio* even into the Marcan text itself. While, on the other hand, we have seen previously that the corresponding Lucan saying is considerably more compressed, besides occupying an entirely different position (xii. 10).

viii. Finally, the few words in Mt xii. 24-30 which remain after deducting those which we have seen to be assignable to Mark and Luke (or their sources) respectively, are just such as would be used by a compiler. For almost all of them are either quite colourless and commonplace, as ἀκούσαντες, and the use of πόλις as a third illustration intermediate between βασιλεία and οἰκία, or else they are such as we know to be characteristic of the same writer in other parts of his compilation, viz. ἐνθυμήσεις, and, at least against Mark, Φαρισαῖοι. The only alteration made by Matthew from his presumed sources which would not come under either of these descriptions is his use of πνεύματι (ver. 28), which might well seem to him a more easy and intelligible expression for the divine power as exercised against demons than δακτύλῳ, which is found in Lk xi. 20, being probably suggested by the language of Ex viii. 19.

These eight observations combine to prove almost irresistibly that Matthew 'conflated' his record of this discourse from two sources, which we have substantially before us in our Luke and Mark. And the insignificance of the only three resemblances which could be found between these two latter, and between them only, shows with almost equal cogency that up to the time of the employment of them by Matthew, they had been quite independent of one another, though they embody traditions either of the same controversy or at least of the same class of controversies.

[1] But see also Dalman, *The Words of Jesus*, E. T., pp. 147 ff.

3. *Luke* xiii. 18, 19.

There remains a passage which is much briefer in itself, and can be treated very much more briefly, than the 'defensive discourse', but which supplies evidence pointing in the same direction. It is the Parable of the Mustard Seed, which Matthew (xiii. 31 f.) and Mark (iv. 30 ff.) place in their collections of seven and three parables respectively, apparently as spoken by the Sea of Galilee somewhat early in the ministry,[1] but which Luke places much later, subjoining it to, and seeming by ἔλεγεν οὖν to connect it with, the deep impression made in a synagogue by the healing of a woman 'which had a spirit of infirmity'. On the other hand, Luke agrees with Matthew in annexing to it the companion Parable of the Leaven—almost the only parable [2] recorded by those two Evangelists but not by Mark, unless we take the Talents and the Pounds, and the Marriage Feast and the Great Supper, as versions of the same two parables respectively.

Here again, as in the last case, it will be observed—

i. That Matthew's language has much in common with Mark only, viz. μικρότερον πάντων τῶν σπερμάτων, ὅταν, μεῖζον τῶν λαχάνων, ὥστε with infinitives instead of finite verbs following καί, besides the unimportant because natural use of forms of the verb σπείρειν instead of Luke's verb βάλλειν, which is much less usual in this particular sense.

ii. That on the other hand Matthew has also not a little in common with Luke only, viz. λαβὼν ἄνθρωπος, αὐτοῦ or ἑαυτοῦ with the same meaning, forms of αὐξάνειν, δένδρον, ἐν τοῖς κλάδοις αὐτοῦ (cf. however, κλάδους in Mk iv. 32), similarities which, though not being very distinctive in

---

[1] Matthew certainly gives this impression, for he introduces it with the words ἄλλην παραβολὴν παρέθηκεν αὐτοῖς λέγων; but Mark's only introductory words are καὶ ἔλεγεν, which do not necessarily imply that it was spoken on that day by the sea-shore.

[2] See p. 127 in this volume.

II. 1. St. Luke's Use of St. Mark's Gospel

themselves severally, are too numerous to have occurred accidentally in this short passage.

iii. That there remains nothing peculiar to Matthew himself except some quite unimportant words of connexion and his usual substitution of τῶν οὐρανῶν for τοῦ Θεοῦ after βασιλεία. These three observations show very distinctly that the various forms of the parable are best accounted for by assuming that Matthew combined the two sources which are substantially preserved for us in our Mark and Luke. But we cannot add so confidently as in the preceding case that these two sources were quite independent of one another. For in the introduction to the parable there is a rather remarkable correspondence in which Mark and Luke stand alone. While Matthew has the simple statement, ἄλλην παραβολὴν παρέθηκεν (cf. Mark's θῶμεν) αὐτοῖς, λέγων ὁμοία κτλ., the others record a doubly interrogative sentence with which the parable was prefaced—

Mk iv. 30	Lk xiii. 18	Is xl. 18	Lk vii. 31
καὶ ἔλεγεν, πῶς ὁμοιώσωμεν τὴν βασιλείαν τοῦ Θεοῦ, ἢ ἐν τίνι αὐτὴν παραβολῇ θῶμεν ;	ἔλεγεν οὖν, τίνι ὁμοία ἐστὶν ἡ βασιλεία τοῦ Θεοῦ, καὶ τίνι ὁμοιώσω αὐτήν ;	τίνι ὡμοιώσατε Κύριον καὶ τίνι ὁμοιώματι ὡμοιώσατε αὐτόν ;	τίνι οὖν ὁμοιώσω τοὺς ἀνθρώπους τῆς γενεᾶς ταύτης, καὶ τίνι εἰσὶν ὅμοιοι ;

I have placed by the side of the Marcan and Lucan verses that verse of 2 Isaiah—a part of the O.T. very familiar to the N.T. writers—because of its remarkable similarity to them in structure and expression, and because there is therefore a possibility that its double interrogation may have become a kind of formula in the introduction of parabolic teaching, and thus may have affected the language of Mark and Luke independently. And I have added in a fourth column the parallel duplication with which Luke introduces the similitude of the Children in the Market-place. Now as to the single question τίνι ὁμοιώσω which we find just below in Lk xiii. 20 and again in Mt xi. 16, there is no doubt that the corresponding query למה הדבר דומה, as quoted by Lightfoot, *Hor. Heb.*, on Mt xiii. 3, or sometimes למה הוא דומה, as found in *Pirqe Aboth*, iii. 27, iv. 27, 28, was both ancient and usual as a Jewish preface to parables. But there does not seem to be evidence for such an habitual use of the double interrogation, so it must be owned that some sort of derivation from one Gospel to the other is a more natural explanation of the coincidence.

We ought, then, in fairness to reckon this introduction to the Parable of the Mustard Seed as forming, together with καλὸν τὸ ἅλας and the use of forms of ἀρτύω in Mk ix. 50, Lk xiv. 34, περίκειται in Mk ix. 42, Lk xvii. 2, and the addition of ἰσχύς in Mk xii. 30, Lk x. 27, a group of five intimations that there had been some kind of bridge of communication between the Marcan and Lucan Gospels as we have them in those parts of the latter Gospel which have now been examined. I have noted in passing ten other similarities or identities between those two Gospels exclusively,[1] but it has seemed to me that all these are expressions which might have suggested themselves, and indeed are likely to have suggested themselves, to the two writers independently as obvious and suitable to the matters which they both had in hand. That, however, as I have admitted, cannot be said of the five similarities which have just been recapitulated. But it does not therefore follow that those coincidences—even if reinforced by any significance that may be thought by any one to attach to the other ten or to some of them—are sufficient to prove any *direct use* of one of these Gospels by the other. Their evidence is much more in favour of there having been some more indirect and

---

[1] These smaller similarities, as well as the five more important ones, have been marked throughout the whole of this Study with Greek letters (α, β, γ, &c.), which have been reserved for this purpose only. So there would be no difficulty in referring back to the places where they are entered.

II. 1. St. Luke's Use of St. Mark's Gospel

casual means by which the words or phrases came across from the one document or line of tradition to the other, for it is most unlikely that the venerated Marcan source, the vehicle of Peter's teaching, would have been put into requisition so seldom and so scantily, if it had been in use at all.[1]

On the whole, then, there seem to be very strong grounds for assuming that Luke's disuse here of his customary Marcan authority was not only comparative but entire, and that even in the thirty-five verses, which are more or less parallel in substance with what we read in our Second Gospel, he was drawing upon a non-Marcan source or sources.

Less positive and more tentative words must be used in any attempt to answer the question which now naturally arises—Can we go any farther than that negative conclusion? Can we indicate with any tolerable amount of likelihood the sources which Luke did use here, as well as the one source which, whether through inability or unwillingness, he did not use? In particular, can we, if we dislike the multiplication of unknown entities, simply attribute a 'Logian' origin to this whole division of his Gospel as it stands, or (if we except certain references to a journey which will be mentioned presently) nearly as it stands? Can Luke have here done nothing more, or very little more, than insert a large block of the work known to Papias as the *Logia*, because he had been unable to find elsewhere appropriate places in which to insert its component parts, and yet he could not bring himself to omit such highly attested materials? Such a view,

---

[1] Another branch of the Synoptic Problem supplies a suggestive parallel to this argument. If indirect and casual transmission, without the use of one Evangelist's work by the other, is accepted as the most reasonable account of the comparatively few sporadic Matthaeo-Lucan peculiarities in many sections of which Mark supplies the groundwork, there seems to be equally good reason for accepting it as the account of the similarly few and sporadic Marco-Lucan peculiarities which we have found here in Luke's great interpolation.

however prima facie improbable, cannot be dismissed as absolutely impossible. And it is a possible view, not only if with Bishop Lightfoot we take the name *Logia* as denoting sacred writings generally, but if, in accordance with a view which now seems more probable, we regard it as meant by Papias to express sayings of the Lord, together with notices of the occasions which led to their being delivered, when such notices were needed for the full understanding of them.[1] For on the whole it is certainly characteristic of this section of the Gospel that it is 'lacking in incident'.[2] Indeed, it may be said that there is really no part of the great interpolation which does not either consist of, or else lead up to, sayings of Jesus, with the single exception of the record of the inhospitable Samaritan village in ix. 51-6, where the shorter and far better attested text ends by only stating that a rebuke was spoken, and without giving any of the words of it. I do not add xi. 53 f. as another exception, because that description of Pharisaic hostility evidently leads up to the warning against Pharisaic leaven in xii. 1, as we may see by disregarding the modern division into chapters and by giving to ἐν οἷς the more simple and natural rendering of 'during which [things]' instead of 'in the meantime'. It must be admitted, however, that the circumstances of the three miracles recorded in xiii. 10-17, xiv. 1-6 (cf. Mt xii. 9-14), and xvii. 12-19 (though in a less degree than the other two) are described more fully than was altogether necessary in order to bring out the force of the sayings for which those miracles respectively supply the occasions.[3]

But there are more serious objections than that to the theory of the use of the *Logia* thus *en bloc* and exclusively of all other authorities. (1) We know that Luke was aware

---

[1] See pp. 105-7, 118, 123 in this volume.
[2] Edersheim, *Jesus the Messiah*, ii. 195.
[3] The same thing may perhaps be said of Luke's record of the healing of the Centurion's servant in an early part of the Gospel (vii. 2 ff.; see p. 119).

of the existence of 'many' attempts to write Gospels, and that these attempts, like his own, were grounded upon original traditions—whether written or oral—which came down from eyewitnesses. From this it seems almost certain that several good sources must have been available for his work; and, if so, it seems very unlikely that he would have confined himself to one of them through nearly one-third of his Gospel. (2) Again, the eight references (ix. 52, 56, 57; x. 1, 38; xiii. 22; xiv. 25; xvii. 11) to a journey or journeys, during which the recorded events are said to have occurred and the recorded discourses to have been spoken, imply more of a connected history that would come under that definition of *Logia* which was above (p. 54) accepted as the most probable, and to which modern opinion seems on the whole to incline. Lk ix. 51 was not entered as a ninth such reference, because it should perhaps be regarded as parallel in substance, though so different in wording, to Mk x. 1 = Mt xix. 1, and therefore as forming a means of introducing the interpolation into the general triple narrative rather than as being part of the interpolated matter.

It would seem, then, that Luke continued here to refer to one or more sources known to him, but completely unknown to us, as well as to the *Logia*, or great *Spruchsammlung* (Q), upon which both he and Matthew so often drew, and that his only change of procedure at chap. ix. 51 lay in his ceasing to use the Marcan document as the framework into which his various extracts were inserted.

What caused that very decided change of procedure it is of course impossible for us to say; but some definite cause for it there must have been. Only conjectures on this point can now be offered, and perhaps they are hardly worth offering. Yet two of them have some plausibility, and the second of them suggests some interesting thoughts.

1. Luke may have drawn up this 'travel-document' with some special purpose before he knew of, or at least before

he began to found a Gospel upon, the Marcan *Grundschrift*, and he may thus have had it ready to his hand for incorporation here. The intention so to incorporate it would probably have affected the arrangement of the previous part of his Gospel in no more than two points: (*a*) it would have caused him to refrain from inserting (or to strike out if he had already inserted) the defensive discourse in a position parallel to that in which Mark places it; and (*b*) he would have had to make a consequent change in the position of the incident of the coming of the mother and brethren, which Mark (iii. 31, and cf. Mt xii. 46) attaches to that discourse, but for which Luke finds a place by subjoining it to the group of parables which forms the body of discourse that comes next in Mark's order (Lk viii. 19 ff.; the matter, however, is complicated by the occurrence of a very similar incident in Lk xi. 27 f., immediately after the 'defensive discourse'). In favour of this supposition that Luke may here have utilized a previously arranged document, it may be suggested that a writer whose *Sparsamkeit*, or economy in the use of his materials with a view to making the best use of his space, often[1] makes him careful to avoid repetitions of identical or similar matter, would hardly have given so fully the closely parallel charges to the Twelve and to the Seventy in chaps. ix and x, if he had drawn up the records of those two missions at or about the same time.

2. Or again, even if Luke was already in possession of the Marcan document upon which he elsewhere places his main reliance as to order, and as to events as distinguished from discourse, he may have deliberately decided to lay it aside here, because for this one portion of his work he may have had other guidance at first-hand towards writing in order

---

[1] See, however, the cautions against exaggerating this tendency in Luke given by Bebb in Hastings's *D. B.* iii. 172 *b*, and by Plummer in *Commentary*, p. xxviii. See also p. 35 above.

(καθεξῆς) as he wished to do, whereas Peter's account only came to him at second-hand, and through a writer who is described to us by Papias (Eus., *H. E.*, iii. 39) as not extending his carefulness and accuracy to the order in which the words and deeds of Christ had occurred. It may be that, at Caesarea or Jerusalem (Acts xxi. 8 ff., 15 ff.) or elsewhere, a more exact and chronological account of this final journey had been supplied to him by one who had at the time of the commencement of that journey become an 'eyewitness and minister of the Word'. And when that suggestion is made, the thought at once arises of that large body[1] of such 'eyewitnesses and ministers' (ὑπηρέται, a word not used of the ministry of the Twelve) who appear for the first time very soon after the beginning of this division of the Gospel (x. 1, and it may be that the preceding verses, ix. 57-62, refer to a sifting of disciples preparatory to this appointment of so many of them to 'preach the kingdom of God'). One would like to think, if one might, that according to the tradition which we first hear from Epiphanius, Luke himself was one of these 'Seventy', and that therefore he himself was the eyewitness through this journey which he describes so minutely, thus supplying to us what would be, in effect though not in form, the most precious of all 'We-sections'. But the distinction which he himself expressly draws between the narrators of whom he was one, and those who were their informants as having been 'from the beginning, eyewitnesses and ministers of the Word',

---

[1] Serious difficulties have been suggested by this mention of the Seventy in Luke x only: but, as Dr. Salmon reminds us, we may accept the statement that such 'supplemental missionaries' (among whom probably such men as Matthias and Joseph Barsabbas and possibly 'Philip the Evangelist' would be numbered) were sent forth at this period, without being equally 'certain ... that their number was exactly seventy or that they were all sent out at one time' (*Human Element in the Gospels*, p. 201). See also Sanday in Hastings's *D. B.* ii. 614 *b*; and König in vol. iii. 563 *a* on the number seventy bearing 'not unfrequently an approximate sense'. For instances of the frequent use of it as to officials in Josephus and elsewhere, see Plummer *in loc.*

has made the acceptance of that tradition all but impossible for us. We must be content to admit with the writer of the Muratorian fragment, 'Dominum tamen nec ipse vidit in carne.' We need not, however, put out of court so decidedly the conjecture that some other disciple, who had been one of the 'Seventy', subsequently supplied Luke with many or most of the materials for his description of this journey, and especially with the order in which events occurred during it. That supposition is at least directly opposed by none, if it is directly supported by none, of our data. In particular it seems to me that there is much less weight than has generally been supposed in the internal evidence against nearly all the sayings and doings here recorded having belonged originally to this late period of the ministry, which according to Luke followed the mission of the Seventy.[1] The most plausible objection is that drawn from one scene (xiii. 10-17) being laid in a synagogue; for it would seem that the use of synagogues for teaching was not now open to Jesus as it had been at first (cf., however, Jn xviii. 20). But even if they were by this time closed to Him in Galilee or parts of it, this need not necessarily have been the case in every outlying place that was visited in the course of this circuitous journey to Jerusalem. So this conjecture as to Luke's informant may at least be borne in mind as giving some interest—though not the interest originally intended—to the appointment of passages referring to the Seventy as the Gospels for St. Luke's Day both in the Western (Lk x. 1-7 or 1-9) and in the Eastern (Lk x. 16-21) Church.

[1] Such evidence is collected by Schmiedel in *Enc. Bibl.* ii. 1873. He there objects to the warning against the plots of Herod Antipas (xiii. 31) that it implies that Jesus was still in Galilee. But Peraea was also under Herod (*ib.* ii. 2030), and part of this period is said in Mk x. 1 and Mt xix. 1 to have been spent beyond the Jordan. See however as to Peraea Mr. Streeter on p. 159 of this volume, and Burkitt, *Gospel History*, &c., p. 96 f.; also Montefiore, *Synoptic Gospels*, ii. 923, 1025, on the different views as to the route to Jerusalem.

II. 1. St. Luke's Use of St. Mark's Gospel

But, indeed, all such conjectures and speculations as have been admitted into these last few paragraphs are easily made too much of, and when that is the case they bring discredit upon the serious study of the Synoptic Problem. They are only harmless if they are clearly and constantly and emphatically distinguished from such conclusions or working hypotheses as are supported by a preponderating, or at least a very substantial, amount of evidence. And that may be safely said of the view that Mark's Gospel was entirely disused as a direct authority by Luke in ix. 51–xviii. 14, whatever source or sources he may have rested upon in its absence.

SYLLABUS

Exceptional character of this 'Great Omission'.

Three proposed ways of accounting for it :—

I. It may have been added by a 'deutero-Mark' after Luke had made his use of Mark's Gospel. The unity of style throughout Mark is shown to be strongly against this solution.

II. Accidental omission must be allowed to be possible.

III. But deliberate omission, owing to a concurrence of various causes, appears to be more probable. This is shown by an examination of the contents of the nine sections which constitute the omitted part of Mark.

2. THE GREAT OMISSION BY ST. LUKE OF THE MATTER CONTAINED IN ST. MARK VI. 45–VIII. 26.

This well deserves its usual name of St. Luke's 'great omission'. It forms a startling contrast with the way in which he has dealt with St. Mark's Gospel up to this point. From the commencement of the Baptist's ministry he has been closely following the order of that Gospel, supplementing it with a good deal of fresh matter (chiefly in what is called his 'lesser interpolation', i. e. Lk vi. 20–viii. 3, see p. 31), but only seldom and briefly making real omissions from it. There are four other apparent omissions, but these are found upon examination to be only cases of supersession by similar matter or of postponements. For the call of the Apostles in Mk i. 16–20 (= Mt iv. 18–22) and the teaching in the synagogue at Nazareth (Mk vi. 1–6 = Mt xiii. 54–58) are superseded by the fuller narratives from a different source, which we find respectively in Lk. v. 1–11 and iv. 16–30; and though the Beelzebub discourse and the Parable of the Mustard Seed disappear from their places in the Marcan order (Mk iii. 22–30 and iv. 30–32), they are only postponed until Luke's 'greater interpolation' or 'Peraean section' (xi. 14–26 and xiii. 18 f.). There remain but three real omissions from Mk i–vi. 44, two of them being made by Matthew also, and being more or less easily explicable, viz. the desire of the 'friends' of Jesus to 'lay hold on him, for they said, he is beside himself' (Mk iii. 20 f.), which considerations of reverence might well cause to be passed over, and the Parable of the Seed growing secretly (Mk iv. 26 ff.), which to those who looked for an early 'consummation of the age' might not commend itself as it does to us; and the third being the details about the Baptist's death and its cause (more briefly given in Mt xiv. 1-12), as to which the fullness with which Mk (vi. 14-29) records them is perhaps more surprising to us, because less accordant with our estimate of the relative importance of things, than Lk's omission of them.[1]

But here there is a sudden change: after adopting for so long, and with such brief and slight exceptions, the substance as well as the order of Mk, Lk suddenly, after the conclusion of the miracle of the Feeding of the Five Thousand (ix. 17), omits 74 verses, or almost exactly one-ninth part of the 661[2] genuine verses of our Second Gospel. And the omission is not only thus great in compass, but it is complete and permanent: that is to say, there are no postponements or reservations of the omitted matter for use on other occasions, except only that the caution against 'the leaven of the Pharisees' (Mk viii. 15 = Mt xvi. 6) re-appears on a later occasion and in a quite different connexion in Lk xii. 1, as a warning against hypocrisy. The reference to washing before meals in Lk xi. 38 f. has been suggested as another exception, but there seems to be very little reason for regarding it as derived from Mk vii. 1 ff.[3]

After Lk has, in ix. 18, resumed the use of Mk, his omissions from it again become brief, no one of them extending over more than a dozen consecutive verses.[4]

---

[1] Luke however had already mentioned the fact of the imprisonment (iii. 19 f.) previously to its actual occurrence, for it must have been subsequent to the baptism of Jesus by John (iii. 21 f.).

[2] This number is arrived at by excluding as probably spurious Mk vii. 16 (in the 'great omission'); ix. 44, 46; xi. 26; xv. 28, as well as the appended verses xvi. 9-20.

[3] The refusal of a sign in Lk xi. 16, 29 ff. is not a case in point, the parallel to it being Mt xii. 38 ff., and not Mk viii. 11 f. = Mt xvi. 1-4.

[4] The omitted incidents, sayings, and important details are as follows, those marked * being omitted by Matthew also:—Mk viii. 32a*; 37; ix. 10-13; 14 b-16*; 23 f.*; 28 f.; ix. 41 (= Mt x. 42); 43, 45, 47, 48; 49*; x. 1-10†; 35-41†; xi. 11*; 12-14; 19-25†; xii. 11; 28-34 (but cf. Lk x. 25-28); xiii. 10; 18; 20; 22 f.; 27; 32; 34-7 (but cf. Lk xii. 36-40); xiv. 3-9†; 27 f.†; 33 f.; 38 b-42†; 50†; 51 f.*; 55-8; 59*; 60; xv. 16 20†; 44 f.*. The probable causes of all the most considerable of these omissions

How are we to account for this one great omission of 74 verses being made? Three ways of explaining it have been propounded:—

I. The omission may have been unavoidable, because this whole division of Mk may not yet have been inserted into that Gospel when Lk used it. To use a now well-known expression, it may have belonged to a 'deutero-Mark'.[1]

A good case could be made for this account of the matter if we could appeal to any appreciable linguistic difference between this one-ninth part of our Mk and the remaining eight-ninths. But we cannot do so. There is a general uniformity of style and wording in the whole Gospel which is sufficient to show that—apart from small additions and modifications—it was composed by one author, or at least was thoroughly worked over by one editor. To say that is not an attempt to deny that there are strong signs of a compiler's hand in our Second Gospel, whether the hand was that of Mark putting together at a later time[2] separate reminiscences heard and perhaps taken down at previous times from St. Peter, or of some second person; the proofs of some such compilation, whether of Aramaic or of Greek materials, are almost irresistible in parts of chapters iii, iv, and ix,[3] and there are phenomena in chapter xiii which have caused Colani's theory of the employment there of 'a little apocalypse' to be welcomed by many scholars.[4] But my contention is that

will appear incidentally as we proceed with the present inquiry (pp. 68-72 *passim*); these are marked † in this list.

[1] So Dr. A. Wright in *Synopsis*², p. lviii, and *Gospel of St. Luke*, p. 83, and elsewhere.

[2] Irenaeus expressly says (iii. 1. 1) that it was after Peter's death that what he had preached was put into writing by Mark; Papias does not specify how soon this was done.

[3] See *Encyc. Bibl.* ii. 1864-7, and Allen's *Commentary on Matthew*, pp. 193, 315.

[4] The case for it is well stated in Charles's *Lectures on Eschatology* (1899), pp. 323-9. See also Mr. Streeter on pp. 179 ff. of this volume.

any such secondary additions and arrangements—or perhaps sometimes derangements[1]—of matter were completed before the Gospel was clothed by some author or editor with the Greek form in which we know it. It is true that the distinctive expressions in Mk are less numerous and outstanding than those in Mt, and to a still greater degree than those in Lk, but still they are quite sufficient to show unity of style and manner—in the narrative nearly everywhere and frequently in the small amount of discourses also. Now on the whole these characteristics occur in the block of 74 verses here omitted by Lk with as much proportionate frequency as they do in the other 587 verses which (with brief and easily explained exceptions) were used by him. Among the proofs, lexical and grammatical, of unity of authorship in this one-ninth and in the other eight-ninths of Mk are the following :—

(a, b) To begin with the two adverbs which are the most conspicuous characteristics of Mk's style in narrative (apart from records of discourse), 5 out of 34 (or approximately one-seventh) of the occurrences of εὐθύς and 5 out of 26 (or approximately one-fifth) of the occurrences of πάλιν are found in this one-ninth part of the Gospel.

(c) Here also belong 18 or 19, being nearly one-seventh, of Mk's 141 historic presents.[2] To show how characteristic of him these are, it may be mentioned that there is only one such present in the division of Mt (xiv. 22–xvi. 12) which is parallel to 62 out of Mk's 74 verses now under consideration (the 12 verses describing two miracles in Mk vii. 31–37 and viii. 22–26 being alone unparalleled in Mt).

(d) Again, as to the imperfects ἔλεγεν and ἔλεγον, which occur 50 times in Mk against 9 times in Mt and 23 times in Lk, there are 6 cases of ἔλεγεν, or nearly one-eighth of the 50, in this division of Mk, while there is not a single case of either the singular or the plural in the corresponding parts of Mt.

(e) Here as elsewhere Mk (like Jn, but very unlike Mt and

[1] As, for instance, the location of the Beelzebub discourse between the two references to the family of Jesus in Mk iii. 21 and 31–35.
[2] A list of these is given in *Horae Synopticae*[2], pp. 144 ff.

II. 2. St. Luke's Use of St. Mark's Gospel

Lk) entirely abstains from ἰδού, with or without καί, in his narrative.[1]

(*f*) And the uncompounded verb πορεύομαι is avoided here, as it is in the rest of the Gospel, with perhaps the exception of ix. 30.

(*g*) Turning now to characteristics of Mk which can be observed in his small amount of discourse as well as in narrative, we find that his habit of generally commencing sentences or clauses with καί, and therefore using δέ comparatively seldom (*Hor. Syn.*[2] p. 150), is kept up here. Out of the 9 sections or sub-sections into which WH divide this part of the Gospel, 7 begin with καί— a proportion which, though it may be exceeded in other parts of Mk, is far greater than would be found in any of the other historical books. And, further, in the portions that can be compared with Mt, we find that clauses which follow a full stop, colon, or note of interrogation are introduced 37 times by καί and only 8 times by δέ in Mk, while in Mt καί is thus used only 16 times and δέ 19 times.[2] And as to Mk's two brief narratives of miracles, for which, as we saw, Mt supplies no parallels, καί is thus used 5 times, and δέ not at all, in each of them.

(*h*) Mk's frequent custom of using duplicate expressions, half of which only is used by the other Synoptists in their parallels, comes out in vii. 15 ἔξωθεν εἰσπορευόμενον, vii. 21 ἔσωθεν ... ἐκ τῆς καρδίας, viii. 17 οὔπω νοεῖτε, οὐδὲ συνίετε; as contrasted with the εἰσερχόμενον, ἐκ τῆς καρδίας, οὔπω νοεῖτε of Mt xv. 11, 19; xvi. 9 respectively.

(*i*) It is notable that ὅ ἐστιν, used by Mk alone among the Evangelists—in introducing an interpretation or explanation—occurs twice out of six times in this division of the Gospel (vii. 11, 34).

(*k*) And διαστέλλομαι, which is almost if not quite peculiar to him (for the reading is doubtful in Mt xvi. 20), occurs here three times out of five.

(*l*) The diminutive θυγάτριον is found both in Mk vii. 25 and previously in v. 23, but nowhere else in the N.T. or the LXX.

Some other instances of consistency in the exclusive or preferential employment of words or phrases might be

---

[1] See J. H. Moulton, *Gram. of N. T. Greek*, i. 11 *note*.
[2] We may notice especially the quasi-adversative καί in Mk vii. 24 *c*, as in xii. 12 *a*.

added:[1] but those already given seem sufficient to establish a moral certainty that this part of Mk was drawn up by the same author or editor as the rest of the Gospel.[2] And from this surely there results a very strong probability that it formed part of the Marcan document which was available for Lk as well as for Mt. Of course we cannot claim that inference as more than a very probable one, for we cannot shut out the two possibilities:

(1) that this section of 74 verses may somehow have dropped off from the MS., as the conclusion seems to have done, though this is much less likely to have happened in the middle than at the end of a book or roll; and
(2) that the author or editor, keeping up exactly the same style, may have chanced to insert this section into the MS. just between the times of it being used by Mt and by Lk—if indeed Mt used it before Lk did, which would not now be considered as certain as it used to be. But these do not seem to me to rank as more than bare possibilities.

II. Considerably more probability attaches to a second theory, viz. that this division of our Second Gospel was contained in Lk's copy of it, but that he accidentally left it unused, having perhaps been misled into doing so by passing on in his MS. from the mention of feeding multitudes in Mk vi. 42-44 to that in Mk viii. 19-21, or from the name Bethsaida in vi. 45 to the same name[3] in viii. 22 (the place being nowhere else mentioned in Mk). I have long thought that this is a more than possible solution; and the evidence for it is greatly strengthened by consideration of the physical difficulties that must have beset compilers and copyists in the first century as compared with our own literary conveniences.[4]

[1] Ἄλαλος and κράβαττος may be specially named; and φέρω where ἄγω might be expected.
[2] It is instructive to observe the contrast with xvi. 9-20, from which Marcan characteristics are almost entirely absent (πρωί and εὐαγγέλιον being the unimportant exceptions).
[3] There is however a Western reading Βηθανίαν.
[4] See Dr. Sanday in this volume, pp. 16 ff.

III. But for those who cannot bring themselves to accept as likely such a prolonged case of omission by homoeoteleuton or by any other accident, there remains a third solution. Lk may have intentionally passed over this whole division of Mk, because its contents seemed to him unsuitable for his Gospel, or at least not so suitable for it as other materials which he had ready for use. And that this may not improbably have been the case as to all, and would almost certainly be the case as to most, of its nine constituent parts,[1] will appear if we consider them with reference to what we can learn elsewhere as to the proclivities and preferences which influenced him in his adoption or rejection of materials.

It will be best to take these nine sections according to the causes which may have led to Lk's omission of them, instead of taking them in the order in which they stand in the Gospel.

(1, 2) Let us begin with the two passages which are absent from Mt as well as from Lk, namely, the two accounts of single miracles of healing in Mk vii. 31–37 and viii. 22–26. Though these accounts are of much interest to ourselves as showing the methods through which Jesus occasionally, and perhaps usually, wrought cures, they would be less well adapted than others for employment by teachers and preachers as proofs of His divine mission in the sense in which St. Peter speaks to the Jews of Him as 'approved (or demonstrated, $ἀποδεδειγμένον$) of God unto you by mighty works and wonders and signs, which God did by him in the midst of you' (Acts ii. 22). These two are the only cases in the Synoptic Gospels in which any other means than laying on of hands is used by Jesus;[2] and the means used in both of them—the application of

---

[1] These form the nine sections numbered 60, 61, and 63–69 in Tischendorf's *Synopsis Evangelica*.
[2] Gould on St. Mark in *Int. Crit. Comm.*, p. 149.

saliva—was so familiar in magic and in medicine, which often were and are closely allied in the East, that it might seem to detract from the exceptional and signal character of the cures.[1] Something of the same effect might be produced by the gradual process of the recovery of sight by the blind man at Bethsaida, as contrasted, for instance, with the case of the man or men at Jericho who 'immediately[2] received sight'. And again a sense of difficulty or painful effort in the Healer might be thought likely to be suggested by the record that He looked up to heaven and 'sighed' or 'groaned'.[3] These considerations might be sufficient to cause the omission of the details of these two miracles by Mt and Lk.[4] And Lk especially, in his readiness to save space by avoiding repetition, would be content with the more impressive and significant healings of a $κωφός$ and of a blind man which he meant to record further on in his Gospel (xi. 14 and xviii. 35-43).

(3, 4, 5, 6) The suggestion as to avoidance of repetition which was thrown out in that last sentence has much more force and importance with reference to four other sections of the omitted part of Mk. Certainly there is some tendency in Lk to pass over incidents similar to those which he has already recorded. No doubt the influence of this tendency has been carelessly exaggerated; and more than one recent writer[5] has warned us against making too much of it, by reminding us that we read in Lk such duplicates as the commissioning of two bands of teachers (ix. 1 ff. and x. 1 ff.), the healing of one leper and of ten (v. 12 ff. and xvii. 12 ff.), two comparisons of the position of the mother of

[1] But there is another case of it in Jn ix. 6. Compare Tac. *Hist.* iv. 81.
[2] Matthew and Mark $εὐθύς$, Luke $παραχρῆμα$.
[3] $Στενάζω$ and $ἀναστενάζω$ are applied to Jesus by Mark only, the former here, and the latter in viii. 12.
[4] Matthew seems to refer in a general way to the first of them, and perhaps to both, in xv. 29-31.
[5] So Bebb in Hastings's *D. B.* iii. 172 f.; Plummer, *Comm. on St. Luke*, p. xxviii, already referred to (p. 56).

II. 2. St. Luke's Use of St. Mark's Gospel 69

Jesus with that of His disciples (viii. 19 ff., xi. 27 f.), two disputes as to who should be the greatest (ix. 46, xxii. 24), besides the three predictions of the Passion and (twice) of the Resurrection (ix. 22, 44, xviii. 31 ff.). But after making all allowances for these and other passages more or less like one another, and also for the briefer 'doublets' in Lk, this tendency is surely traceable in the omissions of the anointing at Bethany (Mk xiv. 3 ff., Mt xxvi. 6 ff.) presumably because of the anointing in the Pharisee's house (Lk vii. 36 ff.), of the incident of the barren fig-tree (Mk xi. 12 ff. and 20 ff., Mt xxi. 18 ff.) because of the parable so closely resembling it (Lk xiii. 6 ff.), of the mocking by Pilate's soldiers (Mk xv. 17 ff., Mt xxvii. 27 ff.) because of that by Herod's soldiers (Lk xxiii. 11).[1] And if there was in his mind any such disposition to abbreviate his Gospel by passing over matter that would add nothing essentially new to it, most certainly this tendency (which has been well expressed by the German word *Sparsamkeit*) would be appealed to and called into exercise as soon as he reached and examined this division of his Marcan MS.

(*a*) Especially this would be the case as to the Feeding of the Four Thousand. So close indeed is this narrative to that of the Feeding of the Five Thousand, that to us it seems less difficult to understand why Lk omitted it than why Mk and Mt give it at such length; they seem to have done so mainly with a view to the distinct references to the two miracles in that rebuke of the Apostles (Mk viii. 19 ff. = Mt xvi. 9 ff.) which they were intending to record, but which we shall see is not retained by Lk.

(*b*) Again, the first narrative omitted, namely the record of a second storm on the lake (Mk vi. 45-52), brings out no new lesson in addition to that contained in the record of the first storm (Mk iv. 35-41), though it is in a different way that the disciples are assured of their Lord's care for them. And, as we shall see presently, the obtuseness of the heart ($καρδία\ πεπωρωμένη$, vi. 52) which Mk here

---
[1] Perhaps we may add the statement by Jesus of the Two Great Commandments (Mk xii. 29-31, Mt xxii. 37-9), which had been attributed by Luke (x. 27) to the inquiring lawyer.

records in connexion with the walking on the water is the kind of trait which Lk does not care to preserve.

(c) Next to this comes a general account of miracles worked on the plain of Gennesaret (Mk vi. 53-6); but if Lk had embodied it in his narrative he would have added but little [1] to the similar account which he had already given in vi. 17-19, founding it upon Mk iii. 7-11.

(d) And if he had retained from Mk viii. 11, 12 the request for and refusal of a sign from heaven, it would practically have been only another account, less full in detail and less appropriate in situation, of the request and refusal which he was intending to give later on (xi. 16, 29 ff.), drawing it, like Mt, from Q [or *Logia*], and subjoining it, like Mt, to the Beelzebub-discourse. Mt, on the other hand, does in his xvi. 1, 4 retain the Marcan narrative, and consequently he has there and in xii. 38, 39 a doublet, which Lk saves some space by avoiding.

(7) Another observable tendency in Lk is to limit the amount of anti-Pharisaic controversy which he preserves. This tendency again must not be exaggerated; for we have to bear in mind the unparalleled reference to the Pharisees as 'lovers of money' in Lk xvi. 14, 15, and the rebukes delivered at the tables of Pharisees in Lk vii. 36 ff. and xiv. 1-14.[2] But it appears very distinctly in the omission from his Sermon (on the Level Place) of the passages against Pharisaic legalism which Mt has in his Sermon on the Mount (v. 20-48, vi. 1-6, 16-18), though the two Sermons have the same general framework. The same tendency appears no less plainly in the absence from Lk of the whole discussion following upon the Pharisees' question about divorce, as related by Mk in x. 2-12 and reproduced by Mt in xix. 3-11.[3] We may therefore attribute to

---

[1] The detail of carrying the sick on beds would have been such an addition; but Luke had already given an instance of this in v. 18.

[2] In Lk xi. 37 ff. there is another case of rebuke at table, but almost the whole of it is also embodied in the public discourse given by Matthew in his chap. xxiii. A. B. Bruce (*Expositor's Gk. Test.* i. 47) suggests that in Luke what is retained of the anti-Pharisaic element 'is softened by being given, much of it, not as spoken *about*, but as spoken *to*, Pharisees by Jesus as a guest in their houses'.

[3] In connexion with Luke's tendency to minimize anti-Pharisaic contro-

II. 2. *St. Luke's Use of St. Mark's Gospel*

the same cause the omission of the primarily anti-Pharisaic discourse, arising from the 'unwashen hands' of the disciples, which we have in Mk vii. 1-23 (followed in Mt xv. 1-20), and in the course of which Jesus spoke words 'making all meats clean' and showing that the only real source of defilement was not physical but moral.

(8) The name 'Pharisees' occurs in yet another of our nine sections of Mk, namely, in the sayings of Jesus which arose out of the Apostles' forgetfulness to take bread with them in the boat (Mt viii. 14-21, preserved substantially in Mt xvi. 5-12). But in that case the reason for Lk's omission of the section does not seem to lie in the caution against 'the leaven of the Pharisees', for he himself records elsewhere (xii. 1), and in a quite different connexion, a like caution—whether it had remained in his mind as a reminiscence of this rejected passage of Mk or whether it was drawn with the following verses (Lk xii. 2-9 = Mt x. 26-33) from Q we cannot say—'Beware ye of the leaven of the Pharisees, which is hypocrisy.' Rather this omission is the result of Lk's tendency to 'spare the twelve'[1]—to say comparatively little as to their faults and failings. Thus, to take only a few prominent instances, Lk passes over both the prediction that they all should be offended (Mk xiv. 27, Mt xxvi. 31), and the fact that after their Master's arrest they all 'left him and fled' (Mk xiv. 50, Mt xxvi. 56); he alone apologetically describes the failure of the three to watch in Gethsemane as a 'sleeping for sorrow' (Lk xxii. 45: contrast Mk xiv. 37, 40 and Mt xxvi. 40, 43), and he considerably abbreviates the narrative as it affects them; he omits the attempt of St. Peter to 'rebuke' his Master

---

versy it is noticeable that certain rebukes which Matthew represents as spoken against Scribes and Pharisees appear in Luke to be addressed to the people generally: compare Lk iii. 7 with Mt iii. 7; Lk xi. 14, 15 with Mt xii. 24; Lk xi. 16, 29 with Mt xii. 38; Lk vi. 39 with Mt xv. 12-14.

[1] A. B. Bruce, *op. cit.*, p. 46, quoting Schanz.

and the stern repulse with which it was met (Mk viii. 32 f., Mt xvi. 22 f.), he has no record of the ambitious request of James and John (Mk x. 35-45, Mt xx. 20-8), contenting himself with the general remark (Lk xviii. 34) that the disciples did not understand the preceding prediction of the sufferings and death of Jesus, instead of showing how these two exhibited their anticipations of an earthly and temporal kingdom. This last instance is particularly interesting to us here, because we find Mt in some degree palliating the two Apostles' conduct by assigning the actual utterance of the request to their mother, while Lk ignores the incident altogether; and we have thus a parallel to the present case, in which Mt softens the language of the rebuke of the twelve in several points, and especially by not preserving the attribution to them of a 'hardened' or blinded heart (πεπωρωμένην καρδίαν, Mk viii. 17),[1] while Lk goes further and removes all possibility of discredit attaching to them by leaving out the whole rebuke and its occasion.

(9) There remains one more of the nine sections which compose the part of Mk omitted by Lk, namely that containing the cure of the Syrophenician woman's daughter in 'the borders of Tyre and Sidon' (Mk vii. 24-30, Mt xv. 21-8). And in this one case it may seem at first sight that the omission of the incident could not be intentional, since the idiosyncrasies and prepossessions of the Third Evangelist would incline him to preserve it in his Gospel. For we rightly regard him as one who, because of his almost certainly Gentile origin and his Pauline associations, would rejoice in the opening of the door of faith to the Gentiles, and who therefore would welcome and emphasize any anticipations of this in the ministry of Christ. Thus we understand his omissions of the limitation of the preaching

[1] On the exact meaning of πωροῦν and πώρωσις, which in the Synoptic Gospels are used only by Mark in iii. 5, vi. 52 (already referred to), and here, see Dean Armitage Robinson in *Comm. on Eph.*, pp. 264 ff., or *Journal of Theol. Studies*, iii. 81 ff.

of the Gospel to the Jews as prescribed in Mt x. 5, 6, and his insertion of the references to the widow of Zarephath and to Naaman the Syrian in Lk iv. 25–7; and his omission of the visit of the Magi (Mt ii. 1 ff.) seems to us only accountable by the supposition that it was unknown to him. How then, we may ask, can he have brought himself to omit these seven verses of Mark, recording as they do the withdrawal of Jesus into a 'frankly pagan'[1] land and a work of mercy wrought in that land[2] in compliance with the request of one of its inhabitants? But if we look closely and carefully into the narrative we may well doubt whether its insertion would have interested, or at any rate whether it would have gratified, Lk's Gentile readers at the time when he compiled his Gospel, and when the claims of the Gentiles to equal rights with Jews were thoroughly established in the Church. It in no way prefigures or anticipates the granting of such rights. For, as Harnack says, neither Mk nor Mt 'leaves it open to question that this incident represented *an exceptional case* for Jesus; and the exception proves the rule'.[3] Mk at once makes it clear that it was for retirement only, and not for the purposes of His ministry that He passed over into that heathen land (ver. 24): when 'he entered into a house there, he would have no man know it', and it was only when 'he could not be hid'[4] that the occasion for the cure was given; the mother's petition is at first refused in terms of which we can only realize the discouragement when we call to mind the ancient and oriental connotation—so different from our own in England now—of the name 'dog'[5]; and, to use Dr. Hort's words, when

[1] Swete, *in loc.*
[2] For it is Matthew only, and not Mark, who says that she came out *from* those borders to make her request: see Allen on Mt xv. 22.
[3] *Expansion of Christianity*, i. 41 (E. T.).
[4] Here is one of those attributions of inability to Jesus which Mark ventures to make, but which did not commend themselves to Luke; cf. Mk vi. 5; xiii. 32 (probably = Mt xxiv. 36); perhaps also i. 45.
[5] See Mt vii. 6, Phil iii. 2 (and Lightfoot on that verse and on verse 8),

at length the boon is 'granted her, nothing is said to take away from its exceptional and as it were extraneous character, it remains a crumb from the children's table'.[1] It would seem then, on consideration of this narrative, that it might be repellent rather than attractive to St. Luke's readers so far as it was taken as bearing on the mutual relations of Jews and Gentiles in the Christian Church; and there seems to have been no other special ground on which he should wish to preserve it, since the case of the Centurion's Servant at Capernaum (vii. 2–10) had already provided him with an instance of a cure being wrought at a distance. We can thus easily understand his omitting this section as well as the other eight, if at this stage of his compilation he began to see the impossibility of compressing his materials within his space,[2] and therefore the necessity of limiting himself to the most important of them, among which he would certainly reckon the incident at Caesarea Philippi, to which he next proceeds.

There seems, then, to be good reason for holding that all the varied matter which happens to come together in Mk vi. 45–viii. 26 is such as Lk, judging from what we otherwise know of him as an author, would be at least not indisposed to pass over. Possibly, indeed, the truth of the case may lie in a combination of the two hypotheses of accident and intention: that is to say, Lk may first have missed this division of Mk by opening his MS. at the wrong place, as above suggested, and in that case, even if he afterwards discovered the mistake and examined the omitted matter, it might seem to him that none of it was so necessary or even suitable for his special purposes that he would care to go back and repair the omission by any subsequent insertions.

2 Pet ii. 22, Rev xxii. 15. I can find no ground for the suggestion that κυνάρια used by Mark and Matthew here implies fondness ('pet dogs', Bruce, *in loc.*) rather than contempt. The only companionable dog seems to be that of Tobias in Tobit v. 16, xi. 4. There is no such friendliness implied in the watch-dogs of Job xxx. 1, Is lvi. 10, 11.

[1] *Judaic Christianity*, p. 34, quoted by Swete.
[2] See Dr. Sanday, p. 25 f., above.

II. 3. *St. Luke's Use of St. Mark's Gospel*

SYLLABUS

Luke does not in his Passion-narrative desert the Second Gospel, but employs it with unusual and remarkable freedom.

This is shown by two contrasts:—

I. The contrast between Luke's use and Matthew's use of Mark's Passion-narrative—

　i. as to verbal similarity,

　ii. as to the introduction of additional matter, and

　iii. especially as to the number of transpositions; and

II. The still more important contrast between Luke's own use of Mark here and elsewhere in those same three respects.

Suggestion that Luke's previous knowledge and use of a Passion-narrative as St. Paul's 'fellow-worker' may have caused him to dispense with the close and constant reference to Mark's Gospel which we find elsewhere.

3. ST. LUKE'S PASSION-NARRATIVE CONSIDERED WITH REFERENCE TO THE SYNOPTIC PROBLEM.

The third of these 'limitations' is of a much less conspicuous kind than the first and second. It is a qualification of, and not an exception to, St. Luke's use of St. Mark's Gospel. But I think that it deserves and will repay consideration. It is to be found in Lk xxii. 14–xxiv. 10, which may be described with sufficient accuracy for our present purpose as St. Luke's Passion-narrative, though it commences with the institution of the Lord's Supper, and includes the visit of the women to the empty tomb. There the Marcan source is not indeed deserted, as it apparently is in the two divisions of Luke already discussed, and in the lesser interpolation which was also referred to (p. 31); nor is its main order departed from, as in Mt viii–xiii, but that source is used with a freedom, as to details both of matter and of order, to which there is no parallel elsewhere in any considerable department of the two Gospels that are founded upon it.

I propose to give proofs of this statement, and then to suggest a certain significance that it seems to have as bearing upon the authorship and composition of the Third Gospel.

That these 123 verses of Passion-narrative are rightly reckoned among those portions of Luke, forming 469 verses out of 1,149, or about two-fifths of the Gospel, which are to be regarded as in some sense founded upon the Marcan basis, will be generally admitted. The proof of this lies not only or chiefly in the main sequence of events, which indeed could not be very different in the Passion-narratives, and which is to a large extent paralleled in the Fourth Gospel

II. 3. St. Luke's Use of St. Mark's Gospel

also, but also and most forcibly in the smaller structural and verbal similarities to Mark (who is here closely followed throughout by Matthew) which appear in such verses as Lk xxii. 18, 22, 42, 46, 47, 52 f., 54 b, 61, 71 ; xxiii. 22, 26, 34 b, 44 f., 46, 52 f. ; xxiv. 6 a.

Our attention, therefore, may be mainly directed to the other task of showing the unusual and remarkable freedom with which Luke here uses his fundamental source. This may be best exhibited by way of contrast (I) with Matthew's procedure in his parallel Passion-narrative, and (II) with Luke's own procedure in the other parts of his Gospel which rest upon the same basis.

I

i. The degrees of closeness with which Mark's wording is followed in any parts of the First and Third Gospels respectively may be ascertained with a very near approach to accuracy by a method which Mr. Rushbrooke's invaluable *Synopticon* makes practicable. There it may be seen how many of the words used in any passage of any one Gospel are reproduced, wholly or in part, in the corresponding passage of any other Gospel. Thus, to take one short verse as an illustration, in Lk xxii. 42, which contains 19 words, 12 words are either wholly or in part printed in red or in spaced type, thus showing that those 12 words are, either in their entirety as $παρένεγκε$ and the 5 following words, or in part as the $θελ$ in $θέλημα$, found also in Mk xiv. 36. Now if we examine in that way both the 123 verses of Luke's Passion-narrative and also the 130 verses of Matthew's parallel narrative, which extend from xxvi. 20 to xxviii. 6, and if we tabulate and compare the results of those examinations, so as to show the amount of agreement with Mark's wording which those narratives respectively show, a very striking contrast presents itself. Matthew's narrative contains 2,083 words; and of these we find that

1,070 words, being about 51 per cent., or a trifle more than half, agree either wholly or in part with the words used in Mark. Luke's narrative contains 1,906 words; but of these only 507 words, being not much more than a quarter, or about 27 per cent., are found either wholly or partially in Mark. That is to say, *Matthew adheres to Mark's language very nearly twice as closely as Luke does*—surely a very notable and significant contrast, as implying very different ways of dealing with the same source. And to those who hold—as it seems to me impossible to avoid holding—that both oral and documentary transmission had shares in the formation of the First and Third Gospels, the natural inference will be that in this part of Matthew the documentary mode of transmission, and in this part of Luke the oral mode, very largely preponderated.

ii. The same inference may be drawn, though less definitely and less directly, if we compare the two Passion-narratives in a less mechanical way, paying attention, not to the amount of verbal alteration from Mark shown in them, but to the amount of distinctly new matter which they respectively add to that source, thus supplying us with additional information. No doubt opinions will differ to a certain extent as to what should thus be classed as distinctly new matter, but I think that in Matthew we may thus label 25 complete verses and 2 half-verses, viz. xxvi. 25, 50 a, 52–4; xxvii. 3–10, 19, 24 f., 43, 51 b, 52 f., 62–6; xxviii. 2, 4, besides a few brief phrases, of which εἰς ἄφεσιν ἁμαρτιῶν (xxvi. 28) is perhaps the most important. In Luke, on the other hand, the new information given us (excluding xxii. 24–7 as being probably transferred from Mk ix. 34 f. and x. 42–5) may be fairly estimated as filling 33 verses and 3 half-verses, viz. xxii. 28 f., 30 (cf., however, Mt xix. 28), 31 f., 35–8, 48 f., 51, 61 a, 67 b, 68; xxiii. 2, 5–12, 15, 27–31, 40–3, 46 b, 48, besides some briefer additions, such as ὡς ἐγένετο ἡμέρα (xxii. 66). There are

II. 3. St. Luke's Use of St. Mark's Gospel

also 3 such verses and 2 half-verses which have not been reckoned here, being those which are double-bracketed by WH as probably insertions by a later hand than Luke's (xxii. 19 b, 20, 43 f.; xxiii. 34 a). And it has not been thought necessary to complicate the comparison by referring to additions to Mark which are identical in Matthew and Luke, for these, so far as they have any importance at all, are limited to two, viz. τίς ἐστιν ὁ παίσας σε; in Mt xxvi. 68, Lk xxii. 64, and ἐξελθὼν ἔξω ... πικρῶς in Mt xxvi. 75, Lk xxii. 62; cf. also Mt xxvii. 54 with Lk xxiii. 47. It may be remarked in passing that the extreme fewness and slightness of these correspondences seems to show that the source (Q or *Logia*) upon which Matthew and Luke had previously drawn so largely did not extend over the period of the Passion.[1]

We have seen, then, that the new or non-Marcan information given in Luke's Passion-narrative only exceeds in amount that given in Matthew's to a comparatively small extent, the proportion between the two being only about four to three (34½ verses against 26, according to the above approximate estimates). That small excess would in itself be hardly worth our notice. But it is certainly important to observe that the difference between the two narratives *as to the way in which the new matter is introduced*, is very much more marked—so much so that in *Synopticon*, while two of its large pages (195 f.) suffice for exhibiting Matthew's 'single tradition', fully five of them (from the middle of p. 227 to the middle of p. 232) are required for Luke's 'single tradition'. The cause of this notable difference is that Matthew's additions are, in nearly every case, simply insertions into the Marcan text—insertions generally made without involving any alterations in that text, though occasionally causing slight modifications of a few words at the points where the older narrative is

[1] See p. 129.

resumed, as in xxvi. 55; xxvii. 11, 26. So it will be found—except only in xxviii. 2-4, where the matter is complicated by the previous notice of the setting of the watch—that if one strikes out with a pen the Matthaean insertions, it will need only a few more strokes of that pen in order to remove the few resumptive words, and thus to make the narrative as consecutive and as intelligible as in the original Marcan text. But the case is very different when we turn to Luke's additions, for we find that the Marcan narrative is in many cases very considerably modified for the sake of them. To work out this point in detail would require more space than can be given here; but striking instances may be seen in the setting and environment of Lk xxii. 31 f., 67 f.; xxiii. 5-12, 40-3. The old and the new matter are so blended that the one is often unintelligible without the other. And therefore it was, for the sake of intelligibility, that it was found necessary to print in *Synopticon* so many Lucan verses which are substantially parallel to Mark, besides those which are simply Lucan additions; and thus, as has been already said, while the proportion of actually new Lucan matter to actually new Matthaean matter is only about four to three, the amount of space required to display them respectively is in the proportion of five to two.

Here again, then, we find in Luke a freedom of adaptation which points to just such modifications and expansions of the Marcan source as would occur in the course of continued oral use of it, while Matthew's procedure is that of a man who adhered as closely as he could—or at any rate very closely—to his Marcan MS., even when he had to make insertions into it.

iii. A third distinction which may be observed between the habits of the two compilers points still more decidedly in the same direction. Transpositions or inversions, both verbal and substantial, of Mark's order are unusually and remarkably frequent in Luke's Passion-narrative. The num-

II. 3. St. Luke's Use of St. Mark's Gospel

ber of them is no less than 12. With the exception of Nos. 1 and 2 in the list, perhaps none of them have any practical importance in the way of giving us different impressions as to the course of events. The others are unimportant in themselves, being chiefly such transpositions of statements as do not necessarily imply any transposition of the facts referred to; but does not their very unimportance make it unlikely that a compiler using a MS. source would have taken the trouble to make such alterations from its order?

The list of the transpositions is as follows (it will be seen that Matthew always follows Mark, except in No. 11, where he does not supply a parallel) :—

1. In Lk xxii. 15-23 the reference to the coming betrayal is recorded *after*, in Mk xiv. 18-25 (so Mt xxvi. 21-9) it is recorded *before*, the institution of the Lord's Supper. This difference is highly important and interesting in its bearing on the question whether Judas was one of those who received the eucharistic bread and wine.

2. (*a*) If the short Western text preferred by WH is adopted in Lk xxii. 17-20, the only cup mentioned is given *before* the bread at the Last Supper (cf. 1 Cor x. 16 and *Didache* 9), and not *after* it, as in Mk xiv. 22-4 (so Mt xxvi. 26-8).

(*b*) If the usual and longer text is there followed, there is a transposition of another kind connected with the institution of the Lord's Supper; for the saying, 'I will not drink from henceforth,' &c., in Lk xxii. 18-20 *precedes*, while in Mk xiv. 22-5 (so Mt xxvi. 26-9) it *follows*, the words of institution.

It is true that both these transpositions are avoided by the arrangement of the narrative in b and c, and very similarly in Syr^{cur} and Syr^{sin}: but almost certainly such arrangement was not original, but made for harmonistic purposes.

3. In Lk xxii. 21-3 the intimation that the traitor would be one who was then present at the table, and the woe pronounced upon him, *precede*, in Mk xiv. 19-21 (so Mt xxvi. 22-4) they *follow*, the questioning of the Apostles as to which of them should be the traitor. It is possible, however, that the questioning among themselves in Luke is to be regarded as an incident distinct from the question 'Is it I?' addressed by them to Jesus in Mark and Matthew.

4. In Lk xxii. 33 f. Peter's denial is foretold *before*, in Mk xiv. 29-32 (so Mt xxvi. 33-5) *after*, the departure from the supper room.

5. In Lk xxii. 56-71 Peter's denials are recorded *before* the examination before the high priest and the mockery by the soldiers there, but in Mk xiv. 55-72 (so Mt xxvi 59-75) *after* those incidents. Here, however, Luke's reason for making the transposition is obvious; it was in order to bring together in his vv. 55 and 56 the statements which Mark separates in his vv. 54 and 66.

6. And in Lk xxii. 63-71 the mockery is related *before*, but in Mk xiv. 55-65 (so Mt xxvi. 59-68) *after*, the examination.

Thus the joint result of the transpositions numbered 5 and 6 is that the three incidents are recorded in these different orders (note yet another arrangement in Jn xviii. 12-27):—

LUKE.	MARK (and MATTHEW).
1. Denials.	1. Examination.
2. Mockery.	2. Mockery.
3. Examination.	3. Denials.

7. In Lk xxiii. 35-8 the superscription on the cross is not mentioned until *after* the reviling and mockery by the rulers and soldiers, though before that by the one malefactor; but in Mk xv. 26-32 (so Mt xxvii. 37-44) the mention of the superscription *precedes* the mockery of

II. 3. *St. Luke's Use of St. Mark's Gospel*

passers-by and chief priests and soldiers, as well as the reproaches of the two malefactors.

8. In Lk xxiii. 36, as has just been said, mockery is ascribed to the soldiers in connexion with offering the vinegar (a connexion perhaps suggested by Ps lxix. 20 f.) when Jesus is on the cross; but mockery from soldiers is only mentioned by Mark at a much earlier stage, viz. in chap. xv. 16-20 (so Mt xxvii. 27-31) referring to the Praetorium. Luke also speaks of Herod's soldiers as mocking (xxiii. 11). Of course it is possible that three distinct incidents, or at least two, may be referred to; but some amount of transposition seems far more probable, judging from the analogy of other cases in which such transferences of words undoubtedly took place.

9. In Lk xxiii. 45 f. the rending of the veil is recorded *before*, in Mk xv. 37 f. (so Mt xxvii. 50 f.) *after*, the death of Jesus.

10. The time of the deposition and burial, viz. the evening of the day of preparation, is only mentioned by Luke (xxiii. 50-4) *after* his account of the request of Joseph and the entombment, but it is named *before* those incidents in Mk xv. 42-6 (so ὀψίας in Mt xxvii. 57). In Luke the notice of time seems also to have reference to the following statement about the women.

11. In Lk xxiii. 56 the preparing of spices and ointments is mentioned *before* the Sabbath is named, and, if we had no other information, we should have supposed that this work was done on the eve of the day of rest; in Mk xvi. 1 the spices are said to have been bought when the Sabbath was *past*. Matthew has no mention of spices or ointments.

12. Luke, in xxiv. 1-10, does not give the names of the women until *after* he has described their visit to the tomb; Mark, in xvi. 1-8 (so Mt xxviii. 1-8), *commences* his account by naming them.

Thus Luke exhibits twelve transpositions from Mark, where Matthew exhibits none. Now such inversions of order are very much more likely to occur in oral than in documentary transmission. The experience of those who have had personal experience of both these methods of reproduction of sources, on the one hand as extempore preachers or teachers, and on the other hand as authors, or even as copyists of extracts into their own notebooks, will have shown them that writers are very unlikely to make changes in the order of the materials before them, except for some special purpose, but that such inversions are constantly occurring in the course of *memoriter* narration and instruction. (See Wright, *New Testament Problems*, pp. 91, 136 f.; also the present writer's *Horae Synopticae*[2], p. 77 f.)

We have seen, then, in three distinct ways, the remarkable freedom with which Luke, as contrasted with Matthew, uses in his Passion-narrative the Marcan *Grundschrift*. And in each case the freedom appeared to be of such a kind as was likely to result from oral use of the source.

II

But perhaps it may be said that there is nothing very surprising or unaccountable in two writers being led by their personal idiosyncrasies, or by the special objects of their literary works, to utilize with very different degrees of closeness a source which lay before them both. Admitting the fact, we may not unreasonably be content to leave it without explanation. But we pass now to what does most certainly call for explanation. We shall see that Luke's free treatment of the Marcan document in his Passion-narrative (xxii. 14 – xxiv. 10) is very strikingly *different from his own treatment of it* in very nearly all the other portions of his Gospel which have any appearance of being grounded on Mark. I say in very nearly all those

II. 3. St. Luke's Use of St. Mark's Gospel

portions, not in quite all of them; for both Matthew's and Luke's narratives of the Baptist's preaching and of the Temptation, though they stand in parallel places to Mark's, and though they embody some matter that seems to be Marcan, contain also a large amount of matter that is not found in Mark. The causes of this cannot be fully discussed here: it may be said, however, as to the Baptist-narrative that there is considerable reason for thinking that there, and probably there only, some of the original Marcan or Petrine matter may have been omitted from our present Mark (so Woods in *Studia Biblica*, ii. 85, 91, 94; cf. Stanton in *Encycl. Brit.* xxix. 41); while of the Temptation-narrative we can only say that in this case the details which the two compilers found in their (? Logian) source happened to be very much larger in quantity than the slight Marcan framework, from which but 13 words are preserved wholly or in part by Matthew, and but 12 by Luke.

i. But let us pass beyond those two more or less preliminary sections, and examine Luke's records of our Lord's actual ministry, from Lk iv. 14 = Mk i. 14 = Mt iv. 12 onwards, so far as they are based on Mark, with a view to comparing them with his Passion-narrative. And first let us apply to them that mechanical and verbal kind of examination with which we commenced our comparison between Matthew's and Luke's Passion-narratives. Now Luke's Ministry-narrative which concerns us consists of 311 verses, which are contained in five sections of the Gospel, namely, Lk iv. 31–44; v. 12–vi. 19; viii. 4–ix. 51; xviii. 15–43; xix. 29–xxii. 13 (I have omitted some single verses such as iv. 14 as being negligible quantities, and I have excluded iv. 15–30 and v. 1–11 as apparently resting upon non-Marcan sources, and being but slightly influenced by Mk vi. 1–6 and i. 16–20). Those 311 verses contain 5,320 words, of which no less than 2,829, being rather more than half of them or about 53 per cent., are also found either wholly or in part in Mark. It should be mentioned in passing that the case is almost the same in Matthew; for those parts of the First Gospel, extending over 477 verses, which refer to the ministry of Jesus and which appear to be founded on the Marcan source, contain 8,180 words, of which 4,173, being a very little more than half, or about 51 per cent., occur either wholly or partially in Mark, so that Matthew adheres to that source to almost exactly the same extent when he is using it with reference to the Ministry and when he is using it with reference to the Passion. But the case is very different as to Luke, with whom we are now concerned: *his* procedure varies very greatly in these two departments of his Gospel. As has just been shown, more than half the words in those five portions of his Ministry-narrative which have a Marcan basis are also found, either entirely or partially, in our present Mark; and it may be added that when we examine those five portions separately, in none of them does the proportion fall below one-half, except very slightly in Lk iv. 31-44 (where the numbers are 126 and 263), while in xviii. 15-43 it rises as high as two-thirds (being 291 words out of 424). How great then is the contrast when we turn to Luke's Passion-narrative, in which we have found (p. 78) that very little more than a quarter of the words (namely, 507 out of 1,906) are wholly or in part identical with words found in Mark. In other words, *the verbal correspondence with the Marcan source is about twice as great in the Lucan account of the Ministry as it is in the Lucan account of the Passion*; and that, as it happens, is almost exactly the same amount of disparity as we found to exist between the Lucan and the Matthaean Passion-narratives when we compared them from this same point of view.

ii. If we turn from the wording to the substance of the two departments of Luke which we are engaged in comparing, we shall find that the *additions to our knowledge*

II. 3. *St. Luke's Use of St. Mark's Gospel*

are considerably less important and less numerous in the Ministry-narrative than in the Passion-narrative, although the former contains 311 verses and the latter only 123. (It must be borne in mind throughout that we are only concerned with those portions of the Ministry-narrative which appear to be founded on Mark and not with the large insertions made from other sources, such as Lk xix. 1–28, besides others already referred to.) In the 311 verses of the Ministry-narrative, there are of course not a few short additions to, and variations from, Mark; but in the great majority of cases these are either (*a*) derived from or suggested by the context, or (*b*) they are the results of Luke's special idiosyncrasies and interests, or (*c*) they are such as an Evangelist might naturally supply as the result of his general knowledge of the habitual tone of the life of Jesus, for instance, the constant recourse to prayer (as in v. 16; vi. 12; ix. 18, 28), or again (*d*) as the result of his general knowledge of the impression made by the Lord's teaching and miracles (as in vi. 11; ix. 43; xviii. 34 (= ix. 45), 43; xix. 37; xx. 26, 39). But to examine and classify all the small Lucan additions would be out of place here; I would mention, however, that in doing so Dr. Wright's edition of *St. Luke's Gospel in Greek*, in which he brackets the apparently 'editorial supplements', is particularly helpful; and I may refer to some suggestions made in *Horae Synopticae*[2], pp. 194 ff. The point before us now is that these small additions do not often contain any substantially new matter, such as would require the hypothesis of a non-Marcan source to account for it. Such really new matter does not seem to me to constitute more than about 17 entire verses, namely, Lk v. 39; ix. 31, 32; xix. 39–44; xx. 18; xxi. 18, 22, 24, 28, 34–6, besides a few short sentences (such as xxi. 11 b) and phrases, and single words. It will be observed that a very large proportion of this new matter is contained in Luke's version of the Prophecy on the Mount in chap. xxi, and seems to be mainly caused (*a*) by the use of Pauline language as in vv. 24,[1] 28, 34-6 (cf. also ver. 18 with Acts xxvii. 34), and (*b*) by Luke's knowledge of the events by which the prophecy had been fulfilled before he wrote, as in vv. 11, 20, 24 (and so also in xix. 43 f.).

But the much shorter Passion-narrative of Luke has been shown (see p. 78) to contain a much larger amount of new matter, namely, about 33 verses and 3 half-verses, besides some more brief and fragmentary additions to our knowledge. Thus it appears that the later of these two departments of Luke which we are comparing, though it extends to only two-fifths of the length of the earlier one (123 verses against 311), contains *nearly twice as much matter*, which seems to imply the use of an additional source or sources besides the Marcan one.

This second contrast, though less capable of clear and incontrovertible statement than those which I place first and third, points in the same direction as they do; for it shows that from Lk xxii. 14 to xxiv. 10 the Evangelist was more ready, or more able, than he had previously been to supplement his Marcan source, not merely with editorial comments and amplifications, but with fresh information.

iii. It will be remembered that the third point of contrast between the Matthaean and the Lucan Passion-narratives lay in the fact that while Luke twelve times transposes the Marcan order, Matthew never does so; and it was pointed out that such transpositions are particularly worthy of notice, because the freedom which they show is so specially symptomatic of oral use of a source, while on the other hand they are the kind of alterations which a copyist is very unlikely to make, however inaccurate he may be in the way of alteration and of omission. Now the occurrence of such

---

[1] The comparison here suggested is that between the last words of the verse and Rom xi. 25. With verse 28 compare the frequent Pauline use of ἀπολύτρωσις, and with verses 34-6 the warnings in 1 Thes v. 3 f.

II. 3. St. Luke's Use of St. Mark's Gospel

changes of order, though not completely absent from Luke's Ministry-narrative, occurs with much greater frequency in his Passion-narrative. For in those 311 verses of the former, which we are now concerned with as being based on Mark, I can find but seven variations from the Marcan order, namely, those which may be seen in—

1. Lk vi. 12–19 compared with Mk iii. 7–19 a.
2. „ viii. 23 „ „ iv. 37, 38.
3. „ viii. 28, 29 „ „ v. 3–8.
4. „ viii. 42 „ „ v. 42.
5. „ viii. 55 b, 56 „ „ v. 42 b, 43.
6. „ ix. 14 a „ „ vi. 44.
7. „ xx. 15 „ „ xii. 8.

The different placing of the coming of the mother and brethren in Lk viii. 19–21 and in Mk iii. 31–5 is not included in this list, because a change of that incident from its Marcan position was necessitated by Luke's omission here of the discourse to which it is appended in Mark.

Of the above seven instances only the first has any intrinsic importance, and there no doubt the transposition of the substance of Mk iii. 7–12 and 13–19 a was intentionally made by Luke, in order to provide an introduction to his Sermon on the Level Place. The other six are trifling alterations of order, which make no difference to our understanding of the narrative, and which therefore no copyist would have been likely to care to make designedly.

Now if the 123 verses of Luke's Passion-narrative contained inversions of Mark's order in the same proportion as the 311 verses of his Ministry-narrative, to which we have now been referring, there would of course only be three such inversions. But we have seen that as a fact there are twelve (see the list of them on pp. 81–3 above). In other words, Luke avails himself of the liberty of transposition *four times as freely* in his Passion-narrative as he does in those narratives of the ministry which are founded upon the same source.

Such are the facts of the case. How are they to be accounted for? How came Luke in his Passion-narrative to deal so freely with his fundamental source, thus differing so remarkably in these respects both from the procedure of Matthew and also from his own procedure in earlier parts of his Gospel?

The well-known theory of Feine and others (see Dr. Sanday in *The Expository Times*, xi. 473 and xx. 112), that Luke had before him some kind of record, or early Gospel, which he used as a third source, in addition to, and frequently in preference to, Mark and the *Logia*, at once suggests itself. And I used to think that the strongest arguments in favour of that theory were to be found in his Passion-narrative. But the closer investigation, of which I have been here summarizing the results, has impressed upon me that such a 'three-document hypothesis', as it may be called, does not give much help towards the interpretation of the phenomena here presented to us. Luke's additions are (unlike Matthew's) so mixed up with the *Grundschrift*, and they have caused alterations and modifications of such kinds, that they suggest a long and gradual conflation in the mind rather than a simple conflation by the pen.

It seems then that more probability would attach to a hypothesis that would represent our author as having been accustomed to make oral use of the materials which he embodies in this part of his Gospel. Now it is something more than a hypothesis, it is the subject of a direct statement in the generally accepted Epistle to Philemon (v. 24), supported by other evidence both external and internal, that St. Luke was a 'fellow-worker' with St. Paul. And if so, he will have been a preacher of Christianity after the Pauline type, and will have been mainly occupied with the Pauline range of subjects. And that range of subjects, so far as we can judge of it from the Apostle's extant Epistles—whether we accept more or fewer of them—and also from the brief reports of his speeches in the Acts, seems to have coincided to a remarkable extent with the matter which we have been considering in Luke's Passion-narrative. For (1) certainly St. Paul's references to the teachings of the Lord during His ministry are much fewer than we should have expected, though sayings are referred to as His in 1 Cor vii. 10, ix. 14, perhaps in 1 Tim v. 18, possibly in 1 Thes iv. 15, and though we find close similarities to His teachings in Rom xii. 14, 17, xvi. 19; 1 Thes v. 2; 2 Thes iii. 3; 2 Tim ii. 12, and though in 1 Tim vi. 3 'the words of our Lord Jesus Christ' are referred to generally as the standard of sound doctrine.[1] And (2) to the acts, including the miracles, of the earlier and ministerial life of Jesus, there are no Pauline references at all either in letters or speeches; for what has been sometimes thought the suspicious similarity between the speeches of Peter and Paul in Acts does not extend to this point, there being no Pauline parallels to Acts ii. 22 and x. 38. 'The Gospel which' Paul 'preached', and wherein he would have his converts 'stand', appears, so far as we can judge from his references to that preaching, to have rested upon the death and resurrection of Jesus Christ as being 'the events instrumental in salvation, the foundation of the new order of grace'. So Wendt well expresses it, where he is pointing out the difference between the predominant aspect of faith in the Pauline Epistles and that in the Johannine discourses, since in the latter belief 'means acceptance of the words of Jesus and observance of His commandments' (*The Gospel of St. John*, p. 198 f., E. T.).[2]

[1] Perhaps, too, St. Paul's appeal to the Corinthians 'by the meekness and gentleness of Christ' (2 Cor x. 1) may imply that they had heard from him the words of Mt xi. 29. On the other hand it should be observed that three of the above references are to the Pastoral Epistles.
[2] See also Menzies, *The Earliest Gospel*, pp. 6 ff.

Thus the Pauline preaching, as contrasted with the substance either of the first three Gospels or of the Fourth, must have been concerned mainly with the Crucifixion and the Resurrection, so far as it consisted in setting forth facts. But as to the Resurrection as a fact there could not be much to say in detail, however important it was as a foundation of doctrine; for the event itself was an invisible one, and the proofs of it would not require repetition, except when doubt or disbelief arose as at Corinth (1 Cor xv. 12). And so the Crucifixion would be thrown into unique prominence as a constant subject of preaching. And accordingly we find St. Paul saying emphatically of himself and his fellow-workers, 'We preach Christ crucified' (1 Cor i. 23; cf. verse 17 and ii. 2).

Now, if this was the case, the story of the Crucifixion, and of the Passion as leading up to the Crucifixion, must have had an intense interest for Christians of the Pauline type. Details about those last days at Jerusalem would be longed for and begged for by them; and, if not St. Paul himself, at least other catechists and teachers such as St. Luke would take pains in order to supply such details, so far as they could gather them, directly or indirectly, from 'eye-witnesses and ministers of the word'. May it not have been thus that the preacher (and perhaps catechist) who afterwards became the Third Evangelist, had for his homiletic purposes gradually supplemented, and in supplementing had to some extent modified and transposed, the generally accepted Marcan record, so far as it related to the Passion and Crucifixion? And so, when he came to this part of his Gospel, he would write down the memories of his past teaching which were impressed upon his mind, without having constant occasion to make direct reference to the Marcan source, as he himself had done in describing those earlier parts of the life of Jesus which were less familiar to him, and as the compiler of the First Gospel

II. 3. St. Luke's Use of St. Mark's Gospel

did in his Passion-narrative as much as in his Ministry-narrative.

Two observations may be added in support of the above suggestion that in xxii. 14–xxiv. 10 Luke may be writing down the substance of what he had spoken as a 'fellow worker' of St. Paul in preaching.

1. The portion of his Gospel which we have found to be characterized by such peculiar freedom in the use of Mark commences with the institution of the Lord's Supper (the next preceding verses having been, as it happens, in unusually close agreement with the Marcan source). Now that incident is also recorded by St. Paul himself (1 Cor xi. 23–5), and indeed it forms the only exception to his silence as to the acts of Jesus which preceded the actual Passion.

2. If we glance at the subjects of Luke's insertions so far as they contain new matter, they seem to be generally of such a kind as would be attractive and interesting when used in preaching. Here again, it is instructive to contrast them in pages 195 f. and 227 ff. of *Synopticon*, or otherwise, with Matthew's insertions of new matter. As to the latter, I do not dwell now upon the remarkable number of difficulties which happen to be suggested by many of them: I only point out that referring as they do very largely to Judas and to Pilate, they offer but little material for instruction as to 'the mind which was in Christ Jesus' when He suffered and died. In proof of this remark, let any preacher of experience, after recalling the two lists of additions made by the First and Third Evangelists respectively, ask himself how often he had made use of the Matthaean additions in comparison with those made by Luke—such as the fuller warning to Simon (xxii. 31–2), the address to the women of Jerusalem (xxiii. 27–31), the story of the penitent robber (xxiii. 39–43). Of course the contrast must not be made too much of: we have one saying from the Cross in Mt and Mk to set against the three found in Lk only (if we

accept as Lucan xxiii. 34 a as well as xxiii. 43 and 46); and Luke's longest insertion, that relating to the appearance before Herod, must be admitted to have been made by him with no homiletic purpose, but to have been a result of his special interest in, and perhaps connexion with, the Herodian family and household (Lk iii. 1, viii. 3, xxiv. 10; Acts xiii. 1). But still the contrast does to some extent exist; and so far as it is recognized, it will add some probability to the suggestion—for it is no more than a suggestion—which has been here put forward to account for the special characteristics of St. Luke's Passion-narrative.

PROBABILITIES AS TO THE SO-CALLED DOUBLE TRADITION OF ST. MATTHEW AND ST. LUKE

SYLLABUS

Explanation of the Title.

I. Reasons for assuming from internal evidence as to this tradition or source—

    1. that it was a written document (Q), and

    2. that it was used by Matthew and Luke independently. Support for these assumptions derived from the statements of Papias as to the *Logia* compiled by Matthew.

II. Classification of all the passages which are more or less parallel in the First and Third Gospels, so as to show three degrees of probability that they were taken from this one written source.

III. The inferences as to (1) the form and (2) the substance of Q which may be drawn from those passages.

IV. Suggestions, mostly conjectural, as to the likelihood or unlikelihood of certain other passages, which are found only in Matthew or only in Luke, having been derived from Q.

PROBABILITIES AS TO THE SO-CALLED DOUBLE TRADITION OF ST. MATTHEW AND ST. LUKE

THE above title seems to require, in two respects, a few words of preliminary explanation.

1. The term 'Probabilities' is used with a very wide range of meaning, so as to cover, in the four divisions into which the Essay falls, these four descending stages: (i) assumptions regarded as sufficiently well founded to serve as bases for discussion, in the course of which they will themselves receive further confirmation; (ii) lists of passages to which an origin may be assigned with various degrees of probability in the usual sense of that word; (iii) inferences from the probably known parts of a document to its general character; and (iv) conjectures for which some grounds are supplied by what has gone before.

2. I have used the phrase 'Double Tradition' because it, (like 'Triple Tradition') has become familiar to English students through its use in Dr. E. A. Abbott's writings[1] and in Mr. Rushbrooke's invaluable *Synopticon*; and it does not, as we shall see that 'Logia' does, beg any question that will come before us. But it is not a satisfactory phrase, for it appears to imply that we attribute to the passages denoted by it the very high value of having been handed

---

[1] See especially *Enc. Bibl.* ii, col. 1773. Of course the term 'Tradition' is not used here (and the words that will be quoted in the text from Dr. Abbott show that he did not use it) as implying the results of oral to the exclusion of documentary transmission. It is used in the wide sense of the Greek παράδοσις, which includes 'transmission orally and by writing (Lid. & Scott, *Lex.*, s. v.). Thus St. Paul speaks of traditions (παραδόσεις) which the Thessalonians had been 'taught whether by word or by epistle of ours' (2 Thes ii. 15). And Josephus twice calls his *History of the Jewish War* a παράδοσις (c. *Apion.* l. ix and x, §§ 50 and 53).

III. Double Tradition of Matthew and Luke

down through two distinct sources. This we know is not the case: it is but one source which we claim for the Double Tradition. And yet we may surely place its contents on a higher level of importance than those of the 'Single Traditions' of St. Matthew or St. Luke,[1] if we can establish for that one source the claim that before the First and Third Gospels were drawn up 'a document containing words of the Lord had existed long enough, and had acquired authority enough, to induce two editors or writers of Gospels, apparently representing different schools of thought and writing for different churches, to borrow from it independently'.[2]

But though this phrase 'Double Tradition of St. Matthew and St. Luke' was used in the title, it will be superseded in the rest of the Essay by the briefer and in most respects[3] equally neutral symbol Q (= Quelle, or source), which has established itself among English hardly less than among German scholars as a convenient designation of the second documentary source (our Gospel of St. Mark being substantially the first) which Mt and Lk[4] are now generally thought to have had before them, and from which they both drew materials for their respective compilations.

[1] Might we not even say than the small 'Single Tradition of St. Mark', since that was (for whatever reasons) ignored or rejected, while what we are calling the 'Double Tradition' was accepted for use, by the two later compilers?

[2] Dr. E. A. Abbott in *Enc. Brit.* x. 801.

[3] The exception is that 'Q' is generally used by scholars as the symbol of a single written source, whereas a 'Tradition' may (as we have seen) be either written or oral, or a compound result of both kinds of transmission. Therefore it was, in order to make no assumption as to the subject-matter of this Essay, that I avoided the convenient 'Q' in my title, though I have to use it so soon as representing a 'working hypothesis'.

[4] Mt and Lk will be used throughout as symbols to denote the editors or compilers to whom the First and Third Gospels in their present forms are due, though in the case of the First Gospel it is now generally admitted (see p. 105 f., *infra*) that his name is unknown to us, while, on the other hand, Harnack (*Lukas der Arzt*, 1906) and others have of late added much strength to the case for assigning the authorship of the Third Gospel, as well as the whole of Acts, to Luke the Physician, St. Paul's companion.

I

Now that description of the purpose served by the supposed Q involves the two large assumptions (1) that a written document was employed, and (2) that such employment of a MS. consisted not in the use of Mt's Gospel by Lk or vice versa, but in the use made by both of them of an authority older than either Gospel. We have therefore to show that these assumptions are so well supported by adequate internal, and perhaps also some external, evidence that we may be justified in using them as bases for further inquiries.

1. The assumption [1] that a *written document of some kind* was used is strongly supported both (i) by general observation of the phenomena broadly presented by the matter common to Mt and Lk, and (ii) by a closer examination of one of these phenomena.

(i) There are many passages, some of them being of considerable length, in which the similarity, even in unimportant details, between the two Gospels seems too great to be accounted for otherwise than by the use of a document. The cumulative force of this argument can only be appreciated after a study of the fifty-four passages which constitute Class A in the lists of the constituent parts of the 'Double Tradition' given below (pp. 113-5). But it may be worth while to refer at once to half a dozen of the instances given there, viz. those numbered 14, 18 (so far as the centurion's words go), 27, 31, 50, 54, and to ask oneself whether the impression of a documentary origin given by them is not practically decisive against an exclusively or almost exclusively oral theory.[2]

[1] As a proof that this, though generally held, is not the universal opinion of the best modern scholars, see Allen's *St. Matthew*, pp. xlv-l of Introduction; and his Essay in this volume.
[2] Among the decreasing number of defenders of such a theory Dr. A. Wright is pre-eminent; see especially his *Synopsis of the Gospels*², pp. xiv ff.

III. Double Tradition of Matthew and Luke 99

(ii) To this broad and general argument drawn from such parallel passages taken as wholes there has to be added another of a more special and minute kind, which will appeal even more convincingly to a careful observer. Particular attention should be paid to certain peculiar or very unusual words or phrases, which seem very unlikely to have been preserved in oral transmission. The scope of the present argument must be cautiously limited: there are some nouns and verbs such as κάρφος, δοκός, διαβλέπω in Mt vii. 3-5 = Lk vi. 41, 42, φωλεός in Mt viii. 20 = Lk ix. 58, σαρόω in Mt xii. 44 = Lk xi. 25, for which no equally forcible and expressive synonym would be likely to suggest itself, and so they would probably be retained even in oral use, though they are very rare in the New Testament and LXX.[1] But there are other phrases for which more familiar substitutes would be easily found, and therefore would be very likely to be introduced in the natural course of oral transmission; e. g. ἐν γεννητοῖς γυναικῶν (Mt xi. 11 = Lk vii. 28), which occurs nowhere else in the New Testament, and in LXX only five times in Job, and for which some such ordinary term as 'men' or 'sons of men' would naturally suggest itself. Still more unaccountable on an oral hypothesis are certain grammatical peculiarities preserved by Mt and Lk, viz. ἱκανός ἵνα, Mt viii. 8 = Lk vii. 6, here only in the New Testament and never in LXX; and in the same saying εἰπὲ λόγῳ, to which construction there seems to be no nearer parallel than Gal vi. 11 γράμμασιν ἔγραψα (cf. Acts ii. 40); φοβεῖσθαι ἀπό Mt x. 28 = Lk xii. 4, here only in N. T., though not infrequent in LXX, especially with προσώπου[2]; ὁμολογεῖν ἐν Mt x. 32 = Lk xii. 8, here only

---

[1] The retention in both Gospels of the elsewhere unknown ἐπιούσιος (Mt vi. 11 = Lk xi. 3) is remarkable, for one might have expected it to be replaced by some more intelligible word which could not be interpreted in so many different senses; but probably it soon became unalterably fixed in both its places by liturgical use.

[2] See J. H. Moulton, *Grammar of New Testament Greek*, p. 102.

in N. T. (for the sense is quite different in Rom x. 9) and not in LXX.[1]

Two remarks have to be made in support of both these applications, the more general and the more special, of the argument just brought forward.

A. The force of that argument is by no means invalidated, though in a slight degree it is weakened, by bringing forward other parallel passages, such as those in lists B and C below (pp. 116-8), which show considerably less prolonged and less precise resemblance between Mt and Lk in their 'double tradition'. To judge mainly from one part of the evidence before us, and to lay comparatively little stress upon the other part of it, is not here the unfair proceeding that it generally is. For it is enough for our present contention if we can show—as I believe will be shown in our Class A—that a considerable number of parallels are so close that a documentary source is the most natural and reasonable explanation of *them*, whatever may be the explanation of other and slighter parallels. We have not to contend that these compilers knew nothing about their subject apart from that one document, nor even that when they were regarding it as their best available source they always did avail themselves of it with uniform care and accuracy. The value set upon exactness of reproduction in copying from written authorities was then very much less high than it is with us,[2] while on the other hand there was more reliance on the storage of memories; and the compilers seem to have been often ready to spare themselves the trouble—a much greater trouble than we, writing at our study tables and within reach of our bookshelves, can easily realize (see pp. 16 ff. of this volume)—of looking up a passage in some MS. when they thought that they had in their minds a knowledge of its substance that would be sufficient for their purpose, whether that knowledge was derived from a recollection of that MS. or from some independent tradition which had previously been impressed upon their memories by that most efficacious of all modes of impression, the habit of teaching it as catechists or otherwise.[3]

---

[1] See Moulton, *op. cit.*, p. 104.
[2] Dr. Salmon has some interesting remarks on this, *Human Element in the Gospels*, p. 5 f.
[3] Thus it is that (as will be noticed again on p. 121) facts and words

III. Double Tradition of Matthew and Luke 101

B. The validity of the argument from similarity of parallel passages which we are now using in one branch—the Logian branch, as it used to be called—of the Two-Document theory, gains support from its validity in the other and less hypothetical branch of that theory, which all agree in calling the Marcan branch. It is of course less hypothetical than the branch before us now, because we have in our hands, substantially if not exactly, the very document which is assumed to have been used by Mt and Lk, or by one or either of them—namely, our canonical Gospel of St. Mark. Now in the passages which are admitted by general consent to be drawn from that document we find just the same two kinds of agreement as we have been noticing in the present case. For in the large amounts of matter common to Mk and Mt and Lk, and to Mk and Mt only, and in the comparatively small amount common to Mk and Lk only, we find

> (i) passages in which not only acts but sayings of Jesus are described to us in words of which a very large proportion are identical (e. g. to take examples only from sayings, Mk ii. 8 b–11 = Mt ix. 4 b–6 = Lk v. 22 b–24; Mk ii. 19 f. = Mt ix. 15 = Lk v. 34 f.; Mk xii. 43 f. = Lk xxi. 3 f.; Mk xiii. 19–23 = Mt xxiv. 21–5); and also
> (ii) the frequent retention by the later Evangelists of Marcan words which, while a Concordance will show them to be very unusual, are by no means irreplaceable (e.g. $\dot{a}\pi a\iota\rho o\mu a\iota$ Mk ii. 20 = Mt ix. 15 = Lk v. 35; $\gamma\epsilon\dot{v}o\mu a\iota\ \theta a\nu\dot{a}\tau o\nu$ Mk ix. 1 = Mt xvi. 28 = Lk ix. 27; $\delta\upsilon\sigma\kappa\dot{o}\lambda\omega s$ Mk x. 23 = Mt xix. 23 = Lk xviii. 24; $\dot{a}\nu\dot{a}\gamma a\iota o\nu$ Mk xiv. 15 = Lk. xxii. 12 instead of the usual $\dot{\upsilon}\pi\epsilon\rho\hat{\omega}o\nu$; and the construction $\dot{\eta}\mu\dot{\epsilon}\rho a\iota\ \tau\rho\epsilon\hat{\iota}s\ \pi\rho o\sigma\mu\dot{\epsilon}\nu o\upsilon\sigma\dot{\iota}\nu\ \mu o\iota$ Mk viii. 2 = Mt xv. 32).[1]

These two classes of similarities between Mk and both or one of the other Synoptists are satisfactorily accounted for by the document which is preserved for us as our Second Gospel: does not this encourage us to believe that the similarities of both these kinds which we find in Mt and Lk only are in like manner to be accounted for by the lost document which we are calling Q?

which must have been constant and prominent parts of elementary Christian teaching seem to be often recorded with less exactness than others which must have been of less importance and less familiarly known.

[1] Other such words could be seen and studied in *Horae Synopticae*[2], pp. 57 ff.

2. In thus speaking of the lost document Q we are making the second of the two assumptions for which the grounds have to be here stated. We are assuming that neither Mt nor Lk drew upon the other's Gospel as his written source, but that they used independently an older document. The following considerations abundantly justify this assumption.

i. We shall see presently that about two-thirds of the parallel passages which give the clearest indications of being drawn from the same document, and a still larger proportion of the other passages which not improbably may be so, are placed differently by Mt and Lk. It seems hardly possible that there could have been this very frequent divergence of order if either of the compilers was using a source which was biographical and chronological to anything like the extent which characterizes our First and Third Gospels: no reason can be given for their thus transposing its contents.

ii. We also observe the significant fact that all those important insertions into the Marcan framework which are called for want of a better name the 'double tradition' of Mt and Lk, are confined to a comparatively few parts of St. Mark's Gospel. We may estimate this fact most clearly by turning to the best known harmony of the Gospels,[1] Tischendorf's *Harmonia Evangelica* which shows us that while there are sixty-eight of his sections which exhibit the use of the Marcan groundwork by both Mt and Lk, there are only ten of them which contain any substantial additions made by both those writers, viz. §§ 14, 15 containing the Baptist's teaching, § 17 containing the Temptation, and §§ 47 (cf. 91) 50, 56, 75, 111, 134, 139 containing discourses of Jesus. In all the other fifty-eight sections,[2] agreements between Mk and Lk only are either entirely absent, or else they are so

---

[1] I believe it is still the best known, though Huck's *Synopse*³ (Tübingen, 1906) is probably now the most satisfactory.

[2] A catalogue of them may be seen in *Horae Synopticae*², pp. 208 ff., paragraphs *a*, *b*, and *c* combined.

III. Double Tradition of Matthew and Luke 103

slight and unimportant that they are quite insufficient to require the use of one Gospel in the other in order to account for them :[1] they are much more reasonably explained either by subsequent harmonizations (whether made intentionally or as the natural result of familiarity with one of the Gospels above the other), or else, and I now think in very many cases, by Mt and Lk having used a copy of Mk in which small alterations and supposed corrections had been already made.[2] But however this may be, the only point before us now is that in all these fifty-eight sections there are absolutely no weighty or lengthy insertions or additions in which Mt and Lk concur. Is it not utterly unlikely that if either of these writers had before him, or at hand, besides his copy of Mk, a completed or nearly completed Gospel (in the sense in which we apply that term to Mt or Lk) he would so entirely or almost entirely have denied himself the use of it during so large a part of his work? Is it not thus practically certain that the only non-Marcan authority available for them was used by them separately, and was a collection consisting mainly (though, as we shall see, not quite exclusively) of sayings of the Lord, which they inserted in various places according to their respective judgements, or their respective stores of independent traditional information?

[It is from the internal evidence supplied by the three Gospels which lie before us that we have drawn the conclusion that Mt and Lk, working in complete distinctness from one another, inserted into the framework of Mk some or all of the contents of a document which was mainly a collection of the sayings of Jesus. Is there any external evidence to support this conclusion? The present writer is

---

[1] Those of them which appear to me least unimportant are collected in *Hor. Syn.*[2], p. 210 f. But the whole of them can be closely examined, and their general slightness realized, in the very full and minute list of them given in Dr. E. A. Abbott's *The Corrections of Mark*, Appendix I, pp. 307 ff.

[2] See Dr. Sanday in this volume, pp. 21-4.

one of those who believe that there is some. As is well known, Papias, who is by far the earliest author who refers to any writings about the life and words of the Lord, mentions two such writings.[1] He may have mentioned others, but Eusebius, to whom we owe most of our earliest 'Reliquiae Sacrae', has only cared to preserve these two notices, the first describing St. Mark's accurate but not chronological record of the reminiscences of St. Peter, and the second consisting only of this one brief sentence, which is evidently connected with something on the same subject that has not been preserved for us, 'So then Matthew composed the oracles in the Hebrew language, and each one interpreted them as he could.'[2]

Two of the questions arising out of this much controverted sentence must be noticed here.

1. First, has it any bearing at all upon our attempt to discover the nature and contents of Q? In favour of a negative answer is the plain declaration that Matthew had written in Hebrew,[3] and that there was no authorized or generally accepted translation of his work, whereas the common matter of Mt and Lk is proved by its verbal similitudes to be drawn from the same Greek source, whether that source be an original composition or a translation. But the force of this argument is broken by the fact that Papias uses the past tense in both parts of his statement; and that would allow for, or possibly might even imply, a subsequent translation, which might have become sufficiently well known to be used by at least the two com-

---

[1] He refers to 'the elder', meaning apparently the Presbyter John, as his authority for either the first part or the whole of his statement about Mark; but whether this reference covers also the statement as to Matthew's work it is impossible to say.

[2] Ματθαῖος μὲν οὖν Ἐβραΐδι διαλέκτῳ τὰ λόγια συνεγράψατο (v. l. συνετάξατο)· ἡρμήνευσε δ' αὐτὰ ὡς ἦν δυνατὸς ἕκαστος, Eus. H. E. iii. 39.

[3] Probably meaning Aramaic. In Wellhausen's *Einleitung*, p. 36 f., may be seen the cases in which the evidence is strongest for Mt and Lk having followed different renderings of the Aramaic text.

pilers with whom we are now concerned. And the amount of difficulty which still remains in Papias's statement that Matthew wrote in Hebrew seems to the present writer to be far outweighed by the broad general correspondence of his two descriptions of the works of Mark and Matthew with the two sources which we find to be treated as of supreme importance by Mt and Lk,[1] though the latter at least knew of many sources. The salient point of the correspondence lies of course in the fact that one of these two sources, i.e. St. Mark's Gospel, contains, as Papias says, both sayings and doings of Christ, while the other, which he ascribes to St. Matthew, has as its main subject sacred utterances (τὰ λόγια), which can only mean those of the Lord.

2. But, secondly, are we justified in saying that sacred utterances would be accepted as the natural and usual connotation of λόγια, when the word was used by Papias without further explanation? Did he mean, and did he expect his readers to understand, that St. Matthew's object in writing was narrower than St. Mark's, and that he designed only to record sayings and discourses of Christ? Probably he did: the amount of that probability cannot be very exactly decided, but certainly the estimate of it has risen of late years in England. Thirty-five years ago, when Bishop Lightfoot wrote on this subject with his usual care and thoroughness, a hopeful endeavour was being made to sustain upon critical and historical grounds the traditional view that our First Gospel came, almost or quite as we have it now, from the hands of 'Matthew the publican', one of the Twelve Apostles. That endeavour is now generally admitted to have failed.[2] Further subsequent study has

[1] This statement is worked out in *Exp. Times*, vol. xii, pp. 72 ff. (see also p. 139).
[2] See among recent English writers, Allen, *St. Matt.* (1907), p. lxxx; Plummer, *St. Matt.* (1909), p. x; Stanton, *The Gospels as Hist. Documents* (1909), ii. 363 f.; H. L. Jackson in *Camb. Bibl. Essays* (1909), p. 442.

shown it to be all but inconceivable that an Apostle should have relied on previous authorities in the way that the composer of the First Gospel unquestionably does, and has brought out other difficulties, both in the way of inconsistencies and of incongruities, which are fatal to the belief in simple Matthaean authorship. But so long as the attempt to support such authorship was being hopefully made by scholars, of course it was of the utmost importance to them to produce evidence that when Papias wrote that 'Matthew composed the *logia*', he meant, or at least may have meant, that the Apostle drew up a biographical memoir such as we now call a Gospel. That this is what he may have meant is all that is claimed by Lightfoot, who only says that the examples brought forward by him show that 'the oracles (τὰ λόγια) can be used as co-extensive with the Scriptures'[1] by Papias, both in the sentence now under discussion and in the title of his five books of Expositions (Λογίων Κυριακῶν Ἐξηγήσεις). But admitting that Lightfoot shows the possibility, does he show any likelihood of this having been so? Certainly he shows that the term had been so used by Philo; but this might be expected of a writer who treated 'all Scripture and every event and person and object contained in it'[2] as material for allegorical and so for spiritual interpretation. And there is no doubt that his wider use of λόγιον and λόγια is to be found in Clem. Alex., Origen, Basil, and other later Greek Fathers. But, excepting Philo, the evidence for it before the date of Papias is but slight, though a tendency to such extension of meaning may be found in Heb v. 12 and still more in Clem. Rom. I. liii (where, however, λόγια are not substituted for γραφαί, but named side by side with them). On the whole, therefore, I think that if a person who has freed himself, as it is not difficult to do now, from all bias on either side will

---

[1] *Essays on Sup. Rel.*, p. 176, reprinted from *Cont. Rev.*, Aug. 1875.
[2] Edersheim in *Dict. Chr. Biogr.* iv. 377.

III. Double Tradition of Matthew and Luke

take concordances and indexes and will examine for himself the 46 places in which λόγιον occurs in the LXX or in the Hexaplaric fragments,[1] the 4 places in the New Testament, the 5 in Clem. Rom. I and II and Polycarp, and the 2 in Justin Martyr, he will come to the conclusion that the sense which a Christian writer of the date of Papias would (apart from any special reason to the contrary) naturally attach to the word is that of a divine or sacred utterance.[2] And this seems to be an opinion widely and increasingly held by recent English writers.[3]

To me it seems impossible to shut out from the mind this testimony of Papias, when one is attempting to estimate the probabilities as to the source which was used by Mt and Mk. But the convenient practice which had grown up of calling it the 'Logian source' has not unnaturally been objected to as 'question-begging',[4] so it has been avoided in this Essay, and the neutral symbol Q has been substituted. And whenever any references are made to the *Logia* compiled by Matthew they have been and will be enclosed in square brackets so that they may interfere as little as possible with the impressions made by the purely internal evidence supplied by the Gospels themselves.]

[1] In no less than 35 of these places λόγιον is the rendering of אִמְרָה or the kindred noun אֵמֶר or אֹמֶר, which can only mean an utterance or speech, while it only 6 times represents the wider term דָּבָר, which is usually rendered by λόγος; these forty-one are the only places in which we can certainly compare it with the Hebrew.

[2] But even if Papias himself applied the word to the complete Gospel which, in his time as in ours, may have been called Matthew's, it is quite possible he may have misunderstood his informant, who was referring to Q. So Harnack suggests, *Sprüche und Reden Jesu*, p. 172 (E. T., p. 248); he regards it as very probable that Q was the work of Matthew.

[3] So Prof. Stanton, *op. cit.*, i. 52-4; Plummer, *St. Matthew*, p. viii; Hastings's *D. B.* iii. 296 (V. Bartlet) and Extra Vol. p. 5 (Votaw); *Encycl. Bibl.* ii. 1810 (Abbott); see also Sanday and Headlam on Rom iii. 2.

[4] As by Dean Armitage Robinson, *Study of the Gospels*, p. 68; cf. Rev. W. C. Allen in *Exp. Times*, xi. 425, and Prof. Burkitt, *Gospel History, &c.*, pp. 124 and 127.

II

Assuming now, at least as a working hypothesis, the use by Mt and Lk independently of a lost document (Q) which consisted mainly of records of discourses, we have to try to ascertain what parallel passages in the First and Third Gospels may be fairly ascribed to this source.

This would be an easy task if all the passages for which parallelism can be claimed were parallel with the closeness which characterizes some of them: in that case we could simply ascribe them all to Q with sufficient probability. But, as we have seen (p. 100), that is by no means the case; we have to admit that there are different degrees of likelihood as to whether such passages came from a written source. Another simple plan would be to confine our attention to the closer parallels, and to dismiss the slighter ones as coming from some 'special source' or oral tradition. But that we should thus be ascribing to Q less than its real importance as a source is suggested by the analogy, already referred to, of the other and less uncertain branch of the 'Two-Document theory'. Even in passages where it is generally admitted that Mt and Lk were using Mk in a written form, we find them suddenly breaking away from the text to which they had been closely adhering; they modify it, they enlarge it, they supplement it, they abbreviate it, they give a different application to its words, they supply different settings and introductions for its sayings; all these things they do, sometimes apart from one another, and sometimes in agreement; sometimes for reasons which we can discover or conjecture, and sometimes when the only assignable cause is a lapse of accurate attention on the part of the copyist, either because he did not think strict accuracy important or because he mistakenly thought he had attained it. See, for instance, the three different applications of εἰς μαρτύριον in Mk xiii. 9, Mt xxiv. 14, Lk xxi. 13, or the variations between Mk vi.

III. Double Tradition of Matthew and Luke

19, 20 and Mt xiv. 5, or between Mk xiv. 71 and Lk xxii. 60.[1] Now if the exactness with which these two compilers adhered to the Marcan source, which may be presumed to have come to them with Petrine authority, was thus intermittent and imperfect, it is unreasonable to suppose that they would adhere more consistently and more accurately to Q [even if it came to them with Matthaean authority].

It seems then that our safest course will be on the one hand to omit none of the passages in Mt and Lk as to which there seems to be any appreciable ground for thinking that the document Q can have been their source, but on the other hand to attempt, in making a catalogue of them, to classify them according to the chief degrees of likelihood that such may have been their origin. Of course such classification can only be tentative, and it must be more or less dependent upon the personal equation of the classifier; but it may have some helpfulness and suggestiveness for students, even if they can only accept it as partially satisfactory to themselves.

In thus beginning by collecting all the parallels for which there is any probability at all of a documentary origin, we cannot do better than adopt as a groundwork the very complete and minute statement of them provided in Mr. Rushbrooke's *Synopticon*.[2] The portions of the

[1] Or again observe the three very different degrees of probability with which Mk ii. 9, 10 = Mt ix. 5, 6 = Lk v. 23, 24, and Mk iii. 28, 29 = Mt xii. 31, 32 = Lk xii. 10, and Mk iv. 24 = Mt vii. 2 = Lk vi. 38 can be alleged as derived from the same written source. The probabilities in these three cases respectively are strong, moderate, and slight, as we shall presently find them to be in the three classes of passages (A, B, C) which we shall be examining as to the likelihood of their origin in Q.

[2] Appendix A, on the 'Double Tradition of St. Matthew and St. Luke', pp. 134–70. I can think of but two little parallels that might perhaps be added, the reference to the close of the Sermon on the Mount in Mt vii. 28 a = Lk vii. 1 a, and the asking for a sign in Mt xii. 38 = Lk xi. 16. It will thus be seen that no account is taken of any passages which do not occur both in Mt and Lk, apart from Mk. And the same course is adopted by Harnack in his proposed reconstruction of Q in *Sprüche und Reden Jesu* (see p. 112,

First and Third Gospels which he there prints side by side for us (or in the cases of Mt xxi. 28-30 and Lk vii. 4 f. and xv. 6 only refers to) occupy about 298 verses (or occasionally parts of verses) in Mt, and about 277 in Lk.[1]

But some of these verses may be at once dismissed from our notice, as for various reasons not bearing on our present purpose.

i. Thus I omit from the following lists the verses, numbering forty-three in Mt and thirty-two in Lk, which contain no words at all which are actually identical in the Greek of the two Gospels. No doubt in some cases (e. g. Mt viii. 13 compared with Lk vii. 10) the substantial agreement of the verses may suggest a common source of some kind, but it does not point at all to a written rather than to an oral source.

ii. On the same ground I omit Mt vi. 34 = Lk xii. 32, and Mt xii. 9 = Lk xiv. 1 because of the extreme slightness of the parallelism in Greek words (only μή in the former, and καί and εἰς in the latter case).

iii. Mt xvi. 2-3 = Lk xii. 54-6 and Mt xxi. 44 = Lk xx. 18 are left out because the genuineness of the passages in Mt is so doubtful.[2]

iv. I also exclude two passages of Mt, viz. vii. 16-18 and ix. 32-4, because the former constitutes a pair of doublets with Mt xii. 33-5, and the latter with xii. 22-4. It seems clear, therefore, that in each of these cases the *two* Matthaean passages can only represent *one* passage in the presumed Q, i. e. in the former case that which is found

below). A very different mode of procedure may be seen in Bernhard Weiss's *Die Quellen der Synoptischen Überlieferung* (Leipzig, 1908). In what he terms the 'Matthäusquelle (Q)' he includes (α) much matter that is found in Mk as well as in Mt and Lk, (β) a good deal that is found in Mt only, and (γ) even some that is found in Lk only. In (β) and (γ) this matter consists largely, though not exclusively, of parables; in (α) there is not a little narrative.

[1] This difference between the numbers of the verses in the two Gospels has of course no significance for us, being merely dependent upon the accident that H. Stephens, in his somewhat hasty and inconsistent division of the New Testament into verses in 1551, made some of them longer in Lk than in Mt.

[2] It is remarkable, by the way, that no more than two passages should have to be excluded on this ground, for it shows how comparatively seldom the temptation to assimilate was yielded to by copyists.

III. Double Tradition of Matthew and Luke

in Lk vi. 43-5, and in the latter case that which is found in Lk xi. 14 f. (It is remarkable that in both cases the passage of Mt which corresponds exactly to Lk in position is less close to it in wording than that which Mt places in another context.)

v. I deduct also from the parallels in *Synopticon* Mt x. 9, 10 a = Lk x. 4, Mt x. 14 = Lk x. 10, 11, Mt xxiii 6, 7 a = Lk xi. 43, Mt xxiv. 26 = Lk xvii. 23, because there are parallels in Mark also which make a non-Marcan origin at least doubtful here (see Mk vi. 8, vi. 11, xii. 38, 39, xiii. 21 respectively). I retain, however, Mt v. 13 = Lk xiv. 34 (the savourless salt), notwithstanding the parallel in Mk ix. 50, because of the probability that the saying may have come down in more than one tradition. And the same probability, largely enhanced by the study of the doublets, especially those in Lk's 'great interpolation',[1] causes the retention of Mt x. 26 = Lk xii. 2 (though similar to Mk iv. 22 = Lk viii. 17) and of Mt x. 38 = Lk xiv. 27 (though similar to Mk viii. 34 = Mt xvi. 24 = Lk ix. 23) and of Mt x. 39 = Lk xvii. 33 (though similar to Mk viii. 35 = Mt xvi. 25 = Lk ix. 24), and of Mt xxv. 29 = Lk xix. 26 (though similar to Mk iv. 25 = Mt xiii. 12 = Lk viii. 18).

After making such deductions the number of verses (or parts of verses[2]) which remain for our consideration as at least possibly constituents of Q would amount to about 236 in Mt and about 225 in Lk. But for our present purpose it will be most convenient to collect these into *passages*—meaning by passages the amounts of matter[3] which we find actually distinct and separate in one or both of the documents before us, or else as to which we can see no positive reason against their having been distinct and

---

[1] See p. 35 of this volume; also *Hor. Syn.*[2], pp. 80 ff., on Doublets.

[2] For, as will be seen in the following lists, only the first parts of Mt x. 8 and 16 and xxiv. 51, and only the second parts of Mt xxi. 31 and Lk xii. 33, are parallel to words in Lk and Mt respectively; and Mt x. 10 and Lk x. 7 and 9 have each to be treated in two separate parts in order to show their verbal correspondence with sentences standing in a different order.

[3] Some of these amounts are smaller than the English word 'passages' usually implies; but we seem to have no such convenient and comprehensive term as the German *Stücke* to express pieces of matter of any size.

separate in the source from which they came. Of these separate or easily separable passages I reckon 84, in all of which, when we take into consideration the substance, their wording, and the positions in which they stand, there is some degree of probability that they rest upon, or at the very least show the influence of, a common written origin.

As an attempt to show the chief degrees of this probability, these 84 passages, instead of being given in one long list, will be sorted into three classes,[1] of which Class A contains 54 passages as to which the probability of derivation from Q seems high. Class B contains 22 passages as to which that probability seems considerable, and Class C contains 8 passages as to which it is but slight, and yet not absolutely negligible. And of course if the fact that the compilers had such a document before them is thought to be established by Class A, the probability that all the items in Class B, and several in Class C, are, if not extracts from, at least reminiscences of the use of that source will be felt to be higher than it would otherwise have been.

The passages which are consecutive in both Gospels will be bracketed together.

By the prefixed asterisk (*) will be denoted the passages which are differently placed or connected in the two Gospels: they amount to 62 out of the 84, being considerably more than two-thirds, which would be 56.

[1] This division of mine into three classes, of which the third is very much smaller than the two others, has much general similarity to Harnack's division of nearly the same matter into two classes with the addition of a brief Appendix. So I should like to explain that mine was completed and typewritten before his *Sprüche und Reden Jesu* reached England early in 1907, and that I have made no alterations in it since then (even when rather inclined to make them), as some readers may perhaps like to compare the two quite independent arrangements. In the notes to this Essay, however, I give some references to Harnack's important and valuable work, naming the pages both of the original and of the Rev. J. R. Wilkinson's English translation (*The Sayings of Jesus*, Williams and Norgate, 1908).

III. Double Tradition of Matthew and Luke

Class A: Passages very probably derived from Q.

No.	St. Matthew.	St. Luke.	Leading words, or general subjects.
1	iii. 7–10	iii. 7–9	The Baptist's preaching { 'Who warned you to flee.' 'Whose fan is in his hand.'
2	iii. 12	iii. 17	
3	iv. 3–11	iv. 3–13	The Temptation.
4	v. 11, 12	vi. 22, 23	'Blessed are ye when men shall reproach you.'
5	*v. 18	xvi. 17	'One tittle shall in no wise pass away from the law.'[1]
6	*v. 25, 26	xii. 58, 59	'Agree with thine adversary.'
7	v. 39, 40, 42, 44–8	vi. 27–30, 32–6	Non-resistance and love to enemies (with much change in order).
8	*vi. 9–13	xi. 2–4	The Lord's Prayer.[2]
9	*vi. 20, 21	xii. 33 b, 34	'Lay up treasure in heaven.'
10	*vi. 22, 23	xi. 34, 35	'The lamp of the body is the eye.'
11	*vi. 24	xvi. 13	'No man can serve two masters.'
12	*vi. 25–33	xii. 22–31	'Be not anxious ... seek his kingdom.'
13	vii. 1, 2	vi. 37, 38	'Judge not ... with what measure ye mete.'[3]
14	vii. 3–5	vi. 41, 42	The mote and the beam.
15	vii. 7–11	xi. 9–13	'Ask and it shall be given ... if ye being evil.'[4]
16[5]	*vii. 12	vi. 31	The golden rule.[5]

[1] Placed in Class A because of the conjunction with Lk xvi. 18; see p. 133 below.

[2] In A chiefly because of the very peculiar word ἐπιούσιος; and Mt's enlargements may easily be due to familiar liturgical use of the prayer.

[3] Cf. Mk iv. 24 b, where the subject is quite different.

[4] The notable variation between ἄρτον—λίθον and ᾠόν—σκορπίον has not seemed quite sufficient to bring the whole passage down to Class B. This is one of some 25 passages in my Class A which Harnack places in his second division (op. cit., pp. 32 ff., E. T. pp. 40 ff.), while there are only 5 passages in my Class B which he places in his first division (pp. 6 ff., E. T. pp. 1 ff.). Thus his list of more important parallelisms between Mt and Lk becomes smaller, and his list of less important parallelisms becomes larger than mine, which constitutes the main difference between the two arrangements.

[5] In this one case the change of position is within the limits of what is probably the same discourse.—For Mt vii. 16-18, which might be expected

S.S.P.

Class A (*continued*).

No.	St. Matthew.	St. Luke.	Leading words, or general subjects.
17	vii. 24–7	vi. 47–9	Houses founded on rock and on sands.
18	viii. 5–10	vii. 1–3, 6–9	Narrative of the centurion.
19	*viii. 11, 12	xiii. 28, 29	'Many shall come from the east and the west.'
20	*viii. 19, 20	ix. 57, 58	'The foxes have holes.'
21	*viii. 21, 22	ix. 59, 60	'Leave the dead to bury their own dead.'
22	*ix. 37, 38	x. 2	'The harvest is plenteous . . . pray ye therefore.'
23	*x. 26–33	xii. 2–9	'Fear them not . . . for there is nothing covered . . .'
24	*x. 34–6	xii. 51–3	Not peace, but division in families.
25	*x. 37	xiv. 26	Preferring father or mother to Christ.
26	*x. 38	xiv. 27	Not bearing the cross.
27	xi. 2, 3, 4–11	vii.18, 19, 22–8	The message from the Baptist, and the declaration of his position.
28	*xi. 12, 13	xvi. 16	Since John 'the kingdom of heaven suffereth violence'. (With change in order.)
29	xi. 16–19	vii. 31–5	The children in the market-place.
30	*xi. 21–4	x. 12–15	'Woe unto thee, Chorazin.' (With change in order as to Sodom.)
31	*xi. 25–7	x. 21, 22	'I thank thee, O Father . . . All things have been delivered unto me.'
32	xii. 22–4	xi. 14, 15	Healing of dumb demoniac. (See also Mt ix. 32, 33, which is closer in wording to Lk.)
33	xii. 27, 28	xi. 19, 20	'If I by Beelzebub, by whom do your sons?'
34	xii. 30	xi. 23	'He that is not with me is against me.'
35	*xii. 33–5	vi. 43–5	The tree known by its fruits. (See also Mt vii. 16–18, which in position is parallel to Lk.)

to be the next entry, see p. 110 above, and Mt xii. 33-5 lower down on this list.

III. Double Tradition of Matthew and Luke

Class A (continued).

No.	St. Matthew.	St. Luke.	Leading words, or general subjects.
36	xii. 39–42	xi. 29–32	Refusal of a sign: Ninevites and Queen of South. (With change of order.)
37	xii. 43–5	xi. 24–6	The return of the unclean spirit.
38	*xiii. 16, 17	x. 23, 24	'Blessed are your eyes... and your ears.'
39	*xiii. 33	xiii. 20, 21	The parable of the leaven.
40	*xviii. 7	xvii. 1	Occasions of stumbling must come.
41	*xviii. 12–14	xv. 4, 5, 7	The lost sheep recovered.
42	*xviii. 15	xvii. 3	'If thy brother sin against thee.'[1]
43	*xviii. 21, 22	xvii. 4	How often to forgive.
44	*xxiii. 4	xi. 46	'They bind heavy burdens on men.' \ Addressed to the 'lawyers' in Lk.
45	*xxiii. 13 [2]	xi. 52	'Ye shut the kingdom of heaven against men.' /
46	*xxiii. 23	xi. 42	'Ye tithe mint and anise.'
47	*xxiii. 25, 26	xi. 39, 41	'Ye cleanse the outside of the cup.'
48	*xxiii. 29–31	xi. 47, 48	'Ye build the sepulchres of the prophets.'
49	*xxiii. 34–6	xi. 49–51	'Behold, I send unto you prophets.'
50	*xxiii. 37–9	xiii. 34, 35	'O Jerusalem, which killeth the prophets.'
51	*xxiv. 27	xvii. 24	'As the lightning... so shall be the coming.'[3]
52	*xxiv. 28	xvii. 37	'Wheresoever the carcase is.'
53	*xxiv. 37–9	xvii. 26, 27	'As the days of Noah, so shall be the coming.'
54	*xxiv. 43–51 a	xii. 39, 40, 42–6	Watchfulness: the faithful and the evil servants.

[1] The words identical in both Gospels are few here; but the connexion with the saying which follows immediately in Lk and soon afterwards (verses 21, 22) in Mt makes a common origin probable. The asterisk is prefixed to Nos. 40, 42, 43, notwithstanding their connexion with one another, because they are placed in Mt xviii before, and in Lk xvii after, the final departure from Galilee; but the accuracy of Lk's chronological arrangement would not be very generally admitted. See, however, p. 57 in this volume. [2] Numbered as verse 14 in WH.

[3] Perhaps the preceding verse (the caution against false reports in Mt xxiv. 26 = Lk xvii. 23) may also have been in Q; but it is not entered here,

Class B: Passages ascribable to Q with a considerable amount of probability.

No.	St. Matthew.	St. Luke.	Leading words, or general subjects.	
1	v. 1, 2, 3, 4, 6	vi. 20, 21, 25 [1]	The beatitudes. (Not including Mt v. 11, 12, Lk vi. 22, 23, which are in Class A.)	
2	*vii. 13, 14	xiii. 23, 24	Entrance by the narrow gate.	
3	vii. 21	vi. 46	Saying 'Lord, Lord', contrasted with doing.	
4	*vii. 22, 23	xiii. 25, 27	The Lord will say, 'Depart from me, ye that work iniquity.' [2]	
5	*x. 7	x. 9 b	Preach that 'the kingdom of heaven is at hand'.	
6	*x. 8 a	x. 9 a	'Heal the sick.'	
7	*x. 10 b	x. 4	Take no shoes. (Compare Mk vi. 9.)	(With numerous changes of
8	*x. 10 c	x. 7 b	'The labourer is worthy of his food,' or 'hire'.	
9	*x. 11	x. 7 a, 8	Remain in the same house.	
10	*x. 12, 13	x. 5, 6	Peace shall rest on the worthy house or man.	
11	*x. 15	x. 12	'More tolerable for the land of Sodom.' (Also in Mt xi. 24.)	
12	*x. 16 a	x. 3	'I send you forth as sheep (or lambs) in the midst of wolves.'	
13	*x. 24, 25	vi. 40	'A disciple is not above his master.' [3]	
14	*x. 39	xvii. 33	'He that findeth,' or 'shall seek to gain, his life'. [4]	
15	*x. 40	x. 16	'He that receiveth,' or 'heareth you'. (See also Mk ix. 37, Mt xviii. 5, Lk ix. 48.)	

because it may have been adopted by Mt and Lk from Mk xiii. 21 as an introduction to the saying about the lightning, although Mt had already used it in his verse 23.

[1] Verse 25 is only included because of the verb πενθήσετε; cf. πενθοῦντες in Mt's verse 4.

[2] Harnack omits these two verses from his list, though admitting that 'a common source lies far in the background' (*op. cit.*, p. 52, E. T., p. 71).

[3] The application is different in the two Gospels, and in Lk the meaning and the relation to the context are obscure.

[4] Mt x. 39 is a doublet with Mt xvi. 25, which stands parallel with Mk viii. 35 and Lk ix. 24, and in very close agreement with them. See *Hor. Syn.*², p. 87.

III. Double Tradition of Matthew and Luke

Class B (*continued*).

No.	St. Matthew.	St. Luke.	Leading words, or general subjects.
16	*xv. 14	vi. 39	The blind guiding the blind.[1]
17	*xvii. 20	xvii. 6	'If ye have faith as a grain of mustard seed.'[2]
18	*xix. 28	xxii. 28, 30	'Ye ... shall sit on ... thrones, judging the twelve tribes'.
19	*xxiii. 12	xiv. 11	'Whosoever shall exalt himself shall be humbled.' (Also in Lk xviii. 14.)[1]
20	*xxiii. 27	xi. 44	Pharisees compared to sepulchres. (See also Mt's verse 28.)[3]
21	*xxiv. 40, 41	xvii. 34, 35	Two men in the field, or bed, two women at the mill.
22	*xxv. 14, 16, 19–29	xix. 12, 13, 15–24, 26	The Parables of the Talents and the Pounds.

Class C: Passages the origin of which in Q is but slightly probable.

No.	St. Matthew.	St. Luke.	Leading words, or general subjects.
1[4]	i. 2–6, 10, 15, 16	iii. 23–5, 31–4	Thirteen names in the Genealogy, out of forty-five names mentioned in Mt and seventy-five in Lk.
2	i. 18, 20, 21, 23, 25	i. 26, 27, 30, 31, 34, 35	Parallels in the pre-Nativity narrative.
3	ii. 22, 23	ii. 39	Removal, or return, to Nazareth in Galilee.
4	*v. 13	xiv. 34, 35	Savourless salt.[5]

[1] Sayings of a proverbial kind, which might have been spoken on various occasions, and might have come down through more than one channel.

[2] The striking expression 'as a grain of mustard seed' occurs only in the two places here referred to; but there is an otherwise similar saying in Mk xi. 23, Mt xxi. 21, which seems to be of Marcan origin. See *Hor. Syn.*[2], p. 89 f., on Doublets.

[3] The detailed application is very different in Mt and Lk, and the passages would have been placed in Class C but for their position with regard to their respective contexts.

[4] Nos. 1, 2, and 3 may be omitted from further consideration, as being quite unlikely to have been in any degree grounded on Q; but the mention of them may serve to remind us that Mt and Lk had some common knowledge of the Christian traditions besides what they drew from Q and from Mk.

[5] Placed in Class C because of the parallel in Mk ix. 50; but see p. 111.

Class C (continued).

No.	St. Matthew.	St. Luke.	Leading words, or general subjects.
5	*vi. 3, 4	xiv. 13, 14	Recompense for alms, or for hospitality.[1]
6	*xii. 10, 11	xiv. 2, 3, 5	Giving help on the Sabbath.
7	*xxi. 31 b–32	vii. 29, 30	The reception of the Baptist by Pharisees, &c., and by Publicans.
8	*xxii. 1–5, 7, 8, 10	xiv. 16–18, 21, 23, 24.	Parables of the Marriage of the King's Son, and of the Great Supper.

III

We have now to endeavour to see, in the third place, what inferences as to the nature and contents of Q we can draw from the above 84 passages which are more or less likely to have been quoted from it.[2] And in order that the very different degrees of that likelihood, and consequently the very different degrees of confidence with which we may allege the passages as grounds upon which to form an estimate of Q, may not be forgotten, the verses taken from Class B will be marked with an obelus (†), and those taken from Class C with a double obelus (‡), in the remaining pages of this essay.

First and foremost the general observation has to be made that in the whole of A and B, which are the two largest as well as the most weighty of the three Classes, containing as they do 76 out of the 84 parallels, there are only two direct exceptions to the general rule that the passages are concerned with sayings of the Lord, accompanied sometimes by the facts which lead up to

---

[1] But the resemblances are very slight, and the passages are only inserted in order not to omit altogether any verbal parallel suggested in *Synopticon*, except those ruled out on p. 110 f.

[2] This is a much more humble and limited task than an attempt to 'reconstruct' Q, which Professor Burkitt justly calls 'futile' (*The Gospel History, &c.*, p. 17; see also pp. 123, 131).

III. *Double Tradition of Matthew and Luke*

them and explain them. These exceptions are the two adjacent records of the Baptist's preaching in Mt iii. 7-10 = Lk iii. 7-9, and Mt iii. 12 = Lk iii. 17; but indeed these records might well have been prefixed to a collection of the Lord's sayings [κυριακὰ λόγια in the narrower sense of the term], as being required in order to explain to readers of Q the references to the Baptist in Mt xi. 2 ff. and Lk vii. 18 ff. and elsewhere.[1] The Temptation-narrative may perhaps occur to us as another exception, but it could only be regarded as coming directly from the Lord, and so might be reckoned as entirely a *logion* of His; and at any rate its chief interest and importance lie in His three sayings contained in it. Again, the narrative of the healing of the centurion's servant is lengthy, but a briefer story than at least Mt gives would be insufficient to bring out the full force of the commendation, 'I have not found so great faith, no, not in Israel.'[2]

Generally, then, our 84 passages support the view that to collect and preserve discourses of Christ was at least the leading purpose of the compiler of Q.

We now turn to see what more special inferences those passages enable us to draw as to (1) the form, and (2) the substance of Q.

I

As to its *form*, the first and most obvious inference is (A) that by far the greater part of it—for almost certainly there is a considerable exception to be allowed for—was drawn up in such a way as to suggest to its readers that little or no

---

[1] So Jülicher, *Introd. to N. T.*, E. T., p. 357.

[2] Even as to Lk's narrative Von Soden says, 'Only once does a saying of the Lord require for its comprehension a more developed story, and this is well told in a style both pleasing and vivid' (*Early Christian Literature*, E. T., p. 132). It is quite possible that the narrative in Q ended with the saying to which it led up, and did not record the cure; for that is related in totally different words by Mt (viii. 13) and by Lk (vii. 10).

importance was to be attached to the chronological or other *order* of its contents. For we have the outstanding fact, shown by the asterisks in our lists, that more than two-thirds of the passages, being 62 out of 84, are differently placed by Mt and Lk. If we take only the most important Class A, this is the case with 37 out of its 54 passages, i.e. with more than five-eighths of them. If we take together the two Classes A and B, which are far more important both in size and substance than C, we find that it is the case with 54 of their 76 passages, which is a proportion slightly exceeding two-thirds.

It may also be specially noticed as a particularly striking proof of the extensiveness of this divergence of order that to every one of the seven discourses which are given at greatest length by Mt (viz. in chaps. v–vii, x, xi, xiii, xviii, xxiii, xxiv–xxv respectively) there are some parallels in Luke's so-called 'Peraean section', or 'great interpolation' (ix. 51–xviii. 14),[1] although there is not one of the seven which is attributed in Mt to the period of the last journey to Jerusalem, for even that in chap. xviii is in xix. 1 expressly dated before the departure from Galilee.

It is thus certain that at least one—and if only one, it would be Mt—of the two compilers took but little account of the order and sequence of Q,[2] save only in the one department of it which was above alluded to as

[1] See E. D. Burton, *Principles of Literary Criticism and the Synoptic Problem* (Chicago, 1904), pp. 38 ff.

[2] Von Soden has made an interesting but not convincing attempt to show that Q is preserved by Lk in the original order in which it was compiled. His principal proof of this is 'the fact that if we simply place together those passages in St. Luke that have close parallels in St. Matthew but are foreign to St. Mark, we find that we have in our hands a collection of sayings systematically arranged according to distinct leading ideas' (*Early Christian Literature*, E. T., p. 129, and see following pages). But is it the fact that we find this? If it were so, would the eschatological warnings be found partly in Lk xii. 35 f., and partly in Lk xvii. 24 ff.? Professor Burkitt, *op. cit.*, pp. 130 f., and Dean A. Robinson, *op. cit.*, p. 87, also think that Lk may have preserved much of Q's order. See the discussion of this point by Mr. Streeter in pp. 141 ff. of this volume.

III. Double Tradition of Matthew and Luke

very probably forming a considerable exception, and which has now to be examined as such.

Certainly it cannot be passed by as an inconsiderable exception, although it only concerns 7 or 8 of the 84 passages before us. We find that in the two Sermons recorded by Mt (v–vii) and Lk (vi. 20–49) respectively, and assigned by them to somewhat different occasions and perhaps (though the mountain and the level place are not irreconcilable) to different places, there is an agreement which cannot be accidental as to four matters of order: that is to say, in both cases the discourse (1) begins with beatitudes, (2) afterwards deals with love to enemies and non-resistance (these two kindred subjects being partially transposed), (3) further on contains cautions against judging others, and (4) concludes with warnings against profession apart from practice—warnings which culminate in a parable drawn from the safe and unsafe foundations of houses.

From this the most obvious, though not quite inevitable, inference is that the Sermon in these four stages lay before both compilers. And that inference is confirmed by the fact that the special formula about Jesus ending His discourses which Mt subjoins to his five most important bodies of sayings (vii. 28; xi. 1; xiii. 53; xix. 1; xxvi. 1) has in this one case a substantial (though not verbal) parallel in Lk vii. 1, 'After He had ended all His sayings in the ears of the people.' Nor is the inference much weakened by the observation that the passages which are thus parallel in position do not correspond to one another in verbal details more closely than others which Mt and Lk place in different situations—indeed (except in the mote and the beam, Mt vii. 3–5 = Lk vi. 41 f.) there is on the whole perhaps less than the usual average of such close verbal correspondence—for this may be only another illustration of the phenomenon already noticed (p. 100) that it is often the most familiar and fundamental matters which are recorded with least of exact agreement, because the Evangelists as teachers had come to know the substance of them so well that they did not always feel the necessity of refreshing their memories of them by constant references to their MSS.

But, as I have said, this inference is not quite inevitable. It is possible that (i) Q may have been throughout a collection of sayings (with introductions where necessary) collected and put together without any reference to chronological or topical order, but that (ii) quite apart from it there might have existed in the Church a well-known tradition that the first great discourse of Jesus dealt successively with the four subjects which have just been named, and that therefore (iii) the compilers of the First and Third Gospels naturally threw into these four stages sayings appropriate to each of them which they independently culled from various parts of Q.

In favour of this suggestion it may be said that it seems to be the simplest way of accounting for the remarkable transpositions of order in the second of these stages (i. e. in Mt v. 39–48 compared with Lk vi. 29–36), and also for the very different placings of the Golden Rule in Mt vii. 12 and Lk vi. 31 (the latter being by far the more appropriate). So I cannot think that it is an altogether negligible suggestion, though no doubt it will seem to most people much more far-fetched than the supposition that the portion of the contents of Q which Mt and Lk agree in embodying in their Sermons was already arranged there in the order in which it was believed to have been spoken.

We may accept then the matter found in both those Sermons as almost certainly forming an exception to what seems to have been the generally non-chronological character of Q.

(B) As we now have the sayings preserved for us by Mt and Lk, a good many of them are accompanied by *introductions*, though very rarely by sequels or statements of results. As to the difficult question whether these sayings

III. Double Tradition of Matthew and Luke 123

as they stood in Q had such introductions—beyond the mere 'Jesus saith' of the first series (1897)[1] of so-called *Logia* found at Oxyrhynchus—we may draw the following inferences:—

(i) Some sayings certainly had them,[2] for both the First and Third Gospels have them almost identically in Mt viii. 19-22 = Lk ix. 57-60 (the two aspirants) and in Mt xi. 2 ff. = Lk vii. 18 ff. (the message from the Baptist and the sayings that followed upon it). The same may be probably said of the expulsion of the dumb spirit in Mt xii. 22 = Lk xi. 14, though the case is complicated here by the admixture of the Marcan narrative with matter from Q. In those two or three instances Mt and Lk retain sayings and introductions together from Q, just as they retain them together from their Marcan source in Mt ix. 14-17 = Lk v. 33-9 drawn from Mk ii. 18-22, in Mt xii. 1-8 = Lk vi. 1-5 drawn from Mk ii. 23-8, and elsewhere.

(ii) No such decided inference can be drawn as to the sayings for which we find introductions supplied by Lk only, as in xi. 1-13, 37-52, xii. 13-34, xiii. 23-7 †, xv. 1-7, xvii. 20-7 and 34 †, 35 †, 37, while only the sayings contained in those passages are given by Mt in one or other of his large bodies of discourse with more or less appropriateness to its general subject. It is easy to say with Loisy and others that Lk 'readily invents the surroundings of the discourses that he

---

[1] In the second series of these sayings (1904) there is a little introduction (His disciples question Him and say, &c.) to the fifth of them, besides the prefatory statement before the first.

[2] *A priori* we might expect this to be the case, as we may see by any collection of sayings intended to exhibit a great personality; there are always some which would not explain themselves without some introductory matter. I will take two instances of very different kinds. In the *Sayings of Muhammad*, edited by Al Suhrawardy (Constable, 1905), I find that of the 451 sayings rather more than one-tenth are introduced by questions, or by brief descriptions of the circumstances under which the Prophet spoke (and about 13 characteristics and anecdotes of him without any sayings are included in the 451). In the *Wit and Wisdom of Samuel Johnson*, selected and arranged by Dr. Birkbeck Hill (Clarendon Press, 1888), there are 887 items, and of these 140, or nearly one-sixth, have some explanatory or introductory matter (most often questions from friends) combined with Johnson's own words, in order to make them intelligible. I have taken no account of the more than 100 footnotes, as many of them are references to books.

repeats'; [1] and it may be admitted that his desire to place things as far as possible 'in order' may have sometimes caused him to adopt without sufficient authority historical occasions which seemed to him suitable for the separate sayings which he wished to locate somewhere. But, judging from the evidence before us in the two Gospels, I cannot think that this chronological tendency in Lk was nearly so strong and effective as the homiletical tendency in Mt to group sayings according to their subjects, and so according to their convenience for teachers. And therefore it seems to me probable that either most or all of the introductions above referred to were drawn with the sayings from Q by Lk, while Mt dropped them out; and also that the exclamations or questions which interrupt discourses in Lk xi. 45, xii. 41, xvii. 37 a (and possibly in xix. 25) were retained from Q by Lk, and not added by him.

(iii) But when allowance has thus been made for those sayings which either certainly or probably had explanatory or chronological introductions prefixed to them in Q, we may safely infer that a very large proportion of sayings stood without them there. Otherwise it would be extremely difficult to account

(a) for the attribution of so many sayings to different occasions and surroundings, as shown by many of the asterisks in our lists,[2] and

(b) for the way in which some of them are strung together [3] with an absence of connexion which baffles the ingenuity of commentators, who have sometimes been unwisely eager to find such links, and

(c) especially for the different turns of meaning which appear to be sometimes given by the two compilers to the same saying, by their adaptation of it to their respective contexts. Thus, for instance, in Mt v. 25, 26 the partially parabolic warning 'Agree with thine adversary, &c.' seems to refer, like the three preceding verses, only or mainly to the danger of remaining unreconciled to our brother

---

[1] Loisy, *The Gospel and the Church*, E. T., p. 71.

[2] See also Dr. A. Wright's *Synopsis*[2], p. xxv, or his *St. Luke*, p. xiii, for instances.

[3] e.g. in parts of Mt's Sermon on the Mount, and in Lk xi. 32-5, xii. 8-12, xvi. 15-18, and xvii. 1-10.

III. Double Tradition of Matthew and Luke 125

men whom we have injured or with whom we have quarrelled; but in Lk xii. 58, 59 it is so linked by γάρ to the foregoing verses there, that it becomes a more general and more completely parabolic warning against unpreparedness for Divine judgement. Again, let us place side by side the following passages:—

Mt x. 26, 27.	Lk xii. 1, 2, 3.
Fear them not therefore: for there is nothing covered, that shall not be revealed; and hid, that shall not be known. What I tell you in the darkness, speak ye in the light: and what ye hear in the ear, proclaim upon the housetops.	Beware of... hypocrisy. But there is nothing covered up, that shall not be revealed: and hid, that shall not be known. Wherefore whatsoever ye have said in the darkness shall be heard in the light; and what ye have spoken in the ear in the inner chambers shall be proclaimed upon the housetops.

Here, by a few modifications of wording, the encouragement to preach boldly which in Mt is given to the Apostles as such, and is grounded upon the universal prevalence and publicity which is assured to their message, appears in Lk as a warning to all Christians against hypocrisy, which would be useless because no concealment or pretence can escape ultimate detection and exposure.[1]

2

From the probable form of Q we turn now to its probable *substance*, or in other words to the presumable character and subjects of the Sayings of Jesus, for the preservation of which we take the document to have been primarily drawn up.

a If its general substance is at all adequately represented to us by the extracts made from it by both Mt and Lk, it consisted mainly of moral and religious teachings, including warnings and encouragements, such as we find addressed to Christ's hearers and especially to His disciples both in the parallel portions of the Sermons on the Mount and on the Level Place, and elsewhere. These are

[1] See Plummer's note on Lk xii. 2, 3.

so numerous that it must be enough to refer to the above lists generally instead of repeating separate references here.¹

b But that Q also contained some warnings addressed to the Jews who were opposing or rejecting Jesus is shown by such passages as Mt viii. 11, 12 = Lk xiii. 28, 29, Mt x. 15 (also xi. 24) = Lk x. 12†, Mt xi. 21-4 = Lk x. 12-15, Mt xii. 39-42 = Lk xi. 29-32, Mt xii. 43-5 = Lk xi. 24-6, Mt xxiii. 37-9 = Lk xiii 34, 35.

c It appears to have also preserved some direct denunciations of the Pharisees in Mt xii. 27, 28 (cf. ver. 24) = Lk xi. 19, 20, Mt xxi. 31b, 32 = Lk vii. 29, 30‡, Mt xxiii. 4-36 *passim* = Lk xi. 39-52 *passim*.

d We infer from Mt x. 7-16 a *passim* = Lk x. 4-12 *passim* † that Q contained some directions that were only or most directly adapted for missionaries and teachers. The latter part of the charge to the Apostles in Mt x, from verse 24 onwards, is not cited here, because the parallels to it in Lk vi. 40†, xii. 2-9 (see above, p. 125), 51-3, and xiv. 26, 27 seem to be addressed to disciples generally, so we cannot say whether they originally formed part of an address to teachers.²

e We infer also from the passages collected by Mt, but placed differently by Lk, in Mt xxiv. 27 = Lk xvii. 24, Mt xxiv. 28 = Lk xvii. 37, Mt xxiv. 37-9 = Lk xvii. 26, 27, Mt xxiv. 40, 41 = Lk xvii. 34, 35†, Mt xxiv. 43-51a = Lk xii. 39, 40, 42-6 that Q included some predictions and warnings as to the coming Parousia.³

f The office and work of the Baptist seem to have been regarded by the compiler of Q as important and interesting for his readers. For, besides the account of John's preliminary preaching in Mt iii. 7-10, 12 = Lk iii. 7-9, 17, there is the long passage in Mt xi. 7-19 (see also xxi.

¹ Compare Harnack, *op. cit.*, p. 173, E. T., p. 251.
² Perhaps the treatment of the two aspirants in Mt viii. 19-22 = Lk ix. 57-60 might also be brought under this heading, for it seems to be a sifting of men with a view to missionary work rather than to ordinary discipleship. It stands in Lk just before the mission of the Seventy, and as to its place in Mt see *Exp. Times*, xii. 472.
³ Jülicher observes that Q ' contains no signs of the writers having witnessed the destruction of Jerusalem ' (*Introd. to N. T.*, E. T., p. 358; and so Von Soden, *op. cit.*, p. 141). The attitude in all the above passages appears to be consistently expectant; and none of the special predictions in Mt xxii. 7b (contrast Lk xiv. 21) and Lk xix. 43, 44 and xxi. 20, which have been suspected of being *vaticinia ex eventu*, are given by both Mt and Lk.

III. Double Tradition of Matthew and Luke 127

31 b, 32 ‡) = Lk vii. 7-19 (see also xvi. 16) dealing with his character and his relation to the Messiah, and introduced by his message from prison.¹

g We pass now to some inferences of a more or less negative kind, i. e. inferences as to the kinds of subject-matter which were either absent from, or but rarely present in Q, so far as we can judge of it from Mt and Lk's employment of it. It is notable that they have drawn from it no long parables, unless we regard the Talents and the Pounds (Mt xxv. 14-30 = Lk xix. 12-27 †), and the Marriage of the King's Son and the Great Supper (Mt xxii. 1-14 = Lk xiv. 16-24 ‡), as derived respectively from the same written source, which seems considerably doubtful as to the first pair, and extremely doubtful as to the second pair of parables.² Setting these aside, the Leaven (Mt xiii. 33 = Lk xiii. 20, 21) and the Lost Sheep are the only two of the parables usually so called (as in Trench's list) which are found both in Mt and Lk, but not in Mk;³ and in Mt xviii: 12, 13 the Lost Sheep would have probably been regarded merely as an interrogative illustration, such as Mt vii. 9, 10 = Lk xi. 11, 12 (fish or serpent, &c.) and Mt xii. 11 = Lk xiv. 5 ‡ (whose sheep or ox shall fall, &c.), and would not have been reckoned as a parable unless Lk (xv. 3-7) had given it to us in a fuller form as one of a connected series of three parables.

But while parables distinguished by their length or by their forming part of a series of parables are thus rare (or in the case of long parables perhaps non-existent) in the discourses attributable to Q, on the other hand those discourses abound in short similitudes and illustrations such as Mt vi. 24; vii. 3-5, 13, 14 †, 24-7; ix. 37, 38; xi. 16-19; xii. 33, 43-5; xv. 14 †, and the Lucan

---

¹ The need in the early Church of information as to the preparatory nature of the Baptist's office and work is shown by Acts xviii. 25 and xix. 3.

² It appears not unlikely that in one or both cases the descriptive language of the more familiar parable (i. e. probably Mt's) was transferred, either intentionally or from force of habit, by teachers to the less familiar one, while the occasions of the two had been different. These two pairs of parables are discussed in Harnack's Appendix, *op. cit.*, pp. 83 ff., E. T., pp. 119 ff.

³ It can be shown, however, that the Parable of the Mustard Seed probably came down in two forms, the one Marcan and the other [Logian or] embodied in Q; see p. 50 in this volume.

parallels. So in this respect they correspond in character with the discourses drawn from the Marcan source, which contain such brief similitudes as those in Mk ii. 19-22; iv. 21; vii. 27; viii. 15; ix. 43 ff., 49, 50; x. 25, 38; xiii. 28, with parallels in Mt and Lk or in Mt only.[1]

h Von Soden when characterizing this source says that in it 'all is original: nothing is borrowed from the Old Testament or from the sayings of the Rabbis'.[2] Without going so far as this as to the use of the Old Testament, we may notice that only one direct quotation from it is preserved by Mt and Lk alone in discourses of Jesus, viz. Mt xi. 10 = Lk vii. 27 ('Behold, I send my messenger, &c.,' Mal iii. 1), and even that prophecy is also given by Mk at the beginning of his Gospel (i. 2). We may, therefore, perhaps say that the sayings preserved in Q were mainly such as brought forward that aspect of the teaching of Jesus which was 'not as the scribes' (Mt vii. 29, Mk i. 22), whose appeals to canonical and other authorities were so constant and so deferential.

But, on the other hand, the language of the Old Testament is frequently embodied in the sayings, as that of Micah vii. 6 in Mt x. 35, 36 = Lk xii. 52, 53, of Isaiah xiv. 13, 15 in Mt xi. 23 = Lk x. 15, of Jer. xii. 7, xxii. 5, and Ps cxviii. 26 in Mt xxiii. 38, 39 = Lk xiii. 35. And there are many allusions to persons and places assumed to be well known in the Old Testament, as Abel, Noah, the Queen of Sheba, Jonah, and apparently the Zechariah of 2 Chron xxiv. 20 f., Sodom, Nineveh, and Tyre and Sidon.

i We cannot assign to Q more than two records of particular miracles, viz. the healing of the centurion's servant in Mt viii. 5 ff., Lk vii. 1 ff., and the healing of a certain dumb demoniac in Mt xii. 22, 23, Lk xi. 14, where in Mk's narrative it is merely implied that healings of that kind had taken place at some time before the 'scribes from Jerusalem' attributed them to the power of Beelzebub (Mk iii. 22). This does not, however, involve the further inference which has been drawn that 'so far as the choice of materials is concerned, little interest is taken in the miraculous'[3] by the compiler of Q, for we have seen the likelihood that no narrative of any kind came within his

---

[1] In the Synoptic Gospels the word παραβολή is sometimes applied to such minor similitudes; see Mk vii. 17 = Mt xv. 15, Mk xiii. 28 = Mt. xxiv. 32 = Lk xxi. 29, Lk v. 36, vi. 39, xii. 41, xiv. 7.

[2] Op. cit., p. 132.   [3] Von Soden, op. cit., p. 133.

III. Double Tradition of Matthew and Luke

scope, except when it was required for the purpose of elucidating the discourses which he gives; and moreover in those discourses the frequent performance of miracles is assumed as a matter of course at least three times—in the message from the Baptist and the reply to it (Mt xi. 2–7 = Lk vii. 18, 23),[1] in the woe pronounced upon Chorazin and Bethsaida (Mt xi. 21–4 = Lk x. 13, 14), and, though more indirectly, in the story of the Temptation, which would be unmeaning to those who did not regard Jesus as possessing miraculous powers. And the appeal to the Pharisees, 'If I by Beelzebub, &c.' (Mt xii. 27 = Lk xi. 19), is so expressed as to imply other successful exorcisms by Him besides that which had just been recorded.

k There seems to be reason for thinking that there was an intention of limiting the collection of sayings in Q to those which were spoken during the period of the Galilean and itinerant Ministry of Jesus, as distinct from the period described in the Passion-narratives. For there are none of our 84 passages which are placed in a later part of the Gospels than Mt xxv or Lk xxi, with the single and slight exception of the promise in Lk xxii. 30† that the Apostles should 'sit on thrones, judging the twelve tribes of Israel' (see Mt xix. 28).

Indeed, Lk xix might have been named[2] instead of xxi as the latest chapter of the Third Gospel in which Q seems to be used; for it is remarkable that there is nothing which is found both in Mt xxiv and Lk xxi apart from Mark, all such parallels to Mt xxiv being drawn from Lk xvii and xii. It is thus generally and almost completely the 'fact that while Mt and Lk each have in their Jerusalem period considerable material not found in Mark, they have no such material in common'.[3]

IV

Having drawn what inferences we can as to the nature and contents of Q [or *Logia*] from the portions of it which

---

[1] Lk's insertion in verse 21 makes it clear that he at least did not regard Jesus as 'speaking not of the physically but of the spiritually blind, lame, leprous, deaf, dead' (Schmiedel, *Enc. Bibl.*, ii. 1883).

[2] We might even have named chap. xvii if it had not been for the one doubtful case of the Parable of the Pounds in xix. 12–27†.

[3] E. D. Burton, *op. cit.*, p. 48. See Harnack, *op. cit.*, pp. 118–21, E. T. pp. 168–72.

we are more or less certain that Mt and Lk have agreed in selecting and preserving for us, we may venture to go a little further. We may find in those inferences grounds upon which to base conjectures as to whether and how far it may be the case that one of these compilers may sometimes have made extracts from parts of that document which the other overlooked or rejected. I use the word 'conjectures' so as to be on the safe side of under-estimating rather than over-estimating the value of any suggestions that will now be made; and no doubt almost all of them might be overthrown by any new knowledge of documents, or any sound arguments drawn from our present knowledge. But the probability (or the reverse) which attaches to the conjectures is of very different degrees; and in some cases it is at least sufficient to warn us against too hastily dismissing the whole of the 'single traditions of St. Matthew and St. Luke' as being necessarily of inferior value [1] to their 'double tradition'. Our present tendency so to depreciate them is not surprising when we consider the difficulties which modern criticism has not unreasonably found in a few parts of both these 'single traditions', and especially in that of St. Matthew; but we need not judge of the whole of either of them by those mere fringes or 'ragged edges', and what has now to be suggested may perhaps help us in keeping up that distinction.

We may enter upon this field of conjecture carrying with us the *a priori* probability that *some* of the contents of Q were omitted both by Mt and Lk, as they almost certainly omitted some of the contents of Mk (see e. g. p. 67 above). It has been assumed indeed [2] that no writer of a Gospel would have omitted from it any well accredited material with

[1] Some very high authorities on the Synoptic Problem hold that Lk had throughout a third source which he preferred both to Mk and to Q; as to the probability that this was the case at least in his 'great interpolation', see p. 56 f. in this volume.

[2] It is laid down as 'a golden rule' by Dr. A. Wright in his *Synopsis of the Gospels*², p. xi, and his *St. Luke*, p. xii; he admits, however, that there may be exceptions to and qualifications of this rule.

III. Double Tradition of Matthew and Luke

which he was acquainted; and perhaps we may allow that no Evangelist would have done so without reluctance and regret, though the apparent adaptations of the two Gospels to different circles of readers may make even this doubtful. But there is reason to think that considerations of space would have forced these two Evangelists to make, whether willingly or unwillingly, a selection of some of their materials to the exclusion of others. It is shown in another of the Essays in this volume (see p. 25 f.) that they probably wrote with the understanding that their Gospels were not to exceed a definite and perhaps conventional size —the size to which Mt, Lk, and Acts[1] approximate. So the question constantly before them would be not whether any of their available materials, but which of them, were to be omitted; and the decision of that question seems to have been left to their own judgements of what should be retained as most valuable for their respective readers, provided only that ample room was reserved for the Passion-narrative to be given fully.

[Those who cannot exclude from consideration the possible or probable identity of Q with the *Logia* of Matthew mentioned by Papias will also be influenced in the same direction by the following considerations:—

(*a*) There will seem to them some unlikelihood that one of the only two written authorities to which Papias—or Eusebius selecting from him—gives this prominence was so brief as to contain only the 236 verses or parts of verses which we have seen to be as high an estimate as can be formed of the matter common to Mt and Lk only (p. 111).

(*b*) They will also see some difficulty in supposing that this comparatively small amount of matter, forming as it does considerably less than a quarter of the 1,068 verses of Mt, could have given the name of St. Matthew to the whole Gospel; and they will feel that the difficulty would be

---

[1] The slight variations in length between the three books might perhaps be accounted for by differences in the handwriting of authors or amanuenses (cf. St. Paul's πηλίκοις γράμμασιν, Gal. vi. 11).

lessened by the supposition that many or all of those other verses in the First Gospel, amounting to about 200,[1] which consist only of sayings and brief narratives connected with sayings, may also have come from the compilation ascribed to Matthew.

(c) And further, if the *Logia* exceeded the narrow limits of the 236 verses, and if it was not known to have been mainly preserved in some well-known Gospel, is it conceivable that so precious a document would have been allowed to perish utterly, leaving no trace (either genuine or apocryphal) either of the original or of any translation?]

It is, then, with more or less prepossession in favour of Mt and Lk separately having preserved some contents of Q which are not found in both their Gospels, that we proceed to form conjectures as to what passages in the two 'single traditions' are more or less likely to have had this origin.

I

The conjecture which is furthest from a mere guess and nearest to an inference is that Mt v. 17–48, the long passage in which the contrast between the Jewish and the Christian law and standard of life is drawn out and illustrated by six examples, was for the most part drawn from Q. For we have two intimations that at least the general framework of that passage was familiar to Lk—possibly of course in some other source known to him and Mt, but far more probably in the Q which they so often used in common.

(i) The first and more direct of these intimations is found in a comparison of Lk vi. 27 with Mt v. 43, 44. In Mt the contrast between the old and the new is clearly expressed, 'Ye have heard that it was said, Thou shalt love thy neighbour and hate thine enemy: but I say unto you, Love your enemies, &c.' Lk, however, for whose Gentile readers the comparative narrowness of the Old Testament

[1] Dr. E. D. Burton, *op. cit.*, p. 41, estimates the number at 230, the difference arising chiefly from the fact that he includes the Parables of the Marriage of the King's Son and the Talents, while I have followed *Synopticon* in regarding them as probably or possibly derived from Q.

III. Double Tradition of Matthew and Luke

precept and the further narrowing of it by later interpretations would have no importance, merely gives the wide Christian standard of duty, 'Love your enemies, &c.' So he, unlike Mt, has no such contrast to express. Why then does he, like Mt, use the adversative particle ἀλλά in his prefatory words, 'But I say unto you which hear, Love your enemies, &c.'? Must it not have been because he had before his eyes or in his memory a source containing the contrast which Mt preserves?[1]

(ii) In Lk xvi. 17, 18 we find these two successive sayings in a discourse directed against the Pharisees, 'But it is easier for heaven and earth to pass away, than for one tittle of the law to fail. Every one that putteth away his wife, and marrieth another, committeth adultery: and he that marrieth one that is put away from a husband committeth adultery.' The juxtaposition of those two sentences—the general declaration of the permanence of the moral law and the warning against a special sin—seems at first sight utterly inexplicable. Yet it may be accounted for not unreasonably if we take it as implying that Lk connected them together because he knew them as part of a discourse in which, as we see in Mt v, the practice of divorce was taken (verses 30-2) as the third of the six illustrations of the principle that, so far from any 'jot or tittle' of the old law passing away, it was to be fulfilled more deeply and more thoroughly than by the righteousness of the Scribes and Pharisees.

On those two special grounds, besides the more general ground that will come before us in a following paragraph (2 *a*), I would place Mt v. 17-48 by itself as a section which we may regard as more likely to have formed part of Q than any other which is found only in a single Gospel.

2

Next to it, but I think at a considerable distance behind it, in such likelihood would come passages which are given only by one of our two Evangelists, but as to which we can

[1] It seems to me to be a much more far-fetched and improbable supposition that Lk was only introducing a contrast between the haters of Christians mentioned five verses previously (vi. 22), and the love that Christians should return for that hatred.

suggest more or less satisfactory reasons for the other one having omitted them.

(a) Thus, especially, we know that Lk omitted the anti-Pharisaic discourses in Mk vii. 1-13 and x. 2-12, which Mt reproduced in chaps. xv. 1-9 and xix. 3-9 respectively. This prepares us to think that Lk may have on the same grounds passed over several anti-Pharisaic passages in Q, while Mt transferred them to his Gospel, so that we find them in the more polemical parts of Mt v. 17-48 just referred to, also in Mt vi. 1-8, 16-18; xv. 12, 13; xxi. 28-32; xxiii. 2, 3, 5, 14-22, 32, 33. Not of course that Lk intended to exclude altogether this controversial element (see p. 70 and such passages as Lk v. 30 ff., vi. 6 ff., xx. 1 ff. drawn from Mk) which was necessarily so prominent in the Master's life and work, but certainly his tendency, as contrasted with Mt's, was to limit the amount of detail concerning it which he might have drawn both from Mk and from Q.

(b) Again, Lk may have omitted as either obscure or uninteresting or even distasteful to his readers the sayings which we read in Mt vii. 6; x. 5, 6, 23; xii. 5, 6, 36, 37 (which might have seemed hard to reconcile with the Pauline doctrine of justification); xviii. 10, 17; xix. 10-12.

(c) Turning now to Mt, he might have omitted the Parables of the Friend at Midnight, the Unjust Steward, and the Importunate Widow (if they were in Q [or *Logia*], which is not very likely) as being liable to give wrong impressions as to the character of the God whom he especially sets forth as the Father.

(d) He might also have passed by as liable to misconstruction among Jewish Christians or as obscure or otherwise unsuitable for the use of the catechists or other teachers whom he had in view, sayings in Q which Lk may have inserted from it in v. 39 (if genuine); vi. 24-6; vii. 40-50; ix. 54-6 (as seemingly disparaging the Old Testament), 61, 62; x. 8; xi. 27, 28, 36; xii. 49.

3

In the third place there is a much larger number of passages found in Mt or Lk but not in both of them, as to which we can only say—and it seems to be just worth saying and illustrating by examples—that the subject-matter of

III. Double Tradition of Matthew and Luke

them is either more or less congruous and *in pari materia* with what we have seen to be the contents of the passages common to both Gospels, and that therefore there is some slight degree of presumption either for or against conjectures that they come from the same source. The degree can only be slight in either direction, for, as has been said, we cannot be confident as to how far we were justified in inferring the character of the whole contents of Q from the parts of it preserved by both Mt and Lk.

The conjectures, such as they are, will be marked by letters in thick type (a, b, &c.), which correspond to those prefixed on pp. 125–9 to the inferences upon which the conjectures are grounded, and which should be referred to in connexion with each of them.

a So far as the rest of Q was homogeneous with the presumed extracts from it in Mt and Lk, it would have consisted mainly of moral and religious teachings for Christians: such we find in Mt v. 5, 7–10, 14, 16, 23 f. (which may be, like the next two verses, an insertion from another part of Q into the framework of v. 17–48); vi. 34; xi. 28–30; xii. 36, 37; xviii. 10, 19 f. only; and other such in Lk x. 38–42; xi. 27 f., 36; xii. 15, 32, 47 f.; xiv. 7–10 and 12–14, 28–33; xvi. 10–12 only.[1]

b But it may also have contained the warnings to opposing Jews which we find in Mt xxi. 43 and in Lk xiii. 1–5, xix. 41.

c And it may have contained even such directly anti-Pharisaic denunciations as Mt only gives in xv. 12 f. and Lk only in xvi. 14 f.

d Nor, again, is there anything at all incongruous with our previous inferences as to Q in the sayings specially addressed to teachers in Mt xxiii. 7 b–10 and in Lk x. 17–20 respectively and independently.

e Nor in the references to the future Parousia which we find in Mt xxiv. 11 f. only, and in Lk xvii. 20–2, 28 f., 32; xxi. 18, 22, 24, 28, 34–6[2] only.

[1] This and the following lists of passages are only given as suggestive, not as positive or exhaustive. And they include a few passages which were also suggested for consideration in the preceding lists.

[2] But the Pauline character of these three verses, when compared with 1 Thes v. 3 f., has to be noticed; of course, however, the language of the

f And the same may be said of the supplementary teaching of the Baptist as to 'the way of righteousness' which Lk alone gives in iii. 10-14.

g On the other hand, the fewness (or possibly absence) of long parables in both Mt or Lk apart from Mk suggests that it was no purpose of the compiler of Q to make a collection of them, and that those which occur in Mt or in Lk only were drawn by those writers from other sources. As to the longer Matthaean parables—the Tares, the Unmerciful Servant, the Labourers in the Vineyard, the Marriage of the King's Son, the Ten Virgins—this conjecture does not seem to be supported by there being anything in their contents which can be distinguished from the tone and substance of Q [or *Logia*]; but some of the longer Lucan parables, and especially the three commencing with the mention of 'a certain rich man' (Lk xii. 16; xvi. 1, 19), do seem to have somewhat of a special character of their own.[1]

To some at least of the shorter parables this conjecture is less applicable. For, among the parables of the Kingdom in Mt xiii, the Hidden Treasure and the Pearl of Great Price may be said to be paralleled in form by the other short Parable of the Leaven, which is found also in Lk xiii. 20 f.; and again the interrogative Parables of the Friend at Midnight (Lk xi. 5 ff.) and the Unprofitable Servants (Lk xvii. 7 ff.), as well as the Lost Piece of Silver (Lk xv. 8 ff.), may be said to suggest by their form the same origin as the Lost Sheep (Mt xviii. 12 ff. = Lk xv. 3 ff.)

And it should be noted that the present conjecture as to the scarcity of what we call parables in Q has no application at all to brief similitudes or apologues or figurative descriptions. We have seen how abundant these are in Q, as also they are in the Marcan source: they may be seen too in the unparalleled parts of Mt, as in v. 14 (city on hill), vii. 6 (dogs and swine), xi. 29 (yoke and burden), xiii. 52 (householder and his treasure), xv. 13 (uprooted plant), xvii. 25 (king's sons and tribute); and in the unparalleled parts of Lk, as in [v. 39 (old wine)], ix. 62 (hand to plough), xii. 47 f. (few or many stripes), xii. 49 (fire on earth), xiv. 28-32 (un-

Epistle might have been grounded on the record which was afterwards embodied in the Gospel.

[1] See also Stanton, *The Gospels as Historical Documents*, ii. 231, on the Lucan parables generally.

III. Double Tradition of Matthew and Luke

finished tower and king's deliberation before war), xx. 18 (falling stone).[1] So it is noticeable that all our authorities for the sayings of Jesus in the Synoptic Gospels, whether we regard them as two or more, agree in ascribing this characteristic of figurative language to them.[2]

h The scarcity of direct quotations from the Old Testament in the 84 passages common to Mt and Lk and presumably drawn from Q suggests that it was probably not from that source that those two writers separately derived the ascription of such quotations to Jesus in Mt ix. 13 and xii. 7 (from Hos vi. 6), xiii. 14 f. (from Is vi. 9 f., which is only referred to and not quoted in the Marcan and Lucan parallels), xxi. 16 (from Ps viii. 2), Lk iv. 18 f. (from Is lxi. 12 and lviii. 6), and xxii. 37 (from Is liii. 12).[3]

We have, however, seen reason (p. 132 f.) for thinking that the six brief texts from the Mosaic law which are brought forward for comment in Mt v. 17-48 may have been found in Q.

i Again, our estimate of the nature of Q formed from the parallel passages in Mt and Lk must incline us to think it improbable that its scope would include the records of single miracles given by Mt only in ix. 27-31, 32-4 (if not a doublet of xii. 22, 23); xvii. 24-7,[4] and by Lk only in v. 1-11; vii. 11-16; xiii. 10-17; xiv. 1-6; xvii. 11-19; xxii. 49-51. But this amount of improbability diminishes in proportion as it seems likely that the narratives were introduced for the purpose of leading up to important *logia* of Jesus.

k Finally, the almost entire absence from Mt and Lk's Passion-narratives of matter which is parallel only in those

---

[1] The parallel in Mt xxi. 44 is probably spurious; to the authorities against it in Tisch's 8th edition Syr^{sin} is to be added.

[2] This is also the case with the Fourth Gospel, as appears especially in Jn ii. 19; iii. 3, 8; iv. 10, 14, 35; v. 35; vi. 27, 32 f.; vii. 37 ff.; viii. 12; ix. 4; x. 1 ff., 7 ff.; xi. 9 f.; xii. 24; xiii. 10; xv. 1 ff.; xvi. 21. So it is also in the Oxyrhynchus Sayings, Series 1, No. 3, and especially No. 5; besides Nos. 1, 6, and 7, which reproduce or expand sayings also preserved in the Synoptic Gospels. The concurrence of all testimonies is remarkable.

[3] But Professor Burkitt (*op. cit.*, p. 202 f.) points out the appositeness and the 'real validity for ourselves to-day' of the references to the Old Testament which are ascribed to our Lord Himself in the Gospels, as distinguished from the use of the Old Testament by 'the early Christians in general, or the First Evangelist in particular'.

[4] Mt xxi. 14 is omitted here as being a more general statement.

two Gospels predisposes us to regard the source which (besides Mk) they had hitherto used in common as not extending over that period so as to supply materials for it. Of course, however, we cannot exclude the possibility that for some reason it ceased at this point to be available for one of the Evangelists, while the other continued the use of it.

IV

ON THE ORIGINAL ORDER OF Q

V

ST. MARK'S KNOWLEDGE AND USE OF Q

VI

THE ORIGINAL EXTENT OF Q

VII

THE LITERARY EVOLUTION OF THE GOSPELS

VIII

THE TRIAL OF OUR LORD BEFORE HEROD

APPENDIX
(*at end of volume*)

SYNOPTIC CRITICISM AND THE ESCHATOLOGICAL PROBLEM

REV. BURNETT HILLMAN STREETER, M.A.

Fellow, Dean and Lecturer in Theology and Classics, of Queen's College, Oxford; Theological Lecturer at Hertford College; Examining Chaplain to the Bishop of St. Albans; *sometime* Fellow of Pembroke College and Theological Lecturer at Jesus College, Oxford.

SYLLABUS

An attempt to show that the very diverse order in which the Q sections appear in Matthew and Luke is no objection to the theory that the bulk of them were derived from a single written source. The diversity is readily explicable on the hypothesis that the original order is that preserved by Luke and that Matthew has altered this in accordance with certain editorial tendencies, which can be clearly traced by studying his treatment of both the Marcan and the peculiar matter which he makes use of.

It is first shown that if attention is concentrated on the more striking sections, there is enough general agreement in the order in which these occur in Matthew and Luke to prove that, at any rate, the bulk of them came from a common source.

The sections differently ordered in the two Gospels fall into three groups :—

(*a*) Matter appearing in Matthew as an expansion of the Great Sermon and the Mission Charge, but in Luke scattered up and down in chapters xi–xvii.

(*b*) Transpositions—in two cases only beyond the immediate context.

(*c*) Seven detached sayings.

The problem is, did these sections come from the same source as those which still show a common order?

Matthew's treatment of Mark shows that he freely altered the original order of at least his principal source. Luke, on the contrary, follows Mark's order closely; certain notable exceptions to this rule are shown to be only apparent. It is, therefore, *a priori*, probable that Matthew would have rearranged the materials from his second source also, and that Luke would not have done so. An examination of the three groups of sections differently placed confirms this :—

The group (*a*) cannot be considered apart from Matthew's marked tendency to group in long discourses sayings on similar topics. Four of these great discourses are examined in detail and shown to be artificial compilations by the editor of materials originally separate, who aimed at giving in five convenient 'Pereqs' the 'New Law'. The presumption is that the present position of the sections in group (*a*) in Matthew is due to the editor and not to his source.

Similarly, an examination of groups (*b*) the transpositions, and (*c*) the detached sayings, proves convincingly in almost every case that the Matthean order is due to the editor. This is not apparently the case with Luke's order, which is therefore presumably as a general rule the order of the original source.

A review of the way in which Matthew and Luke respectively, using Mark as their base, fit into the framework of his story all non-Marcan matter whether Q or otherwise confirms this conclusion.

In conclusion, Harnack's arguments that, on the contrary, the order of Matthew is more original are criticized.

ON THE ORIGINAL ORDER OF Q

HALF a century of critical investigation has made it clear that the parallel matter in Matthew and Luke falls into two parts—a larger part, which is convincingly explained by their use of a common source still substantially preserved in our Second Gospel, and a lesser part, which it seems natural to explain on the same analogy as due to their use of a second common source now lost—which hypothetical source has been conveniently designated by the symbol 'Q'.

Many scholars have, however, felt that the hypothesis that all or even the greater part of the Q matter is derivable from a single documentary source is open to three objections, two of them serious:—

(1) Many of the parallels show an agreement almost word for word, others one close but much less exact, a few present a general agreement combined with much difference in detail. This variation in the degree of agreement has been urged as an argument against derivation from a single written source.

As regards the passages where the differences are great it has weight. But these passages are few in number, and the fact which criticism is called upon to explain, and of which the most natural explanation seems a written source, is that two apparently independent biographers have *so much* that is in *close* agreement. We approach the consideration of the passages where the parallelism is slighter and such as could otherwise have quite well been explained as due to independent tradition of the same discourse, in the light of what we have inferred from the closer parallels. And assuming that they used such a written source, we should expect that they would sometimes reproduce it almost word for word, at other times with considerable freedom, since that is the way we can see they deal with Mark. There are passages where if Mark had been lost Matthew and Luke might seem to be following independent traditions, but where since Mark is not lost we can see they are only independent modifications of his version. The objection, therefore, has no weight except as regards that small minority of the passages where the parallelism is very inexact.

(2) If we allow that this parallel matter may have been all drawn from but a single written source, what intelligible idea can we form of the purpose and aim of such a compilation? It is not a collection of sayings of the Master intended as a kind of manual of Christian ethics, for it includes the Preaching of John the Baptist, the details of the Temptation, the Healing of a Centurion's Servant, the Message of John from prison, &c. On the other hand, it is not a general account of the life and teaching of Christ —a Gospel in the modern sense—for it altogether leaves out the Passion and Resurrection. Considered as a Gospel it is a mere torso.

No more need be said here on this point as the objection is met by the characterization of the purpose and aim of Q (pp. 210–15) which opens the Essay on the Literary Evolution of the Gospels.

(3) The parallel passages in question appear in quite a different order in Matthew and in Luke. At first sight this fact would seem to suggest that what the two writers had in common was a number of short disconnected pieces —whether written or floating in oral tradition—which, assuming they worked independently, they could not but arrange in a different order. If they had used a single written source should we not rather expect them to have reproduced the materials therefrom in something like a uniform order corresponding to that of the original?

This objection loses much of its sting when we notice that,

IV. On the Original Order of Q

if we compare the first thirteen chapters of Matthew and Luke as regards the sections which they derive from Mark, there is found to be an even greater variation in their respective orders. So that if Mark had been lost instead of Q a precisely similar objection would have been made to the hypothesis that these Marcan sections in Matthew and Luke could have come from a single written source.

Further, on closer examination we can detect behind the great variety of order a certain original unity of arrangement, and can usually account satisfactorily for the dislocation it has undergone at the hands of the compilers of our First and Third Gospels.

To show this is the purpose of the present Essay.

If we confine our attention to the more salient features we find that the order of the Q sections in Matthew and Luke is very much the same. Both begin with John's Preaching, the Temptation, a great Sermon, the Centurion's Servant. In Matthew then follow the two would-be followers, Mt viii. 19 f., the saying 'the harvest is plenteous', Mt ix. 37-8, a charge concerning missions,[1] John's Message, Mt xi. 2 f. Luke alters this sequence only by placing John's Message first instead of last. We notice, however, that the Great Sermon and the Mission Charge are expanded by Matthew to more than double the length they have in Luke, and that this expansion is largely effected by the addition of passages which occur elsewhere later on in Luke, scattered up and down in between chapters xi. 1 and xvii. 6. In this fact lies the crux of our investigation. Did these additional passages originally belong to those two great discourses? Or were they originally disconnected and scattered as in Luke? For the moment, however, we postpone its consideration and proceed

---

[1] Appearing in Mt x, conflated with Mark's account of the Mission Charge to the Twelve, in Luke, partly conflated with Mark in ch. ix but chiefly in Lk x as the charge to the Seventy. Cf. p. 173 f.

to notice that if we eliminate from our view those passages, and those only, which occur early in Matthew in these two great discourses, but in Luke scattered in later contexts, there is a broad general agreement in the order of all that remains. The Woes to the Cities, 'I thank thee, Father,' the Beelzebub incident, the sign of Jonah, the Parable of the Unclean Spirit, occur in the same order except that the last two are transposed. Next in Matthew occur the Parables of the Mustard Seed [1] and Leaven, a word about offences, xviii. 7, the Parable of the Lost Sheep, and two words about forgiveness, xviii. 15; xviii. 21. In Luke these occur later, but their order *with regard to one another* is practically the same:—

Matthew.	Luke.
1. Mustard Seed and Leaven, xiii. 31–3.	1. Mustard Seed and Leaven, xiii. 18–21.
2. Concerning Offences, xviii. 7.	2. Lost Sheep, xv. 3–7.
3. Lost Sheep, xviii. 12–14.	3. Concerning Offences, xvii. 1.
4. Forgiveness, xviii. 15 a, 21 b.	4. Forgiveness, xvii. 3, 4.

Passing over these sections what remains appears as follows:—

Matthew.	Luke.
Woes against Pharisees, xxiii. 1–36.	Woes against Pharisees, xi. 39–52.
Jerusalem, Jerusalem, xxiii. 37–9.	The day of the Lord as a thief, and the two Stewards, xii. 39 f.
False Christs and the Parousia, xxiv. 26–8 and 37–41.	Jerusalem, Jerusalem, xiii. 34 f.
The day of the Lord as a thief, and the two Stewards, xxiv. 43 f.	False Christs and the Parousia, xvii. 23–37.
Parable of the Talents, xxv. 14–30.	Parable of the Pounds, xix. 12–27.

The above analysis includes all the Q matter except the doubtful parallel, Marriage of the King's Son, Mt xxii. 2–10 = Wedding Feast, Lk xiv. 16–24, and some seven detached sayings—

[1] For evidence that the Mustard Seed was in Q as well as Mark see the following Essay, p. 172, also Sir J. Hawkins's Essay, p. 50 f. of this volume; so Harnack, *Sayings of Jesus*, English trans., p. 26.

IV. On the Original Order of Q

Mt viii. 11–12 = Lk xiii. 28–9.
Mt xi. 12–13 = Lk xvi. 16.
Mt xiii. 16–17 = Lk x. 23–4.
Mt xv. 14 b = Lk vi. 39 b.
Mt xvii. 20 = Lk xvii. 6 ; cf. Mk xi. 23.
Mt xix. 28 b = Lk xxii. 30 b.
Mt xxiii. 12 = Lk xiv. 11 = Lk xviii. 14.

Thus, except for the matter which Matthew inserts in the Sermon on the Mount and in the Mission Charge, but which Luke has scattered between chapters xi and xvii, and these seven detached sayings, there is enough general agreement in the order of the sections in Matthew and Luke to make it more than probable that at any rate the bulk of these passages come from a single lost source. If so there have been some transpositions and displacements of the original either by Matthew or Luke or by both.

There remains, then, to be asked (1) Did the passages which Matthew gives together in the Sermon on the Mount and the Mission Charge, but which Luke has in various scattered contexts, come from this same source, and if so, what was their original position?

(2) Can we explain the transpositions and displacements just noticed?

(3) Can we account for the seven detached sayings?

One cardinal principle will guide our investigation. It may be presumed that Matthew and Luke would each deal with his second authority in much the same way as he dealt with his first. If, therefore, we study the principles on which they work respectively in dealing with Mark we shall arrive at the principles on which they might be expected to have worked when dealing with Q. How then do they respectively deal with Mark?

Matthew has entirely rearranged the order of practically every section in the first six chapters of Mark. If, therefore, he completely disregards the order of a document relating a series of events, narrated presumably in their historical sequence, we may assume he would be still more indifferent to the original order of a document which was plainly only a loose collection of sayings.

Luke, on the other hand, makes few and trifling alterations of Mark's order. There is apparently one considerable exception to this rule, but it is only apparent. The Great Commandment, x. 25-28, the Beelzebub incident, xi. 14-23, and the Parable of the Mustard Seed, xiii. 18 f., appear in Luke in a context quite different to that which they have in Mark, but, as is conclusively shown in Sir J. Hawkins's Essay (cf. pp. 41 ff. and p. 53 above; cf. also pp. 169 ff.), versions of these incidents occurred in Q as well as in Mark, and Luke seems to follow the version of Q. They appear in his Gospel in the midst of a mass of other material drawn from Q, so that it looks as if he only omits them from the context in which they occur in Mark in order to preserve their original context in Q. The Rejection at Nazareth and the Call of Peter are placed differently than in Mark, but in both cases the story is given in a version other than Mark's. Besides these, until we get to the Last Supper, there is only the trifling displacement of the saying about the True Kindred of Christ, Lk viii. 19-21 = Mk iii. 31-35, an explanation of which is suggested on p. 146. Only in the Passion story from the Last Supper onwards there occurs the quite exceptional series of small transpositions discussed by Sir J. Hawkins and Mr. Bartlet elsewhere, cf. pp. 80 ff. and pp. 331 ff. But we notice that in no case is material removed outside the immediate context.[1]

[1] A few odd *sayings* are given by Luke in different contexts to those in which they appear in Mark, but in most cases it looks as if he is giving the version, and therefore preferably the context, in which the **saying** appeared in Q (cf. Sir J. Hawkins above, p. 38). In some cases we note Luke has omitted the *incident* to which Mark attaches the saying, and is therefore *compelled* to displace the saying if he is to retain it at all; e.g. the saying 'the Kings of the Gentiles', Lk xxii. 25-7, is given in Mark in connexion with the ambitious request of James and John, by Luke (possibly in Q's version) at the Last Supper, but here Luke omits the incident to which Mark attaches it.

IV. On the Original Order of Q

We infer that Luke normally preserves the order of his sources, though in dealing with disjointed sayings we may not, of course, infer he would do this as strictly as in dealing with a sequence of events. It follows that we should *a priori* expect that where Matthew and Luke differ the original order of Q is to be presumed to be that of Luke unless in a particular case a reason to the contrary can be assigned, e. g. a desire to connect with other sayings on a similar topic. A closer examination will confirm this view.

We have seen above that the discrepancy of order of the Q sections in Matthew and Luke is caused by three facts.

(1) Certain matter which occurs in scattered contexts in Luke appears in Matthew as an integral part of the two great discourses, chapters v-vii and chapter x.

(2) Certain other passages are transposed.

(3) The position of some seven detached sayings requires explanation.

These three problems we will proceed to discuss in detail.

Let us first consider the two great discourses, the Sermon on the Mount, Mt v-vii, and the Mission Charge, Mt x. These discourses are elaborately arranged so as to form compendia of maxims on related topics. It seems quite intelligible that an author should wish to bring together all the most characteristic of our Lord's teachings on general Christian Ethics as in Mt v-vii, or Missionary work as in Mt x, and for this purpose should bring together what he found scattered in his source. It is not intelligible that finding them in his source arranged as they are in Matthew, he should scatter them up and down, on no conceivable plan, as they appear in Luke.[1]

Moreover these two discourses do not stand alone in Matthew. It is a marked characteristic of his Gospel to

[1] Had Lk broken up long discourses in order to fit the fragments into appropriate contexts, some would have been found in contexts derived from Mark, but they all appear in a section of the Gospel which draws only from Q and Lk's special traditions.

present the teaching of our Lord in the form of such compendia on related topics—compendia which there is little difficulty in showing were artificially compiled by the editor of the Gospel. Six or, better, five such appear in the Gospel, the fifth and sixth being probably to be reckoned as one—the Great Sermon (chs. v–vii), the Mission Charge (ch. x), Parables of the Kingdom (ch. xiii), Little Ones and Forgiveness (ch. xviii), Woes on the Pharisees (ch. xxiii), and the Last Things (chs. xxiv–xxv).

I owe to Sir J. Hawkins the suggestion that the (late mediaeval) division into chapters helps to blind us to the fact that the author regards ch. xxiii as an introduction to the great Apocalyptic Discourse, chs. xxiv and xxv. The Woes on the Pharisees, the blood of all the righteous from Abel onwards to come on this generation, and the lament over Jerusalem, are a fitting preface to the prophecy of the destruction of the Temple, of the coming of the Son of Man, the Parables of Warning, and the great Judgement-scene.

Five was a conventional number for book-arrangement among the Jews, e. g. the five books of the Law, the five books of the Psalms, the five Megilloth, the five divisions of the Pirque Aboth, &c.[1] It is noticeable also that after each of Matthew's five blocks of discourse occurs a slightly varying formula, καὶ ἐγένετο ὅτε ἐτέλεσεν ὁ Ἰησοῦς . . . (Mt vii. 28; xi. 1; xiii. 53; xix. 1; xxvi. 1),—a formula indicating, be it noted, the *resumption* of a narrative, and therefore due to the editor, though the *first* instance of it, which perhaps suggested to him the others, may have occurred in his source Q, connecting the Great Sermon with the *narrative* of the healing of the Centurion's Servant (cf. Mt vii. 28 = Lk vii. 1). This arrangement of selected sayings of our Lord into five 'Pereqs' cannot be accidental.

In the case of all but the first of these it is demonstrable that the compilation was effected by the editor of the

---

[1] Cf. Hawkins, *Horae Synopticae*², p. 163 f.

IV. On the Original Order of Q

Gospel, and did not exist in his sources. For in these cases Matthew has combined into a single discourse matter which *we know* was originally separate, seeing that part of it occurred in Mark, part in Q, and part in sources of his own. Sometimes he even brings together matter which occurs in *different parts* of Mark and which Luke has kept in their original separation.

(1) Both Mark (vi. 7-11) and Q had Mission Charges. Luke in his chapter ix mainly reproduces Mark; in chapter x he follows Q. Consider now Matthew, chapter x. He starts with matter from Mk vi. 7-11, and weaves into it matter from Q (which appears in Lk x). He continues the discourse with more Q matter (which appears in different, and as far as we could tell by mere inspection neither better nor worse, contexts in Luke), and then—what is most significant—adds a passage from an entirely *different context of Mark* (Mt x. 17-22 = Mk xiii. 9 13), i. e. from Mark's great Apocalyptic discourse, which discourse, when he comes to it, he repeats almost verbatim, but with the omission of these verses, all save the first and last, which cannot well be dispensed with in the original context.[1] He has, therefore, in chapter x brought together into one discourse not only sayings which we may *guess* stood apart in Q (since they so appear in Luke), but matter drawn from a *different* document (Mark), and even drawn from *different parts* of that document.

(2) In ch. xiii we have a collection of seven parables on the Kingdom of Heaven. Since they are derived from Mark, from Q, and from other unknown sources it is clear that they were originally separate, and that their collocation is due to Matthew. It can hardly be an accident that the number in the collection is the sacred number seven.

(3) Chapter xviii is an expansion of Mk ix. 33-47, the

[1] Some critics have supposed this passage stood also in Q. For our argument that its *original* position is in Mark's Apocalypse cf. p. 180. Two verses, however, Mt x. 19-20 = Lk xii. 11-12, may have stood in Q as well as in Mark, cf. p. 37.

incident Mk ix. 38-41, which breaks the continuity of the discourse, being omitted. Into this Marcan section he interpolates xviii. 3-4, from a *different context of Mark*, i.e. Mk x. 15; from Q four passages at different intervals, i.e. xviii. 7, 12-14, 15, and 21 (Offences, Lost Sheep, Forgiveness); and from an unknown source xviii. 10, 16-20, and the Parable of the Unmerciful Servant xviii. 23 ff.

(4) The discourse on the Last Things, Mt xxiv-xxv, is a fourth most instructive instance of Matthew's habit of combining and rearranging passages. xxiv. 1-25 and 29-36 and 42 are from Mark, verses 26-8 and 37-41 occur in Lk xvii. 23-37; thus he combines matter which, as partly from Mark partly from Q, we *know* to have been originally separate. He proceeds to add another extract from Q 43-51, occurring in quite a different context in Luke xii. 39-46, and three parables, ch. xxv, the middle one (the Talents) being probably from Q, the others from an unknown source.

We see too that where appropriateness of subject-matter suggests it Matthew will separate what he found together, as readily as combine what he found apart—

Mt xxiv. 26-7 = Lk xvii. 23-4.
„ xxiv. 28 = „ xvii. 37.
„ xxiv. 37-9 = „ xvii. 26-7.
„ xxiv. 40-1 = „ xvii. 34-5.

We notice that except for the one verse, Mt xxiv. 28 (which Matthew puts at the end of the first part, Luke at the very end of this extract from Q), they are in the same order, and therefore presumably stood together in that order in Q. In Luke xvii *they do so stand*, separated only by verses 28-33, of which 28-30 are doubtless original, as being the second member of the double illustration begun in 26-7 (as in the days of Noah, as in the days of Lot [1]), and the rest *may* be original, or may be derived from Mk xiii. 15-16. That

---

[1] Such double illustrations are a notable characteristic of our Lord's teaching. Cf. p. 173 and p. 195.

IV. On the Original Order of Q

is, in Lk xvii. 23-37, with not more than a verse or two, if anything, interpolated, we have an original section of Q, of which Matthew has transposed one verse, omitted two others, and split up the rest, in order to insert its warning against False Christs immediately after Mark's similar warning, and its affirmation of the unexpectedness of the Parousia after Mark's equivalent statement. We suspect a similar operation if we compare the passages previously discussed, Mt xviii. 7, 15, 21 = Lk xvii. 1, 3, 4. The order of the passages being the same, their conjunction in Luke is more original than their separation in Matthew.

The foregoing examination makes it quite clear that it was Matthew's method deliberately to set about to combine and rearrange into set discourses on related topics matter which he found dispersed, if by so doing he could present it more effectively. We have seen above that Luke has precisely the opposite tendency, a reluctance to part from the order and arrangement of his sources. If so we may fairly assume that the earliest and longest of these discourses, the Sermon on the Mount, contains, like the other four, much that was originally in a different context. We conclude that the Q passages which occur scattered in Lk xi-xvii and collected in Mt v-vii and x are, speaking generally, in a more original connexion in Luke.

We pass on to consider our second problem, the transpositions of Q material in Matthew and Luke. In every case it will appear that they are due to Matthew, but only in the two instances (*a*) and (*b*) has a considerable section been removed to quite a different context.

(*a*) John's Message. Mt xi. 2-19 = Lk vii. 18-35. Here we note :—

(α) The disciples of John are referred as credentials of our Lord's mission to the fact that 'the blind see, the lame walk, lepers are cleansed, the deaf hear, the dead are raised, and the poor have the gospel preached to them'. By placing the incident where he does in his Gospel, Matthew has been able *previously* to give an instance of every one of these cures, and also in the account of the Mission of the Twelve an indication that the people in general have had the Gospel preached to them.

(β) The criticism of the Jewish opposition involved in the Parable of the Children in the Market-place, which concludes the section, forms the transition to that new phase in the Ministry as presented in this Gospel in which the Pharisaic opposition is the outstanding feature. The peculiar appropriateness of its place in Matthew is thus seen to be determined by the editor's own scheme of arranging his materials, not by its original connexion in Q.

(*b*) The short series of parables and sayings beginning with the Parable of the Mustard Seed noticed on p. 144.

The Mustard Seed, as we have seen above—but without its appendix of the Leaven, given by both Matthew and Luke—was in Mark as well as in Q. Matthew follows Mark in connecting it with the Parable of the Sower and making these two the nucleus of his third 'Pereq'. Since Luke here, where Mark and Q overlap, deserts Mark's order, it is presumably because he is adopting the connexion in Q.

The Parable of the Lost Sheep and the sayings on Offences and Forgiveness, as already noted, have been worked by Matthew into the fourth of his five artificially constructed discourses, i.e. ch. xviii, and are therefore not in their original Q context (cf. p. 150).

The remaining transpositions we have to consider are all within the limits of the same general context.

(*c*) Mt iv. 8–9=Lk iv. 5–8 in Matthew appears as the last, in Luke as the second of the Temptations. The 'crescendo' of the allurement in the three Temptations as arranged by Matthew, ending with 'all the kingdoms of the earth and the glory of them', is far more dramatically effective than

IV. On the Original Order of Q

their order in Luke. Luke was sufficient of a literary artist not to spoil such an arrangement if it had occurred in his source—the rearrangement is therefore due to Matthew.

(d) Mt xii. 38–42 = Lk xi. 29–31. 'The sign of Jonah' comes very effectively in Matthew as a reply to a challenge of the Pharisees, provoked by the denunciation which closes the Beelzebub discourse (cf. γεννήματα ἐχιδνῶν, xii. 34). In Luke's order the Beelzebub discourse, the Parable of the Unclean Spirit, and the Sign of Jonah are disconnected utterances. But what the disciples remembered of our Lord's teaching and what was probably recorded in Q would be just such disconnected utterances, being the more striking parts of many separate discourses of our Lord, not a few long connected pieces. We have already seen that the working up of disconnected passages into connected discourses is a characteristic of Matthew, not of his sources. Luke's order is therefore more likely to be original.

(e) Mt xxiii. 37–9 = Lk xiii. 34–5—'Jerusalem, Jerusalem'.

How appropriately placed between the prophecy that 'all the righteous blood shed on the earth from the blood of Abel... shall come upon this generation', and the prophecy of the destruction of the Temple and the universal judgement! Yet seeing the latter prophecy is derived from Mark and the former from Q, we cannot but suspect that the placing is the editor's (cf. also p. 162 f.).

(f) Mt xxiv. 26–8, and 37–41, 43–51. The way in which these are artificially worked by the editor into appropriate contexts in the Marcan Apocalypse has already been pointed out (cf. p. 150 above).

(g) Besides these there occur minor cases of transposition within the limits of a single section. The more important are collected in Hawkins, *Hor. Syn.*[2], pp. 77–80, from which the materials in this paragraph are drawn. Perhaps the most interesting occurs in that portion of the Sermon on the Mount which is paralleled in Luke's Sermon on the Plain, and therefore must have formed part of one continuous discourse in Q (see pp. 161, 189).

 i.e. in Mt v the verses 42, 44, 45 a, 46, 47
  appear in Lk vi as 30, 27, 35 b, 32, 33.

So again in that part of the Mission Charge in Mt x which appears in the Sending of the Seventy in Lk x, we note (cf. below, p. 173) that

 in Mt x the verses 7, 10 b, 11 a, 13, 15, 16 a
  appear in Lk x as 9, 7 b, 10 a, 6, 12, 3.

Again, we notice that transpositions of single words in the same saying are frequent,

 e.g. χιτών and ἱμάτιον in Mt v. 40 = Lk vi. 29.

If we ask whether these minor transpositions of Q material are due to Matthew or to Luke, we again refer to our original canon, how, respectively, do these writers deal with similar material in Mark?

A glance at the list in Hawkins, *op. cit.*, pp. 77–80, gives five instances in which Matthew has made exactly this kind of transposition in discourse material drawn from Mark.

(α) Mk vii. 6–13; Mt xv. 3–9: the quotation from Is xxix. 13, and the reference to Corban.

(β) Mk ix. 12–13; Mt xvii. 12: the rejection of the Son of Man and of Elijah.

(γ) Mk x. 3–9; Mt xix. 4–8: the references to the permission of divorce by Moses and to Gen i. 27.

(δ) In Mt viii. 26 the disciples are rebuked for want of faith *before*, in Mk iv. 39, 40; Lk viii. 24, 25 *after*, the stilling of the storm.

(ε) In Mt xiii. 12 'Whosoever hath, to him', &c., is placed *before*, in Mk iv. 25; Lk viii. 18 it is placed *after*, the explanation of the Parable of the Sower.

The natural inference is that the similar transpositions of Q are due to Matthew rather than to Luke.

If it be urged, on the contrary, that cases are also

IV. On the Original Order of Q

quoted of minor transpositions of Mark's order by Luke, we reply,—

(α) They are confined to the Passion story, where Luke's relation to Mark is quite abnormal, cf. pp. 76 ff.

(β) They are variations in the order in which details are mentioned in describing a scene, not as in Matthew transpositions in the order of sentences in a discourse.

At this juncture we may digress for a moment to consider a point which has a bearing not only on such minor transpositions as we have just been considering, but on the whole question of the literary relation of the first three Gospels.

Sir J. Hawkins argues (cf. pp. 90 ff. above) that the minor transpositions in the Lucan account of the Passion and the enormously diminished proportion of Marcan words actually used is explained by the fact that to Luke as a follower of St. Paul the Passion was the essence of the Gospel Story, and that therefore from frequent retelling the tale in his practical Christian work he knew it by heart and so had no need to keep his eyes on his written authority.[1]

We suspect that the cause of many of Matthew's transpositions of discourse is much the same. Matthew could never have made the elaborate rearrangement of his sources that he has unless he had known his materials almost by heart. 'Matthew' and St. Luke would each have been a catechist before he became an Evangelist, and each would look least closely to his written source where he knew best his materials by heart. In Matthew this would be when he was dealing with the teaching of Christ, wherein to him, next to the hope of the Parousia, lay the essence of 'the Gospel'; to Luke it would have been rather in the Passion story, in incidents like the Rejection of Nazareth, or the Woman

---

[1] This does not mean that added details given by St. Luke are apocryphal, but that from whatever sources they are derived they have been blended with the Marcan account treated as if all was still in a fluid oral state.

that was a Sinner, in parables[1] like the Good Samaritan,
&c., which emphasized that aspect of the Gospel which
was to him most dear (cf. Essay on Literary Evolution
of Gospels, p. 224).

To a similar influence may be ascribed the well-known
modifications in Luke's version of Mark's Apocalypse,
Lk xxi. 5-36 = Mk xiii. The Parousia and its connexion
with the destruction of Jerusalem was too vitally interesting to the early Church not to be the subject of constant
instruction, and in such instruction the interpretation of our
Lord's words would be insensibly blended with the original.
It is thinkable that Luke's version of the Rejection of
Nazareth, the Call of Peter, and the Anointing by a Woman
that was a sinner, in all of which S. Luke's special vocabulary
is unusually preponderant, are similarly catechetical modifications of Marcan stories with an admixture from floating
tradition.

There remains to be dealt with our third problem—the
original position of the seven detached sayings noted on
p. 145. In the case of at least six of them it is quite clear
that at any rate the original position is *not* that given
by Matthew.

(*a*) Mt viii. 11-12 = Lk xiii. 28-9, 'Many shall come from
the East and the West and sit down with Abraham, &c., in
the kingdom.' In Luke this occurs among a number of
apocalyptic sayings, in Matthew in the story of the healing of
the Centurion's Servant, where it gives a universalistic touch
to the incident, which Luke with his special interest would
have been the last to omit if he had found it in his source.

(*b*) Mt xi. 12-13 = Lk xvi. 16. Similarly the saying 'The
law and the prophets were until John' would surely not have
been disconnected by Luke from our Lord's other remarks
about John, and put in a context where it has no con-

---

[1] On the influence of catechetical repetition on the longer parables cf.
p. 198 and p. 200 below.

IV. On the Original Order of Q

ceivable connexion, if he had found it in his source in the context in which it appears in Matthew.

(c) Mt xiii. 16-17 = Lk x. 23-4. 'But blessed are *your* eyes, for they see; and *your* ears,' &c., is most appropriate as a contrast to the unbelievers of the previous verse whose 'hearts were hardened ... that they might not see with their eyes nor hear with their ears', &c. But the preceding verse is a quotation from Isaiah introduced by Matthew to illustrate a passage which he derives from Mark. The insertion then of the passage from Q here is plainly editorial.

(d) Again, Mt xv. 14 b = Lk vi. 39 b, 'blind leaders,' occurs in Luke in the midst of a long extract from Q, in Matthew to illustrate a discussion derived from Mark, a position which cannot be original.[1]

(e) Similarly, Mt xvii. 20 = Lk xvii. 6 (faith as a grain of mustard seed) is most appropriately placed, but it cannot be the original context in Q since the miracle which it illustrates is derived from Mark.

(f) Mt xix. 28 b = Lk xxii. 30 b, 'Ye shall sit on twelve thrones,' occurs in Matthew in a context derived from Mark, in Luke in a context of doubtful origin.

(g) Mt xxiii. 12 = Lk xiv. 11 = Lk xviii. 14, 'Whoso exalteth himself.' In this case we cannot say which context looks more original. The fact that it occurs as a 'doublet' in Luke would incline us to believe that in at least one, if not in both, of the two passages it is in its original context.

We conclude then that whether we examine the six great discourses, the larger or smaller transpositions, or the detached sayings, everything tends to show that Matthew has entirely disregarded the original context of Q, and used it simply as a quarry from which to hew stones for the

[1] Two other sayings in Luke's Great Sermon appear in Mt outside his Sermon, i.e. Lk vi. 40 = Mt x. 24 and Lk vi. 45 = Mt xii. 34 b-35. The latter is discussed in the Additional Note p. 164.

building up of his great discourses and the enlargement and embellishment of the main structure which he takes over from St. Mark.

Making that assumption for the moment it will appear that the way in which the editor of Matthew worked in compiling his Gospel is perfectly natural and intelligible. The narrative portions are practically all derived from Mark,[1] but there is a large number of parables, and much discourse from Q and other sources. Thus his narrative framework is necessarily that of Mark, and the problem of how to distribute so much discourse and parable in this short story was not easy. He solves it, partly by interpolating parables or sayings in the Marcan outline wherever they seemed appropriate, partly by massing them according to subject in these five great compilations we have noticed. The Great Sermon in the shorter form as found in Q gave him both the pattern and the first opportunity of forming a *cento* of our Lord's sayings on related topics by expanding a given nucleus and probably also the formula of resumption with which each concludes (cf. p. 148). The nuclei of the subsequent discourses are given, and their context fixed by discourses in Mark, i. e. the Mission of the Twelve in Mk vi. 7–13, conflated with the Mission Charge of Q (cf. Lk x); Mark's Parable-chapter, iv. 1–34; Mark's Discourse, ix. 33–7, 42–50; Mark's anti-Pharisaic verses, xii. 38–40; and the Apocalypse of Mk xiii. The nuclei of the first two of those centos (ch. v–vii and ch. x) occurred early in Q; if therefore he wanted to expand them with other Q matter he *could* only do so by *anticipating* matter which occurred later in that document. Only in three instances outside those two centos does Matthew *anticipate*

---

[1] The exceptions are—the Infancy, a number of small expansions of the story of the Passion and Resurrection, the miracles, ix. 27–34, which seem to be duplicates of stories from Mark and Q which Matthew repeats again later, the stater in the fish's mouth, the statement that Peter attempted to walk on the water, and the few pieces of narrative which Q supplied.

IV. On the Original Order of Q

sayings, i.e. Mt viii. 11–12 = Lk xiii. 28–9, Mt xi. 12–13 = Lk xvi. 16, discussed above (cf. p. 156), and in the short series of sayings beginning with the Mustard Seed (cf. p. 144 and p. 152).

The problem of fitting the non-Marcan material into the story of Mark was solved by Luke in a different and much simpler way. The Preaching of John the Baptist and the details of the Temptation could of course only come in one place; the Great Sermon and John's Question from Q and some other matter from elsewhere he gets rid of by interpolating them early in Mark's story (Lk vi. 20–viii. 3); the remaining and far larger part he gives in one long interpolation, Lk ix. 51–xviii. 14, as if it all belonged to the last journey from Galilee to Jerusalem, which he conceives as being made through Samaria.[1] Thus, while Matthew follows Mark in giving a Galilean ministry, a period of wandering outside Galilee, and a last week at Jerusalem, Luke gives a Galilean, a Samaritan, and a Jerusalem ministry. For we note that this journeying through Samaria in Luke compensates for the wanderings north and east of Galilee in Mk vi. 45 ff., most of which section Luke entirely omits, while in what he retains he omits the notes of place which show the incidents are outside Galilee, e.g. there is no hint that Peter's confession 'Thou art the Christ' (Lk ix. 18–20) was at Caesarea Philippi.

Outside these three insertions only two fragments of Q are found, i.e. the Parable of the Pounds, xix. 11 f., which

---

[1] It is a mistake to call this the 'Peraean' section, for though Mark makes this journey to have been through Peraea, Luke clearly regards it as through Samaria, ix. 51–3; xvii. 11; hence he places here The Good Samaritan. As a non-Jew he was not sorry to record how the Lord had worked in Samaria (contrast Mt x. 5). It may be, as Burkitt suggests, that our Lord did travel via Samaria Himself, while Peter, Mark's informant, travelled by the ordinary route (cf. Burkitt, *Gospel History*, p. 96, note). An alternative and perhaps more satisfactory explanation is given below, i.e. that the incident of the Samaritan village, Lk ix. 52–56, though omitted by Matthew, was in Q, and that St. Luke not unnaturally inferred that all that followed this in Q took place on a journey through Samaria (cf. p. 191 b).

may have been associated with Jericho in his source (cf. p. 200), and the saying about the Apostles on twelve thrones, xxii. 30 b.

With this simple method of disposing of his materials there was no need for Luke to cut them up and rearrange them as Matthew has done. And that there is no reason to suspect that he has done so gratuitously will further appear from the examination of his 'greater interpolation' in the next Essay. Against this view of the order of Q has lately been opposed the great authority of Harnack, who urges that in two clear and significant instances, and therefore presumably in many others, the order of Matthew is more original than that of Luke. His arguments demand our careful consideration.

The first is stated as follows, p. 174, English translation:—

No.	St. Luke.	St. Matthew.	Leading words, or general subjects.
16	(ix. 2	x. 7	Kingdom at hand.)
17	ix. 57–60	viii. 19–22	Foxes have holes.
18	x. 2	ix. 37–8	The harvest is plenteous.
19	(x. 3	x. 16 a	Sheep and Wolves.)
20	x. 5–6	12–13	Peace to this house.
21	(x. 7 b	10 b	The labourer and his hire.)
22	x. 12	15	'More tolerable for Sodom.'
24	(x. 16	40	'He that heareth you.')
34 a	xii. 2–9	26–33	'There is nothing hidden.'
38	xii. 51, 53	34–6	'I came not to bring peace.'
45	xiv. 26	37	'Hateth not father and mother.'
46	xiv. 27	38	'Take up his cross.'
57	xvii. 33	39	'He that seeketh to save his life.'

Harnack points out that *if the bracketed passages are omitted* the order of the remaining nine sections is identical in both Matthew and Luke. He infers these nine must have stood connected together, as in Matthew, not partly connected and partly dispersed, as in Luke. He has therefore

IV. On the Original Order of Q

to raise doubts whether the four bracketed passages are from the same source as the rest.

But (21), he admits, *must* be from Q, and the occurrence of the others, even though with slight verbal variations, in *the midst of two parallel blocks of Q matter* in Matthew and Luke, makes it hard to believe they are from independent sources. Moreover, wherever we find discourse in Matthew parallel to discourse in Luke or in Mark, a few short sections are differently placed within the limits of the larger sections, e.g. in those parts of the Sermon on the Mount which occur also in Luke's Sermon on the Plain, and which we can therefore be sure stood as one section in Q (cf. above, p. 154). What wonder then if we find three or four verses similarly transposed in the Mission Charge within the original section of Q containing this Charge, i.e. Lk x. 2-16, and parallels in Matthew? Compare again the transpositions in the following parallels: Mt xv. 3-9 = Mk vii. 6-13; Mt xvii. 12 = Mk ix. 12-13; Mt xix. 4-8 = Mk x. 3-9. And it is plain in these latter cases that the transpositions are due to Matthew, for here we have in Mark the original he was working on. The presumption is that in the Great Sermon and in the Mission Charge we are now discussing the transpositions are due to him, and not to Luke.[1] Even in the present chapter, Mt x. 9-10, when he follows Mark, transposes the ῥάβδον with χαλκὸν ἐν ζώναις, and his word for 'sandals' with χιτῶνας. If, therefore, Matthew is here working as he did in the Sermon on the Mount and elsewhere, we may suppose that the original charge in Q was much in the order of Lk x. 2-16, that Matthew transposes a few verses within this section as he has done in the part of the Great Sermon he derived from Q, and then as in the former occasion proceeds to anticipate congruent matter from later parts of Q. As he read through Q to find suitable matter for his second cento he would naturally add such passages

---

[1] Cf. p. 154 above, and Hawkins, *Horae Synopticae*[2], p. 78.

one by one as he came across them unless he had a special reason for rearranging them, and they would therefore naturally appear in the order in which they stood in Q. Thus a closer study shows that the coincidence of order in those sections which Harnack has acutely noticed is no proof of their original contiguity.

Harnack's second argument depends on the ingenious hypothesis that the passage 'Jerusalem, Jerusalem' was the continuation of a quotation from a lost work entitled the 'Wisdom of God' (cf. Lk xi. 49) beginning 'I send unto you prophets', which Matthew mistook for an original utterance of our Lord. It would follow that, as against Luke, Matthew is correct in placing 'Jerusalem, Jerusalem' (Mt xxiii. 37) immediately after the 'The Blood of Abel', &c. (Mt xxiii. 34-6), so as not to divide the quotation into two fragments, though, by omitting the mention of the 'Wisdom of God' preserved by Luke, he in his turn has erred in citing the whole passage as an original saying of Christ. If we accept this view it follows that for once Matthew has preserved the original order and connexion of Q, and Luke departed from it.

It is of course very unlikely that Luke invariably adhered to his general rule, and this case might quite well be the exception, so that even if we accept Harnack's suggestion we need not give up that conclusion as to the order of Q to which all the other facts seem to point. The suggestion, however, ingenious though it is, is not quite convincing. If we read the passage Mt xxiii. 34-9, only prefixing to it Luke's introductory words 'therefore the Wisdom of God said', the first three verses 34-6 do, as various scholars have noticed, read very like a quotation. Verse 39, however, as Harnack admits, is a word of our Lord. The question is do verses 37-8 belong as a conclusion to the first three verses, or do they begin a fresh saying ending with verse 39? We think they begin a fresh saying, for the following reasons:—

(1) Our Lord's way of speaking was so terse and pointed

IV. On the Original Order of Q

(at any rate those sayings of His which have reached us, i.e. those which stuck in the memory of His hearers, are all such) that as a mere quotation 34-8 seems over-long.

(2) The change of tone at verse 37 from fierce proclamation of Divine vengeance to sorrow for the blindness of the sacred city reads as if we have now passed from the lost Jewish Apocalypse to the Master's own thoughts, not like a continuation of the same document.

(3) λέγω γὰρ ὑμῖν, verse 39, follows very awkwardly unless our Lord is Himself the speaker who in verse 37 speaks in the first person. If Matthew is right in his context, and Harnack in his interpretation, the argument would be as follows. Our Lord remarks that the book called the 'Wisdom of God' truly foretells vengeance to fall on this generation, while it laments at the same time the frequent blindness of Jerusalem and consequent desolation of her house, and then adds as His own comment, '*For* I say unto you, Ye shall not see *me* henceforth until ye say, Blessed is he that cometh in the name of the Lord.' The connexion of thought is not obvious.

(4) Harnack's theory, of course, solves the difficulty felt by many that the words 'How often would I' appear to imply previous visits of our Lord to Jerusalem of which the Synoptics elsewhere preserve no record. But even if we lay no stress on the Fourth Gospel it would be strange if the greatest religious genius of His nation had never till the age of thirty made a pilgrimage to the Holy City, nor, when there, felt the hollowness of her religion and yearned to save her. Our Lord's baptism, with which Mark's story begins, was the moment when He felt His own personal call to public work, but it was not the moment when He first felt there was something wrong in the official religion of the day.

(5) A strong reason for supposing the present position of his section in Matthew is editorial has been already given (p. 153 (*e*)).

Studies in the Synoptic Problem

We conclude that Harnack's two instances form no exception to the general rule that it is Luke rather than Matthew who preserves the original order of his authorities, and that his order is to be presumed as Q's order unless for some special reason the contrary appears in some particular instance. Some exceptions there certainly must be, if only because the human mind is incapable of absolute regularity.[1] In no human activity, least of all in literary work, which depends so much on the subtler idiosyncrasies of the mind, is any rule invariably observed. But it is plain that when St. Luke claimed to write καθεξῆς, he meant in the chronological order as determined from his original authorities, and that it is to him rather than to Matthew that we must look if we wish to determine the original order of Q.

[1] e. g. the position of Lk xvi. 13 = Mt vi. 24 seems to be due to the editor.

ADDITIONAL NOTE.

Luke vi

⁴³ Οὐ γάρ ἐστι δένδρον καλὸν ποιοῦν καρπὸν σαπρόν, οὐδὲ πάλιν δένδρον σαπρὸν ποιοῦν καρπὸν καλόν· ⁴⁴ ἕκαστον γὰρ δένδρον ἐκ τοῦ ἰδίου καρποῦ γινώσκεται· οὐ γὰρ ἐξ ἀκανθῶν συλλέγουσι σῦκα, οὐδὲ ἐκ βάτου τρυγῶσι σταφυλήν. ⁴⁵ ὁ ἀγαθὸς ἄνθρωπος ἐκ τοῦ ἀγαθοῦ θησαυροῦ τῆς καρδίας αὐτοῦ προφέρει τὸ ἀγαθόν· καὶ ὁ πονηρὸς ἐκ τοῦ πονηροῦ προφέρει τὸ πονηρόν· ἐκ γὰρ περισσεύματος καρδίας λαλεῖ τὸ στόμα αὐτοῦ.

Matthew vii

¹⁶ Ἀπὸ τῶν καρπῶν αὐτῶν ἐπιγνώσεσθε αὐτούς. μήτι συλλέγουσιν ἀπὸ ἀκανθῶν σταφυλήν, ἢ ἀπὸ τριβόλων σῦκα; ¹⁷ οὕτω πᾶν δένδρον ἀγαθὸν καρποὺς καλοὺς ποιεῖ, τὸ δὲ σαπρὸν δένδρον καρποὺς πονηροὺς ποιεῖ. ¹⁸ οὐ δύναται δένδρον ἀγαθὸν καρποὺς πονηροὺς ποιεῖν, οὐδὲ δένδρον σαπρὸν καρποὺς καλοὺς ποιεῖν.

Matthew xii

³³ *Ἢ ποιήσατε τὸ δένδρον καλὸν καὶ τὸν καρπὸν αὐτοῦ καλόν, ἢ ποιήσατε τὸ δένδρον σαπρὸν καὶ τὸν καρπὸν αὐτοῦ σαπρόν· ἐκ γὰρ τοῦ καρποῦ τὸ δένδρον γινώσκεται. ³⁴ γεννήματα ἐχιδνῶν, πῶς δύνασθε ἀγαθὰ λαλεῖν πονηροὶ ὄντες ; ἐκ γὰρ τοῦ περισσεύματος τῆς καρδίας τὸ στόμα λαλεῖ. ³⁵ ὁ ἀγαθὸς ἄνθρωπος ἐκ τοῦ ἀγαθοῦ θησαυροῦ ἐκβάλλει ἀγαθά· καὶ ὁ πονηρὸς ἄνθρωπος ἐκ τοῦ πονηροῦ θησαυροῦ ἐκβάλλει πονηρά.

Luke's version is supported by Mt vii in three points: (*a*) in context, being placed nearly at the end of the Great Sermon and immediately preceding the saying 'Lord, Lord' (Lk vi. 46 = Mt vii. 21); (*b*) in the addition of the similitude of grapes and thistles, Lk vi. 44ᵇ = Mt vii. 16ᵇ; (*c*) in the form of the sentence about a good tree and good fruit, Lk vi. 43 = Mt vii. 18, contrast xii. 33.

Luke is supported by Mt xii in two points: (*a*) in the addition about the good man and good treasure, and 'out of the abundance of the heart', Lk vi. 45 = Mt xii. 34ᵇ, 35; (*b*) the form of the saying 'a tree is known', Lk vi. 44ᵃ = Mt xii. 33ᵇ, contrast Mt vii. 16 and 20 'ye shall know'.

Thus Lk's general originality is proved as regards both context and form, and it is Mt who has removed the verse Lk vi. 45 = Mt xii. 34ᵇ, 35 from its original context. Cf. *Hor. Syn.*², p. 85.

ST. MARK'S KNOWLEDGE AND USE OF Q

SYLLABUS

In the case of John's preaching, the Temptation, the Beelzebub controversy, the Parable of the Mustard Seed, the Mission Charge, and a number of less striking passages, it is clear that Matthew and Luke had access to a version other than that contained in Mark, i. e. in other words, that in these places Mark and Q overlapped.

A careful examination of the passages shows

(*a*) that the Mark version is usually the shorter, but that the brevity is caused by the omission of features obviously original, so that the Q version is not an expansion of the Mark version, *but Mark may well be a mutilation of Q.*

(*b*) That Mark frequently conflates or connects together sayings which occur in different contexts in Q.

It is inferred that Mark knew Q and quoted therefrom occasionally, but probably only from memory.

It is argued that Mark wrote expressly not to supersede Q, but, since Q contained practically nothing but discourse, to supplement Q with the biographical narrative for which a demand had arisen. Accordingly Mark quotes Q as little as he conveniently can without omitting features which no biography of our Lord could well do without.

The Apocalyptic chapter xiii receives separate treatment. It is not derived from Q, but is a Christian Apocalypse composed to meet a definite crisis but containing a few genuine sayings of our Lord, some of them possibly from Q, along with certain traditional Apocalyptic materials. Its date is the morrow of the Fall of Jerusalem; its main purpose to encourage the despondent by showing that the delay of the Parousia and the intervening events had been foretold by the Master, and especially to warn believers against the false Christs who were expected to precede the Parousia. Matthew's version is derived from Mark, not from another recension of the original 'Little Apocalypse'.

ST. MARK'S KNOWLEDGE AND USE OF Q

THERE are several places where Matthew, Mark, and Luke are all three substantially parallel, but where the variations in detail and additions in which Matthew and Luke agree against Mark are so striking that it is clear they must have derived their versions in part, if not wholly, from some other source than Mark. Using the symbol Q to denote the whole mass of material common to Matthew and Luke not derivable from Mark—a symbol convenient because it begs no questions as to the unity or nature of this source—we may describe the facts noted above by saying that versions of these passages occurred in both Mark and Q.

A close examination of the passages in question seems to make it clear that Mark and Q do not here represent different lines of tradition, but that Mark had knowledge of and made extracts from Q. These extracts are frequently somewhat inexact and suggest quotations from memory from a well-known authority rather than transcriptions of a document actually before the author. The dependence and posteriority of the Marcan version is shown by two constantly recurring sets of phenomena.

(*a*) The Marcan version is almost invariably the shorter, but the brevity is caused by the omission of features in the Q version which are obviously original. The Q version is not an expansion of the Marcan, the Marcan is a mutilation of the Q version.

(*b*) It frequently happens that Mark conflates into a single saying portions of what appear as two separate sayings in Q, or combines into one context sayings which appear apart and in what appear to be more appropriate contexts in Q.

V. St. Mark's Knowledge and Use of Q 167

The matter most characteristic of Mark consists in graphically told anecdote. On the other hand, the matter specially characteristic of Q consists in collections of short sayings, not unlike the Wisdom literature of the Old Testament, and in short parables. It is significant that whenever we find matter of this kind in Mark we usually find that much or all of it is paralleled in Q, and that the Q form seems more original.

We proceed to examine the cases in order.

(1) The substance of John the Baptist's preaching, Mt iii. 7-12 = Lk iii. 7-9, 16-17, makes it quite clear that in Q John had a message of his own—repentance, the wrath to come even upon Abraham's children, the axe at the root of the tree, the threshing floor—in addition to the mere announcement of 'one coming after', which is all that Mark gives, Mk i. 7-8. Now Mk i. 7-8 occurs almost word for word in Mt iii. 11 = Lk iii. 16, but it is clear that Matthew and Luke did not derive the verse from Mark but from the same source whence they derived the preceding and following verses.

[1] Mark i	Matthew iii	Luke iii
	7-10 Γεννήματα ἐχιδνῶν κτλ.	7-9 Γεννήματα ἐχιδνῶν κτλ.
7-8 Καὶ ἐκήρυσσε λέγων, "Ερχεται ὁ ἰσχυρότερός μου ὀπίσω μου, οὗ οὐκ εἰμὶ ἱκανὸς κύψας λῦσαι τὸν ἱμάντα τῶν ὑποδημάτων αὐτοῦ. ἐγὼ ἐβάπτισα ὑμᾶς ἐν ὕδατι, αὐτὸς δὲ βαπτίσει ὑμᾶς ἐν Πνεύματι Ἁγίῳ.	11 Ἐγὼ μὲν βαπτίζω ὑμᾶς ἐν ὕδατι εἰς μετάνοιαν· ὁ δὲ ὀπίσω μου ἐρχόμενος ἰσχυρότερός μου ἐστίν, οὗ οὐκ εἰμὶ ἱκανὸς τὰ ὑποδήματα βαστάσαι· αὐτὸς ὑμᾶς βαπτίσει ἐν Πνεύματι Ἁγίῳ καὶ πυρί. 12 Οὗ τὸ πτύον ἐν τῇ χειρὶ αὐτοῦ, καὶ διακαθαριεῖ τὴν ἅλωνα αὐτοῦ, καὶ συνάξει τὸν σῖτον αὐτοῦ εἰς τὴν ἀποθήκην, τὸ δὲ ἄχυρον κατακαύσει πυρὶ ἀσβέστῳ.	16 Ἐγὼ μὲν ὕδατι βαπτίζω ὑμᾶς, ἔρχεται δὲ ὁ ἰσχυρότερός μου, οὗ οὐκ εἰμὶ ἱκανὸς λῦσαι τὸν ἱμάντα τῶν ὑποδημάτων αὐτοῦ· αὐτὸς ὑμᾶς βαπτίσει ἐν Πνεύματι Ἁγίῳ καὶ πυρί. 17 Οὗ τὸ πτύον ἐν τῇ χειρὶ αὐτοῦ, διακαθᾶραι τὴν ἅλωνα αὐτοῦ, καὶ συναγαγεῖν τὸν σῖτον εἰς τὴν ἀποθήκην αὐτοῦ· τὸ δὲ ἄχυρον κατακαύσει πυρὶ ἀσβέστῳ.

[1] Where Mt, Mk, and Lk *all* contain a passage, but not where it occurs only in Mt and Lk, words in which Mt and Lk agree against Mk are printed in darker type, but there are often further minute agreements in order of words, turn of thought, or parts of words which cannot be conveniently so noted.

For—(a) Matthew and Luke agree against Mark in ἐγὼ μὲν βαπτίζω for ἐγὼ ἐβάπτισα, in αὐτὸς ὑμᾶς βαπτίσει for αὐτὸς δὲ βαπτίσει ὑμᾶς, in placing the announcement of ὁ ἰσχυρότερος between instead of before these two contrasted baptisms, and in the addition of the words καὶ πυρί.

(b) What is still more significant, the subject of the relative οὗ in the verse which follows in Mt and Lk but does not occur at all in Mk (Mt iii. 12 = Lk iii. 17) is contained in this verse which they have in common with Mark. Mt iii. 12 = Lk iii. 17 has no meaning apart from the preceding verse, which therefore must have stood in Q and not have been derived by editors of Mt and Lk from Mark. Thus the verses Mt iii. 11-12 = Lk iii. 16-17, or rather Mt iii. 7-12 = Lk iii. 7-9, 16-17, form one connected whole, of which Mk i. 7-8 is a mutilated fragment.

Again, in all three Gospels John's preaching is introduced by the quotation from Isaiah φωνὴ βοῶντος κτλ. Seeing that in no other case does the editor of Mark himself introduce a quotation or reference to the Old Testament it is probable that this also occurred in Q. Mark alone prefixes to it the quotation from Malachi ἰδοὺ ἐγὼ ἀποστέλλω τὸν ἄγγελον, which is applied to John Baptist in Mt xi. 10 = Lk vii. 27, in the account of John's Message from prison, a passage of Q which does not occur in Mark. It looks as if Mark's double quotation in this passage is a conflation of the two quotations applied to John in two different contexts of Q.

(2) Mark's brief allusion to the Temptation, i. 12-13, is less original than the longer account of Q, Mt iv. 1-11, Lk iv. 1-13. An original tradition is always detailed and picturesque, and would hardly record as does Mark a temptation to do nothing in particular. A later author might well so allude to a story whose details were familiar, but which he could not entirely omit to notice in a life of the Master.

Thus at the outset we are struck by the fact that the

V. St. Mark's Knowledge and Use of Q

first thirteen verses of Mark, so unlike his usual picturesque diffuseness, read like a summary of a longer and fuller account, which the author gives because it had become the recognized introduction to a Gospel writing, but which he hurries through in order to get on to his own special matter.

(3) The Beelzebub controversy, Mk iii. 22–30, Mt xii. 22–32, Lk xi. 14–23.

Mark iii

²² Καὶ οἱ γραμματεῖς οἱ ἀπὸ Ἱεροσολύμων καταβάντες ἔλεγον ὅτι Βεελζεβοὺλ ἔχει, καὶ ὅτι Ἐν τῷ ἄρχοντι τῶν δαιμονίων ἐκβάλλει τὰ δαιμόνια.

²³⁻⁶ Καὶ προσκαλεσάμενος αὐτοὺς ἐν παραβολαῖς ἔλεγεν αὐτοῖς, Πῶς δύναται Σατανᾶς Σατανᾶν ἐκβάλλειν; καὶ ἐὰν βασιλεία ἐφ᾽ ἑαυτὴν μερισθῇ, οὐ δύναται σταθῆναι ἡ βασιλεία ἐκείνη· καὶ ἐὰν οἰκία ἐφ᾽ ἑαυτὴν μερισθῇ, οὐ δυνήσεται σταθῆναι ἡ οἰκία ἐκείνη· καὶ εἰ ὁ Σατανᾶς ἀνέστη ἐφ᾽ ἑαυτὸν καὶ ἐμερίσθη, οὐ δύναται σταθῆναι, ἀλλὰ τέλος ἔχει.

²¹ Ἀλλ᾽ οὐ δύναται οὐδεὶς εἰς τὴν οἰκίαν τοῦ

Matthew xii

²²⁻³ Τότε προσηνέχθη αὐτῷ δαιμονιζόμενος τυφλὸς καὶ κωφός· καὶ ἐθεράπευσεν αὐτόν, ὥστε τὸν κωφὸν λαλεῖν καὶ βλέπειν. καὶ ἐξίσταντο πάντες οἱ ὄχλοι καὶ ἔλεγον, Μήτι οὗτός ἐστιν ὁ υἱὸς Δαβίδ;

²⁴ Οἱ δὲ Φαρισαῖοι ἀκούσαντες εἶπον, Οὗτος οὐκ ἐκβάλλει τὰ δαιμόνια εἰ μὴ ἐν τῷ Βεελζεβοὺλ ἄρχοντι τῶν δαιμονίων.

²⁵⁻⁶ Εἰδὼς δὲ τὰς ἐνθυμήσεις αὐτῶν εἶπεν αὐτοῖς, Πᾶσα βασιλεία μερισθεῖσα καθ᾽ ἑαυτῆς ἐρημοῦται, καὶ πᾶσα πόλις ἢ οἰκία μερισθεῖσα καθ᾽ ἑαυτῆς οὐ σταθήσεται· καὶ εἰ ὁ Σατανᾶς τὸν Σατανᾶν ἐκβάλλει, ἐφ᾽ ἑαυτὸν ἐμερίσθη· πῶς οὖν σταθήσεται ἡ βασιλεία αὐτοῦ;

²⁷⁻⁸ Καὶ εἰ ἐγὼ ἐν Βεελζεβοὺλ ἐκβάλλω τὰ δαιμόνια, οἱ υἱοὶ ὑμῶν ἐν τίνι ἐκβάλλουσι; διὰ τοῦτο αὐτοὶ ὑμῶν ἔσονται κριταί. εἰ δὲ ἐγὼ ἐν Πνεύματι Θεοῦ ἐκβάλλω τὰ δαιμόνια, ἄρα ἔφθασεν ἐφ᾽ ὑμᾶς ἡ βασιλεία τοῦ Θεοῦ.

²⁹ Ἢ πῶς δύναταί τις εἰσελθεῖν εἰς τὴν οἰκίαν

Luke xi

¹⁴ Καὶ ἦν ἐκβάλλων δαιμόνιον κωφόν· ἐγένετο δέ, τοῦ δαιμονίου ἐξελθόντος ἐλάλησεν ὁ κωφός· καὶ ἐθαύμασαν οἱ ὄχλοι.

¹⁵ Τινὲς δὲ ἐξ αὐτῶν εἶπον, Ἐν Βεελζεβοὺλ τῷ ἄρχοντι τῶν δαιμονίων ἐκβάλλει τὰ δαιμόνια.

¹⁷⁻¹⁸ Αὐτὸς δὲ εἰδὼς αὐτῶν τὰ διανοήματα εἶπεν αὐτοῖς, Πᾶσα βασιλεία ἐφ᾽ ἑαυτὴν διαμερισθεῖσα ἐρημοῦται· καὶ δὲ καὶ ὁ Σατανᾶς ἐφ᾽ ἑαυτὸν διεμερίσθη, πῶς σταθήσεται ἡ βασιλεία αὐτοῦ; ὅτι λέγετε ἐν Βεελζεβοὺλ ἐκβάλλειν με τὰ δαιμόνια.

¹⁹⁻²⁰ Εἰ δὲ ἐγὼ ἐν Βεελζεβοὺλ ἐκβάλλω τὰ δαιμόνια, οἱ υἱοὶ ὑμῶν ἐν τίνι ἐκβάλλουσι; διὰ τοῦτο κριταὶ ὑμῶν αὐτοὶ ἔσονται. εἰ δὲ ἐν δακτύλῳ Θεοῦ ἐγὼ ἐκβάλλω τὰ δαιμόνια, ἄρα ἔφθασεν ἐφ᾽ ὑμᾶς ἡ βασιλεία τοῦ Θεοῦ.

²¹⁻² Ὅταν ὁ ἰσχυρὸς καθωπλισμένος φυλάσσῃ

Mark iii	Matthew xii	Luke xi
ἰσχυροῦ εἰσελθὼν τὰ σκεύη αὐτοῦ διαρπάσαι, ἐὰν μὴ πρῶτον τὸν ἰσχυρὸν δήσῃ, καὶ τότε τὴν οἰκίαν αὐτοῦ διαρπάσει.	τοῦ ἰσχυροῦ καὶ τὰ σκεύη αὐτοῦ διαρπάσαι, ἐὰν μὴ πρῶτον δήσῃ τὸν ἰσχυρόν ; καὶ τότε τὴν οἰκίαν αὐτοῦ διαρπάσει.	τὴν ἑαυτοῦ αὐλήν, ἐν εἰρήνῃ ἐστὶ τὰ ὑπάρχοντα αὐτοῦ· ἐπὰν δὲ ἰσχυρότερος αὐτοῦ ἐπελθὼν νικήσῃ αὐτόν, τὴν πανοπλίαν αὐτοῦ αἴρει, ἐφ' ᾗ ἐπεποίθει, καὶ τὰ σκῦλα αὐτοῦ διαδίδωσιν.
	³⁰ Ὁ μὴ ὢν μετ' ἐμοῦ κατ' ἐμοῦ ἐστι, καὶ ὁ μὴ συνάγων μετ' ἐμοῦ σκορπίζει.	²³ Ὁ μὴ ὢν μετ' ἐμοῦ κατ' ἐμοῦ ἐστι, καὶ ὁ μὴ συνάγων μετ' ἐμοῦ σκορπίζει.
		Luke xii
²⁸⁻⁹ Ἀμὴν λέγω ὑμῖν, ὅτι πάντα ἀφεθήσεται τοῖς υἱοῖς τῶν ἀνθρώπων τὰ ἁμαρτήματα, καὶ αἱ βλασφημίαι ὅσα ἂν βλασφημήσωσιν· ὃς δ' ἂν βλασφημήσῃ εἰς τὸ Πνεῦμα τὸ Ἅγιον, οὐκ ἔχει ἄφεσιν εἰς τὸν αἰῶνα, ἀλλ' ἔνοχός ἐστιν αἰωνίου ἁμαρτήματος.	³¹⁻² Διὰ τοῦτο λέγω ὑμῖν, πᾶσα ἁμαρτία καὶ βλασφημία ἀφεθήσεται τοῖς ἀνθρώποις· ἡ δὲ τοῦ Πνεύματος βλασφημία οὐκ ἀφεθήσεται. καὶ ὃς ἂν εἴπῃ λόγον κατὰ τοῦ υἱοῦ τοῦ ἀνθρώπου, ἀφεθήσεται αὐτῷ· ὃς δ' ἂν εἴπῃ κατὰ τοῦ Πνεύματος τοῦ Ἁγίου, οὐκ ἀφεθήσεται αὐτῷ οὔτε ἐν τούτῳ τῷ αἰῶνι οὔτε ἐν τῷ μέλλοντι.	¹⁰ Καὶ πᾶς ὃς ἐρεῖ λόγον εἰς τὸν υἱὸν τοῦ ἀνθρώπου, ἀφεθήσεται αὐτῷ· τῷ δὲ εἰς τὸ Ἅγιον Πνεῦμα βλασφημήσαντι οὐκ ἀφεθήσεται.

Matthew and Luke make four important additions—the fact that the challenge of the Pharisees was evoked by the cure of a dumb demoniac, Mt xii. 22 = Lk xi. 14, and three whole verses, Mt xii. 27, 28, 30 = Lk xi. 19, 20, 23. Of these additions it is indubitable that at least the verses Mt xii. 27–8 and Lk xi. 19–20, 'If I by Beelzebub..., by whom do your sons cast them out?' and 'If I by the finger of God cast out devils...' are original in this context, for they are pointless except as a reply to the challenge, 'By Beelzebub he casts out devils.' But Mt xii. 25–6 = Lk xi. 17–18, which are parallel to Mk iii. 23–36, agree against Mark not only in twelve words (N.B. esp. 'knowing their thoughts') but in the general form and construction of the sentences; they therefore were also in the same source which contained the four additional verses. The same source must also have contained Mt xii. 24 = Lk xi. 15,' By Beelzebub the prince

V. St. Mark's Knowledge and Use of Q

of devils he casts out devils,' the Pharisaic challenge without which the whole discussion has no meaning. Although therefore the verse is found exactly in Mark it must have occurred also in Q.

Accordingly at least Mt xii. 22, 24–8, 30 = Lk xi. 14–15, 17–20, 23 if not more must have stood in Q. But the abbreviated version of Mk iii. 22–6 has such close verbal resemblances in what it has in common with Q, and loses so much force by what it omits from Q, that we can only regard it as a mutilated excerpt from that source.

Again, especially noticeable is the fact that Mark (followed by Matthew, but not by Luke who is using Q alone here) connects with the Beelzebub controversy a saying (Mk iii. 28–9) Blasphemy against the Holy Ghost. Luke in quite a different context (xii. 10) has a *double* saying contrasting the sins of 'a word against the Son' and 'blasphemy against the Spirit'; the same double saying occurs here in Mt xii. 32 and was therefore in Q, but probably as in Luke in a different context. It may be inferred that Mark remembered one half only of the double saying and attached it to what he remembered of the Beelzebub controversy, thus combining fragments of two different passages in Q, which Luke gives in their original separation, but which Matthew, according to his custom, conflates with Mark.[1] The curious phrase Mk iii. 28, τοῖς υἱοῖς τῶν ἀνθρώπων, here only in N.T., is perhaps due to a hazy reminiscence of the τὸν υἱὸν τοῦ ἀνθρώπου of the omitted half of the Q saying.

(4) Mk iv. 21–5 (omitted by Matthew in the parallel context, but reproduced by Luke) consists of five sayings having no internal connexion with one another. A parallel to each of them occurs in both Matthew and Luke in an entirely different context which as a rule looks more original.

iv. 21, 'Light under a bushel,' occurs Mt v. 15 = Lk xi. 33.

iv. 22, 'There is nothing hidden,' occurs as one member

[1] N.B. the way in which Mt xii. 32 fuses together Mk iii. 29 and Lk xii. 10. It throws great light on Matthew's method of conflating the phrasing as well as the matter of his sources.

of one of those antithetical pairs of sayings which are so characteristic both of our Lord's and of earlier Jewish wisdom,' Mt x. 26 f. = Lk xii. 2 f.

iv. 23 ὁ ὦτα ἔχων, occurring three times each in Matthew and in Mark, and twice in Luke, proves nothing.

iv. 24 ἐν ᾧ μέτρῳ μετρεῖτε, is a conflation of Mt vii. 2 = Lk vi. 38 (its original context as shown by its antithesis μὴ κρίνετε in both) with the concluding words of Mt vi. 33 b = Lk xii. 31 b, καὶ προστεθήσεται ὑμῖν.

iv. 25 ὃς γὰρ ἔχει δοθήσεται more appropriately in Q concludes the Parable of the Talents = Pounds, Mt xxv. 29 = Lk xix. 26.

In every case the saying as given by Matthew and Luke is in substance the same as in Mark, but small verbal agreements show they derived it from Q and not from Mark. The whole section is thus clearly a collection of fragments torn from their original context in Q, as if it were a collection of texts quoted loosely from memory.

(5) The Parable of the Mustard Seed. Mk iv. 30-2 = Mt xiii. 31-2 = Lk xiii. 18-19.

Mark iv	Matthew xiii	Luke xiii
30-2 Καὶ ἔλεγε, Πῶς ὁμοιώσωμεν τὴν βασιλείαν τοῦ Θεοῦ; ἢ ἐν τίνι αὐτὴν παραβολῇ θῶμεν; ὡς κόκκῳ σινάπεως, ὅς, ὅταν σπαρῇ ἐπὶ τῆς γῆς, μικρότερον ὂν πάντων τῶν σπερμάτων τῶν ἐπὶ τῆς γῆς, καὶ ὅταν σπαρῇ, ἀναβαίνει, καὶ γίνεται μεῖζον πάντων τῶν λαχάνων, καὶ ποιεῖ κλάδους μεγάλους, ὥστε δύνασθαι ὑπὸ τὴν σκιὰν αὐτοῦ τὰ πετεινὰ τοῦ οὐρανοῦ κατασκηνοῦν.	31-2 Ἄλλην παραβολὴν παρέθηκεν αὐτοῖς λέγων, Ὁμοία ἐστὶν ἡ βασιλεία τῶν οὐρανῶν κόκκῳ σινάπεως, ὃν λαβὼν ἄνθρωπος ἔσπειρεν ἐν τῷ ἀγρῷ αὐτοῦ· ὃ μικρότερον μέν ἐστι πάντων τῶν σπερμάτων, ὅταν δὲ αὐξηθῇ, μεῖζον τῶν λαχάνων ἐστί, καὶ γίνεται δένδρον, ὥστε ἐλθεῖν τὰ πετεινὰ τοῦ οὐρανοῦ καὶ κατασκηνοῦν ἐν τοῖς κλάδοις αὐτοῦ. 33 Ἄλλην παραβολὴν ἐλάλησεν αὐτοῖς, Ὁμοία ἐστὶν ἡ βασιλεία τῶν οὐρανῶν ζύμῃ, ἣν λαβοῦσα γυνὴ ἐνέκρυψεν εἰς ἀλεύρου σάτα τρία, ἕως οὗ ἐζυμώθη ὅλον.	18-19 Ἔλεγεν οὖν, Τίνι ὁμοία ἐστὶν ἡ βασιλεία τοῦ Θεοῦ; καὶ τίνι ὁμοιώσω αὐτήν; ὁμοία ἐστὶ κόκκῳ σινάπεως, ὃν λαβὼν ἄνθρωπος ἔβαλεν εἰς κῆπον ἑαυτοῦ· καὶ ηὔξησε, καὶ ἐγένετο εἰς δένδρον, καὶ τὰ πετεινὰ τοῦ οὐρανοῦ κατεσκήνωσεν ἐν τοῖς κλάδοις αὐτοῦ. 20-1 Καὶ πάλιν εἶπε, Τίνι ὁμοιώσω τὴν βασιλείαν τοῦ Θεοῦ; ὁμοία ἐστὶ ζύμῃ, ἣν λαβοῦσα γυνὴ ἔκρυψεν εἰς ἀλεύρου σάτα τρία, ἕως οὗ ἐζυμώθη ὅλον.

V. St. Mark's Knowledge and Use of Q 173

There are twelve small verbal coincidences between Matthew and Luke against Mark, which show that their version is not derived from him but from Q. What is more important is the fact that in both Matthew and Luke the Parable of the Leaven is appended. Pairs of parables emphasizing different aspects of the same idea are a marked characteristic of our Lord's teaching in all our sources (cf. among others the Hidden Treasure and the Pearl of Great Price in Mt xiii. 44-6 ; the New Patch and the New Wine, Mk ii. 21 f. ; the Tower Builder and King making War, Lk xiv. 28-32). Mark's single parable here is therefore a mutilation of an original pair in Q.

(6) Mk vi. 7-11, Mt x. 1-14, Lk ix. 1-5 ; cf. Lk x. 1-12. A complicated case, for the agreements of Luke with Matthew against Mark occur partly in Lk ix. 1-5, partly in Lk x. 1-12. Matthew as usual conflates Mark and Q, and so for once to some small extent does Luke in ix. 1-5, but Luke also has a version in x. 1-12, much, if not all, of which is Q.

Mark vi

[7] Καὶ προσκαλεῖται τοὺς δώδεκα, καὶ ἤρξατο αὐτοὺς ἀποστέλλειν δύο δύο· καὶ ἐδίδου αὐτοῖς ἐξουσίαν τῶν πνευμάτων τῶν ἀκαθάρτων,

[8-10] Καὶ παρήγγειλεν αὐτοῖς, ἵνα μηδὲν αἴρωσιν εἰς ὁδόν, εἰ μὴ ῥάβδον μόνον· μὴ ἄρτον, μὴ πήραν, μὴ εἰς τὴν ζώνην χαλκόν· ἀλλ' ὑποδεδεμένους σανδάλια· καὶ μὴ ἐνδύσησθε δύο χιτῶνας. καὶ ἔλεγεν αὐτοῖς,

Matthew x

[1] Καὶ προσκαλεσάμενος τοὺς δώδεκα μαθητὰς αὐτοῦ ἔδωκεν αὐτοῖς ἐξουσίαν πνευμάτων ἀκαθάρτων, ὥστε ἐκβάλλειν αὐτά, καὶ θεραπεύειν πᾶσαν νόσον καὶ πᾶσαν μαλακίαν.

[7-8a] Πορευόμενοι δὲ κηρύσσετε λέγοντες ὅτι Ἤγγικεν ἡ βασιλεία τῶν οὐρανῶν. ἀσθενοῦντας θεραπεύετε.

[9] Μὴ κτήσησθε χρυσὸν μηδὲ ἄργυρον μηδὲ χαλκὸν εἰς τὰς ζώνας ὑμῶν, [10] μὴ πήραν εἰς ὁδόν, μηδὲ δύο χιτῶνας, μηδὲ ὑποδήματα, μηδὲ ῥάβδον· ἄξιος γὰρ ὁ ἐργάτης τῆς τροφῆς αὐτοῦ ἐστιν. [11] εἰς ἣν δ' ἂν πό-

Luke ix

[1] Συγκαλεσάμενος δὲ τοὺς δώδεκα ἔδωκεν αὐτοῖς δύναμιν καὶ ἐξουσίαν ἐπὶ πάντα τὰ δαιμόνια, καὶ νόσους θεραπεύειν.

[2] Καὶ ἀπέστειλεν αὐτοὺς κηρύσσειν τὴν βασιλείαν τοῦ Θεοῦ, καὶ ἰᾶσθαι τοὺς ἀσθενοῦντας.

[3-4] Καὶ εἶπε πρὸς αὐτούς, Μηδὲν αἴρετε εἰς τὴν ὁδόν, μήτε ῥάβδον, μήτε πήραν, μήτε ἄρτον, μήτε ἀργύριον, μήτε δύο χιτῶνας ἔχειν. καὶ εἰς ἣν ἂν οἰκίαν εἰσέλθητε, ἐκεῖ μένετε, καὶ ἐκεῖθεν ἐξέρχεσθε.

Luke x

[1] Μετὰ δὲ ταῦτα ἀνέδειξεν ὁ Κύριος ἑτέρους ἑβδομήκοντα, καὶ ἀπέστειλεν αὐτοὺς ἀνὰ δύο πρὸ προσώπου αὐτοῦ εἰς πᾶσαν πόλιν καὶ τόπον οὗ ἔμελλεν αὐτὸς ἔρχεσθαι.

[9] Καὶ θεραπεύετε τοὺς ἐν αὐτῇ ἀσθενεῖς, καὶ λέγετε αὐτοῖς, Ἤγγικεν ἐφ' ὑμᾶς ἡ βασιλεία τοῦ Θεοῦ.

[4-5a] Μὴ βαστάζετε βαλάντιον, μὴ πήραν, μὴ ὑποδήματα· καὶ μηδένα κατὰ τὴν ὁδὸν ἀσπάσησθε. εἰς ἣν δ' ἂν εἰσέλθητε οἰκίαν,... [7] ἐν αὐτῇ δὲ τῇ οἰκίᾳ μένετε, ἐσθίοντες καὶ πίνοντες τὰ παρ' αὐτῶν· ἄξιος γὰρ ὁ

Mark vi	Matthew x	Luke ix	Luke x
Ὅπου ἐὰν εἰσέλθητε εἰς οἰκίαν, ἐκεῖ μένετε ἕως ἂν ἐξέλθητε ἐκεῖθεν.	λιν ἣ κώμην εἰσέλθητε, ἐξετάσατε τίς ἐν αὐτῇ ἄξιός ἐστι, κἀκεῖ μείνατε, ἕως ἂν ἐξέλθητε. εἰσερχόμενοι δὲ εἰς τὴν οἰκίαν ἀσπάσασθε αὐτήν. ¹³ Καὶ ἐὰν μὲν ᾖ ἡ οἰκία ἀξία, ἐλθέτω ἡ εἰρήνη ὑμῶν ἐπ' αὐτήν· ἐὰν δὲ μὴ ᾖ ἀξία, ἡ εἰρήνη ὑμῶν πρὸς ὑμᾶς ἐπιστραφήτω.		⁵ᵇ—⁶ Πρῶτον λέγετ Εἰρήνη τῷ οἴκῳ τούτ καὶ ἐὰν ᾖ ἐκεῖ υἱ εἰρήνης, ἐπαναπαύσ ται ἐπ' αὐτὸν ἡ εἰρήι ὑμῶν· εἰ δὲ μήγε, ἐ ὑμᾶς ἀνακάμψει.
¹¹ Καὶ ὃς ἂν τόπος μὴ δέξηται ὑμᾶς, μηδὲ ἀκούσωσιν ὑμῶν, ἐκπορευόμενοι ἐκεῖθεν ἐκτινάξατε τὸν χοῦν τὸν ὑποκάτω τῶν ποδῶν ὑμῶν, εἰς μαρτύριον αὐτοῖς.	¹⁴ Καὶ ὃς ἐὰν μὴ δέξηται ὑμᾶς, μηδὲ ἀκούσῃ τοὺς λόγους ὑμῶν, ἐξερχόμενοι ἔξω τῆς οἰκίας ἢ τῆς πόλεως ἐκείνης ἐκτινάξατε τὸν κονιορτὸν τῶν ποδῶν ὑμῶν.	⁵ Καὶ ὅσοι ἂν μὴ δέχωνται ὑμᾶς, ἐξερχόμενοι ἀπὸ τῆς πόλεως ἐκείνης τὸν κονιορτὸν ἀπὸ τῶν ποδῶν ὑμῶν ἀποτινάξατε, εἰς μαρτύριον ἐπ' αὐτούς.	¹⁰⁻¹¹ Εἰς ἣν δ' ὁ πόλιν εἰσέλθητε, κ μὴ δέχωνται ὑμᾶς, ἐ ἐλθόντες εἰς τὰς πλα τείας αὐτῆς εἴπατε, Κ τὸν κονιορτὸν τὸν κολ ληθέντα ἡμῖν ἐκ τί πόλεως ὑμῶν εἰς τοὶ πόδας ἀπομασσάμεθ ὑμῖν· πλὴν τοῦτο γινώ σκετε, ὅτι ἤγγικεν βασιλεία τοῦ θεοῦ. ¹² Λέγω ὑμῖν, ὅτ Σοδόμοις ἐν τῇ ἡμέρ ἐκείνῃ ἀνεκτότερον ἔσ ται ἢ τῇ πόλει ἐκείνῃ
	¹⁵ Ἀμὴν λέγω ὑμῖν, ἀνεκτότερον ἔσται γῇ Σοδόμων καὶ Γομόρρων ἐν ἡμέρᾳ κρίσεως ἢ τῇ πόλει ἐκείνῃ. ¹⁶ᵃ Ἰδού, ἐγὼ ἀποστέλλω ὑμᾶς ὡς πρόβατα ἐν μέσῳ λύκων.		³ Ὑπάγετε· ἰδοι ἐγὼ ἀποστέλλω ὑμᾶ ὡς ἄρνας ἐν μέσῳ λύ κων.

Comparing Matthew with the two Lucan passages, it appears at once that Q must have contained six passages not paralleled in Mark. (1) 'Preach the Kingdom is at hand and heal the sick,' Mt x. 7–8 a = Lk x. 9, cf. Lk ix. 2 ; (2) 'The labourer is worthy of his hire,' Mt x. 10 = Lk x. 7 ; (3) 'Into whatever city ye shall enter,' Mt x. 11 = Lk x. 10; (4) 'Your peace be upon the house,' Mt x. 13 = Lk x. 6 ; (5) 'It shall be more tolerable for Sodom than for that city,' Mt x. 15 = Lk x. 12 ; (6) 'I send you as sheep among wolves,' Mt x. 16 = Lk x. 3.¹

But Q must also have contained the substance of the verses which are paralleled by Mark, for

¹ Possibly a seventh, Mt x. 40 = Lk x. 16, 'He that heareth you heareth me, &c.'

V. St. Mark's Knowledge and Use of Q

In Mk vi. 7 = Mt x. 1 = Lk ix. 1, Matthew and Luke agree against Mark in six verbal points.

In Mk vi. 8-9 = Mt x. 9-10, Lk ix. 3 and x. 4, Matthew and Luke agree in adding ἀργύριον and ὑποδήματα, and in giving μήτε ῥάβδον for εἰ μὴ ῥάβδον μόνον, implying in Q a list of requisites similar to Mark's.

Mk vi. 10 = Mt x. 12 = Lk ix. 4 = Lk x. 5 a, or an equivalent indicating entrance of the house, is implied by the subsequent Q verse, Mt x. 13 = Lk x. 5 b-6.

Mk vi. 11 = Mt x. 14 = Lk ix. 5 = Lk x. 10-11. Matthew and Luke agree in the words ἐξερχόμενοι τῆς πόλεως ἐκείνης, κονιορτόν. Also πόλεων is guaranteed as original as against Mark's ἐκεῖθεν, as the next verse, Mt x. 15 = Lk x. 11, has no meaning, unless a city has just been expressly mentioned. Accordingly Mt x. 14 = Lk ix. 5 = Lk x. 10 was derived by the editors from Q not from Mk vi. 11.

Q therefore contained substantially all that Mark gives in much the same language, and in addition six sayings which are intimately connected with them. Again, therefore, Mark's version is a mutilated excerpt of Q.

(7) Mk ix. 42-50, cf. Mt xviii. 6-9. It would appear that this section is a combination of three fragments of Q.

(a) In Lk xvii. 1-2 the saying, 'It is necessary that offences come, but woe to him by whom they come,' is explained by the connected saying, 'it is better for him that a millstone,' &c., apart from which it has little meaning. Mt xviii. 6-7 gives the two sayings in the reverse order but still in connexion, Mk ix. 42 reproduces only one, again breaking up an original pair.

(b) Mk ix. 43-7, 'If thy hand, foot, eye, offend thee,' is substantially reproduced by Matthew twice, i. e. Mt xviii. 8-9, which is in context parallel to this passage of Mark, and with important variations Mt v. 29-30 in the Sermon on the Mount. The natural explanation of the doublet in

Matthew is that in the one case he draws from Mark, in the other from Q.

(c) Mk ix. 50, 'salt,' cf. Lk xiv. 34 = Mt v. 13. Matthew and Luke agree against Mark in the word μωρανθῇ and in adding the idea of casting it away, such a saying therefore stood in Q. Probably however καλὸν τὸ ἅλας (Mark and Luke) stood in Q, for it looks more original than Matthew's ὑμεῖς ἐστὲ τὸ ἅλας τῆς γῆς, which combines with the original saying its homiletic explanation, cf. p. 198 and *Hor. Syn.*², pp. 163 ff.

(8) Mk xii. 38–40, denunciation of the Pharisees, looks like a reminiscence of the long denunciation in Q. Mt xxiii 1–36, cf. Lk xi. 39–52.

The *cumulative* effect of these instances is irresistible, and must establish beyond reasonable doubt that Mark was familiar with Q. Once this is established it is natural to regard as reminiscences of Q certain other passages of a kind which, but for this, might have been regarded as independent versions of sayings of our Lord, e. g. 'The Great Commandment', Mk xii. 28 ff. = Mt xxii. 34 ff. = Lk x. 25 ff., which Sir John Hawkins, p. 41 f. above, has shown was probably contained in both Mark and Q.

For the same reason we may suspect also derivation from Q in the case of the following sayings which exhibit agreements between Matthew and Luke, which show that they knew a version of the saying (i. e. Q's) slightly different from Mark's; though of course in the case of isolated sayings the probability of their being handed down in a similar form by different traditions is much higher than in the case of longer connected passages. In most cases the saying is reproduced twice by Matthew and Luke, once in a form and context resembling Mark and therefore drawn from him, once in a different form; only the latter are here given.[1]

---

[1] For a detailed discussion of these passages showing that Luke derived them from Q not from Mark, not however raising the question of the relation of the Marcan to the Q version, cf. Sir J. Hawkins, pp. 94 ff. above; also *Hor. Syn.*², pp. 83 ff. 'Doublets.'

V. St. Mark's Knowledge and Use of Q

Mk viii. 12,'No sign shall be given,' cf. Mt xii. 39 = Lk xi. 29.
Mk viii. 34, 'take up cross,' cf. Mt x. 38 = Lk xiv. 27.
Mk viii. 38, 'Whoso shall be ashamed of me,' cf. Mt x. 33 = Lk xii. 9, 'Whoso denies me.'
Mk x. 11–12, Divorce, cf. Mt v. 32 = Lk xvi. 18.
Mk x. 31, ' The first shall be last,' cf. Mt xx. 16 = Lk xiii. 30, where the order is reversed.
Mk x. 43–4, cf. Mk ix. 35, 'Whoso would be great,' cf. Mt xxiii. 11 = Lk xxii. 26. N.B. $\mu\epsilon i \zeta \omega \nu$.
Mk xi. 23, Faith, cf. Mt xvii. 20 = Lk xvii. 6, adding ' as a grain of mustard seed '.

We notice that the sixteen passages discussed above are taken from every part of Q, a strong confirmation of the view, still combated by a few critics, that the 'common non-Marcan matter of Matthew and Luke' was derived from a *single written* source. It is highly improbable that the authors of Mark, Matthew, and Luke, writing at different dates and evidently for Churches widely separated in their theological leanings, and probably also in their geographical situation, would yet all three have drawn so extensively from a single source if that common matter had been either a cycle of floating traditions or due to the overlapping of a number of separate written documents.

When once it is realized that Mark used Q, it is impossible not to ask the question whether he may not have derived therefrom more than these sixteen passages. It is probable that to some small extent he did, but to the view put forward by a few scholars that a considerable part of Mark's narrative matter, including some sections at least of his Passion story, was derived from Q, the objections seem fatal. Apart from the subconscious presumption apparently made by some, that if a saying or action is historically genuine it must have been recorded in the earliest written Gospel—the unsoundness of which needs not to be demonstrated—the main arguments for this view are two:

(1) It seems *a priori* improbable that any considerable writing concerned with our Lord could have omitted all reference to His Passion.

(2) The theory would explain the occasional minute verbal agreements between Matthew and Luke in passages where they appear to be following Mark.

The first reason rests on a misconception of the purpose of Q which we deal with in a subsequent essay, cf. p. 214. The second overlooks (*a*) the fact that these agreements are mostly of the nature of grammatical and stylistic refinements on St. Mark's somewhat Aramaic Greek. These are more likely to be due to posterior scribal improvements on the text of Mark, *before* it was used by Matthew and Luke (cf. Dr. Sanday's Essay, p. 21), than to reflect an earlier and therefore presumably even more Aramaic-looking document.

(*b*) In nearly all the passages we have examined, the verbal agreements between Matthew and Luke against Mark are very substantial. Moreover, it was seen that Mark as a rule reproduce Q very freely and often in a much abbreviated form, while Matthew and Luke reproduce Q more exactly and in a longer form than Mark. We may assume, therefore, that if Mark had drawn at all largely on Q in other passages we should have found Matthew and Luke agreeing against Mark in material and conspicuous points. This test, however, breaks down where neither or only one of the two later writers reproduces Mark, and unfortunately this is the case in precisely the only two considerable passages not examined above, where the material consists of discourse rather than narrative, i.e. the Parable of the Seed growing secretly, Mk iv. 26–9, and the Criticism of Pharisaism, Mk vii. 1–23. We hold, therefore, that Mark knew and used Q, but only to a limited extent. The reason he used it so little we endeavour to explain (cf. p. 219) in a subsequent Essay on the Literary Evolution of the Gospels.

The Apocalypse of Mark xiii.

The long discourse Mk xiii demands separate consideration. Some recent scholars have suggested that it is derived from Q, but the hypothesis receives no confirmation from verbal agreements between Matthew and Luke against Mark, nor yet from internal considerations.

The belief entertained in the early Church that our Lord would return visibly on the clouds of Heaven within the lifetime of the first generation, is nowhere definitely expressed in those Apocalyptic sayings of His which are given by Q; much less is His return connected with the Fall of Jerusalem. In Mk xiii He is represented as guaranteeing these views in their crudest and most defined form. The question,[1] therefore, whether this discourse belongs to an earlier or a later source, bearing as it does on the important question, whether such a belief was ever really expressed or entertained by our Lord at all, is one which deserves a detailed investigation.

A discourse thirty-seven verses long at once stands out as unique in Mark. Equally in contrast to Q, and notably to Q's Apocalyptic sections (cf. esp. Lk xii. 35-48, xvii. 22-37), is its systematic and detailed scheme of prediction and its comparative poverty of picturesque metaphor and illustration. It is in fact a complete and carefully articulated Apocalypse of the conventional type, and can therefore only be understood if it is interpreted by the same methods which modern scholarship has found so fruitful when applied to Daniel, Revelation, and the whole mass of non-canonical Apocalyptic literature.

An Apocalypse is normally assigned, not to its true author, but to some great one of the past; Hermas and possibly Revelation are exceptions. There is nothing surprising therefore to find such a prophecy attributed

---

[1] Cf. esp. Schweitzer, 'The Quest of the Historical Jesus.' Cf. also the Appendix to the present volume.

to our Lord. The author usually works upon older Apocalyptic materials of which he deems he has, in an inspired moment, surprised the secret. These he expands and adapts in language of thinly disguised symbolism to show their application to contemporary events. An Apocalypse can therefore, as a rule, be dated by the events it thus reflects. Lastly, it aims at giving the encouragement or warning needed by its readers for a particular crisis. Daniel, for instance, for the crisis caused by the persecution of Antiochus Epiphanes.

Approaching Mk xiii from this standpoint we see at once that it is an Apocalypse pseudonymously put into the mouth of our Lord, doubtless embodying certain older Apocalyptic materials, as well as certain genuine utterances of His, reflecting a series of events important to the early Church, and having two main objects; (*a*) to warn Christians against the Anti-Christs expected to precede the Parousia, and (*b*) to encourage doubters by the assurance that the delays in His coming had been foreseen by the Master and that the recent Fall of Jerusalem is its immediate prelude.

We notice first that the Apocalypse purports to have been delivered *privately* to certain disciples. This is to explain how it is that it has hitherto been unknown to Christians in general—a mark of late date of publication. We are reminded of the secret traditions from particular Apostles produced by the later Gnostics. It is emphasized that the long delay of the Parousia, which was such a difficulty for the Early Church, had been foreseen by the Master and privately explained to an inner circle, οὔπω τὸ τέλος, xiii. 7. He had foreseen the series of persecutions and catastrophes, in each of which as it arrived the faithful had seen the harbinger of that end which never came, ἰδού, προείρηκα ὑμῖν πάντα, xiii. 23. He had given also the reason of His delay. It was that there might be time for the Gospel to be first preached to all the Gentiles,

V. St. Mark's Knowledge and Use of Q

xiii. 10—a reason suggested by the thought in Rom xi (cf. especially verses 11, 12, 25) that the conversion of Israel was predestined, but postponed till the Gentiles had been gathered in. Famines, cf. that in Acts xi. 28, earthquakes as at Laodicea, 61 A. D., or Pompeii in 62 A. D., He had foretold, but these were but the beginnings of the birth-pangs, ὠδίνων, xiii. 9, i.e. of the calamities which it was generally expected would usher in the Messianic Age. He had seen too great world-wide wars, verse 8, as in the year of the four Emperors culminating in the sack of Jerusalem, verses 14–20 - a time in which, 'had not the Lord shortened it, no flesh would have been saved'—all this the Master had foreseen. He had foreseen St. Paul, xiii. 9, accused before the Sanhedrin (εἰς συνέδρια), five times scourged in the Synagogue (εἰς συναγωγὰς δαρήσεσθε), standing before Felix and Festus (ἐπὶ ἡγεμόνων), before Agrippa and Nero (βασιλέων) for His name's sake. He had foretold the horrors of the Neronian persecution when the Christians first arrested informed, as Tacitus relates, on their brethren παραδώσει ἀδελφὸς ἀδελφὸν εἰς θάνατον, verse 12, and Christians were μισούμενοι ὑπὸ πάντων, verse 13, accused, says Tacitus, of 'odium humani generis'. Lastly, He had foreseen one final peril, the false Christs and false prophets, displaying σημεῖα καὶ τέρατα, who might 'deceive even the elect' at the last moment on the very eve of His return.

This last peril is to the author *still in the future* (there is no evidence that it ever did become actual, at least until the Bar-Cochba rising), and to warn his hearers against this is the principal object of the Apocalypse; with this the actual prophecy begins, verses 5–6, with this the series of historical allusions closes, xiii. 21–3. The second object is to encourage those whose hopes are failing. Now at last He is near the doors, xiii. 29. His coming will follow this last tribulation as closely as summer follows the fig-tree's leaves, xiii. 28.

2 Thess ii. 8–12 gives us the key to the author's outlook. The last thing before the Parousia will come the man of

sin, ἐν πάσῃ δυνάμει καὶ σημείοις καὶ τέρασι ψεύδους, 'whom the Lord will slay with the breath of his mouth.' The author is so sure that the end will follow at once after the world-wide horrors of A.D. 69–70 (we must think of Vitellius in Italy as well as Titus in Judaea), that he feels the need of warning lest some false Christ should snatch away some of those who have borne so much and waited so long even at the eleventh hour. So in this hour of supreme expectation and danger, the message once privately given to the four Apostles is published for all, ὃ ὑμῖν λέγω, πᾶσι λέγω, γρηγορεῖτε.

Matthew reproduces Mark xiii with trifling verbal additions, as well as an insertion from Q, Mt xxiv. 26–8, which occurs also in Lk xvii. 23–37. His modifications of the Marcan text as a rule do not suggest greater originality, but one or two have been thought by some critics to show that he had access to a text of the Apocalypse (as some think forming part of Q) in some respects superior to Mark's. In one instance only does this view seem correct, viz. his substitution of εὐθέως for ἐν ἐκείναις ταῖς ἡμέραις of Mk xiii. 24 is probably right, but it is more likely, considering how fond Mark is of the word εὐθύς, that his text has been altered here by later scribes, than that he failed to reproduce his favourite word if it occurred in the source he used. The addition μηδὲ σαββάτῳ, Mt xxiv. 20, is less likely to be original. The interest shown in the career of St. Paul, the Pauline explanation of the delay in the Parousia, the familiarity with the Roman persecution, point away from a Judaistic origin. On the other hand a Judaizing touch not infrequently appears in Matthew's editing of his Marcan source, e.g. he inserts xxiv. 12 against ἀνομία, he transfers the idea 'I was not sent but unto the lost sheep of the House of Israel', suggested doubtless by the source he uses in x. 6, into Mark's story of the Syro-Phoenician, Mt xv. 24, and again he omits Mark's 'the Sabbath was made for man', Mk ii. 27, making the point in his version

V. St. Mark's Knowledge and Use of Q   183

of the story to be merely the right of Messiah *as such* to be Lord of the Sabbath, Mt xii. 8. The reference to Daniel, Mt xxiv. 15, is also editorial, intended to make ἀναγινώσκων refer to the Old Testament, though it doubtless originally meant the present Apocalyptic leaflet. None of the other Matthean variants have the slightest claim to be considered original.

An Apocalypse usually contains older material, so we may perhaps hazard the guess that in xiii. 14 f. we are on the track of the old oracle which Eusebius says induced the Christians to flee to Pella. It is more interesting to inquire whether this chapter reproduces any genuine utterances of our Lord.

Mk xiii. 1-2, 'Not one stone upon another,' is probably genuine and may have been derived from St. Peter's reminiscences, and may have been the saying on which the accusation against our Lord at His trial was based, Mk xiv. 58. In that case the inserted Apocalypse we have been considering does not begin till xiii. 3.

Mk xiii. 11, 15-16 occur attached to Q matter in Lk xii. 11-12 and Lk xvii. 31, and therefore may be from that source, cf. p. 36 and p. 38, on these two passages.

Mk xiii. 21 may be a reminiscence of one half of the Q pair of warning verses, Lk xvii. 23-4 = Mt xxiv. 26-7.

Mk xiii. 28-32. Most of this matter has a genuine look.

Mk xiii. 34-6 looks like a reminiscence of the opening of the Parable of the Talents, Mt xxv. 14-15, cf. especially ἀπόδημος with ἀποδημῶν, conflated with a reminiscence (xiii. 35 b) of Lk xii. 38, which is probably Q.

So far then from being derived from Q, this Apocalypse would appear to be a document of about the year A. D. 70 having, like the rest of St. Mark's Gospel, only a few reminiscences of Q embodied in it.[1]

[1] Mark's genius is that of a narrator not of a προφήτης; moreover, unlike Mt, he has no tendency to build up disconnected sayings into elaborate discourses. He would not have composed the Apocalypse but, accepting it as an authentic word of the Lord, inserted it whole.

SYLLABUS

An attempt, admittedly highly speculative, to ascertain whether any passages peculiar to Matthew or Luke can be referred to Q.

It is briefly shown that Q contained an account of John's preaching, the Baptism and Temptation, the Great Sermon, the Centurion's Servant, and John's Message. Then the main contention is advanced, viz. that the longer interpolation, Lk ix. 51–xviii. 14, is, in the main, an extract of Q expanded by means of a collection of parables peculiar to St. Luke, so that many passages in it, even though not paralleled in Matthew, can be referred to Q.

A difference is noted between the type of parable peculiar to Matthew and Luke and the normal type occurring in Q. The Lucan Parables of the Wedding Feast and the Pounds are probably, but not certainly, derived from the same written source (i. e. Q) as Matthew's similar parables.

Some passages peculiar to Matthew are doubtless also from Q, but these are harder to identify. The question is further complicated by the probability that Matthew and Luke did not know the original Q, but used two differently expanded versions of the original document.

THE ORIGINAL EXTENT OF Q

IF Mark had been lost but Q preserved, and we could therefore only reconstruct Mark by taking all the common matter of Matthew and Luke and deducting that belonging to Q, assigning the rest to the lost (Marcan) document we were reconstructing (the converse of the actual state of things), only those passages of Mark which *both* Matthew and Luke reproduce could have been identified as belonging to this source. But these only amount to about two-thirds of Mark. We infer therefore that the passages which we can *identify as* Q by the fact that *both* Matthew and Luke reproduce them *may* possibly only represent about two-thirds of the original total matter in Q.

It is due to Luke's omissions more than to Matthew's that so large a portion of Mark does not appear in both Matthew and Luke. He omits nearly one-fourth of Mark, and his omissions include discourse matter similar to that of Q, e.g. Mk iv. 26-9; vii. 1-23; ix. 42-50. Matthew omits only about one-twelfth.

If Mark was lost, much of Matthew and a fair amount of Luke, that is now seen to be from Mark, would appear as *peculiar* to Matthew or Luke. Probably therefore much of the peculiar matter of Matthew and a little of the peculiar matter of Luke is from Q, and these *may* amount together to about half as much as what we can now identify as from this source. We say *may* amount to half as much. But if Q was, as we think likely, the work of an original eyewitness and Luke knew this, Luke may have been more chary in discarding from Q than from Mark. Harnack has noted, though perhaps over-estimated, the somewhat critical attitude Luke adopts towards Mark. Matthew, on the other hand, who is interested in making our Lord's sayings into a sort of Christian Law Book (cf. p. 221 f.), may have discarded more of what he deemed irrelevant, so that the proportion of omissions from Q by Matthew and Luke respectively may be more equal than of those from Mark.

The attempt to ascertain which of the passages which now appear as 'peculiar' to Matthew or Luke were derived from Q is naturally one of great interest, but it cannot be too often emphasized that it is at best careful guessing. The results that can be obtained by the most scientific application of critical methods are in this case highly speculative, and lack that objective cogency which we submit attaches to the results attained in the accompanying Essays.

The failure to distinguish clearly between the very varying degrees of probability which belong to different critical conclusions, and the purely subjective character of the arguments sometimes adduced by critics, have to many minds thrown discredit on Synoptic Criticism as a whole, and have produced a general impression that beyond the admitted dependence of Matthew and Luke on Mark the problem is insoluble. What follows therefore is advanced frankly as speculation, but speculation based upon the study of such meagre objective considerations as the materials afford.

It has been shown in the previous Essay that Q contained a much fuller account of the Preaching of John the Baptist than Mark (Mt iii. 7-12 = Lk iii. 7-9, 16-17). The agreement of Matthew and Luke against Mark in the expression περίχωρος τοῦ Ἰορδάνου (Mt iii. 5 = Lk iii. 3) suggests that Q had also a word or two of narrative introduction. In fact since Luke omits Mk i. 5-6, the most striking features in Mark's account, it is probable that he derives nothing at all from Mark, as we saw in the previous Essay was the case with his version of the Beelzebub controversy. In both cases Matthew conflates Mark and Q.

In the account of the Temptation also not only must the

VI. The Original Extent of Q

details, Mt iv. 3-10 = Lk iv. 3-12, being entirely absent from Mark, be referred to Q, but also at least part of the introductory verses Mt iv. 12-13 = Lk iv. 1-2, and also the concluding verses Mt iv. 11a = Lk iv. 13, to which Mk has some equivalent; for

(a) Mk says 'the Spirit drives him', ἐκβάλλει; both Mt and Lk 'he was led (ἄγω) by the Spirit'.

(b) Mt Lk both add ὑπὸ τοῦ διαβόλου.

(c) Mt Lk both add abstention from food during the forty days and consequent hunger.

(d) Mt iv. 11a agrees with Lk iv. 13 against Mark in recording the departure of the Devil.

N.B.—Lk, and so doubtless Q, omits the Marcan detail of a ministry of angels, Mt as usual conflates Mark and Q.

Since Q recorded John's preaching and the Temptation it would be very strange if no mention were made of the Baptism, which is the connecting link between the two. The hypothesis that Q had some account of it receives some confirmation when we notice that Matthew and Luke agree in saying 'the heavens were opened' (ἀνοίγω). Mk has 'He saw the heavens torn asunder' (σχιζομένους). Further, if we accept as original the well attested 'Western' reading of Lk iii. 22, which gives the Voice from Heaven as in Psalm ii. 7, 'Thou art my Beloved Son, this day have I begotten thee,' we can assign no other reason for St. Luke preferring this version to that we find in Mark (and which Matthew reproduces), 'Thou art my Beloved Son, in thee I am well pleased,' except that he found it in Q (cf. Harnack, *op. cit.*, E. T., p. 310). We infer that Q began with an account of John's preaching, the Baptism, and Temptation, which Matthew has conflated with Mark's account, and which Luke gives unconflated but with slight editorial additions.

Next followed, as in Luke, whose order as we have seen in the previous Essay is probably original, the Great Sermon, vi. 20-49, and Centurion's Servant, vii. 2-10, and John's Message, vii. 18-35. Next a large amount of the matter in Luke's longer interpolation, ix. 51-xviii. 14.

Then the Parable of the Pounds, Lk xix. 11-27, if, as we hold, this was derived from the same written source as Matthew's Parable of Talents—a point which will require special discussion—and the half-verse, 'ye shall sit on twelve thrones judging the twelve tribes of Israel,' Lk xxii. 30.

Such is the torso which clearly remains to us of Q. The investigation we are about to undertake may enable us to restore to Q, with some degree of probability, a certain number of other passages which now appear as 'peculiar' to either Luke or Matthew.

Matthew, as we have seen in the previous Essay, mixes his sources, interpolating his non-Marcan matter at innumerable points in the Marcan framework. Luke, on the contrary, likes to follow one source at a time, and that for a considerable time. He interpolates incidents from another source only when from their context they can only come in at that point. For instance, the Zacchaeus incident—and also the Parable of the Pounds which follows, if its introductory verse, xix. 11, is original—only when our Lord is at Jericho, xix. 39-44, only as a sequel to the Triumphal Entry, and of course in the account of the Last Supper, Trial and Crucifixion, where at each stage details are drawn from different sources, he cannot follow one at a time for long. With these exceptions from iv. 31, where he begins to follow Mark, to the Last Supper, xxii, where he cannot help beginning to mix his sources, he has two interpolations only (I speak of interpolations of complete incidents, not of odd verses or editorial comments), but both these are of considerable length, vi. 20-viii. 3 and ix. 51-xviii. 14, and throughout both of these, as is shown in Sir J. Hawkins's Essay, pp. 30 ff., there is, save for a few trifling verbal reminiscences, a complete disuse of Mark as a source.

If, again, we examine these two interpolations, we are

led to infer that here also he has pursued as far as possible his plan of copying one source at a time, interpolating it as little as possible. Both appear to begin with a long extract from Q, followed by matter from another source or sources.

First let us examine vi. 20-vii. 35: the Sermon on the Plain,[1] the Centurion's Servant, the message of John from Prison. It is solid Q, with the one short interpolation, the Widow of Nain, vii. 11-17. The reason of the interpolation is obvious. In vii. 22 John's disciples are referred, for proof of Christ's Messiahship, to various miracles of healing, including raising of the dead, as if they were recent and notorious facts. Luke interpolates the story of the Widow of Nain (N.B. especially vii. 17, the report of it through all Judaea), and the verse vii. 21 ('in that hour he healed many', &c.), probably an editorial inference, to give meaning to this. We have already noticed that apparently for precisely the same reason Matthew interpolates the healing of a leper at the same spot, from Mark, but not in Mark's order, and postpones the account of John's message until he has given a specimen of each kind of the miracles there mentioned before this allusion to them as credentials is made.[2] After the Q matter comes the section vii. 36-viii. 3, derived from other sources.

Examine now the second interpolation, ix. 51-xviii. 14, often miscalled the 'Peraean section' of St. Luke.

First comes the block ix. 51-xii. 59, of which nearly four-fifths, as also occurring in Matthew, is *verifiably* Q, as is the

---

[1] Since two discourses having so much closely parallel as Matthew's Sermon on the Mount and Luke's Sermon on the Plain, both open with Beatitudes, at least the four which they agree in giving must have stood in the original common source. The additional Beatitudes of Matthew and the four contrasted 'Woes' of Luke may have been added either by the Evangelists themselves or by intermediate editors of the somewhat different recensions of Q which they respectively used.

[2] The possibility that Christ Himself meant the words in a metaphorical sense with an intention referring to Isa xxxv. 5 and lxi. 1, does not affect our argument, for in any case neither Evangelist so interpreted them.

case also with all but a few verses of xiii. 18–35. Then follows a mixed section, xiv. 1–xv. 7, containing along with matter not paralleled in Matthew the debatable Parable of the Wedding Feast, the Lost Sheep, and three sayings, xiv. 11, xiv. 26–7, xiv. 34–5, which appear to be from Q.

Then follow three and a half chapters of matter consisting almost entirely of parables peculiar to St. Luke, punctuated at intervals by three short collections of sayings which appear to be from Q, i.e. xvi. 13–18, xvii. 1–6, xvii. 22–37. These parables are mostly longer and of a somewhat different type from the short comparisons which are specially characteristic of Q, a point we shall elaborate later.

The larger interpolation is therefore seen to be based on two main sources, i.e. Q and a Collection of Parables, whether first made by Luke himself or found by him already collected is immaterial. At the beginning of the interpolation he is mainly dependent on Q, and at the end mainly on the Collection of Parables.

The inference at once suggests itself that, except for one or two Lucan interpolations, ix. 51–xii. 59 is a solid transcript of Q much in its original form, of which Matthew has omitted a few sections—an inference which is confirmed by a closer examination of the passages not occurring also in Matthew. In this investigation we will assume, as already proved, the conclusion arrived at by Sir J. Hawkins, pp. 29 ff. above, that the forty verses occurring in this 'longer interpolation', to which Mark has parallel matter, are derived not from Mark but from Q.

The Parables of the Good Samaritan and the Rich Fool are so much of the same character as those of the source of chapters xv–xviii, and the contexts, i.e. the idea of 'My Neighbour', x. 27, the warning against πλεονεξία, xii. 15, which introduces them, are so inviting that we at once suspect these as interpolated into their present place by St. Luke.

VI. The Original Extent of Q

The other passages of the section not paralleled by Matthew are all quite short, and are all passages which for various reasons he may have thought it unnecessary to reproduce. But it should be remembered that though assignable reasons can be shown for most of Matthew's omissions from Mark he sometimes omits without obvious reasons, e. g. the Widow's Mite. The non-insertion by the author of a new work of an incident occurring in a source may be determined by much slighter reasons than the excision by a mere editor from a text he is revising.

ix. 51 is perhaps partly editorial, but the rebuke of James and John, ix. 52-6, for their desire to call down fire on the discourteous Samaritans is probably Q, for two reasons:

(a) It is a notable characteristic of St. Luke to omit or tone down rebukes by our Lord or anything else derogatory to any of the XII.[1] Hence he would not have inserted such an incident from an odd tradition, though he might have retained it if it stood in this place in his second principal source.

(b) If St. Luke found this Samaritan incident at a certain point in Q he might readily have inferred that all that immediately followed in Q also occurred in Samaria. Connecting this with the introductory verse xix. 11 of the Parable of the Pounds, which apparently stood at or near the end of Q, and which dates the parable as spoken near Jerusalem, we have an easy explanation of two remarkable facts: (1) that St. Luke interpolates all the residue of his Q matter into the last journey to Jerusalem, recorded in Mk x; (2) that though Mark clearly makes our Lord journey through Peraea, St. Luke, as in other cases preferring Q to Mark, makes Him go through Samaria (cf. p. 159, note). Matthew's omission of the incident is due to his sharing the tendency to 'spare the Twelve', e.g. in recording the rebuke of these same two Apostles on this same last journey (Mk x. 35 ff.) he places the blame on their mother Salome

[1] Cf. p. 223; also Hawkins, *Hor. Syn.*², p. 121.

and omits the 'hardening of their hearts' recorded in Mk vi. 52; viii. 17.

ix. 61-2 has exactly the same point as the three previous verses, and Matthew, who has a tendency to compress, may have thought this superfluous. Two other cases are noted on p. 195, where he appears to have omitted the second of two similar sayings (cf. also his compression of the threefold illustration, Mk ix. 43, 45, 47, into a twofold, Mt xviii. 8-9).

x. 17-20. The return of the disciples and our Lord's comment thereon, 'I saw Satan fall from Heaven.' Matthew, who conflates the sendings of the Seventy and the Twelve, omits to record the return, given in Mk vi. 30, and therefore omits the occasion for the remarks, supposing them to have stood in Q attached to such a return. He may have found the saying hard because in his own Apocalyptic views[1] the fall of Satan from Heaven was entirely future.

x. 25-8. The Great Commandment was in Q as well as Mark (cf. p. 41 f.).

x. 38-42. Martha and Mary. This probably came in with, and perhaps from the same source as, the preceding Parable of the Good Samaritan, but it *may* have been in Q and omitted by Matthew as likely to suggest that antinomian doctrine of 'salvation without works', which the Church (cf. St. James, whose point of view is akin to St. Matthew) had so soon to fight.

xi. 5-8. The Discourteous Friend, if interpreted as an allegory, as Matthew inclines to interpret the parables, implies God is not anxious to answer prayer but can be worried into it, and may therefore have been omitted. Probably also xviii. 1-8, the Unjust Judge, also stood in Matthew's source and was omitted for the same reason.

xi. 27-8. 'The breast that bare thee.' Matthew has already, xii. 47-50, adopted from Mark a story with exactly the same point, and therefore omits this.

[1] Cf. Appendix, *passim*.

VI. The Original Extent of Q

xi. 53–54, xii. 1, may be merely editorial.

xii. 13–15. 'Who made me a judge?' An apparent disclaimer by Christ which might be misunderstood. N. B. Matthew altered the similar disclaimer in Mark x. 18, 'Why callest thou me good?' to 'Why asketh thou concerning the good?'

xii. 35–8. Matthew has this and more also in his Parable of the Ten Virgins.

It appears then that except for the two Parables of the Good Samaritan and the Rich Fool, and perhaps the story of Martha, ix. 51–xiii. 59 may well be a solid block of Q. xiii. 1–17 we consider later. It may have been interpolated into Q before it came to Luke, but xiii. 18–35 is obviously an extract from Q. It is all paralleled by Matthew (vv. 25–7 vaguely so), except 31–3, 'Go tell that fox,' a passage so un-Lucan in its rough vigour that it is certainly original.

The account of a healing on the Sabbath, which immediately follows, xiv. 1–6, is also probably Q, for Mt xii. 9 f. seems to conflate this story with that which he derives from Mk iii. 1 f. Mt xii. 11 ('the ox or ass in a pit', not in Mark) = Lk xiv. 5, and the form of the questions is influenced from the same source. It is told, not for the sake of the miracle but of the moral, that it is lawful to heal on the Sabbath. It would indeed have been strange if Q had not a word to say on Christ's teaching as to the Sabbath, a point which must have been so important in primitive controversy with Pharisees. Thus St. Luke has three stories of Sabbath cures, all told to bring out the same lesson, vi. 6–11, xiii. 10–17, and xiv. 1–6. The first is from Mark, the second from some special source, the third from Q. Some such story therefore occurred in every form of the earliest Christian tradition.

Chapters xiv and xv raise some interesting and difficult questions, and the solutions here suggested are therefore only tentatively put forward, and are of a far more speculative character than anything heretofore. xiv. 1 makes the incident and discourse following take place at a meal in the house of a Pharisee; xiv. 7-11 is addressed to the guests; 12-14 to the host; and 15-24 in answer to a remark by a guest. Twice before, meals in a Pharisee's house are made the occasion of an incident or discourse (Lk vii. 36; xi. 37), parallels to which are by Mark or Matthew placed otherwise. We suspect therefore that the words in verses 1, 7, 12, and 15 a, which fix all the sections to one such meal, are editorial. But the three sections, vv. 7-11, 12-14, and 15-24, are three sayings concerning banquets, and to this is obviously due their collocation. The question is, did St. Luke find already together *three sayings* about banquets and therefore infer, and add a word or two to indicate, that they were spoken *at* a banquet, or is their collocation also due to him?

Next follow *three sayings* on the cost of following Christ, if, that is, 26-7 be reckoned as a single saying. 26-7 occurs also in Matthew's second cento (ch. x), and is therefore Q. 28-33 are not in Matthew, but obviously stand together as one of those pairs of illustrations so often found in our Lord's teaching. The question is, did they follow 26-7 in Q, or did Luke add them from another source because so appropriate in this context? Next follow *three parables* on God's readiness to forgive sinners—the Lost Sheep, the Lost Coin, the Prodigal Son. The first two seem to form an original pair.

It is quite clear that we are in contact with a case of conscious arrangement: is this due to St. Luke or to his source? Or did Luke find them in his sources as pairs, and by his additions make them into triads? For we notice that each triad of sayings will split into a pair closely related, with a third less closely connected, i.e.:

   xiv. 7-11 + 12-14 *and* 15-24.
   xiv. 28-30 + 31-33 *and* 26-27.
   xv. 3-7 + 8-10 *and* 11-32.

Complementary pairs of parables or illustrations empha-

VI. The Original Extent of Q

sizing slightly different aspects of some idea are a notable characteristic of our Lord's manner of teaching. Such appear, as noticed in a previous Essay, in all our sources, 'The men of Nineveh shall rise in the Judgement . . ., The Queen of the South shall rise in the Judgement . . .'; the Parables of the Mustard Seed and the Leaven, in Q; the New Cloth and the New Wine in Mk (ii. 21); the Pearl of Great Price and the Hidden Treasure, peculiar to Matthew; the Builder of a Tower and the King making War, in the passage under discussion, peculiar to Luke. The Lost Sheep and the Lost Coin form just such a pair, so that we infer that they stood together as such in Q and that Matthew has omitted the latter. Similarly in Lk xvii. 26-30 there is such a double illustration, 'the days of Noah, the days of Lot,' of which only the first member appears in Matthew. We have already (cf. p. 192) seen reason to believe that Matthew has omitted the second member of the pair of sayings, Lk ix. 58-62.

Accordingly, to return to the triads above noticed, we infer that the sources would have presented them as pairs, while the third member of each triad was connected with the pair by an editor, and therefore probably *drawn by him from a different source*. Thus the Lost Sheep and Lost Coin would be both from Q, the Prodigal Son not; the saying xiv. 26-7 is from Q, the Tower Builder and King making War are not, and since the pair xiv. 7-11, 12-14 are not from Q, we should guess that the third member of the triad, the Parable of the Wedding Feast, was from Q, even if a parable closely resembling it did not occur in Matthew as the Marriage of the King's Son, Mt xxii. 1-14.

Many critics, however, think that though Matthew's parable no doubt *ultimately* goes back to the same source as Luke's, his version has too many differences in points of detail to be derivable from the same *written* source. This conclusion we venture to impugn, especially in view of the piece of external evidence that the Wedding Feast stood in Q, deduced from the foregoing analysis of the arrangement in triads. A similar problem is presented by the parallel Parables of the Pounds in Luke and the Talents in Matthew—can these be derived from Q? In both cases we are inclined to attribute the parable to Q for the following reason.

The Parables of our Lord, considered merely in regard to their *form*, fall into two types:

(*a*) The story-parables, such as the Unmerciful Servant or the Prodigal Son—which are equivalent to what in secular writing we call a fable, that is a narrative of imaginary events told for the sake of the moral. These are usually of some length.

(*b*) What we may call the 'analogy-parables'—being either an extended metaphor, 'the Kingdom of Heaven is like unto Leaven,' &c., or illustrations, 'does a man put old wine into new bottles?' These are short and pithy

No doubt it is impossible to draw an absolutely hard and fast line between the two classes. The Lost Sheep in Luke's version might *almost* be classed as a story-parable, in Matthew it appears rather as an 'analogy-parable'. Still the distinction in the main is clear and important.

Examples of both types are found in Mark. The Wicked Husbandmen and the Sower belong to the story type, the Mustard Seed and the New Wine in Old Bottles to the other. It is therefore very remarkable that these two debatable parables, Wedding Feast = Marriage of the King's Son, and Pounds = Talents, are the only instances of the long 'story-parable' which, being reproduced by both Matthew and Luke, can be referred with any cogency to Q.

On the other hand, the great majority of the parables peculiar to either are of this type. One has only to enumerate a few of them, the Good Samaritan, the Prodigal Son, the Unmerciful Servant, the Labourers in the Vineyard, &c., to remind oneself that the originality and spiritual

VI. The Original Extent of Q

insight shown in these are such that we must at once dismiss from our minds the suspicion that this type of parable was not actually used by our Lord, even if we had not the objective evidence of Mark that He used both types. It seems therefore impossible that this type should have been entirely unrepresented in Q, and for this reason we are the more inclined to vindicate for Q at least these two 'story-parables', not, however, forgetting that there may have been others in Q which we cannot now identify, since only one of the later Evangelists has reproduced them.

It seems not unreasonable to surmise that an editor would feel justified in taking more liberties with a parable than with a 'commandment' of the Master, since its bearing lay not in its precise wording but in its general effect, and again more liberties than with the account of an action or scene in His life, drawn from Mark, since the scene or action of the parable was not supposed to be the description of an actual occurrence, and therefore to vary the details was not to distort history. Indeed this is not mere surmise, for Matthew and Luke reproduce the Parables of the Sower and the Wicked Husbandmen with much less exactitude than they do such other utterances of our Lord as are given by Mark.

Making then for the moment the tentative assumption that the Wedding Feast, as it appears in Luke, is approximately in its original form, we see that the operation of certain tendencies elsewhere and everywhere apparent in Matthew will account for the form it takes in his Gospel.

(a) Certain picturesque details are abbreviated or disappear. The excuses (three whole verses in Lk xiv. 18-20), 'I have bought a field . . . a yoke of oxen : married a wife,' are compressed by Matthew (xxii. 5) into, 'One went to his own field, another to his merchandise.' The double gathering into the feast, first of the poor, &c., secondly of any in the highways, is compressed into one. Such compression of narrative—and from the point of view of the editor this type of parable is of the nature of *narrative* rather than of discourse—is a marked characteristic of Matthew, cf. Hawkins, *op. cit.*, p. 158 ff., where illustrations are given of Matthew's compression of matter derived from Q as well as of matter derived from Mark.

(*b*) The other alterations in Matthew appear to be only rather an extreme case of the influence of previous catechetical teaching on the more didactic parts of Matthew, cf. p. 155 above, also Hawkins, *op. cit.*, pp. 163 ff. He has turned the parable into an allegory by combining the story with its moral, which he had doubtless often drawn in oral teaching, by making the Wedding Feast into the Messianic Banquet (cf. γάμος τοῦ ἀρνίου in Rev. xix. 7, 9). God, the King, is the Giver of the feast, it is in honour of His Son, the Christ, but His subjects have ill-treated His messengers, and therefore He slew those murderers and burnt their city, xxii. 6-7—details, not added from some other parable, as Harnack thinks, but reflecting the experience of the early Christian missionaries, and the Fall of Jerusalem, regarded as God's judgement for the deaths of the Messiah and His Apostles; cf. his additions to the Marcan version of the Wicked Husbandmen, xxi. 41 κακοὺς κακῶς κτλ. and xxi. 43, 'the Kingdom shall be taken from them,' &c.; also in xxvii. 25, the inserted 'His blood be on us and on our children'.

Matthew has also appended, as if it were part of the same parable, xxii. 11-14, the Man without a Wedding Garment: this was obviously originally a separate parable, for the King could hardly blame a guest who was brought in from the highways for not having on a wedding garment. The moral of the first parable is that the kingdom would be filled with outcasts rather than with Pharisees and the like; of the second that he who wishes to enter the kingdom must first endeavour to fit himself for it. The two may have formed one of those characteristic pairs

VI. The Original Extent of Q

of parables we have noticed, and the second *may* have been omitted by Luke, who, as a follower of St. Paul, might hesitate to record a parable which *might* be construed as teaching the doctrine of salvation by works.

It will be convenient to consider here the very similar question whether the parable which appears in Matthew as the Talents and in Luke as the Pounds was derived from Q. The very close parallelism between the latter parts of the two parables (Mt xxv. 21, 24–9 = Lk xix. 17, 20–6), and the fact that Matthew and Luke agree in placing them at the end of all the other matter they derived from Q, create a strong presumption that it was derived thence. The different openings require explanation. Harnack adopts the suggestion, originally I believe made by Strauss, that St. Luke has combined two originally separate parables, the Parable of the Pounds (or Talents) and a Parable of the Rebellious Citizens. He urges also that the parallel, Mk xiii. 34, and the fact that Luke only mentions three servants in verses 16–26, though he has spoken of ten just above, shows that Matthew is more original in making the division to be of *all* the property (not of ten minae only) and among three, not ten, servants. In this last point we concur with him, but offer an alternative explanation of the Rebellious Citizens. We suggest that our Lord is not composing a new story, but retelling a well-known incident in the life of Archelaus in such a way as to make it point a double moral, the judgement that was to come firstly upon the professing servants of the Messiah, secondly upon His overt enemies.

In B.C. 4 Archelaus ($εὐγενής\ τις$) went to Rome ($εἰς\ χώραν\ μακράν$) to get his father's will leaving him the kingdom of Judaea confirmed ($λαβεῖν\ ἑαυτῷ\ βασιλείαν$).[1]

---

[1] Unless suggested by some such incident in real life, it seems very strange that a man should be represented as travelling to a distant country in order to get a kingdom in the place he started from.

But the Jews, with whom he was unpopular (οἱ πολῖται αὐτοῦ ἐμίσουν αὐτόν), sent a deputation of fifty members to Rome (ἀπέστειλαν πρεσβείαν ὀπίσω αὐτοῦ) to oppose his claim (οὐ θέλομεν τοῦτον βασιλεῦσαι ἐφ' ἡμᾶς). However he obtained the substance of his claim, the title ethnarch, with the power of king (ἐπανελθεῖν αὐτὸν λάβοντα τὴν βασιλείαν).

While away at Rome to urge his claims (against his brother) we may suppose he must have left some one to administer his revenues and estates, and the princely sums that Matthew mentions, 5 talents, 2 talents, 1 talent, seem more appropriate than the 10 minae in Luke (a talent was about £240, a mina about £4). On his return he would naturally first inquire into the conduct of these administrators and appoint to provincial governments those who had given satisfaction (ἴσθι ἐξουσίαν ἔχων ἐπάνω δέκα πόλεων). In the East the household of the Prince is the regular pathway to office. His next proceeding we can easily guess. He was a Herod, and a few years later was deposed by the Romans, who were none too humanitarian, for his cruelty (πλὴν τοὺς ἐχθρούς μου τούτους, τοὺς μὴ θελήσαντάς με βασιλεῦσαι ἐπ' αὐτούς, ἀγάγετε ὧδε καὶ κατασφάξατε αὐτοὺς ἔμπροσθέν μου).

The parable is dated (xix. 11) as spoken when Christ was near to Jerusalem. Jericho, which He had just passed through, was a city where Archelaus had built many fine buildings which would be shown to pilgrims and his story told. We infer that in position and in the general outline Luke is more original, though Matthew has preserved some details more correctly—the *Talents* and the *three* servants and the entrusting of the *whole* property. Matthew, according to his habit, has cut down pictorial detail which does not assist to make clear the moral; he therefore omits the purpose of the journey, the citizens' embassy, and their subsequent punishment, as obscuring the practical homiletic

VI. The Original Extent of Q

lesson of the parable, that men will be judged according to the use they have made of their Talents.

We return now to consider the Q passages occurring at wide intervals in the remaining portion of Luke's larger interpolation.

xvi. 13, 'Ye cannot serve God and Mammon,' probably owes its position to the occurrence of the word Mammon in the preceding parable.

xvi. 16, 17, 18 are three quite disconnected sayings. No reason for their collocation can be assigned except that they probably stood together in Q, which evidently in many places was a collection of disconnected sayings. Matthew has worked them into appropriate contexts.

We suspect xvi. 15 is also Q, and followed xvi. 13 in the source, verse 14 being editorial, so that xvi. 13-18 is in effect a block of Q, which owes its present position to the appropriateness of its first verse to the context.

xvii. 1-6 is all Q, for although 2 and 6 have parallels in Mark, they are not derived thence by Luke (cf. Sir J. Hawkins's Essay, p. 38 of this vol.).

xvii. 23-4, 26-7, 34-5, 37 b have parallels in Matthew, but the whole section 22-37 is obviously a solid piece of Q. Verses 28-30, 'In the days of Lot,' are the second member of a double illustration, corresponding to 'in the days of Noah', 26-7. 31 and 33, though paralleled in Mark, are not derived from him (cf. p. 36 and p. 38); verse 36 is omitted by the best MSS.

Probably also the passage, xvii. 20-1, which introduces this 'Apocalypse of Q', and the parable xviii. 1-8, which follows, come from the same source, for both are passages which Matthew would almost certainly have omitted, for—

(a) Matthew is the most Apocalyptic of the Gospels,[1] and he would not have understood 'the Kingdom of Heaven cometh not with observation ... for it is ἐντὸς ὑμῶν'. For

---
[1] Cf. Appendix, *passim*.

the same reason he omits Mark's Parable of the Seed growing secretly, which implies a gradual and almost imperceptible coming of the Kingdom.

(b) Matthew treats the Parables as allegories to which every detail has its exact spiritual counterpart; the apparent comparison of God in Lk xviii. 1-8 to an unjust judge unwilling to vindicate the righteous must have perplexed him. St. Luke prefixes a verse, xviii. 1, to point his favourite moral 'pray on', but without this verse we should have inferred from verses 7-8 that it was originally spoken in an Apocalyptic sense. It would have stood in Q between the Apocalyptic passage (Lk xvii. 22-37) and the Parable of the Pounds, and the connexion of xix. 11 b, which introduces the 'Pounds', with xviii. 7-8, the concluding words of the Unjust Judge, is striking. Our Lord has just said 'God will avenge them quickly'; He next speaks 'because they supposed the Kingdom of God should *immediately* appear'.

Thus Q would have ended most appropriately to its purpose (cf. p. 214) with a mass of sayings and parables concerning the Parousia, including Lk xvii. 20-xviii. 8, the Parable of the Pounds, and the promise that the Twelve should sit on twelve thrones judging the twelve tribes of Israel—the original position of which we cannot fix, since both Matthew and Luke insert it in contexts derived from Mark.

To sum up our analysis of St. Luke's longer interpolation. It begins with a long extract from Q, ix. 51-xii. 59, into which are interpolated the Parables of the Good Samaritan, the Rich Fool, and probably the story of Martha and Mary, as well as a few editorial verses. After a short interval a block appears, xiii. 18-xv. 10, which is all Q except the two pairs of sayings, xiv. 7-14 and xiv. 28-33, which however, be it noted, are in their pithy brevity more akin in style to Q than to the long story-parables characteristic of St. Luke's special source. The

VI. The Original Extent of Q

rest of the Q matter appears in the short pieces, xvi. 13-18, xvii. 1-6, and the Apocalyptic section, xvii. 20-xviii. 8. Except for the healing of the Ten Lepers and the analogy-parable, xvii. 7-10, 'we are unprofitable servants,' the rest is all 'story-parables' mostly of considerable length—the Prodigal Son, the Unjust Steward, Dives and Lazarus, the Pharisee and Publican—so that the three last extracts of Q appear to have been saved back in order to break what would otherwise be the monotony of a string of parables.

Burkitt argues that from the account of the Last Supper onwards St. Luke's account of the Passion differs too much from Mark's for us to suppose that he is copying and adopting Mark as heretofore. He suggests that he here follows in the main another written document, and that this document was the end portion of Q. That the original Q contained an account of the Passion so rich in details not in Mark as this, and that Matthew simply neglects it, is in view of Matthew's careful mosaic method of working, and his few omissions from Mark, incredible.[1] It is, however, possible that the version of Q which reached St. Luke had been already expanded to include an account of the Passion. This is possible, but in any case the exceptional preponderance of characteristically Lucan phraseology and the characteristically Lucan unity of feeling and presentment in these chapters show that whether St. Luke got his material from Mark, from oral tradition, or from another written source, or from all three, he turns aside from his document and tells the story in his own words—doubtless as he had often and often told it before to listening pupils. Who would copy from a written page a story he knows by heart? And what Christian does not know the story of the Passion better than any other portion of the Gospel story?[2]

---

[1] The problem why Q had no account of the Passion is discussed on p. 214 f.
[2] Some critics believe that some portion at least of the Passion story as

Since Luke discards so much of Mark which Matthew retains, it may be presumed he would discard something of Q also which Matthew has retained, though not necessarily the same proportion. Can we do anything to identify such passages? Some light may be gained from the study of those passages in Mark which he omits, which are of the *same character* as Q, i. e. which consist of parable or discourse.

These are mainly three: Mk iv. 26 f., the Parable of the Seed growing secretly; vii. 1–23, a discourse on unwashed hands and the Traditions of the Elders; and ix. 42–50 (except that parallels from Q to the first and last verses are inserted in a different context, Lk xvii. 2 and xiv. 34). The most significant of these omissions is vii. 1–23. Its reason is not far to seek, and will give us a hint as to his probable method. St. Luke was evidently writing for a purely Gentile Church, just as Matthew for one mainly Jewish, and our Lord's criticism of Jewish ceremonial and the Rabbinical interpretation of the Law would have little meaning and less homiletic value to a Gentile community. We should not forget that the Jewish and the Gentile worlds at the time of Christ were suffering from opposite diseases— the Jew from too much law, the Gentile from too little. The last three centuries had seen the *growth* of legalism in Judaea and the *decay* of all the old religious and customary sanctions of conduct in the rest of the Mediterranean world. We may perhaps then be justified in inferring that much of the matter in Mt v. 17–42, vi. 1–18, which is really a criticism of Pharisaic Ethics, was found in Q. 'Thou shalt not kill,' 'thou shalt not commit adultery,' did not yet require superseding by a deeper rule in the Gentile world, and there was no need to preach 'Do not your righteousness

given by *Mark* stood in Q, and only cannot be identified as such from the fact that Mark as well as Matthew and Luke has reproduced them. This view is deserving of consideration. The objections to it have been already given (cf. p. 177 f.).

VI. The Original Extent of Q

before men', but rather on the contrary to urge men to set a conspicuous example. So too he may have omitted some of the 'Woes to the Pharisees', which are given by Matthew at so much greater length. And if Luke could discard the Parable of the Seed growing secretly, given in Mark, he *might* have discarded the connected pair of Parables of the Pearl of great price and the Hidden Treasure if they had occurred in Q, which are the only two of the peculiar Matthean parables, as Harnack points out, which have the terse brevity of the parables of Q.[1] All attempts, however, at identifying as originally in Q passages which do not occur in *both* Matthew and Luke, are rendered highly speculative by the following consideration.

The interval of time between the original writing of Q and its use by Matthew and Luke was probably very considerable. And a compilation of this informal description would undoubtedly gather up words of the Master floating in current tradition, especially at an early date, while tradition was fresh. And since the traditions current in one Church would not be the same as those in another, it is highly improbable that the expanded version of Q current in the Church where Matthew worked would be the same as the differently expanded version current where Luke worked. It would seem natural to refer most of the sayings and parables peculiar to Matthew to this origin.[2] Similar additions in the version of Q which reached St. Luke would naturally be looked for in the Q-like passages, xiv. 7-14, 28-33, interpolated into the otherwise solid block of Q in xiii. 18-xv. 10. In that case the first two of the triads of sayings in this section owe their present context not to

---

[1] A fuller discussion of the question whether any of Matthew's peculiar matter can be identified as Q (treated from a slightly different point of view, but arriving at similar results) is found in the previous paper of Sir J. Hawkins, pp. 132 ff.

[2] In that case the edition of Q which Matthew used would have included most or all of the 'Book of Sayings' hypothecated in Mr. Allen's Essay.

St. Luke but to an intermediate editor of Q. The solitary analogy-parable, xvii. 7–10, 'Unprofitable Servants,' which is quite in the style of Q, may be another such early addition. It is even *possible* that xiii. 1–17, which separates the first two great extracts from Q, already stood here in the expanded version of Q which reached St. Luke, for—

(1) xiii. 1–5, Galileans slain by Pilate, &c., is a passage whose detailed allusion to two unimportant local events makes it probable that it was very early committed to writing.

(2) xiii. 6–9, the Parable of the Fig Tree, which may be from Luke's Collection of Parables, *may*, as some have suspected, be the original of which Mark's story of the Cursing of the Fig Tree is a later variant, and if so probably is very early.

(3) xiii. 10–17, a Sabbath Healing, is a type of incident of which Luke has two other cases (Lk vi. 6 ff., xiv. 1 ff.), so that since his *tendency* elsewhere is rather to omit parallel stories occurring in his sources (e.g. Feeding the 4,000, the anointing at Bethany), it is *possibly* more likely that he found it in his source and did not discard than that he interpolated it so near to the other Sabbath Healing of xiv. 1 f., although in its tone and manner it shows the editorial touch of St. Luke, and is therefore more likely to be a favourite story from his own stock of traditions.[1]

Such conclusions are of course highly speculative, but it is at least possible that St. Luke's version of Q contained the bulk of the two blocks ix. 51–xv. 10 and xvii. 1–xviii. 8, and that St. Luke has in accordance with his method incorporated such of his source as he desired to retain with but little interpolation. Thus in both the longer and the shorter interpolations St. Luke is mainly using his version of Q. To this he adds, in the shorter interpolation, the Widow of Nain, the Anointing by the Woman that was a Sinner, and

[1] Cf. p. 193.

VI. The Original Extent of Q

the Parable of the Two Debtors; in the larger interpolation, the Good Samaritan, the Rich Fool, the Prodigal Son, the Unjust Steward, Dives and Lazarus, the Pharisee and the Publican, the incident of the Ten Lepers, and probably Martha and Mary and a Sabbath Healing.

All these additions emphasize aspects of the Gospel in which, as is shown by his selection and treatment of materials elsewhere, St. Luke takes a special interest.[1] They also reflect strongly his characteristic style and vocabulary. We infer that it is more likely that they represent favourite stories selected by him from floating tradition which it was his wont to tell and retell to pupils rather than that he drew them from a third documentary source analogous to Mark or Q.

It is not within the scope of the present essay to consider how far the detailed wording of Q is better preserved by Matthew or by Luke in passages where they differ. For a suggestive and exhaustive attempt to recover the original wording the reader is referred to Harnack's often cited work. We may, however, conclude with some very brief general reflections on this point. Matthew, whose principal interest seems to be didactic, regularly and systematically compresses narrative; for detailed evidence cf. Hawkins, *Horae Synopticae*[2], pp. 158 ff. Luke, though omitting the pure redundancies of Mark's style, compresses little and preserves the liveliness of detail of the original. The presumption, therefore, is that little touches like that introducing the Lord's Prayer, xi. 1, and perhaps the greater detail in parables like the 'Lost Sheep' or 'Wedding Feast' are due to Luke preserving original features. On the other hand many of these additions, cf. those in xiv. 1, 7, 12, 15a noticed on p. 194, or the introduction to the parable, xviii. 1, cf. p. 202, appear to be inferences from the contents of the saying they introduce. Particularly significant is the

---

[1] Cf. the characterization, pp. 222-5 *infra*.

fact that he imports τότε ἔλεγεν αὐτοῖς, Lk xxi. 10, cf. καὶ εἶπε, xxi. 29, into the middle of the Apocalyptic discourse derived from Mark, showing that he likes to divide long pieces of discourse as it were into paragraphs by a word or two of narrative. Luke also re-writes his Marcan matter more than Matthew does, 'Hellenizes' it, so to speak, introducing various improvements in vocabulary and style. This, in spite of the great influence of the LXX on Luke's style and vocabulary, tends on the whole to the loss of something of the Hebraic feeling of the original, which Matthew better retains. Hence in style and feeling Matthew will be something nearer the original. It is doubtless a subconscious recognition of this that has tended to make alike critics and the instinctive feeling of the ordinary Christian look pre-eminently to the Gospel of St. Matthew for the subtler atmosphere of the Master's teaching.

THE LITERARY EVOLUTION OF THE GOSPELS

SYLLABUS

The main position urged in this essay is that the document Q, recovered by critical investigations, the Gospel of St. Mark, and the two Gospels of St. Matthew and St. Luke, form three distinct stages in the evolution of the Gospel writings. Each meets the probable apologetic and practical needs of a different period and presupposes a different background.

Q implies a Palestinian background in the Apostolic age, Mark is Roman and transitional, Matthew and Luke are distinctly sub-Apostolic.

Q was intended not to supersede but to supplement an oral tradition which would have included an account of the Passion—which Q therefore omits. Mark, written later, was intended to supplement Q. Matthew and Luke, on the other hand, aim at completeness, and intend to supersede rather than to supplement earlier writings or traditions.

These conclusions are based partly on the position accorded to John the Baptist, the Parousia, and the Pharisees in the several documents; partly on the absence of a Passion story in Q, and on the fact that Mark several times, but perhaps from memory only, quotes Q; as well as on certain minor considerations.

Analogies are adduced from the early lives of St. Francis, and the nature and significance of the idealizing tendency of Matthew and Luke are also discussed.

THE LITERARY EVOLUTION OF THE GOSPELS

THE early document Q, reconstructed in the preceding critical investigations, belongs to a different age, and is the work of one moving in a quite different atmosphere from that in which were produced the Gospels of St. Matthew and St. Luke. It belongs to the Apostolic Age. The Gospel of St. Mark forms the transition. The two later Gospels belong clearly to the Sub-apostolic period, a period which collected, arranged, and interpreted the relics of a bygone time, which was principally dependent on written records, and whose hold on the living tradition was becoming weak. Both of them attempt, so far as their materials allowed, to give a fairly exhaustive account of the life and teaching of the Master.

Exhaustive is the last word to describe a work like Q, which could omit all mention of the Crucifixion, or even like St. Mark, which gives such scanty fragments of the Master's teaching. These astounding omissions are only conceivable in documents of an earlier age; an age which week by week and day by day expected the Lord's return, and needed not to collect and compile for a posterity which would never be born; an age when the witnesses were so many, and the tradition so vivid, that it was impossible to think of being exhaustive, and he who wrote, wrote only a selection for a special purpose; an age when to put 'the Gospel' in writing meant to compose, not a biography of the Master, but an epitome of His message.

A Christian writer of the first generation is not an historian writing for posterity, for the end of all things is at hand; nor is he a biographer writing with a literary or scientific interest in presenting or analysing an interesting personality.

VII. The Literary Evolution of the Gospels

He is a man with the missionary's passion for souls, striving to bring home to as many as possible, before it is too late, the message, 'Repent ye, for the Kingdom of God is at hand,' with small hope that its preachers should even 'have gone through the cities of Israel till the Son of Man be come,' and repentance be too late, for the Judgement trump has sounded. When such men write, they write with an immediate and a practical purpose.

A brief analysis of the conditions of the first age will show that Q is just the kind of writing we should expect it to produce.

It was as a prophet that our Lord, like John the Baptist, appeared to His contemporaries.[1] Some say He is John arisen, some Elijah, some 'that Prophet', and as a Prophet He spake with authority and not as the Scribes (He is so styled Mk vi. 4; Lk vii. 16, 39; xxiv. 19). It was only quite late in his career that at Caesarea Philippi it flashed upon Peter's mind that He was more than a Prophet, that He was, in fact, the Christ.

The Crucifixion for a moment shook His disciples' faith, the belief that He had arisen again reconvinced them that He *was* the Christ (cf. Rom i. 4). But though He *was* the Christ He had not yet *appeared as Christ*. He had appeared as 'the Prophet like unto me' of whom Moses spoke (Acts iii. 22; vii. 37). His coming *as Christ* was still future, and when this happened there would be no room for doubt, no need for argument or apologetic, no cause to say, 'Lo here or lo there,' for 'as the lightning cometh out of the East and shineth even to the West, so shall be the coming of the Son of Man'. The so-called 'Second Coming' would be the first coming *as Christ*. He had come indeed, but only so far as a Prophet; the message which He preached Himself and which He told His disciples to preach was John's message, 'Repent, for the Kingdom is at hand.'

[1] Cf. *Hibbert Journal*, Oct., 1906.

But this 'repent' meant something more and other than the Pharisaic call, 'If Israel would keep but one Sabbath according to the ordinance the Son of God would appear.' It was a call to a new and deeper righteousness. Of this new righteousness, exceeding that of the Scribes and Pharisees, He had been the Prophet, and on the basis of the righteousness which He had taught as Prophet He would judge the world when He returned as Christ. The main business of the disciples being to prepare men for His coming by preaching this new righteousness, they must before long have needed a selection of the Master's teaching on the nature of this new righteousness, on its relation to that taught by the Scribes and Pharisees, and on the time and manner of His coming. It would never occur to any one to write a biography—'a Gospel' in the later sense. Did they know of biographies of Isaiah, Jeremiah, Ezekiel, and the rest of the prophets? Was it the biographies, was it not rather the epigrammatic sayings of the Rabbis that were cherished in their Schools? It would be on the analogy of books like Isaiah and Jeremiah that Christians would first record the Master's work. And since among the sayings of the more important Old Testament prophets occurs an account of the moment when each received the prophetic call, we rather expect to find that Q begins with a record of this moment in our Lord's life—in His case the Baptism and Voice from Heaven (cf. the previous Essay, p. 187, for proof that Q contained this).

We ought not then to expect to find in Q all that was known of Christ by its author. Q is a selection, compiled for a practical purpose, of those words or deeds of the Master which would give guidance in the actual problems faced by the Christian missionaries. What were these? In Palestine in quite the early years mainly three:—

(*a*) The relation of Christ's teaching to that of John the Baptist.

VII. The Literary Evolution of the Gospels

(*b*) Its relation to the Pharisaic teaching.

(*c*) The problem, if Jesus was really the Messiah, why had He appeared in such dubious guise?

(*a*) The fact that the teaching of John the Baptist had spread as far as Ephesus well in advance of Christianity, the dilemma of the High Priests in face of the question 'The baptism of John, was it from heaven, or from men?' (Mk xi. 29-33) 'since all the people held him to be a prophet', and the probably genuine notice in Josephus (cf. also $\beta\iota\acute{a}\zeta\epsilon\tau\alpha\iota$ Lk xvi. 16 = Mt xi. 12), show that the preaching of John had created a great impression in Palestine, doubtless a greater than the less dramatically ascetic and quieter work of Jesus. The Christian message was so much the same as John's—'Repent ye, the kingdom is at hand'—the call to righteousness, the proclamation of the immediate coming of the Christ—that it was of the utmost importance to make clear the relation between them. Accordingly Q begins with the summary of John's preaching intended to bring out that it was preliminary to, and therefore *an evidence for*, the claims of the One mightier who was to follow. Hence also later on (Mt xi. 2-19 = Lk vii. 18-35), the elaborate report of John's question to our Lord and our Lord's clear definition of the relation of Himself and His teaching to John. John is great but Christ transcends him. To the early Christians it seemed clear that those who had believed that John was a prophet ought to be the first to recognize Him whom John foretold.

(*b*) Outside John's movement, orthodox Pharisaism was the most living religious force in Palestine. What had the Master to say to this? The question is answered by the Beelzebub incident and the Woes to the Pharisees, and probably by much of that matter on this topic in the Sermon on the Mount (and elsewhere in Matthew) which, since Luke omits it, we can only guess to have been in Q.

(c) Lastly, the Christian apologist had daily to meet this objection, 'The Christ should reign in power and glory; how then can this crucified prophet be indeed the Christ?' The account of the Temptation, told no doubt partly as an incident of the Call, is chiefly intended to answer questions such as these. If He was Messiah, why had He not bread to eat? Why did not all Jerusalem see Him borne by angels as He leaped from the temple pinnacle? Why did He not rule all the kingdoms of the earth, a Caesar on the throne of David? This is what Messiah should do. If He was the Christ, why did He not *act* as such? And the answer is the detailed story of the Temptation with its implication— This is precisely what Satan tempted Him to do; but He saw a better way. The same objection is met by the record of our Lord's reply to the question, 'Art thou he that should come, or do we look for another?' concluding with the significant words, 'blessed is he that is not offended in me,' i.e. who does not find the paradox of the humble, toiling, homeless Christ too much for him.

But that is only the first part of the answer, but a part which is given early because it gives the key to the paradox of the New Righteousness—'blessed are ye poor', 'let him take up his cross and follow'. The objection is not finally disposed of till we reach the Apocalyptic matter towards the middle and at the close of the book—Watch, for very soon He will return, and *this* time as Lord and King and Judge, unmistakable and undisguised, 'for as the lightning which lighteneth out of one part under heaven shineth unto the other part under heaven, so shall the Son of Man be in his coming.'

For eighteen centuries the Cross has been the symbol of Christianity, and it seems strange that the earliest 'Gospel' should have told nothing of the Master's Death, or Resurrection. The strangeness disappears if we ask ourselves why it was written at all? Emphatically it was

VII. The Literary Evolution of the Gospels

not written for posterity, for the end of the world was at hand. Nor was it a summary of Christian doctrine to be handed about to casual inquirers like a modern tract. Early Christian teaching, like Jewish, was viva voce. It was from the *living voice* (cf. παρέδωκα 1 Cor xv. 3) that men heard how the Master had been crucified, had risen, had appeared first to Peter, then to the Twelve, &c., and soon would come again to judge. At that period and in that non-literary society of Palestinian peasants *only that was written down which one would be likely to forget*, and that which would be useful for the better instructed leaders to refer to occasionally as an authority on points of detail. No one was likely to *forget* that Christ had died and risen. No one in Galilee or Jerusalem, whether believer, inquirer, or persecutor, but knew something of the Galilean Rabbi who for a time had made such a stir, had been crucified, and of whom at least 500 persons scattered through the land could tell how they had since seen Him alive (1 Cor xv. 6). No painfully decipherable volume could make this tale so vivid as the living voice.[1] The tale was told in every bazaar in Palestine. It was not to retell this tale, but to provide a convenient authority on points *not* of such common knowledge, that Q was written. That is to say, Q is perfectly intelligible as a document written *to supplement* the living tradition of a generation which had known Christ. Within a dozen years after the event something of the kind would be needed. It is not intelligible as a document thirty or forty years later, when the events which Q presupposes as matter of common knowledge were a generation old.

An interesting parallel may be drawn from the records of the life of St. Francis of Assisi. His reception of the Stigmata was, to the minds of his followers, as much the

[1] As late as Papias the living voice was preferred by some as *evidence* to written books.

climax of his life as the Crucifixion was of our Lord's. Yet in the *Speculum Perfectionis*, the earliest collection of his words and acts, it is only alluded to quite casually (cf. *Speculum*, § 99) à propos of certain temptations with which he was harassed, just as in Q the Crucifixion is only hinted at casually (if at all) in the saying, 'He who would be my disciple, let him take up his cross and follow me.' The *Speculum* was written by three companions of St. Francis: is it a rash guess that Q was written by companions of our Lord, and chiefly by that Matthew whose name is given to the expanded edition of it, which stands first in our New Testament? Was it this work that the old elder meant when he spoke to Papias of τὰ λόγια? The editor of our First Gospel shows a special wish to bring Matthew into his story, substituting his name for that of Levi in his original; was this because Matthew's name was already connected with his most valued source? It is a tempting guess; but of this much we can be sure, had Matthew written, it would have been a book like this.

In sharp contrast in many ways to Q is Mark, in its purpose and in the environment it presupposes. We are no longer in Palestine, where the followers of John and of the Pharisees are active religious forces, where every one, friend or foe, had at least heard of the Prophet of Nazareth who was crucified and was said by His disciples to have risen again. We are in Rome, where the general public have never heard of Jesus, where an allusion to Jewish custom requires an explanation (e.g. Mk vii. 3-4), where even the title Christ—in Palestine thrilling with all the magic of a nation's immemorial hope—is to many hardly more than the bizarre conception of a disliked and incomprehensible Oriental tribe, where John Baptist is not even a name, and where lastly we have a *reading public*. Something like a biography is wanted, showing who He

VII. The Literary Evolution of the Gospels

was, how He showed His powers, how He had died and how it was known that He had risen.

In Palestinian Q, John the Baptist looms large, his testimony to our Lord, and our Lord's elaborately reported characterization of him and his work, as that which He Himself only superseded by perfecting, are points of the greatest apologetic value, for in Palestine all 'held John to be a prophet indeed'. In Mark, John is merely the 'messenger sent before thy face' (i. 2), 'the Elijah who must first come' (Mk ix. 11-12).[1] That is to say for Mark the apologetic significance of John's witness to Christ does not depend, as it does in Q, on the acknowledged greatness of John as a prophet, but on the fact that he fulfilled the Old Testament prophecy of the messenger and the Elijah who were to precede the Christ, i.e. Mark addresses a public who know the Old Testament as a venerable and mysterious authority, but are unmoved by the personal prestige of John.

Again, the Temptation, so detailed in Q, is barely alluded to by Mark. Why? We have seen above that the Temptation in Q has no meaning except it be a temptation to live up to a patriotic Jew's nationalistic and political conception of the Messiah. To the average Gentile Christian in Rome this would have little meaning. Q seeks to prove to the Jew that Jesus is Messiah; Mark to the Gentile that He is the 'Son of God' (Mk i. 1). Q tells two or three miracles only (Centurion's servant, a Dumb Demon, and perhaps Lk xiv. 1-6, a Sabbath Cure), and these not for their own sake but for the sake of the sayings they lead up to. In Mark healing miracles abound. Naturally, in the streets of

---

[1] The insertion of the long story of Herodias and the death of John is due to Mark's fondness for a good story, not to its apologetic or practical value, and hence is compressed by Matthew and omitted by Luke; cf. the picturesque details of John's dress and diet, Mk i. 6, which also Luke does not reproduce; cf. the gratuitous story of the young man with a linen garment, Mk xiv. 51-2.

Rome these happened more rarely than in faith-creating Galilee, and they therefore proved more.[1] Probably few in Palestine, except those in high places and the more bigoted Pharisees, ever doubted that Jesus was 'a man of God', but to prove to them that He was more than this, the Christ, required 'a sign from heaven', Lk xi. 16, 'in the depth or in the height,' cf. Isa vii. 11, of a more striking kind than healing some sick and demoniacs—a flight of angels, for instance, to bear Him up when flung from the Temple pinnacle. Miracles of healing and the like therefore were to Q of small apologetic value; not so to Mark.

Lastly, Mark gives in detail the Passion. Some one has even described the Gospel as 'a history of the Passion expanded backwards', so large a proportion of the Gospel deals with that one last week. We trace here the result of greater distance from the events than Q, both in time and in space. Far away is the land where the career of the Nazarene had been a nine days' wonder, discussed in every village. Dead or distant are all those who had ever seen Him. A written account of it all is wanted, more detailed than the catechetical tradition of Mission preachers. We trace also the result of another apologetic interest. In Palestine the Crucifixion of the Messiah, though cancelled, as it were, by the Resurrection, and seen to be after all in accord with Prophecy (Acts ii. 31; iii. 18, &c.), was yet a paradox and a stumbling-block (1 Cor i. 23). The author of Q perhaps was a little glad not to dwell on it. But St. Paul had centred all on the paradox, 'Messiah crucified, the King on the Cross'; and one who had fallen under his influence and was writing for a Church where he had worked, could not but concentrate attention here.

We thought it strange that Q had no Passion story; is

---

[1] 'The sons of the Pharisees,' Matthew xii. 27, and an unknown worker, Mk ix. 38, had this power; cf. also the Jewish exorcists in Acts xix. 13. Its possession therefore proved little.

VII. The Literary Evolution of the Gospels

it not equally strange that Mark has so little of the teaching in which Q is so rich? It can hardly be, as some critics have maintained, that under Pauline influence he laid such stress on the Passion and Resurrection as to lose interest in the teaching. On the contrary, he mentions and emphasizes the great effect of our Lord's teaching much oftener than either Matthew or Luke—the words διδαχή and διδάσκω he uses as often as the two together.[1] Only one explanation seems possible, but that simple and completely satisfactory—the Church for which St. Mark wrote already possessed in writing a convenient summary of the main features of our Lord's teaching, and if so, why may not this writing have been Q? If our characterization of Q above is correct, it was probably written twenty years before Mark, and might well have reached Rome before him.

It does not seem to the present writer probable that Mark worked with a copy of Q unrolled before him, but from time to time, in his account of John's preaching, of the Temptation, the Charge to the Twelve, the Beelzebub controversy, the Parable of the Mustard Seed, and in some minor instances, he has matter parallel to Q, and that usually in a shorter but at the same time a less original-looking form.[2] It would look as if he were quoting Q from memory.

Moreover, if Mark wrote to *supplement* Q, we have a ready explanation of the curious fact noticed in a previous Essay, that while apparently familiar with Q he uses it so little and usually with abbreviation. In writing a life of the Master he could not omit all mention of important facts like John's preaching, the Temptation, the Mission of the Twelve, and the Beelzebub controversy, or give no specimens of the Parables of the Kingdom and other sayings. He gives them, but in as succinct a form as possible.

Just, then, as Q was written to supplement, but not to

---

[1] Cf. the significant facts noted in Hawkins, *Hor. Syn.*², p. 12, διδαχή.
[2] For details see Essay on St. Mark's knowledge of Q.

supersede, a living tradition, so Mark was written to supplement, but not to supersede Q, or some deposit of material very like Q.

Harnack has well pointed out that St. Mark created a new Gospel type, emphasizing the life rather than the sayings. But though he is the transition between Q and the two later synoptics, it is a long step from Mark to Matthew or Luke. These latter aim not at supplementing, but at superseding, previous works. They aim at completeness, beginning with the birth of the Master, and including in one volume His teaching and His life. Their books are conscious works of literary art, and their selection and presentation of detail has been coloured by the apologetic exigencies of a later time. Q is an unordered collection of sayings or incidents, selected because they had vividly impressed the mind of the narrator or had an ethical or apologetic interest for the early community. Mark is a collection of vignettes—scenes from the life of the Master. The oft recurring use of $εὐθύς$ produces an illusory impression that the scenes are all closely connected in time and place, but this is a mere habit of style. The traces of a development which have been noticed in our Lord's Messianic teaching, or in the degree of hostility of the Pharisees, show that the author has some knowledge of the correct order of events, but far too much has been made of this. In the last resort Mark is a series of roughly arranged sketches or reminiscences, exactly as Papias describes it. Matthew and Luke have a more ambitious aim.

Matthew's aim is to give, in one convenient volume, a complete account of our Lord's life, a systematic view of His teaching, and a conclusive proof of His Messiahship; and at every step we feel that he is writing for those to whom Pharisaic Judaism is a very real and potent force, of mixed attraction and repulsion. The genealogy traced from Abraham through David, the messages of angels to Joseph, the birth at Bethlehem, the fulfilment

VII. The Literary Evolution of the Gospels

seen by the evangelist in event after event of the infancy of some Old Testament prophecy, strike the note of apologetic which echoes through the Gospel, as time after time he stops to point out that such a thing occurred 'that it might be fulfilled which was spoken by the prophet'. But Christ is not merely the greater David, He is the greater Moses—the New Lawgiver, who from the mountain—a new Sinai—and on some few other stated occasions gives forth in majestic symmetry the New Law. Above all, He is the Judge that is to come, and that right soon.[1]

In the Sermon on the Mount and the four other great discourses, Matthew has massed together topic by topic, from Mark, from Q, and from his own special traditions, the Master's words on the New Righteousness, the Mission, the nature of the Kingdom, and the Judgement. The loosely arranged *obiter dicta* of Q are selected, re-arranged, systematized, almost made into a code—may one say 'rabbinized'? A striking peculiarity of our Lord's teaching in its original form is that He never once lays down a rule of conduct *as a rule*. His so-called moral precepts suggest principles of right action, they never define cases or classes of right action. 'Turn the other cheek,' 'He that hateth not his father and his mother,' &c., are paradoxes, not meant to be taken literally. They do not aim at giving precise legal rules as to non-resistance or as to the comparative claims of family and religion. They suggest with metaphorical exaggeration general principles by which every age and every individual may be guided in solving the cases which arise. This feature of His teaching was obviously intentional. If once ethics is reduced to a system of rules, the question constantly rises, is such and such an offence 'within the meaning of the act'? *Law* can only be interpreted casuistically,

---

[1] This Apocalyptic aspect of Matthew is treated at length in the Appendix; cf. p. 422 ff.

and on their premises the rabbis were right. Our Lord saw this, and therefore avoided giving any definite precept which His followers might treat as the rabbis did those of Moses. But humanity loves a definite rule, and Peter asks, 'How oft shall my brother offend and I forgive him? Till seven times?' The reply in effect is, 'I give no definite rules—till seventy times seven.' In at least two cases Matthew, or the tradition behind him, has begun to make such rules. In Mt xviii. 15–18 he expands our Lord's general precept on forgiveness in Lk xvii. 3, which merely intends 'strive hard for reconciliation' into a piece of ecclesiastical law. Again in v. 32, and xix. 9, he adds to our Lord's quite general ideal condemnation of divorce, the practical limitation παρεκτὸς λόγου πορνείας, where both Mark x. 11 and Luke xvi. 18 keep the original unexpanded form. The emphasis on the anti-Pharisaic teaching of Christ in Matthew shows who were the keenest foes of the Church he worked in, and his apologetic meets them on their own ground in his appeal to Scripture and his confronting the Old Law with the New.[1]

St. Luke wrote in an atmosphere far different from St. Matthew. He is not writing for men to whom 'Messiah' is a magic word, or to whom religion has always been presented as law. He omits the anti-Pharisaic passage of Mark vii, and cuts short the Woes to the Pharisees of Q which St. Matthew has given at length, and perhaps with additions. He is, moreover, a consummate literary artist. He is writing a biography, avowedly inspired, like a biography by a Tacitus (cf. Tac. *Agric.* 3 fin.) or a Plutarch, with that feeling of *pietas* towards its subject, which antiquity praised in an historian, but which modern scholars with difficulty condone. The artist starts with a definite conception of

---

[1] Cf. Jas i. 25. James is nearer to Matthew than any other book of the New Testament in this conception of Christianity as the New Law; Revelation is the nearest to his Apocalyptic outlook.

VII. The Literary Evolution of the Gospels

that which he is to depict; he selects, he arranges; above all, he ruthlessly discards.

Some things St. Luke discards because he has elsewhere recorded an incident or a saying which teaches the same lesson—Mark's rejection at Nazareth, the anointing at Bethany, the second feeding of the multitude. Others he omits as pure redundancies—the long account of Herodias, the young man with the linen garment. Other incidents he is unwilling to make use of as likely to be laid hold of by religious opponents—the Walking on the Water, which might favour Docetism; the Syrophenician Woman, with its implication that Gentiles were as dogs who could only claim the crumbs of the Master's table, or that the Master could even for a moment grudge His healing; the Cursing of the Fig-tree, as too harsh for the Great Healer. Lastly, from that feeling of *pietas* towards the Twelve—which in the Acts makes him silent about the dispute of Peter and Paul—he will not perpetuate the memory of things like the rebuke 'Retro Satanas', or the un-Christian request of James and John (Mk x. 35 ff.); the protest of all the Twelve that they would never leave Him, and their subsequent desertion (Mk xiv. 31 b, 50); the threefold repetition of their slumber in Gethsemane.[1] St. Luke discards far more of Mark than Matthew, and what he retains he alters far more in the way of verbal improvement; but his literary instinct makes him keep the picturesque touch, the dramatic vividness of his original, in many a place where Matthew has abbreviated them away.[2]

But it is more from what he adds than from what he discards that we see the picture he would paint. The Widow of Nain, the Sinner to whom 'much was forgiven for she loved much', the Good Samaritan, the Rich Fool, the joy

---

[1] Cf. the excuse ἀπὸ τῆς λύπης in Lk xxii. 45, and the toning down of Mk xiv. 29 in Lk xxii. 33.
[2] Cf. Hawkins, *op. cit.*, p. 158, 'The shortening of narratives in Matthew.'

in heaven over one sinner that repenteth, the Prodigal Son, the Samaritan Leper, the Ministering Women, Martha and Mary, the Healing of the ear which Peter had struck off—to name only a few characteristic additions—show his interest in the Gospel as a special message to the sick, to the repentant, and to women.

Such additions of course he did not make from his own imagination. They must have been derived either, like the Marcan and the Q matter, from an earlier written source, or they must represent the traditions which he had himself collected as he wandered in the Churches—most of them perhaps, as Harnack suggests, during his stay along with St. Paul at Caesarea, possibly from Philip's daughters (Acts xxi. 8-10). But whencesoever derived, his *selection* of these particular stories to retell shows his bent of mind. He does not falsify his materials, but discards or includes in subordination to his main conception.

And what is this? To St. Luke Jesus is not primarily the Messiah of Israel, for Israel has by this time finally rejected Him, but the Saviour, the Healer of soul and body for all the world. His genealogy is traced not from Abraham but from Adam, not from the Father of Israel but from the Father of all men. As an infant He was recognized as the Light to lighten the Gentiles; and the prophet who foretold 'the voice of one crying in the wilderness' foretold also, Luke alone notes, that 'all flesh shall see the salvation of God' (Lk iii. 6).

Still more significant is the story of the Sermon at Nazareth and His rejection there. St. Luke knew that this was not the first public act of Christ, for he makes Him allude to previous work at Capernaum (iv. 23), but he puts it before any other act of His public ministrations because he sees in it an epitome of the whole Gospel and the key to its destined reception by Jew and Gentile respectively. Let us examine it more closely. Our Lord begins by proclaiming

VII. The Literary Evolution of the Gospels 225

that this day is fulfilled the great healing prophecy of Isaiah, 'good tidings to the poor, release to the captive, sight to the blind, liberty to the bruised, the acceptable year of the Lord.' But the prophet is not acceptable in his own country. As of old so now. There are sick and needy in Israel as there were in the days of Elijah and Elisha; but the healing and the help will go to the Gentile, as it did of old to Naaman the Syrian and the widow of Sarepta.

Comfort and help to the poor, to the sick, to the repentant, to the Samaritan, and to the Gentile—for St. Luke this is the Gospel—'Blessed are ye poor,' happy Lazarus the beggar, 'to-day is salvation come to this house,' the Prodigal forgiven, the Publican justified, 'for she loved much,' 'and he was a Samaritan,' 'unto all nations beginning from Jerusalem.' In his sequel, the Acts, he carries on the same conception, tracing the gradual widening of the Church from Jew to Samaritan, Samaritan to proselyte, proselyte to heathen; tracing its march from Jerusalem, the capital of Judaism, to Rome, the capital of the world. The last words of St. Paul in Rome (Acts xxviii. 28) significantly re-echo the first words of the Master in Nazareth, 'Be it known therefore unto you (Jews) that this salvation of God is sent unto the Gentiles; they *will* hear.'

The life of St. Francis of Assisi and the early developments of the movement he originated, present many resemblances to the life of Christ and the early history of the Church. It is interesting therefore to notice that the resemblances extend to the early literary records of these two lives. The oldest account of St. Francis is the *Speculum Perfectionis*, which we have already alluded to for the striking analogy it offers to Q's omission of all but a by-allusion to the Passion. Like Q it is an early, naïve, loosely arranged collection of significant incidents and *obiter dicta*. Like Q it has reached us embedded in a later document, from which Sabatier first disentangled it by a process of critical elimination similar to that by which Q has been recovered. Only in the case of the *Speculum* a later discovery has confirmed the critic's conclusions. Next comes the former life of Celano, which, like Mark, is more self-conscious, the first attempt at a biography. Later, the second life of Celano presents a fair parallel to Matthew and Luke, while the still later official life of Bonaventura will to some extent correspond to St. John. All these are more or less self-conscious works of art, written to supply the definitely realized need of the later community—idealization, elimination, systematization, are clearly seen at work.

There is a sense in which each of our first three Gospels is the more original—Mark in that it is the oldest, Matthew and Luke in that they embody a yet older source (Matthew in its more Judaic atmosphere, Luke more nearly in its original informal arrangement). Insomuch as the loss of a single syllable which might throw a ray of light on any act or word of our Lord is to be regretted, we must regret that Q, and possibly some other early writings used by Matthew and Luke, have not been preserved unaltered and entire. Yet perhaps the loss is less than we may think. Who does not feel that St. Mark, the oldest of the Gospels we still have, is the one we could best spare? Without him we should miss the exacter details of a scene or two, a touch or two of human limitations in the Master, or of human infirmity in the Twelve, but it is not from him that we get the portrait of the Master which has been the inspiration of Christendom. A mechanical snapshot is for the realist a more reliable and correct copy of the original than a portrait by Rembrandt. But it cannot give the same impression of the personality behind. The presence of a great man, the magic of his voice, the march of his argu-

VII. The Literary Evolution of the Gospels

ment, have a mesmeric influence on those who hear which is lost in the bare transcript of fragmentary sayings and isolated acts such as we find in Mark or Q. Later on, two great though perhaps unconscious artists, trained in the movement begun by the Master, and saturated by His Spirit, retell the tale, idealize—if you will—the picture, but in so doing make us to realize something of the majesty and tenderness which once men knew in Galilee.

An instance will make this clear. The realist may object that the Sermon on the Mount is not the sermon there delivered, but a mosaic of the more striking fragments of perhaps twenty discourses, and may approve rather of St. Mark or Q because there we have the fragments frankly as fragments. But on the hill or by the lake they were not listened to as scattered fragments, but in the illuminating context, and behind the words was ever the speaker's presence. 'The multitude marvelled as they heard,' says Mark in passages where *his* story leaves us cold. We turn to the arresting cadence of the Sermon on the Mount and it is no longer the multitude but *we* that marvel.

Note.—The special question of the development in the eschatological ideas in the several documents is separately treated in an Appendix to this volume; cf. pp. 425 ff.

SYLLABUS

The trial of our Lord before Herod is not, as some critics think, an apocryphal development of the Passion story. The Massacre of Galileans (Herod's subjects) alluded to in Luke xiii. 1-5 illustrates the incident by supplying a reason for the enmity said to have existed between Pilate and Herod, and a motive for Pilate's not wishing to judge another Galilean without reference to his lawful sovereign.

ON THE TRIAL OF OUR LORD BEFORE HEROD—A SUGGESTION

THIS story is dismissed as a legendary accretion by many critics. This view we challenge, (1) because we can detect no apologetic motive for its growth; (2) because the statement (Lk xxiii. 12) that the incident led to a reconciliation between Pilate and Herod so completely illuminates and is illuminated by certain facts elsewhere recorded.

The instinct of the Church very early divined that it was hopeless to try and overcome the opposition of Judaism, but not so that of the Roman Empire. Tradition, therefore, which is always being modified by the instinct and experience of a community, tends more and more to emphasize the responsibility of the Jews for the blood of Christ and to exculpate the Roman Governor. Thus we find that to the story as told by Mark, Matthew adds the washing of Pilate's hands, Luke his triple attempt (Lk xxiii. 22) to placate the Jews and acquit Christ, while John and the apocryphal Gospel of Peter still further emphasize this idea. But it is not obvious how a trial before Herod comes into line with this tendency.

A decisive consideration, however, emerges if we reflect on the light thrown on the enmity and reconciliation of Pilate by the incident told in Lk xiii. 1-5. Our Lord is informed, as if of a recent event ($ἀπαγγέλλοντες$), of a massacre by Pilate of certain Galileans while offering their sacrifices. Such an event would be bound to produce a protest from Herod, their ruler and natural protector; for though a member of the Herod family might not be overparticular about himself shedding the blood of his subjects on occasion, it was a different thing to stand by and see some one else do this. He was especially bound to protest as they had been massacred while performing their religious duties. After his execution of the Prophet John the Baptist, which, doubtless for political reasons, he had sanctioned with much reluctance (Mk vi. 20, 26), he required a little white-washing in the eyes of his subjects. The absolutism of an Oriental monarch is limited by one thing only—the necessity of appearing as an upholder of the Faith. Even the Hellenizing Herod the Great rebuilt the Temple. The protest against the massacre would therefore have been made sufficiently public, and would annoy Pilate considerably, especially as the Herods had influence in high circles at Rome. We may even conjecture that it was on account of this matter, as well as to attend the Passover, that Herod was in Jerusalem at this time.

Consider the situation. Our Lord is accused to Pilate of agitating to make Himself king. He is a Galilean, and His lawful sovereign, Herod, is at hand. If there is really anything in the charge, Herod may quite well be trusted to deal with a claimant to a kingdom which would include his own, and at any rate there will be no more fuss about Pilate's killing Herod's subjects. Herod, however, had once before (Mk vi. 14) described our Lord as a John Baptist risen again, and had no wish to put to death another popular prophet. If He was really dangerous, Pilate would do it for him. Irritated by the refusal of the prisoner to answer him (xxiii. 9), and to propitiate the priests and scribes, he lets his soldiers mock Him and sends Him back to Pilate, doubtless with a polite disclaimer of any desire to interfere with him in necessary measures for dealing with overt rebellion. Pilate is complimented, Herod's 'face' has been saved by this public acknowledgement of his jurisdiction. They can afford to end a dispute which both parties found embarrassing.

An incident which cannot be explained as an apologetic

VIII. The Trial of Our Lord before Herod

development, and which fits in so well with the historical situation, cannot be dismissed as a legendary accretion. If it be asked, Why, then, does it not occur in Mark? we reply it may well have been unknown to Mark.[1] The Apostles fled at the arrest, all except Peter ; and *he* disappeared after the cock crowed. From Mk xiv. 28 and xvi. 7 it would seem as if he went straight to Galilee. Peter, therefore, and the Apostles were themselves dependent on common report at second hand for subsequent details of the trial. Common report would naturally speak of the important trial before Pilate, which led to the condemnation, not of the trial before Herod (a mere parenthesis in the other trial), which led to nothing. St. Luke, who perhaps ultimately through Manaen, Herod's foster-brother (Acts xiii. 1), or Joanna, Herod's steward's wife (Lk viii. 3 ; xxiv. 10), shows a special interest in and knowledge of the Herods, both in the Gospel and Acts, has here an independent and valuable source of information.

[1] Professor Verrall suggests that Pilate and Herod may have lodged when in Jerusalem in adjoining buildings between which communication was possible without the knowledge of the public.

Note.—The suggestion put forward in this essay has been anticipated by Dr. Arthur Wright, *St. Luke's Gospel in Greek* (London, 1900), p. 203 ; but the coincidence was not noticed until after the essay was in type.

IX

THE BOOK OF SAYINGS USED BY THE
EDITOR OF THE FIRST GOSPEL

X

THE ARAMAIC BACKGROUND
OF THE GOSPELS

THE VEN. WILLOUGHBY CHARLES ALLEN, M.A.
Archdeacon of Manchester and Principal of Egerton Hall;
formerly Fellow and Chaplain of Exeter College

SYLLABUS

1. Criticism of Harnack's reconstruction of Q, pp. 235-40.
2. Some criteria for reconstructing the Source used in the First Gospel, pp. 240-2.
3. Text of the Source so reconstructed, pp. 242-72.
4. Summary of its contents, pp. 272-4.
5. Its characteristics, pp. 274-81.
6. It was not used in its original form by Luke, pp. 281-3.
7. Additional Notes:
    (*a*) Numerical arrangement in the Source, p. 283 f.
    (*b*) Jewish phraseology of the Source, pp. 284-6.

THE BOOK OF SAYINGS USED BY THE EDITOR OF THE FIRST GOSPEL

INTRODUCTION [1]

THE criticism of the Synoptic Gospels seems to have reached this point. It is very generally agreed that Matthew and Luke have edited and enlarged the Second Gospel. The points still debated in this connexion are details. The main fact is, as it would seem, undeniable. There is further a very widely held belief that Matthew and Luke had also before them a second source, consisting mainly of discourses; and for some years attempts have been made to reconstruct this.

It was at one time usual to call this alleged discourse source *the Logia*, but as that term seemed to beg disputable questions connected with a statement of Papias about *the Logia* written by Matthew, recent writers have preferred to adopt for it a colourless symbol Q (=Quelle). Harnack[2] has recently set himself to the reconstruction of Q, and as his results are likely to be widely accepted, it is the purpose of this chapter to offer some criticism of both his methods and his results by way of introducing a reconstruction of a discourse source which was used by the editor of the First Gospel.

A. *Methods.*—Briefly put, his method is to place in the source any section or saying that is found in both Matthew and Luke but not in Mark. The assumption behind this is that wherever two writers agree closely in their records they are borrowing from a common source. As regards this I would only say that I am not prepared to contest

---

[1] A portion of what follows appeared in the *Expository Times* for July, 1909, and is reprinted here by the courtesy of the Editor of that magazine.
[2] *The Sayings of Jesus* (Crown Theological Library).

the general position that the literary agreement between Matthew and Luke in sections common to them is so great that literary dependence in some form must be assumed.

But I would only urge that it does not follow that if these two writers agree closely in many sections all these sections must have come from a single source. They agree, e.g., closely in the case of the Sermon on the Mount. They also agree closely in the account of John's preaching. It does not follow that the sermon and the account of John were found in the same common source. They may have been found there. They may also have been in two separate sources. So far as St. Luke is concerned, he expressly tells us that he was acquainted with the works of many Gospel writers.

On this method of collecting together passages common to Matthew and Luke, in which there is close verbal agreement, Harnack builds up a document which he supposes that these writers used. It contains :—

1. An account of John's preaching.
2. The Temptation and perhaps the Baptism.
3. A good deal of the Sermon on the Mount, followed by the Healing of the Centurion's Servant.
4. The Two Aspirants.
5. Sayings to the disciples about their mission.
6. The discourse about the Baptist, with the two sequels, woes against Bethsaida and Chorazin, and the Thanksgiving to the Father.
7. The Beelzebub section and the sign of Jonah.
8. Woes against the Pharisees.
9. Discourse about the Parousia, and other sayings.

Now, in the first place, a document which contained the material above tabulated would be a very curious sort of Gospel writing. Presumably the purpose of the writer was to collect noteworthy sayings of Christ, and most of the material is of that nature. But what then has the record

IX. Book of Sayings and the First Gospel 237

of the preaching of the Baptist to do in such a work? This would be intelligible enough as an introduction in any historical or biographical narrative of Christ's life, but what has it to do with a collection of Christ's sayings?

Again, the document thus reconstructed contains for the most part sayings or groups of sayings. In the midst of this appears quite unexpectedly a miracle, that of the *Centurion's Servant*. What has this to do in a collection of sayings? A little later there is another miracle, the healing of a dumb demoniac before the Beelzebub discourse. But the two cases are not parallel. Q, as reconstructed by Harnack, contains several instances of a very slight narrative setting to a series of sayings; cf. for example, the *Two Aspirants*, or the *Sending of John's disciples*, or the *Demand for a Sign*. Harnack, by linking together these and one or two other such references to fact, makes up what he calls seven narrative sections, but in reality only one is a narrative section, viz. the *Centurion's Servant*; and the others, including the Beelzebub miracle, are quite different in nature, being not self-contained narratives, but mere allusions to fact which serve as an introduction to a saying or groups of sayings. The narrative of the *Centurion's Servant* is therefore really isolated in Q. And we cannot help asking what right it has to be there. The central point of the story is not Christ's *saying*, 'Not even in Israel have I found such faith' (for as a saying apart from its context that has no meaning), but the *facts* that Christ could heal by a word, and that He had done such a healing for the servant of a centurion.

What has a compilation of discourses in common with a narrative section like this? Or, if the compiler admitted it, then surely his book must have contained other miracles and narratives, and have been of a very different character from the source as reconstructed by Harnack.

Further, Harnack puts into his source eleven instances

of what he calls Parables. But just as he uses the word *narrative* to cover mere references to fact, so he here uses *parable* to cover analogies, similes, &c. Of his eleven cases only four are formal parables. They are the Two Builders, the Leaven, the Mustard Seed, and the Children in the Market-place. The rest are metaphors or allegorical allusions. Now here is a strange thing, that in a document professing to be a collection of some of Christ's sayings there should be only four parables. The inference is obvious. Harnack's reconstructed source is at least incomplete. If there really was a collection of Christ's sayings it must have contained more parables than these four, and those that are missing might very materially affect our judgement of the nature of the document.

And lastly, the reconstructed source brings with it almost as many difficulties as it solves, for it is only possible to explain the text of our two Gospels as reproductions of it by ascribing to the two Evangelists, or to one of them, a freedom of dealing with it which it is hard to reconcile with the probability, admitted by Harnack, that it was of Apostolic origin. How explain, for example, the two presentations of the *Beatitudes* or of the *Lord's Prayer* on the supposition that the Evangelists had before them in an Apostolic document one and the same record of each of these items? Surely the inference here is irresistible that the differences in these sections between the two writers is not due to the fact that they are arbitrarily altering words, which they both had before them in the same form, but that they are reproducing different traditions of the Lord's words.

However, we might perhaps assent that the principle of putting into a common source all that is common to Matthew and Luke alone is not very likely to be far wrong, and that there is some probability that most of the above material occurred in a document lying behind our First and Third Gospels.

IX. Book of Sayings and the First Gospel 239

But two other words of caution are here needed. Before we proceed to discuss the character of this source and its theology we ought to be sure that we really have sufficient data for so doing. This is just where Harnack's method seems to me to break down. (1) We cannot be sure that the source did not contain much more than the material collected above. Either Matthew alone or Luke alone may contain material which belonged to it, or the source may have contained much which neither of these writers have borrowed from it. (2) If so, this lost material, or this material found in only one Gospel, if added to that which Harnack puts into his Q, might very considerably modify our impression of its general characteristics and of its theology.

B. *Results.*—Now Harnack, after reconstructing his document, attempts to characterize its theology, and draws inferences from that as to its date.

There is in it no reference to the Passion. Therefore the central feature of the Gospel message was not Christ as Redeemer, but Christ as Teacher and Prophet of the Kingdom. Therefore the book was compiled before Mark wrote his Gospel, but not too early: otherwise Mark would have used it.

Ramsay[1] tries to improve on Harnack here. He assumes that Harnack's conception of Q is right in the main, but argues that no Christian disciple could have written such a book after Christ's death, or at any rate after Pentecost. It must, therefore, have been composed during Christ's lifetime.

Ramsay is no doubt right that Harnack's Q is inexplicable as a production of a Christian disciple in the first thirty years after the Lord's death, but this fact should lead us not to try and find a possible date during Christ's lifetime for the work, but to ask whether such a document as Har-

[1] *Luke the Physician*, p. 89.

nack gives us ever existed at all. The inference again presses: the source must have contained much more than is given in Harnack's reconstruction, and the missing material might give quite a different character to the work, and make it an intelligible production of the early days of Christianity.

And the data exist for the discovery of the missing material. It is not far to seek, for it lies embedded in the First Gospel. Harnack gives as characteristic features of the source as reconstructed by him, 'Jewish horizon and sentiment' and 'conflict against the Pharisees'. He also says that the conception of the 'Kingdom of God' is that of a future kingdom in Mt viii. 11 = Lk xiii. 28 ; Mt xxiii. 13 = Lk xi. 52; Mt vii. 21 = Lk vi. 46; Mt x. 7 = Lk ix. 2, and Mt vi. 33 = Lk xii. 31; whilst in four other places, viz. Mt xii. 28 = Lk xi. 20 ; Mt xiii. 33, 31 = Lk xiii. 20, 18; Mt xi. 11 = Lk vii. 28, and Mt xi. 12 = Lk xvi. 16, the kingdom is regarded as already present.

Now the exact phrases in these passages are these:—

	Mt			Lk			Harnack		
viii. 11	βασιλεία τῶν οὐρανῶν			βασιλεία τοῦ θεοῦ			βασιλεία τοῦ θεοῦ		
xxiii. 13	,,	,,	,,	otherwise			,,	,,	,,
vii. 21	,,	,,	,,	otherwise			,,	,,	,,
x. 7	,,	,,	,,	βασιλεία τοῦ θεοῦ			,,	,,	,,
vi. 33	βασιλεία			βασιλεία αὐτοῦ			βασιλεία αὐτοῦ		
xii. 28	βασιλεία τοῦ θεοῦ			βασιλεία τοῦ θεοῦ			βασιλεία τοῦ θεοῦ		
xiii. 33	βασιλεία τῶν οὐρανῶν			βασιλεία τοῦ θεοῦ			βασιλεία τοῦ θεοῦ		
31	,,	,,	,,	,,	,,	,,	,,	,,	,,
xi. 11	,,	,,	,,	,,	,,	,,	,,	,,	,,
12	,,	,,	,,	,,	,,	,,	,,	,,	,,

It will be seen that so far as these passages are concerned Matthew eight times has βασιλεία τῶν οὐρανῶν where Luke has βασιλεία τοῦ θεοῦ (if he has any equivalent words), while Matthew only once has βασιλεία τοῦ θεοῦ.

This is one of several cases where Harnack seems to

IX. Book of Sayings and the First Gospel

arrive at faulty conceptions of the theology of Q because he has followed Luke's modifications of the language of Q rather than Matthew's more accurate preservation of it. Another case is that of the phrase ὁ πατὴρ ὁ ἐν τοῖς οὐρανοῖς, from which Harnack everywhere omits the descriptive clause. In this, and in other similar cases, he is removing from the source what were probably some of its most important and striking characteristics. Of course Harnack has an answer to this. He argues that these phrases appear also in passages which are not dependent upon Q, and that they are therefore characteristic, not of Q but of the Editor of the First Gospel. Now the phrases in question, like much else of the terminology of Q, belong to the current Jewish religious language. The terms are technical religious terms. Which is the more likely, that Matthew, writing at a comparatively late date, should have thrust into Mark and into Q a whole series of technical Jewish terms, or that he found them already in his earliest source and was so influenced by them that he used them when rewriting the Second Gospel?

As regards Harnack's distinction between the kingdom as present and future, all the cases, where Matthew has βασιλεία τῶν οὐρανῶν or simply βασιλεία, probably denote the future kingdom, a conception which we shall find to be highly characteristic of Matthew's source. If Matthew has βασιλεία τοῦ θεοῦ in xii. 28, that only shows that the source exceptionally used this phrase, the reason here perhaps being the influence of the preceding πνεύματι θεοῦ.[1]

We find then amongst the characteristics of the source (a) 'Jewish horizon and sentiment'; (b) 'conflict against the Pharisees'; (c) 'the eschatological conception of the kingdom'. Now if we apply these criteria to some of the sayings in Matthew which Harnack does not admit into his source, we shall find that they have a claim to admission there. E. g., v. 20 is anti-Pharisaic; so are vi. 1–18 and

[1] But see below, p. 277, and *St. Matthew*, p. 227.

xv. 12-13. The following are marked by Jewish horizon and sentiment: vi. 10ᵇ 'Thy will be done', vii. 6 'swine' = Gentiles, x. 5ᵇ-8, 23, xv. 23-4, and xxiv. 20; and the following by Jewish phraseology: xvi. 17-19, xviii. 14, 16-20.

In the following pages an attempt has been made to reconstruct the source which was used by the Editor of the First Gospel not simply on the method used by Harnack of throwing into it passages common to Matthew and Luke alone, but on the principle that the sayings in Matthew, over and above those already found in Mark, when put together present us with a homogeneous, consistent, and intelligible work (no doubt only fragmentary). This source was a collection of Christ's discourses and sayings compiled to represent certain aspects of His teaching, and was marked by a very characteristic phraseology.

§ 1. The Text.[1]

A Discourse (Sermon on the Mount).

A. Nine Beatitudes. Mt v. 3-12 (cf. Lk vi. 20-3).

v. 3 Μακάριοι οἱ πτωχοὶ τῷ πνεύματι· ὅτι αὐτῶν ἐστιν ἡ βασιλεία τῶν οὐρανῶν.

4 μακάριοι οἱ πενθοῦντες· ὅτι αὐτοὶ παρακληθήσονται.

5 μακάριοι οἱ πραεῖς· ὅτι αὐτοὶ κληρονομήσουσι τὴν γῆν.

6 μακάριοι οἱ πεινῶντες καὶ διψῶντες τὴν δικαιοσύνην· ὅτι αὐτοὶ χορτασθήσονται.

7 μακάριοι οἱ ἐλεήμονες· ὅτι αὐτοὶ ἐλεηθήσονται.

8 μακάριοι οἱ καθαροὶ τῇ καρδίᾳ· ὅτι αὐτοὶ τὸν Θεὸν ὄψονται.

---

[1] For the sake of convenience the Greek text here printed is taken from *The Greek Testament with the Readings adopted by the Revisers of the Authorized Version*. Words and phrases printed in heavy type seem to be characteristic of the source. But no attempt is here made to reproduce the exact wording of the source as it lay before the Editor of the First Gospel.

IX. Book of Sayings and the First Gospel 243

9 μακάριοι οἱ εἰρηνοποιοί· ὅτι αὐτοὶ υἱοὶ Θεοῦ κληθήσονται.

10 μακάριοι οἱ δεδιωγμένοι ἔνεκεν **δικαιοσύνης**· ὅτι αὐτῶν ἐστιν ἡ βασιλεία τῶν οὐρανῶν.

11 μακάριοί ἐστε, ὅταν ὀνειδίσωσιν ὑμᾶς καὶ διώξωσι, καὶ εἴπωσι πᾶν **πονηρὸν** καθ᾽ ὑμῶν ψευδόμενοι, ἕνεκεν ἐμοῦ.

12 χαίρετε καὶ ἀγαλλιᾶσθε· ὅτι ὁ **μισθὸς** ὑμῶν πολὺς ἐν τοῖς οὐρανοῖς· οὕτω γὰρ ἐδίωξαν τοὺς προφήτας τοὺς πρὸ ὑμῶν.

B. The Old Law and the current 'righteousness' not abolished. Mt v. 17, 20.

17 Μὴ νομίσητε ὅτι ἦλθον καταλῦσαι τὸν νόμον ἢ τοὺς προφήτας· οὐκ ἦλθον καταλῦσαι, ἀλλὰ πληρῶσαι.

20 λέγω γὰρ ὑμῖν, ὅτι ἐὰν μὴ περισσεύσῃ ἡ **δικαιοσύνη** ὑμῶν πλεῖον τῶν γραμματέων καὶ Φαρισαίων, οὐ μὴ εἰσέλθητε εἰς τὴν βασιλείαν τῶν οὐρανῶν.

C. Two series of three examples and illustrations of a new conception of the fulfilment of the Law. Mt v. 21-48.

(a) (1) Murder.

21 Ἠκούσατε ὅτι ἐρρέθη τοῖς ἀρχαίοις, Οὐ φονεύσεις, ὃς δ᾽ ἂν φονεύσῃ, ἔνοχος ἔσται τῇ κρίσει·

22 ἐγὼ δὲ λέγω ὑμῖν, ὅτι πᾶς ὁ ὀργιζόμενος τῷ **ἀδελφῷ αὐτοῦ** ἔνοχος ἔσται τῇ κρίσει.

22 After αὐτοῦ D al S¹ S² add εἰκῇ.

23 ἐὰν οὖν προσφέρῃς τὸ δῶρόν σου ἐπὶ τὸ θυσιαστήριον, κἀκεῖ μνησθῇς ὅτι ὁ **ἀδελφός** σου ἔχει τι κατὰ σοῦ,

24 ἄφες ἐκεῖ τὸ δῶρόν σου ἔμπροσθεν τοῦ θυσιαστηρίου, καὶ ὕπαγε, πρῶτον διαλλάγηθι τῷ **ἀδελφῷ** σου, καὶ τότε ἐλθὼν πρόσφερε τὸ δῶρόν σου.

(2) Adultery.

27 Ἠκούσατε ὅτι ἐρρέθη, Οὐ μοιχεύσεις·

28 ἐγὼ δὲ λέγω ὑμῖν, ὅτι πᾶς ὁ βλέπων γυναῖκα πρὸς τὸ ἐπιθυμῆσαι αὐτῆς ἤδη ἐμοίχευσεν αὐτὴν ἐν τῇ καρδίᾳ αὐτοῦ.

(3) Divorce.

31 Ἐρρέθη δὲ ὅτι Ὃς ἂν ἀπολύσῃ τὴν γυναῖκα αὐτοῦ, δότω αὐτῇ ἀποστάσιον·

32 ἐγὼ δὲ λέγω ὑμῖν, ὅτι πᾶς ὁ ἀπολύων τὴν γυναῖκα αὐτοῦ, παρεκτὸς λόγου πορνείας, ποιεῖ αὐτὴν μοιχευθῆναι· καὶ ὃς ἐὰν ἀπολελυμένην γαμήσῃ, μοιχᾶται.

(b) (1) Oaths.

33 Πάλιν ἠκούσατε ὅτι ἐρρέθη τοῖς ἀρχαίοις, Οὐκ ἐπιορκήσεις, ἀποδώσεις δὲ τῷ Κυρίῳ τοὺς ὅρκους σου·

34 ἐγὼ δὲ λέγω ὑμῖν μὴ ὀμόσαι ὅλως· μήτε ἐν τῷ οὐρανῷ, ὅτι θρόνος ἐστὶ τοῦ Θεοῦ·

35 μήτε ἐν τῇ γῇ, ὅτι ὑποπόδιόν ἐστι τῶν ποδῶν αὐτοῦ· μήτε εἰς Ἱεροσόλυμα, ὅτι πόλις ἐστὶ τοῦ μεγάλου βασιλέως·

36 μήτε ἐν τῇ κεφαλῇ σου ὀμόσῃς, ὅτι οὐ δύνασαι μίαν τρίχα λευκὴν ἢ μέλαιναν ποιῆσαι.

37 ἔστω δὲ ὁ λόγος ὑμῶν, Ναὶ ναί, Οὒ οὔ· τὸ δὲ περισσὸν τούτων ἐκ τοῦ πονηροῦ ἐστιν.

(2) Retaliation.

38 Ἠκούσατε ὅτι ἐρρέθη, Ὀφθαλμὸν ἀντὶ ὀφθαλμοῦ, καὶ ὀδόντα ἀντὶ ὀδόντος·

39 ἐγὼ δὲ λέγω ὑμῖν μὴ ἀντιστῆναι τῷ πονηρῷ· ἀλλ' ὅστις σε ῥαπίζει εἰς τὴν δεξιάν σου σιαγόνα, στρέψον αὐτῷ καὶ τὴν ἄλλην·

40 καὶ τῷ θέλοντί σοι κριθῆναι καὶ τὸν χιτῶνά σου λαβεῖν ἄφες αὐτῷ καὶ τὸ ἱμάτιον·

41 καὶ ὅστις σε ἀγγαρεύσει μίλιον ἕν, ὕπαγε μετ' αὐτοῦ δύο·

42 τῷ αἰτοῦντί σε δίδου, καὶ τὸν θέλοντα ἀπὸ σοῦ δανείσασθαι μὴ ἀποστραφῇς.

For vv. 39, 40, 41, 42, cf. Lk vi. 29, 30, 34.

IX. Book of Sayings and the First Gospel 245

(3) Love to enemies.

43 Ἠκούσατε ὅτι ἐρρέθη, Ἀγαπήσεις τὸν πλησίον σου, καὶ μισήσεις τὸν ἐχθρόν σου·

44 ἐγὼ δὲ λέγω ὑμῖν, ἀγαπᾶτε τοὺς ἐχθροὺς ὑμῶν, καὶ προσεύχεσθε ὑπὲρ τῶν διωκόντων ὑμᾶς·

45 ὅπως γένησθε υἱοὶ **τοῦ πατρὸς ὑμῶν τοῦ ἐν οὐρανοῖς·** ὅτι τὸν ἥλιον αὐτοῦ ἀνατέλλει ἐπὶ **πονηροὺς** καὶ ἀγαθούς, καὶ βρέχει ἐπὶ δικαίους καὶ ἀδίκους.

46 ἐὰν γὰρ ἀγαπήσητε τοὺς ἀγαπῶντας ὑμᾶς, τίνα **μισθὸν** ἔχετε; οὐχὶ καὶ οἱ τελῶναι τὸ αὐτὸ ποιοῦσι;

47 καὶ ἐὰν ἀσπάσησθε τοὺς ἀδελφοὺς ὑμῶν μόνον, τί περισσὸν ποιεῖτε; οὐχὶ καὶ οἱ **ἐθνικοὶ** τὸ αὐτὸ ποιοῦσιν;

48 ἔσεσθε οὖν ὑμεῖς τέλειοι, ὡς ὁ **πατὴρ ὑμῶν ὁ οὐράνιος** τέλειός ἐστι.

For vv. 44, 46–8, cf. Lk vi. 27, 28, 32, 33, 35, 36.

D. Three illustrations of the better 'righteousness' of verse 20. vi. 1–18.

(1) Almsgiving.

vi. 1 Προσέχετε τὴν δικαιοσύνην ὑμῶν μὴ ποιεῖν ἔμπροσθεν τῶν ἀνθρώπων πρὸς τὸ θεαθῆναι αὐτοῖς· εἰ δὲ μήγε, μισθὸν οὐκ ἔχετε παρὰ τῷ πατρὶ ὑμῶν τῷ ἐν τοῖς οὐρανοῖς.

2 Ὅταν οὖν ποιῇς ἐλεημοσύνην, μὴ σαλπίσῃς ἔμπροσθέν σου, ὥσπερ οἱ ὑποκριταὶ ποιοῦσιν ἐν ταῖς συναγωγαῖς καὶ ἐν ταῖς ῥύμαις, ὅπως δοξασθῶσιν ὑπὸ τῶν ἀνθρώπων· ἀμὴν λέγω ὑμῖν, ἀπέχουσι τὸν μισθὸν αὐτῶν.

3 σοῦ δὲ ποιοῦντος ἐλεημοσύνην, μὴ γνώτω ἡ ἀριστερά σου τί ποιεῖ ἡ δεξιά σου·

4 ὅπως ᾖ σου ἡ ἐλεημοσύνη ἐν τῷ κρυπτῷ· καὶ ὁ **πατήρ** σου ὁ βλέπων ἐν τῷ κρυπτῷ ἀποδώσει σοι.

(2) Prayer.

5 Καὶ ὅταν προσεύχησθε οὐκ ἔσεσθε ὡς οἱ ὑποκριταί·

ὅτι φιλοῦσιν ἐν ταῖς συναγωγαῖς καὶ ἐν ταῖς γωνίαις τῶν πλατειῶν ἑστῶτες προσεύχεσθαι, ὅπως ἂν φανῶσι τοῖς ἀνθρώποις· ἀμὴν λέγω ὑμῖν, ὅτι ἀπέχουσι τὸν μισθὸν αὐτῶν.

6 σὺ δέ, ὅταν προσεύχῃ, εἴσελθε εἰς τὸ ταμιεῖόν σου, καὶ κλείσας τὴν θύραν σου πρόσευξαι τῷ **πατρί σου** τῷ ἐν τῷ κρυπτῷ· καὶ ὁ **πατήρ σου** ὁ βλέπων ἐν τῷ κρυπτῷ ἀποδώσει σοι.

(3) Fasting.

16 Ὅταν δὲ νηστεύητε, μὴ γίνεσθε, ὡς οἱ **ὑποκριταί**, σκυθρωποί· ἀφανίζουσι γὰρ τὰ πρόσωπα αὐτῶν, ὅπως φανῶσι **τοῖς ἀνθρώποις** νηστεύοντες· ἀμὴν λέγω ὑμῖν, ὅτι ἀπέχουσι τὸν **μισθὸν αὐτῶν**.

17 σὺ δὲ νηστεύων ἄλειψαί σου τὴν κεφαλήν, καὶ τὸ πρόσωπόν σου νίψαι·

18 ὅπως μὴ φανῇς **τοῖς ἀνθρώποις** νηστεύων, ἀλλὰ τῷ **πατρί σου** τῷ ἐν τῷ κρυπτῷ· καὶ ὁ **πατήρ σου** ὁ βλέπων ἐν τῷ κρυπτῷ ἀποδώσει σοι.

E. But avoid harsh judgements.

vii. 1 Μὴ κρίνετε, ἵνα μὴ κριθῆτε·

2 ἐν ᾧ γὰρ κρίματι κρίνετε κριθήσεσθε, καὶ ἐν ᾧ μέτρῳ μετρεῖτε μετρηθήσεται ὑμῖν.

3 τί δὲ βλέπεις τὸ κάρφος τὸ ἐν τῷ ὀφθαλμῷ τοῦ ἀδελφοῦ σου, τὴν δὲ ἐν τῷ σῷ ὀφθαλμῷ δοκὸν οὐ κατανοεῖς;

4 ἢ πῶς ἐρεῖς τῷ ἀδελφῷ σου, Ἄφες ἐκβάλω τὸ κάρφος ἐκ τοῦ ὀφθαλμοῦ σου· καὶ ἰδού, ἡ δοκὸς ἐν τῷ ὀφθαλμῷ σου;

5 ὑποκριτά, ἔκβαλε πρῶτον τὴν δοκὸν ἐκ τοῦ ὀφθαλμοῦ σου, καὶ τότε διαβλέψεις ἐκβαλεῖν τὸ κάρφος ἐκ τοῦ ὀφθαλμοῦ τοῦ ἀδελφοῦ σου.

Cf. Lk vi. 37, 38, 41, 42.

F. Do not thrust your religion upon others.

6 Μὴ δῶτε τὸ ἅγιον τοῖς κυσί, μηδὲ βάλητε τοὺς

IX. Book of Sayings and the First Gospel 247

μαργαρίτας ὑμῶν ἔμπροσθεν τῶν χοίρων, μήποτε καταπατήσωσιν αὐτοὺς ἐν τοῖς ποσὶν αὐτῶν, καὶ στραφέντες ῥήξωσιν ὑμᾶς.

G. But observe the rule of love.

12 Πάντα οὖν ὅσα ἂν θέλητε ἵνα ποιῶσιν ὑμῖν οἱ ἄνθρωποι, οὕτω καὶ ὑμεῖς ποιεῖτε αὐτοῖς· οὗτος γάρ ἐστιν ὁ νόμος καὶ οἱ προφῆται.

Cf. Lk vi. 31.

H. Beware of false prophets.

15 Προσέχετε ἀπὸ τῶν ψευδοπροφητῶν, οἵτινες ἔρχονται πρὸς ὑμᾶς ἐν ἐνδύμασι προβάτων, ἔσωθεν δέ εἰσι λύκοι ἅρπαγες.

16 ἀπὸ τῶν καρπῶν αὐτῶν ἐπιγνώσεσθε αὐτούς.

21 Οὐ πᾶς ὁ λέγων μοι, Κύριε, Κύριε, εἰσελεύσεται εἰς τὴν βασιλείαν τῶν οὐρανῶν, ἀλλ' ὁ ποιῶν τὸ θέλημα τοῦ πατρός μου τοῦ ἐν οὐρανοῖς.

22 πολλοὶ ἐροῦσί μοι ἐν ἐκείνῃ τῇ ἡμέρᾳ, Κύριε, Κύριε, οὐ τῷ σῷ ὀνόματι προεφητεύσαμεν, καὶ τῷ σῷ ὀνόματι δαιμόνια ἐξεβάλομεν, καὶ τῷ σῷ ὀνόματι δυνάμεις πολλὰς ἐποιήσαμεν;

23 καὶ τότε ὁμολογήσω αὐτοῖς ὅτι Οὐδέποτε ἔγνων ὑμᾶς· ἀποχωρεῖτε ἀπ' ἐμοῦ οἱ ἐργαζόμενοι τὴν ἀνομίαν.

For 21, cf. Lk vi. 46, and for 22 and 23, cf. Lk xiii. 26, 27.

I. Concluding Parable.

vii. 24 Πᾶς οὖν ὅστις ἀκούει μου τοὺς λόγους τούτους, καὶ ποιεῖ αὐτούς, ὁμοιωθήσεται ἀνδρὶ φρονίμῳ, ὅστις ᾠκοδόμησε τὴν οἰκίαν αὐτοῦ ἐπὶ τὴν πέτραν·

25 καὶ κατέβη ἡ βροχὴ καὶ ἦλθον οἱ ποταμοὶ καὶ ἔπνευσαν οἱ ἄνεμοι, καὶ προσέπεσον τῇ οἰκίᾳ ἐκείνῃ, καὶ οὐκ ἔπεσε· τεθεμελίωτο γὰρ ἐπὶ τὴν πέτραν.

26 καὶ πᾶς ὁ ἀκούων μου τοὺς λόγους τούτους, καὶ μὴ ποιῶν αὐτούς, ὁμοιωθήσεται ἀνδρὶ μωρῷ, ὅστις ᾠκοδόμησε τὴν οἰκίαν αὐτοῦ ἐπὶ τὴν ἄμμον·

27 καὶ κατέβη ἡ βροχὴ καὶ ἦλθον οἱ ποταμοὶ καὶ ἔπνευ-

σαν οἱ ἄνεμοι, καὶ προσέκοψαν τῇ οἰκίᾳ ἐκείνῃ, καὶ ἔπεσεν· καὶ ἦν ἡ πτῶσις αὐτῆς μεγάλη.

Cf. Lk vi. 47-9.

A Discourse to the Disciples about their Mission.

ix. 37-8 Ὁ μὲν θερισμὸς πολύς, οἱ δὲ ἐργάται ὀλίγοι· δεήθητε οὖν τοῦ κυρίου τοῦ θερισμοῦ, ὅπως ἐκβάλῃ ἐργάτας εἰς τὸν θερισμὸν αὐτοῦ.

Cf. Lk x. 2.

x. 5ᵇ-8 Εἰς ὁδὸν ἐθνῶν μὴ ἀπέλθητε, καὶ εἰς πόλιν Σαμαρειτῶν μὴ εἰσέλθητε· πορεύεσθε δὲ μᾶλλον πρὸς τὰ πρόβατα τὰ ἀπολωλότα οἴκου Ἰσραήλ. πορευόμενοι δὲ κηρύσσετε λέγοντες ὅτι **Ἤγγικεν ἡ βασιλεία τῶν οὐρανῶν.** ἀσθενοῦντας θεραπεύετε, νεκροὺς ἐγείρετε, λεπροὺς καθαρίζετε, δαιμόνια ἐκβάλλετε· δωρεὰν ἐλάβετε, δωρεὰν δότε.

x. 10ᵇ Ἄξιος γὰρ ὁ ἐργάτης τῆς τροφῆς αὐτοῦ ἐστιν.

Cf. Lk x. 7.

x. 12-13 Εἰσερχόμενοι δὲ εἰς τὴν οἰκίαν ἀσπάσασθε αὐτήν· καὶ ἐὰν μὲν ᾖ ἡ οἰκία ἀξία, ἐλθέτω ἡ εἰρήνη ὑμῶν ἐπ' αὐτήν· ἐὰν δὲ μὴ ᾖ ἀξία, ἡ εἰρήνη ὑμῶν πρὸς ὑμᾶς ἐπιστραφήτω.

Cf. Lk x. 5, 6.

x. 15-16 Ἀμὴν λέγω ὑμῖν, ἀνεκτότερον ἔσται γῇ Σοδόμων καὶ Γομόρρων ἐν ἡμέρᾳ κρίσεως ἢ τῇ πόλει ἐκείνῃ. Ἰδού, ἐγὼ ἀποστέλλω ὑμᾶς ὡς πρόβατα ἐν μέσῳ λύκων· γίνεσθε οὖν φρόνιμοι ὡς οἱ ὄφεις, καὶ ἀκέραιοι ὡς αἱ περιστεραί.

For v. 15, cf. Lk x. 12, and for v. 16, cf. Lk x. 3.

x. 23 Ὅταν δὲ διώκωσιν ὑμᾶς ἐν τῇ πόλει ταύτῃ, φεύγετε εἰς τὴν ἑτέραν. ἀμὴν γὰρ λέγω ὑμῖν, οὐ μὴ τελέσητε τὰς πόλεις τοῦ Ἰσραήλ, ἕως ἂν ἔλθῃ ὁ υἱὸς τοῦ ἀνθρώπου.

It is probable that this discourse in the source contained more than the verses printed above.

For Mt x. 5ᵃ, 9, 10ᵃ, 11, and 14 are borrowed from

IX. *Book of Sayings and the First Gospel* 249

Mk vi. 8-13. But certain modifications of Mark's words in these verses as reproduced by Matthew, and the agreement of Luke in these modifications, suggest that Matthew and Luke are both combining other accounts of the charge with Mark. In the case of Matthew this other account would be the discourse source.

A Discourse about Persecution.

x. 24-41 Οὐκ ἔστι μαθητὴς ὑπὲρ τὸν διδάσκαλον, οὐδὲ δοῦλος ὑπὲρ τὸν κύριον αὐτοῦ. ἀρκετὸν τῷ μαθητῇ ἵνα γένηται ὡς ὁ διδάσκαλος αὐτοῦ, καὶ ὁ δοῦλος ὡς ὁ κύριος αὐτοῦ. εἰ τὸν οἰκοδεσπότην Βεελζεβοὺλ ἐπεκάλεσαν, πόσῳ μᾶλλον τοὺς οἰκιακοὺς αὐτοῦ; μὴ οὖν φοβηθῆτε αὐτούς· οὐδὲν γάρ ἐστι κεκαλυμμένον, ὃ οὐκ ἀποκαλυφθήσεται, καὶ κρυπτόν, ὃ οὐ γνωσθήσεται. ὃ λέγω ὑμῖν ἐν τῇ σκοτίᾳ, εἴπατε ἐν τῷ φωτί· καὶ ὃ εἰς τὸ οὖς ἀκούετε, κηρύξατε ἐπὶ τῶν δωμάτων. καὶ μὴ φοβηθῆτε ἀπὸ τῶν ἀποκτεινόντων τὸ σῶμα, τὴν δὲ ψυχὴν μὴ δυναμένων ἀποκτεῖναι· φοβήθητε δὲ μᾶλλον τὸν δυνάμενον καὶ ψυχὴν καὶ σῶμα ἀπολέσαι ἐν γεέννῃ. οὐχὶ δύο στρουθία ἀσσαρίου πωλεῖται; καὶ ἓν ἐξ αὐτῶν οὐ πεσεῖται ἐπὶ τὴν γῆν ἄνευ **τοῦ πατρὸς ὑμῶν**· ὑμῶν δὲ καὶ αἱ τρίχες τῆς κεφαλῆς πᾶσαι ἠριθμημέναι εἰσί. μὴ οὖν φοβηθῆτε· πολλῶν στρουθίων διαφέρετε ὑμεῖς. πᾶς οὖν ὅστις ὁμολογήσει ἐν ἐμοὶ **ἔμπροσθεν τῶν ἀνθρώπων**, ὁμολογήσω κἀγὼ ἐν αὐτῷ **ἔμπροσθεν τοῦ πατρός μου τοῦ ἐν οὐρανοῖς**· ὅστις δ' ἂν ἀρνήσηταί με **ἔμπροσθεν τῶν ἀνθρώπων**, ἀρνήσομαι αὐτὸν κἀγὼ **ἔμπροσθεν τοῦ πατρός μου τοῦ ἐν οὐρανοῖς**. Μὴ νομίσητε ὅτι ἦλθον βαλεῖν εἰρήνην ἐπὶ τὴν γῆν· οὐκ ἦλθον βαλεῖν εἰρήνην, ἀλλὰ μάχαιραν. ἦλθον γὰρ διχάσαι ἄνθρωπον κατὰ τοῦ πατρὸς αὐτοῦ, καὶ θυγατέρα κατὰ τῆς μητρὸς αὐτῆς, καὶ νύμφην κατὰ τῆς πενθερᾶς αὐτῆς· καὶ ἐχθροὶ τοῦ ἀνθρώπου οἱ οἰκιακοὶ αὐτοῦ. ὁ φιλῶν πατέρα ἢ μητέρα ὑπὲρ ἐμὲ οὐκ ἔστι μου ἄξιος· καὶ ὁ φιλῶν υἱὸν ἢ θυγατέρα ὑπὲρ ἐμὲ οὐκ ἔστι μου ἄξιος· καὶ ὃς οὐ λαμβάνει τὸν σταυρὸν αὐτοῦ καὶ ἀκολουθεῖ ὀπίσω μου, οὐκ ἔστι μου ἄξιος. ὁ εὑρὼν τὴν ψυχὴν αὐτοῦ ἀπολέσει αὐτήν· καὶ ὁ ἀπολέσας τὴν ψυχὴν αὐτοῦ ἕνεκεν ἐμοῦ εὑρήσει αὐτήν. Ὁ δεχόμενος ὑμᾶς ἐμὲ δέχεται, καὶ ὁ ἐμὲ δεχόμενος δέχεται τὸν ἀποστείλαντά με· ὁ δεχόμενος προφήτην εἰς ὄνομα προφήτου μισθὸν προφήτου λήψεται, καὶ ὁ δεχόμενος δίκαιον εἰς ὄνομα δικαίου μισθὸν δικαίου λήψεται.

For v. 24ª, cf. Lk vi. 40; vv. 26-33, cf. Lk xii. 2-9; vv. 34-5, cf. Lk xii. 51-3; vv. 37-8, cf. Lk xiv. 26-7; v. 39, cf. Lk xvii. 33. See *St. Matthew*, p. 111.[1]

It is not likely that the verses printed above all occurred in a block in the source.

In x. 17-22 the Editor of the First Gospel had added to his account of Christ's Charge to the Twelve verses which he borrowed from Mk xiii. 9ᵇ-13 relating to the persecutions which disciples would have to endure in their missionary work. It occurred to him then to add from the discourse source other sayings about persecution. vv. 24-33 may well have stood together in the source. But vv. 34-40 have no particular connexion with the tenor either of the whole chapter (Charge to the Twelve) or of the vv. 24-33 (persecution) which precede them. They may be made up of sayings which occurred in the source as detached sayings or fragments.

A Discourse about St. John the Baptist.

xi. 2-11 Ὁ δὲ Ἰωάννης, ἀκούσας ἐν τῷ δεσμωτηρίῳ τὰ ἔργα τοῦ Χριστοῦ, πέμψας διὰ τῶν μαθητῶν αὐτοῦ εἶπεν αὐτῷ, Σὺ εἶ ὁ ἐρχόμενος; ἢ ἕτερον προσδοκῶμεν; καὶ ἀποκριθεὶς ὁ Ἰησοῦς εἶπεν αὐτοῖς, Πορευθέντες ἀπαγγείλατε Ἰωάννῃ ἃ ἀκούετε καὶ βλέπετε· τυφλοὶ ἀναβλέπουσι, καὶ χωλοὶ περιπατοῦσι· λεπροὶ καθαρίζονται, καὶ κωφοὶ ἀκούουσι· καὶ νεκροὶ ἐγείρονται, καὶ πτωχοὶ εὐαγγελίζονται· καὶ μακάριός ἐστιν, ὃς ἐὰν μὴ σκανδαλισθῇ ἐν ἐμοί. τού-

[1] *International Critical Commentary.*

IX. Book of Sayings and the First Gospel 251

των δὲ πορευομένων ἤρξατο ὁ Ἰησοῦς λέγειν τοῖς ὄχλοις περὶ Ἰωάννου, Τί ἐξήλθετε εἰς τὴν ἔρημον θεάσασθαι; κάλαμον ὑπὸ ἀνέμου σαλευόμενον; ἀλλὰ τί ἐξήλθετε ἰδεῖν; ἄνθρωπον ἐν μαλακοῖς ἠμφιεσμένον; ἰδού, οἱ τὰ μαλακὰ φοροῦντες ἐν τοῖς οἴκοις τῶν βασιλέων εἰσίν. ἀλλὰ τί ἐξήλθετε; ἰδεῖν προφήτην; ναί, λέγω ὑμῖν, καὶ περισσότερον προφήτου. οὗτός ἐστι περὶ οὗ γέγραπται, Ἰδού, ἐγὼ ἀποστέλλω τὸν ἄγγελόν μου πρὸ προσώπου σου, ὃς κατασκευάσει τὴν ὁδόν σου ἔμπροσθέν σου. ἀμὴν λέγω ὑμῖν, οὐκ ἐγήγερται ἐν γεννητοῖς γυναικῶν μείζων Ἰωάννου τοῦ βαπτιστοῦ· ὁ δὲ μικρότερος ἐν τῇ **βασιλείᾳ τῶν οὐρανῶν** μείζων αὐτοῦ ἐστιν.
Cf. Lk vii. 21-8.

Another Fragment about St. John.

xi. 12-15 Ἀπὸ δὲ τῶν ἡμερῶν Ἰωάννου τοῦ βαπτιστοῦ ἕως ἄρτι ἡ **βασιλεία τῶν οὐρανῶν** βιάζεται, καὶ βιασταὶ ἁρπάζουσιν αὐτήν. πάντες γὰρ οἱ προφῆται καὶ ὁ νόμος ἕως Ἰωάννου προεφήτευσαν. καὶ εἰ θέλετε δέξασθαι, αὐτός ἐστιν Ἠλίας ὁ μέλλων ἔρχεσθαι. ὁ ἔχων ὦτα ἀκούειν ἀκουέτω.
For vv. 12-13, cf. Lk xvi. 16.

A third Fragment relating to St. John.

xi. 16-19 Τίνι δὲ **ὁμοιώσω τὴν γενεὰν ταύτην**; ὁμοία ἐστὶ παιδίοις ἐν ἀγοραῖς καθημένοις, ἃ προσφωνοῦντα **τοῖς ἑταίροις** λέγουσιν, Ηὐλήσαμεν ὑμῖν, καὶ οὐκ ὠρχήσασθε· ἐθρηνήσαμεν, καὶ οὐκ ἐκόψασθε. ἦλθε γὰρ Ἰωάννης μήτε ἐσθίων μήτε πίνων, καὶ λέγουσι, Δαιμόνιον ἔχει. ἦλθεν **ὁ υἱὸς τοῦ ἀνθρώπου** ἐσθίων καὶ πίνων, καὶ λέγουσιν, Ἰδού, ἄνθρωπος φάγος καὶ οἰνοπότης, τελωνῶν φίλος καὶ ἁμαρτωλῶν. καὶ ἐδικαιώθη ἡ σοφία ἀπὸ τῶν ἔργων αὐτῆς.
Cf. Lk vii. 31-5.

Woes upon the Cities in which He had preached.

xi. 20-4 Τότε ἤρξατο ὀνειδίζειν τὰς **πόλεις**, ἐν αἷς ἐγένοντο αἱ πλεῖσται δυνάμεις αὐτοῦ, ὅτι οὐ μετενόησαν.

Οὐαί σοι, Χοραζίν, οὐαί σοι, Βηθσαϊδάν, ὅτι εἰ ἐν Τύρῳ
καὶ Σιδῶνι ἐγένοντο αἱ δυνάμεις αἱ γενόμεναι ἐν ὑμῖν, πάλαι
ἂν ἐν σάκκῳ καὶ σποδῷ μετενόησαν. πλὴν λέγω ὑμῖν,
Τύρῳ καὶ Σιδῶνι ἀνεκτότερον ἔσται ἐν ἡμέρᾳ κρίσεως ἢ
ὑμῖν. καὶ σύ, Καπερναούμ, μὴ ἕως τοῦ οὐρανοῦ ὑψωθήσῃ ;
ἕως ᾅδου καταβήσῃ· ὅτι εἰ ἐν Σοδόμοις ἐγένοντο αἱ δυνάμεις αἱ γενόμεναι ἐν σοί, ἔμειναν ἂν μέχρι τῆς σήμερον.
πλὴν λέγω ὑμῖν, ὅτι γῇ Σοδόμων ἀνεκτότερον ἔσται ἐν
ἡμέρᾳ κρίσεως ἢ σοί.
Cf. Lk x. 13-15, 12.

Thanksgiving to the Father.

xi. 25-30 Ἐξομολογοῦμαί σοι, πάτερ, Κύριε τοῦ οὐρανοῦ καὶ τῆς γῆς, ὅτι ἀπέκρυψας ταῦτα ἀπὸ σοφῶν καὶ
συνετῶν, καὶ ἀπεκάλυψας αὐτὰ νηπίοις· ναί, ὁ πατήρ, ὅτι
οὕτως ἐγένετο εὐδοκία **ἔμπροσθέν** σου. πάντα μοι παρεδόθη
ὑπὸ **τοῦ πατρός μου**· καὶ οὐδεὶς ἐπιγινώσκει τὸν υἱόν, εἰ
μὴ ὁ πατήρ· οὐδὲ τὸν πατέρα τις ἐπιγινώσκει, εἰ μὴ ὁ υἱός,
καὶ ᾧ ἐὰν βούληται ὁ υἱὸς ἀποκαλύψαι. δεῦτε πρός με,
πάντες οἱ κοπιῶντες καὶ πεφορτισμένοι, κἀγὼ ἀναπαύσω
ὑμᾶς· ἄρατε τὸν ζυγόν μου ἐφ᾽ ὑμᾶς, καὶ μάθετε ἀπ᾽ ἐμοῦ,
ὅτι πρᾷός εἰμι καὶ ταπεινὸς τῇ καρδίᾳ, καὶ εὑρήσετε ἀνάπαυσιν ταῖς ψυχαῖς ὑμῶν· ὁ γὰρ **ζυγός μου** χρηστός, καὶ
τὸ φορτίον μου ἐλαφρόν ἐστιν.
Cf. Lk x. 21-2.

A Discourse about Beelzebub.

xii. 27-8 Καὶ εἰ ἐγὼ ἐν Βεελζεβοὺλ ἐκβάλλω τὰ
δαιμόνια, οἱ υἱοὶ ὑμῶν ἐν τίνι ἐκβάλλουσι; διὰ τοῦτο αὐτοὶ
ὑμῶν ἔσονται κριταί. εἰ δὲ ἐγὼ ἐν Πνεύματι Θεοῦ ἐκβάλλω
τὰ δαιμόνια, ἄρα ἔφθασεν ἐφ᾽ ὑμᾶς ἡ βασιλεία τοῦ Θεοῦ.
Cf. Lk xi. 19-20.

xii. 30 Ὁ μὴ ὢν μετ᾽ ἐμοῦ κατ᾽ ἐμοῦ ἐστι, καὶ ὁ μὴ
συνάγων μετ᾽ ἐμοῦ σκορπίζει.
Cf. Lk xi. 23.

IX. Book of Sayings and the First Gospel 253

xii. 32 Ὃς ἂν εἴπῃ λόγον κατὰ τοῦ υἱοῦ τοῦ ἀνθρώπου, ἀφεθήσεται αὐτῷ· ὃς δ' ἂν εἴπῃ κατὰ τοῦ Πνεύματος τοῦ Ἁγίου, οὐκ ἀφεθήσεται αὐτῷ.

Cf. Lk xii. 10.

xii. 33-7 Ἢ ποιήσατε τὸ δένδρον καλὸν καὶ τὸν καρπὸν αὐτοῦ καλόν, ἢ ποιήσατε τὸ δένδρον σαπρὸν καὶ τὸν καρπὸν αὐτοῦ σαπρόν· ἐκ γὰρ τοῦ καρποῦ τὸ δένδρον γινώσκεται. γεννήματα ἐχιδνῶν, πῶς δύνασθε ἀγαθὰ λαλεῖν πονηροὶ ὄντες; ἐκ γὰρ τοῦ περισσεύματος τῆς καρδίας τὸ στόμα λαλεῖ. ὁ ἀγαθὸς ἄνθρωπος ἐκ τοῦ ἀγαθοῦ θησαυροῦ ἐκβάλλει ἀγαθά· καὶ ὁ πονηρὸς ἄνθρωπος ἐκ τοῦ πονηροῦ θησαυροῦ ἐκβάλλει πονηρά. λέγω δὲ ὑμῖν, ὅτι πᾶν ῥῆμα ἀργόν, ὃ ἐὰν λαλήσωσιν οἱ ἄνθρωποι, ἀποδώσουσι περὶ αὐτοῦ λόγον ἐν ἡμέρᾳ κρίσεως· ἐκ γὰρ τῶν λόγων σου δικαιωθήσῃ, καὶ ἐκ τῶν λόγων σου καταδικασθήσῃ.

For v. 35, cf. Lk vi. 45.

These verses look like fragments of a longer speech. Probably sayings parallel to Mk iii. 23-9 = Mt xii. 25-6, 29, 31, 32[b] formed part of it.

Discourse in Answer to the Request for a Sign.

xii. 38-45 Διδάσκαλε, θέλομεν ἀπὸ σοῦ σημεῖον ἰδεῖν. ὁ δὲ ἀποκριθεὶς εἶπεν αὐτοῖς, Γενεὰ πονηρὰ καὶ μοιχαλὶς σημεῖον ἐπιζητεῖ· καὶ σημεῖον οὐ δοθήσεται αὐτῇ, εἰ μὴ τὸ σημεῖον Ἰωνᾶ τοῦ προφήτου· ... ἄνδρες Νινευῖται ἀναστήσονται ἐν τῇ κρίσει μετὰ τῆς γενεᾶς ταύτης, καὶ κατακρινοῦσιν αὐτήν· ὅτι μετενόησαν εἰς τὸ κήρυγμα Ἰωνᾶ, καὶ ἰδού, πλεῖον Ἰωνᾶ ὧδε. βασίλισσα νότου ἐγερθήσεται ἐν τῇ κρίσει μετὰ τῆς γενεᾶς ταύτης, καὶ κατακρινεῖ αὐτήν· ὅτι ἦλθεν ἐκ τῶν περάτων τῆς γῆς ἀκοῦσαι τὴν σοφίαν Σολομῶντος, καὶ ἰδού, πλεῖον Σολομῶντος ὧδε. ὅταν δὲ τὸ ἀκάθαρτον πνεῦμα ἐξέλθῃ ἀπὸ τοῦ ἀνθρώπου, διέρχεται δι' ἀνύδρων τόπων ζητοῦν ἀνάπαυσιν, καὶ οὐχ εὑρίσκει. τότε λέγει, Ἐπιστρέψω εἰς τὸν οἶκόν μου, ὅθεν ἐξῆλθον· καὶ ἐλθὸν εὑρίσκει σχολάζοντα, σεσαρωμένον καὶ κεκοσμημένον. τότε πορεύεται καὶ παραλαμβάνει μεθ᾽ ἑαυτοῦ ἑπτὰ ἕτερα πνεύματα **πονηρότερα** ἑαυτοῦ, καὶ εἰσελθόντα κατοικεῖ ἐκεῖ. καὶ γίνεται τὰ ἔσχατα τοῦ ἀνθρώπου ἐκείνου χείρονα τῶν πρώτων. οὕτως ἔσται καὶ τῇ γενεᾷ ταύτῃ τῇ **πονερᾷ**.

Cf. Lk xi. 29-30, 32, 31, 24-6.

A Collection of Parables of the Kingdom.

First Series.
1. The Tares.
2. The Mustard Seed.
3. The Leaven.
    Explanation of the Tares.
Second Series.
1. The Hid Treasure.
2. The Goodly Pearl.
3. The Draw-net.
    Conclusion.

xiii. 24-33, 36-52 Ἄλλην παραβολὴν παρέθηκεν αὐτοῖς λέγων, Ὡμοιώθη ἡ **βασιλεία τῶν οὐρανῶν** ἀνθρώπῳ σπείραντι καλὸν σπέρμα ἐν τῷ ἀγρῷ αὐτοῦ· ἐν δὲ τῷ καθεύδειν τοὺς **ἀνθρώπους** ἦλθεν αὐτοῦ ὁ ἐχθρὸς καὶ ἐπέσπειρε ζιζάνια ἀνὰ μέσον τοῦ σίτου, καὶ ἀπῆλθεν. ὅτε δὲ ἐβλάστησεν ὁ χόρτος, καὶ καρπὸν ἐποίησε, τότε ἐφάνη καὶ τὰ ζιζάνια. προσελθόντες δὲ οἱ δοῦλοι τοῦ οἰκοδεσπότου εἶπον αὐτῷ, Κύριε, οὐχὶ καλὸν σπέρμα ἔσπειρας ἐν τῷ σῷ ἀγρῷ; πόθεν οὖν ἔχει ζιζάνια; ὁ δὲ ἔφη αὐτοῖς, Ἐχθρὸς ἄνθρωπος τοῦτο ἐποίησεν. οἱ δὲ δοῦλοι αὐτῷ λέγουσι, Θέλεις οὖν ἀπελθόντες συλλέξωμεν αὐτά; ὁ δὲ φησίν, Οὔ· μήποτε συλλέγοντες τὰ ζιζάνια ἐκριζώσητε ἅμα αὐτοῖς τὸν σῖτον. ἄφετε συναυξάνεσθαι ἀμφότερα μέχρι τοῦ θερισμοῦ· καὶ ἐν τῷ καιρῷ τοῦ θερισμοῦ ἐρῶ τοῖς θερισταῖς, Συλλέξατε πρῶτον τὰ ζιζάνια, καὶ δήσατε αὐτὰ εἰς δέσμας πρὸς τὸ κατακαῦσαι αὐτά· τὸν δὲ σῖτον συναγάγετε εἰς τὴν ἀποθήκην μου.

IX. Book of Sayings and the First Gospel

Ἄλλην παραβολὴν παρέθηκεν αὐτοῖς λέγων, Ὁμοία ἐστὶν ἡ βασιλεία τῶν οὐρανῶν κόκκῳ σινάπεως, ὃν λαβὼν ἄνθρωπος ἔσπειρεν ἐν τῷ ἀγρῷ αὐτοῦ· ὃ μικρότερον μέν ἐστι πάντων τῶν σπερμάτων, ὅταν δὲ αὐξηθῇ, μεῖζον τῶν λαχάνων ἐστί, καὶ γίνεται δένδρον, ὥστε ἐλθεῖν τὰ πετεινὰ τοῦ οὐρανοῦ καὶ κατασκηνοῦν ἐν τοῖς κλάδοις αὐτοῦ. Ἄλλην παραβολὴν ἐλάλησεν αὐτοῖς, Ὁμοία ἐστὶν ἡ βασιλεία τῶν οὐρανῶν ζύμῃ, ἣν λαβοῦσα γυνὴ ἐνέκρυψεν εἰς ἀλεύρου σάτα τρία, ἕως οὗ ἐζυμώθη ὅλον. ... καὶ προσῆλθον αὐτῷ οἱ μαθηταὶ αὐτοῦ λέγοντες, Διασάφησον ἡμῖν τὴν παραβολὴν τῶν ζιζανίων τοῦ ἀγροῦ. ὁ δὲ ἀποκριθεὶς εἶπεν, Ὁ σπείρων τὸ καλὸν σπέρμα ἐστὶν ὁ υἱὸς τοῦ ἀνθρώπου· ὁ δὲ ἀγρός ἐστιν ὁ κόσμος· τὸ δὲ καλὸν σπέρμα, οὗτοί εἰσιν οἱ υἱοὶ τῆς βασιλείας· τὰ δὲ ζιζάνιά εἰσιν οἱ υἱοὶ τοῦ πονηροῦ· ὁ δὲ ἐχθρὸς ὁ σπείρας αὐτά ἐστιν ὁ διάβολος· ὁ δὲ θερισμὸς συντέλεια αἰῶνός ἐστιν· οἱ δὲ θερισταὶ ἄγγελοί εἰσιν. ὥσπερ οὖν συλλέγεται τὰ ζιζάνια, καὶ πυρὶ κατακαίεται, οὕτως ἔσται ἐν τῇ συντελείᾳ τοῦ αἰῶνος. ἀποστελεῖ ὁ υἱὸς τοῦ ἀνθρώπου τοὺς ἀγγέλους αὐτοῦ, καὶ συλλέξουσιν ἐκ τῆς βασιλείας αὐτοῦ πάντα τὰ σκάνδαλα καὶ τοὺς ποιοῦντας τὴν ἀνομίαν, καὶ βαλοῦσιν αὐτοὺς εἰς τὴν κάμινον τοῦ πυρός· ἐκεῖ ἔσται ὁ κλαυθμὸς καὶ ὁ βρυγμὸς τῶν ὀδόντων. τότε οἱ δίκαιοι ἐκλάμψουσιν ὡς ὁ ἥλιος ἐν τῇ βασιλείᾳ τοῦ πατρὸς αὐτῶν. ὁ ἔχων ὦτα ἀκουέτω. Ὁμοία ἐστὶν ἡ βασιλεία τῶν οὐρανῶν θησαυρῷ κεκρυμμένῳ ἐν τῷ ἀγρῷ, ὃν εὑρὼν ἄνθρωπος ἔκρυψε, καὶ ἀπὸ τῆς χαρᾶς αὐτοῦ ὑπάγει, καὶ πάντα ὅσα ἔχει πωλεῖ, καὶ ἀγοράζει τὸν ἀγρὸν ἐκεῖνον. Πάλιν ὁμοία ἐστὶν ἡ βασιλεία τῶν οὐρανῶν ἀνθρώπῳ ἐμπόρῳ ζητοῦντι καλοὺς μαργαρίτας· εὑρὼν δὲ ἕνα πολύτιμον μαργαρίτην ἀπελθὼν πέπρακε πάντα ὅσα εἶχε, καὶ ἠγόρασεν αὐτόν. Πάλιν ὁμοία ἐστὶν ἡ βασιλεία τῶν οὐρανῶν σαγήνῃ βληθείσῃ εἰς τὴν θάλασσαν, καὶ ἐκ παντὸς γένους συναγαγούσῃ· ἣν ὅτε ἐπληρώθη ἀναβιβάσαντες ἐπὶ τὸν αἰγιαλόν, καὶ καθίσαντες, συνέλεξαν τὰ καλὰ εἰς ἀγγεῖα, τὰ δὲ σαπρὰ έξω έβαλον. ούτως έσται εν τη συντελεία του αιώνος· εξελεύσονται οι άγγελοι, και αφοριούσι τους πονηρούς εκ μέσου των δικαίων, και βαλούσιν αυτούς εις την κάμινον του πυρός· εκεί έσται ο κλαυθμός και ο βρυγμός των οδόντων. Συνήκατε ταύτα πάντα; λέγουσιν αυτώ, Ναί. ο δε είπεν αυτοίς, Διά τούτο πας γραμματεύς μαθητευθείς τη βασιλεία των ουρανών όμοιός εστιν ανθρώπω οικοδεσπότη, όστις εκβάλλει εκ του θησαυρού αυτού καινά και παλαιά.

For the inclusion of the Mustard Seed amongst Parables, although it is found in Mark, see *St. Matthew*, p. 149.

For v. 33, cf. Lk xiii. 20-1.

A Discourse on Forgiveness.

xviii. 15-20 'Εάν δε αμαρτήση εις σε ο **αδελφός** σου, ύπαγε, έλεγξον αυτόν μεταξύ σου και αυτού μόνου· εάν σου ακούση, εκέρδησας τον **αδελφόν** σου. εάν δε μη ακούση, παράλαβε μετά σου έτι ένα ή δύο, ίνα επί στόματος δύο μαρτύρων ή τριών σταθή παν ρήμα. εάν δε παρακούση αυτών, ειπέ τη εκκλησία· εάν δε και της εκκλησίας παρακούση, έστω σοι ώσπερ ο **εθνικός** και ο τελώνης. αμήν λέγω υμίν, όσα εάν **δήσητε** επί της γης, έσται **δεδεμένα** εν τω ουρανώ· και όσα εάν **λύσητε** επί της γης, έσται λελυμένα εν τω ουρανώ. πάλιν λέγω υμίν, ότι εάν δύο υμών συμφωνήσωσιν επί της γης περί παντός πράγματος ου εάν αιτήσωνται, γενήσεται αυτοίς παρά του **πατρός** μου του **εν ουρανοίς**. ου γάρ εισι δύο ή τρείς συνηγμένοι εις το εμόν όνομα, εκεί ειμί εν μέσω αυτών.

For v. 15, cf. Lk xvii. 3, 4.

xviii. 21-35 'Ο Πέτρος είπεν αυτώ, Κύριε, ποσάκις αμαρτήσει εις εμέ ο **αδελφός** μου, και αφήσω αυτώ; έως επτάκις; λέγει αυτώ ο Ιησούς, Ου λέγω σοι έως επτάκις, αλλ' έως εβδομηκοντάκις επτά. Διά τούτο ωμοιώθη η βασιλεία των ουρανών ανθρώπω βασιλεί, ός ηθέλησε συνάραι λόγον μετά

IX. Book of Sayings and the First Gospel

τῶν δούλων αὐτοῦ. ἀρξαμένου δὲ αὐτοῦ συναίρειν προσηνέχθη αὐτῷ εἷς ὀφειλέτης μυρίων ταλάντων. μὴ ἔχοντος δὲ αὐτοῦ ἀποδοῦναι, ἐκέλευσεν αὐτὸν ὁ κύριος αὐτοῦ πραθῆναι, καὶ τὴν γυναῖκα αὐτοῦ καὶ τὰ τέκνα, καὶ πάντα ὅσα εἶχε, καὶ ἀποδοθῆναι. πεσὼν οὖν ὁ δοῦλος προσεκύνει αὐτῷ λέγων, Κύριε, μακροθύμησον ἐπ᾽ ἐμοί, καὶ πάντα σοι ἀποδώσω. σπλαγχνισθεὶς δὲ ὁ κύριος τοῦ δούλου ἐκείνου ἀπέλυσεν αὐτόν, καὶ τὸ δάνειον ἀφῆκεν αὐτῷ. ἐξελθὼν δὲ ὁ δοῦλος ἐκεῖνος εὗρεν ἕνα τῶν συνδούλων αὐτοῦ, ὃς ὤφειλεν αὐτῷ ἑκατὸν δηνάρια, καὶ κρατήσας αὐτὸν ἔπνιγε λέγων, Ἀπόδος εἴ τι ὀφείλεις. πεσὼν οὖν ὁ σύνδουλος αὐτοῦ παρεκάλει αὐτὸν λέγων, Μακροθύμησον ἐπ᾽ ἐμοί, καὶ ἀποδώσω σοι. ὁ δὲ οὐκ ἤθελεν, ἀλλὰ ἀπελθὼν ἔβαλεν αὐτὸν εἰς φυλακήν, ἕως οὗ ἀποδῷ τὸ ὀφειλόμενον. ἰδόντες οὖν οἱ σύνδουλοι αὐτοῦ τὰ γενόμενα ἐλυπήθησαν σφόδρα· καὶ ἐλθόντες διεσάφησαν τῷ κυρίῳ αὐτῶν πάντα τὰ γενόμενα. τότε προσκαλεσάμενος αὐτὸν ὁ κύριος αὐτοῦ λέγει αὐτῷ, Δοῦλε πονηρέ, πᾶσαν τὴν ὀφειλὴν ἐκείνην ἀφῆκά σοι, ἐπεὶ παρεκάλεσάς με· οὐκ ἔδει καὶ σὲ ἐλεῆσαι τὸν σύνδουλόν σου, ὡς καὶ ἐγώ σε ἠλέησα; καὶ ὀργισθεὶς ὁ κύριος αὐτοῦ παρέδωκεν αὐτὸν τοῖς βασανισταῖς, ἕως οὗ ἀποδῷ πᾶν τὸ ὀφειλόμενον. οὕτω καὶ **ὁ πατήρ μου ὁ ἐπουράνιος** ποιήσει ὑμῖν, ἐὰν μὴ ἀφῆτε ἕκαστος τῷ **ἀδελφῷ αὐτοῦ** ἀπὸ τῶν καρδιῶν ὑμῶν.

A Denunciation of the Pharisees.

xxiii. 2-36 Ἐπὶ τῆς Μωσέως καθέδρας ἐκάθισαν οἱ γραμματεῖς καὶ οἱ Φαρισαῖοι· πάντα οὖν ὅσα ἂν εἴπωσιν ὑμῖν, ποιήσατε καὶ τηρεῖτε· κατὰ δὲ τὰ ἔργα αὐτῶν μὴ ποιεῖτε· λέγουσι γὰρ καὶ οὐ ποιοῦσι. δεσμεύουσι δὲ φορτία βαρέα καὶ δυσβάστακτα, καὶ ἐπιτιθέασιν ἐπὶ τοὺς ὤμους **τῶν ἀνθρώπων**· αὐτοὶ δὲ τῷ δακτύλῳ αὐτῶν οὐ θέλουσι κινῆσαι αὐτά. πάντα δὲ τὰ ἔργα αὐτῶν ποιοῦσι πρὸς τὸ θεαθῆναι **τοῖς ἀνθρώποις**· πλατύνουσι γὰρ τὰ φυλακτήρια αὐτῶν, καὶ μεγαλύνουσι τὰ κράσπεδα, φιλοῦσι δὲ τὴν πρωτοκλισίαν ἐν τοῖς δείπνοις, καὶ τὰς πρωτοκαθεδρίας ἐν ταῖς συναγωγαῖς, καὶ τοὺς ἀσπασμοὺς ἐν ταῖς ἀγοραῖς, καὶ καλεῖσθαι ὑπὸ τῶν ἀνθρώπων ῥαββί. ὑμεῖς δὲ μὴ κληθῆτε ῥαββί· εἷς γάρ ἐστιν ὑμῶν ὁ διδάσκαλος· πάντες δὲ ὑμεῖς ἀδελφοί ἐστε. καὶ πατέρα μὴ καλέσητε ὑμῶν ἐπὶ τῆς γῆς· εἷς γάρ ἐστιν ὁ **πατὴρ ὑμῶν, ὁ οὐράνιος.** μηδὲ κληθῆτε καθηγηταί· εἷς γὰρ ὑμῶν ἐστιν ὁ καθηγητής, ὁ Χριστός· ὁ δὲ μείζων ὑμῶν ἔσται ὑμῶν διάκονος. ὅστις δὲ ὑψώσει ἑαυτόν, ταπεινωθήσεται· καὶ ὅστις ταπεινώσει ἑαυτόν, ὑψωθήσεται. Οὐαὶ δὲ ὑμῖν, γραμματεῖς καὶ Φαρισαῖοι, **ὑποκριταί,** ὅτι κλείετε **τὴν βασιλείαν τῶν οὐρανῶν ἔμπροσθεν τῶν ἀνθρώπων·** ὑμεῖς γὰρ οὐκ εἰσέρχεσθε, οὐδὲ τοὺς εἰσερχομένους ἀφίετε εἰσελθεῖν. Οὐαὶ ὑμῖν, γραμματεῖς καὶ Φαρισαῖοι, **ὑποκριταί,** ὅτι περιάγετε τὴν θάλασσαν καὶ τὴν ξηρὰν ποιῆσαι ἕνα προσήλυτον, καὶ ὅταν γένηται, ποιεῖτε αὐτὸν υἱὸν γεέννης διπλότερον ὑμῶν. Οὐαὶ ὑμῖν, ὁδηγοὶ τυφλοί, οἱ λέγοντες, Ὃς ἂν ὀμόσῃ ἐν τῷ ναῷ, οὐδέν ἐστιν· ὃς δ' ἂν ὀμόσῃ ἐν τῷ χρυσῷ τοῦ ναοῦ, ὀφείλει. μωροὶ καὶ τυφλοί· τίς γὰρ μείζων ἐστίν; ὁ χρυσός; ἢ ὁ ναὸς ὁ ἁγιάσας τὸν χρυσόν; καί, Ὃς ἐὰν ὀμόσῃ ἐν τῷ θυσιαστηρίῳ, οὐδέν ἐστιν· ὃς δ' ἂν ὀμόσῃ ἐν τῷ δώρῳ τῷ ἐπάνω αὐτοῦ, ὀφείλει. τυφλοί· τί γὰρ μεῖζον; τὸ δῶρον; ἢ τὸ θυσιαστήριον τὸ ἁγιάζον τὸ δῶρον; ὁ οὖν ὀμόσας ἐν τῷ θυσιαστηρίῳ ὀμνύει ἐν αὐτῷ καὶ ἐν πᾶσι τοῖς ἐπάνω αὐτοῦ· καὶ ὁ ὀμόσας ἐν τῷ ναῷ ὀμνύει ἐν αὐτῷ καὶ ἐν τῷ κατοικοῦντι αὐτόν· καὶ ὁ ὀμόσας ἐν τῷ οὐρανῷ ὀμνύει ἐν τῷ θρόνῳ τοῦ Θεοῦ καὶ ἐν τῷ καθημένῳ ἐπάνω αὐτοῦ. Οὐαὶ ὑμῖν, γραμματεῖς καὶ Φαρισαῖοι, **ὑποκριταί,** ὅτι ἀποδεκατοῦτε τὸ ἡδύοσμον καὶ τὸ ἄνηθον καὶ τὸ κύμινον, καὶ ἀφήκατε τὰ βαρύτερα τοῦ νόμου, τὴν κρίσιν καὶ τὸν ἔλεον καὶ τὴν πίστιν· ταῦτα δὲ ἔδει ποιῆσαι, κἀκεῖνα μὴ ἀφεῖναι. ὁδηγοὶ τυφλοί, οἱ διυλίζοντες τὸν κώνωπα, τὴν δὲ κάμηλον καταπίνοντες. Οὐαὶ ὑμῖν, γραμματεῖς καὶ Φαρισαῖοι, **ὑποκριταί,** ὅτι καθαρίζετε τὸ ἔξωθεν τοῦ ποτηρίου καὶ τῆς παροψίδος, ἔσωθεν δὲ γέμουσιν ἐξ

IX. Book of Sayings and the First Gospel 259

ἀρπαγῆς καὶ ἀκρασίας. Φαρισαῖε τυφλέ, καθάρισον πρῶτον τὸ ἐντὸς τοῦ ποτηρίου καὶ τῆς παροψίδος, ἵνα γένηται καὶ τὸ ἐκτὸς αὐτοῦ καθαρόν. Οὐαὶ ὑμῖν, γραμματεῖς καὶ Φαρισαῖοι, ὑποκριταί, ὅτι παρομοιάζετε τάφοις κεκονιαμένοις, οἵτινες ἔξωθεν μὲν φαίνονται ὡραῖοι, ἔσωθεν δὲ γέμουσιν ὀστέων νεκρῶν καὶ πάσης ἀκαθαρσίας. οὕτω καὶ ὑμεῖς ἔξωθεν μὲν φαίνεσθε τοῖς ἀνθρώποις δίκαιοι, ἔσωθεν δὲ μεστοί ἐστε ὑποκρίσεως καὶ ἀνομίας. Οὐαὶ ὑμῖν, γραμματεῖς καὶ Φαρισαῖοι, ὑποκριταί, ὅτι οἰκοδομεῖτε τοὺς τάφους τῶν προφητῶν, καὶ κοσμεῖτε τὰ μνημεῖα τῶν δικαίων, καὶ λέγετε, Εἰ ἦμεν ἐν ταῖς ἡμέραις τῶν πατέρων ἡμῶν, οὐκ ἂν ἦμεν κοινωνοὶ αὐτῶν ἐν τῷ αἵματι τῶν προφητῶν. ὥστε μαρτυρεῖτε ἑαυτοῖς, ὅτι υἱοί ἐστε τῶν φονευσάντων τοὺς προφήτας. καὶ ὑμεῖς πληρώσατε τὸ μέτρον τῶν πατέρων ὑμῶν. ὄφεις, γεννήματα ἐχιδνῶν, πῶς φύγητε ἀπὸ τῆς κρίσεως τῆς γεέννης; διὰ τοῦτο, ἰδού, ἐγὼ ἀποστέλλω πρὸς ὑμᾶς προφήτας καὶ σοφοὺς καὶ γραμματεῖς· ἐξ αὐτῶν ἀποκτενεῖτε καὶ σταυρώσετε, καὶ ἐξ αὐτῶν μαστιγώσετε ἐν ταῖς συναγωγαῖς ὑμῶν, καὶ διώξετε ἀπὸ πόλεως εἰς πόλιν· ὅπως ἔλθῃ ἐφ' ὑμᾶς πᾶν αἷμα δίκαιον ἐκχυνόμενον ἐπὶ τῆς γῆς, ἀπὸ τοῦ αἵματος Ἄβελ τοῦ δικαίου ἕως τοῦ αἵματος Ζαχαρίου υἱοῦ Βαραχίου, ὃν ἐφονεύσατε μεταξὺ τοῦ ναοῦ καὶ τοῦ θυσιαστηρίου· ἀμὴν λέγω ὑμῖν, ἥξει ταῦτα πάντα ἐπὶ τὴν γενεὰν ταύτην.

For v. 4, cf. Lk xi. 46, for 14 Lk xi. 52, for 23 Lk xi. 42, for 25-6 Lk xi. 39-41, for 27 Lk xi. 44, for 29-33 Lk xi. 47-8, for 34-6 Lk xi. 49-51, for 37-9 Lk xiii. 34-5.

Eschatological Sayings.

xxiv. 10-12 Καὶ τότε σκανδαλισθήσονται πολλοί, καὶ ἀλλήλους παραδώσουσι, καὶ μισήσουσιν ἀλλήλους· καὶ πολλοὶ ψευδοπροφῆται ἐγερθήσονται, καὶ πλανήσουσι πολλούς· καὶ διὰ τὸ πληθυνθῆναι τὴν ἀνομίαν ψυγήσεται ἡ ἀγάπη τῶν πολλῶν.

xxiv. 26-8 Ἐὰν οὖν εἴπωσιν ὑμῖν, Ἰδού, ἐν τῇ ἐρήμῳ
ἐστί, μὴ ἐξέλθητε· Ἰδού, ἐν τοῖς ταμείοις, μὴ πιστεύσητε·
ὥσπερ γὰρ ἡ ἀστραπὴ ἐξέρχεται ἀπὸ ἀνατολῶν καὶ φαί-
νεται ἕως δυσμῶν, οὕτως ἔσται ἡ παρουσία τοῦ υἱοῦ τοῦ
ἀνθρώπου· ὅπου ἐὰν ᾖ τὸ πτῶμα, ἐκεῖ συναχθήσονται οἱ
ἀετοί.

Cf. Lk xvii. 23-4.

xxiv. 30 Καὶ τότε φανήσεται τὸ σημεῖον τοῦ υἱοῦ τοῦ
ἀνθρώπου ἐν τῷ οὐρανῷ· καὶ τότε κόψονται πᾶσαι αἱ
φυλαὶ τῆς γῆς.

xxiv. 37-41 Ὥσπερ δὲ αἱ ἡμέραι τοῦ Νῶε, οὕτως ἔσται ἡ
παρουσία τοῦ υἱοῦ τοῦ ἀνθρώπου. ὥσπερ γὰρ ἦσαν ἐν ταῖς
ἡμέραις ἐκείναις ταῖς πρὸ τοῦ κατακλυσμοῦ τρώγοντες καὶ
πίνοντες, γαμοῦντες καὶ ἐκγαμίζοντες, ἄχρι ἧς ἡμέρας εἰσῆλθε
Νῶε εἰς τὴν κιβωτόν, καὶ οὐκ ἔγνωσαν ἕως ἦλθεν ὁ κατα-
κλυσμὸς καὶ ἦρεν ἅπαντας, οὕτως ἔσται ἡ παρουσία τοῦ
υἱοῦ τοῦ ἀνθρώπου. τότε δύο ἔσονται ἐν τῷ ἀγρῷ· εἷς
παραλαμβάνεται, καὶ εἷς ἀφίεται· δύο ἀλήθουσαι ἐν τῷ
μύλῳ· μία παραλαμβάνεται, καὶ μία ἀφίεται.

Cf. Lk xvii. 26-7, 30, 34-5.

xxiv. 43-51 Ἐκεῖνο δὲ γινώσκετε, ὅτι εἰ ᾔδει ὁ οἰκοδεσπότης ποίᾳ φυλακῇ ὁ κλέπτης ἔρχεται, ἐγρηγόρησεν ἄν, καὶ
οὐκ ἂν εἴασε διορυγῆναι τὴν οἰκίαν αὐτοῦ. διὰ τοῦτο καὶ
ὑμεῖς γίνεσθε ἕτοιμοι· ὅτι ᾗ ὥρᾳ οὐ δοκεῖτε ὁ υἱὸς τοῦ
ἀνθρώπου ἔρχεται. τίς ἄρα ἐστὶν ὁ πιστὸς δοῦλος καὶ
φρόνιμος, ὃν κατέστησεν ὁ κύριος ἐπὶ τῆς οἰκετείας αὐτοῦ,
τοῦ διδόναι αὐτοῖς τὴν τροφὴν ἐν καιρῷ; μακάριος ὁ
δοῦλος ἐκεῖνος, ὃν ἐλθὼν ὁ κύριος αὐτοῦ εὑρήσει ποιοῦντα
οὕτως· ἀμὴν λέγω ὑμῖν, ὅτι ἐπὶ πᾶσι τοῖς ὑπάρχουσιν αὐτοῦ
καταστήσει αὐτόν. ἐὰν δὲ εἴπῃ ὁ κακὸς δοῦλος ἐκεῖνος ἐν
τῇ καρδίᾳ αὐτοῦ, Χρονίζει ὁ κύριός μου, καὶ ἄρξηται τύπτειν
τοὺς συνδούλους αὐτοῦ, ἐσθίῃ δὲ καὶ πίνῃ μετὰ τῶν
μεθυόντων, ἥξει ὁ κύριος τοῦ δούλου ἐκείνου ἐν ἡμέρᾳ ᾗ
οὐ προσδοκᾷ, καὶ ἐν ὥρᾳ ᾗ οὐ γινώσκει, καὶ διχοτομήσει

IX. Book of Sayings and the First Gospel 261

αὐτόν, καὶ τὸ μέρος αὐτοῦ μετὰ τῶν ὑποκριτῶν θήσει· ἐκεῖ ἔσται ὁ κλαυθμὸς καὶ ὁ βρυγμὸς τῶν ὀδόντων.

Cf. Lk xii. 39-46.

xxv. 1-12 Τότε ὁμοιωθήσεται ἡ βασιλεία τῶν οὐρανῶν δέκα παρθένοις, αἵτινες λαβοῦσαι τὰς λαμπάδας αὐτῶν ἐξῆλθον εἰς ἀπάντησιν τοῦ νυμφίου. πέντε δὲ ἦσαν ἐξ αὐτῶν μωραί, καὶ πέντε φρόνιμοι. αἱ γὰρ μωραί, λαβοῦσαι τὰς λαμπάδας ἑαυτῶν, οὐκ ἔλαβον μεθ' ἑαυτῶν ἔλαιον· αἱ δὲ φρόνιμοι ἔλαβον ἔλαιον ἐν τοῖς ἀγγείοις αὐτῶν μετὰ τῶν λαμπάδων αὐτῶν. χρονίζοντος δὲ τοῦ νυμφίου ἐνύσταξαν πᾶσαι καὶ ἐκάθευδον. μέσης δὲ νυκτὸς κραυγὴ γέγονεν, Ἰδού, ὁ νυμφίος· ἐξέρχεσθε εἰς ἀπάντησιν αὐτοῦ. τότε ἠγέρθησαν πᾶσαι αἱ παρθένοι ἐκεῖναι, καὶ ἐκόσμησαν τὰς λαμπάδας αὐτῶν. αἱ δὲ μωραὶ ταῖς φρονίμοις εἶπον, Δότε ἡμῖν ἐκ τοῦ ἐλαίου ὑμῶν, ὅτι αἱ λαμπάδες ἡμῶν σβέννυνται. ἀπεκρίθησαν δὲ αἱ φρόνιμοι λέγουσαι, Μήποτε οὐ μὴ ἀρκέσῃ ἡμῖν καὶ ὑμῖν· πορεύεσθε μᾶλλον πρὸς τοὺς πωλοῦντας, καὶ ἀγοράσατε ἑαυταῖς. ἀπερχομένων δὲ αὐτῶν ἀγοράσαι ἦλθεν ὁ νυμφίος· καὶ αἱ ἕτοιμοι εἰσῆλθον μετ' αὐτοῦ εἰς τοὺς γάμους, καὶ ἐκλείσθη ἡ θύρα. ὕστερον δὲ ἔρχονται καὶ αἱ λοιπαὶ παρθένοι λέγουσαι, Κύριε, κύριε, ἄνοιξον ἡμῖν. ὁ δὲ ἀποκριθεὶς εἶπεν, Ἀμὴν λέγω ὑμῖν, οὐκ οἶδα ὑμᾶς.

xxv. 14-30 Ὥσπερ γὰρ ἄνθρωπος ἀποδημῶν ἐκάλεσε τοὺς ἰδίους δούλους, καὶ παρέδωκεν αὐτοῖς τὰ ὑπάρχοντα αὐτοῦ· καὶ ᾧ μὲν ἔδωκε πέντε τάλαντα, ᾧ δὲ δύο, ᾧ δὲ ἕν, ἑκάστῳ κατὰ τὴν ἰδίαν δύναμιν· καὶ ἀπεδήμησεν. εὐθέως πορευθεὶς ὁ τὰ πέντε τάλαντα λαβὼν εἰργάσατο ἐν αὐτοῖς, καὶ ἐποίησεν ἄλλα πέντε τάλαντα. ὡσαύτως καὶ ὁ τὰ δύο ἐκέρδησεν ἄλλα δύο. ὁ δὲ τὸ ἓν λαβὼν ἀπελθὼν ὤρυξε γῆν, καὶ ἀπέκρυψε τὸ ἀργύριον τοῦ κυρίου αὐτοῦ. μετὰ δὲ χρόνον πολὺν ἔρχεται ὁ κύριος τῶν δούλων ἐκείνων, καὶ συναίρει μετ' αὐτῶν λόγον. καὶ προσελθὼν ὁ τὰ πέντε τάλαντα λαβὼν προσήνεγκεν ἄλλα πέντε

τάλαντα λέγων, Κύριε, πέντε τάλαντά μοι παρέδωκας·
ἴδε, ἄλλα πέντε τάλαντα ἐκέρδησα. ἔφη αὐτῷ ὁ κύριος
αὐτοῦ, Εὖ, δοῦλε ἀγαθὲ καὶ πιστέ, ἐπὶ ὀλίγα ἦς πιστός, ἐπὶ
πολλῶν σε καταστήσω· εἴσελθε εἰς τὴν χαρὰν τοῦ κυρίου
σου. προσελθὼν δὲ καὶ ὁ τὰ δύο τάλαντα εἶπε, Κύριε,
δύο τάλαντά μοι παρέδωκας· ἴδε, ἄλλα δύο τάλαντα
ἐκέρδησα. ἔφη αὐτῷ ὁ κύριος αὐτοῦ, Εὖ, δοῦλε ἀγαθὲ
καὶ πιστέ, ἐπὶ ὀλίγα ἦς πιστός, ἐπὶ πολλῶν σε καταστήσω·
εἴσελθε εἰς τὴν χαρὰν τοῦ κυρίου σου. προσελθὼν δὲ καὶ
ὁ τὸ ἓν τάλαντον εἰληφὼς εἶπε, Κύριε, ἔγνων σε ὅτι σκληρὸς
εἶ ἄνθρωπος, θερίζων ὅπου οὐκ ἔσπειρας, καὶ συνάγων
ὅθεν οὐ διεσκόρπισας· καὶ φοβηθεὶς ἀπελθὼν ἔκρυψα τὸ
τάλαντόν σου ἐν τῇ γῇ· ἴδε, ἔχεις τὸ σόν. ἀποκριθεὶς δὲ ὁ
κύριος αὐτοῦ εἶπεν αὐτῷ, Πονηρὲ δοῦλε καὶ ὀκνηρέ, ᾔδεις ὅτι
θερίζω ὅπου οὐκ ἔσπειρα, καὶ συνάγω ὅθεν οὐ διεσκόρπισα·
ἔδει οὖν σε βαλεῖν τὸ ἀργύριόν μου τοῖς τραπεζίταις, καὶ
ἐλθὼν ἐγὼ ἐκομισάμην ἂν τὸ ἐμὸν σὺν τόκῳ. ἄρατε οὖν ἀπ᾿
αὐτοῦ τὸ τάλαντον, καὶ δότε τῷ ἔχοντι τὰ δέκα τάλαντα·
τῷ γὰρ ἔχοντι παντὶ δοθήσεται, καὶ περισσευθήσεται· τοῦ
δὲ μὴ ἔχοντος, καὶ ὃ ἔχει ἀρθήσεται ἀπ᾿ αὐτοῦ· καὶ τὸν
ἀχρεῖον δοῦλον ἐκβάλλετε εἰς τὸ σκότος τὸ ἐξώτερον· ἐκεῖ
ἔσται ὁ κλαυθμὸς καὶ ὁ βρυγμὸς τῶν ὀδόντων.

For vv. 14-30, cf. Lk xi. 11-28.

xxv. 31-46 "Οταν δὲ ἔλθῃ ὁ υἱὸς τοῦ ἀνθρώπου ἐν
τῇ δόξῃ αὐτοῦ, καὶ πάντες οἱ ἄγγελοι μετ᾿ αὐτοῦ, τότε
καθίσει ἐπὶ θρόνου δόξης αὐτοῦ, καὶ συναχθήσεται ἔμπροσθεν
αὐτοῦ πάντα τὰ ἔθνη, καὶ ἀφοριεῖ αὐτοὺς ἀπ᾿
ἀλλήλων, ὥσπερ ὁ ποιμὴν ἀφορίζει τὰ πρόβατα ἀπὸ τῶν
ἐρίφων, καὶ στήσει τὰ μὲν πρόβατα ἐκ δεξιῶν αὐτοῦ, τὰ
δὲ ἐρίφια ἐξ εὐωνύμων. τότε ἐρεῖ ὁ βασιλεὺς τοῖς ἐκ δεξιῶν
αὐτοῦ, Δεῦτε, οἱ εὐλογημένοι τοῦ πατρός μου, κληρονομήσατε
τὴν ἡτοιμασμένην ὑμῖν βασιλείαν ἀπὸ καταβολῆς
κόσμου. ἐπείνασα γάρ, καὶ ἐδώκατέ μοι φαγεῖν· ἐδίψησα,
καὶ ἐποτίσατέ με· ξένος ἤμην, καὶ συνηγάγετέ με· γυμνός,

IX. Book of Sayings and the First Gospel 263

καὶ περιεβάλετέ με· ἠσθένησα, καὶ ἐπεσκέψασθέ με· ἐν φυλακῇ ἤμην, καὶ ἤλθετε πρός με. τότε ἀποκριθήσονται αὐτῷ οἱ δίκαιοι λέγοντες, Κύριε, πότε σε εἴδομεν πεινῶντα, καὶ ἐθρέψαμεν ; ἢ διψῶντα, καὶ ἐποτίσαμεν ; πότε δέ σε εἴδομεν ξένον, καὶ συνηγάγομεν; ἢ γυμνόν, καὶ περιεβάλομεν ; πότε δέ σε εἴδομεν ἀσθενῆ, ἢ ἐν φυλακῇ, καὶ ἤλθομεν πρός σε ; καὶ ἀποκριθεὶς ὁ βασιλεὺς ἐρεῖ αὐτοῖς, Ἀμὴν λέγω ὑμῖν, ἐφ' ὅσον ἐποιήσατε ἑνὶ τούτων τῶν ἀδελφῶν μου τῶν ἐλαχίστων, ἐμοὶ ἐποιήσατε. τότε ἐρεῖ καὶ τοῖς ἐξ εὐωνύμων, Πορεύεσθε ἀπ' ἐμοῦ, κατηραμένοι, εἰς τὸ πῦρ τὸ αἰώνιον τὸ ἡτοιμασμένον τῷ διαβόλῳ καὶ τοῖς ἀγγέλοις αὐτοῦ. ἐπείνασα γάρ, καὶ οὐκ ἐδώκατέ μοι φαγεῖν· ἐδίψησα, καὶ οὐκ ἐποτίσατέ με· ξένος ἤμην, καὶ οὐ συνηγάγετέ με· γυμνός, καὶ οὐ περιεβάλετέ με· ἀσθενής, καὶ ἐν φυλακῇ, καὶ οὐκ ἐπεσκέψασθέ με. τότε ἀποκριθήσονται καὶ αὐτοὶ λέγοντες, Κύριε, πότε σε εἴδομεν πεινῶντα, ἢ διψῶντα, ἢ ξένον, ἢ γυμνόν, ἢ ἀσθενῆ, ἢ ἐν φυλακῇ, καὶ οὐ διηκονήσαμέν σοι ; τότε ἀποκριθήσεται αὐτοῖς λέγων, Ἀμὴν λέγω ὑμῖν, ἐφ' ὅσον οὐκ ἐποιήσατε ἑνὶ τούτων τῶν ἐλαχίστων, οὐδὲ ἐμοὶ ἐποιήσατε. καὶ ἀπελεύσονται οὗτοι εἰς κόλασιν αἰώνιον, οἱ δὲ δίκαιοι εἰς ζωὴν αἰώνιον.

Fragments inserted by the Editor of the First Gospel in the Sermon on the Mount.

v. 13-16.

13 Ὑμεῖς ἐστε τὸ ἅλας τῆς γῆς· ἐὰν δὲ τὸ ἅλας μωρανθῇ, ἐν τίνι ἁλισθήσεται; εἰς οὐδὲν ἰσχύει ἔτι, εἰ μὴ βληθὲν ἔξω καταπατεῖσθαι ὑπὸ τῶν ἀνθρώπων.

14 ὑμεῖς ἐστε τὸ φῶς τοῦ κόσμου· οὐ δύναται πόλις κρυβῆναι ἐπάνω ὄρους κειμένη·

15 οὐδὲ καίουσι λύχνον καὶ τιθέασιν αὐτὸν ὑπὸ τὸν μόδιον, ἀλλ' ἐπὶ τὴν λυχνίαν, καὶ λάμπει πᾶσι τοῖς ἐν τῇ οἰκίᾳ·

16 οὕτω λαμψάτω τὸ φῶς ὑμῶν ἔμπροσθεν τῶν ἀνθρώ-

πων, ὅπως ἴδωσιν ὑμῶν τὰ καλὰ ἔργα, καὶ δοξάσωσι τὸν πατέρα ὑμῶν τὸν ἐν τοῖς οὐρανοῖς.

These verses are not in Luke's Sermon, but he has a parallel to v. 13 in ch. xiv. 34–5, and a parallel to v. 15 in chs. viii. 16 and xi. 33. If they had stood in the Sermon of the source it is likely that they would also have been in Luke's Sermon.

v. 18–19 Ἀμὴν γὰρ λέγω ὑμῖν, ἕως ἂν παρέλθῃ ὁ οὐρανὸς καὶ ἡ γῆ, ἰῶτα ἓν ἢ μία κεραία οὐ μὴ παρέλθῃ ἀπὸ τοῦ νόμου, ἕως ἂν πάντα γένηται. ὃς ἐὰν οὖν λύσῃ μίαν τῶν ἐντολῶν τούτων τῶν ἐλαχίστων, καὶ διδάξῃ οὕτω τοὺς ἀνθρώπους, ἐλάχιστος κληθήσεται ἐν τῇ βασιλείᾳ τῶν οὐρανῶν· ὃς δ' ἂν ποιήσῃ καὶ διδάξῃ, οὗτος μέγας κληθήσεται ἐν τῇ βασιλείᾳ τῶν οὐρανῶν.

For v. 18, cf. Lk xvi. 17.

For the unsuitability of the verses in their present context see *St. Matthew*, p. 45.

v. 25–6 Ἴσθι εὐνοῶν τῷ ἀντιδίκῳ σου ταχύ, ἕως ὅτου εἶ μετ' αὐτοῦ ἐν τῇ ὁδῷ· μήποτέ σε παραδῷ ὁ ἀντίδικος τῷ κριτῇ, καὶ ὁ κριτής σε παραδῷ τῷ ὑπηρέτῃ, καὶ εἰς φυλακὴν βληθήσῃ. ἀμὴν λέγω σοι, οὐ μὴ ἐξέλθῃς ἐκεῖθεν, ἕως ἂν ἀποδῷς τὸν ἔσχατον κοδράντην.

Cf. Lk xii. 57–9. The connexion of the verses in the Sermon is artificial and literary. See *St. Matthew*, p. 50.

v. 29–30 Εἰ δὲ ὁ ὀφθαλμός σου ὁ δεξιὸς σκανδαλίζει σε, ἔξελε αὐτὸν καὶ βάλε ἀπὸ σοῦ· συμφέρει γάρ σοι ἵνα ἀπόληται ἓν τῶν μελῶν σου, καὶ μὴ ὅλον τὸ σῶμά σου βληθῇ εἰς γέενναν. καὶ εἰ ἡ δεξιά σου χεὶρ σκανδαλίζει σε, ἔκκοψον αὐτὴν καὶ βάλε ἀπὸ σοῦ· συμφέρει γάρ σοι ἵνα ἀπόληται ἓν τῶν μελῶν σου, καὶ μὴ ὅλον τὸ σῶμά σου εἰς γέενναν ἀπέλθῃ.

vi. 7–8 Προσευχόμενοι δὲ μὴ βαττολογήσητε, ὥσπερ οἱ ἐθνικοί· δοκοῦσι γὰρ ὅτι ἐν τῇ πολυλογίᾳ αὐτῶν εἰσακουσθήσονται. μὴ οὖν ὁμοιωθῆτε αὐτοῖς· οἶδε γὰρ ὁ πατὴρ ὑμῶν ὧν χρείαν ἔχετε πρὸ τοῦ ὑμᾶς αἰτῆσαι αὐτόν.

IX. Book of Sayings and the First Gospel

The verses seem out of place in their present connexion in the Sermon. The rest of the context is directed against 'hypocrites', these verses against heathen practices.

vi. 9-13 Οὕτως οὖν προσεύχεσθε ὑμεῖς· **Πάτερ ἡμῶν ὁ ἐν τοῖς οὐρανοῖς**, ἁγιασθήτω τὸ ὄνομά σου· ἐλθέτω ἡ **βασιλεία σου**· γενηθήτω τὸ θέλημά σου, ὡς ἐν οὐρανῷ, καὶ ἐπὶ γῆς· τὸν ἄρτον ἡμῶν τὸν ἐπιούσιον δὸς ἡμῖν σήμερον· καὶ ἄφες ἡμῖν τὰ ὀφειλήματα ἡμῶν, ὡς καὶ ἡμεῖς ἀφήκαμεν τοῖς ὀφειλέταις ἡμῶν· καὶ μὴ εἰσενέγκῃς ἡμᾶς εἰς πειρασμόν, ἀλλὰ ῥῦσαι ἡμᾶς ἀπὸ **τοῦ πονηροῦ**.

Cf. Lk xi. 1-4, where the prayer occurs in quite a different connexion.

vi. 14-15 Ἐὰν γὰρ ἀφῆτε **τοῖς ἀνθρώποις** τὰ παραπτώματα αὐτῶν, ἀφήσει καὶ ὑμῖν ὁ **πατὴρ ὑμῶν ὁ οὐράνιος**· ἐὰν δὲ μὴ ἀφῆτε **τοῖς ἀνθρώποις** τὰ παραπτώματα αὐτῶν, οὐδὲ ὁ **πατὴρ ὑμῶν** ἀφήσει τὰ παραπτώματα ὑμῶν.

vi. 19-34 Μὴ θησαυρίζετε ὑμῖν θησαυροὺς ἐπὶ τῆς γῆς, ὅπου σὴς καὶ βρῶσις ἀφανίζει, καὶ ὅπου κλέπται διορύσσουσι καὶ κλέπτουσι· θησαυρίζετε δὲ ὑμῖν θησαυροὺς ἐν οὐρανῷ, ὅπου οὔτε σὴς οὔτε βρῶσις ἀφανίζει, καὶ ὅπου κλέπται οὐ διορύσσουσιν οὐδὲ κλέπτουσιν· ὅπου γάρ ἐστιν ὁ θησαυρός σου, ἐκεῖ ἔσται καὶ ἡ καρδία σου. ὁ λύχνος τοῦ σώματός ἐστιν ὁ ὀφθαλμός· ἐὰν οὖν ὁ ὀφθαλμός σου ἁπλοῦς ᾖ, ὅλον τὸ σῶμά σου φωτεινὸν ἔσται· ἐὰν δὲ ὁ ὀφθαλμός σου **πονηρὸς** ᾖ, ὅλον τὸ σῶμά σου σκοτεινὸν ἔσται· εἰ οὖν τὸ φῶς τὸ ἐν σοὶ σκότος ἐστί, τὸ σκότος πόσον; οὐδεὶς δύναται δυσὶ κυρίοις δουλεύειν· ἢ γὰρ τὸν ἕνα μισήσει καὶ τὸν ἕτερον ἀγαπήσει, ἢ ἑνὸς ἀνθέξεται καὶ τοῦ ἑτέρου καταφρονήσει· οὐ δύνασθε Θεῷ δουλεύειν καὶ μαμμωνᾷ. διὰ τοῦτο λέγω ὑμῖν, μὴ μεριμνᾶτε τῇ ψυχῇ ὑμῶν, τί φάγητε ἢ τί πίητε· μηδὲ τῷ σώματι ὑμῶν, τί ἐνδύσησθε· οὐχὶ ἡ ψυχὴ πλεῖόν ἐστι τῆς τροφῆς, καὶ τὸ σῶμα τοῦ ἐνδύματος; ἐμβλέψατε εἰς τὰ πετεινὰ τοῦ οὐρανοῦ, ὅτι οὐ σπείρουσιν, οὐδὲ θερίζουσιν, οὐδὲ συνάγουσιν εἰς ἀποθήκας, καὶ ὁ **πατὴρ ὑμῶν ὁ οὐράνιος** τρέφει αὐτά· οὐχ ὑμεῖς μᾶλλον διαφέρετε αὐτῶν; τίς δὲ ἐξ ὑμῶν μεριμνῶν δύναται προσθεῖναι ἐπὶ τὴν ἡλικίαν αὐτοῦ πῆχυν ἕνα; καὶ περὶ ἐνδύματος τί μεριμνᾶτε; καταμάθετε τὰ κρίνα τοῦ ἀγροῦ, πῶς αὐξάνει· οὐ κοπιᾷ, οὐδὲ νήθει· λέγω δὲ ὑμῖν, ὅτι οὐδὲ Σολομὼν ἐν πάσῃ τῇ δόξῃ αὐτοῦ περιεβάλετο ὡς ἓν τούτων. εἰ δὲ τὸν χόρτον τοῦ ἀγροῦ, σήμερον ὄντα, καὶ αὔριον εἰς κλίβανον βαλλόμενον, ὁ Θεὸς οὕτως ἀμφιέννυσιν, οὐ πολλῷ μᾶλλον ὑμᾶς, ὀλιγόπιστοι; μὴ οὖν μεριμνήσητε, λέγοντες, Τί φάγωμεν; ἢ Τί πίωμεν; ἢ Τί περιβαλώμεθα; πάντα γὰρ ταῦτα τὰ ἔθνη ἐπιζητεῖ· οἶδε γὰρ **ὁ πατὴρ ὑμῶν ὁ οὐράνιος** ὅτι χρῄζετε τούτων ἁπάντων· ζητεῖτε δὲ πρῶτον **τὴν βασιλείαν** καὶ **τὴν δικαιοσύνην** αὐτοῦ, καὶ ταῦτα πάντα προστεθήσεται ὑμῖν. μὴ οὖν μεριμνήσητε εἰς τὴν αὔριον· ἡ γὰρ αὔριον μεριμνήσει ἑαυτῆς· ἀρκετὸν τῇ ἡμέρᾳ ἡ κακία αὐτῆς.

For vv. 19-21, cf. Lk xii. 33-4, for 22-3 Lk xi. 34-5, for 24 Lk xvi. 13, for 25-34 Lk xii. 22-31.

vii. 7-11 Αἰτεῖτε, καὶ δοθήσεται ὑμῖν· ζητεῖτε, καὶ εὑρήσετε· κρούετε, καὶ ἀνοιγήσεται ὑμῖν· πᾶς γὰρ ὁ αἰτῶν λαμβάνει, καὶ ὁ ζητῶν εὑρίσκει, καὶ τῷ κρούοντι ἀνοιγήσεται. ἢ τίς ἐστιν ἐξ ὑμῶν ἄνθρωπος, ὃν αἰτήσει ὁ υἱὸς αὐτοῦ ἄρτον, μὴ λίθον ἐπιδώσει αὐτῷ; ἢ καὶ ἰχθὺν αἰτήσει, μὴ ὄφιν ἐπιδώσει αὐτῷ; εἰ οὖν ὑμεῖς, πονηροὶ ὄντες, οἴδατε δόματα ἀγαθὰ διδόναι τοῖς τέκνοις ὑμῶν, πόσῳ μᾶλλον ὁ **πατὴρ ὑμῶν ὁ ἐν τοῖς οὐρανοῖς** δώσει ἀγαθὰ τοῖς αἰτοῦσιν αὐτόν;

Cf. Lk xi. 9-13, where the words occur in a different context.

vii. 13-14 Εἰσέλθετε διὰ τῆς στενῆς πύλης· ὅτι πλατεῖα ἡ πύλη καὶ εὐρύχωρος ἡ ὁδὸς ἡ ἀπάγουσα εἰς τὴν ἀπώλειαν, καὶ πολλοί εἰσιν οἱ εἰσερχόμενοι δι' αὐτῆς· ὅτι στενὴ ἡ πύλη καὶ τεθλιμμένη ἡ ὁδὸς ἡ ἀπάγουσα εἰς τὴν ζωήν, καὶ ὀλίγοι εἰσὶν οἱ εὑρίσκοντες αὐτήν.

Cf. Lk xiii. 24.

IX. Book of Sayings and the First Gospel 267

vii. 16-19 μήτι συλλέγουσιν ἀπὸ ἀκανθῶν σταφυλήν, ἢ ἀπὸ τριβόλων σῦκα; οὕτω πᾶν δένδρον ἀγαθὸν καρποὺς καλοὺς ποιεῖ, τὸ δὲ σαπρὸν δένδρον καρποὺς πονηροὺς ποιεῖ. οὐ δύναται δένδρον ἀγαθὸν καρποὺς πονηροὺς ποιεῖν, οὐδὲ δένδρον σαπρὸν καρποὺς καλοὺς ποιεῖν. πᾶν δένδρον μὴ ποιοῦν καρπὸν καλὸν ἐκκόπτεται καὶ εἰς πῦρ βάλλεται.
Cf. Lk vi. 43-5.

Detached sayings, i. e. sayings which stood in the source in positions which we cannot rediscover.

viii. 11-12 Λέγω δὲ ὑμῖν, ὅτι πολλοὶ ἀπὸ ἀνατολῶν καὶ δυσμῶν ἥξουσι, καὶ ἀνακλιθήσονται μετὰ Ἀβραὰμ καὶ Ἰσαὰκ καὶ Ἰακὼβ ἐν τῇ βασιλείᾳ τῶν οὐρανῶν· οἱ δὲ υἱοὶ τῆς βασιλείας ἐκβληθήσονται εἰς τὸ σκότος τὸ ἐξώτερον· ἐκεῖ ἔσται ὁ κλαυθμὸς καὶ ὁ βρυγμὸς τῶν ὀδόντων.
Cf. Lk xiii. 28-9.

The Editor of the First Gospel has inserted these verses into the narrative of the healing of the centurion's servant.

viii. 19-22 Καὶ προσελθὼν εἷς γραμματεὺς εἶπεν αὐτῷ, Διδάσκαλε, ἀκολουθήσω σοι, ὅπου ἐὰν ἀπέρχῃ. καὶ λέγει αὐτῷ ὁ Ἰησοῦς, Αἱ ἀλώπεκες φωλεοὺς ἔχουσι, καὶ τὰ πετεινὰ τοῦ οὐρανοῦ κατασκηνώσεις· ὁ δὲ υἱὸς τοῦ ἀνθρώπου οὐκ ἔχει, ποῦ τὴν κεφαλὴν κλίνῃ. ἕτερος δὲ τῶν μαθητῶν εἶπεν αὐτῷ, Κύριε, ἐπίτρεψόν μοι πρῶτον ἀπελθεῖν καὶ θάψαι τὸν πατέρα μου. ὁ δὲ Ἰησοῦς λέγει αὐτῷ, Ἀκολούθει μοι, καὶ ἄφες τοὺς νεκροὺς θάψαι τοὺς ἑαυτῶν νεκρούς.
Cf. Lk ix. 57-60.

ix. 13 Πορευθέντες δὲ μάθετε τί ἐστιν, Ἔλεον θέλω, καὶ οὐ θυσίαν.

This saying is inserted by the Editor into Mark's narrative of the controversy about fasting. He inserts it again later (xii. 7) into Mark's account of the controversy about eating on the Sabbath.

xii. 5-7 Οὐκ ἀνέγνωτε ἐν τῷ νόμῳ, ὅτι τοῖς σάββασιν οἱ ἱερεῖς ἐν τῷ ἱερῷ τὸ σάββατον βεβηλοῦσι, καὶ ἀναίτιοί εἰσι; λέγω δὲ ὑμῖν, ὅτι τοῦ ἱεροῦ μεῖζόν ἐστιν ὧδε. εἰ δὲ ἐγνώκειτε τί ἐστιν, Ἔλεον θέλω καὶ οὐ θυσίαν, οὐκ ἂν κατεδικάσατε τοὺς ἀναιτίους. κύριος γάρ ἐστι τοῦ σαββάτου ὁ υἱὸς τοῦ ἀνθρώπου.

This section is inserted by the Editor of the First Gospel into Mark's account of the controversy about eating on the Sabbath.

xii. 11-12 Τίς ἔσται ἐξ ὑμῶν ἄνθρωπος, ὃς ἕξει πρόβατον ἕν, καὶ ἐὰν ἐμπέσῃ τοῦτο τοῖς σάββασιν εἰς βόθυνον, οὐχὶ κρατήσει αὐτὸ καὶ ἐγερεῖ; πόσῳ οὖν διαφέρει ἄνθρωπος προβάτου; ὥστε ἔξεστι τοῖς σάββασι καλῶς ποιεῖν.

This is inserted by the Editor into a narrative recorded by Mark of a healing performed on the Sabbath.
Cf. Lk xiv. 5, xiii. 15.

xiii. 16-17 Ὑμῶν δὲ μακάριοι οἱ ὀφθαλμοί, ὅτι βλέπουσι, καὶ τὰ ὦτα ὑμῶν, ὅτι ἀκούει· ἀμὴν γὰρ λέγω ὑμῖν, ὅτι πολλοὶ προφῆται καὶ δίκαιοι ἐπεθύμησαν ἰδεῖν ἃ βλέπετε, καὶ οὐκ εἶδον, καὶ ἀκοῦσαι ἃ ἀκούετε, καὶ οὐκ ἤκουσαν.

These verses are inserted by the Editor of the First Gospel into Mark's account of Christ's reason for speaking in parables.
Cf. Lk x. 23-4.

xv. 13-14 Ὁ δὲ ἀποκριθεὶς εἶπε, Πᾶσα φυτεία, ἣν οὐκ ἐφύτευσεν ὁ πατήρ μου ὁ οὐράνιος, ἐκριζωθήσεται. ἄφετε αὐτούς· ὁδηγοί εἰσι τυφλοί· τυφλὸς δὲ τυφλὸν ἐὰν ὁδηγῇ, ἀμφότεροι εἰς βόθυνον πεσοῦνται.

Inserted by the Editor into Mark's account of the controversy about eating with unwashed hands.
Cf. Lk vi. 39.

IX. Book of Sayings and the First Gospel 269

xvi. 17-19 Μακάριος εἶ, Σίμων Βὰρ Ἰωνᾶ, ὅτι σὰρξ καὶ αἷμα οὐκ ἀπεκάλυψέ σοι, ἀλλ' ὁ πατήρ μου ὁ ἐν τοῖς οὐρανοῖς. κἀγὼ δέ σοι λέγω, ὅτι σὺ εἶ Πέτρος, καὶ ἐπὶ ταύτῃ τῇ πέτρᾳ οἰκοδομήσω μου τὴν ἐκκλησίαν, καὶ πύλαι ᾅδου οὐ κατισχύσουσιν αὐτῆς. δώσω σοὶ τὰς κλεῖς τῆς **βασιλείας τῶν οὐρανῶν**· καὶ ὃ ἐὰν **δήσῃς** ἐπὶ τῆς γῆς, ἔσται **δεδεμένον** ἐν τοῖς οὐρανοῖς· καὶ ὃ ἐὰν **λύσῃς** ἐπὶ τῆς γῆς, ἔσται λελυμένον ἐν τοῖς οὐρανοῖς.

Inserted by the Editor into Mark's account of St. Peter's confession of faith at Caesarea Philippi.

On these verses see *St. Matthew*, pp. 176-9.

xviii. 7 Οὐαὶ τῷ κόσμῳ ἀπὸ τῶν σκανδάλων· ἀνάγκη γάρ ἐστιν ἐλθεῖν τὰ σκάνδαλα· πλὴν οὐαὶ τῷ ἀνθρώπῳ ἐκείνῳ, δι' οὗ τὸ σκάνδαλον ἔρχεται.

Cf. Lk xvii. 1.

xviii. 10 Ὁρᾶτε μὴ καταφρονήσητε ἑνὸς τῶν μικρῶν τούτων· λέγω γὰρ ὑμῖν, ὅτι οἱ ἄγγελοι αὐτῶν ἐν οὐρανοῖς διὰ παντὸς βλέπουσι τὸ πρόσωπον **τοῦ πατρός μου τοῦ ἐν οὐρανοῖς**.

xviii. 12-14 Τί ὑμῖν δοκεῖ; ἐὰν γένηταί τινι ἀνθρώπῳ ἑκατὸν πρόβατα, καὶ πλανηθῇ ἓν ἐξ αὐτῶν, οὐχὶ ἀφεὶς τὰ ἐννενηκονταεννέα, ἐπὶ τὰ ὄρη πορευθείς, ζητεῖ τὸ πλανώμενον; καὶ ἐὰν γένηται εὑρεῖν αὐτό, ἀμὴν λέγω ὑμῖν, ὅτι χαίρει ἐπ' αὐτῷ μᾶλλον, ἢ ἐπὶ τοῖς ἐννενηκονταεννέα τοῖς μὴ πεπλανημένοις. οὕτως οὐκ ἔστι θέλημα ἔμπροσθεν **τοῦ πατρὸς ὑμῶν τοῦ ἐν οὐρανοῖς**, ἵνα ἀπόληται εἷς τῶν μικρῶν τούτων.

Cf. Lk xv. 3-7.

xix. 11-12 Οὐ πάντες χωροῦσι τὸν λόγον τοῦτον, ἀλλ' οἷς δέδοται. εἰσὶ γὰρ εὐνοῦχοι, οἵτινες ἐκ κοιλίας μητρὸς ἐγεννήθησαν οὕτω· καί εἰσιν εὐνοῦχοι, οἵτινες εὐνουχίσθησαν ὑπὸ τῶν ἀνθρώπων· καί εἰσιν εὐνοῦχοι, οἵτινες εὐνούχισαν ἑαυτοὺς διὰ τὴν **βασιλείαν τῶν οὐρανῶν**. ὁ δυνάμενος χωρεῖν χωρείτω.

On these verses see *St. Matthew*, p. 204 f.

The words are added by the Editor to Mark's account of Christ's teaching about divorce.

xix. 28 Ἀμὴν λέγω ὑμῖν, ὅτι ὑμεῖς οἱ ἀκολουθήσαντές μοι, ἐν τῇ παλιγγενεσίᾳ ὅταν καθίσῃ ὁ υἱὸς τοῦ ἀνθρώπου ἐπὶ θρόνου δόξης αὐτοῦ, καθίσεσθε καὶ ὑμεῖς ἐπὶ δώδεκα θρόνους κρίνοντες τὰς δώδεκα φυλὰς τοῦ Ἰσραήλ.

Inserted by the Editor in Mark's account of Christ's teaching about riches.

xxiii. 37-9 Ἱερουσαλήμ, Ἱερουσαλήμ, ἡ ἀποκτείνουσα τοὺς προφήτας καὶ λιθοβολοῦσα τοὺς ἀπεσταλμένους πρὸς αὐτήν, ποσάκις ἠθέλησα ἐπισυναγαγεῖν τὰ τέκνα σου, ὃν τρόπον ἐπισυνάγει ὄρνις τὰ νοσσία ἑαυτῆς ὑπὸ τὰς πτέρυγας, καὶ οὐκ ἠθελήσατε. ἰδού, ἀφίεται ὑμῖν ὁ οἶκος ὑμῶν ἔρημος. λέγω γὰρ ὑμῖν, οὐ μή με ἴδητε ἀπ' ἄρτι, ἕως ἂν εἴπητε, Εὐλογημένος ὁ ἐρχόμενος ἐν ὀνόματι Κυρίου.

Added by the Editor at the end of the chapter of denunciation upon the Pharisees, ch. xxiii.

Cf. Lk xiii. 34-5.

Other Parables.

xx. 1-15. Labourers in the Vineyard. Ὁμοία γάρ ἐστιν ἡ βασιλεία τῶν οὐρανῶν ἀνθρώπῳ οἰκοδεσπότῃ, ὅστις ἐξῆλθεν ἅμα πρωῒ μισθώσασθαι ἐργάτας εἰς τὸν ἀμπελῶνα αὐτοῦ. συμφωνήσας δὲ μετὰ τῶν ἐργατῶν ἐκ δηναρίου τὴν ἡμέραν ἀπέστειλεν αὐτοὺς εἰς τὸν ἀμπελῶνα αὐτοῦ. καὶ ἐξελθὼν περὶ τὴν τρίτην ὥραν εἶδεν ἄλλους ἑστῶτας ἐν τῇ ἀγορᾷ ἀργούς, κἀκείνοις εἶπεν, Ὑπάγετε καὶ ὑμεῖς εἰς τὸν ἀμπελῶνα, καὶ ὃ ἐὰν ᾖ δίκαιον δώσω ὑμῖν. οἱ δὲ ἀπῆλθον. πάλιν ἐξελθὼν περὶ ἕκτην καὶ ἐννάτην ὥραν ἐποίησεν ὡσαύτως. περὶ δὲ τὴν ἑνδεκάτην ἐξελθὼν εὗρεν ἄλλους ἑστῶτας, καὶ λέγει αὐτοῖς, Τί ὧδε ἑστήκατε ὅλην τὴν ἡμέραν ἀργοί; λέγουσιν αὐτῷ, Ὅτι οὐδεὶς ἡμᾶς ἐμισθώσατο. λέγει αὐτοῖς, Ὑπάγετε καὶ ὑμεῖς εἰς τὸν ἀμπελῶνα. ὀψίας δὲ γενομένης λέγει ὁ κύριος τοῦ ἀμπελῶνος τῷ ἐπιτρόπῳ αὐτοῦ, Κάλεσον τοὺς ἐργάτας, καὶ ἀπόδος

IX. Book of Sayings and the First Gospel 271

αὐτοῖς τὸν μισθὸν ἀρξάμενος ἀπὸ τῶν ἐσχάτων ἕως τῶν πρώτων. καὶ ἐλθόντες οἱ περὶ τὴν ἐνδεκάτην ὥραν ἔλαβον ἀνὰ δηνάριον. καὶ ἐλθόντες οἱ πρῶτοι ἐνόμισαν ὅτι πλείονα λήψονται· καὶ ἔλαβον καὶ αὐτοὶ ἀνὰ δηνάριον. λαβόντες δὲ ἐγόγγυζον κατὰ τοῦ οἰκοδεσπότου λέγοντες ὅτι Οὗτοι οἱ ἔσχατοι μίαν ὥραν ἐποίησαν, καὶ ἴσους ἡμῖν αὐτοὺς ἐποίησας τοῖς βαστάσασι τὸ βάρος τῆς ἡμέρας καὶ τὸν καύσωνα. ὁ δὲ ἀποκριθεὶς εἶπεν ἑνὶ αὐτῶν, Ἑταῖρε, οὐκ ἀδικῶ σε· οὐχὶ δηναρίου συνεφώνησάς μοι; ἆρον τὸ σὸν καὶ ὕπαγε· θέλω δὲ τούτῳ τῷ ἐσχάτῳ δοῦναι ὡς καὶ σοί. οὐκ ἔξεστί μοι ποιῆσαι ὃ θέλω ἐν τοῖς ἐμοῖς; ἢ ὁ ὀφθαλμός σου **πονηρός** ἐστιν, ὅτι ἐγὼ ἀγαθός εἰμι;

Added by the Editor in Mark's account of Christ's teaching about riches to explain πολλοὶ δὲ ἔσονται πρῶτοι ἔσχατοι καὶ ἔσχατοι πρῶτοι.

xxi. 28-32. Parable of the Two Sons. Ἄνθρωπος εἶχε τέκνα δύο· καὶ προσελθὼν τῷ πρώτῳ εἶπε, Τέκνον, ὕπαγε, σήμερον ἐργάζου ἐν τῷ ἀμπελῶνι. ὁ δὲ ἀποκριθεὶς εἶπεν, Οὐ θέλω· ὕστερον δὲ μεταμεληθεὶς ἀπῆλθε. καὶ προσελθὼν τῷ δευτέρῳ εἶπεν ὡσαύτως. ὁ δὲ ἀποκριθεὶς εἶπεν, Ἐγώ, κύριε· καὶ οὐκ ἀπῆλθε. τίς ἐκ τῶν δύο **ἐποίησε τὸ θέλημα** τοῦ πατρός; λέγουσιν, Ὁ πρῶτος. λέγει αὐτοῖς ὁ Ἰησοῦς, Ἀμὴν λέγω ὑμῖν, ὅτι οἱ τελῶναι καὶ αἱ πόρναι προάγουσιν ὑμᾶς εἰς τὴν βασιλείαν τοῦ Θεοῦ. ἦλθε γὰρ πρὸς ὑμᾶς Ἰωάννης ἐν ὁδῷ **δικαιοσύνης**, καὶ οὐκ ἐπιστεύσατε αὐτῷ· οἱ δὲ τελῶναι καὶ αἱ πόρναι ἐπίστευσαν αὐτῷ· ὑμεῖς δὲ ἰδόντες οὐδὲ μετεμελήθητε ὕστερον, τοῦ πιστεῦσαι αὐτῷ.

xxii. 2-14. The Marriage Feast. Ὡμοιώθη ἡ **βασιλεία τῶν οὐρανῶν** ἀνθρώπῳ βασιλεῖ, ὅστις ἐποίησε γάμους τῷ υἱῷ αὐτοῦ, καὶ ἀπέστειλε τοὺς δούλους αὐτοῦ καλέσαι τοὺς κεκλημένους εἰς τοὺς γάμους· καὶ οὐκ ἤθελον ἐλθεῖν. πάλιν ἀπέστειλεν ἄλλους δούλους λέγων, Εἴπατε τοῖς κεκλημένοις, Ἰδού, τὸ ἄριστόν μου ἡτοίμακα· οἱ ταῦροί μου καὶ τὰ σιτιστὰ τεθυμένα, καὶ πάντα ἕτοιμα· δεῦτε εἰς τοὺς γάμους.

Οἱ δὲ ἀμελήσαντες ἀπῆλθον, ὁ μὲν εἰς τὸν ἴδιον ἀγρόν, ὁ δὲ ἐπὶ τὴν ἐμπορίαν αὐτοῦ· οἱ δὲ λοιποὶ κρατήσαντες τοὺς δούλους αὐτοῦ ὕβρισαν καὶ ἀπέκτειναν. ὁ δὲ βασιλεὺς ὠργίσθη, καὶ πέμψας τὰ στρατεύματα αὐτοῦ ἀπώλεσε τοὺς φονεῖς ἐκείνους, καὶ τὴν πόλιν αὐτῶν ἐνέπρησε. τότε λέγει τοῖς δούλοις αὐτοῦ, Ὁ μὲν γάμος ἕτοιμός ἐστιν, οἱ δὲ κεκλημένοι οὐκ ἦσαν ἄξιοι· πορεύεσθε οὖν ἐπὶ τὰς διεξόδους τῶν ὁδῶν, καὶ ὅσους ἂν εὕρητε καλέσατε εἰς τοὺς γάμους. καὶ ἐξελθόντες οἱ δοῦλοι ἐκεῖνοι εἰς τὰς ὁδοὺς συνήγαγον πάντας ὅσους εὗρον, πονηρούς τε καὶ ἀγαθούς· καὶ ἐπλήσθη ὁ γάμος ἀνακειμένων. εἰσελθὼν δὲ ὁ βασιλεὺς θεάσασθαι τοὺς ἀνακειμένους εἶδεν ἐκεῖ ἄνθρωπον οὐκ ἐνδεδυμένον ἔνδυμα γάμου· καὶ λέγει αὐτῷ, Ἑταῖρε, πῶς εἰσῆλθες ὧδε μὴ ἔχων ἔνδυμα γάμου; ὁ δὲ ἐφιμώθη. τότε ὁ βασιλεὺς εἶπε τοῖς διακόνοις, Δήσαντες αὐτοῦ πόδας καὶ χεῖρας ἐκβάλετε αὐτὸν εἰς τὸ σκότος τὸ ἐξώτερον· ἐκεῖ ἔσται ὁ κλαυθμὸς καὶ ὁ βρυγμὸς τῶν ὀδόντων. πολλοὶ γάρ εἰσι κλητοί, ὀλίγοι δὲ ἐκλεκτοί.

Cf. Lk xiv. 15–24.

§ 2. CONTENTS OF THE SOURCE.

The Source as reconstructed above contained:—

1. A discourse on the relation of Christ's disciples (*a*) to the Mosaic Law, (*b*) to the current Pharisaic religion (Sermon on the Mount).
2. A discourse to the disciples about their mission.
3. A discourse about the persecution which they would meet with. This may or may not have formed part of the preceding.
4. A discourse about John the Baptist.
5. Woes upon the cities in which Christ had preached.
6. Thanksgiving to the Father.
7. A discourse on the charge that He cast out devils by the help of Beelzebub.
8. A discourse in answer to the request for a sign.

IX. Book of Sayings and the First Gospel

9. A collection of Parables of the Kingdom.
10. A discourse and Parable about Forgiveness.
11. A denunciation of the Scribes and Pharisees.
12. Eschatological Sayings and Parables.
13. A number of detached sayings which the Editor of the First Gospel has inserted partly into Mark's narratives, partly into the longer discourses mentioned above.
14. Three other Parables.

It will no doubt be objected to the above reconstruction that critical reasons make it certain that Matthew and Luke had a common source (for at least the Sermon on the Mount) in which the Sermon was followed by the Miracle of the healing of the Centurion's Servant, and that this narrative therefore ought to find a place in any reconstruction of the source. On this see *St. Matthew*, p. 73.

I would only add here that if the reconstruction attempted above gives at all a true idea of the source, it is almost impossible that the miracle formed part of it. For (1) a miracle would be quite out of place in a collection of discourses and sayings such as the above; (2) the miracle has none of the features which are collected below as characteristic of the source. Mt viii. 11-12 do contain such features, but, as the absence of these verses in Luke's account of the miracle shows, they are not an integral part of the narrative but have probably been inserted here by the Editor of the First Gospel from the source.

Matthew and Luke may very well have obtained this miracle from a common source, but, if so, that source must have been some other Gospel writing than the book of discourses which has been constructed above, and which the Editor of the First Gospel used so freely.

For somewhat similar reasons I have omitted from the source the records of John's preaching and of the Temptation and Baptism of Christ. Matthew and Luke may have had a common source for these, but, if so, it must have been some writing other than the discourse source above reconstructed. The strongly anti-Pharisaic character of the account of the Baptist's preaching, iii. 7-12, would indeed suit the discourse source well enough. But what has this account of the Baptist to do in a book containing sayings of Christ? Moreover these sections, viz. the Baptist's preaching, Mt iii. 1-12, the Baptism, iii. 13-17, and the Temptation, iv. 1-11, have characteristics of their own which sharply differentiate them from the source, e.g. the historic presents in narrative, iii. 1, 13, 15; iv. 5, 8ᵇ, 11. On the one hand, these cannot be due to the Editor, who systematically obliterates the historic presents in Mark (except λέγει -ουσιν) some sixty-nine out of seventy-nine times. On the other, these historic tenses are quite foreign to the source, for its narrative sections, viz. the Parables, and e.g. xi. 2-4, 20; xii. 38; xiii. 51, contain no such tenses (λέγει -ουσιν excepted). The inference is that in iii. 1-12, 13-17; iv. 1-11, the Editor is using sources other than his discourse source. The phrase ἡ ἁγία πόλις, iv. 5, links these narratives with xxvii. 50-4, which certainly did not come from the discourse source.

iii. 12 might well be a fragment of the discourse source on the ground of δικαιοσύνη (see below), but this must remain uncertain.

§ 3. CHARACTER OF THE SOURCE.

The disciples of Christ, as they are presupposed in these sayings, are Jews. This is implied throughout the book rather than anywhere expressly stated. The contrast is that of Christian Jews versus the official Judaism of the day, and not that of Gentiles versus Jews. Official Judaism, as represented by the Scribes and Pharisees, is everywhere condemned. It is a purely formal religion, vi. 1-18; xxiii. 4-11, 27-8. Its leaders reject Christ and attribute His miracles to Beelzebub, x. 25; xii. 27-37. They will also

IX. Book of Sayings and the First Gospel

persecute His disciples, x. 24-9. But though they regard themselves as the true heirs of the kingdom, viii. 12, they will be expelled from it, and Christ's disciples will be seen to be the rightful inheritors, xiii. 38.

The Christian disciples are spoken of as a society of people characterized by spiritual qualifications, v. 3-9, persecuted, reproached, and evil spoken of, v. 10-11. They are still subject to the Law[1] of Moses, v. 17-20, but are to avoid the current unspiritual interpretation of it, and, by penetrating more deeply into its religious implications, are to aim at a righteousness which is to be greater than that of the Scribes and Pharisees, v. 21. They are to preach the 'kingdom of the heavens' 'to the lost sheep of the house of Israel', x. 6, not to Gentiles or Samaritans, x. 5^b.

The horizon of the community of Christ's disciples is everywhere assumed to be the coming of the 'kingdom of the heavens'. Of this it is said that it belongs to the 'poor in spirit', v. 3, and to those who are 'persecuted for righteousness' sake', v. 10. They who 'do the will of the Father who is in the heavens' will enter into it, vii. 21. It will come at the 'end of the age', xiii. 40, when the wicked will be cast out and the righteous will shine forth, xiii. 41-3. The doctrine about the kingdom is far-reaching and deeply penetrating, xiii. 31-3. Men will give up everything else for it, xiii. 43-6. The disciples are to pray for its coming, vi. 10.

Beyond the statement that it will come at the 'end of the age', xiii. 40, nothing is said explicitly as to the period and manner of its coming.

But there is another series of statements which throws light upon this. In x. 23 we read that the missionaries

[1] Characteristic of this source is the representation of Christ as sanctioning divorce for adultery in accordance with the Law. Influenced by this the Editor has made Mk x. 1-12 unintelligible by introducing this sanction into it, Mt xix 3-9.

would not have finished the cities of Israel until the Son of Man should come. Again, in xiii. 41 we read that at the 'end of the age' the Son of Man will send forth His angels. A little later, in xix. 28, we hear of the 'regeneration' when the Son of Man will sit upon the 'throne of his glory', or of the Son of Man coming in His glory, xxv. 31. This coming is called 'the parousia of the Son of Man', xxiv. 27, 37, 39.

That the 'coming of the kingdom' and the 'coming' or 'parousia' of 'the Son of Man' are equivalent terms is clear from the section xxv. 31-46. There the Son of Man comes in His glory with all His angels, 31. Three verses later He is called the 'king', 34, and bids the elect 'inherit the kingdom prepared for you from the foundation of the world'.

That the Editor of the First Gospel identified the coming of the kingdom and the coming of the Son of Man is shown by the fact that under the influence of this idea he has substituted for Mark's phrase 'the kingdom of God come with power', Mk ix. 1, the words 'the Son of Man coming in his kingdom', xvi. 28. The Jewish horizon of these statements about the kingdom comes out very clearly in xix. 28, where it is said that when the Son of Man sits upon the 'throne of his glory' the disciples will 'sit on twelve thrones judging the twelve tribes of Israel'.

Of course it may be argued that in the case of some of the parables, e.g. the Leaven and the Mustard Seed, it is more natural to interpret 'the kingdom of the heavens' as the Christian Church, or the Christian system, or the spiritual forces behind Christianity.

But the point is that in dealing with the phrase *in the source* we are not asking what the phrase originally meant as used in these parables by Christ, nor what the phrase might connote (it may of course in such a parable as the Mustard Seed denote anything that anybody cares to read

IX. Book of Sayings and the First Gospel 277

into it), but what it meant, first to the compiler of the source, and secondly to the Editor of the First Gospel who used that source. To both these writers the phrase signified, as the whole tenor of their writings shows, 'the coming kingdom of the Son of Man'.

The source, then, is characterized by a very primitive type of doctrine. Christ is the 'Son of Man', or the 'king' of the coming kingdom. He is also the 'Son' of God who alone can reveal the Father, xi. 25-7. He was greater than Jonah, xii. 41, or Solomon, xii. 42, greater also than the Temple, xii. 6.

Primitive too and very Jewish is much of the phraseology of the source. Characteristic here are:

(1) ἡ βασιλεία τῶν οὐρανῶν, 22 times. This always signifies the coming kingdom. See *St. Matthew*, pp. lxvii-lxxi, and on xi. 12 see *St. Matthew*, pp. 116-17. Whether the phrase here is part of a comment by the Evangelist, or whether he records it as an utterance of Christ borrowed from the source, it can only denote the coming kingdom, treated with violence in the person of its representatives (just as we might say that 'Free Trade' or 'Compulsory Service' is badly treated) or making great progress amongst men. Twice in the source, viz. xii. 28 and xxi. 31, occurs ἡ βασιλεία τοῦ θεοῦ. In xii. 28 it has a meaning different to that of ἡ βασιλεία τῶν οὐρανῶν, and the Editor, who would certainly have substituted the latter phrase if it had been possible, has retained the phrase of the source. In xxi. 31 the same inference is to be drawn, ἡ βασιλεία τοῦ θεοῦ stood in the source, and the Editor retained it because he felt that ἡ βασιλεία τῶν οὐρανῶν, in the sense (eschatological) which he understood it to have everywhere else, would not be suitable here. See *St. Matthew*, p. 227.

(2) ὁ υἱὸς τοῦ ἀνθρώπου, 13 times.

(3) ὁ πατὴρ ὁ ἐν τοῖς οὐρανοῖς, 13 times, not elsewhere. See *St. Matthew*, p. 44.

(4) ὁ πατὴρ ὁ οὐράνιος, 5 times, and ὁ ἐπουράνιος, xviii. 35, not elsewhere.

(5) πατήρ = God, followed by a possessive pronoun, 10 times.

(6) συντέλεια τοῦ αἰῶνος, xiii. 39, 40, 49.

(7) παρουσία, xxiv. 27, 37, 39.

(8) ἐκεῖ ἔσται ὁ κλαυθμὸς καὶ ὁ βρυγμὸς τῶν ὀδόντων, 6 times, once in Luke.

(9) δικαιοσύνη, in *Sayings* attributed to Christ, 6 times, not in Mark or Luke.

(10) μισθός, in *Sayings* attributed to Christ, 10 times, in Mark once, in Luke 3 times.

The above are all Jewish in phrase and in idea.

More isolated Jewish phrases or ideas are the following:—

(11) 'dogs' and 'swine', vii. 6, as metaphors for Gentiles or unbelievers.

(12) 'yoke', xi. 29-30, of a body of teaching, as in the Jewish phrase 'yoke of the law' or 'yoke of the kingdom', not in Mark or Luke.

(13) 'flesh and blood', 'gates of Hades', 'bind and loose', xvi. 17-19, not in Mark or Luke.

(14) 'scribe' of Christian teachers, xiii. 52, cf. xxiii. 34, not in Mark or Luke.

(15) οἱ δίκαιοι = the elect, xiii. 43, 49; xxv. 37, 46, not in Mark or Luke.

(16) τὸ σκότος τὸ ἐξώτερον, viii. 12; xxii. 13; xxv. 30, not in Mark or Luke.

(17) θρόνος δόξης, xix. 28, xxv. 31.

(18) ποιεῖν τὸ θέλημα, 3 times, once in Mark, not in Luke.

Other characteristic words of the source are:—

ὑποκριτής, 14 times (especially of the Pharisees), Mark once, Luke 3 times.

ἐθνικός, 3 times, not in Mark or Luke.

ἔμπροσθεν, in *Sayings* attributed to Christ, 13 times, not in Mark in sayings, 5 times in Luke.

IX. Book of Sayings and the First Gospel 279

ὁμοιόω, 8 times, Mark once, Luke 3 times.

ἀδελφός (figurative), v. 22 (twice), 23, 24, 47 ; vii. 3, 4, 5 ; xviii. 15 (twice), 21, 35 ; xxiii. 8 ; xxv. 40, not in this sense in Mark, in Luke 6 times, of which 4 are parallel to Mt vii. 3–5 ; xviii. 15.

πονηρός, 23 times, twice in Mark, 12 times in Luke, especially ὁ πονηρός = the devil, xiii. 19, 38, and perhaps v. 37 ; vi. 13, not in Mark, in Luke only perhaps in xi. 4 = Mt vi. 13.

συνάγω, in *Sayings* attributed to Christ, 13 times, not in Mark, 4 times in Luke.

ἑταῖρος, xi. 17 (?) ; xx. 13 ; xxii. 12, not in Mark or Luke.

οἱ ἄνθρωποι, 23 times (viii. 27 is different), elsewhere in the First Gospel ix. 8, and from Mk, xvi. 13, 23 ; Mark 4 times, Luke 8 times.

ἀνομία, 4 times, not in Mark or Luke.

I have purposely omitted from the above any great use of xvi. 17–19, on account of the difficulty of these verses.

The problem of this passage consists in the fact that we have here combined—

(*a*) an unusual number of purely Jewish expressions in a few lines, σὰρξ καὶ αἷμα (Gal i. 21 looks like a reference to this saying. Heb ii. 14 is different), ὁ πατήρ ὁ ἐν τοῖς οὐρανοῖς, πύλαι ᾅδου, the 'binding' and 'loosing', ἡ βασιλεία τῶν οὐρανῶν, perhaps also the contrast ' earth—heaven '; cf. vi. 10.

(*b*) The occurrence of ἐκκλησία and an impression that in these verses ' kingdom of the heavens ' and ' church ' are used as equivalent terms.

The Jewish terminology would suggest a very early date for the words. On the other hand, if ' church ' and ' kingdom ' are equivalent, the words can hardly have been written until late in the first century or even after its close.

The question therefore is, Ought an impression, made

perhaps wrongly by the juxtaposition of two phrases, to outweigh the positive evidence of the Jewish phraseology which suggests a Palestinian origin and date for the verses?

The mere use of ἐκκλησία ought to cause no difficulty. St. Paul's letters are evidence that within thirty years of Christ's death this term was the natural one to apply to any community of Christ's disciples. Further that Christ should have spoken of His disciples as forming a community, school, guild, society, congregation of some sort, marked off from their Jewish fellow countrymen by their belief in Him as the Son of Man, is intelligible and natural.

So that when His words were put into Greek, ἐκκλησία (probably on account of its usage in the LXX for the congregation of Israel) was a very natural term to select as the rendering of the Aramaic original, whatever that may have been.

But is the ἐκκλησία identical with the 'kingdom of the heavens'? If so, the words cannot have stood in the source. There seems little reason for this identification. See *St. Matthew*, p. 177. The ἐκκλησία here and in xviii. 17 is the body of Palestinian adherents of Christ. The 'kingdom of the heavens' is as elsewhere the coming kingdom for which they were waiting. Just as all the Apostles are to sit on twelve thrones in that kingdom, acting as judges, xix. 28, so St. Peter is to have legal authority in it. But if this authority of his is to be exercised in the coming kingdom, how can it be said to be exercised 'upon earth'? The answer is that there is nothing in the source which suggests that the coming kingdom of the heavens would be anywhere else than upon earth.

Thus here as elsewhere in the source we find ideas about the kingdom which are primitive and Palestinian. They remind us of the early days of the Church at Jerusalem when, as the writer of the Book of the Acts narrates, St. Peter took the lead in Church matters.

IX. Book of Sayings and the First Gospel

We must leave undeveloped the later history of this primitive book of Christ's sayings. The question whether Mark had read it is too difficult to be discussed here. If, as seems probable, he drew from it some of the sayings which he recorded, then we ought to add to it some at least of the sayings which are found in Matthew and Mark. I have omitted these from the preceding reconstruction solely because, so far as Matthew is concerned, it is certain that he had them before him in Mark, and uncertain whether they occurred also in the discourse source.

A little later than the date of the composition of St. Mark's Gospel the Editor of the First Gospel took this work and the book of discourses, and wove them together.

How greatly he was influenced by the discourse source his Gospel shows. In the spirit of v. 17-20 he cannot think that Christ, as St. Mark would seem to suggest, abolished the Mosaic distinctions between clean and unclean meats (see *St. Matthew*, p. 167 note).

Influenced by v. 32 he has removed the impression left by Mk x. 8-11 that Christ had set aside the Mosaic sanction of divorce.

And under the influence of the discourse source he everywhere alters Mark's 'kingdom of God' into 'kingdom of the heavens' (Mt xix. 24 = Mk x. 25 is a possible exception).

Nor can we here discuss the question whether St. Luke ever saw this book of discourses. If it has been rightly reconstructed above it is hardly likely that he was acquainted with it. He certainly has in his Gospel much that ultimately came from it. But St. Luke knew many Gospel writings, i. 1, and it is probable that some of these had already borrowed largely from the discourse source. In that case St. Luke's acquaintance with it was only indirect.

In conclusion it will be seen that the source reconstructed above is a source for the First Gospel, not for the Third. On the same kind of principle, i. e. of putting together passages homogeneous in character, and characterized by a special phraseology, it might be possible to reconstruct for the Third Gospel one or more sources in addition to Mark. But these sources would not be the same source that we have constructed for the First Gospel, though one or more of them might contain matter parallel to that found in the source of the First Gospel.

The argument of the previous pages has, I hope, shown that by putting together passages which occur in the First Gospel, exclusive of the passages there borrowed from Mark, a book of sayings is obtained, characterized by a uniform phraseology and a distinctive theology. The fact that St. Luke records many parallel sayings does not lead to the conclusion that he used the same source, because, in the form in which he gives them, they are often different in phraseology, in context, and sometimes in meaning. These differences suggest that he borrowed them from sources other than that employed in the First Gospel. If it be said that the language is often remarkably similar in the two Gospels the answer is that (*a*) Similarity of language does not always prove identity of source. If Mark's Gospel had been lost, and we now attempted to reconstruct it out of the First and Second Gospels, identity of language, and agreement in omission and insertion, would lead us to place in our reconstructed Mark a number of phrases which as a matter of fact do not belong to Mark, and to omit some of Mark's most strikingly characteristic phrases and sections. This fact alone shows how precarious is the method of reconstructing a common source out of the First and Third Gospels on the ground of agreements in language. A Mark reconstructed on this principle would be very unlike our Mark. (*b*) In sayings of Jesus much identity of language was to be expected even though the immediate sources from which they were taken were widely different. E.g. the Lord's Prayer must have

IX. Book of Sayings and the First Gospel

been widely current in the Greek-speaking Churches, probably before any Greek Gospel was written. But there is no evidence that any form of it had any variant for the remarkable ἐπιούσιος. (c) There is some probability that at least some part of the identity of language between the First and Third Gospels is due to assimilation of one Gospel to the other.

If it be said further that the suggestion in the foregoing pages that the Editor of the First Gospel drew directly from an Apostolic book of sayings, and that the Editor of the Third Gospel procured some of the same sayings not directly from the source, but indirectly through other writers, cannot be right because the language of a saying in Luke seems sometimes more original than the language of the parallel saying in Matthew, the answer is that Luke's occasional priority in respect of language does not affect the argument. E.g. it is urged that Luke's πτωχοί (vi. 20) is more original than Matthew's πτωχοὶ τῷ πνεύματι (v. 3). That, if it be true, only shows that the Editor of our First Gospel has sometimes modified the language of his source, and that the saying in question has eventually reached Luke in an unmodified form. Πτωχοί may have stood in Greek or in its Aramaic original in Mt's source. But 'Matthew' when writing the First Gospel may well have known that the Palestinian 'poor' = 'godly, oppressed poor' would be misleading unless interpreted to Greek readers. And indeed there is some probability that the single word in the saying as it eventually reached Luke misled him, or had previously misled the writer of the book from which he borrowed the saying.

Additional Notes.

Numerical Arrangement in the Source.

Nine Beatitudes, v. 3–12.
Three times ἐρρέθη, v. 21, 27, 31.

Again three times ἐρρέθη, v. 33, 38, 43. This second series is introduced by πάλιν.
Three examples of Pharisaic 'righteousness', vi. 2, 5, 16.
Three aspirations in the Lord's Prayer, vi. 10.
Three petitions in the Lord's Prayer, vi. 11-13.
Three times μὴ φοβηθῆτε, x. 26, 28, 31.
Three times οὐκ ἔστιν μου ἄξιος, x. 37-8.
Three sayings about 'receiving', x. 40-2.
Three parables—'Tares', 'Mustard Seed', 'Leaven', xiii. 24-33.
Three parables—'Hid Treasure', 'Goodly Pearl', 'Draw-net', xiii. 44-50.
Three eschatological parables, xxiv. 43-xxv. 30.

The Jewish character of the language of the Source.

The few illustrations given are selected on the ground that they are easily verifiable by readers unacquainted with Hebrew.

δικαιοσύνη. Harnack remarks that 'this Evangelist has also a preference for the conception δίκαιος (δικαιοσύνη)'. But with the exception of iii. 15 δικαιοσύνη occurs only in passages which come from the source. It is unnecessary to illustrate the Jewish atmosphere of this conception.

μισθός. Here, too, illustration would be superfluous. Cf. *St. Matthew*, p. 42.

ζυγός. Cf. *Mechiltha*,[1] p. 15, 'He who transgresses one commandment breaks the Yoke and destroys the Covenant,' and *Sayings of the Jewish Fathers*,[2] iii. 8, 'Whoso receives upon him the Yoke of Torah.'

ποιεῖν τὸ θέλημα. Cf. *Mechiltha*, p. 37, 'to do the will of Him who spake and the world was'; p. 57, 'that the reward of those who do His will might be great'; p. 124, 'when the Israelites do the will of God, His name will

---

[1] *Mechiltha, übersetzt von J. Winter und A. Wünsche.* Leipzig, 1909.
[2] Edited by C. Taylor.

IX. Book of Sayings and the First Gospel

be made great in the world'; p. 305, 'to increase the reward of those who do His will'; and pp. 86, 119, 125, 129, 338, 340.

Cf. also *Sayings*, v. 30, quoted below.

ἐθνικός. The original was probably גוי, which in Biblical Hebrew means 'nation', but in Rabbinic Hebrew = 'nicht-Jude': see Levy, *Neuhebräisches und Chaldäisches Wörterbuch*.

ὁμοιόω. For this word in connexion with parables see *St. Matthew*, p. 119.

ἡ βασιλεια τῶν οὐρανῶν. In Jewish literature מלכות שמים denotes God's supreme authority, and this can of course be regarded from many points of view. It may be an ideal realized in partial measure by all who submit themselves to the divine will, or in Jewish language 'take upon themselves the yoke of the kingdom'. Or from another point of view it is the divine will which, as a matter of fact, is supreme, in spite of all appearances to the contrary, and although this supremacy is recognized only by the godly. Or it may be regarded from the point or view of that moment in the future when this supremacy will be recognized universally by all men. In the New Testament ἡ βασιλεία τοῦ θεοῦ has all these meanings, but in our source ἡ βασιλεία τῶν οὐρανῶν seems always used in the eschatological sense. 'The kingdom of the heavens' is not yet. It is imminent and will be inaugurated when the Son of Man comes with the clouds of the heavens. See, for the Rabbinic teaching about the kingdom, Schechter, *Some Aspects of Jewish Theology*, cc. 5-7, and more especially for its eschatological aspects Volz, *Jüdische Eschatologie*, pp. 299 ff.

ὁ πατὴρ ὁ ἐν τοῖς οὐρανοῖς. Cf. *Mechiltha* (ed. Winter und Wünsche), p. 7, 'the Israelites ... lift up their eyes to their Father who is in the heavens'; p. 149, 'The Israelites humbled themselves before their Father who is in the heavens'; p. 213, 'my Father who is in the heavens'.

Sayings of the Jewish Fathers (ed. Taylor), v. 30, 'R. Jehudah ben Thema said, Be bold as a leopard, and swift as an eagle, and fleet as a hart, and strong as a lion, to do the will of thy Father which is in heaven.'
If the ὁ ἐν τοῖς οὐρανοῖς is, as Harnack and others think, 'a liturgical addition' the addition must have been made by the writer of the source, not by Matthew. But there is no reason why Christ should not have used expressions characteristic of the devotion of His age.

ἀδελφός, in a figurative sense, is characteristic of all Jewish literature.

σὰρξ καὶ αἷμα, a frequent phrase in Jewish writings.

'bind' and 'loose' also frequent.

For the 'rock' of xvi. 18 cf. the passage quoted by Schechter, p. 59, 'When he perceived that Abraham would one day arise he said, Behold I have found the petra on which to build and base the world.'

The proverb ᾧ μέτρῳ μετρεῖτε μετρηθήσεται ὑμῖν, vii. 2, is frequent in Midrashic literature, cf. *Mechiltha*, pp. 76, 79, 126, 128, 133, 173.

The antithesis, heaven—earth, vi. 9; xvi. 19; xviii. 18, 19, is frequent in Jewish writings, and this is also the case with that other antithesis 'in secret—openly', vi. 4. Cf. *Mechiltha*, p. 44, 'He who practises anything in secret the Holy One, blessed be He, makes him known openly'; p. 193. 'If thou callest in secret I will answer thee in publicity.'

Some of the language, however, is akin rather to the Apocalyptic style.

ἡ συντέλεια τοῦ αἰῶνος. See *St. Matthew*, p. 153.

ὁ υἱὸς τοῦ ἀνθρώπου. See *St. Matthew*, p. lxxi.

ὁ κλαυθμὸς καὶ ὁ βρυγμὸς τῶν ὀδόντων. See *St. Matthew*, p. 78.

τὸ σκότος τὸ ἐξώτερον, ib.

θρόνος δόξης. See *St. Matthew*, p. 183.

THE ARAMAIC BACKGROUND OF THE GOSPELS

SYLLABUS

1. Various opinions as to the language spoken by Christ, p. 288 f.
2. Some data, pp. 289–91.
3. Some probabilities, p. 291 f.
4. Language in which the Gospels were written, pp. 292–5:
    (*a*) St. Luke in Greek.
    (*b*) St. Mark in Aramaic.
    (*c*) St. Matthew in Greek.
5. Aramaisms in St. Mark, pp. 295–9.
6. Alleged Aramaisms in the Sayings common to St. Matthew and St. Luke, pp. 299–304.
7. Evidence alleged to prove that Christ spoke in Aramaic, pp. 304–6.
8. Conclusions, p. 306.
9. Notes, pp. 307–12.

THE ARAMAIC BACKGROUND OF THE GOSPELS

THE question as to the language spoken by our Lord has been much debated during the last century and a half. In 1767 a Neapolitan named Diodati tried to prove that at the Christian era Greek was the only language spoken in Palestine.[1] Five years later a reply appeared from the pen of De Rossi,[2] who held that at this period the Hellenistic language was not current in Palestine, and that Christ spoke Syro-Chaldee. He was followed in 1798 by Pfannkuche,[3] who came to the same conclusion. Five years later a more moderate view was put forward by Prof. Paulus of Jena, who held that Aramaic was the current language in Palestine in the time of Christ, but that Greek was so commonly spoken that Christ may have employed it.[4] Since this date it has been commonly accepted that Aramaic was the popular language of Palestine in the lifetime of Christ. This has been argued at length by Dalman,[5] Neubauer,[6] Meyer,[7] Zahn,[8] and Schürer,[9] and is assumed for Jerusalem by so eminent an authority as Wellhausen,[10] as well as by the host of writers on the New Testament who, knowing no Aramaic, are dependent here upon what they suppose to be expert

---

[1] *De Christo graece loquente exercitatio.* Neap., 1767.
[2] *Della lingua propria di Cristo e degli Ebrei nazionali della Palestina da' tempi de' Maccabei.* Parma, 1772.
[3] *Ueber die Palästinische Landessprache in dem Zeitalter Christi und der Apostel*, in Eichhorn's *Allgemeine Bibliothek*, vol. viii. Leipzig, 1798. Translated in Clark's *Biblical Cabinet*, vol. ii. Edin. 1833.
[4] *Verosimilia de Iudaeis Palaestinensibus Iesu atque etiam Apostolis non Aramaea dialecto sola, sed Graeca quoque Aramaizante locutis.* Jenae, 1803.
[5] *Words of Jesus.* Edin. 1902.
[6] *Studia Biblica*, i. Oxford, 1885.
[7] *Jesu Muttersprache.* Leipzig, 1896.
[8] *Einleitung in das Neue Testament.*
[9] *Jewish People in the Time of Christ*, II. i. 8. Edin. 1901.
[10] *Einleitung in die drei ersten Evangelien*, s. 14.

X. The Aramaic Background of the Gospels

authority. In favour of Greek as the language of Christ there are only two well-known names. In 1862 Dr. Roberts believed that he had proved 'beyond the reach of all reasonable objection, and from the undeniable facts of the New Testament history, that Greek and not Hebrew was the common language of public intercourse in the days of Christ and his Apostles';[1] and in 1891 Dr. T. K. Abbott[2] came to the conclusion that 'the admitted facts are quite reconcilable with the supposition that Aramaic was but little used, and by a minority; and are not reconcilable with the supposition that Greek was not generally familiar'.[3]

The following facts seem to be provable :—

(a) From the period of the exile to the Christian era Hebrew gradually ceased to be the language of ordinary life in Palestine, whilst it still continued to be the language of the schools and of sacred literature.

The following are written in Hebrew :—

c. 520, Haggai and Zechariah.

c. 450, Malachi, Isaiah lvi-lxvi (?).

c. 300, Chronicles, Ezra, Nehemiah (parts of Ezra are in Aramaic).

c. 170, Daniel (partly in Aramaic).[4]

The following were probably written in Hebrew, but are now extant in Greek :—

Ecclesiasticus, Pre-Maccabean.

Judith, Maccabean (?).

1 Maccabees, first cent. B. C.

---

[1] *Discussions on the Gospels*, p. 298. London, 1862. Reissued in 1888 as *Greek the Language of Christ and His Apostles*. See also *A Short Proof that Greek was the Language of Christ*. London, 1893.

[2] *Essays on the Original Texts of the Old and New Testaments*, No. 5, p. 182. London, 1891.

[3] See also Dr. Moulton's *Grammar of New Testament Greek*, p. 8. 'That Jesus Himself and the Apostles regularly used Aramaic is beyond question, but that Greek was also at command is almost equally certain.'

[4] The Hebrew Books of Ruth, Canticles, Esther, Ecclesiastes, Jonah, Job, and portions of the Psalter and the Book of Proverbs are of uncertain date, but all probably post-exile.

Psalms of Solomon, first cent. B. C.
Baruch i–iii. 8, date doubtful.
Testaments of the Twelve Patriarchs, second cent. B. C. (?).
The following may have been written in Hebrew, but are now extant only in other languages:—
Book of Jubilees, second cent. B. C.
Book of Enoch, first cent. B. C. (?).[1]

(*b*) After the return from captivity Aramaic gradually made its way in Palestine until it superseded Hebrew as the language of everyday life. For the proofs see Dalman, pp. 2 ff.; Schürer, II. i. 8 ff. It seems to have been little used for literary purposes in the pre-Christian and early post-Christian period. Parts of Ezra and Daniel are in Aramaic, and Marshall[2] believes that Tobit and Baruch iii. 9–iv. 4 were originally written in this language. Further, Josephus states that he first wrote his *Jewish War* in Aramaic.

(*c*) From the period of Alexander (c. 320) Greek culture found its way increasingly into Palestine. For proofs see Schürer, II. i. 11 ff. It is doubtful how far it was used by Palestinian Jews for literary purposes. The Wisdom of Solomon and 2, 3, and 4 Maccabees were probably written in Egypt, but the place of writing of the following is uncertain:—

Tobit, 200–100 B. C. (?).
The Greek Esdras before Josephus.
The Greek additions to Esther and Daniel.[3]
The Prayer of Manasses, date uncertain.
The Epistle of Jeremiah, date uncertain.

If it cannot be proved that any of these books were written in Palestine, or that the translators of 1 Maccabees, Judith,

---

[1] For evidence in favour of Hebrew originals of these books and of the *Testaments* see the editions of Dr. Charles.

[2] *Dict. Bib.*, articles *Tobit, Baruch*.

[3] The date of these additions is quite uncertain. Marshall, *Dict. Bib.*, argues for an Aramaic original of *Bel and the Dragon*.

X. The Aramaic Background of the Gospels

Psalms of Solomon, and the Testaments of the Twelve Patriarchs were Palestinians, it must yet remain possible that this was the case. That books were written in Greek by Palestinians is also made probable by the reference in early Christian writers to lost works of Jewish writers in Greek. Such were Theodotus, who wrote a poem on Sichem in hexameters (second cent. B.C.?); Philo, an epic poet (second cent. B.C.?); Ezekiel, a dramatic poet (second cent. B.C.?); Justus of Tiberias, an historian known to Josephus; Eupolemus, an historian (second cent. B.C.).[1]

Thus the evidence for any Palestinian Greek literature in the pre-Christian period seems to be slight, and mainly inferential. But we are not much better off in the case of Aramaic Palestinian literature in this period. And for the last century B.C. and first century A.D. the evidence for Hebrew Palestinian literature is of the nature of probability that books now extant in other languages were originally written in Hebrew.

Still more doubtful is the extent to which Greek was understood and spoken in Palestine in everyday life at the Christian era.[2] Schürer, who holds that 'Aramaic was in the time of Christ the sole popular language of Palestine', is nevertheless constrained to admit that 'a slight acquaintance with Greek was very widely diffused, and that the more educated classes used it without difficulty'; 'there must have been not infrequently the necessary acquaintance with the Greek tongue';[3] and Dalman, whilst arguing that 'Aramaic was the everyday speech of the Jewish people at this period', adds the significant qualification, 'in so far at least as it was not Greek.'[4]

It seems to be probable that in the last century B.C. and first century A.D. Hebrew, Aramaic, and Greek might be,

[1] On these writers see Schürer, II. iii. 222 ff.
[2] The best account of the spread of Greek in Palestine is perhaps to be found in Zahn, *Einleitung*, i. 24 ff.
[3] II. i. 9, 48.   [4] *W. J.*, p. 7.

and were, all alike used for literary purposes. Further, that for purposes of social intercourse Hebrew was dead except amongst the learned in the Jewish Rabbinical Schools. Aramaic was the language proper of Palestine, and the lower classes, especially in the villages, may have spoken it alone. But in view of the wide diffusion of Greek culture and religion since Alexander the Great, and the presence of large numbers of Greeks and Hellenistic Jews in the larger cities, it would have been easy for any intelligent Jew to acquire a smattering of Greek sufficient for purposes of conversation with Greeks whom he met in the Greek-speaking cities or with Hellenistic Jews who had settled in Palestine. The question whether Christ Himself spoke Greek can hardly be settled by arguing from general probabilities as to the spread of the Greek language in Palestine. To answer it we must interrogate the written records of His life and words.

And in dealing with these our question becomes a double one. The first three Gospels are written in Greek. (1) Was that their original language, and are they based on Greek sources? (2) Apart from the question of the language of the first Gospel writings, did Christ speak in Aramaic or in Greek?

The case of St. Luke is the easiest and may be taken first. It is written in Greek, and is largely based on Greek sources. That is to say, the compiler had before him a Greek Gospel practically identical with our St. Mark. He has also a good many sayings which are also found in St. Matthew. Whatever St. Matthew may have done, St. Luke no doubt drew them from a Greek source or sources. The rest of the Gospel of St. Luke was probably also based on Greek sources. The first two chapters, which are strongly marked by Hebraisms (not Aramaisms), have often been thought to be translation work of a Hebrew original. But it is equally possible that they were pur-

X. The Aramaic Background of the Gospels 293

posely written in the style of the Greek version of the Old Testament. St. Luke's language, generally speaking, in the Gospel is tinged with Hebraisms, but these need not anywhere be signs of translation work. Conscious imitation of the Septuagint will quite adequately account for them.

The case of the Second Gospel is rather different. This too is extant in Greek, and in the judgement of most modern writers that was the original language. The Greek of the Gospel is coloured by Aramaisms (not Hebraisms). So long ago as 1902 I ventured to suggest that the only adequate explanation of this foreign element is that the Gospel is a translation of an Aramaic original.[1] Recently this opinion has received the weighty corroboration of the judgement of Wellhausen. It is not sufficient to say that the writer may have been an Aramaic-speaking Jew who was not very adequately equipped with a knowledge of Greek, and that he was writing in Greek matter which had come to him orally in Aramaic. The evidence rather suggests, as Wellhausen points out, a translator of an Aramaic document who sometimes misinterprets by translating too literally.

On the original language of the First Gospel much has been written, but the investigations of the last century of criticism seem to have proved beyond reasonable doubt that the Gospel was written in Greek, and is based at least in part upon Greek sources. Like St. Luke, the author had before him a Gospel practically identical with our St. Mark. And he also has a good many sayings which in substance are also found in the Third Gospel.

It may be still debated whether these sayings lay before St. Luke and the author of the First Gospel in the same form and language. A comparison of the sayings common to the two writers does not suggest that the two writers were translating an Aramaic document. The present writer

[1] *Expository Times*, xiii. 328 ff.

believes that the author of the First Gospel had such a document (a collection of discourses by the Apostle Matthew) before him (either in a Greek translation or in the original Aramaic), and that St. Luke became acquainted with some of its contents when they had been translated into Greek and had become scattered in oral transmission or in the process of incorporation into other writings. (See pp. 281 ff.)

Thus an examination of the first three Gospels suggests the conclusion that they are at least in part based upon earlier Aramaic Gospel writings. The evidence for an original Aramaic Mark is perhaps slight, that for an Aramaic collection of discourses written by Matthew the Apostle rests upon the well-known evidence of Papias.[1] Meanwhile the conclusion so reached is perhaps surprising. In view of the fact that most of the extant Palestinian literature of a religious nature seems to have been written in Hebrew, we might have expected those who first attempted to record the words and works of the Messiah to have adopted this language.[2] The fact that they did not do so is probably due to many causes arising out of the circumstances of the early Palestinian Churches. By the time that the first written records were made, the gulf between the Jewish Christians and their compatriot Jews had probably widened. There may have been some sort of feeling that for records of Christ's life in Hebrew the use of the sacred language of Judaism would seem too much like

---

[1] Cited by Eus., *H. E.*, iii. 39. *Hebrew* in this passage may mean *Hebrew* or Aramaic. See Dalman, *W. J.*, p. 6, Zahn, *Einl.*, i. 18. It is possible that Papias identified τὰ λόγια with our First Gospel, but as Harnack points out (*Sayings*, p. 248) the informant of Papias may have known better.

[2] Attempts to show that the earliest Gospel writings were in Hebrew have not proved very successful. See Dalman, *W. J.*, 43 ff. Briggs (*Ethical Teaching of Jesus*, 4, 5) holds that the *Logia* was written in Hebrew, and that the narratives of the Infancy in Mt and Lk rest upon Hebrew originals. But the Hebraistic colouring of Lk i, ii may well be due to imitation of the Greek of the Septuagint, and elsewhere both the linguistic features of the Gospels and also general considerations favour Aramaic against Hebrew.

X. The Aramaic Background of the Gospels

an attempt to identify Christianity with the religion of the Scribes and Pharisees. Still more powerful would be the fact that Palestinian Christianity included in its membership many by whom Hebrew would be little understood. There were many Hellenists living in Palestine, of whom some would have some knowledge of Aramaic whilst others may have been acquainted only with Greek. There were many Galileans to whom again Aramaic would be acceptable. And there were no doubt others, e.g. at Antioch, to whom Greek would have been still more intelligible even if they understood any Aramaic at all. It was no doubt the increasing numbers of this element in Palestine itself and the needs of the growing Greek-speaking Churches in Asia Minor and Greece that led to the compilation of Greek Gospels. If St. Mark ever existed in Aramaic it must very soon have been translated. St. Matthew and St. Luke knew it only in a Greek translation. And the same is true of the Aramaic collection of discourses. It is possible that the writer of the First Gospel had seen the original Aramaic, but St. Luke (even if he had before him the complete collection at all and not rather excerpts from it which had passed into other writings) certainly knew its contents in a Greek form.

Aramaisms in St. Mark.

(1) The frequent historic presents (about 150). In *Expository Times*, xiii. 329, I suggested that these were due to translation of Aramaic participles. About seventy-one of these are cases of λέγει or λέγουσιν. Wellhausen, *Einleitung*, p. 16, says: 'Bei λέγει ist auch das Praesens historicum wichtig, das in diesem Falle noch beliebter ist als sonst. Man darf darin aramäischen Einfluss erkennen.'

(2) The use of ἤρξατο (-αντο) with an infinitive about twenty-six times. This might be Hebrew as well as Ara-

maic. Dalman, *W. J.*, 27, says, 'the Palestinian Jewish literature uses the meaningless " he began" in the same fashion.'

(3) The frequent use of ὅτι after verbs of 'saying'.

(4) The frequent use of πολλά as an adverb = the Aramaic סגי. So now Wellhausen. See e. g. on Mk i. 45 'πολλά adverbial wie saggi ; bei Mk beliebt '.

(5) Mk iv. 8 ἐν...ἐν...ἐν. The MSS. offer many combinations of εἰς and ἐν. Due to translation of חד or חד ב. Wellhausen says, ' ἐν τριάκοντα καὶ ἐν ἑξήκοντα καὶ ἐν ἑκατὸν bedeutet dreissigmal oder dreissigfach wie chad schib'a (Dan iii. 9 eins sieben) ἑπταπλασίως' (*Einl.*, p. 31). I gave this reference in *Expository Times*, xiii. 330.

(6) Mk vi. 22 τῆς θυγατρὸς αὐτῆς (A. C. αὐτοῦ ℵ B). In *Expository Times*, xiii. 330, I suggested that this was due to mistranslation of an Aramaic original. Wellhausen on vi. 17 says, ' αὐτός weist nach aramäischer Weise vor auf 'Ηρώδης. Ebenso vi. 22 αὐτῆς τῆς 'Ηρωδιάδος.'

(7) Mk iii. 28 τοῖς υἱοῖς τῶν ἀνθρώπων is a pure Aramaism = τοῖς ἀνθρώποις.

(8) Mk xii. 28 πάντων. The masculine is probably due to mistranslation of the neutral Aramaic.

(9) Mk i. 23, v. 2 ἐν πνεύματι ἀκαθάρτῳ = 'possessed by an unclean spirit '. The difficult ἐν is probably due to mistranslation.

(10) Mk viii. 24 ὅτι, mistranslation ד = οὕς.

(11) Mk vi. 8, 9 εἰ μή and ἀλλά are probably both due to misreading of ולא, ' and not,' as אלא = 'sondern '.

(12) In *Expository Times*, xiii. 329, I urged that the tautology and fullness of expression which is so striking a feature of Mark's style is thoroughly Semitic in character. See now on this Wellhausen, *Einleitung*, p. 17 f.

For the following I am indebted to Wellhausen :—

(13) Mk i. 7 οὗ ... αὐτοῦ ' ist semitisch '.

(14) Mk i. 8 ἐβάπτισα ' ebenso das Präteritum (ich taufe euch da eben) '.

X. *The Aramaic Background of the Gospels* 297

(15) Mk i. 34 'D: καὶ τοὺς δαιμόνια ἔχοντας ἐξέβαλεν αὐτὰ ἀπ' αὐτῶν. Durchaus semitisch'.
(16) Mk i. 35 ἐξῆλθεν καὶ ἀπῆλθεν. See *Einleitung*, p. 17.
(17) Mk ii. 4 ἀπεστέγασαν τὴν στέγην. Wellhausen points out that after this clause ἐξορύξαντες seems pointless. He suggests that ἀπεστ. κτλ. is a misrendering of schaqluhi or arîmuhi leggara, which in this context meant 'they brought him up to the roof'.
(18) Mk ii. 7 λαλεῖ βλασφημεῖ for λαλεῖ βλασφημῶν due to translation of two Aramaic participles.
(19) Mk ii. 10 ὁ υἱὸς τοῦ ἀνθρώπου literal translation of the Aramaic phrase = 'man'. So ii. 28.
(20) Mk ii. 22 ' εἰ δὲ μή ist vellâ (sonst)'.
(21) Mk iii. 4 ' σώζειν ist das jüdisch aramäische אחי'.
Einleitung, p. 33.
(22) Mk v. 41 For ταλιθα D. has ραββι θαβιτα. Wellhausen thinks that the original was ραβιθα the feminine of râbiâ = 'maiden'.
(23) Mk vii. 21-23 τῶν ἀνθρώπων...τὸν ἄνθρωπον. Both are renderings of nâsha.
(24) Mk vii. 30 ' βεβλημένον ist r'mê = liegend '.
(25) Mk vii. 31. Sidon is an error for Saidan = Bethsaida. It had occurred to me before I saw Wellhausen's note that διὰ Σιδῶνος might be a misrendering of לבית צידא.
(26) Mk x. 22 ἦν γὰρ ἔχων = the Aramaic qnê hvâ.
(27) Mk xiv. 8 ' ἔσχεν trägt den Sinn von eschk'chat und klingt lautlich daran an; προέλαβεν μυρίσαι sieht vollends nach einem Aramäismus aus'.
(28) Mk xv. 13 'Das aramäische Äquivalent für πάλιν bedeutet nicht bloss *abermals*, sondern auch *weiter, darauf*. Es könnte hier vielleicht im Griechischen *hingegen, hinwieder* heissen'.
(29) The order verb-subject: 'Diese Wortstellung, von der sich bei Markus nur wenige Ausnahmen finden, ist semitisch, nicht griechisch,' *Einleitung*, p. 19.

Other cases may be gleaned from Wellhausen's commentary on Mark or from his *Einleitung*, pp. 14 ff.

The impression which St. Mark makes as being a translation of our Aramaic original is one which derives its strength not so much from a number of isolated points as from the style and sentence-construction taken as a whole. The Gospel has a Semitic atmosphere about it to an extent which is not true of the other two Synoptic Gospels. In part single sentences or phrases are Semitic in character and might be retranslated into either Hebrew or Aramaic. But it is the specifically Aramaic colouring that predominates. It is just this fact that makes any attempt at retranslation so precarious and uncertain. For we know unhappily very little of the actual Aramaic idiom spoken in our Lord's lifetime. The extant Aramaic literature is either too early, as e.g. the Aramaic sections of Ezra and Daniel, or too late, as e.g. the Palestinian Aramaic literature of the post-Christian period or the Meshnic Aramaic, to be any very precise guide. Wellhausen thinks that the Aramaic section in Daniel stands nearest to the Aramaic of Christ's time. Dalman believes that 'the Targum of Onquelos and the Palestinian Talmud and Midrash remain our most important criteria'. But Wellhausen objects that the Targums as translations are strongly hebraized, and that the Palestinian Talmudic Aramaic is too specifically Rabbinic.

Even if the proofs that St. Mark's Gospel was originally written in Aramaic were more convincing than they are it is probable that no competent Aramaic scholar would venture to retranslate it into the original in view of the very great ignorance that we are in as to the exact nature of the idiom and vocabulary of the Aramaic spoken in Palestine in the first century. The most that can be done is to point out the probability that the Greek of the Gospel reflects an Aramaic background and to make tentative suggestions here and there as to the probable wording of an

X. The Aramaic Background of the Gospels

Aramaic phrase or two. See further on this subject, Wellhausen, *Einleitung*, pp. 38 ff.

Aramaisms in the Collection of Discourses.

Since this source has to be reconstructed out of St. Matthew and St. Luke it is not unnatural that critical writers should differ largely in their attempts to refashion it. The usual method of doing so is to work upon the principle that all passages common to Matthew and Luke and not in Mark may be supposed to have come from the discourse collection. This principle underlies Harnack's reconstruction.[1] Weiss[2] enlarges his reconstructed collection of discourses by putting into it sections common to all three Evangelists, on the principle that Mark had already borrowed from it, and that sections so borrowed lay before Matthew and Luke in duplicate, both in the original document and in Mark.

I have elsewhere[3] tried to show that the First Gospel is our best authority for the contents of this discourse source, and that we should probably assign to it most of the sayings and parables peculiar to this Gospel together with some of the sayings which are found also in Luke either in substance or in close verbal agreement, on the ground of similarity in certain characteristics to the sayings peculiar to Mark.

But without attempting to settle the exact contents of this collection we may ask whether in passages assigned to it by recent writers there are any traces of an Aramaic original. The following is a gleaning from some recent works, with no attempt at completeness, of supposed traces of such an Aramaic background.

Mt xxiii. 25 ἔσωθεν δὲ γέμουσιν.

---

[1] *Sprüche und Reden Jesu.* Leipzig, 1907.
[2] *Die Quellen der synoptischen Überlieferung.* Leipzig, 1908.
[3] *St. Matthew,* Intern. Crit. Comm., pp. xli ff.

Lk xi. 39 τὸ δὲ ἔσωθεν ὑμῶν γέμει.

Wellhausen, *Einleitung*, p. 36, argues that Luke is right here, and that Matthew's γέμουσιν should be in the second person. The error is due to mistranslation of a participle. But αὐτοῦ in Mt xxiii. 26 shows that Matthew interprets the whole saying as a contrast between the outside of the vessels and their contents which are impure because the product of avarice (ἁρπαγῆς καὶ ἀκρασίας). On the other hand Luke's ὑμῶν is inconsistent with his context. Without it the contrast is as in Matthew between the contents of the vessels and their exterior. This is also the meaning of vv. 40, 41. With ὑμῶν the contrast in v. 39 is between the ceremonial cleanness of the vessels and the moral uncleanness of their possessors.

Wellhausen tries to introduce consistency into St. Luke by transposing ἔσωθεν and ἔξωθεν in v. 40, by interpreting ὁ ποιήσας in the sense of 'cleanse', and by supposing that δότε ἐλεημοσύνην in v. 41 is a mistaken misreading of דכו = καθάρισον as in Matthew for זכו, which is supposed to mean 'give alms'.

It must, however, remain doubtful whether the two points of divergence in which Wellhausen appeals to an Aramaic original are not rather due to different interpretation of a saying which lay before the two Evangelists in slightly different forms.

Matthew interprets the whole saying with reference to the Jewish casuistical distinctions between clean and unclean utensils. Ceremonial cleansing of a vessel could not really make it clean if it was used to contain that which was procured by immoral means. If the vessels were used only to contain things rightly obtained ceremonial cleansing would be unnecessary. St. Luke, on the other hand, interprets the whole passage with primary reference not to the Jewish casuistic rules about vessels, but to the persons of the hearers. 'They laid great stress on the cleansing of vessels whilst

X. The Aramaic Background of the Gospels

their own hearts were evil. The same God who made the vessel made also their inner being and would require purity in the one as much as in the other. Let them give alms of the contents of the vessels and they need not trouble so much about ceremonial cleansing.'

It is quite possible that Luke had the saying before him much as it stands in Matthew, and that to widen its atmosphere from a purely Jewish to a more universal one he has inserted ὑμῶν in v. 39, has also perhaps inserted v. 40, and has paraphrased καθάρισον by δότε ἐλεημοσύνην in v. 41.

Mt v. 11 εἴπωσιν πᾶν πονηρὸν καθ' ὑμῶν.
Lk vi. 22 καὶ ἐκβάλωσιν τὸ ὄνομα ὑμῶν ὡς πονηρόν.

Wellhausen (ibid.) argues that behind these two sentences lies an Aramaic phrase which might literally have been rendered by ἐκβάλωσιν ὑμῖν ὄνομα πονηρόν. But whether in Aramaic or in Greek this strikes one as being less probable than either of the two phrases in the Gospels. Still in view of the remarkable verbal agreement in the rest of the passage the appeal to an Aramaic original to explain variations in this sentence is plausible.

Mt v. 12 τοὺς πρὸ ὑμῶν = Lk vi. 23 οἱ πατέρες αὐτῶν.

Wellhausen (ibid.) says that these variants go back to *daq' damaihon* and *daq' damaikon*. This is plausible.

Mt x. 12 ἀσπάσασθε αὐτήν = Lk x. 5 λέγετε· εἰρήνη τῷ οἴκῳ τούτῳ.

Wellhausen (ibid.) urges that the Lucan form is presupposed also in the following words in Mt x. 13. He means, I suppose, that the original Aramaic has been literally given by Luke, and abbreviated by Matthew into ἀσπάσασθε. This is possible.

Mt xi. 19 ἔργων = Lk vii. 35 τέκνων.

Meyer[1] suggests as originals עבידתהא, עבדהא. But עבדהא does not immediately suggest τέκνων. Moreover, it is questionable whether τέκνων is not the right reading in

---

[1] *Jesu Muttersprache*, p. 82.

both Gospels. In Matthew it is read by $B^2 D$ al $S^1 S^2$ a c k against ℵ B * $S^{3,4}$ Codd ap Hier for ἔργων, which seems therefore to have no testimony prior to the fourth century. If τέκνων is original in Matthew, ἔργων is due not to an Aramaic original, but to a Greek copyist who substituted it as easier than τέκνων. ℵ has it also in Luke.

Mt xxi. 31 προάγουσιν ὑμᾶς εἰς τὴν βασιλείαν τοῦ θεοῦ.
Lk vii. 29, 30 ἐδικαίωσαν ... τὴν βουλὴν τοῦ θεοῦ.

Meyer, p. 86, regards these two phrases as parallels, though they appear in very different contexts. He thinks that Matthew's βασιλείαν is a translation of מילכתא = 'counsel', misread as מלכותא = 'kingdom', and that προάγουσιν and ἐδικαίωσαν are variant translations of יכון. But it is doubtful whether this verb could possibly be rendered by προάγουσιν.

The above are some of the most striking cases where variants in passages common to Matthew and Luke have been traced to a common Aramaic original. I must confess that they do not seem to me, either singly or collectively, to be at all convincing.

Many variants in such passages *might*, it is true, be different translations of a Semitic original, e.g.:—

Mt v. 25 ὑπηρέτῃ	= Lk xii. 58 πράκτορι
v. 26 κοδράντην	xii. 59 λεπτόν
v. 39 στρέψον	vi. 29 πάρεχε
vi. 28 καταμάθετε	xii. 27 κατανοήσατε
vii. 11 ὄντες	xi. 13 ὑπάρχοντες
vii. 13 πύλης	xiii. 24 θύρας
vii. 25 βροχή	vi. 48 πλημμύρας
vii. 27 πτῶσις	vi. 49 ῥῆγμα
x. 16 πρόβατα	x. 3 ἄρνας
x. 28 δυνάμενον	xii. 5 ἐξουσίαν ἔχοντα
xi. 8 οἴκοις τῶν βασιλέων	vii. 25 βασιλείοις
xi. 17 ἐκόψασθε	vii. 32 ἐκλαύσατε
xxiv. 43 εἴασεν	xii. 39 ἀφῆκεν
xxiv. 45 δοῦλος	xii. 42 οἰκονόμος
xxiv. 45 οἰκετείας	xii. 42 θεραπείας
xxiv. 45 τροφήν	xii. 42 σιτομέτριον

X. The Aramaic Background of the Gospels 303

In others it seems rather probable that Luke has substituted a word exegetical of the variant which Matthew has, e. g. :—

Mt v. 46 ἀσπάσησθε	= Lk vi. 33 ἀγαθοποιῆτε
v. 48 τέλειοι	vi. 36 οἰκτίρμονες
vi. 12 ὀφειλήματα	xi. 4 ἁμαρτίας
vii. 11 ἀγαθά	xi. 13 πνεῦμα ἅγιον
x. 34 μάχαιραν	xii. 51 διαμερισμόν
xxiii. 34 γραμματεῖς	xi. 49 ἀποστόλους

whilst in others there are variations more serious in character, or omissions or additions on the part of one or other Evangelist, or so striking a variation in meaning, that it is very difficult to suppose that the two Evangelists could be translating from the same Aramaic document, or indeed using a common Greek course, e. g. :—

Mt v. 15. Luke, in viii. 16, adds σκεύει, and has κλίνης for μόδιον. In xi. 33 he has μόδιον, but prefixes εἰς κρύπτην. Matthew has at the end καὶ λάμπει πᾶσιν τοῖς ἐν οἰκίᾳ. Luke, ἵνα οἱ εἰσπορευόμενοι τὸ φῶς βλέπωσιν.

Mt vii. 9. Lk xi. 12 adds the clause about the egg.

Mt x. 29 two sparrows; Lk xii. 6 five sparrows.

Mt v. 3-12 = Lk vi. 20-23. Matthew has nine blessings Luke, four blessings and four woes.

Mt vi. 9-13 = Lk xi. 1-4. Matthew is longer.

{ Mt xxiii. 14 κλείετε τὴν βασιλείαν τῶν οὐρανῶν.
{ Lk xi. 52 ἤρατε τὴν κλεῖδα τῆς γνώσεως.

{ Mt xxiii. 23 ἄνηθον καὶ τὸ κύμινον.
{ Lk xi. 42 πήγανον καὶ πᾶν λάχανον.

{ Mt xxiii. 23 τὸν ἔλεον καὶ τὴν πίστιν.
{ Lk xi. 42 τὴν ἀγάπην τοῦ θεοῦ.

Mt xxiii. 25-26 = Lk xi. 39-41. In Matthew the contrast is between the exterior of the vessels and their contents, in Luke between the inner immorality of the hearers and their zeal for ceremonially cleansing the outsides of vessels.

Mt xxiii. 27 = Lk xi. 41. In Matthew the Pharisees are compared to whitened tombs, in Luke to unwhitened tombs.

Mt xxiv. 40 ἀγρῷ = Lk xvii. 34 κλίνης.

These and similar divergences, combined with the

frequently quite different situation and context in which sayings are placed, make it very difficult to believe that Matthew and Luke are translating from a common Aramaic document, or indeed using a common source, whether Aramaic or Greek. It is, of course, quite possible, though detailed proof can I believe not be given (the argument must be based on the general Aramaic ring of the sayings), that the passages common to Matthew and Luke are all ultimately drawn from an Aramaic collection of sayings. It is possible that either Matthew or Luke (Matthew more probably) used this source and translated it. But if so, in order to account for the variations between the two Evangelists, other translators must have done the same work and the sayings thus translated must have passed through several stages of transmission in Greek, and probably been diffused into several sources before they reached the other Evangelist (probably Luke).

To our first question therefore the answer must be that there is some evidence that the Gospels are based at least in part on Aramaic sources. So far as Mark goes the evidence is the Aramaic atmosphere that surrounds the Greek in which it was written. For Matthew and Luke the evidence is that on the one hand the sayings common to them seem to be derived ultimately from a common source, and on the other that Papias seems to bear witness to such a source, and says that it was written in Aramaic. This suggests an answer to the second question. If the earliest Gospel documents, the Second Gospel, and Matthew's collection of discourses, were written in Aramaic, there is a presumption that that is the language which Christ habitually used. Is there any other evidence to this effect? And upon this point reference is generally made to the passages in the Gospels which contain Aramaic words or expressions as uttered by Christ. They are the following:—

(1) Mk v. 41 ταλιθα κουμ (see above, p. 297).

X. The Aramaic Background of the Gospels

It is, however, not a little remarkable, on the assumption that Christ habitually spoke in Aramaic, that this particular phrase should have been preserved. Its retention would be explained in a much more obvious and striking way if Christ habitually spoke Greek and had here departed from His usual custom to speak to the child in the only language known to her.

(2) Mk iii. 17 Βοανηργές.

The retention of this name would be equally intelligible whether Christ spoke usually in Aramaic or in Greek. But it perhaps lends weight to the theory that He spoke in Aramaic.

(3) Mk vii. 34 ἐφφαθά.

Here as in No. 1 the retention of the Aramaic word is more easily explained if Aramaic was not the language ordinarily spoken by Christ, but was employed by Him here exceptionally. The reason cannot of course be determined, but possibly the man to whom the words were uttered understood no other language.

(4) Mk xv. 34 ελωι ελωι λαμα σαβαχθανι (λαμα B D, λεμα א C L, σαβαχθανι E F K L, σαβακτανει א, ζαφθανει D, ζαβαφθανει B). The Greek editor of Mark has slightly Hebraized the verse in λαμα for λεμα and in ελωι for αλαι, but σαβαχθανι is wholly Aramaic. A great deal of stress has been laid on this verse by those who maintain that Jesus spoke Aramaic only. But as Abbott justly remarks, 'the argument is deprived of all weight by the fact that the words are a quotation.'

In view of Mark's statement that some of those who stood near could either really misunderstand the cry to be a call for Elias or distort it into an appeal to Elias by way of a mocking joke, it is difficult not to believe that Christ quoted the Psalm in Hebrew, Éli Éli lama azabhtani. In that case the source of Mark, whether an original Aramaic Mark or St. Peter speaking in Aramaic, has Aramaized the words for the benefit of a circle to whom Aramaic would be familiar rather than Hebrew. If the words were originally uttered in Hebrew they throw no light upon the language usually used by Christ, but only prove that He was acquainted with the Hebrew Scriptures and could quote them when He pleased.

(5) Some Aramaic phrases in sayings of Christ which have been translated into Greek in our Gospels have already been noticed on pp. 295-7. Note especially here Mk iv. 8 and iii. 28. There are also in His sayings several Aramaic or Hebrew words which have been simply transliterated. Such are ῥακά Mt v. 22, μαμωνᾶς Mt vi. 24, Lk xvi. 9, ἀμήν, ἀββᾶ Mk xiv. 36, κορβᾶν Mk vii. 11, γέεννα, βεελζεβούλ Mt x. 25, xii. 27, but these throw little light upon the question of the language generally spoken by Him because they are most of them words which might well have been borrowed by a Greek-speaking Jew from Hebrew or Aramaic.

The conclusions to be drawn from the facts now stated seem to be the following :—

(*a*) There seems to be some evidence that our present Synoptic Gospels are based at least in part upon Aramaic originals. If so, it is more probable than not that the earliest Gospel writings were written in Aramaic because Christ spoke in Aramaic.

(*b*) The Aramaic words retained in His sayings in a Greek transliteration are on the whole most easily explained from the same fact, though one or two of them, e. g. ταλιθα κουμ and εφφαθα, would be more strikingly explained on the assumption that He spoke Greek.

(*c*) One or two Aramaic idioms translated into Greek, e. g. Mk. iii. 8, iv. 28, suggest Aramaic as His habitual language.

(*d*) The Cry upon the Cross, Mk xv. 34, points to an acquaintance by Him with the Hebrew Scriptures.

NOTE

NOTE

Some inferences as to the historical character of some expressions of Christ which are based upon examination of their supposed Aramaic originals.

ὁ υἱὸς τοῦ ἀνθρώπου.

Some extravagant hypotheses have been based upon the supposed Aramaic original of this phrase.

It is said with justice that the original would be בר אנשא, but it is further said, as e. g. by Wellhausen, that this really means not 'the Son of Man' but 'der Mensch' (so de Lagarde, Lietzmann, Schmidt). For 'the Son of Man', see Dalman, p. 239.

It has been further argued that in the mouth of Christ 'der Mensch' was simply an equivalent of the pronoun of the first person, or that the phrase was not used by Christ Himself but invented for Him in the Christian Church.

Wellhausen,[1] for example, argues as follows:—

(1) ὁ υἱὸς τοῦ ἀνθρώπου is a translation of Barnascha.

(2) Barnascha can only mean ' der Mensch '.

(3) As attributed to Christ it can only mean the Messiah. But how can this be?

(4) It was not a standing Messianic title.

(5) It came into use in the Church when the expectation of His return grew up. He must, they thought, have foretold this, but they shrank from representing Him as saying in plain terms, ' I shall appear as Messiah in glory.'

Consequently they put into His mouth the words, ' The Man of whom Daniel spoke will appear in the clouds of the heaven.'

This was soon interpreted as equivalent to ' I will return '. The next stage was to make the Son of Man the subject in the prophecies of death and resurrection where it be-

---

[1] *Das Evangelium Marci*, pp. 65 ff.

X. The Aramaic Background of the Gospels

comes necessarily a designation of Christ Himself. Finally, the phrase was introduced into non-eschatological sayings, where it becomes equivalent simply to 'I'.

Now Wellhausen is a brilliant philologist, but he is often a very bad interpreter, and his exposition of the development of this phrase in the Church is contrary to all the evidence.[1]

In the first place, so far from there having been a tendency to introduce the phrase into Christian theology, there seems to have been a directly contrary tendency to avoid it. In what other way can we explain its almost entire absence from the writings of the New Testament outside the Gospels?

Secondly, the phrase is used in passages of eschatological and of non-eschatological import, which so far as any evidence goes are equally early in respect of attestation; e.g. if it be said that Mark is the earliest strata of Gospel tradition the phrase occurs there in x. 45 in a non-eschatological context side by side with its occurrence in eschatological passages. Or if it be said that passages common to Matthew and Luke are drawn from a source which is as early as Mark and of as good authority, there too we find the phrase in contexts of both characters (see Harnack, *Sprüche und Reden Jesu*, p. 165). In fact there is not a shred of evidence that the phrase in non-eschatological passages is later than it is in eschatological contexts.

If we are dealing with the evidence of the New Testament and not trying to force speculative theories into it, we shall reconstruct the history of the phrase 'Son of Man' on lines quite different to Wellhausen's fantastic edifice.

It may be quite true that ὁ υἱὸς τοῦ ἀνθρώπου is a translation of בר אנשא.

---

[1] It is satisfactory to find Harnack (*Sprüche*, p. 169) expressing himself decisively in favour of the genuineness of the phrase: *dass Jesus sie gebraucht hat ist sicher.*

It may be true again that ברנאשא can only mean 'the man', 'der Mensch'.

But if so that only proves that Christ when He wished to say 'the בר אנש of Daniel' must have given this allusion by intonation or emphasis.

Or else He used some other phrase to express His meaning, for it surely cannot be argued that Aramaic is a language so inadequate that when He wished to convey the conception 'the בר אנש of Daniel' He could not do so.

The evidence of the Gospels, whether of Mark the earliest of our Gospels, or of the alleged discourse source lying behind Matthew and Luke, or of the editors of Matthew and Luke or of St. John, is all in the same direction. Christ used the phrase of Himself, and probably, though this is a controversial point, did so to suggest that in His person would be fulfilled the prophecy of Daniel, not however limiting the phrase to sayings where this would be immediately suggested, but employing it in passages of quite general import. The Christian Church of the New Testament period seems to have avoided the phrase for reasons which need not be discussed here. But this reserve is itself a proof of the antiquity and genuineness of the Gospel passages in which it occurs.

My Father.

It has been denied that Christ could speak of God as His Father in any exclusive sense on the ground that in the Aramaic of His period אבא, which means 'the Father', had become the regular form for 'my Father'.

Dalman[1] admits that in all cases where the Gospels have 'my, your, thy, their Father' there is no certitude that Jesus used the appellation of Father without addition. In Jewish phraseology it would have the addition of 'which is in heaven'. Schmidt[2] puts the case rather differently:

---
[1] *Words*, p. 192.   [2] *The Prophet of Nazareth*, p. 154.

X. *The Aramaic Background of the Gospels*

'Jesus said neither "my Father" nor "your Father", but "the Father who is in heaven".'

It has therefore been argued on the ground of language that Christ could not have used the phrase 'my Father' in any exclusive sense.

But here again the Aramaic scholars seem too much inclined to underrate the possibilites of the Aramaic language. It has been shown that in the Aramaic of the period אבא was used indiscriminately for 'the Father' and 'my Father', to the exclusion of אבי 'my Father' from ordinary use. That is to say that in addressing his earthly father the Jew felt that there was no need to express the personal pronoun. The personal relation was assumed. Still less need, perhaps, was there to express the pronoun in addressing or speaking of God the common Father of all men.

But what is there here to conflict with the evidence of the Gospels that Christ spoke of God as 'my Father'? Surely the language is not so inadequate to express personal relations that if He wished to break away from the common usage and to say 'my Father' instead of 'the Father', He could not have found words to do so.

It may, perhaps, be argued that there is every probability that if He had adopted the current form of expression, and said 'the Father', the Gospel writers would have introduced the 'my' when translating into Greek, and that the supposition that He did use 'the Father' is not only in itself probable, but is confirmed by the occurrence of $ἀββᾶ$ in Mk xiv. 36.

Let us grant it. But it still remains true that He thought and spoke of God as His Father in a unique sense, because both Mark and the alleged discourse source of Matthew and Luke, that is to say the two earliest strata of Gospel writings, preserve words in which He spoke of Himself and of God as 'the Son—the Father'.

In view of modern attempts to represent Mt xi. 25-27 as a Christian hymn put into the mouth of Christ, it is refreshing to find Harnack[1] defending their authenticity. Indeed, since they occur in Matthew and Luke, they have exactly as much claim to historicity as any other saying recorded in common by those writers; and the objections brought against them are the subjective kind of argument which when unsupported by any concrete evidence introduces hopeless chaos into the criticism of the Gospels, and brings lasting discredit upon it.

The particular expression 'the Son, the Father' which occurs here is further supported by Mk xiii. 32, and is consequently as strongly supported as any other saying ascribed to Christ in the Gospels. It implies consciousness of a unique relationship to God, and that relationship, as the context suggests, consisted of fullness of revelation.

Now since Christ spoke words like these, what possible objection can there be to the evidence of the Gospels that He also used the expression 'my Father' and avoided the corresponding 'our Father'? Mt vi. 9 is of course not a case in point, as the 'our Father' there is put into the mouth of Christ's disciples. The linguistic argument breaks down because the Lord may very well have chosen to avoid the current use of the ambiguous אבא, and to substitute אבי or אבא with a separate possessive pronoun. And this finds some support in the fact that in Jewish writings of the second century we find 'my Father (אבי) who is in heaven', side by side with 'thy, his, our, your, their Father who is in heaven'. See the instances quoted in Dalman, *Words*, pp. 186 ff., and in *St. Matthew*, Intern. Crit. Comm., p. 44.

[1] *Sprüche und Reden*, pp. 189 ff.

XI

THE SOURCES OF ST. LUKE'S GOSPEL

Rev. J. VERNON BARTLET, M.A., D.D.
Professor of Church History in Mansfield College, Oxford

SYLLABUS

The current Two-Document theory is open to question. The differences in the Logian element of Matthew and Luke demand fuller scope for the Oral factor.

I. Yet Luke used a second written source besides Mark, and our problem is to define its character.

(i) The test of *style* points to the Jewish-Christian or Hellenistic nature of Luke's special source (S).

(ii) Characteristic *ideas* confirm this, e.g. the notion of 'fulfilment', Messiah, &c.

Analysis of certain sections in this light :—The Epileptic Boy (ix. 37-43^a); Peter's Confession; the non-use of Mk vi. 45-viii. 26; the Feeding of the 5,000 (ix. 10^b-17); and especially the Mission of the Twelve.

Hence the basal Apostolic tradition (Q), implied even by Mark, was used by Luke in an independent form (QL) already embedded in his 'special source' (S); while Q itself included the 'Logia'. This seen in the Great Sermon, the Message of the Baptist and Jesus' response, and the Parable of the Sower.

The question whether one 'special source' will explain all Luke's non-Marcan matter, to be answered in the affirmative : e.g. for the Sermon at Nazareth, the incident at Nain, &c.

These results apply also to the Passion story, on the view that this also stood in Q as far back as we can trace it : detailed proof. Further, it is there even clearer than elsewhere that the continuous twofold special material in Luke (S + QL), apart from Mark, lay before the Evangelist already unified in an order fixed by the witness of a single authoritative informant.

Traces of independent historical witness peculiar to Luke's narrative, both before the Passion (xviii. 15-xxi. 38) and after (ch. xxiv).

Luke's 'Great Insertion' (ix. 51-xviii. 14) best explained on the above theory : The 'Peraean' Ministry; the Mission of the Seventy (special relation of Luke's informant to their circle) ; the Lucan Parables, their setting and special features.

Exact form of Luke's special source : its probable place of origin among Palestinian Hellenists ; its Johannine elements ; Luke's editorial handling of it.

II. Objections met.

Professor Stanton's kindred view.

Merits of the theory. Diagram.

THE SOURCES OF ST. LUKE'S GOSPEL

THIS essay is of the nature of 'a minority report'. Its germ has been present to the writer's mind for some years, in fact ever since he reached the conclusion, when working on the First Gospel for Dr. Hastings's *Dictionary of the Bible*, that the First and Third Evangelists cannot have used the same document for the non-Marcan element common to them. This conviction soon coalesced with another, namely, that Luke largely follows a written source peculiar to himself, which appears most clearly in what is called his 'great interpolation' amid the Marcan framework (ix. 51–xviii. 14) and in his story of the Passion and Resurrection. These two convictions have gradually shaped themselves into the theory of Luke's sources, and incidentally of the whole Synoptic problem, which it is the aim of this essay to unfold in some detail.

My main divergence from the theory underlying most of the essays in this volume consists in a rejection of the current 'Two-Document hypothesis'. That our Mark was used in the two other Synoptic Gospels, I firmly believe, and so far agree with the current documentary hypothesis. On the other hand, I cannot see that the common use of a second document, whether by Matthew and Luke alone or by Mark also, is probable : and so far I concur not only with Archdeacon Allen,[1] but also with the resistance to the dominant Documentary theory made by the upholders of the Oral hypothesis.[2] Accordingly, I would offer my

---

[1] Mr. Allen argues, indeed, for a *written* 'discourse source' or Q as used by our Matthew—an hypothesis which does not seem to me proven : but he also inclines to the view that 'St. Luke's acquaintance with it was only indirect', viz. through sources which 'had already borrowed largely from the discourse source' (p. 281).

[2] Dr. A. Wright, the most vigorous among living English exponents of

own hypothesis—which is primarily a sort of 'Two-Document' theory of Luke's Gospel alone—to the consideration of both schools as possibly affording the principles of an *eirenicon* between them.

I.

The first and main point must be to justify the belief that Luke uses a second written source, alongside and indeed in preference to Mark, and gradually to define its nature. The criteria to be used are twofold, those of language and those of ideas; but the two lines of evidence converge on the same point, namely, clear trace of Judaeo-Christian origin as compared with the style and mode of thought of the Third Evangelist himself. Here, as in all else bearing on Luke's sources, the analogy afforded by his other book, the Acts, must be used as far as may be.

(i) As regards *style*, the problem is not nearly so simple as it might at first seem, judging from the generally pure Greek of Acts, particularly its second half. For in Luke's Gospel other factors than his own free style enter in to a far greater degree, causing an intimate blending of Semitic and Greek features. The most authoritative discussion of this occurs in G. Dalman's examination [1] of the Semitic element in the Synoptic Gospels, where he distinguishes carefully between (1) Hebraisms and Aramaisms, (2) original and secondary Hebraisms. As regards (1) he finds that 'we must class as distinct Aramaisms the redundant ἀφείς (καταλιπών) and ἤρξατο, as well as the adverb εὐθύς (παραχρῆμα). The use of εἶναι with the participle to represent an historic tense is Aramaic rather than Hebrew. ... The genuine Hebraisms are the phrases connected with πρόσωπον, the construction ἐν τῷ with the infinitive, the emphasizing of the verb by its cognate substantive [e.g. ἐπιθυμίᾳ ἐπεθύμησα

---

this theory, seems prepared to believe that Mark was used by our Matthew and Luke, though possibly 'in its oral stage' (*St. Luke's Gospel in Greek*, p. vii).

[1] *The Words of Jesus*, 17 ff.

XI. The Sources of St. Luke's Gospel

Lk xxii. 15], and the formulae καὶ ἐγένετο, ἐλάλησεν λέγων, ἀποκριθεὶς εἶπεν.' As to the distribution of these, he finds no special preponderance of Aramaisms in Luke, but only of Hebraisms. Further, these can nearly all be regarded as secondary Hebraisms, due to the action of the Septuagint upon the style of Luke or his Hellenistic sources. This is particularly the case in the stories connected with the Nativity in chs. i–ii, which keep very close to Old Testament models, whether this be due primarily to the source here followed by Luke or to Luke himself, who has a subtle instinct for the fitness of things in matter of style. Dalman sums up on the style of the Synoptists generally, in the thesis (p. 42): 'the fewer the Hebraisms, the greater the originality (of the tradition) ; the more numerous the Hebraisms in any passage, the greater the interference of Hellenistic redactors.' Thus we need not be surprised if Luke 'does not shrink from using those Hebraisms which are most foreign to the feeling of the Greek language' (p. 38). He consciously writes his Gospel on the lines of the Greek Bible ; and so far from shunning this feature already present in his sources, he seems even to adopt favourite terms and idioms from them or their fountain-head, when he has occasion to add anything in his own words.

A striking instance is the Old Testament expression, ' And it came to pass . . .,' which occurs in Luke in three forms,[1] two of them borrowed in all probability from the LXX. In the full Lucan type of this construction, in all its varieties, ' It came to pass ' (ἐγένετο) is followed first by a note of time or occasion and then by a verbal clause. In the two Hebraistic or LXX species of it, the verb is finite, with or without καί (or ἰδού) preceding ; in the more Greek or Lucan variety, since it alone is found in Acts (for v. 7 is a very

---

[1] Compare J. H. Moulton, *Grammar of New Testament Greek*, Prolegomena, pp. 15-17; also H. St. John Thackeray, *Grammar of the Old Testament in Greek*, pp. 50-2.

doubtful exception), the verb is an infinitive. Taking the LXX varieties first, we find that (*a*) the finite verb follows directly on the qualifying clause denoting the occasion in some twenty-two cases, eight [1] of which occur in chs. i–ii; while (*b*) καί precedes the verb in some eleven cases (including xxiv. 15 where the reading is doubtful), but is absent from chs. i–ii.

In the body of the Gospel the distribution is as follows:—
(*a*) without καί, vii. 11; ix. 18, 28, 33, 37; xi. 1, 14, 27; xvii. 14; xviii. 35; xix. 29; xx. 1; xxiv. 30, 51.
(*b*) with καί, v. 1, 12, 17; viii. 1, 22; ix. 51; xiv. 1; xvii. 11; xix. 15; xxiv. 4, 15 (?).

Here, broadly speaking, there is nothing to suggest different sources as explaining these two varieties. When, moreover, we observe that, save in two cases where καί is followed by ἰδού, it is always followed by αὐτός or αὐτοί, we are led to suspect that καί has a sort of demonstrative force, analogous in fact to καὶ ἰδού. That is to say, αὐτός (αὐτοί in xiv. 1) is used to define more accurately, or more emphatically in the case of Jesus Himself (save xix. 15), who is the subject of the verb following. In this case the καί preceding, taken in connexion with 'And it came to pass', seems to add a certain emphasis [2] of dignity. It seems, too, as if the preface 'And it came to pass...' was secondary,[3] the original tradition having simply 'And he', or 'And, lo', as the case might be. Thus in ch. v we have

---

[1] i. 8, 23, 41, 59; ii. 1, 6, 15, 46.
[2] Compare vii. 12, 'Now as he approached the gate of the city, *and lo*, there was borne forth one dead' (cf. Acts i. 10): also ii. 21 καὶ ὅτε ... καὶ ἐκλήθη, and 27 f. (next note).
[3] In ii. 27 f. we have καὶ ἐν τῷ εἰσαγαγεῖν .... καὶ αὐτός without ἐγένετο, cf. 21; and its almost entire absence from the other Synoptics confirms such a view. In the (*a*) type it occurs in Mk i. 9; iv. 4 (but not in the parallels in Luke and Matthew); while in Matthew it is found only in his special formula 'And it came to pass when Jesus finished ... he ...' (vii. 28; xi. 1; xiii. 53; xix. 1; xxvi. 1), traceable to the Evangelist himself (so Dalman, *op. cit.*, p. 41). Similarly the (*b*) type is found outside Luke only in Mt ix. 10, in the form καὶ ἰδού, seemingly suggested by Mark's καὶ

XI. The Sources of St. Luke's Gospel

'Now it came to pass, whilst the crowd pressed on him...
and he was standing by the lake of Gennesaret' (v. 1);
'And it came to pass, whilst he was in one of the cities,
and, lo, a man full of leprosy' (v. 12); 'And it came to pass
on one of the days, and he was teaching' (v. 17). Possibly
here καὶ ἐγένετο stood in Luke's source in the first case,
while in the other two he himself added[1] it (along with
a vague note of time or place), in order to maintain the
elevated or archaic style. A parallel case to such following
of a lead in his source seems to meet us in the next chapter,
where the third or more Greek type of construction after
ἐγένετο occurs in three[2] successive sections, the first being
parallel to Mk ii. 23 καὶ ἐγένετο αὐτὸν ἐν τοῖς σάββασιν
διαπορεύεσθαι. These are the only cases of this Greek usage
in Luke's Gospel (against sixteen in Acts), with the exception of iii. 21, which is parallel to one of Mark's two instances
of the (a) type. It looks, then, as if Luke here took the
suggestion as to the use of ἐγένετο from Mark, but in combining his two sources (there are signs of more than Mark
in the Baptism section) changed the construction to his own
natural Greek type in first using ἐγένετο..., in the body of
his Gospel, as distinct from chs. i–ii. This makes the
occurrence in the next ἐγένετο passage (v. 1) of the LXX
(b) type rather less likely to be due to Luke himself.[3] But,
once started on this LXX style for the Ministry by his
special source, he continues throughout his Gospel with the

γίνεται κατακεῖσθαι αὐτόν (cf. Mt xviii. 13, and Lk xvi. 22). Finally
Mark has, in addition to this imperfect example, the third or properly Greek
type, with the infinitive, in ii. 23 (to be quoted in the text).

[1] The parallel to v. 12 in Mt viii. 2 is simply 'And, lo, a leper...';
and ἐν μιᾷ τῶν ἡμερῶν in v. 17 is like the vague ἐν μιᾷ τῶν πόλεων in v. 12,
while the paratactic nature of the rest of the verse suggests something like
iv. 14 f. as the original basis: cf. xix. 1 f.

[2] It is worth noting, too, that in all of these, and also in iii. 21, we get δέ
and not καί, the more Hebraic conjunction, with ἐγένετο.

[3] Yet in view of ἐγένετο δέ, not καὶ ἐγένετο, it is possible that Luke did add
ἐγένετο (to make a more striking fresh beginning) to καὶ ἐν τῷ ... καὶ αὐτός
in his source, a sentence exactly analogous to ii. 27: cf. xiv. 1 f.

two LXX types, save for ch. vi, where Mark diverts him for a moment, early in his task. Henceforth he adheres to them, sometimes perhaps adopting[1] them from his source, sometimes adding them to make the opening of sections less abrupt and the narrative more dignified—especially in the case of the καὶ αὐτός type (e. g. viii. 1). That καὶ αὐτός itself (where αὐτός does not mean 'himself', but 'he') is not Luke's own style, seems to be proved by its absence from Acts (see *Horae Synopticae*[2], 41 f.).

Whilst, then, in view of Luke's manifest intention to relate the Gospel story in a biblical style kindred to its contents, and one more or less traditional in connexion with its transmission, we cannot argue that the occurrence of ἐγένετο in the constructions examined proves his use in any given case of a Jewish-Christian source; still he may well have received the impulse to use the less purely Greek forms of the construction under the influence of one or more Jewish-Christian sources. This applies specially to chs. i-ii, where one form of this construction alone is found. As for the body of his Gospel, the use of the other form, with καὶ αὐτός in the apodosis, was at least suggested and facilitated, if not by actual cases in a source, then by the way in which the structure of sentences,[2] especially at the opening of sections, lent itself to the elevated form of diction introduced by ἐγένετο. There are other linguistic criteria which point in the same direction. Thus Dr. J. H. Moulton,[3] who reduces

---

[1] ix. 28, 33, xi. 1 (in 14 all the construction save ἐγένετο occurs also in Mt ix. 32 = his Q), xvii. 14, xviii. 35, xxiv. 30, 51 (?), may be examples of this for (a); while v. 1, xix. 15 (in a parable, without αὐτός), xxiv. 4, 15 (?), may be original cases of (b). In cases like xiv. 1, we may suspect that ἐγένετο, &c., has transformed a more paratactic construction, like 'And he entered... and they...'

[2] e. g. ἐν τῷ with an infinitive, recalling a similar Hebrew construction with ב (perhaps represented also by Matthew's ὅτε ἐτέλεσεν κτλ.), followed by καὶ αὐτός or καὶ ἰδού.

[3] *Op. cit.*, pp. 14 ff., cf. p. 226. So, too, Thackeray, *op. cit.*, p. 53, cites the Hebraic use 'he added and' in xix. 11, xx. 11 f., with two types of construction.

XI. The Sources of St. Luke's Gospel

'Semitisms' in Luke to a minimum, still sees in his use with 'inordinate frequency' of the imperfect of 'to be' with a participle, in the pleonastic use of 'began' (e.g. iii. 8, contrasted with Mt iii. 9), and in certain other pleonasms, evidence of fidelity to Greek sources more Semitic in style than anything he would of himself have written.

Under this head of Hebraic pleonasms we may reckon parallelism, a feature which, as going deeper than mere language, is the less likely to be due to Luke. This criterion serves to indicate the presence alongside Mark of a second source in certain cases where proof of it on other grounds is not conclusive. Take for example Lk ix. 43^b-45, a passage of central importance as connected with others both in form and in idea. Here verse 44 opens with words to which Mark affords no parallel,[1] 'Do ye set in your ears these sayings,' a phrase Semitic rather than Greek in its concreteness, and such as would hardly occur to Luke of his own motion. It has, moreover, a parallel in the Eschatological Discourse, 'Set, then, in your hearts not to premeditate' (xxi. 14). Hence, when we find also in ix. 45 a case of Hebrew parallelism not in Mark, we may be fairly sure that Luke has here a second source at his disposal, which may also account for his omission of explicit reference to Jesus' death (in Mark ix. 31), whereas in the later passage xviii. 31–34 such a reference occurs. This passage itself, while parallel to Mk x. 32-34, adds in ver. 34 a case of triple[2] parallelism similar in substance to that just cited, while it also clothes part of the reference to the Passion in a form differing[3] from Mark's, namely, 'All

---

[1] The emphasis which they add suggests what is borne out by Lk ix. 22, which is quite parallel to Mk viii. 31 (esp. if ἀναστῆναι be preferred in Luke, ἐγερθῆναι being an assimilation to Matthew), viz. that ix. 44 f. introduce the first reference to the Passion in Luke's second source. That parts of Lk ix. 22-27 were absent from this source, is likely enough from the doublets found in xvii. 25, 33, xii. 8 f.

[2] Notice, too, the καὶ αὐτοί with which the verse opens.

[3] So, too, the addition of καὶ ὑβρισθήσεται, between two kindred words.

things that are written through the prophets shall be accomplished' (τελεσθήσεται).

(ii) But in these two passages, the last in particular, we have already passed to the second class of criteria for Jewish-Christian sources behind Luke—that of *ideas*. For the notion that the disciples' obtuseness to the forecasts of the Passion was due in part to Divine action, is an Hebraic one: witness the explanation of the crowd's dullness in relation to Christ's parables (Mk iv. 11 f. and parallels). This notion, however, occurs also in Lk xxiv. 16, 'But their eyes were holden, that they should not recognize him,' and xxiv. 45, 'Then opened he their mind, that they might understand the Scriptures.' Then again, the reference to the fulfilment of Scripture in Jesus' career, especially its suffering and death, connects xviii. 33 with several other passages in Luke (e.g. xxiv. 25-27, 44-46), some of which are sayings of Jesus Himself and indubitably not due to Luke. Specially noteworthy are xii. 50, 'I have a baptism to be baptized with, and how am I straitened until it be accomplished'; xiii. 32, 'and the third day I am consummated' (τελειοῦμαι); and xxii. 37, 'For I say unto you, that this which is written must be accomplished in me (δεῖ τελεσθῆναι ἐν ἐμοί), namely, And he was reckoned with transgressors: for that which concerneth me hath accomplishment' (τέλος). Whether ix. 31, 'who ... spake of his decease which he was about to fulfil (πληροῦν) in Jerusalem,' is also due to a source, may be held more doubtful, as it is comment, not a saying of Jesus: but probably it is not Luke's own (cf. κατὰ τὸ ὡρισμένον, xxii. 22). The section on the Transfiguration contains other traces too of a second source, both in style (e. g. the frequency of ἐν τῷ with infinitive, ix. 29, 33, 34, 36, and καὶ αὐτοί introducing a case of identical parallelism, 36) and

seems too otiose to be Luke's own idea; whereas in his second source it may have stood alone.

XI. The Sources of St. Luke's Gospel   323

in substance. Under the latter head come not only 31 f., but also the idea of 'My Chosen' (ὁ ἐκλελεγμένος), as distinct from 'My Beloved' in Mark and Matthew, as an epithet of Messiah. This Jewish conception meets us again in the Trial before the Sanhedrin in xxiii. 35, where Luke has 'the Elect one' (ὁ ἐκλεκτός), again independently of Mark and Matthew. All these phenomena suggest the presence in various parts of Luke of *a source parallel with Mark even in sections which at first sight appear dependent on Mark alone*: and this result will be found to prove the best working hypothesis in every part of his Gospel.

Let us take as another instance the section between the Transfiguration and the warning as to the coming Passion, that dealing with the Epileptic Boy (ix. 37–43^a). Its close, describing the effect upon the spectators, is peculiar to Luke, and leads on by contrast to the warning words to the disciples which occupy the next section. Other independent features are (1) the form of vv. 38 f., 'Lo, a man ... shouted out (ἐβόησεν) ... I beseech thee to look upon my son (cf. Mt xvii. 15, 'pity my son,' whereas Mk ix. 17 has 'I brought my son to thee'), because he is my only child (μονογενής, as in vii. 12, viii. 42—in a section with like marks of independence); and, lo, a spirit taketh him and he suddenly crieth out [1] ... and hardly departeth from him, contorting (συντρῖβον) him'; (2) 'And as he was yet a coming' (42^a), in contrast to Mark's account, both in form and idea; (3) the addition in 42^b, 'and restored him to his father.' With these we might reckon the agreement with Matthew in v. 41 also, in adding 'and perverse', save that the reading is not quite above suspicion of assimilation. But in any case the facts are enough to suggest that Luke used a second source which, like Mark, represented the form which the common apostolic tradition (Q) assumed in the memory and teaching of some oral evangelist of the

[1] This can hardly be based on Mark, who refers to the spirit as 'dumb'.

first generation. Such a special source (S) best explains both the additions in the passages examined and also the omission of what comes between them in Mk ix. 9-13, although its matter—especially 'And how is it written of the Son of man, that he should suffer many things and be set at nought?'—was quite congenial to Luke, as we have seen already. The same theory seems to hold good also of the section which precedes[1] the Transfiguration, that on Peter's Confession, which would surely form part of the common apostolic tradition (Q). Here the opening situation diverges from Mark unaccountably, save on our hypothesis. Note too οἱ ὄχλοι, instead of οἱ ἄνθρωποι, in Jesus' question; προφήτης τις τῶν ἀρχαίων ἀνέστη, where Mark has εἷς τῶν προφητῶν; and τὸν Χριστὸν τοῦ θεοῦ,[2] where Mark has σὺ εἶ ὁ Χριστός. These, and the more marked divergences in Matthew, all point in the same direction.

This brings us to one edge of the first of the two chief breaks in Luke's parallelism to Mark. Here it helps us to account for the non-use of Mk vi. 45-viii. 26, if we may suppose that Luke's other source had nothing parallel to this section. Besides, in the Feeding of the Five Thousand (ix. 10ᵇ-17), the last section before the break, the presence of a second source can be traced in many deviations from Mark (partly shared by Matthew), which, though sometimes slight, are hard to account for otherwise (comp. B. Weiss, *Die Quellen des Lukas*, 180 ff.). The like is true of the vv. 7-10ᵃ, dealing with Herod's opinion about Jesus[3] and the Return of the Twelve 'Apostles', whose mission has just been described. Their charge on that occasion

---

[1] Perhaps more immediately in S, since much of vv. 22-7 can be explained from Mark alone: see previous note.

[2] In Lk iv. 41 Jesus is described simply as τὸν Χριστόν.

[3] One notes here the same phrase, προφήτης τις τῶν ἀρχαίων ἀνέστη, already noticed in ix. 18-20; while v. 9 in its peculiarities connects naturally with the episode of Herod in the Passion story, especially xxiii. 8 (cf. also viii. 3).

XI. *The Sources of St. Luke's Gospel* 325

calls for careful study, since upon our view of its relation to that given to the Seventy, a chapter later in Luke, much depends. That Luke's 'special source' contained both of these commissions in terms having much in common,[1] is the hypothesis which seems best to fit all the facts. Here observe (1) the contradiction of Mark's 'save only a staff' by Luke's 'neither a staff', in agreement not only with Matthew (= his Q) but also *e silentio* with Lk xxii. 35, *which refers back to the mission of the Twelve* and also explicitly forbids the use of sandals (so Matthew here), a point on which Luke here tacitly deserts Mark (cf. Lk x. 4); (2) other agreements with Matthew (= Q) rather than Mark, viz. the *oratio recta* throughout, and the phrases εἰς ἣν ἄν (Mark ὅπου ἄν), ὅσοι (Matthew ὅς, Mark ὅς . . . τόπος), ἐξερχόμενοι . . . τῆς πόλεως ἐκείνης (Mark ἐκπορευόμενοι ἐκεῖθεν), κονιορτόν (Mark χοῦν), which is also the form in x. 11[2]; (3) certain cases of similar agreement and disagreement in the preface to the Commission itself. We will place the three accounts side by side :—

Mk vi. 7, 8ᵃ.	Lk ix. 1-3ᵃ.	Mt x. 1, 5ᵇ.
(1) Καὶ προσκαλεῖται τοὺς δώδεκα, (2) καὶ ἤρξατο αὐτοὺς ἀποστέλλειν δύο δύο, (3) καὶ ἐδίδου αὐτοῖς ἐξουσίαν τῶν πνευμάτων τῶν ἀκαθάρτων.	Συνκαλεσάμενος δὲ τοὺς δώδεκα ἔδωκεν αὐτοῖς δύναμιν καὶ ἐξουσίαν ἐπὶ πάντα τὰ δαιμόνια καὶ νόσους θεραπεύειν, καὶ ἀπέστειλεν αὐτοὺς κηρύσσειν τὴν βαυ. τ. Θεοῦ καὶ ἰᾶσθαι.	Καὶ προσκαλεσάμενος τοὺς δώδεκα μαθητὰς αὐτοῦ ἔδωκεν αὐτοῖς ἐξουσίαν πνευμάτων ἀκαθάρτων ὥστε ἐκβάλλειν αὐτὰ καὶ θεραπεύειν πᾶσαν νόσον καὶ πᾶσαν μαλακίαν.
(4) Καὶ παρήγγειλεν αὐτοῖς . . .	καὶ εἶπεν πρὸς αὐτούς . . .	. . . παραγγείλας αὐτοῖς λέγων.

[1] Some assimilation of language between them would easily go on in tradition.

[2] Luke also has ἀποτινάσσετε (ἀπό), as compared with Mark's ἐκτινάξατε . . . τὸν ὑποκάτω, though he has no bias against Mark's verb; witness its use in the same connexion in Acts xiii. 51, xviii. 6. This suggests the same source which in Lk x. 11 uses the kindred form ἀπομάσσεσθαι. Note too εἰς μαρτύριον ἐπ' αὐτούς (Mark αὐτοῖς, as Lk v. 14). Finally Lk ix. 6 hardly seems based on Mk vi. 12 alone; it rather recalls ix. 1ᶜ, Mt x. 1ᵃ.

Note (1) the agreement against Mark's order for clause (3), and the divergence of all three in clause (2)—Matthew having no trace of it here (only in v. 5), while Luke omits the detail δύο δύο, though he has its equivalent in the sending of the Seventy ; (2) the agreement against Mark in the reference to 'treating disease', which is enforced again by Luke's κηρύσσειν τ. β. τ. θ. καὶ ἰᾶσθαι ; (3) as regards Luke alone, the presence of δύναμιν before ἐξουσίαν (cf. iv. 36, v. 17, vi. 18, x. 19, and xxiv. 49, for its presence in S), ἐπὶ πάντα τὰ δαιμόνια instead of τῶν πν. τ. ἀκαθάρτων (cf. x. 17 and viii. 27, 29 f., 33, 35, 38), and the reference to 'preaching the Kingdom of God' (supported by Mk vi. 12, Mt ix. 35, x. 7, and Lk x. 9, 11 : see also viii. 1).

These phenomena surely presuppose other forms of the same basal tradition (Q) which lies behind Mark as influencing both Luke and Matthew, and are not satisfied by any theory of mere editorial freedom in dealing with Mark's text. And this seems to hold good in almost every section where Luke runs parallel with Mark, though space forbids our continuing detailed analysis back through chaps. iii–viii. In Luke, moreover, the independent traits have often, as we have seen, affinity with sections peculiar to that Gospel. Hence *the form in which this parallel tradition lay before our Evangelist seems already incorporated in his 'special source'.* But, as we have just found in the case of the Charge to the Twelve, as well as in other sections where we traced an element common to Matthew and Luke alone, *this parallel tradition* may itself have *included the original didactic element* which has often been segregated, more or less sharply, from the narrative element so predominant in Mark, and styled the *Logia* or Collection of Sayings. To the justification of this further suggestion we must now direct our analysis.

This brings us to the Great Sermon and its setting in

XI. The Sources of St. Luke's Gospel

our Gospels. The matter is complicated by the way in which these vary at this point, Mark making the appointment of the Twelve the sole event on the Mount, while Matthew postpones all mention of it to the time of their actual sending forth (x. 1 ff.). It is, however, pretty clear that Matthew has placed his Sermon at an artificially early point in his narrative for special reasons connected with the structure of his Gospel. Hence we cannot safely infer that his form of Q diverged in this respect from Luke's narrative, in which the appointment of the Twelve immediately precedes the Sermon. Nor is there any reason to doubt that this was the case in Q as known to Mark, for he passes over also the kindred body of discourse on occasion of the Baptist's message to Jesus. In Luke, however, even when we eliminate—to the easing of the syntax in vi. 13-19—all that may fairly be due to Mark, we get a simple and fitting preface to Luke's form of the Sermon, with certain features all its own. In the first place, the order in which the ministry to the great crowds from a distance is recorded differs; next, the motive of Jesus' ascent of the Mount, as giving Him privacy at a time of great popularity (in order to prepare for the grave step of choosing His inner circle of personal disciples and helpers), is specified in Luke alone, in terms of much verisimilitude[1]; then, the slightly different order and form of the names of those chosen; then, the descent to a 'level place', where assembled 'a great crowd of his disciples' (note this recognition of the wider sense of the term), as well as a great multitude of others (as in Mark): and finally, 'And he ($\kappa\alpha\grave{\iota}$ $\alpha\grave{\upsilon}\tau\acute{o}s$), lifting up his eyes on his disciples, began to say . . .' This, the immediate prelude to the Sermon, coincides so far with Mt v. 1 f.,

[1] 'He went forth (Mark, ' goeth up,' as Luke in ix. 28) to the mountain to pray, and he was passing the whole night in prayer to God; and when it was day . . .' The references in Luke to Jesus as praying were already in his source, to judge from v. 16, xi. 1 (cf. ix. 18, 28), and the *absence* of such reference in iv. 42, where Mk i. 35 has it.

'And ... his disciples came to him; and opening his mouth, he began to teach them, saying ...' So, too, its epilogue in Lk vii. 1, 'As soon as he fulfilled all his words into the ears of the people, he entered into Capernaum,' agrees in substance with the epilogue in Mt vii. 28ª, along with the opening clause of viii. 5. These probably stood together in Matthew's Q, but were separated to admit matter found in Mk i. 22, 40-4 [1] (the cleansing of the leper, being in Mark, too, the immediate antecedent of an entrance into Capernaum, ii. 1). Here, then, we seem to trace a common tradition behind Luke and Matthew, apart from Mark. But as in both it leads at once to the incident of the Centurion's servant, common in substance but widely differing in form, we reach two results: (1) the Logian element was not, as far back as we can trace it, a mere collection of discourse, but included consecutive narrative at the heart of which lay some characteristic saying of Jesus; (2) the forms in which the Q tradition, embracing this Logian element, was known to Luke and Matthew were far from the same.

The second of these important conclusions is confirmed by the next large Logian pieces, the Message of the Baptist and Jesus' reply and comments (Lk vii. 18-35, Mt xi. 2-19), and the Parable of the Sower and its interpretation. In the latter case, indeed, we may add, as a third form of Q, the type of tradition lying behind Mark: [2] and the like threefold form of Q seems best to explain the relations of the three Synoptics [3] for the Ministry of John the Baptist, the Baptism, and the Temptation. As regards the application of (1) to the problem of Luke's sources, *the main*

---

[1] Mt viii. 1 seems a mere editorial echo of iv. 25.

[2] Probably Lk viii. 16-18, to which there are doublets in the peculiar parts of Luke (xi. 33, xix. 26), represent Mark as coloured by remembrance of the language of such doublets. If so, vv. 19-21 may have followed in Luke's source on the Parable of the Sower.

[3] Mark represents a modified form of Q^{mk}, Luke = Mark + S (including its Q), Matthew = Mark + Q^{mt}.

XI. The Sources of St. Luke's Gospel

question still remaining is whether a 'special source' (S), embodying its own form of Q with other traditions peculiar to itself, will explain all his non-Marcan material, or whether, on the other hand, Luke has fitted traditions collected by himself independently into the framework of Mark or S, or of both. In this connexion the Sermon at Nazareth, the raising of the Widow's Son at Nain, and the Woman in the Pharisee's house invite attention.

Luke's decisive setting aside of Mark's placing of the visit to Nazareth, and his use of the sermon there as a sort of 'frontispiece' to the story of the Ministry, point strongly to its having so stood in his other source. This is confirmed by the very form 'Nazara' (instead of Mark's 'Nazaret', i. 9, also in Lk i-ii, Mt ii. 23 ; in Mt xxi. 11, Acts x. 38 our texts have 'Nazareth'), which seems the more vernacular form, but occurs elsewhere only at the same point in Matthew (iv. 13, probably = his Q). It is not what we should expect from Luke himself ; and the simple style of the opening, 'And he came to Nazara' (cf. the similar εἰσῆλθεν εἰς Καφαρναούμ in vii. 1, which we have traced to Q), and indeed of the whole verse where 'and' is the only conjunction and is thrice repeated, suggests a primitive type of narrative like the Q tradition. Again, the saying in iv. 24, 'Verily I say unto you, No prophet is acceptable in his native place,' occurs in a form differing from that in Mark and Matthew in a way characteristic of the Q element in Luke's S, viz. the use of ἀμήν, which is alien to Luke's style (occurring only here and in xii. 37, xviii. 17, 29, xxi. 32, xxiii. 43, against 13 times in Mark). Finally, both the style of iv. 14[b], 15 καὶ φήμη ἐξῆλθεν καθ' ὅλης τῆς περιχώρου περὶ αὐτοῦ, καὶ αὐτὸς ἐδίδασκεν ἐν ταῖς συναγωγαῖς αὐτῶν, δοξαζόμενος ὑπὸ πάντων (which connects the incident with Jesus' return from the Temptation into Galilee), and their parallels with Matthew (ix. 26 καὶ ἐξῆλθεν ἡ φήμη αὕτη εἰς ὅλην τὴν γῆν ἐκείνην, iv. 23 καὶ περιῆγεν ἐν ὅλῃ τῇ Γαλειλαίᾳ, διδάσκων ἐν ταῖς συναγωγαῖς αὐτῶν, cf. ix. 35ᵇ), confirm the view that they were the equivalent in S (Q) for the quite differently worded general statement in Mk i. 14ᵇ, which Luke ignores. Such a general preface in S satisfies the requirements of the reference in the Sermon itself (iv. 23) to deeds at Capernaum; while this again prepares for the examples belonging to that centre of His early ministry (cf. Mt iv. 13) which follow in Lk iv. 31–44. These probably formed part of S as well as Mark, for the differences in form (especially in the true text) cannot all be explained as editorial changes from Mark. Particularly is this so in vv. 42–4, where it is 'the crowds' themselves that find Jesus and are answered in words differing a good deal in form from Mark, and where 'Judaea', in the wide sense, appears instead of 'the whole of Galilee' as the sphere of His ministry. On this section follows naturally the Calling of Simon, the name by which Peter regularly appears in the Q or S element in Luke; while 'the Lake' (of Gennesaret), the style of the inland Sea of Galilee found also in viii. 22 f., 33, is a description suggesting a form of tradition current near the real sea, e. g. at Caesarea (see below).

As regards the two other special incidents, before and after the Message of John in Lk vii. 18 ff., there is no sign that they belong to another circle of tradition from that of Luke's continuous 'special source'. The mention of the obscure city of Nain points to early Palestinian *provenance*; and the closing sentence, 'And this account touching him (i.e. 'A great Prophet is arisen among us') went forth in the whole of Judaea and all the region round about,' is all of a piece with v. 15, 'And the account touching him went abroad yet more,' and the reference in iv. 44 to Palestine as 'Judaea'. How naturally such a section leads up to the Message from John, and to the allusion in Jesus' reply to the raising of the dead as among the signs which should resolve John's doubts, is obvious: such a connexion may have arisen in

XI. The Sources of St. Luke's Gospel

tradition quite as easily as in Luke's own mind. Similarly with the episode of the woman that was 'a sinner', illustrating the description of Jesus as 'Friend of tax-collectors and sinners', which closes the same section (vii. 34). We may even add to this natural chain of sequence the short summary of Jesus' now more itinerant ministry (viii. 1-3) which makes special mention of the devoted service of other grateful women, some of whom are named. For the substance of this, too, may well have stood in Luke's special source.

The presumption, then, is that a large part, at any rate, of S lay before Luke already unified in tradition with his Q material (QL). Such a presumption is greatly strengthened by consideration of the much-debated question whether Q included any part of the Passion narrative. Those who take the negative side point to the way in which the element common to Matthew and Luke, apart from Mark, abruptly disappears or at least dwindles at the point where the public ministry closes, on the eve of the Last Supper. But granting that a Q element apart from Mark is no longer so apparent, this is only what one would expect in any case, seeing that the didactic element proper, as contrasted with that inherent in the personal story of Jesus and His companions, necessarily shrinks to slight dimensions at this point. Accordingly, any tradition going beyond what is embodied in Mark's account of the last two days of Jesus' earthly career would naturally appear only at a few points.

Are there, however, any traces whatever of Q continuing side by side with Mark in either Matthew or Luke, or in both together? We will first take the latter form of the question, as likely to yield the most decisive answer, if the affirmative be the true one at all. Now the Trial before the Sanhedrin is a point at which the life of Christ emerges once more into publicity; so that the more exoteric Q tradition might be expected *a priori* to re-emerge at this stage, as continuing that story of the conflict between Jesus and His chief opponents in which Q seems to have aimed at instructing its hearers. There in the dialogue between the High-priest and Jesus, which forms the heart of the incident, not only does Luke show traces of partial independence of Mark—this in itself might be due to S, Luke's special source—but the same is true of Matthew. Here are the main peculiarities in Mt xxvi. 63 f.: '*I adjure thee by the living God* (cf. xvi. 16) *that thou tell us if* thou art the Christ, the Son of *God*' (Mark has 'the Blessed'[1]). Jesus *saith* (λέγει, the historic present, which Matthew usually changes when it occurs in Mark, who here has εἶπεν), *Thou sayest it; howbeit I say unto you* (πλὴν λέγω ὑμῖν), *from henceforth* (Luke ἀπὸ τοῦ νῦν, cf. xxii. 18) . . .' The words in italics themselves suggest a parallel source influencing Matthew's use of Mark; and this impression grows when we note that πλὴν λέγω ὑμῖν is a Q phrase, found also in Mt xi. 22, 24 (where Lk x. 11, 14 also has πλήν, a particle found only in Sayings in Luke's Gospel, while in Acts and Mark it occurs only as a preposition, save as πλὴν ὅτι in Acts xx. 23), xviii. 7 (= Lk xvii. 1), and xxvi. 39 (= Lk xxii. 42). This last passage carries back the presumption of the influence of Q to the scene in Gethsemane likewise, since not only does πλήν there occur both in Matthew and Luke, but Lk xxii. 39-52 (including the Arrest) is full of deviations from Mark. Matthew's account, too, of the second prayer of Jesus in Gethsemane (xxvi. 42), its added words to Judas, 'But Jesus said to him, Friend, (do) that for which thou art come' (v. 50ᵃ), and the account of the cutting-off of the ear of the High-priest's servant (vv. 51-4), with its individual sayings— all point to the influence of a source of knowledge beyond

---

[1] A markedly Jewish title which Matthew, who had just used the Hebraic 'living God', would hardly tone down to 'God'; on the other hand, 'the Son of God' is found also in Lk xxii. 70, as though this were the common Q wording here. Luke also supports Matthew in what follows next, having '*Ye say* that I am', against Mark's simple 'I am'.

XI. The Sources of St. Luke's Gospel

Mark. That this was none other than the Q tradition, in the form current in Matthew's circle, is in itself probable, and is rendered more so by repeated use of the historic present, the distribution of which in our Gospels is striking[1] and probably significant. As a rule Matthew, where parallel to Mark, changes the latter's historic presents into past tenses. Even where he adopts any of them, it is very sparingly, and these usually words descriptive of conversation (e.g. viii. 4; ix. 6, 9; xii. 13; xiv. 17; xxii. 20): nor is it certain in all of these cases that Matthew is using Mark alone,[2] since in xxii. 21 we find two historic presents ('They say "Caesar's". Then saith he to them') where Mark has aorists. Yet in the ten verses, Mt xxvi. 36-45, there occur no less than eight cases, out of a total of twenty-one cases of all kinds in which Matthew agrees with Mark in using the historic present. Further, another occurs five verses earlier, in the prediction of Peter's denial, and is followed by one peculiar to Matthew (v. 35, where Mark has ἐλάλει). This again points to Q as influencing Matthew's narrative, as does also the fact that it omits a notable feature in Mark, viz. the prediction that before the cock should crow *twice* Peter should deny thrice (xiv. 30, cf. 72).

But if Q contained any part of the Passion story, it must have contained it all in outline, seeing that it hangs together. This is borne out by positive evidence elsewhere. For Matthew, although he tends to avoid historic presents where he is not influenced by the Q tradition,[3] has 'he

[1] See *Horae Synopticae*[2], 1909, pp. 143-9.

[2] The cases of pure narrative are in introductions to sections which may well have stood in Q, and where, moreover, the parallel with Mark is not verbal (ix. 14; xv. 1; xvii. 1 *bis*; xxii. 16; xxvii. 38): so that here, too, the tense may not be due wholly to Mark's influence. This view finds further confirmation in the fact that the one passage in Luke in which the historic present occurs with τότε (as often in Matthew) is xi. 24-26, the picture of the Demon cast out and returning, which appears also in Matt. xii. 43-45, and so probably belongs to Q.

[3] Note that in ch. xvii. 2-xxii. 15, while Matthew does not reproduce one of Mark's 26 historic presents, he has some 19 cases of 'he saith', 'they say', independent of Mark. The same independent usage is seen in the

saith' also in the course of Peter's denials (xxvi. 71)—a section which has special features ('Jesus the Galilaean', 'the Nazaraean', 'thy speech makes thee manifest', the omission of 'a second time', besides more dubious points); in the examination before Pilate (xxvii. 13, 22, verses between which comes a good deal special to Matthew, but implying at least an oral context similar to that in Mark, e.g. 19, along with 24); and in the Appearance of the risen Jesus to the women in xxviii. 10. When we look for similar traces of the Q type of tradition in Luke, they are forthcoming. Thus Jesus' words to the 'daughters of Jerusalem' are quite in its style, including the use of πλήν (xxiii. 28), and τότε (v. 30), which also seems characteristic of QL.[1] We have already seen reason to trace QL as underlying Lk xxii. 35, while πλήν occurs twice in xxii. 21 f., in the heart of the Lucan account of the Last Supper, in which there is throughout much independence of Mark. Indeed this applies to the whole of ch. xxii, being traceable in such verses as 3[a], 'Now *Satan entered into* Judas' (cf. 31 f.), 4[b] 'and captains' (cf. 52), 6[b] 'apart from crowd' (ἄτερ, cf. 35), 8-10[a] 'Peter and John' and matters of form, 14-23 (both in substance and order[2]); 24-30 (with parallels[3] in Mk x. 41-5 = Mt xx. 24-8, cf. Mk ix.

accounts of John and the Baptism of Jesus (iii. 1, 13, 15), the Temptation (iv. 5 f., 8 *bis*, 10 f.), the Centurion of Capernaum (viii. 7), the Two Aspirants (viii. 20, 22, 26), the Two Blind Men (ix. 28 *bis*), and other passages (xiii. 51; xiv. 31; xv. 12, 33 f.; xvi. 15)—most, if not all, of which probably belonged to Q. The historic present also occurs some 17 times in Matthaean parables, xii. 44 f. (Lk xi. 24-6); xiii. 28 f., 44 *ter*; xviii. 32; xx. 6-8 *quater*; xxii. 8, 12; xxv. 11, 19 *bis*.

[1] Especially as seen in its occurrences in discourse in Luke, some 13 out of a total of 15 cases. Of the other two, xxi. 10, 'Then he said to them,' occurs amid discourse; and xxiv. 45, 'Then opened he their mind to understand the Scriptures,' is closely related to what looks like Q matter. Note also in xxiii. 43 ἀμήν, found in Luke only 5 other times (iv. 24; xii. 37; xviii. 17, 29; xxi. 32), against 13 in Mark and 30 in Matthew, and so probably adopted by him only from his special source.

[2] Luke's order is psychologically superior, passing only after the Supper to the topic of betrayal (cf. Jn xiii. 21 ff.).

[3] That Luke is here independent of Mark is proved not only by the

XI. The Sources of St. Luke's Gospel

35, Mt xxiii. 11; Mt xix. 27 f., i.e. Q tradition variously placed); 31-4, 'Simon, Simon, behold, Satan asked, &c.'; 35-8, the new need of equipment; and the sections examined above. The differences extend even beyond the verses indicated, and are not to be explained as merely due to Luke's stylistic method. Further, there are analogous, though far slighter, marks of another narrative than Mark as known to Matthew, even in the first half of its corresponding chapter.

All this points to Q as in some form including the Passion story, so full of sayings bearing on Jesus the Messiah and His Mission. When, however, we add the striking diversity of Luke's order both in chapter xxii and in the whole Passion story, it is most probable that his Q matter had already taken its place in the contexts in which it actually occurs in his pages, i.e. without reference to the Marcan narrative. This seems a more natural solution than that put forward quite tentatively by Sir J. C. Hawkins at the end of Essay II in this volume. The one thing which remains obscure is the relation of Luke's non-Marcan matter at this point to what we have called his special source of information (S), as distinct from QL. To that source it is usual to assign most of those episodes which have no parallels in Mark or Matthew (assumed to contain between them practically all the common Apostolic tradition, Q), such as the raising of the Widow's Son at Nain, the scene in the house of Simon the Pharisee, and some passages in Luke's 'Great Insertion' already examined. But it is clear that if we isolate such S sections, they do not form or even suggest a continuous whole such as we should expect to find in a written document or primitive Gospel. Accordingly we

difference of form, but also by his not using Mk x. 45, which speaks of the Son of Man giving His life 'a ransom for many'—the verse of all others which he might have been thought sure to seize and work in somewhere. That he does not do so, should deter us from assuming that Luke anywhere detaches verses from their context in Mark in an arbitrary fashion.

seem faced by these alternatives: either (1) Luke was there using a series of disconnected anecdotes written down in his notebook from the lips mainly of a single early witness—for they betray even in Luke's re-writing of them a Judaeo-Christian manner not his own, and even the stamp of a single mind rather than a circle of tradition; or (2) these ancedotes came to him already associated with the form of Q tradition which we have called QL, the local type familiar to the witness from whom he derived also the distinctive S element. In the former case Luke must himself have written down in his notebook the QL type of local tradition, and then woven in the various anecdotes at a later date, possibly only when writing his Gospel by the aid of Mark. In the latter, QL and S were already fused together in the narrative which Luke derived from his special informant (= S), and which he committed at the time to his notebook. We have already argued as regards the part of Luke's Gospel prior to the Great Insertion, that the latter is the more probable view. But even if this were otherwise, it would remain quite possible, and even probable, that the Passion narrative and its sequel lay before Luke in a form differing from the foregoing just in this, that all that his informant (= S) knew touching this, the final stage, had been given to Luke as an articulated story, wherein the order was determined by the knowledge of this witness himself, and so was the real historical order in a sense unparalleled in the rest of Luke's non-Marcan data. The natural, psychological sequence here visible bears out this view, and indeed suggests that the author of the S element is now speaking as an 'eyewitness' or as an associate of such, and so reproduces the local form of the current Apostolic tradition (QL) in its real historic setting. This would explain the freedom with which the Marcan narrative (also embodying a certain amount of Q matter) is ignored and at times traversed.

XI. The Sources of St. Luke's Gospel

But in fact these phenomena of independent historical witness underlying the Lucan narrative are not confined to the Passion. They extend beyond it on both sides, so far as the history lies in Jerusalem and the immediate vicinity.[1] Let us first take what of this precedes the Passion.

From the point at which Luke runs parallel with Mark after the Great Insertion (xviii. 15 ; Mk x. 13), his sources seem to be as follows:—

xviii. 15–17. Children brought to Jesus . . . . . Mark, ? S[2]
    18–30. The Rich Ruler's question, &c. . . . S[3]
    31–34. Warning as to the Passion . . . . . S[4]
    35–43. Blind man at Jericho . . . . . . S[5]
xix. 1–10. Zacchaeus of Jericho . . . . . . S[6]
    11–28. Parable of Money as a trust . . . . S
    29–36. The Colt procured for Jesus' entry . . Mark (S)[7]
    37–44. Approach to Jerusalem, &c. . . . . . S
    45–48. Cleansing of the Temple . . . . . S[8] (Mk)
xx. 1–8. Question as to Jesus' authority . . . Mark, S
    9–19. Parable of the Vine-dressers and the Heir S[9], Mark

[1] It is noteworthy that out of some 20 sections in which Sir J. C. Hawkins (*Horae Synopticae*[2], pp. 210-11) discerns variations from Mark common to Luke and Matthew, such as seem to point to a second common source (of some kind) fall between Lk xxi. 37 and xxiv. 9. This suggests that the evidence for the Q tradition behind Mark as influencing these two Gospels in some way, is specially manifest for the final Jerusalem days.

[2] Note καὶ τὰ βρέφη, Mark παιδία (also used by Luke in Jesus' rebuke) ; note also προσεκαλέσατο (αὐτά), and ἀμήν, which Luke would probably avoid (in favour of ἀληθῶς, cf. ix. 27, xii. 44, xxi. 3), if using Mark only.

[3] Note especially ἄρχων, ἐν (τοῖς) οὐρανοῖς, the order μὴ μοιχεύσῃς, μὴ φονεύσῃς, also ἀμήν (see note 2).

[4] The divergent form of 31ᵇ, cf. xxii. 37 ; καὶ ὑβρισθήσεται; v. 34, cf. ix. 45.

[5] The difference of locality, οἱ προάγοντες in 32, all 43ᵇ ; cf. Mt also for its Q, e. g. in δύο, and 33 f.

[6] The seeming lack of connexion with what follows is probably due to the reason for the parable given in 11ᵇ, which may be Luke's own addition. Originally the connexion of thought was simply the true use of money as a trust, whereas 11ᵇ turns attention to a secondary feature of the parable, absent from Matthew's version.

[7] To judge from Matthew's independence here, his Q also had this section.

[8] Matthew also deserts Mark's order here and supports Luke's, owing to his Q.

[9] Here again Matthew's independence, like Luke's, points to a second

338   *Studies in the Synoptic Problem*

```
xx. 20-26. Question as to the Census-money  . .  S¹, Mark
    27-38. The Sadducees put a test question  . .  S, Mark
       39. Certain Scribes approve Jesus' answer .  S²
       40. Questioners now silent . . . . . .  Mark
    41-44. Jesus puts a question as to Messiah . .  S
    45-47. Warning against the Scribes . . . .  S³, Mark
xxi. 1-4. The Widow's Mites . . . . . . .  Mark, (S)⁴
    5-36. Eschatological Discourse . . . . .  S⁵, Mark
    37 f. Jesus' haunts during these days . . .  S
```

As for what follows the Passion, there are traces here also of a source other than Mark, but embodying much the same tradition as to both the Burial⁶ (xxiii. 50-6) and the Resurrection (ch. xxiv). In the latter case we have signs of independent developments of the fundamental tradition (Q) in all three Gospels, especially as to the angelic manifestation at the tomb. That known to Mark makes the women see, on entering the rock-tomb, 'a youth seated on the right hand, arrayed in a white robe' (στολή); that followed by Matthew (QM) represents 'the angel of the

---

source. In connexion with Luke's variations in v. 19, where he has λαόν, while Mark has ὄχλον, note the reference to 'the people' (λαός) as a prime factor of the situation in Jerusalem which marks Luke's account throughout. From xviii. 43 onwards λαός occurs some 15 times in this connexion, but only once in Mark—in a passage which confirms its historical fitness (xiv. 2 = Mt xxvi. 5; cf. xxvii. 25, 64)—although Mark uses 'crowd' in some of the same passages (xi. 32; xii. 12, 37; xv. 8, 11, 15). In Luke's narrative it occurs in cases that cannot be due to himself, and points to a consecutive second source running through these closing chapters.

¹ In xx. 20ᵇ the use of 'righteous' suggests the same source as is used in xviii. 9. Matthew also shows signs of Q, including historic presents in xxii. 20.

² Here S's tradition deviated from Mark (cf. x. 25 ff.) and led directly to what we find in Lk xx. 41, 'And he said to *them*.' As to 41-44, the deviations in Matthew also suggest the presence of more than Mark (i. e. Q).

³ Note 'to the disciples', supported by Mt xxiii. 1.

⁴ Note ἀναβλέψας (cf. xvi. 23), πενιχράν, εἰς τὰ δῶρα.

⁵ Luke's eschatological discourse has its own opening and ending, and much else due to a non-Marcan source.

⁶ Note Luke's characterization of Joseph, especially as δίκαιος, cf. xxiii. 47, xx. 20; xviii. 9; ii. 25; i. 6, 17, and other features not paralleled in Mark, e. g. as to the Tomb, and in 56ᵇ, 'and they rested on the sabbath according to the precept.'

XI. The Sources of St. Luke's Gospel 339

Lord' as seated on the stone which he had rolled away, his raiment (ἔνδυμα) 'white as snow' and 'his countenance as lightning'; while Luke's source (S) says 'two men came upon them (ἐπέστησαν) in dazzling apparel' (ἐσθῆτι ἀστραπτούσῃ, cf. Matthew ὡς ἀστραπή). The setting being thus different and pointing to second sources as used by both Matthew and Luke, it is natural to suppose that the difference in words uttered was also due to these sources. Thus Luke's special source already omitted reference to any coming appearance in Galilee, pointing on the one hand backwards to the predictions of the Passion and Resurrection (in terms of ix. 44; xviii. 33: cf. xxiv. 44-6), and on the other hand leading up, by the report carried to 'the eleven and all the rest', to the appearance in Jerusalem which follows in xxiv. 36 ff. This, then, seems to have been the immediate sequel in the common Jerusalem form of the Apostolic tradition as known to S; but to judge from the way in which it is linked on to the close of the episode of the Two Disciples going to Emmaus (xxiv. 33-5), the latter incident was added to the common tradition by the author of S himself, out of his own special knowledge. Yet the language and ideas of the two sections are perfectly homogeneous alike with each other and with the references to the fulfilment of prophecy in Jesus' whole career, which enter again and again into the substance of the narrative of the Ministry, and this too in passages belonging clearly to the QL matter (ix. 31, 44; xii. 50; xviii. 31; xxii. 37: cf. xiii. 32), as well as to that more peculiar to S (iv. 21). Thus, once again, we have grounds[1] for asking whether QL was not already fused with the special S matter in the document used by Luke. If we look to certain S sections in the Lucan narrative prior to Jesus' arrival at Jerusalem, we may hesitate

---

[1] We may add that ἀμήν, which is found in xii. 37; xviii. 17, 29; xxi. 32 (i.e. 4 out of the Luke's 6 cases), occurs in iv. 24; cf. the remaining case, xxiii. 43.

between this theory and one which regards Luke as having himself fitted such sections, received as detached episodes, into the fairly consecutive QL tradition, along with Mark. But in view of the seeming historical unity of the two elements in the last stage of Jesus' ministry, which we have been tracing, it is best to assign their unity throughout—or at most with rare exceptions—to the mind from which Luke derived his non-Marcan material as a whole.

Having now tested Luke's narrative on both sides of its central and most distinctive part (ix. 51–xviii. 14), where we had in Mark one of his sources before us for comparison, we can the better approach the so-called Great Insertion in the Marcan type of framework. Will our theory of a single 'special source' in addition to Mark still meet the case? That the conditions are not the same is evident on the very face of the narrative. There is a comparative lack of indications of *historical* sequence and circumstance, as evidenced by place-names and definite notes of transition from stage to stage of a developing ministry—whether as regards Jesus' self-manifestation or the attitude of different classes in Israel to Him and His message. The fact is that the development of the Galilaean ministry has already passed its crisis before the point at which the Great Insertion comes in. In other words, His ministry in the more populous parts of provincial Israel was practically over, when Jesus left Galilee proper and began to journey—still through Herod's territory, though now East of Jordan—towards Jerusalem at a time when the Passover was already approaching. This, at least, is the impression conveyed by the Synoptic narrative as a whole. But Luke's Great Insertion gives us the impression that much more took place at this juncture than we should gather from Mark, ere His journey developed into the prophetic Progress with which all our

XI. *The Sources of St. Luke's Gospel* 341

Gospels picture Jesus as actually approaching David's city.

Here two questions need to be kept apart; the correctness of this impression, and the source to which it is due in Luke's Gospel. It is with the latter alone that we are directly concerned. Yet the two blend intimately at one point at least, namely the very opening of the Great Insertion, where we read of the mission of the Seventy, a definite historical event, and one which presupposes a rather systematic ministry on the line of Jesus' route itself. This opening part of the Peraean ministry we shall examine with some care, before discussing the material in ix. 51–xviii. 14 as a whole, to the very fullness of which—rather than the nature of the Ministry itself, even including that of the Seventy—is due our feeling that it should represent the traditions of a fairly prolonged activity.

The actual point of departure in Luke's Peraean section corresponds to Mk x. 1 : 'And . . . he cometh into the borders of Judaea and beyond Jordan ; and there come together again multitudes unto him, and as he was wont he again began to teach them.' This points back by the repeated use of 'again' to the period of retirement with the inner circle, for the purpose of teaching them apart as to the issues of His coming visit to Jerusalem. Now, having finished 'teaching his disciples' (ix. 31), He resumes His usual teaching of the multitudes, as He makes His way towards Jerusalem on the eastern side of Jordan where Peraea, a part of Herod Antipas's tetrarchy of Galilee, bordered on Judaea proper. The language of Mark itself suggests a leisurely progress, including something like a ministry in that region. This is obviously how Luke understands the matter, referring back to this historical situation at two points (xiii. 22 ; xvii. 11) in the lengthy account he believes himself in a position to give of Christ's teaching during this period. To judge from independent features in Lk ix. 51ᵇ, 52ᵃ, he had a second source which gave what looked like the beginning of this journey, before Jesus had crossed Jordan, while He was on the borders of Galilee and Samaria. It told a story occasioned by the sending of messengers ahead, to prepare people hitherto unfamiliar with the prophet of Nazareth for his arrival amongst them ; and it was the fact that they entered a Samaritan village, in the region where Galilee and Samaria were in contact, that led to the incident (ix. 52-6) which caused the sending of these messengers to be remembered in some line of Christian tradition, apparently rather a direct [1] one. It is in logical continuation of this narrative, that we get in x. 1 the record of a more organized sending forth of such forerunners as have just been spoken of. But we have no sure means of judging whether the intervening three examples (two in Mt viii. 19 ff.) of would-be personal disciples [2] (ix. 57-60) originally came here in the special source, or were placed here by Luke himself.

What, then, is the value of Lk x. 1 ? [3] Does it represent true tradition, or only a later conception? In its favour is the temporary nature of the commission as defined in the verse itself—partly on the lines of ix. 52, which most accept as historical, and partly on those of the commission to the Twelve. The contrary impression, viz. that a secondary permanent apostolate is attributed to the Seventy, is largely due to the degree to which the charge in x. 2 ff. is a *replica* of that to the Twelve, as found in ix. 1-6 (comp. Mk vi. 7-12). But (1) we need not wonder if there has been some assimilation of traditions in two cases so similar in the main;

[1] One lying too before Luke in writing: witness the early order 'James and John', which was changed in Luke's own day owing to James's death and John's later prominence (cf. Acts i. 13, and the reversal of Mark's order in Lk viii. 51 ; ix. 28).

[2] The very urgency of Jesus' demands best suits a late and critical stage in His ministry.

[3] Its present wording probably owes something to Luke, e. g. ἀνέδειξεν ὁ κύριος, possibly ἑτέρους ; but that is all.

www.ingramcontent.com/pod-product-compliance
Lightning Source LLC
Chambersburg PA
CBHW052137300426
44115CB00011B/1410

Vitellius, 182.
Volz, B., 285.
Von Soden, Freiherr, 30, 119 f., 126, 128.
Votaw, C. W., 107.

Wattenbach, W., 17.
Weiss, B., viii, xvi, xx, xxiii, 110, 299, 324, 357, 361.
Weiss, J., xxi, xxiii, 357, 425.
Wellhausen, J., 104, 288, 295-301, 308.
Wendling, E., xxiv, 390-421.
Wendt, H. H., 91.

We-sections, 57.
Westcott and Hort's text, 25, 65, 79, 81, 115, 346.
Western readings, 66, 187.
Widow's mite, 338.
Wilkinson, J. R., 112.
Williams, N. P., references to, vii, x, xxii, 13.
— essay by, 389-421.
Winter and Wünsche, 284 f.
Woods, F. H., 34, 85.
Wrede, W., 398.
Wright, A., xxiii, 63, 85, 87, 124, 130, 315.

II. Subject-Index

Ramsay, Sir W.M., xxiv, 14, 239 f., 375.
Ramses II, Pharaoh of Exodus, 369.
Ramses III, Pharaoh of Exodus, 370.
Resurrection, predictions of, 69.
— appearances, 334.
— narrative of, 338 f., 361, 395.
Roberts, A., 289.
Robinson, J. Armitage, 72, 107, 120.
Rushbrooke, W. G., 47, 96, 109 et al.

S. *See* Essay XI.
Sabatier, P., 226.
Salmon, G., 57, 100.
Samaritan, 353.
— village, hospitable, 54.
Sanday, W., references to, vii, 57, 66, 90, 103, 107, 178.
— preface by, vii–xxvii.
— essay by, 3–26.
Sanhedrin, 395.
Saxon Chronicle, 381 f.
Schanz, P., 71.
Schechter, S., 285 f.
Schmidt, N., 308, 310.
Schmiedel, P. W., 129.
Schürer, E., 44, 48, 288, 290 f.
Schweitzer, A., 179, 425.
Seed growing secretly, parable of, 61.
Septuagint, 32, 37, 40, 99 f., 107, 208, 293 f.
— influence on Luke, 280, 317 ff.
Sermon on the Mount (or level plain), xv, xxii, 70, 124, 147–52, 158, 161, 175, 187, 189, 213, 221, 242 ff., 272 ff., 326–8.
Seti II, 370.
Seventy, the, appointment of, 57 f., 143, 154, 325, 341 ff.
Shema, 43, 44.
Simon the Pharisee, 335.
Simpson, D. C., xxvi.
Smith, W. Robertson, 375.
Son of God in Q, 332.
Son of Man, meaning of, 308–10.
— the Son, the Father, 310–12.
Sower, parable of, 328, 362.
Special source, xix.
Speculum perfectionis, 215 f., 225 f.
Spiegelberg, W., 369.
Stanton, B. H., xi, xxi, xxiii, xxv, 85, 105, 107, 136, 345, 348 f., 356–8, 362.
Stephens, H., 110.
Storm, stilling of, 395.
Strauss, D. F., 199.
Streeter, B. H., references to, vii, x f., xii, xv–xviii, xxi, xxiii, 11, 120.
— essays by, 141–231.
— appendix by, 423–36.
Synagogues, Christ forbidden, 68.
Synoptic Gospels, conditions under which written, 11 ff.
— not exactly histories, 14.
Syriac Sinaitic, 44, 47, 81, 137.
Syrophoenician woman story, 399.
Swete, H. B., 73, 74.

Tacitus, 68, 181, 222.
Talmud, Palestinian, 298.
Taylor, C., 284, 286.
Tel-el-Amarna Tablets, 369.
Temptation, xvii, 85, 102, 113, 119, 129, 142 f., 152, 159, 168, 186 f., 214, 217, 219, 236 f., 273 f., 328, 334, 361.
Thackeray, H. St. John, 317, 320.
Theodotus, 291.
Theological Studies, Journal of, 72.
Thorpe, B., editor of *Saxon Chronicle*, 381.
Three-stratum hypothesis, xxv, 390 ff.
Thucydides, 25.
Tischendorf's *Synopsis Evangelica*, 47, 67, 102.
Titus, 182.
Tobit, 74.
Tomb, angels at, 338 f.
Tradition, meaning and use of term, 96.
— 'Double,' 96–7, 130.
— 'Single,' 130.
Turner, C. H., 20, 44.
Twelve, The, 342–4.
Two-document hypothesis, xi, xix, 3, 315, 389.
Tyrrell, G., 425.
τότε, 334.

Veil, rending of, 83.
Verrall, Professor, 231.
Virgil, 18.

454   II. Subject-Index

Matthew, Gospel of (continued)—
— interest in Judas and Pilate, 92.
— rabbinization of Christ's teaching, 221 f.
— Matthaeo-Lucan peculiarities, 35.
— method of conflation, 171, 173.
Matthias, 57.
Mechilta, 284–6.
Megilloth, the five, 148.
Menzies, A., 91, 390.
Merenptah, 369 f.
Meyer, A., 288, 301 f.
Meyer, E., 369.
Miketta, 369.
Milligan, G., 355.
Milligan and Moulton, 39, 65.
Mimes of Herodas, length of, 26.
Möller, 371.
Moses, 154, 370.
Moulton, J. H., 99 f., 289, 317, 320.
Muhammed, Sayings of, 123.
Muratorian fragment, 58.
Mustard seed, parable of, 50–3, 127.

Nain, 329, 330, 335, 352.
Nazareth, rejection at, 155.
— sermon at, 329 f., 352.
— form of name, 329.
Neubauer, A., 288.
Nöldeke, Th., 374.

Odyssey, length of, 25 f.
Old Testament, allusions in Q, 128.
'Omission, the great,' 61–74.
— its extent, 62.
— ways of explaining its origin, 63–74.
Onquelos, Targum of, 298.
Oral tradition, 4 f., 96–8, 315, 351, 359 f.
Origen, 106.
Orr, Jas., 367, 371, 373.
Oxyrhynchus, 123, 137.

Papias, 53, 57, 63, 104–7, 131, 215 f., 294, 304, 359, 362, 370.
Parables, type of, 196.
Parousia, 135, 144, 155 f., 180 ff.
Passion, predictions of, 69, 339.
— narrative of, in Lk, 75–94, 137 f., 146, 155, 218, 315, 324; in Matt., 158; in Q, 177–9, 203,
361; in Wendling's hypothesis, 395.
Pauline influence in Luke, xiii. 88, 90–4, 134, 135, 155, 218; in Mk, 399.
Paul's allusion to Christ's life and teaching, 90 f.
Paulus, H. E. G., 2 8.
Pella, 183.
Peraean Section, 191. *See also* Luke's Greater Interpolation.
'Pereqs,' arrangement into five, 148, 152.
Persecution, Neronian, 181.
Peter, St., as Mk's informant, 13, 57, 63, 85, 104, 305, 356, 389.
— call, 352.
— confession, 159, 269, 324.
— rebuke, 71.
— denial, 82, 333.
— name, 330.
— preparing Passover, 353.
Petrie, Flinders, 369.
Pfannkuche, 288.
Pharisee's house, 329, 352.
Pharisees, xv, 62, 70 f.
Philip the Evangelist, 57, 351 f., 360.
— his daughters, 224, 353.
Philo, 106.
— poet, 291.
Pilate, trial before, 228–231.
Plummer, A., 10, 32, 44, 56, 57, 68, 105, 107, 125.
Polycarp, 107.
Praetorium, 83.
Prayer, recourse to, in Lk, 87
— Lord's, 99, 113.
πλήν, 332, 334.

Q, 4, 12, 13, 20, 33, 39, 47, 55, 70, 71, 97–130, 131–8, 315, 323 f., 326, 425–36 [*cf. sub* Logia, L].
— latest chaps. in Mt and Lk of use of, 129, 331–5.
— date of, 371.
— phrases, 332.
— historic presents in, 333 f.
— Apocalypse in, *see sub* Apocalyptic Sayings.
— Logia, xiv.
QL type, 335.

Rabbis, 212.

II. Subject-Index 453

Kenyon, F. G., 25 f.
König, E., 57.
Kuenen, A., and theory of Hexateuch, 371, 373.
καθεξῆς, 354.

L, title of document, 4. *See also* Logia *and* Q.
Lagarde, P. de, 308.
Lake, K., 371.
Lawyer's Question, 41-5.
Lenwood, F., viii.
Levy, J., 285.
Lieblein, 369.
Lietzmann, H., 308.
Lightfoot, J. B., 54, 73, 105 f.
Liturgical usage, influence of, 99, 113, 286.
Logia, 53 ff., 70, 85, 90, 104, 106 f., 119, 127, 216, 235, 294, 352, 357, 362.
— *see sub* Q *and* L.
— of Oxyrhynchus, 123.
Loisy, A., 124, 425.
Lord's Prayer, 282.
Lord's Supper, 81, 93, 188, 334, 396.
Luke, author of third Gospel, 97.
— his economy for space sake in use of material, 56.
— knowledge of many previous Gospels, 55.
— information gained from Philip at Caesarea or Jerusalem (*see sub* Philip), xxi, 57.
— at Caesarea, 351.
— not outside Palestine, 353.
— his advantages less than those of Josephus, 13 f.
— ἀμήν, alien to style of, 329.
— vocabulary, 332.
Luke, *Gospel of:*
— characteristics of, 13.
— object of its being written, 222 f.
— for Gentiles, 204.
— Pauline influence upon, *see sub* Paul.
— influences of LXX upon, 208, 293 f.
— original language of, 292 f.
— historic presents in, 333.
— Hellenization of Marcan matter, 208.
— attitude adopted to disciples, 223.

— Greater interpolation into Mark's order, $9^{51}-18^{14}$, 25-59, 130, 160, 189 ff., 335, 340.
— Lesser interpolation into Mark's order, $6^{20}-8^3$, 31-3.
— Great omission of contents of Mark $6^{45}-8^{26}$, 61 74, possibly due not to
  (1) Non-existence of Mark at time, 63-6;
  nor (2) accidental oversight, 66;
  but to (3) deliberate omission, 67-74; in order
  (*a*) to avoid miracles achieved by material means, 68 f.;
  (*b*) to prevent undue repetition, 68-70;
  (*c*) to limit anti-Pharisaic controversy, 70 f.;
  (*d*) to spare the Twelve, 71 f.
Luke's Day, St., Gospels for, 58.

Mark, Gospel of:
— number of verses in, 3.
— length of, 25 f.
— secondary features in, 9 f.
— original language of, 293 ff.
— object of its being written, 14, 220.
— relation to St. Peter's teaching, 13, 57.
— date of, 385 f.
— and Ur-Marcus, 21, 63 ff., 289-421.
— used by Matt and Luke, 3, 9, 29 ff.
— present recension not known to Matthew and Luke, 21 f.
— historic presents in, 64, 295.
— arguments against Deutero-Mark, 64 ff.
— Wendling's hypothesis as to, 389-421.
Marquart, J., 370.
Marshall, J. T., 290.
Matthew, Gospel of:
— original language of, 293.
— based on St. Mark and Q, 13.
— object of its being written, 14, 220 f.
— length of, 25 f.
— historic presents in, 274, 333.
— collection of material into five blocks, 30.
— principal interest, 207.

II. Subject-Index

Delitzsch, F., *Babel und Bibel*, 372.
De Rossi, G. B., 288.
De Wette, 373.
Deutero-Mark, 63.
Didache, 81.
Diodati, 288.
Divorce, 70, 275.
Dobschütz, E. von, xxvi, 432.
Document, Two, theory, 389.
Doublets, 34–7, 111, 117, 137, 157 f., 172, 175 f., 328; in O.T., 382 f.
Driver, S. R., 377.
Duplicate expressions, 65.
Dürr, Alphons, xxvi.

Edersheim, A., 54, 106.
Eerdmans, B. D., 369 f., 373 ff.
Elijah, 154.
Emmaus, disciples going to, 339.
Enc. Biblica, 63.
Epiphanius, 57.
Eschatological discourse, *see sub* Apocalyptic.
1 Esdras, 381.
4 Esdras, 49.
Eupolemus, 291.
Eusebius, 104, 183, 294.
Ewald, H., 373.
Evangelists, conditions under which they wrote, 11 ff.
— not copyists but historians, 12.
— use of books and freedom of transcription, 16.
Expos. Times, 105.
Ezekiel, poet, 291.

'Father of' men, applied to God, 37; the Father, *see sub* Son.
Feeding of 4,000, 401.
— 5,000, 401.
Feine, P., xxi, 90, 357.
Fig-tree, 401.
Francis, St., of Assisi, 215 f., 225 f.

Gethsemane, prayer in, 332.
Gnostics, secret tradition of, 180.
Gould, E. P., 67.
Gunkel, H., 372.

Habiri, relation to Israelites, 369.
Harnack, A., xvii, xxi, 73, 97, 107, 109, 112, 113, 116, 126 f., 129, 144, 160–4, 185, 187, 199, 205, 207, 220, 224, 235–42, 284, 286, 294, 299, 309, 312, 355.
Hawkins, Sir John, references to, vii, ix f., xii–xv, xviii f., xxiii–xxv, 3, 4, 5, 10, 13, 34, 35, 64, 65, 84, 87, 101–3, 111, 116 f., 144, 153, 160–4, 176, 188, 190 f., 201, 198, 205, 207, 223, 320, 333, 335, 337, 376, 430, 432.
— essays by, 29–138.
Hebrews, Gospel according to, 359, 361.
Herod the Great, 230.
Herod, his soldiers, 83.
— Luke's interest in, xiv, 94, 229–31.
Herodotus, 25.
Hexateuch, xxiii.
Hibbert Journal, 211.
High Priest, 82.
Historic Presents, *see sub* Matt., Mk, Lk.
Horae Hebraicae, 52.
Horae Synopticae, *see references sub* Hawkins.
Hort, F. J. A., 73 f.
Huck, A., viii, 102.
Hupfeld, H., 373.
Hyperides, length of, 26.

Iliad, length of, 25 f.
Imperfect, use of, 64.
Irenaeus, 63.

Jackson, H. L., 105.
Jairus's daughter, 394.
James and John, their request, 72, 401.
James, Epistle of, 222.
Jeremias, A., 372.
John the Presbyter, 104.
Johns, C. H. W., Babylonian influences, 372.
Johnson, Samuel, Wit and Wisdom of, 123.
Jonah, sign of, 144, 153.
Joseph of Arimathaea, 83.
Joseph Barsabbas, 57.
Josephus, 95, 213, 290.
— advantages over St. Luke, 14.
Judas, 82, 93.
Jülicher, A., 119 f.
Justin Martyr, 107.
Justus of Tiberias, 291.

II. SUBJECT-INDEX

Abbott, E. A., 10, 19 f., 21, 96 f., 103, 107.
Abbott, T. K., 289, 305.
Addis, W. E., references to, xxxiii f.
— essay by, 367–86.
Allen, W. C., references to, vii, xi, xv, xvii–xix, xxiii, 3, 4, 30, 43, 63, 105, 107, 205, 315.
— essays by, 233–312.
Amenhotep II or III, 369.
Antiochus Epiphanes, 180.
Apocalypse, Little, 63, 148 f., 156, 158, 179–183.
Apocalyptic Sayings in Q, 179, 201–3, 207, 214.
— evolutionary stages of, 425–36.
Apostles, Teaching of, 362.
Aramaic background, xviii f.
— Original of Gospel, 104, 359, 386.
Archelaus, 199.
Aspirants, the two, 334, 434 f.
Astruc, 373.
ἀληθῶς, 337.
ἀμήν, 329, 334, 337, 339.
ἀπ' ἄρτι, 430.
ἄτερ, 334.

Bacon, B. W., 361.
Badcock, C., viii, xxii.
Bäntsch, B., 372.
Baptism, xviii.
Baptist, xviii.
— preaching of the, 85, 102, 113, 119, 126 f., 136, 142 f., 328, 334.
— message from, 114, 123, 129, 142, 151 f., 159, 168, 187 ff., 328, 361.
— death, 61 f., 230, 394.
— Christ's relation to, 212.
Bar-cochba, 181.
Bartlet, J. Vernon, referred to, vii, xi f., xv, xix–xxiii.
— essay by, 315–63.
Basil, St., 106.

Beatitudes, xxii, 21, 189, 238, 242 ff.
Bebb, Ll. J. M., 56, 68.
Beelzebub, defence against charge of, 45–9, 64, 70, 114, 128 f., 146, 153, 169, 213, 219, 400 f.
Beissel, S., 18.
Betrayal, the, 334.
Birt, Th., 17, 25.
Bleek, F., 373.
Blessing of children, 401.
Blind Men, the two, 334.
Book Rolls, method of transcribing from, 17 f.
— length of, 25.
Box, square, for book roll, 17.
Briggs, C. A., 294.
Bruce, A. B., 70, 71, 74.
Burial, 338.
Burkitt, F. C., 107, 118, 120, 137, 159, 203.
Burney, C. F., 361.
Burton, E. D., 120, 129, 132.

Caesarea Philippi, 159, 211, 401.
Cambridge Biblical Essays, 105.
Canister, for book roll, 17.
Capernaum, events at, 390 f.
Catechist, 155.
Celano, Thomas of, 226.
Centurion's servant, healing of, 54, 74, 114, 119, 128, 142 f., 148, 156, 187, 217, 236 ff., 328, 334, 357, 361.
Charles, R. H., 44, 63, 290.
Cleansing the Temple, 401.
Clem. Alex., 106.
Clem. Rom., 106 f.
Cleophas, 352.
Colani, T., 63.
Colenso, Bishop, 368.
Corban, 154.
Cross, bearing the, 382.

Dalman, G., 49, 288, 290 f., 294, 308, 310, 312, 316–18.
De Lagarde, P., 308.

I. Index of Scripture References

S. JOHN
ii. 19	137
iii. 3, 8	137
iv. 10, 14, 35	137
v. 35	137
vi. 27, 32 f.	137
66	41
vii. 37 ff.	137
viii. 12	137
ix. 4	137
6	68
x. 1 ff., 7 ff.	137
xi. 9 f.	137
xii. 24	137
xiii. 10	137
21 ff.	334
xv. 1 ff.	137
xvi. 21	137
xviii. 12–27	82
20	58
61	41
xix. 26 f.	353
xx. 14	41
31	14

ACTS
i. 10	318
13	342
21	344
ii. 21, 27 ff.	318
22	67, 91
31	218
40	99
iii. 18	218
22	211
vii. 27	211
viii. 1, 5	350
14, 25	353
14 ff.	353
x. 38	91, 329
xi. 28	181
xiii. 1	xiv, 94
xviii. 25	127
xix. 3	127
13	218
xx. 23	332
xxi. 8–10	224
8 f.	57, 351
15 ff.	57
xxiv. 27	xxi
xxvii. 34	88
xxxviii. 28	225

ROMANS
i. 4	211
iii. 2	107
23 ff.	399
x. 9	100
xi. 25	88, 181
25 f.	398
11 f.	181
xii. 14, 17	91
xvi. 19	91

CORINTHIANS
1 Cor.
i. 17	92
23	92, 218
ii. 2	92
vii. 10	91
ix. 14	91
x. 16	81
xi. 23–5	93
xv. 3 f.	215
6	215
12	92
52	431

2 Cor.
x. 1	91

GALATIANS
i. 21	279
ii. 10	360
vi. 11	99, 131

PHILIPPIANS
iii. 2, 8	73

COLOSSIANS
iv. 6	40

THESSALONIANS
1 Thess.
iv. 15	91
16	431
v. 2	91
3 f.	88, 135

2 Thess.
ii. 8–12	182
iii. 3	91

TIMOTHY
1 Tim.
v. 18	91
vi. 3	91

2 Tim.
ii. 12	91

PHILEMON
24	xiii. 90

HEBREWS
ii. 14	279
v. 12	106
ix. 26	432

JAMES
i. 25	222

PETER
2 Peter.
ii. 22	74

REVELATION
xvii. 16	48
xviii. 16, 19	48
xix. 7, 9	198
xxii. 15	74

I. Index of Scripture References

S. Luke xix. 26 . 34,	xxii. 4 . . 334	xxii. 64 . . 79
111, 117, 172,	6 . . . 334	66 . . . 78
328, 383	8–10 . . 334	67 f. . 78, 80
28 . . . 346	8 . . . 353	69 . . . 430
29–xxii. 13 . 85	14–xxiv. 10 , xii,	70 . . . 332
29–36 . . 337	76–94	71 . . . 77
29 . . . 318	14–23 . . 334	xxiii. 2 . xiv, 78
37–44 . . 337	15–23 . . 81	5–12 . 78, 80
37 . . . 87	15 . . . 317	7 . . . 346
39–44 . 87, 188	17–20 . . 81	8 . . . 324
41 . . . 135	17–19 . . 8	9 . . . 230
43 f. . 88, 126	18–20 . . 81	11 . . 69, 83
45–8 . . 337	18 . . 77, 332	12 . . . 229
xx. 1–8 . . 337	19 . . . 79	15 . . . 78
1 ff. . . 134	20 . . . 79	22 . . 77, 229
1 . . . 318	21–3 . . 82	26 . . . 77
9–19 . . 337	21 f. . . 334	27–31 . 78, 93
9 . . . 348	22 . . 77, 322	28 . . . 334
11 f. . . 320	24–8 . . 334	30 . . . 334
15 . . . 89	24–7 . . 78	34 . . 77, 79, 94
18 . 87, 110, 137	24 . . 34, 69	35–8 . . 82
19 . . . 338	25–7 . 146, 434	35 . . . 323
20–44 . . 42	26 . . . 177	36 . . . 83
20–6 . . 338	28 f. . . 78	39–43 . . 93
20 . . . 338	28 . . . 117	40–3 . 78, 80
26 . . . 87	30 . 78, 117, 129,	43 . 94, 329, 334,
27–38 . . 338	145, 157, 160,	339
35 . . . 325	188, 426	44 f. . . 77
39 . . 87, 338	31–4 . . 335	45 f. . . 83
40 . . . 338	31 f. . 78, 80, 93,	46 . . 77, 78, 94
41–4 . . 338	334	47 . . 79, 338
41 . . . 338	33 . . . 223	48 . . . 78
45–7 . . 338	33 f. . . 82	50–6 . . 338
46 . . . 35	34 . . . 337	50–4 . . 83
xxi . . . 88	35–8 . 78, 335	52 f. . . 77
1–4 . . 338	35 . 35, 334, 343	56 . . 83, 338
3 . . . 337	37 . 137, 322, 337,	xxiv . . . 338
5–36 . 156, 338	339	1–10 . . 83
10 . . 207, 334	39–52 . . 332	4 . . 318, 320
11 . . 87 f.	42 . . 77, 332	6 . . . 77
13 . . . 108	43 f. . . 79	9 . . 337, 344
14 . . . 321	45 . . 71, 223	10 . . xiv, 94
14 f. . . 35	46 . . . 77	15 . . 318, 320
18 . . 87 f., 135	47 . . . 77	16 . . . 322
20 . . 88, 126	48 f. . . 78	19 . . . 211
22 . . 87, 135	49–51 . . 137	21 . . . 126
24 . . 87 f., 135	51 . . . 78	25–7 . . 322
28 . . 87 f., 135	52 . . . 334	30 . . 318, 320
29 . . 128, 207	52 f. . . 77	33–5 . . 339
32 . 329, 334, 339	54 . . . 77	33 . . . 344
34–6 . 87 f., 135	56–71 . . 82	36 ff. . . 339
37 . . . 337	60 . . . 109	44–6 . 322, 339
37 f. . 338, 352	61 . . 77, 78	45 . . 322, 334
xxii . . . 334 f.	62 . . . 79	49 . . . 326
3 . . . 334	63–71 . . 82	51 . . 318, 320

S.S.P.   G g

448 I. Index of Scripture References

S. Luke xiv.	12–14		xvi. 18	xvii. 38 f., 113,	xvii. 34	. . 303
	135, 194 f.			133, 177, 201,	34 f.	117, 123, 126,
12	. . 194, 207			222, 412		150, 201, 260
13 f.	. . . 118		19 .	. . 136	36 .	. . 30, 201
15–24	. 194, 272		19 ff.	. . . 348	37 .	115, 123, 124,
15 .	. 194, 207		22 .	. . . 318		126, 150, 201
16–24	. 127, 144		23 .	. . . 338	xviii. 1–8	. 192, 201 f.
16–18	. . . 118		xvii. 1–xviii. 8	. 206	1 .	. 202, 207
16 ff.	. . . 348		1–10	. . . 124	2 .	. . . 348
18–20	. . . 197		1–6	190, 201, 203	2 ff.	. . . 348
21 .	. . . 118		1 .	115, 144, 151,	7 .	. . . 353
23 f.	. . . 118			269, 332, 346	7 f.	. . . 202
25–7	. . . 193		1 f..	. . . 175	9 .	. . . 338
25 .	. 55, 346		2 .	. 38, 40, 52,	10 .	. . . 348
26 .	114, 126, 160			201, 204	10 ff.	. . . 348
26 f.	. 190, 194,		3–24	. . . 260	14 .	34, 117, 145,
	195, 250		3 .	115, 144, 151,		157
27 .	35, 111, 114,			222, 256	15–43	. . 85 f.
	126, 160, 177		4 .	. 115, 144,	15–17	. . . 337
28–33	135 f., 194,			151, 256	15 .	. . . 337
	202, 205		6 .	38, 39, 117, 145,	17 .	329, 334, 339,
28–32	. . . 173			157, 177, 201		432
34 .	. 38, 40, 52,		7–10	. 203, 205	18–30	. . . 337
	176, 204		7 ff.	. . . 136	18 .	. . . 42
34 f.	117, 190, 264		11–19	. 137, 358	22 .	. . . 6
xv–xviii	. . . 190		11 .	55, 159, 318,	29 .	329, 334, 339
xv	. . . 348			341, 346	31–4	. 69, 337
1–7 .	. . . 123		12–19	. 54, 68	31 .	. 337, 339
2 .	. . . 349		14 .	. 318, 320	32 .	. . . 337
3–7 .	127, 136, 144,		16 .	. . . 350	33–5	. . . 339
	194, 269		20–xviii. 8	. 202 f.	33 .	. 321 f., 339
3 .	. . . 349		20–7	. . . 123	33 f.	. . . 337
4 f..	. . . 115		20–2	. . . 135	34 .	72, 87, 821, 337
7 .	. . . 115		20 f.	. 201, 433	35–43	. 68, 337
8–10	. . . 194		21 f.	. . . 115	35 .	. 318, 320
8 ff.	. . . 136		22–37	. 190, 201 f.	43 .	. 87, 337 f.
11–32	. . . 194		23–37	144, 150, 182 f.	xix .	. . . 129
11 ff.	. . 348 f.		23 .	38, 41, 111, 115	1–28	. . . 87
23 f.	. . . 349		23 f.	. 150, 201	1–10	. . . 337
32 .	. . . 349		24 .	115, 126, 426	1 .	. . . 120
xvi. 1 .	. 136, 346		24 ff.	. . . 120	1 f.	. . . 319
1 ff.	. . . 348		25 .	. . . 321	11–28	. . . 337
9 .	. . . 306		26–30	. . . 195	11–27	. . . 188
10–12	. . . 135		26 .	. . . 426	11 .	188, 191, 200,
13–18	190, 201, 203		26 f.	. 115, 150,		202, 320, 337
13	113, 164, 201, 266			201, 260	11 f.	. . . 159
14 .	. . . 201		28–33	. . . 150	12–27	127, 129, 144
14 f.	. 70, 135		28–30	. 150, 201	12 f.	. . . 117
15–18	. . . 124		28 f.	. . . 135	12 ff.	. . . 348
15 .	. 201, 347		30 .	. . . 260	15–24	. . . 117
16 .	114, 127, 145,		31 .	38, 183, 201	15 .	. 318, 320
	156, 159, 201, 213,		32 .	. . . 135	16–26	. . . 199
	240, 251, 427		33 .	35, 111, 116,	17 .	. . . 199
17 .	39, 113, 133,			160, 201, 250,	20–6	. . . 199
	201, 264			321, 412	25 .	. . . 124

I. Index of Scripture References 447

S. Luke xi. 14 f.	71,	xi. 53 f.	. 54, 193	xii. 53	. .	45
	114, 171	xii. 1–3	. . 125	54–6	. .	110
14 ff.	. . 347	1 .	38, 54, 62, 71,	57–9	. .	264
15 .	45–9, 170		193, 346, 412	58 .	. .	302
16 .	46, 62, 70, 71,	2–9 .	71, 114, 126	58 f.	. 113,	125
	109, 218	2 .	35, 111, 160,	59 .	. .	302
17–23	. 45–9		250	xiii. 1–17	. 193,	206
17–20	. . 171	2 f. .	. 125, 172	1–5 .	135, 206,	229
17 .	. 45, 170	4 .	. . 99	6–9 .	. 69,	206
18 .	45, 46, 170	5 .	. . 302	10–17	54, 58,	137,
19 .	. . 129	6 .	. . 303		193,	206
19 f.	47, 114, 126,	8–12	. . 124	15 .	. .	268
	170, 252, 413	8 .	. . 99	18–xv. 10	. .	205
20 .	49, 240, 427	8 f. .	. . 321	18–35	. 120,	193
21 f.	. . 48	9 .	. 35, 177,	18–21	. .	144
22 .	. . 45		426, 429	18 .	. 51,	240
23 .	47, 114, 170 f.,	10 .	38, 40, 45, 49,	18 f.	50–3, 61,	146,
	252, 412		109, 253		172,	427
24–6	115, 126, 254,	11 f.	35, 37, 149,	20 .	. 240,	427
	333		183	20 f.	. 115,	127,
25 .	. . 99	12 .	. . 37		136,	256
27 .	. . 318	13–34	. . 123	22–7	. .	123
27 f.	56, 69, 134 f.,	13–15	. 193, 348	22 .	55, 341,	346
	192	15 .	. 135, 190	23 f.	. 116,	427
29–32	. 115, 126	16–21	. . 348	24 .	. 266,	302
29–31	. . 153	16 .	. . 136	25 .	. .	116
29 .	71, 177, 412	16 ff.	. . 348	26 f.	. .	247
29 f.	. 46, 254	22–31	. 113, 266	27 .	. .	116
29 ff.	. 62, 70	22 .	. . 346	28 .	. .	240
31 .	. . 254	27 .	. . 302	28 f.	114, 126,	145,
31 f.	. . 8	31 .	32, 172, 240	156,	159, 267,	426
32–5	. . 124	32 .	. 110, 135	30 .	. 38,	177
32 .	. . 254	33 .	. 111, 343	31–3	. .	193
33 .	35, 171, 264,	33 f.	. 113, 266	32 .	. 322,	339
	303, 328, 383	34 .	. . 153	34 f.	115, 126,	144,
34 f.	. 113, 266	35–8	. . 193		153, 259,	270
36 .	. . 134 f.	35 ff.	. . 120	35 .	. .	128
37 .	. . 194	36–40	. . 62	44 .	. .	334
37–52	. . 123	37 .	329, 334, 339	xiv., xv.	. . 193	f.
37–44	. . 70	38 .	. . 183	1–xv. 7	. .	190
38 f.	. . 62	39–46	. 150, 261	1–14	. .	70
39–52	126, 144, 176	39 .	. . 302	1–6 .	54, 137,	193,
39–41	. 250, 303	39 f.	115, 126, 144		206,	217
39 .	. 115, 300	40 .	. . 426	1 .	110, 193,	194,
41 .	. 115, 303	41 .	. 124, 128		207, 318,	320
42 .	115, 259, 303	42–6	. 115, 126	1 f. .	. .	319
43 .	. 35, 111	42 .	. . 302	2 f. .	. .	118
44 .	. 117, 259	44 .	. . 337	5 .	118, 127,	193,
45 .	. . 124	47 f.	. . 135 f.			268
46 .	. 115, 259	49 .	. 134, 136	7–14	. 202,	205
47 f.	. 115, 259	50 .	. . 339	7–11	. . 194	f.
49–51	. 115, 259	51–3	. 114, 126,	7–10	. .	135
49 .	. . 162		160, 250	7 .	128, 194,	207
52 .	115, 240, 259,	51 .	. . 303	11 .	34, 117,	145,
	303, 427	52 f.	. . 128		157,	190

446   I. Index of Scripture References

S. Luke viii. 28 f.	89	ix. 51–xviii. 14	. xii,	x. 9	. 111, 116, 154,
29 f.	. . 326	29–31, 37–59, 120,			174, 326
33 .	. 326, 330	159, 189 f., 315,		10 .	35, 154, 174 f.
35 .	. . 326		340, 358	10 f.	. 111, 175
38 .	. . 326	51–xii. 59	189 f.,	11 .	. 35, 174 f.,
42 .	. 89, 323		202		325 f., 332
46 .	. . 7	51–xv. 10	. 206	12–15	. 114, 126
55 f.	. . 89	51–x. 42	. 346	12 .	116, 126, 154,
ix .	. . 149	51–6	. . 54		160, 174, 248,
1–6	. . 342	51–3	. . 159		252, 343
1–5	35, 68, 173–5	51 .	. 55, 191,	13–15	. 252, 343
1–3	. . 325 f.		318, 346	13 f.	. . 129
1 .	. 75, 343 f.	51 f.	. . 342	14 .	. 332, 343
2 .	160, 174, 240	52–6	159, 191, 342	15 .	. . 128
3–5 .	. . 35	52 .	. . 342	16–21	. . 58
3 .	. . 175	52 f.	. . 346	16 .	. 116, 160
4 .	. 37, 175	52 ff.	. 350, 347	17–20	. 135, 192,
5 .	. . 175	54–6	. . 134		343 f., 433
6 .	. . 325	54 .	. . 353	17 .	. . 326
7–10	. . 324	56 f.	. . 55	19 .	. . 326
7 .	. . 6	57–62	. 57, 345	21–4	. 343 f.
9 .	. . 324	57–60	. 123, 160,	21 .	114, 252, 343 f.
10–17	. . 324		267, 342	21 ff.	. . 343
10 .	. . 344	57 .	. . 346	23 f.	. 115, 145,
12–17	. . 418	57 f.	. . 114		157, 268
14 .	. . 89	58–62	. . 195	25–37	. 346–8
17 .	. . 62	58 .	. . 99	25–8	41–5, 62, 146,
18–22	. . 418	59 f.	. . 114		176, 192, 347
18–20	. 324, 159	60 .	. . 114	27	43, 44, 52, 69, 190
18 .	62, 87, 318,	61 f.	. 134, 192	28 .	. 43, 347
	327	62 .	. 41, 136	29–37	. . 358
22–7	. 321, 324	x .	149, 158, 344	33 ff.	. . 350
22 .	. 69, 321	1–12	. 173–5	38 .	. 55, 346
23 .	. 35, 111	1–11	. 35, 68	38 ff.	. . 345
24	35, 111, 116, 412	1–9 .	. . 58	38–42	. 135, 192
26 .	. 35, 429	1–7 .	. . 58	38 .	. 55, 354
27 .	. 337, 429	1 .	55, 57, 341	42 .	. . 354
28 .	87, 318, 320,	1 ff.	. . 343	xi–xvii	. . 151
	327, 342	2–16	. 161, 343	1–13	. . 123
29 .	. . 322	2–12	. . 343	1–4	. 265, 303
31 .	. 322, 339	2 .	114, 160, 248	1	207, 318, 320, 327
31 f.	. 87, 323	3 .	116, 154, 160,	2–4	. . 113
33 .	318, 320, 322		174, 248, 302	3 .	. . 99
34 .	. . 321 f.	4–12	. . 126	4 .	. 279, 303
36 .	. . 322	4 .	35, 111, 116,	5–8 .	. . 192
37–43	. . 323		175, 325, 343	5 ff.	. . 136
37 .	. . 318	5 35, 175, 301, 325		9–13	. 113, 266
38 f.	. . 323	5 f. .	. 116, 160,	11–28	. . 262
42 .	. . 323		175, 248	11 f.	. . 127
43–5	. . 321	6 .	. 154, 174	12 .	. . 303
43 .	. . 87	7 .	35, 37, 111,	13 .	. 302 f.
44 .	69, 321, 339		116, 154, 160,	14–26	. . 61
45 .	87, 321, 337		174, 248	14–23	146, 169–71
46 .	. 34, 69	7 f. .	. . 116	14 .	68, 111, 123,
48 .	. . 116	8 .	. . 134		128, 170, 318, 320

I. Index of Scripture References

S. Luke iii. 16	167	vi. 12-19	31, 89	vii. 6	99
16 f.	167 f., 186	12	87	7-19	127
17	113, 119, 168	17-viii. 3	357	10	110, 119, 357
19 f.	62	17-19	70	11-17	189
21	319	18	326	11-16	137
21 f.	62	20-viii. 3	31-3,	11	318
22	187		61, 159, 188	12	318, 323
23-38	353	20-49	121, 181	16	211
23-5	117	20 f.	242, 303	17	189
31-4	117	20	283	18-35	151, 188, 213, 328
iv. 1-13	168	20 f.	116		
1 f.	187	22	133, 301	18-23	129
3-13	113	22, 23	113, 116	18	129
3-12	187	23	301	18 f.	114
5-12	8	24-6	134	18 ff.	119, 123, 330
5-8	152	25	116	21-8	251
11	187	27-30	113	21	189
13	187	27	132, 154	22-8	114
14	85	27 f.	245	22	189, 427
14 f.	319, 329	29-36	122	25	302, 427
15-30	85	29	154, 244, 302	27	32, 128, 168
16-30	61	30	154, 244	28	99, 240
18 f.	137	31	113, 122, 247	29 f.	118, 126, 302
21	339	32-6	113	31-5	114, 251
23	224, 330	32	154, 245	31	51
24	329, 334, 339	33	154, 245, 303	32	302
25-7	73	34	244	34	331
31-44	85 f., 330	35	154	35	301
31	188	35 f.	245	36-viii. 3	189
36	326	36	303	36-50	358
41	324	37 f.	113, 246	36	194
42-4	330	38	32, 109, 172	36 ff.	33, 69, 70
42	327	39	71, 117, 128, 145, 157, 268	39	211
44	330			40-50	134
v. 1-11	61, 85, 137	40	116, 126, 157, 250	41 f.	113
1	318-20			viii. 1-3	331, 358
7	317	41 f.	99, 121, 246	1	318, 320, 326
12-vi. 19	85	43-6	164	3	xiv, 94, 324
12-14	68	43-5	111, 114, 164, 267	4-ix. 51	85
12	318 f.			14	6
14	325	43	164	16-18	328
15	330	44	164	16	7, 35, 264, 303, 383
16	87, 327	45	157, 164, 253		
17	318 f., 326	46	116, 164, 240, 247	17	35, 111
23 f.	109			18	34, 111, 154, 383
30 ff.	134	47-9	114, 248		
33-9	123	48	302	19-21	69, 89, 146, 328
36	128	49	302		
39	87, 136, 300 f.	vii. 1-3	114, 128	19	8
40	300 f.	1	109, 121, 148, 328 f.	19 ff.	56
41	300 f.			22	318
vi. 1-5	123	2-10	54, 187	22 f.	330
6-11	193, 206	4-6	357	23	89
6 ff.	134	4 f.	110	24 f.	154
11	87	6-9	114	27	326

444   *I. Index of Scripture References*

S. Mark xii. 13-37	42	xiv. 8	.	. 297	xv. 17	.	393, 394
18–27	. . 434	10 f.	.	. 391	19 .	.	. 394
20 .	. . 6	12–xv. 8 .		. 393	26–32	.	. 82
24 .	. . 434	12 ff.	.	394, 405	28 .	.	. 62
28–34	. 41, 62,	15 .	.	. 101	34 .	.	. 305
	176, 346	17–21	.	. 396	36 .	.	6, 394
28 .	. 296, 347	18–25	.	. 81	37 f.	.	. 83
29–31	. . 69	19–21	.	. 82	40–xvi. 8		. 393
30 .	. 43, 44, 52	22–5	.	81, 391	42–6	.	. 83
32 .	. . 347	22–4	.	. 81	44 f.	.	. 62
33 .	. 43, 44	27 .	.	. 71	xvi. 1–8	.	. 83
34 .	42, 347, 428	27 f.	.	. 62	1 .	.	. 83
37 .	. . 338	28 .	.	. 231	5 .	.	. 393
38–40	158, 176, 412	29–32	.	. 82	7 .	.	. 231
38 f.	. . 35	29 .	.	. 223	9–20	.	62, 66
xiii	. xxv, 156, 158,	30 .	333, 394, 405				
	179–83, 413, 416 f.,	31 .	.	. 223		S. LUKE	
	419, 421, 428, 430	33 f.	.	. 62	i, ii	. 292, 294, 317–	
1 f.	. . 183	35 .	.	. 394		20, 329, 353	
4–37	. . 397	36 .	77, 306, 311		1 .	.	. 281
5 f.	. . 181	37 .	.	. 71	2 f. .	.	. 351
7 .	. . 180	38–42	.	. 62	3 .	.	. 35
8 .	. . 181	40 .	.	. 71	6 .	.	. 338
9–13	. . 149	47 .	.	. 393	8 .	.	. 318
9 .	. 108, 181	49 .	.	. 7	17 .	.	. 338
10 .	. 62, 181	50 .	62, 71, 223		23 .	.	. 318
11 .	35, 37, 183	50 f.	.	. 393	26 f.	.	. 117
12 .	. . 181	51 f.	.	62, 217	30 f.	.	. 117
13 .	. . 181	53 .	.	. 395	34 f.	.	. 117
14–20	. . 181	53 f.	.	. 406	39 .	.	. 353
14 f.	. . 183	55–65	.	. 82	41 .	.	. 318
15 f.	38, 150, 183	55–64	.	. 395	59 .	.	. 318
18 .	. . 62	55–8	.	. 62	65 .	.	. 353
19–23	. . 101	56–72	.	. 82	ii. 1	.	. 318
20 .	. . 62	56 .	.	. 406	1 f.	.	. 13
21–3	. . 181	58 .	.	. 183	6 .	.	. 318
21 . 38, 41, 116, 183		59 .	.	. 62	15 .	.	. 318
22 f.	. . 62	60 .	.	62, 406	21 .	.	. 318
23 .	. . 180	61 .	.	. 406	22 .	.	. 346
24 .	10, 182, 385	62 .	.	406, 430	25 .	.	. 338
25–7	. . 431	63 .	.	. 406	27 .	.	. 319
27 .	. . 62	68 .	.	. 405	27 f.	.	. 318
28–32	. . 183	71 .	.	. 109	37 .	.	. 353
28 .	. 128, 181	72 .	.	333, 394	39 .	.	. 117
29 .	. . 181	xv. 1–5	.	. 406	46 .	.	. 318
32 .	. 62, 73, 312	2 .	.	. 406	iii–viii	.	. 326
34–7	. . 62	3 .	.	. 406	1 .	.	. 94
34–6	. . 183	4 .	.	. 406	1 f.	.	xiv, 13
xiv. 1–xv. 37	. 391	5 .	.	. 406	3 .	.	7, 186
1 .	. . 7	8 .	.	. 338	6 .	.	. 224
1 f. .	. . 391	11 .	.	. 338	7–9 .	113, 119, 126,	
2 .	. . 338	13 .	.	. 297		167 f., 186	
3–9 . 33, 62, 69, 396		15 .	.	. 338	7 .	.	. 71
3–7 .	. . 391	16–20	.	62, 83	8 .	.	. 321
8–xvi. 7 .	. 397	17–20	.	. 69	10–14	.	. 136

I. Index of Scripture References 443

S.Mark vi. 19f.	7,108f.	viii. 17	65, 72, 192	ix. 49 .	. 62, 128
20 .	. . 230	19–21	. 66, 69	50 . 38,	40, 52, 117,
22 .	. . 296	19 f.	. . 418		128, 176
26 .	. . 230	22 .	. . 66	x .	. . 149
30 .	. 192, 344	22–6	. 64, 67	1–44	. . 391
31–4	. . 21	24 .	. . 296	1–12	. . 275
31 .	. . 402	27–37	. . 391	1–10	. . 62
32–4	. . 391	27–33	. . 418	1 .	. 55, 341
34 .	. . 405	27 .	. . 401	2–12	xvii, 70, 134
35–44	. . 418	29 .	. 21, 409	3–9	. 154, 161
37 .	. . 7	31–x. 45 .	. 397	8–11	. . 281
38 ff.	. . 394	31 .	. . 321	11 . 38,	39, 222, 412
39 .	. 393, 394	31 ff.	. . 397	11 f.	. . 177
42–4	. . 66	32 .	. . 62	13–16	. . 401
44 .	. . 89	32 f.	. . 72	13 .	. . 337
45–viii. 26	xii, xxv,	34 .	. 35, 177	15 .	. 150, 432
	10, 24–6, 324,	35–45	. . 72	17 .	. . 42
	397, 417, 421	35 .	35, 116, 412	18 .	. 8, 193
45–52	. 69, 159	37 .	. . 62	21 .	. . 6
45 .	. . 66	38 .	35, 177, 428 ff.	22 .	. . 297
47 ff.	. . 402	ix. 1 .	101, 276, 325,	23 .	. . 101
52 .	69, 72, 192		429 f.	25 .	. 128, 281
53–6	. . 70	2–8 .	. . 392	25 ff.	. . 338
vii. 1–23	71, 178, 185,	3 .	. . 393	31 .	. 38, 177
	204	9–13	. . 324	32–4	. . 321
1–13	. . 134	9 .	. . 409	35–45	. 192, 435
1 ff.	. . 62	10–13	. . 62	35–41	. 62, 223
3 f. .	. . 216	11 f.	. . 217	35 .	. . 401
6–13	. 154, 161	12 f.	. 154, 161	38 .	. . 128
11 .	. . 306	14–x. 52 .	. 392	41–5	. . 334
15 .	. . 65	14–16	. . 62	42–5	. 78, 434
16 .	. . 62	17 .	. . 323	43 f.	. . 177
17 .	. . 128	19 .	. . 21	45	309,335,399,411
21–3	. . 297	23 f.	. . 62	xi. 1–10	. . 392
21 .	. . 65	31 .	. 321, 341	2 ff.	. . 394
23 .	. . 65	33–50	. . 412	3 .	. . 6
24–30	. . 72	33–47	. . 149	8 .	. . 394
24 .	65, 173, 401	33–7	. . 158	11–44	. . 397
25 .	. . 65	33 .	. . 401	11 .	. . 62
27 .	. . 128	34 f.	. . 78	12–14	. 62, 69
29 ff.	. . 402	35 .	. 177, 334	15–xiii. 36	. 391
30 .	. . 297	37 .	. . 116	15–33	. 401, 414
31–7	. 64, 67	38–41	. . 150	15–17	. . 401
31 .	. . 297	38 .	. . 218	18–26	. . 401
34 .	. . 305	41 .	. . 62	19–25	. . 62
viii. 1–9	. . 418	42–50	. 158, 175,	20–5	. . 69
1 ff.	. . 402		185, 204	23 .	38, 39, 117,
2 .	. . 101	42 . 38,	40, 52, 175		145, 177
2 f. .	. . 419	43 .	. 62, 192	26 .	. . 62
4 .	. . 419	43 ff.	. 128, 175	27–33	. 213, 401
11 f.	. 46, 62, 70	44 .	. . 62	27 .	. . 401
12 .	7, 21, 68, 177,	45 .	. 62, 192	32 .	. . 338
	412	46 .	. . 62	xii. 8 .	. . 89
14–21	. . 71	47 .	. . 192	11 .	. . 62
15 .	38,62,128,412	47 f.	. . 62	12 .	. 65, 338

442 I. Index of Scripture References

S. Matthew xxvii.	57	83
62–6	.	78
64	.	338
xxviii. 1–8	.	83
2	.	78
4	.	78
10	.	334

S. MARK

i. 1–ii. 20	.	396
i–vi. 44	.	61
1	.	217
2	32, 128,	217
4–14	.	392
5 f.	.	186
6	217,	394
7	.	296
7 f.	.	167 f.
8	.	296
8 f.	.	296
9	318,	329
10	.	394
12 f.	.	168
13	.	394
14	85,	330
16–38	.	390
16–20	61, 85,	405
22	128,	328
23	.	296
25	.	395
34	.	297
35	297,	327
39–44	.	391
40–4	.	328
45	73, 296,	402
ii. 1–iv. 33	.	391
ii	.	391
1	.	328
4	.	297
7	.	297
8–11	.	101
9 f.	.	109
10	.	297
13	.	405
18–22	.	123
19–22	.	128
19 f.	.	101
20	.	101
21 f.	.	173
22	.	297
23–8	.	123
23	319,	405
27	.	183

iii. 1–5	.	391
1 f.	.	193
4	.	297
5	.	72
6–19	.	396
7–19	31,	89
7–12	.	89
7–11	.	70
8	.	306
9	.	296
9 ff.	.	402
10–20	.	415
11 f.	.	415
13–19	.	89
15–17	.	414
17	.	305
19–21	.	21
20 f.	61,	391
20–35	400,	413
21–5	.	416
21	45, 64,	391,
	400 f., 413,	414
22–30	61, 169–	70,
	347, 413,	414
22–7	.	45–9
22–6	.	171
22	45,	128
23–iv. 34	.	397
23–36	.	170
23–9	.	253
23–6	.	21
24 f.	.	45
26	.	45
27	45,	48
27–33	.	414
28	171, 296,	306
28 f.	38, 48,	109,
	170,	171
29	.	40
30	.	46
30–2	.	416
31–5	. 45, 64,	89,
	146,	391
31 . 56, 400 f.,		414
33	.	415
iv	.	414
1	.	405
1–34	.	158
1–32	.	413
1–9	.	391
4	.	318
8 . 296,		306
11	.	411
11 f.	.	322
11 ff.	.	410

iv. 12	.	398
19	.	6
21–5	.	171 f.
21 . 7, 35, 128,		171
22	35,	171
23	.	172
24 . 32, 109,		113,
		172
25	. 154,	172
26–9	178, 185,	391,
		432
26–8	.	61
26 f.	.	204
28	.	306
30–2	21, 50–3,	61,
		172
30	.	51
32	.	50
33	.	391
35–vi. 44	392,	395
35–41	.	69
35 ff.	394, 395,	402
37	.	394
37 f.	.	89
39 f.	.	154
v. 1 ff.	.	394
2	.	296
3–8	.	89
11 ff.	394,	405
30	.	7
36	.	401
41	297,	304
42	.	89
42, 43	.	89
vi. 1–13	.	397
1–6	61,	85
1 ff.	.	402
2–5	.	402
3	.	8
4	.	211
5	.	73
6–11	.	35
7–13	21,	158
7–12	.	342
7–11	. 149,	173–5
7	. 175,	344
7 f.	.	325
8 f.	. 175,	296
9	.	116
10	. 37,	175
11	.	175
12	. 325 f.,	344
14–29	.	62
14	. 6,	230
17	.	296

I. Index of Scripture References

S. Matthew xxii. 7	126	xxiv. 2	. . 7	xxv. 29	. 111, 172
		9 .	. . 35	30 .	. . 278
7 f. .	. . 118	11 f.	. . 135	31–46	. 262 f., 276,
8 .	. . 334	12 .	. . 182		431
10 .	. . 118	13 .	. . 35	31 .	. 276, 278
11–14	. . 198	14 .	. . 108	34 .	. . 276
12 .	. 279, 334	15 .	. . 183	37 .	. . 278
13 .	. . 278	17 f.	. . 38	40 .	. . 279
15–46	. . 42	20 .	. 182, 242	46 .	. . 278
16 .	. . 333	21–5	. . 101	xxvi. 1	121, 148, 318
20 .	. 333, 338	23 .	38, 41, 116	5 .	. . 338
21 .	. . 333	26–8	144, 150, 153,	6 ff.	. 33, 69
25 .	. . 6		182, 260, 430	20–xxviii. 6	. 77
34–40	. 42, 176	26 .	. 111, 115	21–9	. . 81
37–9	. . 69	26 f.	. 150, 183	22–4	. . 82
37 .	. . 44	27 .	115, 126, 276,	25 .	. . 78
xxiii .	. 120, 148		278, 426	26–9	. . 81
1–36	. . 144	28 .	115, 126, 150	26–8	. . 81
1 .	. . 338	29–36	. . 150	28 .	. . 78
2–36	. 257–9	29–31	. . 431	31 .	. . 71
2 f. .	. . 134	29 .	10, 385, 431	33–5	. . 82
4–36	. . 126	30 .	. 260, 431	35 .	. . 333
4–11	. . 274	31 .	. . 431	36–45	. . 333
4 .	. 115, 259	32 .	. . 128	39 .	. . 332
5 .	. . 134	36 .	. . 73	40 .	. . 71
7–10	. . 135	37–51	. . 430	42 .	. . 332
8 .	. . 279	37–41	144, 150, 153,	43 .	. . 71
11 .	. 177, 335		260	50 .	. 78, 332
12 .	117, 145, 157	37–9	115, 126, 150	51–4	. . 332
13 .	115, 240, 427	37 .	276, 278, 426	52–4	. . 78
14–22	. . 134	39 .	. 276, 278	56 .	. . 7, 71
14 .	. 259, 303	40 .	. . 303	59–75	. . 82
21 f.	. . 115	40 f.	117, 126, 150	59–68	. . 82
23 .	115, 259, 303	42 .	. . 150	63 f.	. . 332
25 .	. . 299	43–51	115, 126, 150,	64 .	. . 430
25 f.	115, 259, 303		153, 260 f.	68 .	. . 79
26 .	. . 300	43 .	. . 302	71 .	. . 334
27 .	117, 259, 303	43 f.	. . 144	75 .	. . 79
27 f.	. . 274	44 .	. . 426	xxvii. 3–10 .	. 78
28 .	. . 117	45 .	. . 302	13 .	. . 334
29–33	. . 259	51 .	. . 111	19 .	. 78, 334
29–31	. . 115	xxv .	. 430 f.	22 .	. . 334
32 f.	. . 134	1–12	. . 261	24 .	. . 334
34–9	. . 162 f.	5 .	. . 386	24 f.	. . 78
34–6	115, 162, 259	11 .	. . 334	25 .	. 198, 338
34 .	. 278, 303	14–30	. 127, 144,	27–31	. 69, 83
37–9	115, 126, 144,		261 f.	37–44	. . 82
	153, 259, 270	14 .	. . 117	38 .	. . 333
37 .	. . 162	14 f.	. . 183	43 .	. . 78
38 f.	. . 128	14 ff.	. . 348	49 .	. . 7
39 .	. . 162 f.	16 .	. . 117	50–4	. . 274
xxiv–xxv	120, 148, 150,	19–29	. . 117	50 f.	. . 83
	430	19 .	. 334, 386	51 .	. . 78
1–25	. . 150	21 .	. . 199	52 f.	. . 78
1 .	. . 7	24–9	. . 199	54 .	. . 79

I. Index of Scripture References

S. Matthew xiii. 12 . . . 111, 154
14 f. 137
16 f. . . . 115, 145, 157, 268
19-23 101
19 279
22 6
24-33 . . . 254 f., 284
24-30 . . . . 431 f.
28 f. 334
31-3 144
31 240
31 f. 50-2, 172, 427
33 . 115, 127, 240, 256, 427
34 199
35 183
36-52 . . . 254-6
36-43 431
38 . . . 275, 279
39 278
40 . . . 275, 278
41-3 432
41 276
43-6 275
43 278
44-50 284
44-6 173
44 334
47 f. 431
49 278
49 f. 431
51 . . . 274, 334
52 . . . 136, 278
53 . 121, 148, 318
54-8 61
55 8
xiv. 1-12 62
2 6
5 . . . . 8, 109
17 333
22-xvi. 12 . . . 64
31 334
xv. 1-20 71
1-9 134
1 333
3-9 . . . 154, 161
11 65
12-14 71
12 334
12 f. . . 134 f., 242
13 136
13 f. 268
14 117, 127, 145, 157

xv. 15 128
19 65
21-8 72
22 73
23 f. 242
24 . . . 10, 183
29-31 68
32 101
33 f. 334
xvi. 1-4 62
1 . . . . 46, 70
2, 3 . . 46, 110
4 . 7, 46, 70, 382, 412
5-12 71
6 . . 38, 62, 412
9-12 69
9 65
13 279
15 334
16 332
17-19 242, 269, 278 f.
20 . . 65, 116
22 f. 72
23 279
24 . . . 111, 382
25 . . . 111, 412
27 . . . . 429 f.
28 . 101, 276, 429 f.
xvii. 1 333
2-xxii. 15 . . 333
12 . . . 154, 161
15 323
20 . 39, 117, 145, 157, 177
24-7 137
25 136
xviii . 115, 120, 148 f., 175
3 432
3 f. 150
5 115
6-9 175
6 . . . 38, 40
6 f. . . . 175
7 . 115, 144, 150 f., 269, 332
8 f. . . 175, 192
10 . 134 f., 150, 269
12-14 115, 136, 144, 150, 269, 348
12 f. . . . 127
13 . . . . 278 f.
14 242
15-20 . . . 256
15-18 . . . 222

xviii. 15 115, 144, 150 f., 256, 279
16-20 . 150, 242
17 . . 134, 280
19 f. . . . 135
21-35 . . 256 f.
21 . 144, 150 f., 279
21 f. . . . 115
23 f. . . . 135
23 ff. . . . 150
32 334
35 . . . 278 f.
xix. 1 . 55, 121, 148, 318
3-11 70
3-9 . . 134, 275
4-8 . . 154, 161
9 . 38, 39, 222, 383
10-12 . . . 134
11 f. . . . 269
16 42
17 8
20 6
23 101
27 f. . . . 334
28 . 78, 117, 129, 145, 157, 270, 276, 278, 426
30 38
xx. 1-15 . . . 270 f.
6-8 334
13 279
16 177
20-8 72
24-8 334
xxi. 3 6
11 329
14 137
16 137
18 ff. 69
21 . 38, 39, 117
28-32 . 134, 271
28-30 . . . 110
31 . 111, 277, 302
31 f. . 118, 126 f.
41 198
43 . . 135, 198
44 . . 110, 137
xxii. 1-14 127, 195
1-5 118
2-14 . . . 271 f.
2-10 . . . 144
2 ff. . . . 348
5 197
6 f. 198

I. Index of Scripture References

```
S. Matthew ix. 37 f.        x. 34    .    .    303    xii. 9-14   .   .    54
       114, 127, 143, 160       34 f.   .    .    250         9 .    .   .   110
       42-50    .   .   175     35  .   .    .     45         9 f.   .   .   193
   x    .   120, 147, 158,      35 f.   .    .    128        10 f.   .   .   118
                       194      37  .   114, 160, 248        11  .   .   127, 193
   1-14    .   .   173-5        37 f.   .    250, 284        11 f.   .   .   268
   1    .   .   175, 325        38  .  111, 114, 160,        13  .   .   .   333
   1 ff.   .   .   .   327                   177, 382        17-20   .   .   307
   5-8    .   .   242, 248      39  .  111, 116, 160,        19  .   .   .   307
   5    .   159, 248, 275,                   250, 412        22-32   .   169-171
                 325, 326       40-2    .    .    284        22-4    .   110, 114
   5, 6    .   .   73, 134      40  .   .   116, 160         22  .   .   123, 170 f.
   6    .   .   183, 275        42  .   .    .     62        22 f.   46, 120, 137
   7-16    .   .   .   126     xi    .   .    .    120       22 ff.  .   .    45
   7    .   116, 154, 160,      1    .   121, 148, 318       24-30   .   46, 47, 49
                 240, 326       2-19    .   151, 328         24-8    .   .   171
   7 f.   .   .   .   174       2-11    .    250 f.          24  .   71, 126, 170
   8    .   .   111, 116        2-7 .   .    .    129        25  .   .   .    45
   9    .   .   .   .   111     2-4 .   .    .    274        25 f.   .   170, 253
   9 f.   .   161, 175, 248     2 f.    .   114, 143         26  .   .   .    45
  10    .   111, 116, 154,      2 ff.   .   119, 123,        27-37   .   .   274
               160, 174, 248                213-78           27  .   29, 218, 306
  11    .   37, 116, 154,       4-11    .    .    114        27 f.   47, 114, 126,
                 174, 248       5   .   .    .    427                170, 252, 413
  12    .   .   175, 301        7-19    .    .    126        28  .   240, 277, 427
  12 f.   116, 160, 248         8   .   .    .    302        29  .   .   .   253
  13    .   .   154, 174       10   .   32, 128, 168         30  .   47, 114, 170 f.,
  14    .   111, 175, 248      11   .   99, 240, 427                    252, 413
  15    .   116, 126, 154,     12-15   .    .    251         31 f.   38, 48, 109,
               160, 174 f.     12   .   213, 240,                    170, 253, 427
  15 f.   .   .   .   248                   277              32  .   40, 171, 253
  16    .   111, 116, 154,     12, 13   114, 145, 156,       33-7    .   .   253
               174, 302                     159, 427         33-5    35, 110, 114,
  17-22    .   149, 250        16-19   114, 127, 251                      164
  19 f.   .   .   .   149      16   .   .    .     52        33  .   .   127, 164
  20    .   .   .   .    37    17   .   .    279, 302        34 f.   .   157, 164
  22    .   .   .   .    35    19   .   .    .    301        35  .   .   164, 253
  23    .   134, 242, 248,     20-7    .   .    343 f.       36 f.   .   .   134 f.
              275, 385, 429    20-4    .   .    251 f.       38-45   .   .   253 f.
  24-41    .   .   249 f.      20   .   .    .    274        38-40   .   46, 62
  24-33    .   .   .   250     21-4    114, 126, 129         38  .   71, 109, 153,
  24-9    .   .   .    275     22   .   .    .    332                     274
  24 f.   116, 126, 157        23   .   .    .    128        38 f.   .   .    70
  25    .   .   274, 306       24   .   116, 126, 332        39-42   .   115, 126
  26-33   71, 114, 160,        25-30   .    .    252         39  .   177, 382, 412
                  250          25-7    .   114, 277          41  .   .   .   277
  26    .   .   111, 284       28-30   .    .    135         41 f.   .   8, 277
  26 f.   .   125, 172         29   .   .    91, 136         43-5    115, 126 f.,
  28    .   99, 284, 302       29 f.   .    .    278                     333
  29    .   .   .   303       xii. 1-8   .    .    123       44  .   .   .    99
  31    .   .   .   284        5-7 .   .    .    268         44 f.   .   .   334
  32    .   .   .    99        5 f.    .    .    134         46  .   .   .    56
  33    .   177, 426, 429      6   .   .    .    277         47-50   .   .   192
  34-40    .   .   .   250     7   .   .   137, 268         xiii  .   120, 136, 148 f.
  34-6    .   114, 160         8   .   .    .    183         3   .   .   52, 275
```

I. Index of Scripture References

S. Matthew v–vii. . 120 f., 147
- 1–4 . . . 116
- 1 f. . . . 326
- 3–12 . 242, 283, 303
- 3–9 . . . 275
- 3 . . 275, 283
- 5 . . . 135
- 6 . . . 116
- 7–10 . . . 135
- 10 . . . 275
- 10 f. . . . 275
- 11 . . . 301
- 11, 12 . 113, 116
- 12 . . . 301
- 13–16 . . 263 f.
- 13 . 38, 111, 117, 176, 264
- 14 . . . 135 f.
- 15 . 171, 264, 303
- 16 . . . 135
- 17–48 . xv, 132 f., 134 f., 137
- 17–42 . . 204
- 17–20 . 275, 281
- 17 . . . 243
- 18 . 39, 113, 264
- 18 f. . . . 264
- 20–48 . . 70
- 20 . . 241, 243
- 21–48 . . 243–5
- 21 . . 275, 283
- 22 . . 279, 306
- 23 f. . . 135, 279
- 25 . . . 302
- 25 f. 113, 124, 264
- 26 . . . 302
- 27 . . . 283
- 29 f. . 175, 264
- 30–2 . . 133
- 31 . . 283, 412
- 32 . xvii, 39, 177, 222, 281, 383
- 33 . . . 284
- 37 . . . 279
- 38 . . . 284
- 39–48 . . 122
- 39–42 . . 244
- 39 . . . 302
- 39 f. . . 113
- 40 . . . 154
- 42 . . 113, 154
- 43 . . . 284
- 43 f. . . 132
- 44–8 . . 113

v. 44 . . 154, 245
- 45 . . . 154
- 46–8 . . 245
- 46 . . 154, 303
- 47 . . 154, 279
- 48 . . . 303
- vi. 1–18 204, 241, 274
- 1–8 . . 134
- 1–6 . 70, 245
- 2 . . . 284
- 3 f. . . 118
- 5 . . . 284
- 7 f. . . . 264
- 9–13 113, 265, 303
- 9 . . . 312
- 10 . 242, 275, 279, 284
- 11–13 . . 284
- 11 . . . 99
- 12 . . . 303
- 13 . . . 279
- 14 f. . . 265
- 16–18 70, 134, 246
- 16 . . . 284
- 19–34 . 265 f.
- 19–21 . . 266
- 20 f. . . 113
- 22 f. . 113, 266
- 24 . 113, 127, 164, 266, 306
- 25–34 . . 266
- 25–33 . . 113
- 28 . . . 302
- 33 . 32, 172, 240
- 34 . . 110, 135
- vii. 1–5 . . 246
- 1 f. . . 113
- 2 . 32, 109, 172
- 3–5 . 99, 113, 121, 127, 279
- 6 . 73, 134, 242, 246 f., 278
- 7–19 . . 267
- 7–11 . 113, 266
- 9 . . . 303
- 9 f. . . . 127
- 11 . . . 302 f.
- 12 . 113, 122, 247
- 13 . . . 302
- 13 f. 116,127,266,427
- 15–23 . . 247
- 16–21 . . 164
- 16–19 . . 267
- 16–18 35, 110, 114, 164

vii. 16 . 113, 164
- 18 . . 113, 164
- 20 . . . 164
- 21 . 116, 164, 240, 247, 275
- 22 f. . . 116, 247
- 24–7 . 114, 127, 247 f.
- 25 . . . 302
- 27 . . 128, 302
- 28 . 109, 121, 148, 318, 328
- 29 . . . 128
- viii–xiii . 29 f., 76
- 1 . . . 328
- 2 . . . 319
- 4 . . . 333
- 5–10 . 114, 128
- 5 . . . 328
- 7 . . . 334
- 8 . . . 99
- 11 . . . 240
- 11 f. 114,126,145, 156,159,267, 273,426
- 12 . . 275, 278
- 13 . . 110, 119
- 19–22 123, 160, 267
- 19 f. . . 114, 143
- 19 ff. . . 342
- 20 . . 99, 334
- 21 f. . . . 114
- 22 . . . 334
- 26 . . 154, 334
- 27 . . . 279
- ix. 4–6 . . 101
- 4 . . . 47
- 5 f. . . 109
- 6 . . . 333
- 8 . . . 279
- 9 . . 38, 333
- 10 . . . 318
- 13 . . 137, 267
- 14–17 . . 123
- 14 . . . 333
- 15 . . . 101
- 26 . . . 329
- 27–34 . . 158
- 27–31 . . 137
- 28 . . 320, 334
- 32–4 46, 110, 137
- 32 . . . 320
- 32 f. . . 114
- 33 . . . 320
- 34 . . . 46
- 35 . . 326, 330

I. INDEX OF SCRIPTURE REFERENCES

GENESIS
i. 1–ii. 4 . . 373
ii. 4–iii end . 373
iv. 1 . . . 378
vi. 13–viii. 22 . 377
   13–22 . . 377
vii. 6, 9, 11, 13–
   16, 18–21, 24 . 377
viii. 1, 2, 3–5,
   13–19 . . 377
xxvii. 23, 27 f. . 375
xxviii. 20 f. . 375
xlix . . . 382

EXODUS
i. 11 . . . 369
iii. 13 f. . . 378
viii. 19 . . 49
xx. 22–xxiii . 379
xxi. 24 . . 383
xxxiv. 2, 3, 14, 17,
   19, 21–3, 25–7 379

LEVITICUS
v. 18, 21 ff. . . 385

NUMBERS
xv. 37–41 . . 43
xxi. 14 f., 17 f.,
   27–30 . . 382
xxiii. 24 . . 382

DEUTERONOMY
vi. 4–9 . . 43
   5 . . . 43 f.
xi. 13–21 . . 43
xxxii . . . 382
xxxiii . . . 382

KINGS
4 (2) xxiii. 25 . 43 f.

CHRONICLES
1 Chron. xxi. 28–
   xxviii. 1 . . 381
2 Chron. xxiv. 20 f. 128

JOB
xxx. 1 . . . 74

PSALMS
iii–xli . . . 383
xiv . . . 383
xxxi. 1–3 . . 383
xl. 13–17 . . 383
xlii–lxxxix . . 383
l. (li) 13 . . 37
liii . . . 383
lxix. 20 f. . . 83
lxx . . . 383
lxxi. 1–3 . . 383
lxxxiv–lxxxix . 383
cxviii. 26 . . 128

PROVERBS
x–xxii. 16 . . 383
xxii. 17–xxiv. 22 . 383
xxiv. 23 f. . . 383
xxv–xxix . . 383

ISAIAH
vi. 9 f. . . . 137
vii. 11 . . 218
xiv. 13, 15 . . 128
xxxv. 5 . . 189
xl. 18 . . . 51
liii . . . 411
   12 . . . 137
lvi. 10 f. . . 74
lviii. 6 . . 137
lxi. 1 . . . 189
   12 . . . 137
lxiii. 10 f. . . 37

JEREMIAH
xii. 7 . . . 128
xxii. 5 . . 128

DANIEL
iii. 96 (29) . . 40

HOSEA
vi. 6 . . . 137

AMOS
iv. 11 . . . 375

MALACHI
iii. 1 . . 32, 128

S. MATTHEW
i. 2–6 . . . 117
   10 . . . 117
   15 f. . . 117
   18 . . . 117
   20 f. . . 117
   23 . . . 117
   25 . . . 117
ii. 1–12 . . 73
   22 f. . . 117
   23 . . . 329
iii. 1–12 . . 274
   1 . . 274, 334
   5 . . 7, 186
   7–12 167, 186, 274
   7–10 113, 119, 126
   7 . . . 71
   9 . . . 321
   11 . . . 167 f.
   12 . 113, 119, 126,
         168, 274
   13–17 . . 274
   13 . . 274, 334
   15 . 274, 284, 334
iv. 1–11 . 168, 274
   3–11 . . 113
   3–10 . . 187
   5–10 . . 8
   5 . . 274, 334
   8 . . 274, 334
   8 f. . . 152
   10 f. . . 334
   11 . . 187, 274
   12 . . . 85
   12 f. . . 187
   13 . . . 329 f.
   18–22 . . 61
   23 . . . 329
   25 . . . 328
v–viii . . . 158

seized upon and amplified this element in His teaching, and slowly modified the tradition of His actual language into accord with their own interpretation? But the process was not allowed to go on unchecked. Two great religious geniuses, St. Paul and the author of the Fourth Gospel, stemmed the tide, and by a counter evolution brought back the Church to profounder and more spiritual conceptions; which, though often expressed in terms of a Hellenized philosophy foreign to the Master's own environment, surely present some aspects of His mind which in the Synoptic Gospels are almost buried under the picturesque materialism of Jewish Eschatology.

It was a profound belief of both these men that the Spirit of the Master was still with them when they taught and wrote. Criticism has not proved that they were mistaken.

rests all on the broad principle that a God to whom persons are dear is a God whose own nature guarantees to them eternal life.

A third incident (Mk x. 35-45)—the reply to James and John, 'to sit on my right hand and my left is not mine to give'—has been taken by some to imply a tacit acceptance of the detail of the Messianic picture of the Kingdom implied in the request. But consider the reply as a whole, 'Ye know not what ye ask. Can ye drink of the cup that I drink, and be baptized with the baptism that I am baptized with?' 'We can.' 'Ye shall drink of the cup and be baptized with the baptism, but to sit on my right hand and on my left is not mine to give.' Is the element of conscious metaphor and symbol present when He speaks of the Cup and the Baptism, but absent when He speaks of His right hand and His left in the Kingdom?

No passage in the Gospels seems to cast more light than this on His real attitude to the Apocalyptic Hope. He does accept the Kingdom and the place for Himself therein implied by the request, but He does it in the half-playful spirit of one who speaks to little children about great things which he feels to be too great for himself, much more for them, to fully comprehend, and is fain to use the old simple words whose face meaning he has himself transcended only in the sense that he realizes that all words are inadequate, and that there are things which the greatest can see only 'in a glass darkly'.

Not only in Religion, equally in Philosophy, Literature, Art, even sometimes in Science, the rule holds good that the great man is only partially understood by his followers. Some one-sided aspect of the Master's thought is seized upon by his admirers, and by a change of emphasis what was almost an accident in his conception becomes an essential tenet of his School. What wonder then if the early disciples of our Lord, steeped in Jewish Apocalyptic thought, solution; it is however clear that the nearer we get to Him the greater is the emphasis on the present, the gradual, and the internal aspects of the Kingdom, and the greater the reserve with which the detail of contemporary Apocalyptic is endorsed.

Jewish Apocalyptic, albeit bizarre to modern eyes, was no ignoble thing. The eternal optimism, which is of the essence of true religion, expresses itself in different forms in different epochs. To men appalled alike by the corruption and by the irresistible might of Roman civilization, and inheriting the previous religious history of Israel and her prophets, it was an heroic confidence in the Divine intention to regenerate the world that found its most natural expression in terms of the Messianic hope apocalyptically conceived.

On the side of this spirit of triumphant and confident faith our Lord placed Himself definitely and unreservedly. But many of its material hopes clashed with His sense of ultimate values, cf. Mk x. 42-5 with Lk xxii. 25-7. Many of its detailed expectations ran counter to the sense which all great teachers have of the infinity and inscrutability of the Divine, and of the futility of making our conceptions the measure of God's activities, cf. especially Mk xii. 24.

Three incidents in His career markedly illustrate this general attitude.

In the wilderness there is presented to His mind under its various forms the contemporary Messianic ideal on its more political and worldly side. Accepting the Messiahship He yet sees Temptation in some aspects of the ideal.

Near the end the Sadducees (Mk xii. 18-27) try to pose Him by challenging the Messianic hope on another of its many sides—the Resurrection. Again He accepts the ideal, while rejecting the limitations, of contemporary Apocalyptic. He turns away from the flesh and blood environment presupposed in His opponents' objection, and (*b*) Two cases have been noticed in a previous essay where it would appear that Matthew has omitted sayings in Q implying a *present* Kingdom which Luke still preserves, i. e. Lk x. 17-20, 'I saw Satan fall from Heaven' (cf. p. 192, above), and Lk xvii. 20-1, 'The Kingdom of God cometh not with observation ... for it is ἐντὸς ὑμῶν' (cf. p. 201).

The above sketch is far from exhaustive, but it suffices to show clearly that in the series Q, Mark, Matthew, there is a steady development in the direction of emphasizing, making more definite, and even creating, sayings of our Lord of the catastrophic Apocalyptic type, and of thrusting more and more into the background the sayings of a contrary tenor.

But what right have we to assume that the process had not already begun even before Q crystallized the tradition into writing. The sayings preserved in Q were not taken down at the time by a shorthand writer; they had lived for many years in the memory of the disciples. The human memory retains little that it does not transmute, and the more interesting the thing remembered and the more often it is repeated to others, the more inevitably does it become coloured by the idiosyncrasy of the teller. Hence a tendency which continued to modify the record of our Lord's sayings even after they had been reduced to writing cannot but have operated previously when memory was unchecked by the written document.

The argument, however, must not be pushed to the length of entirely eliminating the Apocalyptic element from the authentic teaching of our Lord. The beliefs of the early Church may have modified and did modify the records of His utterances, but it is too great a paradox to maintain that what was so central in the belief of the primitive Church was not present, at least in germ, in what the Master taught. The problem does not admit of any cut and dried strophic interpretation (cf. esp. vv. 41-3) given to the two parables which *are* explained acquires an enhanced significance as showing the 'tendency' of the author or the tradition behind him.[1]

(*f*) Mk x. 15 = Lk xviii. 17 = Mt xviii. 3.

Mark x	*Luke* xviii	*Matthew* xviii
[15] Ἀμὴν λέγω ὑμῖν, ὃς ἐὰν μὴ δέξηται τὴν βασιλείαν τοῦ Θεοῦ ὡς παιδίον, οὐ μὴ εἰσέλθῃ εἰς αὐτήν.	[17] Ἀμὴν λέγω ὑμῖν, ὃς ἐὰν μὴ δέξηται τὴν βασιλείαν τοῦ Θεοῦ ὡς παιδίον, οὐ μὴ εἰσέλθῃ εἰς αὐτήν.	[3] Ἀμὴν λέγω ὑμῖν, ἐὰν μὴ στραφῆτε καὶ γένησθε ὡς τὰ παιδία, οὐ μὴ εἰσέλθητε εἰς τὴν βασιλείαν τῶν οὐρανῶν.

The phrase δέξηται τὴν βασιλείαν, in which Luke supports Mark, implies a present Kingdom. Matthew omits the whole verse in the context parallel to Mark, and inserts it xviii. 3, but significantly alters this particular phrase.[2]

(*g*) In Matthew also we find constantly repeated certain Apocalyptic phrases, e.g. the expression συντέλεια τοῦ αἰῶνος, used by him five times, not elsewhere in the Gospels, and once only in the N. T. in Heb. ix. 26 with plural αἰώνων. Also the phrase 'Weeping and gnashing of teeth' occurs six times in Matthew and only once in Luke, and not elsewhere in the N. T.

But Matthew not only heightens the Apocalyptic effect of the materials before him, he also has a tendency to omit sayings inconsistnt with the view of the Kingdom as entirely future and catastrophic.

(*a*) He omits the Parable of the Seed growing secretly (Mk iv. 26-9), and substitutes for it, in the same context, the Parable of the Tares [3] (Mt xiii. 24-30), with its Apocalyptic explanation.

[1] It is not certain that these parables were spoken in at all an eschatological sense, cf. von Dobschütz, *The Eschatology of the Gospels*, p. 84, a book which only reached me after this was printed.

[2] This instance I owe to Sir J. Hawkins.

[3] I owe to Sir John Hawkins the observation that Matthew's Parable of the Tares is coloured by reminiscences of the omitted Parable of the Seed growing secretly. N.B. especially καθεύδειν, βλαστᾶν, πρῶτον, χόρτος, σῖτος, καρπός, θερισμός. Some of these could be accounted for from similarity of subject-matter, but hardly so many in so short a space. It cannot, therefore, be said that the Seed growing secretly was not in the text of Mark used by Matthew.

of ch. xxv ending with the dramatic picture of the Great Assize.[1]

(d) But Matthew not only adds weight to Mark's Apocalypse by adding fresh materials so as to more than double its length; he also embellishes what he takes over from Mark with details from the conventional stock of Apocalyptic ideas.

Mark xiii	*Matthew* xxiv
²⁵⁻⁷ Καὶ οἱ ἀστέρες ἔσονται ἐκ τοῦ οὐρανοῦ πίπτοντες, καὶ αἱ δυνάμεις αἱ ἐν τοῖς οὐρανοῖς σαλευθήσονται· καὶ τότε ὄψονται τὸν υἱὸν τοῦ ἀνθρώπου ἐρχόμενον ἐν νεφέλαις μετὰ δυνάμεως πολλῆς καὶ δόξης. καὶ τότε ἀποστελεῖ τοὺς ἀγγέλους, καὶ ἐπισυνάξει τοὺς ἐκλεκτοὺς αὐτοῦ ἐκ τῶν τεσσάρων ἀνέμων, ἀπ' ἄκρου γῆς ἕως ἄκρου οὐρανοῦ.	²⁹ᵇ Καὶ οἱ ἀστέρες πεσοῦνται ἀπὸ τοῦ οὐρανοῦ, καὶ αἱ δυνάμεις τῶν οὐρανῶν σαλευθήσονται· ³⁰ καὶ τότε φανήσεται τὸ σημεῖον τοῦ υἱοῦ τοῦ ἀνθρώπου ἐν τῷ οὐρανῷ· καὶ τότε κόψονται πᾶσαι αἱ φυλαὶ τῆς γῆς, καὶ ὄψονται τὸν υἱὸν τοῦ ἀνθρώπου ἐρχόμενον ἐπὶ τῶν νεφελῶν τοῦ οὐρανοῦ μετὰ δυνάμεως καὶ δόξης πολλῆς. ³¹ καὶ ἀποστελεῖ τοὺς ἀγγέλους αὐτοῦ μετὰ σάλπιγγος φωνῆς μεγάλης, καὶ ἐπισυνάξουσι τοὺς ἐκλεκτοὺς αὐτοῦ ἐκ τῶν τεσσάρων ἀνέμων, ἀπ' ἄκρων οὐρανῶν ἕως ἄκρων αὐτῶν.

N.B. the additions of v. 30 a and the σάλπιγξ in 31 (cf. 1 Thess iv. 16, 1 Cor xv. 52).[2]

(e) Matthew alone gives, with their interpretation annexed, the two Parables of the Tares, xiii. 24–30 (explained 36–43), and of the Drag-net, xiii. 47–8 (explained 49–50). No explanation (except that of the Sower, which he takes over from Mark) is given of the other 'Parables of the Kingdom' in this chapter, i.e. of the Mustard Seed and Leaven, the Hidden Treasure and Pearl of Great Price. These last four seem, on the face of them, to be incompatible with an entirely future and catastrophic conception of the Kingdom. Hence the highly Apocalyptic and cata-

---

[1] The authenticity of the parable (Mt xxv. 31-46) *as a whole* seems guaranteed by internal considerations, but much of the detail in its Apocalyptic setting, especially v. 31, is probably a later development. The parables were especially liable to slight modifications, cf. pp. 197 f.

[2] The added εὐθέως of Mt xxiv. 29a may be a heightening of Apocalyptic effect, or it may have stood originally in Mark also and have fallen out of his text.

N.B. Matthew changes the vague 'Kingdom coming' to the more definite 'Son of Man coming in his Kingdom'. Luke supports Mark, thus guaranteeing the present text of Mark as original.

(c) Mk xiv. 62 = Mt xxvi. 64 = Lk xxii. 69. Our Lord's reply to High-priest.

Mark xiv	Matthew xxvi	Luke xxii
⁶² Ὁ δὲ Ἰησοῦς εἶπεν, Ἐγώ εἰμι· καὶ ὄψεσθε τὸν υἱὸν τοῦ ἀνθρώπου καθήμενον ἐκ δεξιῶν τῆς δυνάμεως καὶ ἐρχόμενον μετὰ τῶν νεφελῶν τοῦ οὐρανοῦ.	⁶⁴ Λέγει αὐτῷ ὁ Ἰησοῦς, Σὺ εἶπας· πλὴν λέγω ὑμῖν, ἀπ' ἄρτι ὄψεσθε τὸν υἱὸν τοῦ ἀνθρώπου καθήμενον ἐκ δεξιῶν τῆς δυνάμεως καὶ ἐρχόμενον ἐπὶ τῶν νεφελῶν τοῦ οὐρανοῦ.	⁶⁹ Ἀπὸ τοῦ νῦν δὲ ἔσται ὁ υἱὸς τοῦ ἀνθρώπου καθήμενος ἐκ δεξιῶν τῆς δυνάμεως τοῦ Θεοῦ.

But the disciples were not present at the trial, and must have been dependent on the version of the trial circulated by His enemies. And since it was for the 'blasphemous' admission that He was the Christ that He was condemned, we may be pretty sure that the Apocalyptic terms of that admission at least suffered no toning down.[1]

In Matthew the tendency to fill in the details of the picture and emphasize the Apocalyptic side of the eschatology is still more marked.

Two instances have been already noted: (a) his modification (Mt xvi. 27) of Mk viii. 38; and (b) the similar but slighter modification (Mt xvi. 28) of Mk ix. 1.

(c) A more conspicuous example is his further development of the Apocalypse of Mk xiii into Mt xxiv and xxv. Its length and importance is increased by the addition of the most Apocalyptic sections of Q (Mt xxiv. 26-8, 37-51), which in their new context take on a more catastrophic shade, and by the three Apocalyptic parables

---

[1] Sir J. Hawkins suggests to me that ἀπ' ἄρτι Mt = ἀπὸ τοῦ νῦν Lk perhaps points to some such expression having dropped out of the text of Mark. As both these phrases mean 'henceforth' rather than 'immediately' it would seem that even here room is left for a non-catastrophic coming.

Synoptic Criticism and Eschatology

Luke xii

⁹ Ὁ δὲ ἀρνησάμενός με ἐνώπιον τῶν ἀνθρώπων ἀπαρνηθήσεται ἐνώπιον τῶν ἀγγέλων τοῦ Θεοῦ.

Matthew x

³³ Ὅστις δ' ἂν ἀρνήσηταί με ἔμπροσθεν τῶν ἀνθρώπων, ἀρνήσομαι αὐτὸν κἀγὼ ἔμπροσθεν τοῦ πατρός μου τοῦ ἐν οὐρανοῖς.

Mark viii

³⁸ Ὃς γὰρ ἂν ἐπαισχυνθῇ με καὶ τοὺς ἐμοὺς λόγους ἐν τῇ γενεᾷ ταύτῃ τῇ μοιχαλίδι καὶ ἁμαρτωλῷ, καὶ ὁ υἱὸς τοῦ ἀνθρώπου ἐπαισχυνθήσεται αὐτόν, ὅταν ἔλθῃ ἐν τῇ δόξῃ τοῦ πατρὸς αὐτοῦ μετὰ τῶν ἀγγέλων τῶν ἁγίων.

Matthew xvi

²⁷ Μέλλει γὰρ ὁ υἱὸς τοῦ ἀνθρώπου ἔρχεσθαι ἐν τῇ δόξῃ τοῦ πατρὸς αὐτοῦ μετὰ τῶν ἀγγέλων αὐτοῦ, καὶ τότε ἀποδώσει ἑκάστῳ κατὰ τὴν πρᾶξιν αὐτοῦ.

Luke ix

²⁶ Ὃς γὰρ ἂν ἐπαισχυνθῇ με καὶ τοὺς ἐμοὺς λόγους, τοῦτον ὁ υἱὸς τοῦ ἀνθρώπου ἐπαισχυνθήσεται, ὅταν ἔλθῃ ἐν τῇ δόξῃ αὐτοῦ καὶ τοῦ πατρὸς καὶ τῶν ἁγίων ἀγγέλων.

N.B. Mark adds to Q ὅταν ἔλθῃ ἐν τῇ δόξῃ τοῦ πατρός. Mt xvi. 27 develops still further, and, *omitting* the first half of the saying, 'Whoso is ashamed of me,' &c., in which originally lay its whole point, further elaborates the eschatological residue, καὶ τότε ἀποδώσει ἑκάστῳ κτλ., thus completely changing the whole character of the saying, dropping its moral, and making it into a purely Apocalyptic prophecy. The series Lk xii. 9, Mk viii. 38, Mt xvi. 27 gives in epitome the eschatological evolution in the Gospels.

(*b*) Mk ix. 1.

Mark ix

¹ Καὶ ἔλεγεν αὐτοῖς, Ἀμὴν λέγω ὑμῖν, ὅτι εἰσί τινες ὧδε τῶν ἑστηκότων, οἵτινες οὐ μὴ γεύσωνται θανάτου, ἕως ἂν ἴδωσι τὴν βασιλείαν τοῦ Θεοῦ ἐληλυθυῖαν ἐν δυνάμει.

Matthew xvi

²⁸ Ἀμὴν λέγω ὑμῖν, εἰσί τινες τῶν ὧδε ἑστηκότων, οἵτινες οὐ μὴ γεύσωνται θανάτου, ἕως ἂν ἴδωσι τὸν υἱὸν τοῦ ἀνθρώπου ἐρχόμενον ἐν τῇ βασιλείᾳ αὐτοῦ.

Luke ix

²⁷ Λέγω δὲ ὑμῖν ἀληθῶς, εἰσί τινες τῶν ὧδε ἑστηκότων, οἳ οὐ μὴ γεύσονται θανάτου, ἕως ἂν ἴδωσι τὴν βασιλείαν τοῦ Θεοῦ.

Note Mark's phrase ἐληλυθυῖαν ἐν δυνάμει, which seems to *limit* the coming to a catastrophic manifestation, and the date limit. Q never dates.[1]

---

[1] It is hazardous, since it is absent from Lk, to refer to Q the saying, Mt x. 23, 'Ye shall not finish the cities of Israel before the Son of Man come.' It can hardly, however, belong to the latest development of the tradition, and was probably found by 'Matthew' in the already expanded version of Q which reached him; cf. p. 205.

Parable of the Seed growing secretly (if indeed this was not already in Q, cf. p. 178 fin.), or like the reply to the Scribe, 'Thou art not far from the Kingdom of God,' Mk xii. 34, and other passages, but the dominant note has changed.

The amount of space given by St. Mark to our Lord's teaching is so small as to constitute one of the problems of Synoptic criticism (cf. p. 219). But explain this how we may, the length and elaborate character of the Apocalypse of ch. xiii shows the importance assigned to it by the author—naturally, if the end of the world is coming in a few months, details on that subject are of surpassing interest.

Mark xiii dominates the eschatology of the Second Gospel, and through him that of the two later Gospels, which so largely depend on Mark, especially that of Matthew. It is the citadel of the extreme eschatological school of interpretation. Hence the question how far it fairly represents the mind of our Lord is crucial. The question is discussed at length in an earlier essay (cf. pp. 179 ff. above), so that the results there arrived at may be here assumed, viz. that very little of that discourse can reasonably be regarded as authentic teaching of Christ, the rest is in the ordinary manner of Jewish and Christian Apocalypse.

In three passages outside ch. xiii the catastrophic coming of the Kingdom or of the Son of Man is alluded to with a detail not found in Q.

(a) Mk viii. 38, a specially interesting case.

A similar saying occurs in Matthew and Luke not only in the context parallel to Mark, but elsewhere in a slightly different form, so that it is evident that the saying was in Q as well as in Mark (cf. p. 177), and was doubtless derived by Mark from Q, but slightly changed in passing through his mind.

We have also Matthew's further modification of the Marcan form, so that the alterations, made almost unconsciously as they doubtless were, are most significant.

There is a second and equally important point in Q's eschatology. Sayings which appear to imply a catastrophic coming of the Kingdom are rare in Q. The eschatological sayings *characteristic* of Q are rather those that imply a Kingdom which is in some sense already present and which will increase by a gradual growth.

(*a*) 'If I by the finger of God,' &c., ἄρα ἔφθασεν ἐφ' ὑμᾶς ἡ βασιλεία, Lk xi. 20 = Mt xii. 28.

(*b*) John's question 'Art thou he that should come?' is answered by a list of tokens of the actual presence of the Kingdom, 'the blind see,' &c., Lk vii. 22 = Mt xi. 5.

(*c*) So the obscure phrase 'From the days of John', βιάζεται, whatever its exact meaning, seems to imply a present kingdom, Lk xvi. 16 = Mt xi. 12. Cf. also 'He that *is* least in the Kingdom of Heaven *is* greater than he,' Lk vii. 28 = Mt xi. 11.

(*d*) Again, the Parable of the Mustard Seed (Lk xiii. 18–19 = Mt xiii. 31-2) is meaningless unless it is intended to expressly enforce the idea of a gradual growth.[1]

(*e*) Still more markedly the Parable of the Leaven (Lk xiii. 20 = Mt xiii. 33) expounds the Kingdom, at least in one of its aspects, as an influence slowly pervading society.

(*f*) Such too is the more natural interpretation of 'Strive to enter in by the strait gate', Lk xiii. 24 = Mt vii. 13. Cf. also 'Ye have not entered in yourselves, and have prevented those that were entering', Lk xi. 52 = Mt xxiii. 13.

Thus in Q, while the catastrophic eschatology is undoubtedly present, it is vague and undefined. The eschatology which is really characteristic of Q is of a different kind.

Passing on to Mark we find that in his eschatology, as in other respects, he belongs to the transitional stage; cf. the Essay, 'The Literary Evolution,' &c., p. 210, above. The non-catastrophic view is even reinforced by sayings like the

---

[1] This occurred in Q as well as in Mark, cf. p. 172.

conformed to the Apocalyptic picture which was cherished by the early Church.[1]

It is undeniable that language of a definitely Apocalyptic type is already present in Q.

'In an hour when ye think not the Son of Man cometh,' Lk xii. 40 = Mt xxiv. 44.

'As the lightning, when it lighteneth out of the one part under heaven, shineth unto the other part under heaven, so shall the Son of Man be in his day,' Lk xvii. 24 = Mt xxiv. 27.

'As it came to pass in the days of Noah, even so shall it be also in the days of the Son of Man,' Lk xvii. 26 = Mt xxiv. 37.

'Ye shall sit on thrones judging the twelve tribes of Israel,' Lk xxii. 30 = Mt xix. 28.

It may be argued that these and similar sayings (e.g. Lk xii. 9 = Mt x. 33; Lk xiii. 28-29 = Mt viii. 11-12) already imply all the essential elements of the catastrophic eschatology in Matthew or in the Epistles to the Thessalonians; and that the clouds of glory, the attendant angels, the darkened sun and moon, the falling constellations, the trumpet blast, the throne of judgement, the dating within the lifetime of the Twelve, given in the later documents, do no more than fill in the detail of the picture already implied in Q.

But the notable fact about Q's presentation is precisely that this filling in of detail still remains to be done. Vagueness and reserve are the characteristic notes of the Apocalyptic sayings of Q, a vagueness and reserve in such marked contrast to the definiteness and elaboration already assumed by the early Christian theology when St. Paul wrote to the Thessalonians, and probably long before, that it can hardly be without significance.

---

[1] This does not apply to Luke, in whom a slight, but only very slight, tendency to tone down eschatological language can be detected, doubtless the result of Pauline influence.

APPENDIX

SYNOPTIC CRITICISM AND THE ESCHATOLOGICAL PROBLEM

IT would be outside the scope of the present volume to discuss at large the great problem, forced acutely upon the attention of scholars by the writings of Johannes Weiss, Schweitzer, Loisy, and Tyrrell, as to how far the Apocalyptic eschatology of the primitive Church really represented the mind of Christ. But it will not be inappropriate to consider briefly what light is thrown on the question by the critical investigation of the sources of the Gospels.

The gradual evolution of Christian eschatology in the writings of St. Paul and St. John is a commonplace to all students of the New Testament. The Christian hope, first finding its expression in crude Apocalyptic like that of the Epistles to the Thessalonians, insensibly changes its emphasis, passes through the mysticism of the Epistles of the Captivity, and culminates in the Johannine doctrines of the Spirit and Eternal Life.

The critical recognition of the priority of Q to Mark and of Mark to Matthew makes it clear that there was taking place in other circles of the Church during the same period *an evolution in the contrary direction.* The Apocalyptic element in Mark has a precision and detail not found in Q, in Matthew is seen a still further development. The eschatological language of the Master becomes more and more

SYLLABUS

Three clearly marked stages in the development of the Eschatological Teaching ascribed to our Lord are found respectively in Q, Mark, and Matthew.

In Q the emphasis is rather on the conception of the Kingdom, as already present and to be extended by a process of gradual growth. Sayings implying that its appearance is future and catastrophic also occur, but they are not elaborated into any detail.

In Mark—especially in ch. xiii—the emphasis is on the future catastrophic conception, which is worked out with much detail of the conventional Apocalyptic type.

In Matthew the detail is still further elaborated, and both by what he adds and what he omits the catastrophic conception is enhanced.

The same tendency was no doubt in operation before even Q was written down, but some residuum of Apocalyptic eschatology in the authentic teaching of Christ is required to explain the beliefs of the early Church.

Jewish Apocalyptic was the expression, determined by local and temporary conditions, of certain of the essential elements of Religion. Three incidents are quoted to show how our Lord, while adopting the ideals of Apocalyptic, endorsed with reserve the details of their contemporary expression.

The tendency in the early Church to conform His teaching more closely to Apocalyptic standards was arrested by St. Paul and St. John, who brought back the Church to a position nearer that of the Master Himself.

APPENDIX

SYNOPTIC CRITICISM AND THE ESCHATOLOGICAL PROBLEM

Rev. BURNETT HILLMAN STREETER

string of disconnected sayings, probably in order to illustrate his central conception of Jesus as the Son of God, but without any idea of writing an exhaustive biography and without feeling himself obliged to reproduce all the material with which he was acquainted.

4. Some time later the original Gospel was enlarged by the addition of ch. vi. 45 – viii. 26, and of ch. xiii (the Apocalyptic passage). For these sections the editor may have used a later form of Q, which by this time had hardened into a collection of discourses, not improbably including a good deal of narrative setting. Thus in the last thirty years of the first century A.D. the Gospel was current in at least three recensions, viz. :—

(a) Our present Gospel without either the great interpolation or ch. xiii (the original form).

(b) Our present Gospel without the great interpolation (the form used by Luke).

(c) Our present Gospel as it stands (the form used by Matthew).

It is possible that (b) and (c) may be second and third editions of the Gospel published in his later years by St. Mark himself; and there is some linguistic and stylistic evidence for this view, which does not, however, amount to proof.[1] We do not wish to exclude the possibility of the presence of other and more minute redactional additions, but on the whole, and with the exception of the two important sections mentioned above, we find ourselves able at the close of the inquiry to join in the aspiration *requiescat Urmarcus*.

---

[1] The evidence with regard to the great interpolation is summarized by Sir John Hawkins in his Essay 'St. Luke's Use of St. Mark's Gospel', pp. 63-5.

Source' in Mark xiii seem to offer two obvious crevices into which the scalpel of literary criticism may find an entrance. The conclusion suggested is that a redactor (possibly Mark himself, as we saw above) coming into possession, we know not how, of a number of incidents more or less loosely connected by the 'Bread-*motif*', inserted them into the proto-Mark at a point which seemed appropriate, namely after the Feeding of the Five Thousand. This is confirmed by the fact that these sections certainly do seem to be characterized by that geographical and chronological indefiniteness which Wendling notes as a feature of the 'Evangelist's' work. It is extraordinarily difficult to construct a consistent scheme out of the geographical notices given: if one tries to work them out, the impression produced is that of an apparently motiveless ferrying backwards and forwards over the lake (*ein seltsames Hin- und hergondeln*, Wendling). Here again the author seems to be reproducing not the living tradition of eye-witnesses, but fragments of fixed records, long before committed to writing, in which the geographical notices have remained as it were fossilized.

The results of our inquiry may be briefly summarized as follows:—

1. The distinction drawn by Wendling between M^1 and M^2, the earlier and the later constituents of the proto-Mark, seems to have disappeared. Though ingenious, it appears unnecessary, and accordingly, by the law of parsimony, probably baseless.

2. The attribution of dogmatic interests to M^3 seems equally groundless. Consequently a great portion of the material condemned by Wendling as 'redactional additions' on the ground of its alleged doctrinal tendency will have to be re-transferred to the original narrative.

3. The original compiler of the Petrine memoirs (=John Mark?) drew upon Q in one of its primitive forms as a

XIII. The Origin of St. Mark

upon written records. The reason for supposing the 'Four Thousand' scene to be a doublet of the 'Five Thousand' is, not the assumption that such an event could only have occurred once, but the extreme difficulty of supposing that the memory of the first miracle could have been erased from the minds of the disciples so soon after its occurrence as to leave them in the state of perplexity depicted in ch. viii. 4. There we are told that the Lord called His disciples and said (vv. 2, 3), 'I have compassion on the multitude, because they have been with me now for three days, &c.'; to which the disciples return the helpless answer (v. 4), 'Whence can one satisfy these men with bread here in the wilderness?' Now if the miracle of the Five Thousand had previously occurred, surely the obvious reply would have been 'Work a miracle, as thou didst when thou feddest the Five Thousand'. To suppose that they had forgotten the first incident seems to postulate an almost incredible dullness on the part of the disciples. The considerations just adduced are equally cogent, whatever view be taken of the objective truth of the narratives. Again, the practical identity of content taken together with the diversity of detail seems to show that we have here two streams of tradition flowing ultimately from the same objective fact (whatever that may have been). And though we agree with Wendling in considering the later scene to be a doublet of the first, we cannot follow him in supposing that the 'Four Thousand' incident was deliberately concocted by the redactor on the basis of the 'Five Thousand' scene. Such a procedure seems entirely motiveless now that we have eliminated the supposition of doctrinal interests on the part of the redactor. The more probable conclusion is that the first account comes from the Petrine tradition and the second from some other source, possibly Q (= the Matthaean tradition?).

This doublet and the emergence of the 'Apocalyptic

It is a remarkable fact that all these sections, except No. 11,[1] are reproduced by Matthew, and that all without exception are omitted by Luke.[2] The latter has followed Mark more or less faithfully up to the Feeding of the Five Thousand (Mk vi. 35-44 = Lk ix. 12-17). He then leaves out these eleven sections and goes straight on with the Messianic confession of St. Peter (Mk viii. 27-33 = Lk ix. 18-22). This is the more surprising as these sections include the story of the Syrophoenician woman's daughter, which St. Luke, the disciple of St. Paul, would naturally have welcomed as illustrating his master's favourite thesis 'to the Jew first, and then to the Greek'. The simplest explanation appears to be that St. Luke omitted them because they were not in his copy of St. Mark.

We have also to observe that these sections contain what appears to be a genuine doublet, viz. the account of the Feeding of the Four Thousand (viii. 1-9). This seems to be an independent version of the events narrated in vi. 35-44 (the Feeding of the Five Thousand), which has however been worked over by an editor and assimilated in language and schematic arrangement to the first account. There can be no doubt, however, that the editor regarded the two accounts as two separate incidents, for he carefully distinguishes them in the words attributed to our Lord, ch. viii. 19, 20, 'When I broke the five loaves amongst the 5,000, how many baskets full took ye up? and when the seven loaves amongst the 4,000, how many hampers full ...?' and this would suggest that the interpolation of these sections took place (late in the history of the Gospel) at a time when the living memory of eyewitnesses had almost died out and been replaced by dependence

---

[1] And possibly No. 7; see Sir John Hawkins's Essay, 'St. Luke's Use of St. Mark's Gospel,' p. 68, note 4.

[2] This is the more striking when we remember that 'Matthew has a much stronger tendency than Luke to shorten narratives and in this respect to depart from the model of Mark' (*Horae Synopticae*, 1910 edition, p. 129).

and are willing to admit that sources are not to be multiplied *praeter necessitatem*, there seems no reason why we should not suppose that the Apocalyptic passage is drawn from one of the (probably) numerous forms of Q current in the first century. It seems probable that Q began as a series of Logia loosely strung together, in course of time attracting to itself other floating material, and gradually becoming systematized and hardened into discourses, until we meet it in the period of Gospel-formation (A.D. 70-100) as a 'Halbevangelium' (Jülicher) containing not merely discourse matter but also a certain amount of narrative setting. In that case the Q sayings already enumerated would come from an earlier, the Apocalyptic passage from a later form of Q. It would follow from this that the Q sayings were worked into the original narrative by St. Mark, the first editor of the Petrine recollections, and that the 13th chapter was added some years later, possibly by St. Mark himself—for we must always remember the possibility that 'Urmarcus' and our present Gospel may be simply shorter and longer recensions of the same work by the same author.

We have now to consider the passage vi. 45-viii. 26, which Wendling calls the 'great interpolation' of M^3, comprising the following sections:—

    1. The Walking on the Lake.
    2. Return to Gennesaret—healings.
    3. Question of hand-washing.
    4. 'Corban.'
    5. That which defileth a man.
    6. The Syrophoenician woman.
    7. Healing of deaf and dumb man.
    8. Feeding of the Four Thousand.
    9. Demand for a sign.
    10. 'The leaven of the Pharisees.'
    11. The blind man at Bethsaida.

(vv. 21-5), and the Parable of the Mustard Seed (vv. 30-2) are drawn from Q. The identity of the content of these passages with that of the corresponding sections in Mt and Lk compels us to assume a common source for them, whilst the divergence in expression forbids us to suppose that the other two Evangelists were simply copying Mark.

The above seem to be some of the most certain instances of the use of Q by 'Mark'. A much longer and fuller list will be found in Mr. B. H. Streeter's Essay ('St. Mark's Knowledge and Use of Q'), based upon proofs more minute and exhaustive than can be given here. I cannot feel, however, that the theory which sees in Mk xiii a Jewish or Jewish Christian Apocalypse pseudonymously attributed to our Lord rests upon any sure foundations. This hypothesis, commonly associated with the names of Colani and Weiffenbach, seems open to the same objections which we brought against Wendling's supposition of a 'Messiasgeheimnistheorie'. It certainly provides an explanation of the facts: but is there any proof that this explanation is the true one? May not the 'Little Apocalypse' theory be merely another case of Ptolemaic astronomy? It cannot of course be denied that Mark xiii is thoroughly Apocalyptic in tone and colour, reproducing the conventional signs of the end which were commonplaces of the current eschatological literature. Nor can it be denied that this chapter, consisting as it does of a long connected discourse, in sharp contrast to the terse and pithy aphorisms strung together in chapter iv, seems to stand out by itself as a distinct and separate whole. But all that these facts warrant us in concluding is that in Mark xiii we have to deal with an 'Apocalyptic Source'. There is no proof, so far as I know, that Mark xiii ever existed as a separate document, and to suppose that our Lord 'could' not have used the language attributed to Him here is surely to beg the question. If we leave out of sight for a moment *a priori* considerations of this nature,

3. The Seed growing in Secret.
4. The Mustard Seed.

The sources of this group are indicated by Wendling as follows :—

M¹. The Parable of the Sower.
  The Seed growing in secret.
M³ or 'Ev'. The explanation of the 'Sower' parable (vv. 10-20).
  The Lamp and the Measure.
  The Mustard Seed.

Now the assignment of vv. 10-20 to the latest stratum is based mainly upon the supposition of a 'Messiasgeheimnistheorie' in the mind of a later redactor. We have seen however (p. 410) that there is every reason to suppose the 'Messianic mystery' to be an objective fact rather than a dogmatic theory ; and if this be so, these verses must be assigned to the primitive narrative or 'Urmarcus'. The contradiction which has been alleged to exist between vv. 11, 12

ἐκείνοις δὲ τοῖς ἔξω ἐν παραβολαῖς τὰ πάντα γίνεται, ἵνα βλέποντες βλέπωσι καὶ μὴ ἴδωσι κτλ.

and v. 33

τοιαύταις παραβολαῖς πολλαῖς ἐλάλει αὐτοῖς τὸν λόγον, καθὼς ἠδύναντο ἀκούειν (M¹),

which are said to assign different and contradictory reasons for the parabolic form of teaching, will disappear. The second passage states the reason for parables, viz. a desire to adapt the teaching to the receptivity of the hearers : the first states the effect which as a matter of fact was produced upon them, and this effect, by a characteristic flash of brilliant paradox, is spoken of as the aim and object of the teaching. However, Wendling seems to me to have succeeded in showing that the simile of the Lamp and the Modius, with the chain of sayings which is attached to it identified with the 'Mother and Brethren' of v. 31: but whether they are or not, there is no reason for postulating a later interpolator for vv. 22–30. If we assume that the two visits (narrated in vv. 21 and 31) are identical, the Beelzeboul incident becomes a digression, designed to heighten the reader's expectancy, in the manner which Wendling has already noted as characteristic of M^2, and which we may confidently assert to be characteristic of the original St. Mark, now that the distinction between M^1 and M^2 has been abolished. If, however, they are not identical, Wendling's argument at once falls to the ground. In either case, the use of Q in this passage is to be attributed not to a later redactor, but to the original editor of the Petrine memoirs himself.

It is perhaps not out of place to observe here that similar considerations apply to another alleged instance of M^3's mechanical method of interpolation, xi. 15–33 (the withering of the Fig-tree), which has been already considered above (p. 401). It may be conceded at once that the insertion of the Fig-tree incident dislocates the natural sequence of events, which should run—

vv. 15–17. Jesus cleanses the Temple;

vv. 27–33. The priests demand His authority for so doing: but there is no reason why we should attribute this dislocation to a later redactor rather than to the original Mark, especially when we remember that according to Papias (*ap.* Euseb. *H. E.* iii. 39) St. Mark wrote οὕτως ... ὡς ἀπεμνημόνευσε and ἀκριβῶς ... οὐ μέντοι τάξει. This conclusion remains unaffected even if we concede further that the Fig-tree incident is a parable from Q which has been mistaken for history.

(*b*) The parables contained in the fourth chapter of St. Mark's Gospel are four in number, namely:—

    1. The Sower.

    2. The Lamp and the Measure.

XIII. The Origin of St. Mark

But the admission that in some way and at some time 'Mark' used Logia from Q at once raises the question, To what source are we to assign the following sections—

(*a*) The Beelzeboul incident (iii. 22–30);
(*b*) The Parables (iv. 1–32);
(*c*) The Synoptic Apocalypse (xiii)?

(*a*) The Beelzeboul section, on which Wendling's comments have been already given (p. 400), is substantially the same in all three Gospels. We notice, however, that Matthew and Luke agree against Mark,

(1) in making the healing of a dumb man the occasion of the incident;
(2) in inserting the retort εἰ ἐγὼ ἐν B. ἐκβάλλω τὰ δαιμόνια, οἱ υἱοὶ ὑμῶν ἐν τίνι ἐκβάλλουσιν; εἰ δὲ ἐν πνεύματι (Lk δακτύλῳ) θεοῦ ἐγὼ ἐκβάλλω τὰ δαιμόνια, ἄρα ἔφθασεν ἐφ' ὑμᾶς ἡ βασιλεία τοῦ θεοῦ (Mt xii. 27, 28 = Lk xi. 19, 20, verbally identical: note that Mt does not follow his usual custom of writing ἡ βασ. τῶν οὐρανῶν instead of ἡ βασ. τ. θεοῦ);
(3) in inserting the saying ὁ μὴ ὢν μετ' ἐμοῦ κατ' ἐμοῦ ἐστιν, καὶ ὁ μὴ συνάγων μετ' ἐμοῦ σκορπίζει (Mt xii. 30 = Lk xi. 23, verbally identical).

Whilst, however, Matthew is roughly in accord with Mark in placing the scene at Capernaum, just before the 'Mother and Brethren' incident, Luke inserts it in quite a different connexion, as an event of the journey which forms the background of the great Lucan interpolation. From these facts we conclude, not that Matthew and Luke are copying Mark, but that all three are using a common source, i.e. Q—Mark probably using an earlier, Matthew and Luke a later and expanded form of the document. It does not however follow that we can accept Wendling's account (given above, p. 400) of the genesis of the passage Mk iii. 20–35. It is doubtful whether those who are called in a curiously vague phrase οἱ παρ' αὐτοῦ (v. 21) are to be

abstracted from such hypotheses Wendling's argument at once assumes the form of a vicious circle, which may be expressed as follows: 'These doctrines are of later date, because the earliest sections of Mark do not contain them: but these same sections are shown to be the earliest by the fact that they do not contain these doctrines.'

So far, we have found that the presence or absence of 'doctrine' constitutes no sound criterion of the age and authenticity of the Marcan sections. What judgement are we to pass upon the other tests employed by our author? We may say at once that in a general sense the use of Q by the author or final redactor of Mark seems to be now well established (for proofs see Mr. Streeter's Essay, V, p. 165). When scholars like Loisy, Bousset, B. Weiss, Bacon, and (since 1907) Harnack agree in maintaining this position, we may be fairly sure of being on safe ground. The following passages are declared both by Loisy and Wendling to be either drawn from or based upon Q :—

Chapter viii. 12. Why doth this generation seek after a sign? (= Mt xii. 39, xvi. 4; Lk xi. 29).
viii. 15. The leaven of the Pharisees (= Mt xvi. 6; Lk xii. 1).
viii. 35. He who wishes to save his life shall lose it (= Mt x. 39, xvi. 25; Lk ix. 24, xvii. 33).
ix. 33–50. Teaching given by our Lord during His last stay at Capernaum.
x. 11. Divorce (= Mt v. 31; Lk xvi. 18).
xii. 38–40. Denunciation of the Scribes.

This list certainly does not exhaust the number of instances in which 'Mark' (or the final redactor) appears to have used Q; it can only claim to represent cases in which such use seems fairly clear. And it must be remembered that we are in no way prejudging the question whether these Sayings were taken from Q and worked up into the primitive narrative by 'Urmarcus' or whether they were added to the 'Urbericht' at some later period by a redactor.

was not so taken at all, it did leave them worse, and that in proportion to the opportunities they had of really understanding it.'[1]

If the facts are interpreted in this simple and natural manner, the whole hypothesis of a deliberate construction of incidents designed to support a 'Messiasgeheimnistheorie' and a 'Verstockungstheorie' falls to the ground. Similar considerations apply to the rejection of certain sections solely or mainly on the ground that they embody the Pauline doctrines of the Atonement and the Church. Granted the initial assumption that Jesus could not have applied the 53rd chapter of Isaiah to Himself or regarded His coming Death as in some sense a Ransom for humanity, the hypothesis of a deliberate construction of incidents designed to support these doctrines certainly holds the field. Granted the further assumption that He could not have formed an inner circle of Twelve to be His companions and the instruments for continuing His work after His departure—granted also that He could not have taken any interest in the welfare of Gentiles—it is certainly most natural to suppose that the account of the Call of the Twelve is a piece of incipient sacerdotal dogma disguised as history and designed to glorify the origins of the Apostolic College, and that the incidents of the Syrophoenician's daughter and the strange wonder-worker who 'followed not us' (= St. Paul?) are fictions composed to justify the Pauline movement towards a Universal as opposed to a purely Jewish Christian Church. But here again the grounds on which these assumptions are based do not seem to be purely 'philological' in nature.[2] At any rate, when

---

[1] W. Sanday, reviewing Jülicher's *Die Gleichnisreden Jesu*, J.T.S., Jan. 1900. For a further comment on ch. iv. 11 see below, p. 415.

[2] It is of course quite possible that the *form* of the saying x. 45 (λύτρον ἀντὶ πολλῶν) may be coloured by Pauline phraseology: but that is a very different thing from saying that its *content* comes from St. Paul and not from our Lord.

to the winds with the open confession, 'Art thou the Christ, the Son of the Blessed? I am; and ye shall see, &c.' We may admit also that the use of the title 'Son of Man' may have been dictated by this policy of 'reserve' or 'economy': those hearers whose spiritual eyes were open would doubtless think of the heavenly being depicted in the Similitudes of Enoch, whilst for the careless and unspiritual it would be an insoluble enigma. But the defenders of the 'Messiasgeheimnis' theory have never given a satisfactory reply to the question, Why may not all this have been actually the case? Why assume it to be the artificial construction of a later redactor? It will be found, I think, that the positive arguments for the theory rest upon assumptions regarding the intrinsic possibility of such an event as the Walking on the Sea—assumptions which are not of a purely literary or critical nature. On the other hand, the supposition that, in tracing the gradual unveiling of the Messianic mystery, we are dealing with fact and not with fiction seems to possess a considerable degree of *a priori* probability. It is, I suppose, generally admitted that Jesus considered Himself to be the Messiah, and that His conception of the Messiahship was diametrically opposed to the prevailing expectation of an earthly kingdom. He never attempted to be a Theudas or a Barkocheba. Otherwise the history of the first century A.D. would be unintelligible. This being so, what more likely than that He should have employed the method of 'economy' in unfolding His Ideas of His Kingdom and His own Messianic nature? From this point of view the words of our Lord (ὑμῖν τὸ μυστήριον δέδοται τῆς βασιλείας τοῦ θεοῦ· ἐκείνοις δὲ τοῖς ἔξω ἐν παραβολαῖς τὰ πάντα γίνεται· ἵνα βλέποντες βλέπωσι καὶ μὴ ἴδωσι κτλ., iv. 11 ff.) fall naturally into their place in the scheme of His teaching. His 'simple and yet profound teaching left men either better or worse according as it was apprehended and taken to heart. If it theory of the 'Messianic mystery': hence the term 'Son of Man' is peculiar to these sections. (*b*) The Pauline doctrines of the Atonement and of the Church.

2. The use of isolated sections from 'Q'.
3. Geographical and chronological indefiniteness.
4. Complete lack of humour, dramatic feeling, and poetic imagination.
5. Mechanical methods of interpolation.

With regard to these points we may offer the following considerations. It is undoubtedly the fact that the Gospel, as we possess it, represents the Lord as concealing the mystery of His Person from the people, and gradually revealing it to the inner circle of the Twelve. We can trace a definite advance and evolution of the idea of His Personality in the minds of the chosen few. All the time that the Messianic secret was being veiled from the gaze of the common folk, the disciples were being allowed to see more and more of it, until the process of their education culminates in Peter's confession at Caesarea Philippi (viii. 29). This event marks the close of the first and the opening of the second period in the progressive revelation; 'from that time forth' the Lord begins to prophesy His future Passion. Now that the conviction of His Messiahship is firmly rooted in their minds, He unveils a further aspect of the 'Messiasgeheimnis' by putting before them the conception of the suffering Son of Man. But towards the multitude the veil of impenetrable secrecy is still maintained. The Transfiguration is immediately followed by the stern command ἵνα μηδενὶ διηγήσωνται ἃ εἶδον (ix. 9). However, as the drama advances, the secret gradually leaks out. The blind man at Jericho hails Jesus as the 'Son of David'; the triumphal entry into Jerusalem implies the popular ascription to Him and His own acceptance of Messianic attributes; and finally, in the Sanhedrin, all secrecy is flung

one another in the mind of St. Peter or of the author of the Gospel, so that, for instance, he puts the same phrase οὐκ ἀποκρινῇ οὐδέν into the mouths both of the high-priest and of Pilate—with perfect simplicity and *naïveté*.

And, although I have not space to examine all the alleged $M^1 = M^2$ doublets, I think it will be found that they all rest upon the two assumptions noted before, viz. that only one of a pair of more or less similar incidents can be authentic, and that it is impossible for the same author to be at one time terse and prosaic, at another time poetic and graceful. Both of these assumptions will, I think, be admitted to be highly precarious and indeed unnecessary. And the fact that the characteristically Marcan words and phrases collected in *Horae Synopticae* are found to be more or less equally distributed over the alleged M^1 and M^2 narratives, seems to show that there is no reason for supposing the primitive 'Urbericht' to come from more than one hand.[1]

IV

We now come to the broad and striking distinction which Wendling alleges to exist between 'Urmarcus' and the 'Redactional Additions' of Ev or M^3. Here again it is obviously impossible to examine Wendling's theory in every detail of its application to the Marcan text, so that (as in the case of M^1 and M^2) we must content ourselves with the consideration of the principal canons by which he discerns the later from the earlier strata, and of one or two typical instances of their employment. The main characteristics which, according to him, stamp the M^3 sections as the product of a later age are as follows:—

1. An apologetic purpose, viz. the defence of (*a*) the

[1] For details, see *Horae Synopticae*, 1910 edition, p. 144 ('List of 151 Historic Presents in Mark'), pp. 12, 13 ('Words and Phrases characteristic of St. Mark's Gospel').

fanatical populace in the unemotional phrase περισσῶς ἔκραξαν, and the word φραγελλώσας is almost shocking in its apparent want of pathos or sympathy. On the other hand, the Sanhedrin-section depicts the tragedy with high poetic feeling. Every detail is sketched with loving care, the whole scene with its lights and shadows forming a Rembrandt-like picture: 'Wie sorgfältig ist die Verleugnung des Petrus vorbereitet, und mit welcher Liebe ist die Szene der Verleugnung selbst ausgemalt! Nur die Hand eines dichterisch nachempfindenden Schriftstellers konnte den tragischen Gehalt dieses Vorgangs so erschütternd zum Ausdruck bringen.' The conclusion is that the Pilate-section comes from M^1, and that the Sanhedrin-section is a free creative imitation, composed on the basis of the older narrative by M^2.

In this argument, again, we seem to detect Wendling's characteristic assumption of the uniqueness of every genuine incident of our Lord's life. The parallelism, which looks at first sight so imposing, is only arrived at by altering the order of verses in, and omitting all the characteristic matter of, the second section. If we compare the two scenes as they stand all that can be proved is—

(1) the greater wealth of detail in the Sanhedrin-scene;
(2) the recurrence of certain *motif*-phrases of the Sanhedrin-section in the Pilate-section.

Assuming then that both were written by the same author, these phenomena would be amply explained by supposing—

(1) that the author had fuller information about the trial before the Sanhedrin than about the Pilate-scene (this would only be natural if his knowledge were derived from St. Peter, who, according to the story, was present in the high-priest's palace during the trial, but did not attempt to enter Pilate's residence);
(2) that the two narratives had subconsciously reacted upon

if we are prepared to say that the non-miraculous incidents are *eo ipso* more primitive than the miraculous, and this would beg a great number of questions which do not come either within the sphere of the literary critic in general or of this Essay in particular. Space forbids us to examine all the instances which Wendling gives of $M^1 = M^2$ doublets; but one of the most important may be briefly touched upon, viz. the Process before the Sanhedrin (ch. xiv. 53 ff.), which is said to be a doublet of the Trial before Pilate (ch. xv. 1-5).

The main argument for considering the two Trial-scenes to constitute a doublet rests upon an alleged parallelism between them—an identity of ground-plan. This is exhibited by Wendling in the form of a scheme, which I reproduce:—

Trial before Pilate.	*Trial before Sanhedrin*
xv. 2 καὶ ἐπηρώτησεν αὐτὸν ὁ Πειλᾶτος σὺ εἶ ὁ βασιλεὺς τῶν Ἰουδαίων;	xiv. 61 πάλιν ὁ ἀρχιερεὺς ἐπηρώτα αὐτὸν καὶ λέγει αὐτῷ σὺ εἶ ὁ Χριστὸς ὁ υἱὸς τοῦ εὐλογητοῦ;
ὁ δὲ ἀποκριθεὶς αὐτῷ λέγει· σὺ λέγεις.	62 ὁ δὲ Ἰησοῦς εἶπεν ἐγώ εἰμι.
3 καὶ κατηγόρουν αὐτοῦ οἱ ἀρχιερεῖς πολλά.	56 πολλοὶ γὰρ ἐψευδομαρτύρουν κατ' αὐτοῦ
4 ὁ δὲ Π. πάλιν ἐπηρώτησεν αὐτὸν οὐκ ἀποκρίνῃ οὐδέν; ἴδε πόσα σου κατηγοροῦσιν.	60 καὶ . . . ὁ ἀρχιερεὺς . . . ἐπηρώτησεν τὸν Ἰησοῦν λέγων οὐκ ἀποκρίνῃ οὐδέν; τί οὗτοί σου καταμαρτυροῦσιν;
5 ὁ δὲ Ἰησοῦς οὐκέτι οὐδὲν ἀπεκρίθη ὥστε θαυμάζειν τὸν Π.	61 ὁ δὲ ἐσιώπα καὶ οὐκ ἀπεκρίνατο οὐδὲν . . .
	63 ὁ δὲ ἀρχιερεὺς διαρρήξας

These two sections, in spite of this striking parallelism, differ nevertheless in respect of style and narrative method. The Pilate-section is dry, terse, and business-like in its method of stating the facts. The author describes the shouts of the scientific order) than those depicting Him as the wonder-working Son of God; and though we do not doubt his sincerity when he says that for his inquiries 'ist keine theologische oder religionsgeschichtliche Richtung irgendwie massgebend gewesen', yet we cannot help feeling in his work the subconscious influence of a very definite Christology.

We may point out, moreover, that some of the characteristics noted above do not prove very striking on close examination. The mention of the swine at Gerasa (v. 11 ff.), of the paschal lamb (xiv. 12 ff.), of the cock-crow (xiv. 30, 68) which reminded St. Peter of the Lord's prophecy of his denial, does not necessarily show a particular interest in zoology on the part of the author of those sections: it is difficult indeed to see how he could have avoided mentioning them, if he was going to relate the incidents in which they occur at all. The same considerations apply to 'M^2's' alleged interest in plants and in costume. As for his love of colours and landscape painting, the same characteristics appear in the sections assigned by Wendling to M^1; for instance, the lake and the fishing boats (i. 16-20, ii. 13, iv. 1, vi. 34), the corn-fields (ii. 23), &c.

The other arguments adduced by Wendling seem equally inconclusive. The organic connexions between M^1 and M^2 sections, which he treats as proofs of the exquisite literary craftsmanship with which M^2 disguises his sutures, might just as well be taken to prove that no such sutures exist. Nor does Wendling's theory of 'doublets' carry much conviction with it. It seems to be based on the assumption that every genuine utterance of Christ and every genuine incident of His life must necessarily have been unique. If He is said to have used the same word (the Aramaic equivalent of πεφίμωσο or φιμώθητι) to a demoniac and to the waters of the lake, one saying must be a 'doublet' of the other. Such an assumption could only be established latter distinction first. The general argument for M^2 is, briefly, this: certain sections of the 'Urbericht' are distinguished by the following characteristics, viz. :—

1. Poetic and dramatic feeling.
2. Freshness and vividness of narrative colouring.
3. Sympathy with nature.
4. Interest in animals, plants, colours, costumes, &c.
5. Interest in the miraculous, and a tendency to regard Jesus exclusively as a great Wonderworker than as a Prophet.

It follows (Wendling would say) that these brilliant sections which stand out so sharply from the more sober-coloured background of the main narrative must be considered as editorial additions (M^2) with which an earlier and simpler book (M^1) has been overlaid. But there seems no obvious reason why we should not explain the characteristics summarized above as proceeding not from difference of authors but from difference of subject-matter. Such incidents as the Baptism, the Transfiguration, and the Arrest in Gethsemane (assigned by Wendling to M^2) obviously lend themselves to pictorial and dramatic treatment in a way which would not be possible to the Healing of Peter's wife's mother and the Call of Levi. It seems purely arbitrary to assume that a single author must write on the same level of poetic feeling, sprightliness, and humour all the way through; at any rate, on such an assumption it would not be difficult to detect Macaulay[1] the historian and Macaulay[2] the poet behind the famous 'History of England'. The contention that the presence of 'nature-miracles' indicates a later document begs a good many questions with which the literary critic as such has no concern. Wendling assumes throughout his work that sections representing our Lord simply as the human Prophet must necessarily be the earlier, *because* the more reliable (an inversion of the true

II

Such, in outline, is Wendling's theory, and it cannot be denied the merit of ingenuity and plausibility. We may admit at once that it gives a consistent explanation of the facts; the only question is whether the explanation is the true one. The phenomena of the Gospel can certainly be deduced (with a little goodwill) from the 'Three-Stratum Hypothesis' if we are given liberty to postulate any conceivable combination of the three strata; but, none the less, the genetic history of those phenomena may have been in actual fact completely different. A striking parallel to all such hypothetical constructions is afforded by the Ptolemaic system of astronomy. Given the geocentric hypothesis, and given also liberty to add epicycle to epicycle *ad infinitum*, the most intricate movements of the heavenly bodies could be 'explained' in accordance with the Ptolemaic presuppositions: but we know now that, in spite of the ingenuity and coherence of these 'explanations', the geocentric theory was fundamentally untrue. After reading Wendling's book, one's first feeling is, 'This theory may be true; but then so may any other theory.' One's next thought is, 'After all, does the theory really fit the facts? or have they to be forced into a Procrustean mould in order to be explained?' And a little consideration will show, I think, that a great deal, if not all, of Wendling's elaborate structure will have to be dismantled.

III

It is claimed that the distinction between the redactional additions of 'Ev' and the 'Urbericht' ($M^1 + M^2$) is that which leaps most immediately to light on first inspection, being much more obvious and more tangible than the distinction between M^1 and M^2. We shall therefore be following the line of least resistance if we examine the has none of his predecessor's imagination and humour, none of his faculty for visualizing the incident which he describes and making it live over again before his eyes ; hence the details of his pictures are vague, cloudy, and confused. When he does attempt to set his imagination to work, he merely succeeds in being fantastic or grotesque ; for this, Wendling compares the incident of the walking on the lake (ch. vi. 47 ff.), a doublet of the stilling of the storm (ch. iv. 35 ff.), and the healing at a distance (ch. vii. 29 ff.). Hence he is obliged to rely upon purely external imitation ; he takes over simply the outward husk, the words and phrases of his original, often without understanding the inner meaning (cf. i. 45, iii. 9 ff., vi. 1 ff., 31, viii. 1 ff., and others quoted by Wendling, *Entstehung*, p. 236). Occasionally words used in the original appear in 'Ev's' sections with quite different meanings (i. 45, vi. 2-5, &c.). In short, his tendency is to generalize and coarsen the *motifs* and incidents taken over, to heighten the miraculous element, to weaken the fresh natural colours of the original, and to combine the smaller fragments into conglomerates or pieces of literary mosaic-work.

Altogether, the work of 'Ev' produces a general impression of uncertainty and vagueness. 'Man hat an manchen Stellen das Gefühl, dass der Ev nicht erzählt, sondern konstruiert.' His geographical and chronological notices are hazy and indefinite, being apparently based upon the schematic introduction of certain stock *motifs* (ὄρος, οἰκία, προσκαλεσάμενος, καθίσας). Two of his incidents, the cursing of the fig-tree and the widow's mite, are probably parables which have in course of time crystallized into history. From all these considerations it follows that the redactor's additions are of even less historical value than the M² sections, being simply fictions designed to turn the naïve primitive account of the sayings and doings of Jesus into a dogmatic Christological treatise.

XIII. The Origin of St. Mark

insert between vv. 21 and 31 the 'Beelzeboul' scene, which has absolutely no connexion with it, thus giving us *two* visits of the relatives instead of one, and destroying the whole point and sting of the reply τίς ἐστιν ἡ μήτηρ μου καὶ οἱ ἀδελφοί μου ; A second striking instance of this procedure is found in chapter xi. 15-33, which may be schematically represented as follows:—

From M¹, where they form a continuous narrative.
- (1) vv. 15-17. Jesus cleanses the Temple:
  [*Insertion by* 'Ev' vv. 18-26—*the withered fig-tree*]
- (2) vv. 27-33. The priests forthwith demand His authority for so doing.

Here again the insertion destroys the natural connexion of (1) and (2), and compels its author to postpone (2) (the demand for 'authority') to the next day. The interpolator then attempts to conceal the suture by the feeble and colourless *motif* καὶ ἐν τῷ ἱερῷ περιπατοῦντος αὐτοῦ [ἔρχονται πρὸς αὐτὸν οἱ ἀρχιερεῖς . . . κτλ.], v. 27. Wendling gives a list of twelve passages, of which the two quoted above are the most conspicuous instances, where this mechanical process of splitting old sections and inserting new matter has taken place.

Like his immediate predecessor, M², the 'Evangelist' has a great fondness for doublets, sometimes reproducing isolated sentences and ideas, sometimes whole incidents from the narrative (M¹ + M²) which lay before him. For instance, the Feeding of the Four Thousand is an artificial construction, imitated from the Feeding of the Five Thousand (M²); the strife 'who should be first' amongst the disciples (ch. ix. 33) is a generalized doublet of the scene 'Grant us to sit the one on thy right hand, the other on thy left, &c.' (ch. x. 35, M¹), the picture of the child set in the midst (v. 36) being taken from the section on the Blessing of the Children (ch. x. 13-16, M¹). The journey to Tyre (ch. vii. 24) is a doublet of that to Caesarea Philippi (ch. viii. 27). But his doublets are far less convincing and successful than those of M². He

the Twelve, is really the figure of St. Paul, idealized and projected backwards into the life of Christ.

The literary methods of 'Ev' are in striking contrast with the dramatic art of his predecessor, M^2. He is a dogmatic theologian of a 'high and dry' type; consequently all his additions are mechanical insertions, displaying no organic connexion with their context, and no sense of literary or dramatic appropriateness. His is a clumsy hand, hacking, hewing, and mortising indiscriminately. One of his favourite methods is to take a section of the composite narrative ($M^1 + M^2$), split it into two halves, and insert a construction of his own between them, doing his best to smooth over and obliterate all traces of the sutures; an excellent example of this is to be found in ch. iii. 20-35 (the attempt of His friends to arrest Him as a madman; the incident 'How can Satan cast out Satan'; and the visit of His mother and brethren). In the primitive Mark-Gospel (M^1), which at this point has been left untouched by M^2, the narrative originally ran:—

(v. 21) καὶ ἀκούσαντες οἱ παρ' αὐτοῦ ἐξῆλθον κρατῆσαι αὐτόν· ἔλεγον γὰρ ὅτι ἐξέστη· (v. 31) καὶ ἔρχονται ἡ μήτηρ αὐτοῦ καὶ οἱ ἀδελφοὶ αὐτοῦ, κτλ. to the end of v. 35.

This (according to Wendling) forms a simple and natural incident. His family (οἱ παρ' αὐτοῦ) hearing of the crowds which throng His footsteps come to the conclusion that He is mad, and, under the leadership of Mary, set off for Capernaum with the object of putting Him under restraint. Arrived before the house in which He is teaching they send in a message, apparently as a stratagem to lure Him out into the open air where they can lay hands upon Him. Jesus sees through the design, is deeply wounded by His relatives' misunderstanding, and returns a crushing reply in which He disowns His family in favour of all who do God's will (ἀποκριθεὶς αὐτοῖς λέγει· τίς ἐστιν ἡ μήτηρ μου κτλ.). The Evangelist tears asunder the incident in order to to the disciples, explaining to them the inner meaning of the enigmatic teaching just given to the multitude; and he seems to feel the necessity of placing the scene of this esoteric teaching indoors.

In the second place the 'Evangelist' in common with St. Paul and the Pauline school generally felt himself obliged to offer some explanation of our Lord's death upon the Cross. In the eyes of a first-century Jew the shameful death of Jesus was a direct contradiction of His claims to Messiahship; the Cross was 'to the Jews a stumbling-block, and to the Gentiles foolishness'. Hence arose the doctrine of the Atonement, which surmounted the difficulty by representing the Death of Christ as an expiatory sacrifice or ransom for humanity. This theory, which owed its origin mainly to St. Paul, was used by the Evangelist as a basis for the construction of incidents and scenes. In order to illustrate it he turns the last journey up to Jerusalem into a deliberate and conscious journey to death. No less than three definite predictions of His own death are attributed to the Messiah, and in x. 45 the fully developed Pauline doctrine of the ἀπολύτρωσις (Rom iii. 23 ff.) is crystallized into an aphorism and put into the mouth of Jesus; 'The Son of Man came not to be ministered unto, but to minister, and *to give his life a ransom for many.*'

Lastly, the final redactor was in close sympathy with the Pauline doctrine of the complete equality of Jew and Gentile, circumcised and uncircumcised, within the pale of the Christian Church. Accordingly, with the view of gaining support for this tendency, he makes the Messiah take a long journey outside the borders of the Holy Land, into the territory of Phoenicia, where one of His most striking miracles is performed upon a Gentile child. This journey has the effect of still further widening the geographical horizon of the Gospel. And the mysterious wonder-worker, who cast out demons in the name of Jesus but followed not

The final redactor to whom, according to Wendling, we owe these sections, is a theologian, in sharp contrast to M¹ the historian and M² the poet. Practically all his additions have been made in the interests of a theory. The main doctrinal ideas underlying this redactional matter are three in number:—

(1) The doctrine of the 'Messianic mystery'.
(2) The doctrine of the Atonement.
(3) The Pauline doctrine of the Church.

The first of these doctrines, according to our author (who is in this matter implicitly following Wrede, *Das Messiasgeheimnis in den Evangelien*), arose from the necessity felt by early Christian apologists for explaining the apparent failure of our Lord's mission to the Jews, the chosen people. It taught, briefly, that the Jews had rejected His claims to Messiahship partly owing to a 'judicial blindness' (compare St. Paul's argument in Rom xi. 25, 26), and partly owing to the (alleged) fact that Jesus had followed the deliberate policy of concealing from them His true Messianic nature, which He revealed only to the inner circle of His disciples. Hence it was that He adopted the parabolic form of teaching, in order that 'seeing they might see and not perceive, hearing they might hear and not understand, lest they should be converted and be forgiven' (iv. 12). Only to the faithful few is it given to know the mystery of the kingdom of God (*ibid.*). Hence also come the severe, almost fierce commands to the demons and the recipients of healing not 'to make him known'. But the 'Evangelist' cannot deny himself the pleasure of depicting his divine hero as surrounded by throngs of listeners seeking for instruction, or sick demanding cure; and so he is obliged to make the recipients of miraculous healing disobey the injunction to silence, and spread the fame of the Messiah far and wide.

In accordance with this theory all 'Ev's' incidents show a tendency to end up with an esoteric discourse addressed

XIII. The Origin of St. Mark

    Promiscuous healings and exorcisms.
    Call of the Twelve.
iii. 23–iv. 34. *Opponents and Disciples.*
    Self-defence against 'Beelzeboul' accusations.
    Initiation of the Twelve into the mystery of the parabolic form of teaching.
vi. 1–13. *Failure at Nazareth and success in distant regions.*
vi. 45–viii. 26. The 'Great Interpolation'. *Journeys, Miracles, and Controversies.*
    Dominating *motifs*:
        (a) The Mystery of the Bread and the disciples' want of understanding.
        (b) The relations of Jesus with Jews and Gentiles.
    Events:—
        1. Walking on the lake.
        2. Promiscuous healing (Gennesareth).
        3. Discourses about clean and unclean.
        4. Exorcism of Syrophoenician woman's daughter.
        5. Healing of a dumb man (Decapolis).
        6. Feeding of the Four Thousand.
        7. Pharisees demand a sign (Dalmanutha).
        8. Remarks on the miracle of the bread (on the voyage).
        9. Healing of blind man (Bethsaida).
viii. 31–x. 45. *The Journey to Death at Jerusalem and the Destiny of the Son of Man.*
        1. Sufferings, Death, Resurrection.
        2. Hints for the life of the Church.
        3. Second coming and future reign.
xi. 11–44. *Three visits to the Temple.* ['Ev' introduces division of Temple-scenes into three days.]
    First look round.
    The barren fig-tree.
    Small interpolations (The stone which the builders rejected; 'Thou lookest not on the countenance of man'; Love better than burnt-offering).
    Warning against scribes: the widow's mite.
xiii. 4–37. *Prophecy about the last Things.*
xiv. 8–xvi. 7. *Small and unimportant Interpolations.*
    e.g. the prophecies; the false witnesses; the Roman centurion at the Cross.

Supper at Jerusalem (xiv. 17–21) is a doublet, consciously constructed, of M¹'s Last Supper, which takes place at Bethany (xiv. 3–9). In the same way M² has doubled the Trial of Jesus, the Mocking, the drink given at the Crucifixion, the derision of the passers-by, and the death-cry. But in all his borrowing and doubling of older sections and sentences, the freshness and force of the original is carefully preserved; the picture never becomes vague, undecided, or generalized—a strong contrast, as we shall see, to the procedure of M³ or 'Ev', the final redactor.

In general, the impression which one gains from Wendling's account of M² is one of a writer of great literary and dramatic power, who was interested more in pictorial and dramatic effect than in strict objective truth; who aimed, in fact, at composing an historical romance, comparable to Philostratus' life of Apollonius of Tyana, rather than a scientific biography.

We now have a continuous narrative, M¹ + M², consisting of the 'Urmarcus' or primitive Mark (M¹) as worked over and interpolated by M². In this form the Marcan source was known to and used by St. Luke. But after the appearance of St. Luke's Gospel, and before the publication of Matthew, the document fell into the hands of a third writer denoted by the symbols of M³ and 'Ev', under whose hands it assumed its present form. The sections assigned by Wendling to the final redactor are as follows (printed at length in *Urmarcus*, pp. 60–71, 'Zusätze des Evangelisten.' It will be observed that they constitute between a third and a half of the Gospel):—

i. 1–ii. 20. *Small and mainly unimportant additions.*
    Foreword; contents of the preaching of Jesus; driving out of Demons; He becomes well known against His will; the Pharisees; presages of death.

iii. 6–19. *The Crowds of Hearers and the Chosen Few.*
    Flight from the crowds—in vain.

prosaic events narrated by M^1; he is the first to give us prodigies and nature-miracles, and a narrative of the Resurrection.

The manner in which he handles the primitive Mark-Gospel or 'Urmarcus' deserves special note. The main additions which he makes to the body of the work are three in number, viz. the Prelude or Preparation for the Appearance of the Messiah prefixed to the beginning, the account of the Passion and Resurrection dovetailed into the end of the primitive Gospel, and the large section iv. 35-vi. 44 inserted into the body of the work, and containing a collection of prodigies or 'wonderful works'. But the fundamental ground-plan of the old book, M^1, has not been altered, though its historical and geographical horizon has been materially widened. And his method of redaction is characterized in a high degree by the same sense of dramatic propriety and historical realism which we have noted above. He is no mechanical interpolator of disconnected and meaningless fragments; all the connexions of his plot are *organic*, each situation leading naturally on to the next (cf. the structure of the Prelude :— John the Baptist preaches on the banks of the Jordan; Jesus arrives, is baptized, receives the illapse of the Spirit, is 'driven' into the wilderness, and so on. His faculty of creative imitation is shown in the account of the process in the Sanhedrin (xiv. 53, 55–64), which is a literary construction based upon a free treatment of the trial before Pilate, which he found in M^1. In composing his narrative of the stilling of the storm (iv. 35 ff.) his innate sense of dramatic effect has led him to take over the stern command φιμώθητι from M^1 (i. 25, where it is addressed to the evil spirit), and to transfer its application to the winds and waves. This process of free creative imitation is seen very clearly in the Passion-narrative as given by M^2, which is very largely built up of doublets of incidents and *motifs* already existing in M^1. For instance, the Last

seeking for artistic effect, he delights to sketch in a few vivid strokes the changing landscape which forms the background of his drama (e.g. iv. 35 ff., the storm-lashed waters of the lake; v. 1 ff., the precipitous coast of Gerasa, the tombs on the hill-side, and the city in the distance; ix. 2, the mount of Transfiguration with the clouds sailing past its summit). Most of his incidents take place in the open air. He frequently mentions plants and animals (i. 6, 10, 13; v. 11 ff.; vi. 38 ff.; xi. 2 ff.; xiv. 12 ff., 30, 72, animals; vi. 39; xi. 8; xv. 17, 19, 36, plants), and betrays a special interest in costume (e.g. John's garment of camel's-hair, the glistening robes of the transfigured Lord, the σινδών of the young man in Gethsemane, &c.). And he is fond of heightening the vividness of his pictures by the use of adjectives and adverbs, e.g. iv. 37 μέγας (λαῖλαψ, λίθος, &c.) and xiv. 35 μικρόν (προσελθών).

Together with this naïve delight in the sights and sounds of the natural world he has a keen appreciation of dramatic effect. He knows how to awaken the expectancy and excitement of his readers by dropping some casual hint, or narrating some secondary scene, which brings the crux of the situation into clearer relief; for instance, the actual raising of Jairus's daughter is deferred, and the interest and suspense of the reader correspondingly heightened, by the insertion of subordinate incidents—the healing of the issue of blood, the arrival of the messengers with the news of the death, the expulsion of the professional mourners. Often this same feeling of suspense and curiosity is produced by the insertion of a short historical excursus explaining the situation, into the midst of the incident which he has begun to narrate; cf. the account of the Herodias intrigue, which for a short time 'holds up' the development of the final tragedy of John the Baptist's life. And in general his choice of incidents is inspired by a love of the sublime and miraculous, in contrast to the more homely and, so to speak,

xiv. 12–xv. 38 (parts of: for sections in these chapters belonging to M¹ see p. 391). *The Last Day of Jesus' Life.*
Marvellous discovery of the upper room furnished.
Prophecy of betrayal, desertion, denial.
Victory over the fear of death, in Gethsemane.
Futile attempt at assistance, then—the Lord completely forsaken.
Condemnation by the chiefs of the hierarchy.
Peter's denial.
Mocking by Roman soldiers.
Additional sufferings in the hour of death:—the spiced drink, the partition of the garments, mocking repetition of the prophecy of the destruction of the Temple, the death-agony, the last insult (the drink of sour wine).
Accompanying natural portents.
xv. 40–xvi. 8. *Witnesses for the Death, Burial, and Resurrection.*

This second writer, M², is characterized by Wendling as the 'poet', in contrast with M¹, the 'historian'. Like his predecessor, he is interested only in the work of narration; he has no dogma or theory to defend. But he differs widely from M¹ in respect of style and method. The primitive Gospel which lay before him was terse and unadorned to the point of dryness; but the additions and interpolations with which he has embellished the original narrative are instinct with freshness, originality, life, and colour. He has the true poetic faculty of visualizing a scene, making it live before him in imagination, and then pouring it out on paper in vivid hues and lightning strokes of the brush. His pictures are no vague impressionistic blurs, but careful studies characterized by an almost photographic distinctness and a wealth of clear-cut individual detail. To him, in fact, and to him alone, is due that peculiar quality of freshness and objectivity which distinguishes the Second Gospel from the other two. He has a marked sympathy with nature; he alone mentions colours—green vi. 39, white ix. 3, xvi. 5, red xv. 17, and, without consciously been the earliest record of our Lord's life to appear in written form. The ground-plan of the narrative is simple: the incidents group themselves under three heads, viz.:

1. Capernaum.
2. Journeys (to Caesarea Philippi and Jerusalem).
3. Jerusalem.

The theatre of the action is thus comparatively restricted: the two fixed points round which the drama plays are Capernaum and Jerusalem. We may note that the only miracles which it contains are works of healing.

This primitive Mark-Gospel, with its naïve historical interest and its complete lack of doctrinal tendency or literary craftsmanship, not many years after its first appearance, was worked over by a later writer, M^2, who made it the basis of his own narrative. The sections which Wendling assigns to M^2 are as follows (printed at length in small type in Wendling's *Urmarcus*, pp. 42–60):—

i. 4–14. *Preparations for the Appearance of Jesus.*
    John the Baptist and his prophecy of the Messiah.
    The Baptism.
    The Temptation in the Wilderness; John delivered up.

iv. 35–vi. 44. *Wonderful Works.*
    Control of the powers of Nature.
    Hosts of evil spirits vanquished.
    Healing of an incurable disease (the woman with an issue of blood).
    Raising of a dead child (Jairus's daughter).
        Digression;—The impression produced on Herod: narration of the end of John the Baptist.
    Miraculous feeding of the Five Thousand.

ix. 2–8. *The Transfiguration.*

ix. 14–x. 52. *Other Wonderful Works.*
    Healing of an epileptic boy.
    Healing of a blind man at Jericho.

xi. 1–10. *Triumphal entry into Jerusalem.*
    Marvellous discovery of the colt.
    Popular homage to the son of David.

XIII. The Origin of St. Mark

i. 39–44. *Preaching Tour in Galilee.*
    Healing of leper.

ii. 1–iv. 33 (parts of: see pp. 396, 397). *Sojourn in Capernaum.*

Chapter ii, with the exception of a few words.
{ Preaching in a house; healing of lame man.
Preaching on the shore; call of Levi; eating with publicans and sinners; question of fasting; the Sabbath walk through the cornfields. }

  iii. 1–5. The healing of withered hand; question of healing on Sabbath.
  iii. 20, 21, 31–5. The mother and brethren.
  iv. 1–9, 26–9, 33. Preaching from boat; Parables.

vi. 32–4, viii. 27–37. *Journey to the North.*
  Voyage (to Bethsaida); preaching in desert.
  Journey to Caesarea Philippi; 'Whom say men that I am?'

x. 1–44. *Journey to Jerusalem.*
  Discourse during the journey (on the kingdom of God); the children; the rich man; the sons of Zebedee.

xi. 15–xiii. 36. *Appearance in the Temple.*
  Cleansing of the Temple—Discourse.
  Questions on—
    His authority (Parable of Vineyard).
    The Tribute.
    The doctrine of the Resurrection.
    The chief commandment.
  Discourse (Is the Messiah David's Son?).
  Prophecy of destruction of the Temple.

xiv. 1–xv. 37 (parts of: see p. 393). *Persecution and Death.*
  Plot of Sanhedrin.
  Last meal at Bethany; anointing.
  Treachery of Judas.
  The 'words of remembrance' (i.e. what was later interpreted as the institution of the Eucharist).
  Arrest; flight of disciples; mocking.
  Trial before Pilate; condemnation; walk to place of execution.
  Crucifixion; derision; death.

These sections, according to Wendling, form a fairly continuous and intelligible Gospel, which may, indeed, have examine it, in the hope that some positive conclusions may emerge in the course of the argument. For this purpose I have selected the 'Three-Stratum Hypothesis' (*Dreischichtshypothese*) which was first propounded by E. Wendling in his brochure *Urmarcus* (Tübingen, J. C. B. Mohr, 1905), and has been more recently developed at length in his larger work *Die Entstehung des Marcusevangeliums*, both because of the extreme interest and acuteness of the literary analysis by which the theory is supported, and because of the favour which it seems to have received from English students of the origins of St. Mark.[1]

I

Wendling's theory may be summarized as follows. Our present Gospel is composed of three strata or layers, contributed by three different authors, whom he calls M^1, M^2, and M^3, or Ev (= Evangelist). The earliest stratum, the work of M^1, constitutes the kernel of the book, and shows manifest signs of derivation from a source in close proximity to the actual facts: the identification of this primitive source with the Petrine recollections or memoirs is neither affirmed nor denied. M^1 is primarily a historian: he has no doctrinal or other axe to grind, and his style is distinguished by clearness, simplicity, and pregnant brevity. To this source are assigned the following sections (printed at length, in large type, in Wendling's *Urmarcus*, pp. 42-60):—

Chapter i. 16-38. *First appearance in Capernaum.*
    Call of the two pairs of brothers.
    Preaching and casting out of demon in the synagogue.
    Healing of Peter's mother-in-law.
    Healing of many sick persons in the evening.
    Withdrawal into privacy in the morning.

[1] As for instance from Professor Menzies, *Review of Theology and Philosophy*, July, 1909.

THE ORIGIN OF ST. MARK

THE inquiry which we propose to pursue in this essay treats of one aspect of the ultimate problem raised by the commonly accepted 'Two-Document theory', viz. the investigation of the 'sources of sources'. The assumption that one of the main sources of the present Synoptic Gospels is to be identified with our St. Mark, or something very like it, is almost universally accepted, even by those who do not subscribe to the other part of the theory, which postulates a written original for the non-Marcan matter common to Matthew and Luke. It follows that the so-called 'Triple Tradition' has been reduced to a 'Single Tradition', and that many incidents of the Gospel story, for which it was formerly supposed that we possessed three independent and converging testimonies, can now be based only on the authority of St. Mark. Consequently it is of the highest importance that we should know exactly how much St. Mark's authority is worth. Is the Second Gospel, as we have it, a literary unity, coming almost immediately from the lips of St. Peter, the spokesman of the Apostolic band, and consequently possessing first-hand authority in all its parts? or is it a composite work with a long and complicated literary history behind it, the product of several epochs of primitive Church life and thought, containing a kernel of Petrine tradition, but including layers of legendary embellishment and theological fiction? It is quite impossible within the limits of a single essay to discuss adequately the various replies which have been given to these questions; and it therefore seems best to take one definite theory of the genesis of St. Mark's Gospel and

SYLLABUS

Introductory: the problem stated.

I. Wendling's 'Three-Stratum Hypothesis'—M^1 the historian M^2 the poet, and M^3 or 'Ev', the theologian: extent and characteristics of the three strata: M^1's terseness, M^2's imaginative style and interest in the miraculous, M^3's doctrinal ideas—the 'Messiasgeheimnistheorie', the Atonement, and the Church: M^3's redactional methods: two typical instances of their employment (the Beelzeboul incident and the Withering of the Fig-tree).

II. General doubts regarding the whole theory.

III. Examination of the distinction between M^1 and M^2: Wendling's arguments inconclusive: examination of the two trial-scenes (an alleged $M^1 = M^2$ doublet): conclusion—Urmarcus at least (i.e. everything prior to M^3) is a literary unity.

IV. Examination of the distinction between Urmarcus and M^3's Redactional Additions: M^3's supposed dogmatic interests: Why should not the concealment of the Messianic mystery have been a fact? Similar considerations applied to the doctrines of the Atonement and the Church: the 'doctrinal' argument against the alleged M^3 sections really a *petitio principii*. However, the use of Q by the author of the Second Gospel seems fairly certain: discussion of the Beelzeboul incident, the Parables, and the Eschatological Discourse. The 'great interpolation' (vi. 45–viii. 26): the Feedings of the Five Thousand and of the Four Thousand: they appear to constitute a genuine doublet: Conclusion: Wendling seems to have made out his case with regard to the 'great interpolation'.

General conclusion: the Second Gospel seems to have gone through three recensions (all possibly coming from the same hand), viz.:—

(a) The earliest—without the 'great interpolation' or the 'Eschatological Discourse' (ch. xiii).

(b) The second recension (used by Luke) without the 'great interpolation' but including ch. xiii.

(c) The third recension (used by Matthew) = Mark as it stands.

XIII

A RECENT THEORY OF THE ORIGIN OF ST. MARK'S GOSPEL

REV. NORMAN POWELL WILLIAMS, M.A.

Chaplain Fellow of Exeter College, Oxford

ἐκείνων). Here St. Matthew seems to be using an archaic source which did not, however, represent his own view, as is plain from Mt xxv 5 (χρονίζοντος τοῦ νυμφίου) and xxv. 19 (μετὰ δὲ πολὺν χρόνον). It is, however, admitted that St. Mark wrote at latest soon after the final victory of Titus, so that his Gospel belongs, as has been already said, to the sub-Apostolic age. Now it is on this oldest narrative that Matthew and Luke build their own Gospels. As a rule they follow the order, and incorporate most of the matter, of Mark: when they adopt some other order or make notable omissions we can generally see the motive they had for their deviation. Add to this that behind our oldest Gospel lies the collection of the Lord's sayings, which is used at all events in Matthew and Luke. Further that Matthew's, and still more Luke's, use of the Marcan document certainly justifies our confidence that they are honest and competent in their use of other documents now lost, or of material drawn from oral tradition. Those, however, are matters beyond our present scope. We conclude with the remark that our authorities for our Lord's life and words transcend immeasurably our authorities for the life and work of Moses. In one point only is the advantage the other way. We have in the Gospels to recognize the probability of an Aramaic background, so that the words of the Lord are accessible to us only in a translation. To this of course the Hexateuch offers no parallel.

mentioned by Ezekiel and prominent in P, are to some extent the provision. In this respect a study of the different strata of P is well worth while: the trespass offering, originally intended as atonement for unintentional offences (Lev v. 18), is extended (Lev v. 21 ff.) to deliberate transgression. All this and much else of the same sort is instructive enough to the student of religious history, nor should we forget that P preserves some ancient usages. But P has really nothing to tell us of the central figure in his work, i. e. of Moses. Nor do we get much nearer to him by the help of J and E. Just as P throws light on the changes produced by the exile, so do they on the early history of the kingdom. Nor can it be alleged with any show of reason that by the division of the Hexateuch into its component documents we have gained four witnesses instead of one. That of course would be a gain if the documents, in their account of Moses and his work, differing perhaps on many details, agreed in the main features of the picture which they draw of the Patriarchs and Moses. At most this can be said of J and E, and even they are too far removed from the scenes which they portray to be of much value as witnesses. Our real knowledge of Hebrew history begins with the Judges. The existence of Moses and the mighty work he did in binding them to the worship of one God, and that a righteous God who had delivered them from their oppressors, are, as I believe, assured facts. But that is all or nearly all that we know of him.

Contrast with this the results of criticism as applied to the Synoptic Gospels. The earliest narrative of our Lord's life is our Second Gospel, possibly written after the destruction of Jerusalem in A. D. 70. That St. Mark wrote after the event may perhaps be regarded as a legitimate inference from Mk xiii. 24 (ἐν ἐκείναις ταῖς ἡμέραις) compared with Mt xxiv. 29 [1] (εὐθέως δὲ μετὰ τὴν θλῖψιν τῶν ἡμερῶν

---

[1] See also Mt x. 23.

come unto thee and bless thee.' The Deuteronomist, on the contrary, begins his legislation (xii) with the strict and reiterated injunction that sacrifice must be confined to the single place 'which Jehovah your God shall choose out of all your tribes'. The passage just quoted from Exodus insists that the altar, wherever it may be erected, is to be of earth or else of unhewn stone; the same Book of Exodus, in xxvii. 1 f., directs that the altar of burnt-offering be built of shittim wood with a network of brass.

Very noteworthy is the contrast between the way in which the editors of the Hexateuch use and arrange their sources. In the Pentateuch[1] it is the latest and most unhistorical of the documents at his command which the final editor has chosen to be the framework into which all the other documents are fitted. It is P which regulates the chronology. It is a main object of the editor to keep P intact. How anxious he is to do so may be seen in Gen xix. 29. We have had the whole story of Lot's deliverance from Sodom as told in JE: the catastrophe is over and the cities are destroyed by fire. Still, after all, the dry summary of P is appended: 'It came to pass, when God destroyed the cities of the plain, that God remembered Abraham, and sent Lot out of the midst of the overthrow, when he overthrew the cities in the which Lot dwelt.' Here and there P had to lose something but not much. Now there is a great deal which we may thankfully learn from P. It throws a flood of light on the religious views of the Jewish reformers under Ezra and Nehemiah. It enables us to understand the way in which the distinction between priests and Levites, the office and power of the high-priest, were developed after the exile. More than that, it bears witness to that sense of sin which had been deepened by the exile and for which the trespass and sin-offering, first

---

[1] Pentateuch, not Hexateuch, for though P is used in Joshua it does not supply the basis of the book.

XII. Criticism of the Hexateuch, etc.

on divorce (xix. 9 ; v. 32)? Why does St. Luke repeat twice over the saying about the setting of a light upon a candlestick (viii. 16 ; xi. 33), the maxim, 'He who hath, to him it shall be given' (viii. 18 ; xix. 26), &c.? The answer is plain, when we find that the words in question or their equivalents also occur in St. Mark, so that we are led naturally to the conclusion that St. Matthew and St. Luke repeat themselves, because they used or remembered first one and then another source in which the words were given. The nearest parallel which the Old Testament offers to this occurrence of doublets is met with in the Psalms and in the Book of Proverbs. We may, for instance, be sure that the second great collection of Psalms, xlii–lxxxix, in which lxxxiv–lxxxix form an appendix, was published independently of the prior collection, viz. iii–xli. The reason is that Psalm liii is a doublet of Psalm xiv, Psalm lxx of Psalm xl. 13–17, and Psalm lxxi. 1–3 of xxxi. 1–3. Similarly it may be proved that the Proverbs of Solomon x–xxii. 16 formed a collection independent of Prov xxv–xxix, which are also attributed to Solomon, and that the Maxims of the Sages (xxii. 17–xxiv. 22) once formed a booklet of their own apart from the still smaller collection of such Maxims in xxiv. 23–34. The Hexateuch abounds with doublets, but they are far more numerous and on a much larger scale than anything to be met with in the Synoptics. Here it must suffice to mention a few out of many. We have, as has been said above, two accounts of the Creation ; two accounts of Hagar's removal from Abraham's house, of the origin of the name Beersheba, of the revelation of the divine name Jehovah. In the legislative portions a double and often contradictory treatment of the same subject is still more frequent and striking. According to Ex xxi. 24 an altar may be erected in various places, and this permission is followed by the promise, 'In all places where I record my name, I will differ very much, each containing matter peculiar to itself. Only one MS. contains the story of the Battle of Hastings. The Chronicler quotes at length several poems without affording any clue to their origin. The Chronicle then, like the Hexateuch, is the slow growth of centuries; it belongs to more than one kingdom; it contains, though here we are anticipating a subject to be discussed presently, at least one notable doublet, for five of the six MSS. place the murder of Cynewulf under the year 755 and again (this time rightly) under the year 784. Lastly, the quotation of poems has an interesting parallel in similar quotations by the oldest writers in the Hexateuch. Of these the most important is the so-called Blessing of Jacob in Gen xlix. It is very likely that in its original form the poem is anterior to the rise of the Monarchy under Saul, though it has suffered serious alteration. Its moral and religious ideals differ in a striking manner from those of the Prophets. Benjamin is glorified, though he lives by rapine and murder; Jehovah helps Israel in war and blesses it with fruitfulness, but nothing is said of any moral bond between the nation and its God. We have similar poetic insertions in the fragment from the 'Book of the Wars of Jehovah' (Num xxi. 14, 15), in the 'Song of the Well' (Num xxi. 17, 18), in the quotation from 'the poets' (המשלים Num xxi. 27–30) which probably referred originally to the victories of Israel under Omri over Northern Moab, in the Prophecies of Balaam (Num xxiii. 24). Less ancient are the 'Blessing of Moses' (Deut xxxiii) and the 'Song of Moses' (Deut xxxii). Further we may compare the fragments of old Jewish-Christian psalmody which survive in the Gospel according to St. Luke.

The great argument for the severance of documents is the occurrence of doublets. Why, for example, does St. Matthew repeat twice over our Lord's dicta on the sign of Jonah (xvi. 4; xii. 39), on bearing the cross (xvi. 24; x. 38),

XII. Criticism of the Hexateuch, etc. 381

his own views are often in manifest opposition to the authorities which he follows. Thus in 1 Chron xxi we have an account of David's sin in numbering the people. The first twenty-seven verses are based on 2 Sam xxiv, with important modifications, the most notable being that the Chronicler attributes David's temptation to Satan, whereas the older and more naïve writer referred it to God. Then in verse 28–xxviii. 1 we have a characteristic addition by the hand of the Chronicler himself. In some other places the older sources are reproduced verbally. So again the Greek Ezra (1 Esdras in our English Apocrypha) is, with the exception of iii. 1–v. 3, taken bodily from the canonical book of Ezra with excerpts from Chronicles and Nehemiah. Nay, in the historical annals of our own land we have an example of the way in which a document of the first importance could be pieced together without the faintest regard to literary ownership and unity as we now understand them. The *Saxon Chronicle* relates the history of Britain from the invasion of Britain by Julius Caesar to the accession of Henry II in 1154. 'It affords,' says Mr. Thorpe, who edited it for the Master of the Rolls' Series, 'no information as to its several writers.' For the first 500 years it gives information of no independent value drawn from Latin authors. After that it follows Bede, adding, however, some original matter. From the birth of Alfred in 849 to his death it is a document of the first rate, and, though this does not admit of positive proof, it is quite likely that this part of the work was written or at least edited by Alfred himself. But the later part of the history also has elements of high value. It is, e.g., impossible to doubt that the vivid picture of William the Conqueror is from the hand of a contemporary. As a whole the Chronicle belongs to South England, but the Worcester MS. contains a long insertion which is undoubtedly derived from Mercian and Northumbrian sources. The six MSS.

of Mosaic legislation. He insists, e. g., on the strict limitation of the priesthood to those Levites and to those only who could claim descent from Aaron. Here he directly contradicts Deuteronomy. Moreover, it is demonstrable that the most striking points in his legislation were unknown till the time of Ezekiel, who, in 571, sketched a plan of ritual reform. In fact, Ezekiel is the father of the sacerdotal law. His proposed code is one in spirit, though it differs in detail from that which occupies most of the middle books in the Pentateuch. Only Ezekiel promulgates as new, rules which the Priestly Code puts back to the time of Moses at the very birth of the Hebrew nation. Probably Ezra who, as has been said, promulgated, also compiled it. Finally the various documents J, E, D, P, were united into one book, which is known to us as the Pentateuch.[1] When was this final step taken? Not later than 330 B.C., for then at all events, if not a century before, the Samaritans received the Pentateuch in Hebrew and substantially in its present form.

Both the Hexateuch and Gospels, then, are composite in a high degree. Against J, E, D, P, on the one side, we have to set the Marcan source, the non-Marcan source Q, and other special documents and traditions used by Matthew and Luke. Some have felt a difficulty in supposing that great books arose in this mechanical way and that one anonymous writer borrowed without acknowledgement from an older writer also anonymous. Whatever we might have expected *a priori*, there can be no reasonable doubt that this has taken place both in the Hexateuch and the Gospels. Nor is this surprising. Any one can see for himself that the Chronicler has inserted in his own work, and that without acknowledgement, whole sections of historical matter from Genesis, Samuel, and Kings, although

---

[1] Not the Hexateuch. P supplies the framework of the first five books, but not of Joshua—though it is of course partly embodied in Joshua.

XII. Criticism of the Hexateuch, etc. 379

Each is a narrator and not a lawgiver, though each incorporates a brief code (the Elohist in Ex xx. 22-xxiii, the Jahvist in portions of Ex xxxiv, perhaps 2, 3, 14, 17, 19ᵃ, 21-3, 25-7). Each wrote long after the tribes had been knit together in national life and after the division of the Southern from the Northern Kingdom, yet before even the Northern Kingdom had reached the brink of ruin. We cannot fix precisely the dates of publication. It may, however, be considered certain that the Jahvist wrote between 900 and 700 B.C., and it is generally admitted that the Elohist wrote somewhat later than the Jahvist. He belonged to the Northern Kingdom, and there are plausible reasons in support of the conjecture that he flourished in the long and prosperous reign of Jeroboam II, i. e. circ. 782 to 743 B.C. It can be shown that J and E were united by an editorial hand into a single history. In this process each source lost something, for though Oriental writers were tolerant of doublets, even they must set limits to the repetition of the same story with minor discrepancies. It is quite possible that the Elohist began with an account of Creation, and that this part of his work was displaced by the corresponding section of the Jahvist.

In 622 B.C. a momentous change occurred in the religious history of Israel. The legislative portion of the Book of Deuteronomy discovered in that year and accepted as a canonical book, in reality as the first canonical book, limited sacrifice to the one central shrine at Jerusalem. In 444 or thereabouts a further and no less momentous change occurred. In that year Ezra proclaimed the law which he had brought with him from the land of exile. This 'Priestly' document, known to modern scholars as P, professes to give the history of Israel from the Creation to the conquest. In reality its compiler is occupied throughout with the history of sacred institutions, with the abstinence from blood and with circumcision, above all with the minutiae

The underlined verses represent the Flood as lasting a full year; it is not till 150 days have passed, that the waters begin to decline. According to the verses which are not underlined, the seven days of preparation are followed by forty days of rain; nothing is said about 'the fountains of the great deep' which were broken up from below. After three periods of seven days each the flood abates. The underlined verses ignore, those not underlined accentuate, the distinction between clean and unclean beasts and the sacrifice which Noah offers on leaving the ark. Surely this illustration of critical method is convincing. Observe that it deals quite successfully with verses which have to be divided between two distinct and contradictory sources.

We may now proceed to give a more general view on the points of contrast between the criticism of the Hexateuch and of the Synoptics. Clearly in each case we are dealing with composite documents. The two oldest documents in the Hexateuch are those of the Jahvist and Elohist. The former is so called because he uses the name Jehovah from the beginning. For example, he puts the words 'I have gotten a man with the help of Jehovah' (Gen iv. 1) into Eve's mouth.[1] The Elohist on the contrary implies (Ex iii. 13 f.) that this name was first revealed to Moses shortly before his return from Midian to Egypt. There are other differences between the two writers. The Elohist is less anthropomorphic and generally substitutes revelation by dreams or angels for the immediate apparition of Jehovah. The Jahvist shows a special interest in the Kingdom of Judah, to which he in all probability belonged. Thus he dwells on Abraham's stay at Hebron, and in the story of Joseph he assigns the first place among the Patriarchs to Judah. Still the two writers are closely allied in spirit.

[1] The meaning, however, of the words translated 'with the help of' is very doubtful. Perhaps we should read with Onkelos 'from Jehovah'.

however, is not the chief point. 'The style of P,' says Dr. Driver, 'stands apart not only from that of J, E, and D, but also from that which prevails in any part of Judges, Samuel, and Kings, and has substantial resemblances only with that of Ezekiel.' No wonder then that it is much easier to distinguish P than it would have been to recover Mark, had it disappeared, as a separate book, by an examination of our First and Third Gospels. Let us suppose that Mark had been preserved only in Matthew and Luke, and that these last had been compiled about 350 A.D. in that intensely controversial and theological age which followed the Nicene Council. Would it have been so difficult to recover the text of Mark then? Nor do we think that critics need apologize for assigning one half-verse to one document and another half-verse to another document. True, it is sometimes difficult to make an accurate and complete separation between J and E; but if we find a half-verse in the style of J or E followed by another half which deals with the same subject in the spirit and style of P, there need be no difficulty in assigning each half-verse to its proper source. After all, the reader, if comparatively a stranger to critical analysis, may easily convince himself that the critical method may, and at least in some instances does, attain absolute success. Let any one take Gen vi. 13–viii. 22 and underline vi. 13–22; vii. 6, 9, 11, 13–16, except the last clause of 16; 18–21, 24; viii. 1–2, except the last clause of 2; 3^b–5; 13–19. He will find that he has two narratives before him. They have suffered a little in the process by which they have been welded together, but they can be easily distinguished, and on the whole each is complete and consistent with itself; each is distinct both in matter and form from the other. The verses not underlined use the name Jehovah; the verses underlined only speak of Elohim. The verses underlined, and only they, reckon by the years of Noah's life, by months and by days.

understood him, thought that the severance of documents could not be carried out in detail. Sir William M. Ramsay's argument is interesting for our present purpose, because he connects it directly with the documents of the Synoptic Gospels. Supposing, he says, that St. Mark's Gospel as a separate book had perished, we could not have recovered it from a critical examination of Matthew and Luke, although we know that all of it except some fifty verses at most out of 661 verses are to be found there. The parallel is surely misleading in an extraordinary degree. The Synoptists wrote within a decade or two of each other; P is separated from J and E by two or three centuries. Again, the view which the Synoptists take of our Lord's history and teaching is in all essential points the same; P differs from his predecessors through and through. J gives one account of the Creation; P another and a contradictory one. According to J and E the Patriarchs make sacrifice habitually and at various shrines in Canaan; according to P they never sacrifice at all, and this for the very good reason that as yet God had appointed no priests, set apart no altar, prescribed no ritual. According to J the distinction between clean and unclean meats is primaeval and is taken for granted in the story of the Flood; P makes it a matter of direct institution. Instances might be multiplied indefinitely. Passing to the linguistic differences we find, as we should expect, that St. Mark has peculiarities of his own. Sir John Hawkins (*Hor. Synopt.*², p. 12 f.) has collected forty-one words or phrases which are either found in Mark alone, or which occur in Mark oftener than in Matthew and Luke together. Similarly Dr. Driver (*Introduction to O. T.*, pp. 123f.) has gathered together words and phrases characteristic of P as compared with those of the other documents. No one can examine the two lists without seeing at once that the diversity of style in the Hexateuch has no real analogy in the Synoptics. This,

Hexateuch. The present writer believes that Dr. Eerdman's exegesis is often fanciful and misleading. Who for example can believe that when Amos (iv. 11) writes 'I have overturned [some] among you as when Elohim overthrew Sodom and Gomorrha', he means that Jehovah had nothing to do with the destruction of these cities, and intends by Elohim a god or gods distinct from Jehovah (*Alttestamentliche Studien*, p. 36)? Few will acquiesce in his interpretation of Gen xxvii. 28, 'The smell of my son is as a field which Jehovah' (i. e. the rain-god) 'has blessed, and may Elohim' (i. e. gods of all sorts) 'give it of the dew of heaven.' It has been argued, as we venture to think rightly, that Gen xxvii is composite, because the blessing of Jacob by Isaac occurs twice in verses 23 and 27. We cannot escape from this difficulty by translating the same Hebrew word 'welcomed' in v. 23 and 'blessed' in v. 27. It is unreasonable to infer from Gen xxviii. 20, 21 that Jacob, on condition of receiving protection on his way from the gods in general, vows to choose Jehovah as his own special God. An examination of the new theory would take a great deal of space, nor is this a fitting occasion to deal with it in detail. Scholars have not had time as yet to give an opinion upon it. Dr. Eerdmans has not extended his analysis beyond Genesis, and the learned author himself does not seem to expect any great success for the present.

But if we are able to distinguish the documents enumerated above and to ascertain their general characteristics, are we also able to carry out the process thoroughly and assign each verse or half-verse to its proper source? Sir William M. Ramsay (*Luke the Physician*, &c., pp. 74 ff.) has recently expressed his belief that critics have been over-confident in their attempts to assign each verse or half-verse to this or that source, and he appeals to private conversations with Dr. Robertson Smith, who, as Sir William M. Ramsay

used to be called the 'Grundschrift', but is now generally known as P. It is the framework into which all the other documents of the Pentateuch have been fitted, and to which other documents, when need arises, have to give way. We have it nearly complete, and its limits were fixed by Nöldeke in 1869. We have, therefore, four documents to deal with. Two of them are occupied with the general history of the Patriarchs and their descendants. These are the Jahvist (J) and an Elohist, two authors whose main interest is in history rather than in legislation (E). Next we have in Deuteronomy (D) a legislation which stands by itself. Lastly we have the more elaborate legislation with narration designed to introduce and explain it (P). For a century and more D has been relegated to the time of Josiah or at the earliest of Manasseh. The school of Wellhausen has accepted on the whole the distinction between the documents attained by the patient labour of a long line of scholars. It has, however, transposed the order of the documents. It places P after Deuteronomy and after the exile. Till very lately we might have claimed the practically unanimous consent of scholars to the summary which has just been given. If, however, Dr. Eerdmans is right, we must believe that the criticism of the Hexateuch from its very outset has been following an *ignis fatuus*. For the most part it has been labour in vain. Eerdmans entirely repudiates the view that Genesis is composed of J, E, and P. Dismissing or almost dismissing literary criticism, he places first those legends in Genesis which are frankly and consistently polytheistic, next those which recognize Jehovah as one among many gods, and last of all legends which have been monotheistic from the beginning. This is quite different from the use of the divine names made by Astruc and his successors. Those who accept this view will object *in limine* to any comparison we can make between the documents of the Synoptics and the

'the priority of the Prophets to the Levitical law' (and this is the hinge on which the documentary question turns) 'has been proved up to the hilt for any thinking and unprejudiced man who is capable of examining the character and value of the evidence'. One name remains to be mentioned, that of Dr. Eerdmans, the pupil and successor of Kuenen at Leyden. He is by no means a conservative or a reactionary, and stands as far removed from Dr. Orr as Wellhausen himself. He maintains, however, that the whole criticism of the Hexateuch from its first start in 1753, when Astruc published his *Conjectures sur les Mémoires originaux dont il paroît que Moïse s'est servi pour composer le livre de la Genèse*, has been on a wrong track. Astruc laid the chief stress on the use of the divine names Jehovah and Elohim, and pointed out that there are two accounts of Creation, viz. one in Gen i. 1–ii. 4^a, and another in ii. 4^b to the end of chapter iii. Great advance has been made since then, but no critic has abandoned Astruc's method. The document has been found to run through the Pentateuch, and Bleek showed in 1822 that the Book of Joshua is the natural continuation of the history which begins in Genesis. Ewald and others traced the various documents through the whole of the Hexateuch, i. e. through the Pentateuch and Joshua, while De Wette in 1805 and 1806 called attention to the peculiar style and character of Deuteronomy. Hupfeld in 1853 completed the dissection of the Hexateuch by demonstrating that there are two writers who use the divine name Elohim and never employ that of Jehovah before the time of Moses.[1] We have, therefore, a writer who gives the account of the Creation in Gen i-ii. 4^a, recounts the gradual institution of religious institutions in Israel, and ends by relating the conquest and partition of Canaan among the tribes. This document

---

[1] The difficulty is increased by the fact that the Elohist uses the word Elohim even after the revelation of the name Jehovah to Moses.

(*Problem of the O. T.*, 1906), for though it has found enthusiastic welcome in certain circles, it has made no way, so far as we are aware, among Hebrew scholars. It does not even represent a serious reaction. It is far otherwise with the change of view which has taken place on the subject-matter of the Hexateuch. Gunkel in his brilliant commentary on Genesis (1901) has made a most reasonable and fertile distinction between the age of the documents and that of the various myths, legends, and fragments of history, written or unwritten, which these documents embody. A somewhat similar line of inquiry, with special reference to the connexion between Hebrew and Babylonian religion and ethics, has been pursued by a number of scholars. Prominent among them are Frederic Delitzsch, whose lectures on *Babel und Bibel* were delivered in 1902 and published in an English version by Mr. Johns of Cambridge in 1903. More valuable and cautious are the investigations of A. Jeremias (*Das alte Testament im Lichte des alten Orients*, 1905), Bäntsch (*Hebräischer Monotheismus*), and Dr. Burney in the *Journal of Theological Studies* for April, 1908. If these eminent scholars are right—the present writer ventures to express his own conviction that they have failed to prove their case—the belief in the gradual evolution of Hebrew religion would have to be abandoned. Monotheism, or at least Monolatry (i.e. the worship and public recognition of one, only God), would take its place at the beginning of Hebrew religion (i.e. in the time of Abraham), and we should have no further reason for refusing to accept the Decalogue as the work of Moses. Obviously, the questions at issue here are of the very highest importance. They do not, however, affect the point which concerns us at present, viz. the severance of the documents. On the contrary Bäntsch is himself a distinguished scholar of the Wellhausen school, while Dr. Burney in the essay to which we have already referred affirms that

XII. Criticism of the Hexateuch, etc.

or even the main features of such a life out of his own imagination. Besides St. Mark we have a collection of the Lord's Sayings freely used in our First and Third Gospels. This collection, generally known as Q, can hardly have been compiled after the destruction of Jerusalem, and Prof. K. Lake, in a recent number of the *Expositor*, has given strong reasons for putting it a decade or even two decades earlier. We may hold with a fair degree of confidence that it belongs to the Apostolic and not, like our Second Gospel, to the sub-Apostolic age. Of course, even a contemporary document may be wilfully mendacious or hopelessly inaccurate and fanciful. But no competent judge will relegate the Synoptic Gospels to such a class. Consequently there is no reason to apprehend that any candid examination of the Gospels will in the end prove destructive, even in that modified sense of the term according to which the criticism of the Hexateuch may be described as to a certain extent destructive. This will become clearer when we examine the points of union and of contrast between the criticism of the Hexateuch and that of the Synoptics. But before entering on this, the central part of the matter, it will be well to answer, so far as we can, two preliminary questions: first, how far are we justified in taking for granted that the theory of Wellhausen, Kuenen, and their school on the composition of the Hexateuch is still generally accepted? And next, supposing that this theory of the documents is right in the main, is it possible to separate the original documents and so recover them in their pristine form?

Undoubtedly changes have occurred which affect the criticism of the Hexateuch. It would be strange indeed if all subsequent investigation had simply acquiesced in the results attained by Wellhausen and his school and composed itself comfortably to sleep. We may, I think, dismiss the extreme conservatism of Möller (*Are the Critics right?* Engl. Transl., 1903) in Germany and Dr. Orr in Scotland

the Exodus in Merenptah's reign, and understand by the Israel of the inscription tribes akin to the Hebrews, which last never were in Egypt at all. This last supposition is held in a more distinct form by Marquart (*Chronol. Untersuchungen*). He believes that the tribe of Joseph alone, and not the Leah tribes, were settled for a time in Egypt or on its north-eastern borders and quitted them in the epoch of disturbance which intervened between Seti II and Ramses III. No one can be certain as yet that he has found a way out of this perplexing labyrinth. Let us for the moment put the date of Moses as far down as we can, say about 1250, or even with Eerdmans (*Vorgesch. Israels*, p. 74) about 1150 B. C. Even then the oldest document of the Hexateuch, that of the Jahvist, is separated by several centuries from the Mosaic age. Possibly even six centuries may have intervened between Moses and the earliest record of his life accessible to us. Contrast this with the Gospels as related to our Lord's life. Nobody doubts the date at which all the records place our Lord's death. It is at least an uncontroverted fact that He is said to have suffered under Pontius Pilate in the reign of Tiberius. Moreover, we have a narrative of our Lord's life, substantially identical with our Second Gospel, and committed to writing within a generation after Christ's death. It is not the work of an eyewitness, but there is no reason to doubt and strong reason to accept the early tradition (Papias *apud* Euseb. *H. E.* iii. 39) that Mark was the companion and 'interpreter' of St. Peter, and derived from him his knowledge of Christ's words and deeds. The historical character of Mark's narrative is attested partly by the fact that it was written when some of those who had been 'ministers and eyewitnesses of the word' still survived, partly by the naturalness of the picture which it presents and the absolute impossibility that any man, even if he had the genius of Shakespeare, could have produced such a life

XII. Criticism of the Hexateuch, etc. 369

worked is unknown even approximately. For long the popular theory has been that Ramses II (circ. 1340-1273) was the Pharaoh of the oppression. The supposition was plausible. We read in Ex i. 11 that the Hebrews were employed as serfs in building Pithom and Raamses, and there is evidence that those cities (Pitum and Ramses) were built under Ramses II. Moreover, his long reign of sixty years and more is well suited to the events as given in Exodus. The Exodus was placed under his successor Merenptah. But in 1896 Flinders Petrie discovered a pillar erected by Merenptah in his fifth year, which makes the favourite theory untenable, at least without serious modification. The most important words stand thus on the inscribed slate: 'Libya has been wasted: the land of the Hittites is quieted. . . . Ascalon is led away: Gezer is taken: Jenucam is annihilated. Israel is wasted: it is left without fruit of the field.' So far then from crossing the Red Sea and becoming wanderers in the wilderness under Merenptah we find the Israelites in his reign already settled in Canaan and leading an agricultural life. No wonder that scholars since Petrie's discovery have been driven in diverse directions. Miketta (*Pharaoh des Auszugs*, 1903) and Lieblein (*Soc. Bibl. Archaeol.* xx) carry the Exodus back to Amenhotep II or III, about the middle of the fifteenth century B.C. If the Habiri mentioned in the Tel-el-Amarna tablets dating from circ. 1400 B.C. are Hebrews, this theory would find some confirmation, but any such identification is extremely precarious. Meyer (*Die Israeliten*, p. 224 f.) supposes that the Hebrews were the Bedouins on whom Seti I made war, and places the Hebrew invasion of Palestine under the immediate predecessors of this same Seti I (circ. 1350 B. C.), when Egypt was in confusion and distress. So far the dates given are early. Flinders Petrie, however (*Hist.*, vol. iii), and Spiegelberg[1] (*Aufenthalt Israels in Aegypten*) place

[1] Known to me only through Eerdmans.

ciples and was conducted on methods which had only to be applied with like thoroughness to the New Testament to work like havoc.' This argument, familiar enough forty or fifty years ago in the days of 'Essays and Reviews' and Bishop Colenso's work on the 'Pentateuch', is now seldom heard from scholars. Still it is heard, as the words quoted from Dr. Orr suffice to prove.

Now it is certain that the principles of criticism are always and everywhere the same. Either these principles are unsound and should therefore be entirely dismissed, or they are valid and must be applied without fear or favour. No document can claim exemption from critical sifting; the reverence of ages, the intrinsic beauty of the narrative, the depth and sublimity of the lessons it enforces, can of themselves make no difference here; the results of critical inquiry once established by proof, must needs be accepted, even if they seem to endanger the very basis of religion and morality. It is indeed scarcely necessary to say that religion and morality rest on foundations which never can be shaken, and that the discovery of new truths may strengthen but cannot by any possibility undermine the structure. That, however, is not the point which concerns us here. Rather we would urge the fact that the uneasiness to which reference has been made arises from a confusion between critical method and the subject-matter with which the critic has to deal. No doubt the method of inquiry must always conform to the same essential rules. If, however, the matter subjected to criticism be different, the result will be different also, just as the same acid produces different effects when applied to different colours. Taking then the earliest portions of the Hexateuch and the Gospels we naturally begin by asking what extent of time separates them from the alleged facts. As regards the Hexateuch, we at once come face to face with the difficulty that the date at which Moses is said to have lived and

THE CRITICISM OF THE HEXATEUCH COMPARED WITH THAT OF THE SYNOPTIC GOSPELS

VAGUE ideas on the relations between Old and New Testament Criticism have prevailed in the popular mind. Hence misunderstandings have arisen, apt to create a prejudice against historical inquiry on the one hand and historical Christianity on the other. Thus Biblical scholars, especially those of the English type, have been accused of timidity and inconsequence. They are willing enough, so their adversaries allege, to apply historical method in all its vigour and rigour to the examination of the Old Testament, but they stop short of a sudden, and shrink from subjecting the Gospel records to the same inexorable tests. There has been, and still perhaps is, an uneasy feeling abroad that criticism has reduced the traditional accounts of early Israel to the legendary level, and that a like fate must in the end overtake the presentation of our Lord's life and teaching as it lies before us in the Gospels. Nor is this view wholly confined to those who have but vague impressions on the trend of Biblical criticism. No candid person will deny that Dr. Orr has a detailed acquaintance with the literature of the subject; yet he warns us (*Problem of the Old Testament*, p. 477) that we cannot reasonably abandon the Biblical tradition on Abraham and Moses, unless we are also prepared to part with Christ and the Gospels. 'The fact is becoming apparent,' he says, 'even to the dullest, which has long been evident to unbiased observers, that much of the radical criticism of the Old Testament proceeded on prin-

SYLLABUS

The principles of criticism whether applied to the Old or New Testament are identical.

But the subject-matter in each case is very different.

The date of Moses most uncertain, but he must have lived at least several centuries before any record of his life, which has reached us, came into being. Contrast with this the proximity of St. Mark's Gospel and of Q to the events which they attest.

The present position of criticism of the Hexateuch. The uncritical conservatism of Möller and Orr. New views on the early date of Monolatry. Eerdmans' rejection of critical principles accepted ever since Astruc published his book on the composition of Genesis in 1751.

Sir W. M. Ramsay's protest against the claim of Hexateuch critics to determine in the minutest details the extent of the several documents. The misleading nature of the parallel which he draws. The minute severance of documents in the Hexateuch justified by an examination of the story of the Flood as given in Genesis.

General sketch of the documents in the Hexateuch and their characteristics.

Both Hexateuch and Gospels of composite origin. Similar composite origin can be proved in case of Chronicles, 1 Esdras, and may be illustrated from the Saxon Chronicle.

Doublets the best clue to diversity of documents. Doublets in Synoptic Gospels, Psalms, and Proverbs.

The compiler of the Hexateuch had no documents near to the time of Moses, and he makes his latest document the framework in which he sets and to which he adapts all his earlier material. The Synoptic Evangelists, on the contrary, base their narratives on Mark, their earliest document for the life of Christ. Matthew and Luke also build on Q, which may belong to the Apostolic age. But a peculiar difficulty arises in the Gospels from the fact that there must have been an Aramaic background.

XII

THE CRITICISM OF THE HEXATEUCH COMPARED WITH THAT OF THE SYNOPTIC GOSPELS

REV. WILLIAM EDWARD ADDIS, M.A.

Vicar of All Saints, Ennismore Gardens, S.W.

XI. The Sources of St. Luke's Gospel

The following diagram may help to put the gist of this essay clearly before the reader's mind.

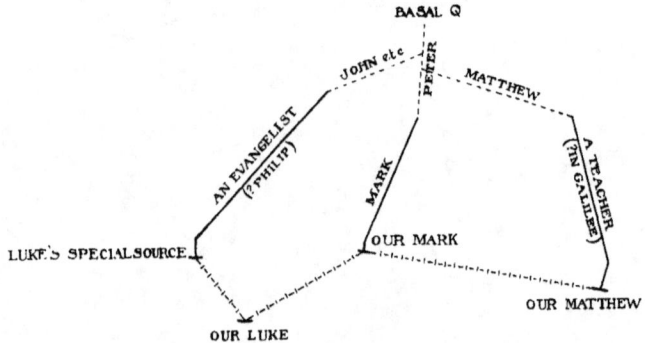

Here .... represents a special line of the oral apostolic tradition (Q).
_____ represents the 'author' of a written Gospel (embodying other elements than his special form of Q).
—·—·—·— represents a written Gospel as source of a later one.

The opposite impression as to the nature of Q, even in its oral stage, rests on little save a dubious reading of Papias's reference to 'the *Logia*' compiled by Matthew, and the form in which the teaching of Jesus appears in our First Gospel. But this is probably a secondary and 'rabbinizing' form [1]—to use a convenient phrase—i. e. a product of the practice of Christian instruction and apologetic in certain Palestinian circles. Thus Q as known to the author of our Matthew (QM), whether oral or written, was very different in form from Q as known—orally, as it seems—to Mark (QMk), or again to the author of Luke's special source (QL).[2]

(*c*) The theory of Luke's 'special source', as sketched above, is also on the lines most applicable to his sources in Acts. It correlates itself, moreover, with the Hellenistic side of the Judaean Church, just as Matthew's Q seems connected with the Hebraic.

(*d*) Finally, our theory can claim partial support from some of the other essays in this volume. For certain of their observations point, on the one hand, away from a written source common to Matthew and Luke, and on the other hand towards a special source for Luke in which much of the Q element stood already incorporated.

---

[1] Jesus' teaching was set forth as a New Law (*Thora*). Compare the spirit of the so-called *Teaching of the Apostles*, ch. viii, as to Fasting and Prayer.

[2] These are practically distinguished even by Prof. Stanton, e. g. pp. 370 f.; cf. 26, note 6. The parable of the Sower affords a good case in point.

defining his attitude to it, so as not to seem to cast any reflection upon it too. This leads naturally to a second merit in our theory.

(*b*) It involves what seems also the simplest and most adequate account of the whole Q element in the Synoptic problem, including the phenomena of Mark. Analogy again, particularly that of the earliest forms of the Franciscan tradition, does not favour the view that the original cycle of apostolic tradition (Q) took the form of a mere summary of Jesus' Sayings, with a bare minimum of historical setting. It consisted rather of *Memorabilia* of His life and ministry, as of the Prophet of the Kingdom in word and deed,[1] in such a way as to convey a real image of His personality, as it had impressed leading Apostles like Peter and the sons of Zebedee. As Prof. B. W. Bacon well observes:—

'Whatever of Q has passed into either Matthew or Luke *through the medium of Mark* will fail to appear. And it is precisely the narrative element or elements . . . which would suffer this fate. It becomes therefore largely a *petitio principii* to argue from the paucity of narrative of Q *thus reconstructed* (i. e. after the elimination of the Mark element in Matthew and Luke) that it was not, like our gospels,[2] a story of the "sayings and doings", but merely a manual of the "teachings" of Jesus' (*American Journal of Theology*, xii. 653).

To this I may add, on my theory of Luke's special source as largely parallel with Mark where Luke's own Gospel is so, that we have here in a slightly different form positive traces of Q as used by that source. Further, the form of the *Gospel according to the Hebrews*, so far as known to us, supports the above view of Q.

---

[1] B. Weiss approaches this conception of Q as furnishing a series of typical anecdotes, each with one striking saying at least at its centre, common to all our three Gospels.

[2] Admitting that Q began with narrative—the work of the Forerunner, the Baptism, and Temptation—and included stories such as the Healing of the Centurion's servant, it is hard to see why it should not have included the Passion and Resurrection. 'The writer (or teacher) who begins his work as a story, and ends it as a homily, . . . is a curiosity' (Bacon, l.c.).

regards Mark, such deviations at once cease to be difficulties, since those which are not purely stylistic in nature, whether conscious or involuntary, nor even cases of a change of order tending to greater clearness of narration,[1] may have existed originally in a document composed without any reference to Mark. As to the Q element in Matthew, our theory gives adequate flexibility for the widest deviation, by leaving more to the unconscious factor operative in different local traditions[2] prior to incorporation in our Gospels. Thus the Q element in Luke came to him already in its present setting, in his primary source, to whose author it was known in an oral form differing as much from the form found in Matthew as does that in Luke's own work. That the author of Matthew knew Q in written rather than oral form, as even Mr. Allen maintains, I am as little concerned on my theory of Luke to deny, as he is to assert that Q was known to Luke[3] (or his special source) in the same or indeed in any written form. Nevertheless I am not convinced that there ever was a written 'book of discourses' that has perished. Analogy is against the idea that an Apostle himself committed to writing, at so early a date as is requisite, a record of his oral teaching. Nor do I think that Luke would have written as he does in his preface, had there been a work by one of the Twelve already in wide and honoured circulation: he would have felt the need of

in teaching. Our theory also explains most naturally the deviations from Mark *common to Luke and Matthew*, as due to their use of Q, though not in identical forms (hence their agreements are not more numerous).

[1] These are of course hard to distinguish from cases due to another order in the second source, where its presence may otherwise be suspected.

[2] Thus the affinity between poverty and 'faith', and the duty of using one's goods entirely as in trust for those in need—so much more marked in Luke than in Matthew—seem characteristic of the Judaean Church as reflected in Gal. ii. 10, the Epistle of James, and the early chapters of Acts (cf. x. 2). This points to the home of S, and turns our mind once more to the Hellenistic circle of Philip at Caesarea.

[3] See p. 281. 'It is hardly likely that he was acquainted with it', i.e. the 'book of discourses' used by our Matthew.

tolic tradition (Q) is conceived to have passed over into written form. I can see no evidence that Q was ever written down before it was so in Luke's S. That even the first evangelist embodies Q in oral rather than written form seems the more probable view on internal evidence. Probably his Q was of a type connected in some way with the Apostle Matthew, since this is implied alike by the title of our First Gospel and by the tradition in Papias (though there the emphasis falls on the language of Matthew's collection of *Logia* rather than on their reduction to writing). But it is hard to believe that an actual apostolic writing would have been suffered to perish among Jewish Christians of all types (even after being used in the composition of later Gospels), especially in those conservative circles where the *Gospel according to the Hebrews* was later the only one in use. Either, then, this gospel itself embodied the Aramaic work of Matthew to which the tradition in Papias really refers, or Matthew never committed his oral teaching to writing. In neither case is there cogent reason for assuming any document as entering into the development of our Synoptic Gospels prior to Mark, on the one hand, and Luke's special source on the other. Each of these may well contain in rather different form the common apostolic tradition, both narrative and didactic, as known to their respective authors.

It remains only to sum up the main merits of the above special 'Two-Document theory' of Luke's Gospel.

(a) First and foremost, it is the simplest explanation of the highly complex phenomena in question, and at the same time the most adequate. It does away with the need for finding many and various motives, more or less problematical, for what are usually assumed to be Luke's editorial changes, even in little things, from Mark[1] or Matthew's Q. As

[1] These would often be quite unconscious, since Luke's memory would be filled with the wording of Q as embodied in S, through constant use of it

Lk ix. 51–xviii. 14. But just as *some of the earlier sections* of the document *have been introduced* into the Synoptic outline [1] *before the first of these two insertions*, so likewise *a few have been given after the second of them.*'

'The evangelist himself has added *a few passages*,[2] *gathered by him probably from oral tradition*. In particular the accounts of incidents in the history of the Passion and Appearance of the Risen Christ, peculiar to this Gospel, owe (it would seem) their written form to him. . . .'

'Our third evangelist had besides *a narrative of the Birth and Infancy* of John the Baptist and of Jesus, which was *composed in Palestine*, but which was probably a separate writing . . .'

Here the great element common to Prof. Stanton and myself is the belief that (α) a single document 'supplied the greater part of the non-Marcan matter' in Luke's Gospel for the whole Ministry; (β) this embodied a form of Q differing considerably from that known to Matthew, and even to Mark; (c) the matter additional to the original form of Q which this enlarged document contained, represented traditions current 'somewhere in Palestine', and in southern Palestine. Our differences turn on (α) the stage at which the various forms of Q passed into written form; (β) the 'few passages' added by the evangelist himself from oral tradition, including some in the history of the Passion and Resurrection. As to the Nativity narratives in chaps. i–ii (and the connected Genealogy), neither of us sees clear evidence for including it in Luke's 'special source', though it too was composed in Palestine.

Thus the one difference in principle between my theory and that of other upholders of Luke's 'special source' as an expanded form of Q, lies in the point at which the original apos-

---

[1] This bears also on certain striking divergences of Luke from Mark in narratives where they are parallel, as though Luke had a second form of the original apostolic tradition here before him.

[2] e.g. the episode of Zacchaeus (cf. *op. cit.*, p. 238), and within the two 'Insertions' vii 36–50; viii. 1–3; x 29–37; and possibly xvii. 11–19 (p. 229). Yet see above.

XI. The Sources of St. Luke's Gospel

cussion is the most important that has appeared for a long time, at least in English, it may be well to place before the reader his summing up, and then define exactly the seeming advantages of the theory already outlined. Here is his theory in his own words (p. 239 f.), the italics being added to indicate the main points in common.

'For his account of the Ministry of Jesus our third evangelist used, besides the original (or approximately the original) Gospel by Mark, *one other principal source*, namely, *an expanded form of the original Greek Logian* document [1] . . . With a copy of the latter as a foundation, a good deal of other matter was embodied, *somewhere in Palestine*,' if not in Jerusalem.

'*The additional matter* may have been derived to some extent from the Aramaic Collection of Logia, which had not been fully rendered before. But besides this it *comprises many parables*, which corresponded (there is no reason to doubt) with Aramaic originals, but *which had been told orally* and in greater or less degree shaped anew, before they were committed to writing. *Some of the few incidents added may also have been first current as traditions in the community* where the document was produced.'

'*This* document has *supplied* the *greater part of the non-Marcan matter* in the Gospel *from the beginning of the Synoptic outline* onwards. And it is natural to conjecture that *the peculiarities* of the third Gospel *in passages which have* on the whole close *parallels are* in some instances *due to it*, e. g. . . . a portion of the account of the Centurion's servant (Lk vii. 4–6ᵃ, 10). Most of the matter from it has been given in two sections, Lk vi. 17–viii. 3, and

---

[1] I should say 'tradition', owing to the wide divergences between the Logian element in Luke and Matthew, which seem to preclude a common document of any kind. But the point is secondary to the general idea of the single source here defined, an idea common to C. Weizsäcker (in his *Untersuchungen über die evang. Geschichte*, 1864, pp. 205 ff.), P. Feine (*Eine vorkanonische Überlieferung des Lukas*, 1891), J. Weiss in the eighth edition of Meyer's *Kommentar* on Luke (1892), and W. Soltau, *Unsere Evangelien*, 1901, though some of them think that Luke also made use of the same written Q as Matthew. Feine thought too that Luke used what he calls 'the Synoptic basal document' (*Grundschrift*), mainly narrative in character, as distinct from the Logia (*Redequelle*) conceived on old-fashioned lines—as though exclusively didactic in form, whereas B. Weiss and others have made it probable that the original common apostolic tradition (Q) contained a fair amount of narrative as setting for striking sayings.

history. It was just in this respect too that he felt himself to possess special advantages, in that his efforts to trace the actual course of things had been conducted under most favourable conditions. What those conditions were he does not say: they certainly did not consist in the number of written sources at his disposal. We should rather gather that his advantage lay in the direct way in which the original facts, as handed down by eyewitnesses who afterwards ministered the Message to others, had reached him. This condition would be completely satisfied supposing that, in addition to Mark's Petrine form of the apostolic tradition (which may not yet have been current where Luke was writing), he possessed a series of written memoranda taken down years before from the lips of one who had been perhaps in part an eyewitness, but at any rate an early associate of eyewitnesses. For *the special accuracy* of such materials he was *able personally to vouch*, from what he knew of their immediate source, as well as from other early witness. Among his grounds for assurance on this point he may have included the large support given, as to contents and order, by so weighty a narrative as the Gospel of Mark, also written by one he knew well. But the very fact that he often sets aside Mark's order for that of his special source, suggests that his grounds of confidence in this latter on other and more direct evidence must have been in themselves conclusive. In any case there is no reason to include this source among the 'many' written narratives current in the region where he was writing, narratives which he hopes by its help to supersede.

The first draft of this essay was already complete when Prof. Stanton's judicial examination of the subject[1] rendered a fresh testing of the matter desirable. On the whole his results do not differ widely from my own. But as his dis-

---

[1] *The Gospels as Historical Documents*, Part II, pp. 220-322 in particular.

XI. The Sources of St. Luke's Gospel

that the theory reduces Luke's part in his Gospel to a minimum, viz. the blending of his two authorities, and the smoothing of the style of the whole into something like unity, as well as conformity to the literary and other requirements of his own circle of readers. This many will feel contrary to their previous impressions of the purport of Luke's own preface. But does that preface really suggest anything as to Luke's use of written sources at all? Here are his words in a form which aims at rather more exactitude than would be in place even in our Revised Version.

'Forasmuch as many have taken in hand to draw up a narrative concerning the facts that are matter of full conviction among us Christians (τῶν πεπληροφορημένων ἐν ἡμῖν πραγμάτων), according as they were handed down to us by the original witnesses and servants of the Message (οἱ ἀπ' ἀρχῆς αὐτόπται καὶ ὑπηρέται γενόμενοι τοῦ λόγου); it seemed good to me also, as having investigated[1] (παρηκολουθηκότι, i.e. having by inquiry accompanied in mind) from an early date all things with accuracy (ἄνωθεν πᾶσιν ἀκριβῶς), to write for you in orderly fashion, most excellent Theophilus, that thou mightest recognize as touching the doctrines (λόγων) in which thou wast instructed their secure nature.'

Luke's object was to confirm trust in the Christian doctrines (λόγοι) by setting the Christian facts (πράγματα) of deed or word in the convincing light of ordered sequence, instead of more or less haphazard presentation of anecdotes and sayings. It was the partial and uncoördinated character of the existing narratives accessible to converts or inquirers, especially in the region where Luke is writing,[2] that prompted him to supply one which could appeal to the Greek sense of rational order and development, as belonging to genuine

---

[1] Dr. G. Milligan tells me that this sense, to 'investigate' a matter, is supported by the papyri, where it has in one case τῇ ἀληθείᾳ after it.

[2] This may have been the province of Asia (so Harnack for Acts), where a rank growth of Gospel-narratives may well have arisen of which no specimens survive.

they move, as well as by their close affinity of language and idea with other parts of Luke's special matter, notably in his last chapter.

Finally as to the degree of editorial adaptation which S may have undergone in being worked into Luke's Gospel, it seems to have been inconsiderable and due mainly to concern for ordered sequence (καθεξῆς), to which the Evangelist attached such value for his reader. This would naturally show itself at the opening of sections, and in a lesser degree at their close. There is, however, no clear proof that Luke made up even so much setting without seeming warrant in his sources, one or both. His use of Mark discountenances any such suggestion.[1]

II

To such a theory of the sources of Luke's Gospel two initial objections occur readily. In the first place the large extent of 'the special source', far larger than has usually been supposed by those who assume its existence at all. But such an objection loses point once it is granted that Mark, with which our source is on this showing often closely parallel, was itself based on an apostolic tradition already stereotyped in its salient features, at any rate as current in the Jerusalem Church.[2] It simply becomes a matter of evidence in detail touching divergence amid agreement between Mark and Luke, throughout the sections where they are parallel. The second *à priori* objection would be,

in the Gospels (Lk x. 38, 42, as an exception, only confirms the point, on our view of S).

[1] The scope of this essay does not require examination of such editorial or literary changes in detail as Luke may have made in S, as he certainly made them in Mark. His enhancement of the Biblical style of the narrative by the frequent insertion of 'And it came to pass . . .' has been noted: the only other instance of heightening the dignity of the story which need here be alluded to, is Luke's apparent substitution or addition of the title 'the Lord' in solemn contexts.

[2] The tradition as known to our Matthew might differ a good deal, as being current later and in quite a different part of Palestine.

with Peter in the early chapters of Acts, which probably embody traditions from the same source as the special element in Luke's Gospel, that fact may reflect a special interest on Philip's part in this apostle, which seems to come out also in the specification of Peter and John as the two disciples sent to prepare for the Passover in Lk xxii. 8, as well as later to inspect Philip's work in Samaria (Acts viii. 14 ff.). The same result emerges from a consideration of the intimate domestic picture of Martha and Mary, who also enter largely into the Johannine Gospel, and of the story illustrating Jesus' attitude to Samaritans (ix. 54, cf. the Parable of the Good Samaritan, and the episode of the Grateful Samaritan), read in the light of John's mission to the Samaritans in Acts viii. 14, 25. Even the special sympathy with women traceable in several episodes in Luke's Gospel, may be correlated with what we read of John in connexion with the mother of Jesus (Jn xix. 26 f.), although there was doubtless a selective affinity between such traditions and Philip, the father of four prophetic daughters, and indeed Luke himself. Still it need not be assumed that all the elements of Luke's special source belong to the same stratum of Gospel tradition. Some may go back to early Jerusalem days: others may have reached its narrator only in Caesarea or its region, and have undergone some changes in transmission. But none suggest an origin outside Palestine. This is true even of the most special group of all Luke's peculiar traditions—and which need not belong to his 'special source' at all—those touching the nativity of Jesus and His Forerunner, including the Genealogy in iii. 23-38. These too are in any case of Palestinian origin, to judge by their local colour[1] and the circle of interests within which

---

[1] e. g. the allusive phrase 'the Hill country' (ἡ ὀρεινή, i. 39; cf. 65); the order in the expression 'night and day', in ii. 37, contrasted with that in xviii. 7; the use of 'brought him up' without specifying Jerusalem, if (as argued above) εἰς Ἱεροσόλυμα be secondary; and also the use of Μαριάμ prevailing in chaps. i-ii, in contrast to Μαρία, the more Greek form usual

Caesarea, this time to remain there some two years, or a considerable portion of that period. In every particular that occurs to one's mind in thinking of the special matter in Luke's Gospel, including the ways in which its Q element diverges from that preserved in Matthew,[1] the special tradition of Philip—associate of apostles and other personal disciples of Jesus in Jerusalem—as that tradition would shape itself in his mind and speech in Caesarea, seems to suit the conditions of the case.[2] If not himself an eye-witness of Jesus' last days in Jerusalem, he would have just the perspective which the 'special source' seems to have had. For its narrative of the Jerusalem ministry is not only full and intimate,[3] but is also markedly consecutive, whereas it lacks close historical connexion for the matter prior to that period, even though its pictures are vivid and seem largely derived from eye-witnesses. Philip would naturally hear first-hand touching the sending of the Seventy and their return; for some of these would be his intimates in the early years at Jerusalem, before the Hellenists were scattered through Stephen's liberal interpretation of Messiah's message. The Evangelist of Samaria was, too, the most likely of media for traditions touching Jesus and Samaritans.

As to the earlier Galilaean days, touching which the 'special source' seems to have contained detached but vivid stories—the Sermon at Nazareth, the call of Simon, the incident at Nain, the Woman at the Pharisee's feast—we may even suggest the apostle through whom Philip was able to enrich his tradition with matter so congenial to his own spirit and conception of the Gospel. If John is associated

---

[1] That the Lucan *Logia* should as a rule be less modified and added to in substance by the unconscious action of tradition, but on the other hand should less faithfully preserve the original Semitic form – as many scholars believe – is just what one would expect of a tradition current in Hellenistic Caesarea about A. D. 57 or 58.

[2] Observe e. g. the confident allusion to Cleopas as one of the two going to Emmaus.

[3] e. g. the note as to Jesus' daily habits in xxi. 37 f.

XI. The Sources of St. Luke's Gospel

S as *the tradition collected in a single Judaeo-Christian mind*, embodying the common apostolic tradition (Q) along with other elements peculiar to its own personal information, and as probably written down by Luke himself more or less in the language [1] of this 'minister of the word', as he responded to Luke's special inquiries (Lk i. 2 f.). Thus S was a peculiar form of written memoirs [2] elicited by our Third Evangelist *ad hoc*, not immediately for the literary purpose to which he finally put it, but rather as a permanent record of the most authentic tradition to which it had been his lot to obtain access, for use in his own work as an evangelist or catechist of the oral Gospel. No wonder, then, if it had large affinity with his own conception of the Gospel, while it was often clothed in phrases and conceptions which were more Jewish than those native to his own mind (as shown by those parts of Acts where he is writing most freely).

When we have so stated the matter, we are already hovering on answers to further queries. In view of what we know of Luke's history from Acts, we can hardly doubt that it was while with Paul in Caesarea (the only place in Palestine where he ever had leisure for such a task), that he made his careful inquiries and wrote down his 'special source'—possibly, too, any other traditions that he may have worked up later along with it in his Gospel. Nor need we doubt as to the witness from whose lips he would by preference gather his traditions for committing to writing. It would be he whom Luke singles out for emphatic notice as the host of Paul and himself at Caesarea, when on their way to Jerusalem, and characterizes as 'Philip the Evangelist' (Acts xxi. 8 f.). With him he would cultivate the closest relations when a few weeks later he found himself again in

---

[1] This would account fully for the blending of non-Lucan and Lucan style.
[2] Analogous to Luke's own Travel-diary which seems to lie behind parts of his book of Acts.

substance and form, have been already prepared for easy assimilation into the work of such an Evangelist as Luke: hence the special difficulty of distinguishing in detail what may or may not be due to his 'special source' or to his editorial hand.[1]

So far we have, for the most part, left over the question as to the exact form in which S came to Luke. That it lay before him in a written shape when he compiled his Gospel, hardly needs arguing further. Still we have to face the objection that a Gospel-writing of such high authority, to judge from Luke's use of it, could hardly fail—once it passed into circulation—to leave some trace of itself on tradition or even on our Matthew, seeing that it would be almost certainly of Palestinian origin. If, however, it never passed into circulation, but was known only to Luke, then it must either have been written by its author for him, in response to his inquiries, or by Luke himself, virtually from his informant's lips. For had he not written it down on the spot, as it were, the Jewish tone and phrasing so noticeable in its underlying texture would not have been preserved by him, a Gentile Christian. Thus these two alternatives come to very much the same thing in the end. The body of tradition cannot have been reported to Luke by a number of persons in different circles and at very different dates. It is all too homogeneous in spirit, form, phraseology, and in its special interests, shown in the matter most peculiar to it, e. g. that touching Samaritans (ix. 52 ff.; x. 33 ff.; xvii. 16; cf. Acts viii. 1, 5 ff.) Its homogeneity is too great to be the product even of a single circle of tradition. It bears the impress of a single selective and unifying mind, other than and prior to that of the Evangelist himself, though one congenial to his own. In other words, we can best conceive

---

[1] This consideration renders of doubtful value much even of Professor Stanton's careful linguistic analysis in pp. 291-312.

XI. The Sources of St. Luke's Gospel

of standpoint and feeling between it and the foregoing, especially in 'Rejoice with me, for I have found ... (the) lost' (cf. xv. 23 f., 32)—in direct antithesis to the attitude of Jesus' critics in xv. 2—forbids the idea that the conjunction of the third or most distinctively S parable was Luke's own device.[1]

As regards the special character of the parables distinctive of Luke, a word more may be said. Professor Stanton observes (p. 231) that these 'contain, strictly speaking, no reference to the Kingdom of God.... They teach moral and spiritual lessons, applicable under all circumstances ..., and the main consideration in each case is the practical inference to be drawn by individuals'—even when the future Kingdom of God is in question. Again, in form and imagery, 'they are concerned with human emotions and motives, inner debatings and actions, which are vividly described; they are in fact short tales of human life.' They require 'no separate interpretation', but 'bear their moral on the face of them'. As Professor Stanton further remarks: 'Different kinds of parables spoken by Christ, as well as different parts of His Teaching more generally, may have had a special interest and attraction for particular individuals or portions of the Church, and so may have been separately collected and preserved.' This fully accords with the suggestions made above, when speaking of the Seventy. Both the Lucan parables and his whole teaching as to riches and the breadth of Christ's Gospel towards sinners, tax-collectors, and Samaritans, suggest that Luke's special tradition had passed through the medium of some Hellenistic circle of Palestinian Christianity, which has acted by selective affinity on its contents, and has to some extent influenced its language and style. If so, it would in both respects, in

---

[1] The fact that xv. 3 runs 'He spoke to them this parable', rather than 'these parables', will not bear pressing, as though in the source only one parable followed originally, i. e. xv. 4 ff.

reached Luke already united, in a seemingly original manner, with a section of his form of Q (QL). That is, QL was here, too, one with S, and not distinct from it in tradition.[1] But further, seeing that not only in its spirit but also in the very formula with which it opens, 'A certain man' (ἄνθρωπός τις), this parable is closely linked to a series of the most distinctive Lucan parables (xii. 16 ff.; xiv. 16 ff.; xv. 11 ff.; xvi. 1 ff., 19 ff.; xix. 12 ff.; cf. xviii. 2 ff., 10 ff.), it is natural to infer that they, too, came to Luke already united with his QL matter in the special source. Two of them (xiv. 16 ff., xix. 12 ff.) have substantial parallels, yet with differences showing distinct lines of tradition, in Mt xxii. 2 ff.; xxv. 14 ff. But in no case does a non-Lucan parable open with 'A certain man' (cf. 'A certain judge', 'Two men', Lk xviii. 2, 10), although all three Gospels agree in the opening, 'A man planted a vineyard' (xx. 9). Yet even here it is to be noted that they do not agree exactly, Luke having ἄνθρωπος ἐφύτευσεν ἀμπελῶνα, Mark ἀμπελῶνα ἄνθρωπος ἐφύτευσεν, Matthew ἄνθρωπος ἦν οἰκοδεσπότης ὅστις ἐφύτευσεν ἀμπελῶνα. It looks, then, as if the Lucan form of opening to so many parables were a mannerism of the S type of tradition, whether it was transmitting common Q matter (QL) or parts of the apostolic tradition peculiar to itself (S proper).

Another case of the blending of these two streams in S, analogous to that afforded by x. 25-37, may be seen in the three parables of Lk xv. The first of these, which opens with 'What man of you?', has a parallel in Mt xviii. 12-14, 'What think ye? If any man have' (ἐὰν γένηταί τινι ἀνθρώπῳ): then the extra element in Q as known to Luke (QL) reveals itself in the second parable on similar lines, 'Or what woman': and finally, the third opens in characteristic S form, with 'A certain man had two sons'. Yet the affinity

[1] This runs counter to Professor Stanton's finding as regards this parable (*op. cit.*, p. 229), but has analogy in the connexion of xii. 13-15 and 16-21 (where note the Jewish idea in ἀπαιτοῦσιν).

XI. The Sources of St. Luke's Gospel

the question as to one's neighbour arises out of the maxim of Jesus in v. 28, i.e. ' Love thy neighbour as thyself, and thou shalt live '. The words of transition, moreover, ' But he, wishing to justify himself . . .,' have a parallel in words of Jesus (xvi. 15) presumably belonging to Luke's Q element, ' Ye are they who justify themselves before men.' Further, the dialogue in which the moral of the parable is applied at the close, presupposes just such a situation as is described in the foregoing encounter with the Lawyer. Accordingly the whole section, Lk x. 25-37, may have stood as a unit[1] in a single source here drawn on. This would also explain why Luke places vv. 25-8 far out of its context in Mark, a transposition which would not otherwise readily occur to him, and which he would hardly venture on without objective warrant (comp. xi. 14 ff. in the face of its parallel in Mk iii. 20-30) ; for there is nothing in what precedes or follows to suggest placing vv. 25-8 alone here. But if these verses formed a unit with the parable of the Good Samaritan in his source, there is some fitness in this unit standing (as it may have stood already in S) near to words in which Jesus shows His attitude to Samaritans (ix. 52 ff.). Indeed, this juxtaposition may even be true to facts.

Be this as it may, we must go behind Luke to his source for Lk x. 25-37 ; and this has important consequences. It means that a parable, regarded as among the most distinctive of Luke's Gospel, and so as belonging to his ' special source ' —if one source contained the bulk of such peculiar matter—

---

[1] It has also internal verisimilitude, since it was more like Christ's method to give His questioner positive instruction in the larger spirit of the precept of Love to one's neighbour, than to send him away merely baffled in his attempt to trip up the prophet of Nazareth (implied by Mk xii. 34 and made explicit in Luke and Matthew). But if so, Luke's setting is better than Mark's, since Jesus would hardly have put the lesson in a form so offensive to Pharisaic feeling at so critical a moment as His final visit to Jerusalem. Perhaps Mark's order was caused by the feeling that καλῶς διδάσκαλε (xii. 32) in the scribe's mouth was connected with the διδάσκαλε, καλῶς εἶπας, in which Q (see Lk xx. 39, cf. Mk xii. 28[b]) described the attitude of his class to Jesus' answer to the Sadducees.

to his readers. So, too, in the use of his special source between ix. 51–xviii. 14 he may at times go beyond it in specifying those addressed (e.g. in xii. 1, 22; xvi. 1; xvii. 1); and he certainly seems once [1] at least to enhance the quasi-historic setting of this whole section, by inserting a reminder that Jesus is to be thought of as still on His way up to Jerusalem. 'And *it came to pass, when on the way to Jerusalem, that* he (καὶ αὐτός) was passing between Samaria and Galilee' (xvii. 11). Yet even here he is only following a hint of his source in ix. 51,[2] if not again in xiv. 25 (συνεπορεύοντο δὲ αὐτῷ ὄχλοι πολλοί). On the whole, then, the position of this Great Teaching Section in the setting of a prolonged journey, resting on a basis of fact preserved in ix. 51–x. 42 in particular, was a form of narration due to S itself.

But what of the Parables so distinctive of this section? Were they already part of S as they now stand in Luke, or did he fit them in to their present setting from elsewhere? The section, x. 25–37, is crucial for the relation of these Parables to the QL element in S. In the first place there is good reason, derived partly from Luke's own differences from Mark (xii. 28–34) and partly from the divergences in Matthew (in some cases agreeing with Luke's), to believe that the Scribe's question as to the Great Commandment stood in Q as well as in Mark. In the second place, it is in Luke united closely with the parable of the Good Samaritan, peculiar to this Gospel. It is often assumed, indeed, that this conjunction is due to Luke himself; but this is rather a violent theory, in view of the natural way in which

---

[1] Probably again in xiii. 22, xix. 28, in both of which Westcott and Hort read Ἰεροσόλυμα, the more Greek form found in Luke's Gospel only here and in ii. 22; xxiii. 7 (a parenthetic note by Luke writing as Greek to Greeks).

[2] καὶ αὐτὸς τὸ πρόσωπον ἐστήριξε τοῦ πορεύεσθαι εἰς Ἱερουσαλήμ. Note that πορεύεσθαι seems a favourite word of Luke's S, e.g. 52 f., 57, in the same context. It is probable, then, that both ix. 57 and x. 38 ἐν τῷ πορ. αὐτούς, without ἐγένετο) are also due to S.

other hand fresh types of spiritual receptivity would be represented by certain of the wider circle of witnesses, some of whom may, for instance, have been more cultivated in mind and more liberal in sympathies, especially towards a class like the Samaritans, than the framers of the official tradition. Through some such witnesses, say those with whom a Hellenist member of the Jerusalem Church would find most in common, distinctive traditions such as mark Luke's 'Great Insertion' would be most likely to survive and take on a special shape. Finally, one or more of such members of the original 'Seventy' may well have been disciples won early in this Journey, men like those whose call is recorded in Lk ix. 57-62.

One who moved in such circles, and was also in personal contact with the Twelve themselves,—c. g. Peter and James and John, perhaps the last in particular (cf. the intimate story of Martha and Mary, x. 38 ff.)—would gradually gather much the sort of traditions, more or less grouped according to affinities of idea, that we find in Lk ix. 51–xviii. 14. It looks, too, as if the historical order were best preserved at its beginning, but soon fades away, to be followed by a series of sections more or less loosely linked together in groups, the links between the several groups being specially loose, where they exist at all. That these links belonged for the most part to the 'special source', prior to its incorporation into what aimed definitely at being a connected narrative like Luke's Gospel, is rendered most probable by a *comparison with Luke's method when dealing with Mark*,[1] which lies before us much as he used it. For there 'our third Evangelist is careful not to create connexions in time which he did not find in his source', although he may add explanatory touches in the introductory matter, derived from what follows, to make the situation clearer

---

[1] This is so well argued by Professor Stanton in *The Gospels as Historical Documents*, Part II, pp. 228 f., that it is needless here to labour the point.

referred to the Galilaean ministry [1] and the Twelve (as Mt xi. 20-7 suggests). Indeed it looks as if Lk x. 21-2 (24) originally belonged to the conversation between Jesus and the Twelve on their return, as referred to in Mk vi. 30 = Lk ix. 10. As to vv. 17-20 themselves, the disciples' crowning joy in their power over demons follows well on v. 9, where power over sickness alone had been mentioned in their Charge, and corresponds to what we read of in Mk vi. 7; Lk ix. 1, as a notable feature in the charge to the Twelve.

If we have been right in judging as historical the mission of the Seventy heralds of Jesus' coming, on His journey towards Jerusalem, it will have an important bearing on the origin of certain parts of Luke's 'special source'. For this episode was no part of the common Apostolic tradition (Q). Nay, more, since it records actual words spoken by Jesus touching the success of their mission—words to which there is no extant parallel in the story of the Twelve—we are warranted in supposing that the tradition came through some one in specially close touch with the second circle of Jesus' personal followers, 'the rest' spoken of in Lk xxiv. 9, cf. 33, to whom reference is made in Acts i. 21 in connexion with the filling of the gap in the inner circle of the Twelve. Such a man would meet in early Jerusalem days some who had served among the Seventy, and so hear and preserve their special traditions. But the limitations of traditions so obtained are as obvious as their value. They would lack much that belonged to the official tradition of Jesus' ministry, particularly the early stereotyping of its order by constant use, and in connexion with this the preservation of certain details of place and time not really essential to the spiritual value of each incident. On the

[1] This is probably true also of a good deal of what follows in the Great Insertion, which contains (especially after ch. x) what S had collected without being able to assign it a definite place in the familiar framework of Apostolic tradition (Q).

XI. *The Sources of St. Luke's Gospel* 343

(2) something of this may be the result of Luke's own ordering activity. He may have attached to this sending out of temporary heralds of Jesus' approach words found in the charge to the Twelve in his S, which he did not use (though they influenced his use of Mark) in the former connexion, owing to Mark being there available. This would accord with the allusion to the Twelve, in terms of what we find in x. 4, which occurs in xxii. 35, 'When I sent you forth without purse (βαλλάντιον, cf. xii. 33) and wallet and shoes, lacked ye anything?' It is just possible that this form of commission was addressed both to the Twelve and the Seventy, as reported in S. But it cannot there have been addressed to the Seventy only, as in Luke. Hence the QL type of cross-reference in xxii. 35 cannot have been inserted by Luke, but was already part of S—a result which makes QL in ix. 1 ff. or x. 1 ff., or in both, also part of S.

As to the exact contents of the Charge in x. 2–16, which perhaps already formed a unit in QL (or S), vv. 13–15 have been artificially attracted by affinity between v. 14 and v. 12; and as in Matthew also (xi. 20–7) what we find in vv. 13–15 immediately preceded what follows in vv. 21 ff.—linked, too, by the same formula 'in that hour' (season)—it is natural to conclude that it was so also in QL. Whence, then, came vv. 17–20, which record the return of the Seventy and make this 'the hour' when vv. 21 f. (or even 21–4, as in Luke) were spoken? Surely they must have been introduced by the mind which brought vv. 13–15 into connexion with x. 2–12, since without them the connexion of what we have shown to be their sequel in Q (as proved by Mt xi. 20–7)—especially in the Lucan form, 'In that hour he *exulted* ... and said,'—is far less natural than with them. The whole combination probably took place in the mind of the author of S rather than in Luke's, even though it be incorrect, in so far as vv. 13–15, 21–2 (24) historically